MULTIPLE NATIONALITY AND INTERNATIONAL LAW

Developments in International Law

VOLUME 57

The Titles published in this series are listed at the end of this volume.

Multiple Nationality and International Law

ALFRED M. BOLL

Foreword
by
Judge Kenneth Keith

MARTINUS NIJHOFF PUBLISHERS
LEIDEN / BOSTON

A C.I.P. record for this book is available from the Library of Congress.

Printed on acid-free paper.

ISBN-13:   978 90 04 14838 3
ISBN-10:   90 04 14838 8

Printed and bound in The Netherlands.

Remembering
Jeannette Waddell Fournier (1955–2006)

American by birth and Swiss by marriage, Jeanie Fournier was a brilliant and devoted nurse, public health specialist, and humanitarian diplomat who inspired various generations of workers dedicated to serving the victims of conflict. Born in Ohio, she joined the International Committee of the Red Cross (ICRC) in 1980 as an American Red Cross nurse working on the Thai-Cambodian border. With her Swiss husband Henry and while raising their children Katherine and Matthieu, she subsequently served the ICRC in various capacities in Gaza, Kinshasa, Harare, Jakarta, and Beirut. She was killed on a field mission in the Casamance region of Senegal when her vehicle struck a landmine. She will be remembered for her commitment to humanitarian work, and represented the best of both her countries of nationality.

Contents

Foreword

Nationality plays a central role in national and international law and practice. States in principle are obliged to allow their nationals to enter their territory and in general not to limit their right to leave. Nationals owe allegiance to their state of nationality and may be subject to its jurisdiction even when outside its territory. Those duties may include service in the armed forces of the State, in peace as well as in war. The State also has the right, if not the duty, to present claims at the diplomatic level to protect the rights and interests of its nationals. Individuals increasingly have the right under treaties negotiated by their states to bring claims for instance about investments directly against other states.

Although nationality has those and other important consequences, States have considerable freedom, long recognized in treaty, their practice and court decisions, in formulating their nationality laws. The 1930 Hague Convention on conflict of nationality laws declares that it is for each state to determine under its own law who are its nationals. It also recognizes that that freedom is subject to limits set by conventions, international custom and recognized principles of law. Conventions adopted in the last 50 years impose restrictions relating to statelessness, the nationality of married women, discrimination against women, and children of diplomatic and consular officials but the freedom is still extensive.

That freedom, as well as the legal restrictions, appear in the law and practice of many states in recognizing or conferring dual nationalities. This may occur at birth where the parents have different nationalities and the laws of those two states recognize nationality by descent or where the birth is in a third state which confers nationality on the basis of birth there; or it may occur at a later time where, following migration or adoption, a foreign national seeks or obtains the local nationality. Another important source of multiple nationality is the break up of empires and of other states, a frequent occurrence over the last century.

Dr Alfred Boll, in a meticulous comprehensive study based on a valuable collection and analysis of state practice, treaties, court decisions and scholarly writing, addresses the modern day phenomenon of multiple nationality. That phenomenon, he says, is a reality and he is concerned with the consequences of that reality. Those consequences are to be found in the law and practice of 45 states along with that of another 30 summarised in the extensive appendix. As he so clearly shows, state practice does not reject multiple nationality although a small number of states do reject it, but with important qualifications.

The continuing and growing significance of the issues which Dr Boll considers so carefully appears in the recent work of the International Law Commission on the effect of succession of states on nationality and diplomatic protection (the latter completed just this year), in changes in national law about multiple nationality (with a number removing certain bars on it) and in the work of international courts and tribunals in which nationality is an issue. This book will provide continuing assistance to those engaged in those and related activities.

The study also provides important contexts for possible future developments such as possible limits on the freedom of states to present or not the claims of their nationals at the diplomatic level. Another context is the burgeoning law of international human rights which may, depending on particular treaty obligations, enable individuals to make claims at the international level without reference to nationality. The duty to protect regardless of states and by reference to need has of course long been established in the Geneva Conventions of 1864 and later, a body of law for which Dr Boll as an official of the International Committee of the Red Cross had responsibility when he undertook the research and analysis underlying this important work.

Kenneth Keith
Wellington and The Hague
September 2006

Preface and Acknowledgements

This book is based on a thesis presented in 2003 at the University of Sydney for the degree of Doctor of Juridical Studies. The material has since been revised and updated. The author is indebted to his adviser, Professor Ivan Shearer, then Challis Professor of International Law at the University of Sydney Faculty of Law, now Professor Emeritus, for his invaluable guidance and insights in the preparation of this text.

The author's interest in multiple nationality, the development of related state practice, and the effects of this most interesting body of law, is the result of personal and family experience. Such experience includes various migrations across national boundaries in both trying and happy circumstances, and the treatment of family members as nationals or non-nationals by the governments involved. Such treatment led the author to question issues related to multiple nationality not only in personal terms, but more generally in relation to the respective rights, requirements and responsibilities of governments and the individuals whom they protect (or over whom they claim personal jurisdiction), or who seek protection from them. The author's previous employment, involving the implementation and dissemination of international humanitarian law, contributed to this interest by fostering an examination of ideas surrounding the relationship between the individual and the collective generally, and international legal systems of protection for the individual.

This study is not focused on questions surrounding the desirability of multiple nationality. It is neither the author's intention to argue that national legal orders directly or indirectly allowing for multiple nationality are inherently either a positive nor a negative thing, nor that states which attempt to discourage multiple nationality thereby deny individuals what might be considered human, or equal, rights. The tension between the rights of the individual and the requirements of the state is, however, inherent in the subject matter. Likewise, the study does not argue that states should adopt a particular stance toward multiple nationality. Rather, it presents a case that the existence of multiple nationality is not to be avoided, that multiple nationality has in practice become the norm rather than the exception, and that this in turn has particular and important consequences for international law and the nature of the relationship between states.

The author would like to thank his thesis examiners, Ryszard Piotrowicz, Professor of Law, University of Wales, Aberystwyth, and Andrew Byrnes, Professor of Law, University of New South Wales, Sydney, for their valuable comments. Thanks are likewise due to Terry Carney, Professor of Law at the University of Sydney, Christophe Swinarski, Visiting Professor of Law, Cardinal Stefan Wyszyński University, Warsaw, and Dr Cameron Spenceley, who read various parts of the text and whose suggestions were helpful and much appreciated. Professors Hilary Charlesworth and William Maley of the Australian National University, Canberra, and Dr Eduardo Valencia-Ospina also provided valuable suggestions. Various informal conversations with members of the consular and diplomatic corps, and various government officials, in different places over time also greatly assisted the author in understanding national policies and laws. The author also heard many personal and family histories that could not be included herein, which provided useful background information, as well as an important reminder of the human emotion and practical problems faced by individuals that underpin the subject matter.

Inspiration and enthusiasm come from many sources, including those important people in our lives who guide us, accompany us on our journey, and brighten our days. In this sense I wish to mention my parents John and Ruth Boll-Senn, Ernest and Ursula Strauss-Senn, Edward C. W. Lee, and José J. Alcaide Román. The tumultuous life experiences of my grandparents, Fritz and Auguste Boll-Rohrmüller, and my grandmother's sense of humanity and dedication to social justice, have informed my own views of the importance of systems of protection for the individual vis-à-vis the state, and nationality's importance and relevance. Lastly, I wish to honour Elisabeth Quiel, a single woman of modest means who as a hunchback faced social stigma, and whose life might otherwise remain unmentioned in the public domain. When her elderly Jewish (German) employer of several decades was expelled from her nursing home during the National Socialist regime, she did her best to visit her and continue to care for her, at considerable personal risk. Her example of bravery and dedication inspires the conviction that the individual can contribute to the common good through even the smallest act, and even in the direst of circumstances.

The author would also like to thank the staff at the various libraries where he conducted his research, in particular the Max-Planck-Institut für ausländisches öffentliches Recht und Völkerrecht (Heidelberg), as well as the Library of the University of Sydney Faculty of Law; the State Library of New South Wales; Bibliothèque de la Faculté de droit de l'Université de Genève; Bibliothèque de l'Institut universitaire de hautes études internationales, Genève; Biblioteca de la Facultad de Derecho de la Universidad Complutense (Madrid); the Library of the Victoria University of Wellington Law Faculty (New Zealand), the United Nations Library (Geneva), the Memorial and Law Libraries at the University of Wisconsin-Madison, and the Joseph Regenstein Library and D'Angelo Law Library at the University of Chicago.

The views expressed herein are of course the author's and do not necessarily represent those of his current employer the United States Department of State, or previous employer, the International Committee of the Red Cross.

Alfred Boll
Washington, May 2006

Chapter 1

The Context and Significance of Multiple Nationality

In 1926 Théodore Baty wrote a treatise entitled *La double-nationalité est-elle possible?*[1] The title suggests not only the enquiry to be undertaken, but the underlying notion, prevalent at the time, that dual or multiple nationality was an aberration to be avoided at worst, and eliminated at best.[2] Without seeking to belittle or minimise Baty's analysis or underlying premise, one of the ideas on which this study is based is that multiple nationality is not only possible, but a reality that affects millions of individuals world-wide, as well as their governments.[3]

---

[1] *Is dual nationality possible?* Théodore Baty, "La double nationalité est-elle possible?" *Revue de droit international et de législation comparée* (1926), vol. 7, 622–632. Baty argues that although *jus sanguinis* and *jus soli* are the two accepted bases for attribution of nationality, only the latter is a valid criterion in international law for a state to exercise diplomatic protection of an individual, and that in any case diplomatic protection cannot be exercised by a state solely on the basis of a jus sanguinis relationship.

[2] Bar-Yaacov states that "[i]t is a widely held opinion that dual nationality is an undesirable phenomenon detrimental both to the friendly relations between nations and the well-being of the individuals concerned". Nissim Bar-Yaacov, *Dual nationality* (London: Stevens & Sons Ltd., 1961), 4.

[3] Aleinikoff and Klusmeyer cite "tens of millions" of multiple nationals, including 25 percent of all Australians. T. Alexander Aleinikoff and Douglas Klusmeyer, "Plural nationality: facing the future in a migratory world," in *Citizenship today. Global perspectives and practices*, ed. T. Alexander Aleinikoff and Douglas Klusmeyer (Washington: Carnegie Endowment

Unless specified otherwise, the term "nationality" is used herein to signify the quality of the legal relationship between an individual and the state which regards him or her as its national, or such status of the individual, following the conventional terminology used in international law. It is to be regarded as wholly distinct from the meaning given to "nationality" when referring to members of a national or ethnic group, or people, unrelated to a state-subject of international law. The term "citizenship" is sometimes used as a synonym by commentators and in municipal legislation, but should be distinguished. The usage of these and other related terms is explained, compared and defined in detail in chapter two.

This book addresses not just "dual nationality" but any "multiple nationality", although the former category is certainly more representative as far as the number of persons it affects. An analysis of multiple nationality will allow for consideration of all issues related to dual nationals, while delineating the enquiry as far as the relevant issues in international law in the most appropriate and flexible sense.

The contention that states have always been opposed to the possession of more than one nationality by individuals, or that multiple nationality has invariably been seen as undesirable, is belied by historical evidence. Claims to personal jurisdiction over individuals through imposition of nationality, notwithstanding competing claims, have been relatively common since the emergence of the relationship or status of nationality in modern international law. Likewise, claims that the nature of nationality in international law calls for exclusivity are contradicted by past and present state practice. In current practice, states' policies and laws regulating nationality continue to produce instances of multiple nationality, and international and municipal efforts to avoid or eliminate it have been largely unsuccessful. Barring a concerted and comprehensive harmonisation of municipal laws regulating nationality with the specific aim of its elimination, the existence of multiple nationality would seem to be inevitable due to operation of national laws. Indeed, a general trend is observed indicating increasing acceptance of multiple nationality in national legislation, policies,

---

for International Peace, 2001), 63–88, 79. A 1976 report to the Australian Parliament states that "the large migration programme followed by Australia since the end of World War II has resulted in a large proportion of the 1,069,500 people granted Australian citizenship also being classified as dual nationals by virtue of the domestic legislation of their former homelands". Joint Committee on Foreign Affairs and Defence (Australia), "Dual nationality (report from the Joint Committee on Foreign Affairs and Defence)", (Canberra: Parliament of Australia, 1976), 18. It is difficult to judge the accuracy of statistics, or to obtain information on the number of multiple nationals in relation to most countries. Even national governments find it difficult to ascertain how many of their nationals possess the nationality of another country, especially in countries where renunciation of a previous nationality is not a condition of naturalisation. "It would not be possible or viable for the Home Office to collect information on the number of United Kingdom citizens with dual nationality as part of the process of applying for citizenship, since it would not be possible to determine the number of persons who renounced or retained their previous nationality". Reply of Angela Eagle to Mr Gordon Prentice, United Kingdom Parliament (internet), http://www.parliament.the-stationery-office.co.uk/pa/cm200102/cmhansrd/vo011203/text/11203w29.htm, consulted on 17 January 2003.

and treaty obligations. The development of national and international human rights norms and law has also influenced this area of the law.

The implications of this increasingly common phenomenon are important for states, in terms of how they manage their bilateral and multi-lateral legal relations. Specifically, the consequences of state practice toward multiple nationality on the international plane bear on the principles of international law that govern nationality, and the essence of nationality itself in international law. The issues raised are equally important for individuals. Rather than concentrating their efforts on eliminating or encouraging multiple nationality, it behoves governments to understand its nature and consequences on the international level in context, and to manage their relations bearing this reality in mind. Along these lines, although the subject is taken up in chapter four, this study does not concentrate on the question of whether multiple nationality is a good or a bad thing for states or individuals, but on the consequences in international law of what is a reality.

This book examines current state practice toward multiple nationality, and draws conclusions about the effects in international public law of that practice. It attempts to take changes in state practice over time into account, and provides an historical overview of attitudes toward multiple nationality. This study does not concern itself with the effects of state practice on "private international law", also known as conflicts of law.[4]

The appendix on state practice covers 75 countries. The basis for the conclusions in chapters five and six is an examination of national legislation and policy regarding multiple nationality that takes 45 of these states and territories into account, constituting a representative sample of states. This is expanded upon below. Although it might be tempting to regard it as such, the enquiry is not one involving the discipline of comparative law per se. The author's aim is not to compare states' practices with regard to multiple nationality or in terms of their systems of law, but to examine whether general trends can be observed in state practice as a whole, and to draw conclusions about the effects of such practice in international law. Nevertheless, the very nature of examining the same criteria within a group of similarly placed subjects would on its face seem to be a comparative one, and comparative legal scholarship and ideas are instructive, and have been taken into account.

This study seeks to delineate the effects of state practice in light of *opinio juris* in terms of the rules of international law related to nationality, opinion which is far from uniform, and thereby discern the value, significance and nature of nationality, as well as its consequences, on the international plane. In this sense, it separates the legal consequences of nationality on the international and municipal planes, and presents

---

[4] For a treatise on multiple nationality and conflicts of law, see Rainer Hausmann, "Doppelte Staatsbürgerschaft für Ausländer: Auswirkungen im Internationalen Privat- und Verfahrensrecht", paper presented at the Hohenheimer Tage zum Ausländerrecht 1999 und 5. Migrationspolitisches Forum, Klaus Barwig, G. Brinkmann, K. Hailbronner, B. Huber, C. Kreuzer, K. Lörcher, C. Schuhmacher eds., (Hohenheim: Nomos Verlagsgesellschaft, 1999), 163–188.

arguments related to the nature of obligations of loyalty and the nature of allegiance on both the municipal and international planes, as well as the rights of citizenship in relation to nationality.

A. MULTIPLE NATIONALITY AND EMOTION

The analysis of state practice toward multiple nationality in chapters five and six is not centered around arguments as to what states' policies toward multiple nationality should or should not be. The analysis of state practice and its effects in international law attempts to avoid completely arguments surrounding issues that contain an element of emotion such as national identity, appropriate levels of immigration, and the determination of the national interest in terms of the politics of nationality, citizenship and immigration.[5]

Nevertheless, it cannot be ignored that it is exactly such issues with "emotional" in addition to "practical" content that seem to be the pivotal questions for many when dealing with the topic of multiple nationality. This is because nationality is itself intimately bound-up with individual and collective identity, and the social consequences of group membership, in addition to its political, economic and other consequences. Thus in addition to what may be labelled objective or quantifiable considerations in

---

[5] These are highly emotive issues with important ramifications. For example, the International Organisation for Migration estimated that remittances from the 175 million emigrants spread around the world to their home countries could amount to €243 Billion in 2004. "Remessas mundiais de emigrantes podem atingir 243 mil milhões de euros", Lusa: Agência de Notícias de Portugal, 2004 (internet), www.lusa.pt/print.asp?id=SIR-6189151 consulted 14 July 2004. There is a plethora of views regarding state and individual interests in relation to the movement of people, which are influenced by "emotional" and other factors. Noting the dire straits that propel people to move from developing to developed countries, the economic need for such workers in the developed world, as well as increasing hostility to immigration, *The Economist* argues that migration must be carefully managed so that voters see it is in their interest. The magazine's editors propose a common labour market for the developed world, and that as far as migration from "poor" countries is concerned, that preference be given to people from culturally similar backgrounds. "Race and religion must be a part of the public discussion of migration. To pretend that they do not affect attitudes makes policy more restrictive than it should be". "Opening the door. Whom to let in to the richer countries and why", *The Economist*, 2 November 2002, 11. Others contend that migration constitutes a brain drain that damages the poorest countries. Celia W. Dugger, "'Brain drain' is damaging world's poorest countries, study shows", *International Herald Tribune*, 26 October 2005, 3. The United Nations Global Commission on International Migration, established to debate and consider the ramifications of international migration and policy issued a report in 2005 to serve as a guide for the formulation of migration policies. United Nations. Global Commission on International Migration, Report, October 2005 (internet), http://www.gcim.org/en/finalreport.html consulted on 1 March 2006.

relation to the ingredients and consequences of nationality, there is undoubtedly an element of human emotion linked to group membership, centred around ideas and feelings of inclusion and exclusion, which is subjective and hardly quantifiable. Such emotion may have influenced the decision of Denmark's Prince Henrik's "to head home to France to 'reflect on life' after 30 years as prince consort . . . 35 years after he gave up his nationality, his religion, his language – and even changed his name from Henri to Henrik to marry Queen Margrethe II" after a perceived snub that he said "was a sign of the Danes' unwillingness to accept him as one of their own".[6]

Many of the individual and collective interests related to nationality might in fact be characterised as possessing both objective and subjective elements: at least one of the consequences of nationality (at least what appears upon first reflection – dealt with in chapter three – to be a consequence of nationality), namely loyalty, is clearly not just a legal standard; it is an emotional one as well.[7]

The subject of multiple nationality thus raises the issue of whether, notwithstanding any relevant legal classification, an individual can, or should be considered as

---

[6] Agence France Presse, "Royal cheesed off in Danish blue," *The Australian*, 7 February 2002, 7.

[7] Justice Gaudron of the High Court of Australia, in describing the situation of elected Member of the Australian Parliament Mrs Hill as a dual British and Australian national, stated "[h]owever, it does appear that Mrs Hill understood that, at all relevant times from the grant of citizenship, her sole loyalty was to Australia". *Sue v Hill and Another*, (1999) 163 ALR 648, 677. Referring to Mrs Hill's "understanding" may indicate a feeling held subjectively, but the statement taken overall might also be interpreted to indicate that the judge regarded Mrs Hill's naturalisation as establishing a legal standard whereby Mrs Hill's "sole loyalty" *should* be to Australia. In either case the comment is *obiter dicta*. There is no question however, that Mrs Hill's naturalisation in Australia did not terminate her British nationality. If loyalty is a consequence of nationality, Justice Gaudron's statement may indicate the Court's view of Mrs Hill's obligations as an Australian, but this is not to say that the United Kingdom might not equally hold Mrs Hill to an obligation of loyalty as a consequence of nationality. Ideas of allegiance and an obligation of loyalty as a consequence of nationality are discussed in chapter three. The author's view that loyalty is best conceived of as a consequence of nationality under municipal law as opposed to international law has previously been published in Alfred Boll, "Nationality and obligations of loyalty in international and municipal law", The Australian Year Book of International Law (2004), vol. 24, 37–63. The plea made by *Miss World 2002*, Azra Akin, a national of Turkey who grew up in Denmark, in favour of Turkey's inclusion not only in the European Union, but in a European identity, might reflect loyalty to her country of nationality, or perhaps it evidences a personal identity that has successfully bridged or combined national identities. See Elaine Sciolino, "Visions of a Union: Europe Gropes for an Identity", *The New York Times*, 15 December 2002, 11. Opposition to migration and membership in society often involves a perceived threat to the group. The value of expressions of group identity, and participation in such expression, should not be underestimated. One supporter of the murdered Dutch politician, Pim Fortuyn, who favoured an end to immigration to the Netherlands stated, "people feel they are losing their own identity, . . . these [Muslims] are people who don't sing along with the national anthem". Peter Fray, "The new infidels", *The Sydney Morning Herald*, 11–12 May 2002, 36.

belonging to (and beholden to), more than one state on the plane of emotion and identity. There are of course countless examples from all walks of life and areas of the law about how people have been included in or excluded from society generally, or from smaller groups, and the reasons for those decisions and the interests behind them. But the desire to delineate clearly groups and their members would seem to be a common one, as is advocacy for exclusivity as far as group membership.[8] On the other hand, it is not uncommon for individuals to wish to hide membership in a group based on its treatment in wider society.[9]

In terms of multiple nationality, its acceptance or incorporation into the legal order might be said to reflect a view of general inclusiveness, whereas its rejection seems to be a sign of exclusivity, whatever the underlying reason. Chapter four provides an outline of views and treatment of multiple nationality advocating both exclusivity, and inclusiveness in the field of nationality, ostensibly based on objective criteria. On the plane of emotion, or in terms of the "emotional" component to such views, the reasoning behind exclusivity might in part reflect a perception that as individuals derive benefits from nationality, it is unfair for the same person to receive more than the normal benefit, an idea perhaps akin to jealousy.[10] Of course benefit or special

---

[8] Deciding who should be included in a particular group is a common area of controversy, especially when the criteria for delimitation are unclear or involve multiple membership. One example is the participation of transgender athletes in the *Sydney 2002 Gay Games*, where a person who underwent surgery to become a woman was allowed to play on both the men's and the women's teams, amid controversy "about who[m] they should be competing against". Louise Perry, "Mixed feelings on player hitting for both sides," *The Australian*, 5 November 2002, 5.

[9] This was or is the case for many Australians with Aboriginal ancestry. See Leisa Scott, "Dark secrets, white lies," *The Weekend Australian Magazine*, 2 March 2002. Likewise in the USA, the number of Native Americans counted in census figures between 1990 and 2000 increased by at least 26%. As birth rates cannot account for this figure, it must be due in great part to increased self-identification by individuals, perhaps related to greater acceptance of Native Americans in wider society. See United States Census Bureau. "Difference in population by race and hispanic or latino origin for the US: 1990 and 2000", 2004 (internet), http://www.census.gov/population/cen2000/phc-t1/tab04.pdf, consulted 1 March 2006.

[10] Keskin argues that that such arguments have been central to German opposition to multiple nationality. "Ähnlich wird bei der Auseinandersetzung um die Doppelstaatsbürgerschaft argumentiert, die Einwanderer würden hierdurch privilegiert, weil sie sowohl im Einwanderungs' als auch im Herkunftsland staatsbürgerliche Rechte erlangen würden". Hakkı Keskin, "Staatsbürgerschaft im Exil", paper presented at the conference: Doppelte Staatsbürgerschaft – ein europäischer Normalfall?, (Berlin: Senatsverwaltung für Gesundheit und Soziales, 1989), 43–54, 43. (Author's translation: *Similarly it is argued in relation to multiple nationality that immigrants would thereby be privileged, as they would have the rights of citizenship in both the country to which they immigrated as well as in their country of origin.*) García Moreno links traditional Mexican opposition to multiple nationality to nationalism, while not specifically labelling the related concerns practical or emotional. "El derecho positivo mexicano no es ajeno a dicha consideración negativista acerca de la doble nacionalidad, siendo explicable el

treatment may be the result of a foreign link unconnected to multiple nationality as such.[11]

The world of professional sporting does seem to provide many examples of athletes whose relationship to their nationality, or nationalities, evinces an attitude directed at enhancing their careers as opposed to emotional considerations.

> *There are countless examples of players changing nationalities whether for lifestyle, political or career purposes. Monica Seles won Wimbledon as a Yugoslavian but now plays as an American. Greg Rusedski was born in Montreal and only took out British citizenship at the age of 22. Martina Navratilova won her first grand slams as a Czech, yet at the age of 44 is still playing occasional doubles tournaments as an American. Mary Pierce considers herself French despite growing up in Canada and residing in Florida. Mark Philippoussis spent more time in Florida than in his native Melbourne, while Pat Rafter has for many years listed Bermuda as his residence for tax reasons. . . . In logistical terms, it will be a relatively seamless transition for Jelena Dokic of Australia to become Jelena Dokic of Yugoslavia.[12]*

---

nacionalismo que permea a toda la legislación, resultado de duras y dolorosas experiencias históricas". Víctor Carlos García Moreno, "La propuesta sobre doble nacionalidad", paper presented at the conference: La doble nacionalidad (Ciudad de México: Miguel Ángel Porrúa Librero-Editor, 1995), 173–181, 175. (Author's translation: *Mexican law is not free from said negativist consideration in relation to dual nationality, which is explained by the nationalism that permeates all (Mexican) legislation, which is the result of difficult and painful historical experience.*)

[11] An example is the long delay in extradition proceedings when "disgraced Mexican pop idol Gloria Trevi" was extradited from Brazil to Mexico "to face charges of kidnapping young girls and forcing them into sex with her manager . . . Brazil's Supreme Court authorised extradition . . . in December 2000. Five months later, Trevi became pregnant – a fact used by her lawyers to keep her in Brazil, which traditionally refuses to send home foreigners with Brazilian-born children". Richard Boudreaux, "Fallen rock star flies home to face the music in sex scandal", *The Sydney Morning Herald*, 23 December 2002, 7. It was not any possible multiple nationality of Trevi's child that delayed her extradition, but its Brazilian nationality as such, from which she derived a direct benefit. Another example is benefits derived from a spouse's nationality, without necessarily involving multiple nationality. For example, Semyon Yukovich Mogilevich, a reputed underworld figure who reportedly acquired Israeli nationality as a Jewish emigrant from Russia, subsequently migrated to Hungary by marrying a Hungarian national, frustrating law enforcement authorities. Michael Binyon, "Mob boss outsmarted KGB, ripped off Jews. The Mr Biggest of the Moscow underworld has had a chequered career", *The Australian*, 24 August 1999, 12.

[12] Chip Le Grand, "Pragmatism takes hold in nationality stakes. Adopting a new country is a common occurrence in world tennis", *The Weekend Australian*, 20–21 January 2001, 34. It is to be assumed that many of the changes in nationality referred to actually involve the acquisition of another nationality without losing the prior one, resulting in the multiple nationality of the sportsman or sportswoman. The poaching of athletes by countries is also common. *The Economist* claimed that "Stephen Cherono, a Kenyan runner, is, for example, said to have been promised $1,000 a month for life to become a Qatari named Saif Saeed Shaheen. Rich countries are not the only buyers. A Cuban-born triple jumper, Yamile Aldama, was prevented from

The emotional component to an obligation of loyalty has already been mentioned: if nationals owe other members of the group (as yet unspecified) duties, how can these be performed if similar duties are owed to another collective?[13] Similarly, emotion and attachment clearly play a role in the individual confronted with a choice of nationality.[14]

Turning to states whose policies toward multiple nationality might be said to reflect inclusiveness, such policies might also reflect the effects of subjective identity and

---

competing for Britain because she could not get British citizenship in time, though she lives in London. So Ms Aldama went to Khartoum to become Sudanese in two days". "For a wreath, a flag – or cash?", *The Economist*, 14 August 2004, 23.

[13] In terms of emotion, Keskin argues that "[i]nnere Bindungen und Loyalitäten gegenüber dem Staat und der Gesellschaft können nicht per Gesetz verordnet werden. Sie sind vielmehr das Ergebnis eines gleichberechtigten und akzeptierten Lebens in einer Gesellschaft von Mehrheit und Minderheiten". Keskin, "Staatsbürgerschaft im Exil", 52. (Author's translation: *Inner ties and loyalty to the state and society cannot be decreed by law. Rather, they are the result of equal rights and acceptance in life within a society made up of the majority and minorities.*) Ideas of loyalty as a consequence of nationality are increasingly being discussed in the framework of human rights, such as in courses at the University of Chicago. "Multiple nationality is not just cultural. . . . It's a new way of looking at nationality and citizenship, calling into question the traditional position that a citizen's loyalty cannot be shared". "Human-rights course offers a close look at worldwide violations", *University of Chicago Magazine*, December 1998, 8–9, 9.

[14] "Das Haupthindernis bei der Annahme der deutschen Staatsbürgerschaft, ist ohne Zweifel die erzwungene Ablösung von der Staatsangehörigkeit des Herkunftslandes. . . . Der Einbürgerungswillige befürchtet also, trotz Verlustes seiner emotionalen Bindungen, bei Verzicht auf seine ehemalige Staatsbürgerschaft eine fehlende Akzeptanz in der neuen Heimat und Gesellschaft. Er hat Angst, in diesem Falle nichts mehr zu besitzen, keinen Boden mehr unter seinen Füssen zu haben. Er befürchtet, dass er von seinen Verwandten und ehemaligen Freunden, die in der Tradition der Mittelmeerländer trotz langjähriger Trennung nicht verloren gehen, nicht verstanden zu werden". Keskin, "Staatsbürgerschaft im Exil", 48. (Author's translation: *The main obstacle to the adoption of German citizenship is without a doubt the forced detachment from the citizenship of the country of origin . . . The individual ready to seek naturalisation fears, in spite of [in addition to, sic.] the loss of his emotional ties, a lack of acceptance in his new home and society upon renunciation of the former nationality. He is afraid in this situation of not possessing anything anymore, of being out of his depth. He is afraid of not being understood by his relatives and former friends, who, as is the case in Mediterranean countries, are still friends notwithstanding the long period of separation.*) In 2005 the German Foreign Minister requested lists of Turkish citizens resident in Germany who had applied for Turkish passports, referring to a "bad situation" should dual nationality encumber electoral results. "Dupla cidadania complica relações entre Ancara e Berlim", *Público* (Lisboa), 13 April 2005, 17. García Moreno also attributed the traditional reticence of Mexicans to become naturalised in the United States to both emotional and practical reasons: "por razones personales, o afectivas y debido a que algunos de ellos poseen propiedades". García Moreno, "La propuesta sobre doble nacionalidad", 177. (Author's translation: *for personal or emotional reasons, and due to the fact that some of them own property.*) Mexico thereafter changed its nationality law such that naturalisation abroad does not provoke a loss of Mexican nationality.

emotion.[15] They are certainly influenced, and in some cases dictated by, ideas of human rights, a topic that is taken up in chapter four. But why does one state's national identity seem to incorporate a notion of exclusiveness akin to "if you're one of them you can't be one of us", while another's posits, "you're one of us, regardless if you're one of them"? One may enquire why states adopt a particular attitude, but the question of which position it is in states' best interest to adopt is perhaps even more important in terms of policy.[16]

It would seem that in any case states are increasingly sensitive to any intimation that policies excluding multiple nationality amount to a denial of human rights. The Turkish ambassador to the United Nations in Geneva was quick to contradict a sentence in the report submitted by the United Nations' Special Rapporteur on contemporary forms of racism, racial discrimination, xenophobia and related intolerance, which stated that Turkish nationality law did "not allow dual nationality". Turkey requested that its letter be "circulated as an official document of the current session of the Commission on Human Rights".[17]

Rather than concentrating on whether multiple nationality is desirable or not, this book seeks to put such arguments into the context of international law and the reality of state practice. In the author's opinion questions of the desirability of multiple nationality largely miss the point: multiple nationality is a reality that must be dealt with as such.[18]

---

[15] Such as the notion of *Auslandschweizer* or "Swiss Abroad" which indicates emotional and political recognition of emigrants' place in the home country. The sentiment expressed in this sense matches Swiss legal practice, which accepts and incorporates multiple nationality to a great extent.

[16] It is tempting to reflect on the ideas of the German sociologist Ferdinand Tönnies related to what he termed "Gemeinschaft", or community, and "Gesellschaft", or society, the former being closer to family relations, whereas the latter can approximate the state, and how interrelated groups determine or manage their respective interests as they overlap or come together. See generally Ferdinand Tönnies, *Community and civil society*, ed. José Harris, trans. José Harris and Margaret Hollis (Cambridge: Cambridge University Press, 2001).

[17] Economic and Social Council United Nations, Commission on Human Rights, "Letter dated 25 March 1996 from the Permanent Representative of Turkey to the United Nations Office at Geneva addressed to the Chairman of the Commission on Human Rights", E/CN.4/1996/153, (Geneva: United Nations, 9 April 1996).

[18] While it might be argued that the author's starting point, which essentially constitutes an assumption that multiple nationality is inevitable, or its elimination highly improbably, amounts to a position that is favourable to multiple nationality, this is not the case. The assumption itself is tested in the survey of state practice, which is also structured so as to discern certain nuances in the acceptance or rejection of multiple nationality. Hansen and Weil cite arguments surrounding the inevitability of multiple nationality as being "in favour" of multiple nationality. Randall Hansen and Patrick Weil, "Introduction. Dual citizenship in a changed world: immigration, gender and social rights", in *Dual nationality, social rights and federal citizenship in the U.S. and Europe. The reinvention of citizenship*, ed. Randall Hansen and Patrick Weil (New York: Berghahn Books, 2002), 9.

B. THE SIGNIFICANCE OF NATIONALITY

This book seeks to build on existing studies of dual or multiple nationality and related treatises on nationality itself. It is the author's belief that some areas of disagreement with such works can often be related to the justified question, *'why should we care?'* as well as to specific developments in international law.

The most common point of departure for studies of multiple nationality has concentrated on the interests of the states affected, as opposed to those of the individual. In his significant work on dual nationality published in 1961, Nissim Bar-Yaacov introduces his subject as follows:

> *Nationality is a legal and political tie which binds individuals to a State and renders them subject to its personal jurisdiction. The present meaning of nationality is associated with the establishment of sovereign States, and denotes the sum of obligations – or allegiance – which an individual owes to a State.*[19]

This statement (it is taken up again in the conclusions herein) approaches the subject matter in terms of what the State demands of its nationals, rather than what the individual may demand of the State as a consequence of the link of nationality. Similarly in terms of multiple nationality, when individuals' interests have been considered, they have been seen in terms of the problems caused by more than one state attributing its nationality to the individual, rather than the benefits derived from it. Military service is an oft-cited example. These issues are dealt with in the following chapters. More recently, however, scholars have concentrated on the issue of multiple nationality both in terms of state interests as well as those of the individual with a relationship to a particular state.

As the analysis of state practice herein does not concentrate on what state policy toward multiple nationality should be, but on what current practice is and its consequences in international law, contemplating the wider issues beyond the scope of the questions posed seems unnecessary, even inadvisable. It is submitted however, that adopting the notion that both states and individuals have interests in multiple nationality as a conceptual point of departure may have a direct bearing on the conclusions to be drawn about the effects of state practice. This should be clearly exposed at the outset. It is the author's view that this starting point is unavoidable. It is a consequence of the developments in international law regarding the individual's relationship to his or her own state, and to the state generally, over the past fifty or so years, since the Universal Declaration of Human Rights. This is, however, not necessarily to argue that individuals have per se become subjects of international law.[20] Never-

---

[19] Bar-Yaacov, *Dual nationality*, 1.

[20] Brownlie argues that "[t]here is no general rule that the individual cannot be a 'subject of international law', and in particular contexts he appears as a legal person on the international plane. At the same time to classify the individual as a 'subject' of the law is unhelpful, since this may seem to imply the existence of capacities which do not exist and does not avoid the

theless, commentators would generally seem to agree that the traditional exclusion of the individual from the sphere of international law entirely is no longer tenable. Already in 1950 Sir Hersch Lauterpacht wrote that

> *The claim of the State to unqualified exclusiveness in the field of international relations was tolerable at a time when the actuality and the interdependence of the interests of the individual cutting across national frontiers were less obvious than they are today. It is this latter fact which explains why the constant expansion of the periphery of individual rights – an enduring feature of legal development – cannot stop short of the limits of the State. What is much more important, the recognition of the individual, by dint of the acknowledgment of his fundamental rights and freedoms, as the ultimate subject of international law, is a challenge to the doctrine which in reserving that quality exclusively to the State tends to a personification of the State as being distinct from the individuals who compose it, with all that such personification implies. . . . International law, which has excelled in punctilious insistence on the respect owed by one sovereign State to another, henceforth acknowledges the sovereignty of man. For fundamental human rights are rights superior to the law of the sovereign state.*[21]

Multiple nationality affects both states and individuals in important ways and has consequences for both. It goes to the heart of questions surrounding the relationship of the individual to the state, the traditional notion of states' power over individuals and their right (or obligation) to represent their nationals' interests, as well as all the rights, privileges and duties ascribed to nationality by states. A grant of nationality, or its denial (for example to be deprived of one's nationality on the basis of the avoidance of multiple nationality) has important practical as well as emotional consequences for the individual. In this sense multiple nationality is important not only because it brings together issues of states' and individuals' interests, but because the issue of nationality is itself such an important one. The link between the state and

---

task of distinguishing between the individual and other types of subject." Ian Brownlie, *Principles of public international law*, Fifth ed. (Oxford: Clarendon Press, 1998), 66. "He probably is in particular contexts, although some would say that this is true only when he has true procedural capacity." Brownlie, *Principles of public international law*, 605. Shaw, however, cites the "ultimate concern for the human being" as the "essence of international law", remarking that 19th century positivist theories "obscured this and emphasised the centrality and even exclusivity of the state in this regard. Nevertheless, modern practice does demonstrate that individuals have become increasingly recognised as participants and subjects of international law. This has occurred primarily but not exclusively through human rights law." Malcolm N. Shaw, *International law*, Fourth ed. (Cambridge: Cambridge University Press, 1997), 183. In his synthesis of the development of the individual's position in international law, Cassese maintains that while "individuals possess a limited locus standi in international law" as well as "a limited legal capacity" they nevertheless possess international legal status. Antonio Cassese, *International law* (Oxford: Oxford University Press, 2001), 85.

[21] Hersch Lauterpacht, *International law and human rights* (London: Stevens, 1950), quoted in Henry J. Steiner and Philip Alston, *International human rights in context – law politics morals*, Second ed. (Oxford: Oxford University Press, 2000), 147.

the individual that is defined by nationality is still a supreme one, if perhaps no longer an all-encompassing one.

Returning to the question posed by Baty cited at the outset of this chapter (*is dual nationality possible?*), his answer also largely depicts the importance of the individual's relationship to the state only in terms of state to state relations, rather than the broader context of the rights and emotions associated with a relationship of nationality. For the world of international law and relations in 1926, the question and analysis was neither naïve nor arrogant. It did not perceive that there might be other issues involved. For the world of 2006, his view of the importance of multiple nationality in terms only of state interests (leaving Baty's legal interpretation aside) seems barely to scratch the surface of the issues raised, or at least to dismiss other issues such as rights and relationships too quickly.

The spirit underlying Baty's argument (that nationality is not – or should not be – important to the individual) however, is not without supporters today, albeit with a diametrically opposed focal point. While not arguing that nationality is unimportant, Schnapper claims that its value in the European Union is diminished by the divorce of what is usually seen as among the consequences of nationality, the participation in local, national, and supranational political and economic life, from the status itself, accompanied by the creation of a supra-national identity.[22] While Baty seemed to ignore the individual, Schnapper seems ready to write-off the state, at least in the context of the European Union. Such arguments might be compared to or associated with arguments that the state as an entity is in decline (an argument not made herein).[23]

Weil and Hansen reject Schnapper's arguments (espoused, they say, in sociological circles) that the extension of economic and social rights to legal permanent residents in the European Union reduces the value of nationality, and that trans-national migration is weakening the legal link between individual and state.[24] They point out that although permanent residents in many countries benefit from rights normally accorded to citizens, these vary greatly from state to state and can be changed at will. The status is thus ill-suited to espousing rights against the state based on the relationship itself. In affirming that the status of citizenship (nationality) is the nexus between the individual and the collective in the form of the state, they point out that the very fact that certain citizens may be deprived of certain rights does not diminish the value of citizenship itself, in fact, it emphasises its importance.[25] These ideas are discussed in the following chapter.

---

[22] Dominique Schnapper, *Qu'est-ce que la citoyenneté?* (Paris: Gallimard, 2000), 246–61.

[23] See generally, Martin van Creveld, *The rise and decline of the State* (Cambridge: Cambridge University Press, 1999).

[24] Patrick Weil and Randall Hansen, "Citoyenneté, immigration et nationalité: vers la convergence européenne," in *Nationalité et citoyenneté en Europe*, ed. Patrick Weil and Randall Hansen, *Collection "Recherches"* (Paris: Éditions La Découverte, 1999), 9–28, 10.

[25] Ibid.

C. MULTIPLE NATIONALITY IN INTERNATIONAL LAW

In addition to its value in terms of the relationship between the individual and the state, it is clear that the status or relationship of nationality has an important place in, and ramifications for, the law of nations. Nationality is one of the fundamental bases upon which states found their standing vis-à-vis other states on the plane of international law.

It has been stated that international law in respect of nationality is in many respects uncertain. Brownlie says that the lack of criteria in international law regarding nationality produces a "structural defect . . . in certain types of doctrine concerning nationality".[26] Chapter three will expand on these issues. The International Court of Justice defined nationality in the *Nottebohm* case as

> . . . *a legal bond having as its basis a social fact of attachment, a genuine connection of existence, interests and sentiments, together with the existence of reciprocal rights and duties. It may be said to constitute the juridical expression of the fact that the individual upon whom it is conferred, either directly by the law or as the result of an act of the authorities, is in fact more closely connected with the population of the State conferring nationality than with that of any other State.*[27]

The Court made this statement after restating the rule that it is up to "each sovereign State, to settle by its own legislation the rules relating to the acquisition of its nationality".[28] The Court declined to address whether "international law imposes any limitations on [the state's] freedom of decision in this domain".[29] It stated that whether nationality is effective vis-à-vis other states in international law, however, is a completely separate question. One aim of the survey of state practice herein is to examine the extent to which the ICJ's definition of nationality is challenged or reinforced by the current practice of states in terms of multiple nationality. If effective nationality on the international plane means that an individual is more closely connected to one state than to any other, what about a world in which individuals increasingly have legal ties to more than one state, such legal status being built into national legislation and policy?

---

[26] Brownlie, *Principles of public international law*, 69.

[27] *Nottebohm Case (second phase), Judgment of April 6th, 1955*, I.C.J. Reports (1955) 4, 23. Randelzhofer does not consider that the ICJ in fact intended this to be a general definition of nationality, and says it is limited to the issue of "diplomatic protection in the particular case of conferrment of nationality by naturalization". Albrecht Randelzhofer, "Nationality", in *Encyclopedia of Public International Law*, ed. Rudolf Bernhardt and Max Planck Institute for Comparative Public Law and International Law, vol. 8, (Amsterdam: Elsevier, 1985), 416–424, 421. Most authors however do cite it as a general definition.

[28] *Nottebohm Case (second phase), Judgment of April 6th, 1955*, 20.

[29] Ibid.

Aside from prompting us to enquire about the definition of nationality at international law, state practice toward multiple nationality also raises issues of subjective judgment as far as recognising a claim of nationality at international law. In declining to allow Liechtenstein to protect its national Mr Nottebohm against Guatemala, the state of his long-term residence, the Court had posed the following question:

> At the time of his naturalization does Nottebohm appear to have been more closely attached by his tradition, his establishment, his interests, his activities, his family ties, his intentions for the near future to Liechtenstein than to any other State? . . . Naturalization is not a matter to be taken lightly. To seek and to obtain it is not something that happens frequently in the life of a human being. It involves his breaking of a bond of allegiance and his establishment of a new bond of allegiance.[30]

Yet if naturalisation does not in fact involve breaking a bond of allegiance, either from the standpoint of the state of original nationality or that of the state whose nationality is acquired, does it not give rise to questions as to the nature of the act and the quality of the relationships involved? This is discussed in chapter three.

Lastly, the final two chapters herein address the issue the Court declined to take-up in *Nottebohm*, whether international law itself imposes limits on states' regulation of nationality, through the examination of state practice vis-à-vis multiple nationality.[31]

D. SOVEREIGNTY AND THE NATURE OF THE STATE

In addition to raising the question as to the development of general principles of law in the area of nationality, state practice related to multiple nationality arguably raises fundamental questions regarding state sovereignty and the equality of states, and perhaps even regarding the nature of the state itself.[32]

The generally accepted legal criteria for statehood are found in Article 1 of the Montevideo Convention on Rights and Duties of States:[33]

> The State as a person of international law should possess the following qualifications: (a) a permanent population; (b) a defined territory; (c) government; and (d) capacity to enter into relations with the other states.[34]

---

[30] Id., 24.

[31] The question whether international law imposes limits on states' regulation of nationality is the subject of the comprehensive work by Donner. Ruth Donner, *The regulation of nationality in international law*, 2nd ed. (Irvington-on-Hudson (USA): Transnational Publishers Inc., 1994).

[32] Brownlie remarks that issues related to the sovereignty and equality of states are incidents of statehood rather than being related to the origins and continuity of statehood. Brownlie, *Principles of public international law*, 70.

[33] See Id., 69.

[34] Convention on Rights and Duties of States, Seventh International Conference of American States, Montevideo, Uruguay, 26 December 1933 (entered into force: 26 December 1934).

Although some writers take issue with this expression of conditions,[35] for our purposes here we are only concerned with the first criterion, namely that of a permanent population. Whereas borders define territory, nationality would seem to be the most obvious criterion as far as defining a state's permanent population. Some authors seem to support this idea:

> *Nationality rests with territory at the heart of the definition of the nation-state. If territory determines the geographical limits of state sovereignty, nationality determines its population. Beyond these limits one finds foreign land, foreign sovereignty, and foreigners.*[36]

and

> *The State population is the most important element of the notion of the State, because territory and government must serve the welfare of the population. The State itself is an organization whose primary task is to support human beings. Membership in the State population is determined by domestic laws on nationality, international law leaves it to the discretion of every State to define the nature of nationality.*[37]

Crawford disagrees, stating

> *The rule under discussion requires States to have a permanent population: it is not a rule relating to the nationality of that population. It appears that the grant of nationality is a*

---

[35] Brownlie notes that "it is not more than a basis for further investigation. As will be seen, not all the conditions are peremptory, and in many case further criteria must be employed to produce a working legal definition of statehood". Brownlie, *Principles of public international law*, 70.

[36] Patrick Weil, "Access to citizenship: a comparison of twenty-five nationality laws," in *Citizenship today. Global perspectives and practices*, ed. T. Alexander Aleinikoff and Douglas Klusmeyer (Washington: Carnegie Endowment for International Peace, 2001), 17–35, 17.

[37] Rudolf Bernhardt, ed., *Encyclopedia of public international law*, vol. 4 (Amsterdam: Elsevier, 2000), 601. Other general statements support the idea that a state's population is more than just the persons present on a specified territory, but linked to laws and the structure and purpose of society. In this regard, under "Idea of the State", a well-known manual of international law terminology states, "[t]he population of a State consists of one or several nations i.e. stable human groups bound together not for any special purpose like an economic or professional organisation, but for all purposes hence the State is called civitas perfecta – community of people living under the same laws". Isaac Paenson, *Manual of the terminology of public international law (law of peace) and international organizations* (Brussels: Bruylant, 1983), 54. Vattel also links the nature of the State to the act of political (and perhaps legal) association: "When men, by the act of associating together, form a State or Nation, each individual agrees to procure the common good of all, and all together agree to assist each in obtaining the means of providing for his needs and to protect and defend him. It is clear that these reciprocal agreements can only be fulfilled by maintaining the political association. The whole Nation is therefore bound to maintain it; and since its maintenance constitutes the self-preservation of a Nation, it follows that every Nation is bound to preserve its corporate existence". Emmerich de Vattel, *The law of nations or the principles of natural law applied to the conduct and to the affairs of nations and of sovereigns*, trans. Charles G. Fenwick, 1758 ed., vol. 3 (Washington: The Carnegie Institution of Washington, 1916), 13.

matter which only States by their municipal law (or by way of treaty) can perform.
Nationality is thus dependent upon statehood, not the reverse.[38]

He points to the fact that persons can be considered nationals of a state for the purposes of international law under the doctrine of the effective link, even if they do not possess nationality under a state's municipal laws. Is it possible that state practice toward multiple nationality, by raising questions related to the doctrine of the effective link, may thus also influence views of the condition or status of the state's population in terms of the essence of the state itself?[39]

In addition to prompting reflection as to the nature of the state in terms of its population, multiple nationality raises issues as to the power, and obligations, of the state vis-à-vis other states. Donner states that

---

[38] James Crawford, *The Creation of States in International Law* (Oxford: Clarendon Press, 1979), 40.

[39] Arguments supporting Crawford's view might be discerned from the situation of the Vatican City State, which may in fact constitute a particularly apt example, as the constitution of its population is unique, yet there is no question as to the existence of the state as far as its treatment as such by other states. De La Brière argues that the Vatican possesses a territory, a population, exclusive jurisdiction over its population, legislative, judicial and executive power, an armed force to ensure public order, telecommunications' autonomy, and its own currency, the distinctive elements by which a state is recognised. Labelling the state *sui generis*, de la Brière approves of the characterisation of the Vatican's nationality as a "nationalité de fonction" (*functional nationality*), and also seems to regard nationality as a consequence of the existence of the state. Yves De La Brière, "La condition juridique de la Cité du Vatican", in *Recueil des Cours*, vol. 33 (Paris: Librairie du Recueil Sirey, 1930), 114–163, 119–124. Thus, although the Vatican's population and the identity of those who possess its nationality cannot be characterised as stable, as the individuals who compose it change, the positions they occupy within the hierarchy of the Holy See are permanent, leading to a conclusion that "permanent population" in the Vatican's case has to do with presence and function, as opposed to identity or personality. It is important that this question not only be viewed in theoretical, but in practical terms as well. Okafor, writing about what he labels a crisis of legitimate statehood, or structural legitimacy, in post-colonial African states, notes the socio-cultural fragmentation of such states, and argues that "governments have all-too-often been able to rely on international law to provide powerful rationalisations, justifications and excuses for their attempts at coercive nation-building . . . [which] have in far too many cases had a negative effect on the peace and development of the post-colonial African state". Obiora Chinedu Okafor, *Re-defining legitimate statehood, Developments in international law* (The Hague: Martinus Nijhoff Publishers, 2000), 181. The question behind this reflection is whether states that have been established without a genuine act of political association (perhaps a political as opposed to contractual *meeting of the minds*) should be regarded as states in the first place. In this sense Okafor discusses the "effectiveness principle" citing Crawford for the proposition that "where a state actually exists, the legality or legitimacy of its creation must be a purely abstract question since the law must take account of the new situation despite its legality". Okafor, *Re-defining legitimate statehood*, 65. quoting Crawford, *The Creation of States in International Law*.

The extent of a State's rights to determine to whom its nationality may be granted, or from whom withdrawn, is dependent on the definition of State sovereignty and, consequently, of what matters fall within domestic jurisdiction.[40]

The limits to state discretion in the field of nationality will be discussed in chapter three. It remains to be asked, however, whether state practice toward multiple nationality influences the contours of state sovereignty itself, beyond the reserved domain of nationality.[41]

Brownlie states that

The principal corollaries of the sovereignty and equality of states are: (1) a jurisdiction, prima facie exclusive, over a territory and the permanent population living there; (2) a duty of non-intervention in the area of exclusive jurisdiction of other states; and (3) the dependence of obligations arising from customary law and treaties on the consent of the obligor".[42]

In this expression, sovereignty is essentially related to territory, yet

On the basis of the internationally recognized principle of personality, the link of nationals to their own State has predominance over possible links with other States.[43]

Nationality itself thus raises a more generalised issue, namely the exercise of state power over individuals based on two discrete links: territorial presence and legal status.[44]

The question is presented to what extent state practice vis-à-vis multiple nationality influences a state's jurisdiction over its own and other nationals, in relation to its obligation not to intervene in areas of exclusive jurisdiction of other states, both in territorial and in personal terms.

---

[40] Donner, *The regulation of nationality in international law*, 29.

[41] Brownlie says "As a separate notion in general international law, the reseved domain is mysterious only because many have failed to see that it really stands for a tautology. However, if a matter is prima facie within the reserved domain because of its nature and the issue presented in the normal case, then certain presumptions against any restriction on that domain may be created". Brownlie, *Principles of public international law*, 294.

[42] Id., 289.

[43] Bernhardt, ed., *Encyclopedia of public international law*, 602.

[44] In some states, nationality status itself must be the result of a territorial link (if not territorial presence), even if that link may prove superficial or illusory. In Switzerland, the Constitution of 1848 set out three separate categories of legal classifications: Gemeindebürgerrecht, Kantonsbürgerrecht, and Schweizerbürgerrecht. (Author's translation: *communal (or municipal) citizenship, cantonal citizenship, and Swiss citizenship.*) Only the last could be considered Swiss nationality on the international plane, but it was dependent on cantonal citizenship, which was in turn dependent on being accepted into a community or "Gemeinde" (literally, 'congregation'). Problems ensued when persons naturalised on a cantonal level did not have a specific local link. See Eduard Hiss, *Geschichte des neuern Schweizerischen Staatsrechts*, vol. 3 (Basel: Verlag von Helbing & Lichtenhahn, 1938), 259–60. Swiss nationality is still possessed by virtue of a specific territorial link to a canton and municipality.

A final note in relation to sovereignty and nationality is perhaps required by the situation of those independent and sovereign states whose constitutional structures share the same natural person as head of state, such as the United Kingdom, Canada, Australia and New Zealand, among others. This is important because such countries seem to express sovereignty (or at least the executive power of the state) in the form of this physical person, and may even assign an amount of personal judgment to her constitutional role. In the Australian context, it is widely debated whether the Queen or the Governor-General appointed on the advice of her Australian ministers, holds reserve powers attributed to her personally by virtue of being the office-holder. A plurality of justices in *Sue v Hill* pointed out that section 59 of the Australian Constitution "provides for disallowance by the Queen of any law within one year of the Governor-General's assent. The text of the Constitution is silent as to the identity of the ministers upon whose advice the monarch is to act in these respects".[45]

The assumption that such a person would possess the nationality of the state in question seems natural and perhaps even unavoidable, yet whether Elizabeth II, as Queen of Australia under the Australian Constitution possesses, or can possess, Australian nationality, is unclear. Likewise the question whether Elizabeth Windsor, as a natural person (assuming that the person can be separated from the office, or the Crown),[46] is an Australian national, is posed. There are persuasive arguments that in both cases she in fact is not to be considered an Australian national (the constitutional position of Queen does not seem to bear a link to nationality as such, and there is no evidence that as an individual natural person she possesses Australian nationality, although Brownlie cites a "general rule that a Head of State has the nationality of the State represented").[47]

---

[45] *Sue v Hill and Another*, (1999) 163 ALR 648, 669. A manual of Australian constitutional law labels the Queen's function as "primarily ceremonial", but acknowledges that "whether the monarch can ever lawfully act independently of advice is unclear, though in practice such action has sometimes occurred". Tony Blackshield, George Williams, and Brian Fitzgerald, *Australian constitutional law and theory. Commentary and materials* (Annandale (NSW): The Federation Press, 1996), 1–2.

[46] In 1897 Neubecker concluded that the nature of sovereignty meant that the person of the Sovereign could not be divorced from the position: "Eines nur ist dabei vergessen oder unberücksichtigt gelassen: das ist die Souveränetät der Königin Viktoria. Die Königin Viktoria kann nach dem Begriffe der Souveränetät nicht fremde Unterthanin sein, also hier Coburgerin: sie gehört als englische Königin einzig und allein dem englischen Staate an". Friedrich Karl Neubecker, "Thronfolgerecht und fremde Staatsangehörigkeit. Ist die Zugehörigkeit eines regierenden deutschen Fürsten zu einem fremden Staatsverband vereinbar mit den Normen des Staats- und Völkerrechts?" (Inaugural-Dissertation, Königliche Friedrich-Wilhelms-Universität zu Berlin, 1897), 2. (Author's translation: *Only one thing has thereby been forgotten or left unconsidered, that is the sovereignty of Queen Victoria. According to the concept of sovereignty Queen Victoria cannot be a foreign subject, in this case a subject of Coburg. As English Queen she belongs only and exclusively to the English State.*)

[47] Ian Brownlie, "The relations of nationality in public international law", *The British Yearbook of International Law*, (1963) vol. 39, 284–364, 309. In *Sue v Hill*, Justices Gleeson,

Assuming the Queen's Australian Office involves the exercise of personal judgment or even power, it is difficult to separate the individual from the office itself, and in this case, the Queen's nationality becomes relevant. Countries such as Australia and Canada may in fact have a constitutional interest in naturalising, or otherwise legislatively or judicially defining Elizabeth Windsor and the heirs to the throne or regal office as a national, although to do so against her will would be a breach of international law. This is discussed in chapter three.[48]

Whether or not possession of the nationality of the states of which Elizabeth Windsor is head of state would have any effect on the context of the personal powers she has, or may have, is unclear. But it is certainly a topic that should provoke reflection. In concluding arguments related to the divisibility of the Crown in the British Commonwealth, O'Connell states:

> *That the Crown is no longer one juristic being cannot dissolve or even loosen the bond between the sovereign and her several independent communities: on the contrary, the Queen's altered titles, emphasising her separate relationship to each Dominion, can only have the effect of making her more personally intimate to her several organized communities, with a consequent greater participation by them in the common life of which she is representative.[49]*

Formal possession of the nationality of the states she represents would arguably serve to emphasize such personal intimacy, and reinforce her duties as head of state in each state's municipal law. Duties to the state as a consequence of nationality are discussed in chapter three. The attribution of nationality to individuals who at some point

---

Gummow and Hayne of the High Court of Australia held that "the circumstance that the same monarch exercises regal functions under the constitutional arrangements in the United Kingdom and Australia does not deny the proposition that the United Kingdom is a foreign power . . . Australia and the United Kingdom have their own laws as to nationality so that their citizens owe different allegiances. The United Kingdom has a distinct legal personality". *Sue v Hill and Another*, 675. This plurality distinguished five separate uses of the expression "the Crown", only one of which relates to the "person occupying the hereditary office". The justices cite the statement by British Justices May and Kerr that "[i]t is settled law that, although Her Majesty is the personal sovereign of the peoples inhabiting many of the territories within the Commonwealth, all rights and obligations of the Crown- other than those concerning the Queen in her personal capacity – can only arise in relation to a particular government within those territories. The reason is that such rights and obligations can only be exercised and enforced, if at all, through some governmental emanation or representation of the Crown". *Sue v Hill and Another*, 664.

[48] There are precedents for naturalisation in the royal context. The German (Saxon) husband of Britain's Queen Victoria, a reigning German Prince, was naturalised in Great Britain on 24 January 1840, in anticipation of their marriage on 10 February the same year. Neubecker, "Thronfolgerecht und fremde Staatsangehörigkeit. Ist die Zugehörigkeit eines regierenden deutschen Fürsten zu einem fremden Staatsverband vereinbar mit den Normen des Staats- und Völkerrechts?", 2.

[49] D. P. O'Connell, "The Crown in the British Commonwealth", *The International and Comparative Law Quarterly* (1957) vol. 6, no. 1, 103–125, 125.

become monarchs is also common. Neubecker already in 1897 cited the British statutory provision of 1705 attributing British nationality to all Protestant descendants of the Electress Sophie, which at the time included the German Emperor and other European heads of state,[50] and currently includes Queen Beatrix of the Netherlands.[51]

The subject of the nationality and possible multiple nationality of reigning princes seems to have been of great importance at several points in the 19th century, albeit in the more complicated political context of subject status and sovereignty. For example, in the context of the succession to the throne of Sachse-Coburg-Gotha in 1893 by Alfred, Duke of Edinburgh and of Sachse-Coburg-Gotha, Queen Victoria's second son, Neubecker outlines the political and legal controversy in Germany and England at the time, over whether a reigning German Sovereign might also be considered another state's subject.[52] Queen Beatrix's dual Dutch and British nationality seems to be a matter of discomfort for the Netherlands' government, whose current policy maintains that limits on multiple nationality should be imposed.[53]

These questions are not raised glibly. If for instance, Elizabeth Windsor were indeed a multiple national of Australia, Canada, Barbados, Papua New Guinea, the Solomon Islands, the United Kingdom, and so on, which depends on the municipal

---

[50] Neubecker, "Thronfolgerecht und fremde Staatsangehörigkeit. Ist die Zugehörigkeit eines regierenden deutschen Fürsten zu einem fremden Staatsverband vereinbar mit den Normen des Staats- und Völkerrechts?", 13.

[51] H. U. Jessurun d'Oliveira, "Onze koningin heeft twee nationaliteiten. Kan dat nog wel?", *HP/De Tijd*, 16 December 2005, 22–28. The statute was abrogated by the British Nationality Act (1948). Id., 23. This means that Beatrix' children Crown Prince Willem-Alexander and his two brothers are British citizens by descent, but her grandchildren would, absent other conditions for attribution of British nationality, not be British. Id., 26. Jessurun d'Oliveira points out that due to their mother Princess Máxima's Argentine nationality, the Crown Prince's children may, however, opt for Argentine nationality upon reaching the age of majority. In this case they would lose their Netherlands' nationality, and place in the line of succession. Id., 28.

[52] He concludes that this could never be the case due to the position of Sovereign as such: "Der Herzog Alfred ist deutscher Souverän und kann als solcher nicht Unterthan einer fremden Macht, eines anderen Staates sein". Id., 15. Author's translation: *Duke Alfred is a German Sovereign and as such cannot be the subject of a foreign power, of another State*. Arguing that this position automatically terminated Alfred's British nationality, Neubecker nevertheless has to deal with the fact that the UK still seemed to regard the Prince as its national. He argues that even if England did give the Prince certain rights, that rights as such don't create a subject, only duties, and the Prince had none of the latter, as a German Sovereign. Neubecker, "Thronfolgerecht und fremde Staatsangehörigkeit. Ist die Zugehörigkeit eines regierenden deutschen Fürsten zu einem fremden Staatsverband vereinbar mit den Normen des Staats- und Völkerrechts?", 14. This is arguably an exclusive view of the multiple nationality that the Prince probably did possess in terms of the two countries' municipal laws. In regard to the Austrian nationality of the Prince of Thurn and Taxis, see Hans Kelsen, *Beiträge zur Kritik des Rechtsgutachtens über die Frage der Österreichischen Staatsbürgerschaft des Fürsten von Thurn und Taxis* (Zagreb: Jugoslovenska Stampa, 1924).

[53] Jessurun d'Oliveira, "Onze koningin heeft twee nationaliteiten. Kan dat nog wel?", 25.

law of each country in question, this would surely reflect an attitude by those states vis-à-vis multiple nationality and perhaps even sovereignty.

Lastly, anticipating further issues in relation to jurisdiction, while Elizabeth II, Queen of Australia, and Head of State, might be termed or regarded as the outward expression of Australia's sovereignty, that is not to say that Australia, in relation to the natural person Elizabeth Windsor as a national of the United Kingdom (again, assuming she is a national of the United Kingdom), is not in a position to exercise personal jurisdiction over her for certain purposes. This is because personal jurisdiction over individuals can be exercised over certain categories of non-nationals as well as nationals, an issue discussed in chapters three and four.

E. AN ANALYSIS OF STATE PRACTICE TOWARD MULTIPLE NATIONALITY

Multiple nationality is produced by the complementary effects of two or more distinct municipal legal systems, when each attributes its state's nationality to the same individual. Although a state may have defined a general position on the desirability of multiple nationality in laws and pronouncements on policy, this is not always of relevance in practical terms, as far as the existence of the status itself, due to the operation of municipal legislation. Although a state may postulate that it is opposed to multiple nationality, or claim that it will not allow it, depending on its own laws regulating the acquisition and loss of nationality, it may in fact tolerate classes of citizens with multiple nationality to varying degrees. Likewise, a state may officially accept that its citizens be multiple-nationals in terms of stated policy and doctrine, yet have municipal legal provisions that effectively eliminate or discourage such a status.

Importantly, generalisations about state practice often prove to be overly simplistic, or even wrong.[54] Maintaining that states either accept or reject multiple nationality is to ignore that state practice evinces a nuanced spectrum of attitudes toward multiple nationality, rather than black and white clearly demarcated extremes. This is a central tenet herein, and the research undertaken reveals some of the gradation in such attitudes.

---

[54] Illustrating how different perceptions of a nation's attitude towards multiple nationality can be, in a colloquium organised by the Mexican Congress on the possible amendment of Mexican nationality law to "allow" dual nationality, García Moreno lists Germany as among the countries which "accept and recognise" dual nationality. Víctor Carlos García Moreno, "La propuesta sobre doble nacionalidad", paper presented at the conference: *La doble nacionalidad* (Ciudad de México: Miguel Ángel Porrúa Librero-Editor, 1995), 173–181. Whether this is correct or incorrect is a matter of opinion, as in 1999 Germany did amend its nationality laws to tolerate multiple nationality among a bigger group of persons than had previously been the case. Germany, however, remains one of the countries with a strong (legally defined) principle of avoidance as far as its nationals possessing more than one nationality.

It is a generally accepted rule of international law that "[i]n principle, questions of nationality fall within the domestic jurisdiction of each state".[55] This statement, objections to it, and its consequences in terms of multiple nationality and otherwise, will be explored in chapters three and four. As it is the accepted general rule, it is the starting point from which any examination of state practice regarding multiple nationality must emanate, involving firstly an analysis of municipal as opposed to international law.

In order to establish current state practice, this study will focus on the specific rules regulating nationality provided in municipal legislation, which directly or indirectly produce or frustrate the production of multiple nationality, in addition to related government policy. Where possible, evidence of changes in national attitudes toward multiple nationality will also be sought. The specific factors bearing on multiple nationality which will be examined in states' municipal legislation and policy are outlined below. Such policy analysis includes issues such as state practice in terms of the diplomatic protection of multiple nationals, as an *ingredient* in the study, as opposed to ascertaining the effects of overall state practice on the ability and right of states to extend diplomatic protection to their nationals, which is taken up in terms of conclusions.

The author's preliminary question, what is current state practice toward multiple nationality, is much the same as that asked by Bar-Yaacov some forty years ago. Although Bar-Yaacov claimed not to approach the subject with preconceived ideas as to the desirability or undesirability of multiple nationality, by characterizing it as a "problem", he in fact did have a pre-conceived notion of the phenomenon in terms of its negative consequences for the individual and the state.[56]

Even if it is accepted that Bar-Yaacov intended to approach his subject dispassionately, the analytical approach he adopted arguably did not allow for a comprehensive assessment of state practice. Bar-Yaacov's work contains an historical survey of the development of the municipal legislation on nationality of France, the Soviet

---

[55] Manley O. Hudson, special rapporteur of the International Law Commission, quoted in Ian Brownlie, *Principles of public international law*, Fifth ed. (Oxford: Clarendon Press, 1998), 385.

[56] Bar-Yaacov's "prime objective has been to clarify the status of dual nationality in international law and the attitudes of States as reflected in their legislation and practices, and to offer any results that such a study might provide – whether relating to the desirability or undesirability of dual nationality, or to the means by which the problem could, fully or partially, be solved, or to the notion of nationality in general." Nissim Bar-Yaacov, *Dual nationality*, (London: Stevens & Sons Ltd., 1961), xi. Further, in the introduction to his text, after enumerating the "unfortunate position of dual nationals", Bar-Yaacov writes "the suggestion is occasionally put forward, that dual nationals are in a particularly favourable position because they may enjoy the benefits of the nationality of two States without fulfilling duties to either. The 'advantage' of such a situation should not be exaggerated." Bar-Yaacov, *Dual nationality*, 4–5. His introduction omits considerations related to why such a status might be of importance to the individual, aside from mentioning unethical misrepresentation for personal gain.

Union, the United Kingdom, and the United States, in addition to the nationality laws then in force in Bolivia, Japan and Sweden. As in the current study, Bar-Yaacov considered that the sample of states surveyed should be a representative one, which he defined as one which "provide[s] adequate representation of the principal systems of regulating nationality as well as an indication of the political, demographic and legal factors underlying their adoption".[57] It is the author's proposition, presented below, that in terms of presenting a representative sample of states from which general practice can be deduced, this approach does not go far enough in terms of its analysis or its content.

The conclusions herein are not based on a comprehensive review of the national legislation and policies of all states. Indeed, Donner notes that "a comparative study of the nationality laws and regulations of the States making up the international community of today . . . would be foredoomed to failure".[58] Given the task involved in ensuring that states' legislation and policy are reviewed comprehensively and competently, this would certainly seem to be the case. As the scope of this study is however restricted to certain provisions within national laws and policy which relate to the production, elimination and treatment of multiple nationality specifically, it is submitted that the study can be both representative, and not of an impossible magnitude.

The conclusions herein are based on 45 jurisdictions, from which the author seeks to extrapolate generally in order to deduce state practice. It is therefore paramount that the sample of states selected for analysis be representative of state practice vis-à-vis nationality generally, in terms of the various factors that influence states in enacting legislation on nationality and which bear on the possible multiple nationality of their citizens. Notwithstanding its limitation to 45 jurisdictions, almost one fourth of the world's independent states are subjects of the present analysis.[59]

The author does not seek to approach the topic from a particular paradigm or ideology. Thus no particular theoretical framework (positivist, feminist, critical legal theory, or similar) underlies the analysis, although elements of these methodologies may be adopted.[60] This again is a consequence of the fundamental limitation of the

---

[57] Id., 6.

[58] Ruth Donner, *The regulation of nationality in international law*, 2nd ed. (Irvington-on-Hudson (USA): Transnational Publishers Inc., 1994), xvi–xvii.

[59] As of 1 January 2006 there were 191 states members of the United Nations or parties to the Statute of the International Court of Justice. Only the Cook Islands, Niue (both associated states of New Zealand) and the Vatican City State arguably constitute states not members of the United Nations or party to the ICJ's Statute. Cook Islands' nationality is discussed in chapter four. See United Nations, List of member states (internet), http://www.un.org/Overview/growth.htm, consulted on 15 January 2006, and International Court of Justice, Bases for jurisdiction of the Court (internet), http://www.icjcij.org/icjwww/ibasicdocuments. htm, consulted on 15 January 2006.

[60] It should be noted that the author accepts Hart's positivist doctrine that "developed municipal legal systems contain a rule of recognition specifying the criteria for the identification of the laws which courts have to apply". Herbert Lionel Adolphus Hart, "The concept of law – postcript", ed. Penelope A. Bulloch and Joseph Raz (Oxford: Clarendon Press, 1994), 246. Not

question posed. Rather than asking why states legislate in a particular fashion, this study seeks only to identify how they in fact legislate, from which practical conclusions regarding the effects of this practice in international law can be drawn, without the use of any particular "lens" other than that of international law.[61] In this sense, the study's approach is based principally on municipal law in force.

1. Selection of state-sample

It is of great consequence to the validity of this study that the sample of states selected for analysis be representative of state practice generally. In this sense a random sample of states must be rejected specifically because it can be argued that there are identifiable factors that influence state policy on nationality and multiple nationality. These factors may be readily evident from government statements, or implicit in terms of the pressures brought to bear on governments in the creation of a legislative framework.

There are many factors that implicitly influence states in determining who is to be regarded as a national or admitted to nationality. Most are arguably products of aspects of each nation's historical, political, and economic development, and demographics, although emotive factors related to national identity cannot be discounted and can play a crucial role. Evidence of such varying factors can be found in international law itself, in terms of what the International Court of Justice called the impossibility "for any general agreement to be reached on the rules relating to nationality".[62]

Part of the difficulty in identifying such motivating factors is that governments do not typically define the motives behind their nationality laws, or rules relating to multiple nationality. Points of departure can be deduced, however, from the factors which arguably create a state interest, whether political, social, juridical or other, in the attri-

---

to do so would be to postulate that it is impossible to know the consequences of laws, let alone their contents. Hart defends positivism against critics by pointing out that the theory "makes no claim to identify the point or purpose of law and legal practices as such; so there is nothing in my theory to support Dworkin's view, which I certainly do not share, that the purpose of law is to justify the use of coercion". Id., 248. Indeed, if the central question posed in this study were "why do states legislate the way they do?", or "what should state practice be?", the underlying purpose of the law and legal practices would be of central importance to the arguments submitted.

[61] For challenges to the interpretation of international law in terms of its nature and workings from the critical legal studies' school, see Wade Mansell, "Pure law in an impure world", in *The critical lawyers' handbook 2*, ed. Paddy Ireland and Per Laleng, *Law and Social Theory* (London: Pluto Press, 1997), 30–45; Sol Picciotto, "International law: the ligitimation of power in world affairs", in *The critical lawyers' handbook 2*, ed. Paddy Ireland and Per Laleng, *Law and Social Theory* (London: Pluto Press, 1997), 13–29.

[62] *Nottebohm Case (second phase), Judgment of April 6th, 1955*, I.C.J. Reports (1955) 4, 23.

bution of nationality to individuals, as well as related pressures on states in terms of controlling or interacting with persons with a relationship to the state or its people, or persons without such a relationship.

1.1   Factors underpinning or influencing legislation on nationality

O'Leary identifies several factors in terms of both inclusion and exclusion: political participation and the rights of citizenship[63] (Davis adds that this is "to access the resources of the state");[64] an "historic-biological aspect of nationality" linked to "lineage and belonging to a geographical entity", which emerges in modern times in the attribution of nationality through *jus sanguinis* and *jus soli*;[65] a sociological dimension encompassing the "cultural, historical and social aspects of state membership" which cannot be expressed through law alone;[66] protection of economic interests;[67] historical background of the state and related development of the law;[68] immigration/emigration and movement of persons.[69]

---

[63] Síofra O'Leary, *The evolving concept of community citizenship – from the free movement of persons to Union citizenship* (The Hague: Kluwer Law International, 1996), 7. Along these lines, Pickus argues for example that the process of naturalisation (nationality laws) in the United States should "adequately incorporate newcomers, strengthen citizenship, [and] foster self-government". Noah M. J. Pickus, "To make natural: creating citizens for the twenty-first century," in *Immigration and citizenship in the twenty-first century*, ed. Noah M. J. Pickus (Lanham: Rowman & Littlefield, 1998), 108.

[64] Uri Davis, *Citizenship and the State – a comparative study of citizenship legislation in Israel, Jordan, Palestine, Syria and Lebanon* (Reading (UK): Garnet Publishers, 1997), xiv.

[65] O'Leary, *The evolving concept of community citizenship – from the free movement of persons to Union citizenship*, 6.

[66] Id., 6–7.

[67] Id., 9.

[68] Id., 12.

[69] Id., 9 and 13. O'Leary cites historical influences on the U.K. and Ireland which produce privileged treatment for each others' nationals, adding "Irish nationality law is also very liberal, which can be explained in terms of its large emigrant community and, to a certain extent, by the fact that Ireland has never been a traditional destination for immigration". O'Leary, *The evolving concept of community citizenship – from the free movement of persons to Union citizenship*, 13. Weil and Hansen go further, stating "à travers l'Europe, les politiques de l'immigration sont aussi devenues les politiques de la nationalité". (Author's translation: *Across Europe immigration policies have also become nationality policies.*) Patrick Weil and Randall Hansen, "Citoyenneté, immigration et nationalité: vers la convergence européenne," in *Nationalité et citoyenneté en Europe*, ed. Patrick Weil and Randall Hansen, *Collection "Recherches"* (Paris: Éditions La Découverte, 1999), 9–28, 9. They explicitly postulate that two factors have led to changes in European nations' municipal nationality laws: (1) massive immigration to Europe after the Second World War, and (2) the need to integrate an often growing population of resident foreigners. Id., 11 and 18–21.

Masing emphasises factors related to identity and self-perception of a collective political entity, as well as migration.[70] He states that the principle of avoidance of multiple nationality was in and of itself a decisive factor in the revision of German nationality law, in relation to the incorporation of immigrants into German nationality.

In the context of the Middle East Davis cites the relative secularization of the state and the

> *supremacy of the democratic state (and citizenship of the democratic state) over national identity or confessional identity . . . the secular state that defines the boundary of its polity in geographical terms – not in ethnic terms.*[71]

He makes the point that inclusion or exclusion of specific groups can be behind nationality laws.

> *By instituting a two-tier citizenship, one jinsiyya ("passport citizenship") and the other muwatana ("democratic citizenship"), it was possible for legislators of at least two states in the region (Jordan and Israel) to create large constituencies – that is, large Palestinian constituencies – that can only be characterized by the surreal Orwellian designation as "pretend citizens" or "part citizens". These are citizens (they have valid full-term passports), and they have no rights or they have only part rights.*[72]

Spiro cites geopolitical issues. In relation to what he views as an historical aversion to dual nationality, and in relation to nationality generally, he refers to a general background of "the anarchical context of the state system, one in which no superior authority imposed order and in which each nation's fortune faced constant threat from other states in a zero-sum world".[73] Along related lines, albeit not regarding multiple nationality, Kymlicka argues that "[s]ince the Cold War, ethno-cultural conflicts have become the most common source of political violence in the world, and they show no sign of abating". He cites clashes between minority and majority ethnic groups

---

[70] Johannes Masing, *Wandel im Staatsangehörigkeitsrecht vor den Herausforderungen moderner Migration* (Tübingen: Mohr Siebeck, 2001), 1–2 and 73–77. He notes the public emotion and discussion surrounding the revision of German nationality law in 2000, notwithstanding that administrative and citizenship rights, as well as issues of immigration, have little to do with the law of nationality in Germany. Nevertheless, he also characterizes the law reform as "prinzipielle Antwort auf die Herausforderungen der Migration". (Author's translation: *the main response to the challenges of migration.*) Ibid.

[71] Davis, *Citizenship and the State – a comparative study of citizenship legislation in Israel, Jordan, Palestine, Syria and Lebanon*, xv–xvi.

[72] Id., 7–8. Likewise, the position of the more than three million "British Nationals (Overseas)" should be considered, whose nationality derives from an association with the United Kingdom's (until 1997) Crown Colony of Hong Kong. Their status as nationals of the UK does not give rise to anything other than diplomatic protection (outside Hong Kong and China). The UK's treatment of its nationals in Hong Kong is discussed in chapter four.

[73] Peter J. Spiro, "Dual nationality and the meaning of citizenship", *Emory Law Review*, vol. 46, no. 4, 1412–1485, 1417–1418.

within states as the "greatest challenge facing democracies today".[74] He also mentions the state's treatment of national minorities, ranging from physical elimination, coercive assimilation, political and economic discrimination, to protection by law, as having produced different political policies at different times.[75] It is not unwarranted to extrapolate from this to the domain of nationality.

As opposed to a view of an anarchical state system, Weil and Hansen demonstrate that the political process of European integration and the notion of European Union (EU) citizenship, combined with immigration to EU states, has led to de-facto harmonisation of municipal laws on nationality. They note that this has taken place notwithstanding that the process of European integration has not formally involved the harmonisation of EU states' respective municipal laws on nationality.[76]

In discerning other factors that influence states in relation to the attribution or withdrawal of their nationality, it might seem tempting to take the specific areas of national legislation or international relations that are affected by the attribution of nationality, or multiple nationality, into account. This might include areas such as taxation, military service by individuals, consular protection, and so on. These areas might be considered to amount to the accepted or standard powers of states over their nationals, and the rights that individuals (nationals) have vis-à-vis their governments. It is unclear, however, whether these areas by themselves create a state interest in legislating one way or another as regards nationality or multiple nationality. All that is clear is that these are areas of the law that affect individuals who are nationals or multiple nationals, and the state's relationship to such persons.

Likewise, examination of prevailing doctrine on nationality, as far as it can be defined, might lead to conclusions regarding state interests in legislating in a particular manner or adopting a particular policy. Thus Spiro effectively argues that a 'world view' (or theoretical paradigm) can influence particular policy and laws vis-à-vis nationality: the doctrine of permanent or indelible allegiance to a territorial sovereign, with its medieval roots, directly affected British and American policy and law into the late 19th century, leading to tensions and even war between the two states (the US being a destination country for European immigrants) over issues of nationality.[77]

---

[74] Will Kymlicka, *Multicultural citizenship – a liberal theory of minority rights* (Oxford: Clarendon Press, 1995), 1.

[75] Id., 2.

[76] Weil and Hansen, "Citoyenneté, immigration et nationalité: vers la convergence européenne", 25–26. de Groot concludes that there is no movement toward a European nationality as such and that nationality law remains firmly in the hands of EU member states. G.-R. de Groot, "Towards a European Nationality Law", Electronic Journal of Comparative Law, vol. 8.3, October 2004 (internet), http://www.ejcl.org/83/art83–4.html, consulted 1 March 2006. In this sense the EU citizenship provided for in the Treaties of Maastricht (1992) and Amsterdam (1997) and in the Draft Constitutional Treaty (2003) does not replace member states' nationality laws. Ibid.

[77] Spiro, "Dual nationality and the meaning of citizenship", 1422–1424. This is explored in detail in chapter four.

Lawrence, writing in 1895, confirmed that

> *Till recently the law of Great Britain embodied the doctrine of inalienable allegiance; and*
> *one of the chief causes of the war with the United States in 1812 was the rigor with which*
> *that doctrine was applied by her government. British cruisers took from American vessels*
> *on the high seas naturalized American citizens and impressed them for service in the*
> *Royal Navy, on the grounds that they were British subjects by birth and that no forms*
> *gone through in America could divest them of their British nationality.*[78]

To assume however, that state motivation or interest is always defined by or enunci-
ated through prevailing doctrine or law, would seem too strong. Again taking the doctrine of perpetual allegiance as an example, while its application declined throughout
the 19th century, some states still continued to place limits on expatriation, such as
expatriation conditional on the fulfilment of military service.[79] Thus, examination of
the state interest in nationality, taking the doctrine of perpetual allegiance as a starting point, would result in a limited and time-based picture unable to be divorced from
other factors. It is thus submitted that neither an examination of prevailing doctrine,
nor areas of law or international relations affected by multiple nationality, will by
itself suffice to discern state interest in legislating on questions of nationality.

1.2 General categories adopted to identify a representative sample of states

The author does not wish to pretend that the short survey above of writers from various fields is either comprehensive or definitive. It is not possible to know the exact
reasons why states legislate in one way or another on nationality, or to ascribe the
appropriate level of importance to any given factor or influence. To do so would be
akin to possessing a formula to describe and predict the political process with cer-
tainty. The enumeration of issues above is also not to argue that any one or more of
the factors mentioned is currently applied by states, but simply that these are factors
which have been ingredients in states' perceptions of their interests in terms of nationality and multiple nationality.[80]

---

[78] T. J. Lawrence, *The principles of international law*, ed. Percy H. Winfield, 7th ed.
(London: Macmillan & Co., 1895), 205.

[79] Such as France until 1945. Spiro, "Dual nationality and the meaning of citizenship", 1424.

[80] In this regard see also generally Théodore Baty, "La double nationalité est-elle possible?",
Revue de droit international et de législation comparée, (1926) vol. 7, 622–632; Rogers
Brubaker, *Citizenship and nationhood in France and Germany* (Cambridge (Massachusetts):
Harvard University Press, 1992); William Rogers Brubaker, "Citizenship and naturalization:
policies and politics," in *Immigration and the politics of citizenship in Europe and North
America*, ed. William Rogers Brubaker (Lanham: University Press of America, 1989), 99–127;
William Rogers Brubaker, "Introduction," in *Immigration and the politics of citizenship in
Europe and North America*, ed. William Rogers Brubaker (Lanham: University Press of
America, 1989), 1–27; Marco Cuniberti, *La cittadinanza – Libertà dell'uomo e libertà del cit-
tadino nella constituzione italiana*, vol. 18, *Diritto e Istituzioni Richerche Dirette da Giorgio
Berti* (Verona: Casa Editrice Dott. Antonio Milani, 1997); Laurie Fransman, "The case for

Taking these considerations as a starting point, four general categories are proposed in relation to a state's relationship to natural persons and its decisions on inclusion and exclusion in terms of nationality. These have in turn guided the selection of the state sample proposed herein:

(1)   the movement of persons between states;
(2)   the historical political and legal position of the state (including economic and geographic considerations) within the international community and its relationship to other states;
(3)   the ethnic (or similar category of identification) and demographic composition of nation states and relevant international connections;
(4)   the national legal system and factors that influence it.

In order to identify a sample of states that takes the above-mentioned general criteria into account, the subsequent sub-headings related to the general categories are proposed. Following the factors mentioned above, they are intended to be purely indicative of trends and influences on states in matters of the relationship between states and natural persons, in order to ensure that the sample of states presented is in fact representative of state practice in matters of nationality.

Thus, the sample should include states: (specific parameters where present are defined below)

(1)   that have experienced an historical influx of immigrants,
(2)   that have experienced an influx of other people/groups,
(3)   that have had an historical outflow of people/emigrants,
(4)   that are former colonies or were ruled by another power,
(5)   that are former colonisers or held trust territories,
(6)   that lost territory to neighbours,
(7)   that acquired/gained territory from neighbours,
(8)   that have common law, civil law, Islamic, and "socialist" legal systems,
(9)   that have a significant[81] minority ethnic group or groups,
(10) whose own predominant ethnic or other group is present in another country,
(11) where a significant number of citizens / former citizens or their descendants live abroad,

---

reform of nationality law in the United Kingdom," in *Citizenship and nationality status in the new Europe*, ed. Síofra O'Leary and Teija Tiilikainen (London: Sweet & Maxwell, 1998), 123–147; Tomas Hammar, "State, nation, and dual citizenship," in *Immigration and the politics of citizenship in Europe and North America*, ed. William Rogers Brubaker (Lanham: University Press of America, 1989), 81–95; Yasemin Nuhoglu Soysal, *Limits of citizenship – migrants and postnational membership in Europe* (Chicago: The University of Chicago Press, 1994); Ineta Ziemele, "The citizenship issue in the Republic of Latvia," in *Citizenship and nationality status in the new Europe*, ed. Síofra O'Leary and Teija Tiilikainen (London: Sweet & Maxwell, 1998), 187–204.

[81] Significance may be seen not only in numbers overall, but in terms of economic or political clout or power.

(12) whose own minority ethnic or other group is present in another country,
(13) whose international legal personality is either called into question or limited,
(14) at various stages of economic development,
(15) with various sizes of land mass,
(16) with various sizes of population,
(17) with various levels of population density,
(18) that attribute nationality according to (i) parentage (*jus sanguinis*), (ii) place of birth (*jus soli*).

The author acknowledges that it is possible to take issue not only with the factors themselves, but with the countries selected to fit into them.

Whether or not a country falls into the above-listed considerations depends on subjective judgments over which there can be considerable disagreement: the time frame considered and a judgment of proportions (e.g. "an historically large influx or outflow of immigrants/emigrants or others"), political and historical views (e.g. "territory lost/gained from a neighbour"), among many other factors, and relative judgments (developing status, size of population). For example, in the heading "own minority ethnic group also present in another country" the author has chosen to include Fiji, taking the Indo-Fijian population into account as a distinct ethnic minority as it is perceived as such, although it is made up of Fijian nationals who in most cases have no specific ties to the subcontinent. Germany has however not been included in this category, even though its resident ethnic Turkish population is a notable minority, as the majority remain non-nationals.

To take such considerations into account, in terms of immigration, two separate sub-headings are proposed, "countries with an historical influx of immigrants" for countries which have or had a stated program or policy of permanent settlement, and "countries which experienced an influx of other people/groups" for nations without an express political goal of incorporating and accepting newcomers into national life. The subjectivity of the placement of states into these headings is clear: does the migration to France of Italians and Poles in the 1930s place France in either of these two groups? The author's classification in this sense is based on whether such migration arguably still influences French thinking on nationality. Current or very recent trends are also avoided in terms of inclusion in categories, as it is doubtful whether municipal legislation will reflect them. For example, Argentina has traditionally been, and seen itself as, a country to which people immigrated, yet has seen large outflows of emigrants in recent years.[82] The decision to categorise countries accordingly clearly involves subjective judgment.

The author has included countries and territories in relevant sub-headings based on a subjective impression attributable to the place itself, and generally excluding external views of the same question. For example, Venezuela is included in the list of

---

[82] Harris Whitbeck, *Struggling economy fuels Argentine emigration*, Cable News Network CNN, 23 July 2001 (internet), http://www.cnn.com/2001/WORLD/americas/07/23/argentina.migration, consulted 1 March 2006.

countries that "lost territory to a neighbouring state", as it maintains a territorial claim over territory held by Guyana. It is to be assumed that Guyana does not share that view.[83] Much that may seem self-evident is not devoid of controversy. It is indeed easy to take issue with these categories, and the states selected to fit them, but it is submitted that in the aggregate, the considerations factored together, combined with the relatively large number of states/territories included, has produced a balanced and representative sample of states.

Other factors that might arguably be relevant to the four main categories, such as religion and ideology in relation to states, have been omitted, although it is submitted that the sample of states presented represents sufficiently diverse groups within each. At the same time, since the end of the Cold War, ideology as such would seem to play a smaller role in national legal approaches. In this sense the categories of states adhering to or influenced by English Common Law, European Civil Law (Napoleonic Code) and Islamic Law are considered, in addition to "socialist" law. On the national level "ideology" arguably includes the legal basis for the relationship between the individual and the state and the development of notions of the rights of individuals vis-à-vis the state. It is submitted that such considerations are inherently difficult to quantify; they might be incorporated through inclusion of states which have and have not adhered to universal and multi-lateral human rights treaties. In this sense the state sample is also largely representative.

Although the author has attempted to guarantee geographic representation in the survey, there is no prima facie indication that geography per se plays a role in national legislation and views on nationality other than the influence of geography on the various factors outlined above. Such a premise may however be questioned; thus an attempt has been made to ensure that the countries selected within the above-listed criteria come from all the world's regions. Likewise, it is unclear whether a country's size and population or its level of economic development plays a role; thus the sample also includes developing and developed countries, and considers both size and population.

2. State sample adopted

The survey of national legislation and policy includes the following 45 states and territories:

Argentina, Australia, Brazil, Canada, China (People's Republic of), the Cook Islands, Egypt, Fiji, France, Germany, Hungary, India, Indonesia, Iran, Ireland, Israel, Italy, Ivory Coast, Japan, Kenya, Korea (Republic of), Latvia, Malaysia, Mexico, Morocco,

---

[83] Safraz W. Ishmael, *The beginning of the Guyana-Venezuela border dispute*, Guyana news and information (internet), http://www.guyana.org/features/guyanastory/chapter52.html, consulted 1 March 2006.

the Netherlands, Nigeria, the Philippines, Portugal, Romania, the Russian Federation, Singapore, South Africa, Spain, Switzerland, Syria, Taiwan,[84] Thailand, Turkey, the United Kingdom, the United States of America, Uruguay, Venezuela, Zimbabwe, and the Hong Kong Special Administrative Region (SAR) of the People's Republic of China.

GEOGRAPHICAL DISTRIBUTION	COUNTRIES / TERRITORIES SURVEYED
Americas (7)	Argentina, Brazil, Canada, Mexico, Uruguay, USA, Venezuela
Europe (14)	France, Germany, Hungary, Ireland, Italy, Latvia, the Netherlands, Portugal, Romania, the Russian Federation, Spain, Switzerland, Turkey, the United Kingdom
Asia (11)	PRChina, Hong Kong, India, Indonesia, Japan, Korea, Malaysia, the Philippines, Singapore, Taiwan, Thailand
Africa (6)	Ivory Coast, Kenya, Morocco, Nigeria, South Africa, Zimbabwe
Pacific (3)	Australia, Cook Islands, Fiji
Middle East (4)	Egypt, Iran, Israel, Syria

CONSIDERATIONS	COUNTRIES / TERRITORIES SURVEYED
Historical influx of immigrants (11)	Argentina, Australia, Brazil, Canada, Israel, Mexico, Singapore, South Africa, USA, Uruguay, Venezuela
Historical influx of other people (16)	Fiji, France, Germany, Hong Kong, Italy, Latvia, Malaysia, the Netherlands, Portugal, Russian Federation, Spain, Switzerland, Taiwan, United Kingdom, Zimbabwe

---

[84] The inclusion of Taiwan, or the "Republic of China" (ROC) as its authorities define the territory (herein referred to as "Taiwan") in this survey does not imply that the author wishes to take a stand on issues relating to the government and legal personality of the State of China. Rather, Taiwan's laws are examined solely in relation to the system by which they claim to regulate and attribute nationality and policies related to multiple nationality. This does not imply that the ROC is or is not a state, or that ROC practice can necessarily be seen as contributing to a survey of state practice. Its inclusion in the survey is to be seen from the standpoint of practical interest, especially in relation to overseas Chinese communities, and the policy of the People's Republic of China (PRC).

(cont.)

CONSIDERATIONS	COUNTRIES / TERRITORIES SURVEYED
Historical outflow of people/emigrants (24)	China, Cook Islands, Germany, Hong Kong, Hungary, India, Iran, Ireland, Israel, Italy, Japan, Korea, Latvia, Mexico, the Netherlands, the Philippines, Portugal, the Russian Federation, South Africa, Spain, Switzerland, Taiwan, Thailand, United Kingdom.
Former colonies/ruled by other power (29)	Argentina, Australia, Brazil, Canada, Cook Islands, Egypt, Fiji, Hong Kong, India, Indonesia, Ireland, Israel, Ivory Coast, Kenya, Korea, Latvia, Malaysia, Mexico, Morocco, Nigeria, the Philippines, Singapore, South Africa, Syria, Taiwan, Uruguay, USA, Venezuela, Zimbabwe
Former colonisers/held trust territories (11)	Australia, France, Germany, Italy, Japan, the Netherlands, Portugal, South Africa, Spain, United Kingdom, USA
Territory lost to neighbour(s) (11)	China, Germany, Hungary, India, Italy, Japan, Mexico, Romania, Russian Federation, Thailand, Venezuela
Territory gained from neighbour(s) (2)	France, USA
Common law system (15)	Australia, Canada, Cook Islands, Fiji, Hong Kong, India, Ireland, Kenya, Malaysia, Nigeria, Singapore, (South Africa), United Kingdom, USA, Zimbabwe
Civil law system (28)	Argentina, Brazil, China, Egypt, France, Germany, Hungary, Indonesia, Israel, Italy, Ivory Coast, Japan, Korea, Latvia, Mexico, Morocco, the Netherlands, the Philippines, Portugal, Romania, Russian Federation, Spain, Switzerland, Taiwan, Thailand, Turkey, Uruguay, Venezuela
Islamic legal system or influence (5)	Egypt, Iran, Malaysia, Morocco, Syria
Significant minority ethnic group or other groups (11)	Fiji, Indonesia, Israel, Latvia, Malaysia, the Philippines, Romania, Singapore, South Africa, Switzerland, Thailand
Own predominant ethnic or other group also present in another country (12)	Cook Islands, Germany, Hungary, Ireland, Israel, Korea, Malaysia, Mexico, Romania, Russian Federation, Singapore, Syria
Significant number of citizens/former citizens or their descendants live abroad (28)	China, Cook Islands, France, Germany, Hong Kong, Hungary, Iran, Ireland, Italy, Japan, Korea, Latvia, Mexico, Morocco, the Netherlands, the Philippines, Portugal, Romania, Russian

(cont.)

CONSIDERATIONS	COUNTRIES / TERRITORIES SURVEYED
	Federation, Singapore, South Africa, Spain, Switzerland, Taiwan, Thailand, Turkey, United Kingdom, Venezuela
Own minority ethnic/other group of citizens is also present in another country (18)	China, Fiji, Indonesia, Israel, Italy, Japan, Kenya, Latvia, Malaysia, Romania, Russian Federation, Singapore, South Africa, Switzerland, Thailand, UK, USA, Zimbabwe
International legal personality is either called into question or limited (3)	Cook Islands, Hong Kong, Taiwan
Developed (members of the OECD plus Hong Kong, Singapore, Taiwan)[85] (21)	Australia, Canada, France, Germany, Hungary, Ireland, Italy, Japan, Korea, Mexico, the Netherlands, Portugal, Singapore, Spain, Switzerland, Turkey, UK, USA
Developing (not members of the OECD) (24)	Argentina, Brazil, China, Cook Islands, Egypt, Fiji, India, Indonesia, Iran, Israel, Ivory Coast, Latvia, Malaysia, Morocco, Nigeria, Philippines, Romania, Russian Federation, South Africa, Syria, Thailand, Uruguay, Venezuela, Zimbabwe
Large area (over 7 million km²) (6)[86]	Australia, Brazil, Canada, China, Russian Federation, USA
Small area (under 50,000 km²) (9)	Cook Islands, Fiji, Hong Kong, Israel, Latvia, Netherlands, Singapore, Switzerland, Taiwan
Large population (over 100 million)[87] (9)	Brazil, China, India, Indonesia, Japan, Mexico, Nigeria, Russian Federation, USA
Small population (under 10 million) (8)	Cook Islands, Fiji, Ireland, Israel, Latvia, Singapore, Switzerland, Uruguay
High population density (over 200 persons per km²)[88] (11)	Germany, Hong Kong, India, Israel, Japan, Korea, the Netherlands, the Philippines, Singapore, Taiwan, UK

---

[85] For complete list of members see Organisation for Economic Co-operation and Development (OECD), http://www.oecd.org/document/58/0,2340,en_2649_201185_1889402_1_1_1_1,00.html (internet), consulted on 1 March 2006.

[86] For country areas in square kilometres see Central Intelligence Agency (CIA), *The world factbook 2006* (internet), http://www.cia.gov/cia/publications/factbook/index.html, consulted 1 March 2006.

[87] Ibid.

[88] Population Density. Wikipedia (internet), http://en.wikipedia.org/wiki/Population_density, consulted on 1 March 2006.

(cont.)

CONSIDERATIONS	COUNTRIES / TERRITORIES SURVEYED
Low population density (under 20 persons per km²) (5)	Argentina, Australia, Canada, Russian Federation, Uruguay
Attribute nationality including "pure" jus soli (7)	Argentina, Brazil, Canada, Mexico, Uruguay, USA, Venezuela
Attribute nationality only according to jus sanguinis or some variation thereof (37)	(all others)

3. The "nationality" to be examined

States sometimes have more than one formal category (status or class) of nationality. The United Kingdom, for example, has been characterised as having six categories of nationality.[89] In terms of state practice, each formal category of nationality must be considered in relation to multiple nationality. Although the rights attached to these formal categories may vary, their inclusion guarantees the survey's integrity.[90]

It might be argued that should a state treat a group of its nationals so differently from another group of nationals in terms of rights vis-à-vis the state, they should be looked at as possessing different categories of nationality, regardless of form. Although certainly important, this proposal is not relevant for the present study, as long as the state's practice in terms of multiple nationality is the same for all sub-groups. General issues surrounding the rights which commonly attach to nationality (i.e. "citizenship" versus "nationality") will be discussed in the next chapter. Fionda recalls in a general sense that the law often treats children as a category apart, and that note should be taken of this.[91]

4. Note on the effects of residence and other factors

As outlined above, there are ways in which states can encourage individuals to become nationals or to give up that status, such as creating incentives for permanent

---

[89] Laurie Fransman, British nationality law (London: Butterworths, 1998), xiii.

[90] For example, nationality without the inherent right of entry or abode (as in the case of "British Nationals (Overseas)" is of very different value both in terms of the obligations of the state and the rights of the individuals affected, from nationality with such associated rights (British citizenship). Yet in terms of state practice regarding multiple nationality, the quality of the nationality may or may not be important.

[91] Julia Fionda, "Legal concepts of childhood: an introduction," in Legal concepts of childhood, ed. Julia Fionda (Oxford: Hart Publishing, 2001), 3–17, 5.

residents to become naturalized citizens.[92] Although they may influence the decisions made by individuals in relation to their nationality, these factors do not in themselves affect state practice toward multiple nationality, and thus do not need to be taken into account in the survey.

Likewise, in the context of naturalisation, it should be noted that being excluded from seeking nationality, or being allowed to seek it, does not by itself necessarily relate to state practice vis-à-vis multiple nationality. Only when a specific condition of naturalisation is renunciation of a previous nationality, or when a consequence of naturalisation is deprivation of a previous nationality, is naturalisation relevant to state practice vis-à-vis multiple nationality. The issues involved should not be confused, although access to naturalisation is highly debated in many countries. Although the question of access to naturalisation is labelled crucial to both individuals and states, it complements, but does not contribute to, policy related to multiple nationality. It is thus not per se an "ingredient" in the present study. Preventing persons or groups of persons from being naturalised, or placing conditions on naturalisation, may reflect views of the essence of the state and its interests, but does not show practice that must be taken into account here.[93]

5. Review of municipal legislation

It is important to emphasise that the municipal laws reviewed are not related principally to multiple nationality, but to nationality itself. This is because multiple nationality is not granted or taken away by municipal law: only one state's nationality is treated, a fundamental rule of international law being that one state cannot regulate another's nationality, only its own. This is not the same as when states treat an individual as possessing a particular nationality for their own internal purposes.[94] The review of legislation must thus concentrate on the ways in which states attribute their nationality, and the ways in which such nationality is lost.

---

[92] As is arguably the case in Australia, where permanent resident visas are not renewed unless the holder has spent two of the previous five years in Australia, the same period of time required for naturalization. Should there be a chance that an individual with "permanent residence" might leave Australia at some time, only naturalisation guarantees that he or she will be able to return to Australia as a permanent resident, although there are provisions allowing for some discretion in this regard. See Department of Immigration & Multicultural Affairs (Australia), *Permanent resident travel – frequently asked questions,* (internet), http://www. dimia.gov.au/faq/perm_res/02.htm, consulted 1 March 2006.

[93] Weil and Hansen list the right to naturalisation given to "second generation" immigrants in most European Union countries as constituting one of the principal points of convergence of municipal legislation on nationality in the EU. Weil and Hansen, "Citoyenneté, immigration et nationalité: vers la convergence européenne", 13.

[94] "Von dem Grundsatz, dass jeder Staat nur seine eigene Staatsangehörigkeit regeln kann wird eine Ausnahme für die Regelung einer "funktionellen" oder "fiktiven" Staatsangehörigkeit

An analysis of each state's legislation on the attribution/acquisition and withdrawal/loss of its nationality will in and of itself reveal an attitude vis-à-vis multiple nationality. For example, whether naturalisation in another state provokes an automatic loss of nationality, whether there are legal provisions to avoid such loss in certain cases, whether proof of loss of a previous nationality (or only a pledge to renounce such nationality) is a condition of naturalisation, or whether a state legislates that its nationality will be lost if another nationality is possessed beyond a certain age, are all relevant to state practice in terms of how it directly facilitates or frustrates the possession of more than one nationality by an individual. All can be seen from the examination of the laws of a single state.

Another such example is when a state attributes its nationality by means of both *jus soli* and *jus sanguinis*, meaning that its contingent of multiple nationals will be greater than if it applied only one of the two most common modes of attribution. Yet another illustration is the provision (now inapplicable for most practical purposes) in United States law that the act of voting in a foreign election constitutes an "expatriating act" and results in automatic loss of United States nationality. In practical terms, the cohort of persons likely to vote in an election may be expected to be nationals of the country concerned (although as discussed in chapter two, this is changing in the context of the European Union). The US provision thus seems particularly targeted at US multiple nationals, and at the elimination of such multiple nationality by a withdrawal of US nationality. Such a measure may not seem particularly harsh, as voting is generally purely a matter of individual choice. Pity however the Australian-American dual national who (if the US law were enforced without other considerations) would be faced with the choice of losing her/his US nationality, or breaking Australian law, as voting is compulsory in Australia. There are many such considerations.

When the pictures obtained from various countries' legislation are juxtaposed, an image of the complementary effects of states' municipal legislation will emerge. This is especially important as far as discerning the extent to which multiple nationality exists in reality, notwithstanding the fact that the people whom it affects may be

---

gemacht. So haben die Einwanderungsgesetze der USA zeitweilig bestimmt, welche Personen im Sinne dieser Gesetze Staatsangehörige von bestimmten Auswanderungsländern waren. Damit wurde aber nicht eine fremde Staatsangehörigkeit geregelt, sondern die Feststellung hatte nur innerstaatliche Bedeutung". (Author's translation: *An exception to the principle that each state may only regulate its own nationality is made for the rule regarding "functional" or "fictitious" nationality. Along these lines, immigration legislation in the United States from time to time held which persons were deemed to have emigrated from which countries. A foreign nationality was not thereby regulated, as the determination was meaningful only in a municipal sense.*) Wolfgang Hannappel, *Staatsangehörigkeit und Völkerrecht – Die Einwirkung des Völkerrechts auf das Staatsangehörigkeitsrecht in der Bundesrepublik Deutschland*, ed. Dieter Henrich, Erik Jayme, and Fritz Sturm, vol. 27, *Schriftenreihe der Wissenschaftlichen Gesellschaft für Personenstandswesen und verwandte Gebiete M. B. H.* (Frankfurt am Main: Verlag für Standesamtswesen, 1986), 24–25.

unaware that they are in fact multiple nationals, or that they could be multiple nationals, for instance if they applied for a passport to which they have an entitlement under a state's municipal law, not thereby losing their existing nationality.

A template onto which provisions of each state's municipal legislation on nationality must be drafted focusing on the acquisition and loss of nationality in municipal law, in order for individual state practice to be compared and its overall effect in international law understood. While many existing reviews of municipal legislation on nationality do use similar templates, other reviews are simply compilations of nationality legislation.

Several factors must be taken into account. States' laws regulating the acquisition and loss of nationality are varied in form and scope.[95] They range from the exceptionally detailed as in the case of Germany, to expressions of general policy to guide authorities, as in the People's Republic of China and even to a certain extent in its Hong Kong Special Administrative Region. Likewise, states and writers may use different terms to describe essentially the same legal act or procedure, the terms expatriation and denationalisation often overlap for example, or are used with slightly different shades of application. It is thus important that the underlying event and its legal consequences be clearly understood, and categorised systematically, as states may view the underlying occurrence differently in terms of its legal consequences or context. For example, some states may provide for resumption of nationality, or reintegration, whereas others may provide the same underlying right to ex-nationals, but regard or classify the process as naturalisation. While the review undertaken should adopt each state's own characterisation of the legal consequences of the act undertaken, it cannot ignore the larger context, and must attempt to group situations together whenever justifiable, in order to facilitate comparison and review. This is discussed further below, in terms of the modes of acquisition and loss of nationality.

The starting point for any template would seem to be a review of the principal modes for the grant and withdrawal of nationality. But to do so would be to forget that there may be states with various categories of nationality, or which pass as nationality, which must be examined separately. Thus, only once the existence or not of such categories has been ascertained, should each state's modes of attribution and withdrawal of nationality be examined, separately for each category of nationality. Three sources have been used by the author in the construction of a template: the modes discussed by authors on nationality in relation to international law, the modes used in existing reviews of municipal legislation on nationality,[96] and modes found in

---

[95] Already demonstrated by the survey of laws and practice related to nationality carried out by Sieber in 1907. In carrying out his study, Sieber does not seem to have created a template to be used for all states, but tailored his study according to how the laws of each country addressed the subject. There are many variations on many themes. See J. Sieber, *Das Staatsbürgerrecht im internationalen Verkehr, seine Erwerbung und sein Verlust*, vol. 1 (Bern: Verlag von Stämpfli & Cie., 1907).

[96] Those reviewed by the author, incorporating collections of laws on nationality and studies of nationality practice related especially to the situation of women, include: Ibrahim Abdul-

municipal legislation itself when it proposes an additional category not previously identified. This is not to say that the author has identified and incorporated all modes of attribution and withdrawal of nationality, but that the desired template should include the principal modes as well as leaving some latitude for other modes that retain some significance generally, not just in relation to a particular state.

Karim Alghasi, "Die Staatsangehörigkeit in den Bundesstaaten, im Staatenbund und in der Staatengemeinschaft, angeführt als Beispiel: Die Staatsangehörigkeit in den arabischen Staaten", dissertation presented at the Julius-Maximilians-Universität Würzburg (Würzburg, 1965); Carlos Arellano García, "Los peligros de la doble nacionalidad", paper presented at the conference: *La doble nacionalidad* (Ciudad de México: Miguel Ángel Porrúa Librero-Editor, 1995); Nissim Bar-Yaacov, *Dual nationality*, (London: Stevens & Sons Ltd., 1961); Dennis Campbell and Susan Meek, eds., *International immigration and nationality law*, vol. 1 (The Hague: Kluwer Law International, 2001); Bernard Dutoit and Simon Affolter, *La nationalité de la femme mariée*, vol. 1: Europe de l'Est et pays de l'ex-URSS, Supplément 1989–1997 (Genève: Librairie Droz, 1998); Bernard Dutoit and Catherine Blackie, *La nationalité de la femme mariée*, vol. 3: Amérique, Asie, Océanie, Supplément 1980–1992 (Genève: Librairie Droz, 1993); Bernard Dutoit et al., *La nationalité de la femme mariée*, vol. 2: Afrique (Genève: Librairie Droz, 1976); Bernard Dutoit, Daniel Gay, and Terrence Vandeveld, *La nationalité de la femme mariée*, vol. 3: Amérique, Asie, Océanie (Genève: Librairie Droz, 1980); Bernard Dutoit and Denis Masmejan, *La nationalité de la femme mariée*, vol. 2: Afrique, Supplément 1976–1990 (Genève: Librairie Droz, 1991); Bernard Dutoit and Christine Sattiva Spring, *La nationalité de la femme mariée*, vol. 1: Europe – supplément 1973–1989 (Genève: Librairie Droz, 1990); Richard W. Flournoy, Jr. and Manley O. Hudson, eds., *A collection of nationality laws of various countries as contained in constitutions, statutes and treaties* (London: Oxford University Press, 1929; reprint, Littleton: Fred B. Rothman & Co., 1983); Karl Gläser, *Erwerb und Verlust der Staatsangehörigkeit in Hispano-Amerika*, ed. Richard Schmidt, *Abhandlungen des Instituts für politische Auslandskunde an der Universität Leipzig* (Leipzig: Universitätsverlag von Robert Noske, 1930); Randall Hansen and Patrick Weil, "Introduction: citizenship, immigration and nationality: towards a convergence in Europe?", in *Towards a European nationality*, ed. Randall Hansen and Patrick Weil (Houndmills: Palgrave, 2001), 1–23; Hellmuth Hecker, *Das Staatsangehörigkeitsrecht des anglophonen Afrika*, vol. 38, *Sammlung geltender Staatsangehörigkeitsgesetze* (Frankfurt am Main: Alfred Metzner Verlag, 1981); Hellmuth Hecker, *Das Staatsangehörigkeitsrecht des nicht-anglophonen Afrika*, vol. 39, *Sammlung geltender Staatsangehörigkeitsgesetze* (Frankfurt am Main: Alfred Metzner Verlag, 1982); Hellmuth Hecker, *Das Staatsangehörigkeitsrecht von Australien und Ozeanien*, vol. 37, *Sammlung geltender Staatsangehörigkeitsgesetze* (Frankfurt am Main: Alfred Metzner Verlag GmbH, 1980); René Hegi, "La nationalité de la femme mariée", thesis presented at the Université de Lausanne (Lausanne: Imprimerie La Concorde, 1954); Ko Swan Sik, ed., *Nationality and International Law in Asian Perspective* (Dordrecht: Martinus Nijhoff Publishers, 1990); Atsushi Kondo, ed., *Citizenship in a global world. Comparing citizenship rights for aliens* (Houndmills (UK): Palgrave, 2001); Ernest Lehr, *La nationalité dans les principaux états du globe (acquisition, perte, recouvrement)*, (Paris: A. Pedone, 1909); André Liebich, "Plural citizenship in post-Communist states", *International Journal of Refugee Law*, (2000) vol. 12, no. 1, 97–107; Julius Magnus, ed., *Tabellen zum internationalen Recht. Zweites Heft. Staatsangehörigkeitsrecht* (Berlin: Verlag von Franz Vahlen, 1926); A. Peter Mutharika, *The regulation of statelessness under international law*, June 1989 ed. (Dobbs Ferry: Oceana Publications, Inc., 1989); Thomas

Oppenheim notes that there are no specific rules of international law regarding the criteria for acquisition of nationality, just common modes thereof.[97] The same basically holds true for modes of loss of nationality, although as will be outlined in chapter three, the freedom of states in matters of loss may be more limited.[98]

The main modes for acquisition of nationality include (1) birth through jus soli, (2) birth through jus sanguinis, (3) naturalisation, (4) resumption/reintegration, (5) by transfer of territory, (6) acquisition of domicile with the intention of establishing a permanent residence (*animo manendi*), (7) service to the state, and (8) changes in civil status provoked by a relationship to a national (adoption, legitimation, affiliation, marriage), sometimes called by "registration". These are relatively straightforward.

Oppermann and Ahmad Yousry, eds., *Das Staatsangehörigkeitsrecht der Arabischen Staaten*, vol. 15a, *Sammlung Geltender Staatsangehörigkeitsgesetze* (Frankfurt am Main: Alfred Metzner Verlag, 1964); Durward V. Sandifer, "A comparative study of laws relating to a nationality at birth and to loss of nationality", *The American Journal of International Law*, (1935), vol. 29, 248–279; Gustav Schwartz, *Das Recht der Staatsangehörigkeit in Deutschland und im Ausland seit 1914*, ed. Heinrich Titze and Martin Wolff, *Rechtsvergleichende Abhandlungen* (Berlin: Verlag von Julius Springer, 1925); Sieber, *Das Staatsbürgerrecht im internationalen Verkehr, seine Erwerbung und sein Verlust*; Edgar Tomson, *Das Staatsangehörigkeitsrecht des frankophonen schwarzen Afrika*, ed. Forschungsstelle für Völkerrecht und ausländisches öffentliches Recht der Universität Hamburg, vol. 28, *Sammlung Geltender Staatsangehörigkeitsgesetze* (Frankfurt am Main: Alfred Metzner Verlag, 1967); Verlag für Standesamtswesen GmbH, *Ausländisches Staatsangehörigkeitsrecht*, ed. Verlag für Standesamtswesen GmbH, vol. 6; *Kleine Fachbibliothek für Verwaltung und Recht* (Frankfurt am Main: Alfred Metzner Verlag, 1955); Verlag für Standesamtswesen GmbH, *Ausländisches Staatsangehörigkeitsrecht*, 2 vols., *Leitfaden für die Standesbeamten* (Baden-Baden: Verlag für Behördenbedarf, 1955); Patrick Weil, "Access to citizenship: a comparison of twenty-five nationality laws," in *Citizenship today. Global perspectives and practices*, ed. T. Alexander Aleinikoff and Douglas Klusmeyer (Washington: Carnegie Endowment for International Peace, 2001); Patrick Weil and Randall Hansen, eds., *Nationalité et citoyenneté en Europe* (Paris: Éditions La Découverte et Syros, 1999); Peter Weis, *Nationality and statelessness in international law* (Alphen aan den Rijn: Sijthoff & Noordhoff, 1979).

[97] Robert Jennings and Arthur Watts, "Oppenheim's International Law", (London: Longman, 1992), 869.

[98] Weis disagrees with the author's view: "To sum up: the right of a State to make rules governing the loss of its nationality is, in principle – with the possible exception of the prohibition of clearly discriminatory deprivation – not restricted by international law, unless a State has by treaty undertaken specific obligations imposing such restrictions". Weis, *Nationality and statelessness in international law*, 126. However, he does go on to say that "Brownlie has stated correctly that deprivation of nationality must be regarded as illegal if it is part and parcel of a breach of an international duty". Weis, *Nationality and statelessness in international law*, 123. Weis argues that "[i]t is not by denationalisation as such, but only by the denial of residence or of admission, that a State can cast a burden upon other States; it may thereby infringe their right to regulate the admission and residence of aliens and thus violate their territorial supremacy". Weis, *Nationality and statelessness in international law*, 126.

In terms of the desired template, a useful contrast is to compare these categories to those used by Magnus in 1926,[99] whose review of national legislation is also based on a template, as well as other compilations of nationality legislation.[100] A perusal of these studies indicates that the above-listed categories do include all major modes of acquisition of nationality, but cautions that there may be additional relevant considerations, such as in relation to persons who are affected by others' nationality status[101] or acquisition of nationality, and when states provide what many label an option of nationality. The latter category is difficult to categorise, as the underlying option may be expressed in various ways, and be related to the acquisition, retention, or loss of nationality. For example, Sandifer, writing in 1935, points out that under various countries' legislation, options exist (or in most cases, as will be seen, existed) to renounce nationality acquired by *jus soli* in favour of one acquired *jus sanguinis*; for children born abroad to opt for their parents' nationality; for children born in a state of alien parents to opt for its nationality; and for dual nationals to renounce one nationality in favour of the other.[102] The template must therefore include variables as to whether attribution of nationality is in any way conditioned in relation to possible multiple nationality. Along similar lines, it is clear that an important consideration in relation to multiple nationality is whether loss of an existing nationality is a condition of acquisition of the new nationality. This must also be considered in relation to each mode examined.

Other factors that Magnus and others take into account in their review of municipal legislation are arguably less important, or even irrelevant, such as when naturalisation is facilitated for certain persons and thus subject to different conditions from naturalisation generally, and the categories of persons granted such rights or entitlements to seek naturalisation. Such categories include entitlements to seek naturalisation based on: (a) previous national status (as opposed to resumption or reintegration);

---

[99] Magnus, ed., *Tabellen zum internationalen Recht. Zweites Heft. Staatsangehörigkeitsrecht.*

[100] See the following inserts (with years of publication indicated in parenthesis) in *Juris-Classeur Nationalité*, ed. Michel Verwilghen and Charles L. Closset, *Collection des Juris-Classeurs* (Paris: Éditions du Juris-Classeur): Stefania Bariatti, "Nationalité: Italie", (1994); Octavian Capatina, "Nationalité: Roumanie", (1996); Pierre Corboz, "Nationalité: Suisse", (1997); Philippe de Patoul, Tony O'Connor, and John G. Fish, "Nationalité: Irlande", (1984); Hugues Fulchiron and Savinien Grignon Dumoulin, "Nationalité: France," (1997); Louis Kim-Ukkon, "Nationalité: Corée (République de)", (1997); Ko Swan Sik and J. Van Rijn van Alkemade, "Nationalité: Pays-Bas", (1984); Elisa Pérez Vera and José-María Espinar y Vicente, "Nationalité: Espagne", (1993); Anne-Françoise Ravet-Gobbe, "Nationalité: Portugal", (1983); Fouad Abdel-Moneim Riad, "Nationalité: Egypte", (1985).

[101] Especially women historically, and children. Weil notes however that "[e]ach of the twenty-five countries that had a provision for automatic acquisition of citizenship through marriage in its legislation has repealed it within the past forty years". Weil, "Access to citizenship: a comparison of twenty-five nationality laws", 28.

[102] Sandifer, "A comparative study of laws relating to a nationality at birth and to loss of nationality", 249–61.

(b) immigration; (c) descent from a national; (d) membership in national / ethnic group; (e) naturalisation of family member extended to others; (f) marriage; (g) adoption; (h) service to state; (i) purchase of territory. As long as the effects of, and conditions precedent to, naturalisation in relation to the nationality of other states are taken into account, no reference need be made to the categories of people entitled to seek naturalisation in the template.

Considerations in relation to transfer of territory as a means of acquisition and loss of nationality are arguably different in substance and context from other modes of acquisition. The situations contemplated include (1) secession of territory, or cession of part of territory where the former state continues to exist, including newly independent states, (2) the dissolution of a state where the former state ceases to exist, and (3) the unification of two states. As these situations are rare at the current time, they are thus atypical of state practice as a whole. It might also be suspected that policies in relation to the retention or loss of nationality in such contexts might have less to do with multiple nationality as such, than with the political and emotional context and interests related to the underlying event. However, while state practice toward multiple nationality in the context of transfer of territory may represent an atypical situation, it nevertheless is state practice vis-à-vis multiple nationality, and should be considered. The sample of states includes several states which have recently undergone such transfers of territory and populations, as well as many states that have experienced such transfers both within the (relatively) recent and distant past.

Common modes of loss of nationality mentioned include: (1) release or renunciation, (2) deprivation, and (3) expiration.[103] Authors, however, construct various categories for modes of loss, and do not necessarily agree when the underlying act that provokes the loss, either by the individual or the state, falls into one category or the other. Weis, for example, says

> *substitution, i.e., automatic loss of nationality upon acquisition of another nationality, may be regarded as a special mode of loss of nationality, since it takes place by operation of law (without any act either on the part of the State or on the part of the individual) as a result of the acquisition of another nationality, in those states which recognise it in their legislation.*[104]

In the author's opinion, it is arguably more apt to classify the automatic loss of nationality upon acquisition of another as a kind of deprivation.[105] To argue that the operation of law is not an act of the state is to ignore that it is the state that makes, implements and enforces the law, or that such processes take place under the state's

---

[103] Ivan A. Shearer, *Starke's International Law*, 11th ed. (London: Butterworths, 1994), 311. Weis views expiration as a kind of denationalisation. Weis, *Nationality and statelessness in international law*, 116.

[104] Weis, *Nationality and statelessness in international law*, 116.

[105] Donner does as well, see Ruth Donner, *The regulation of nationality in international law*, 2nd ed. (Irvington-on-Hudson (USA): Transnational Publishers Inc., 1994), 122.

auspices. It also does not seem plausible to argue that such loss necessarily ensues from the act of the individual in acquiring the new nationality, as the acquisition of the second nationality may have been involuntary. This was often the case for women upon marriage, as many states' laws made the extension of the husband's nationality automatic upon the event, meaning the performance or registration of the marriage.[106] To claim that women consented to such "substitution" as opposed to being deprived of their nationality, in the author's opinion reflects an unwarranted assumption in relation to the individual's will, and thus an incorrect characterisation of the legal process involved. It is argued that adopting this view reflects current standards of human rights as far as the influence of individual will on the state's actions, but it is clear that this was not the case historically. Germany's Constitutional Court held in 1990 that the effect of a statutory provision according to which Germans could request retention of German nationality, such that naturalisation elsewhere would not provoke loss of nationality, was that the withdrawal of German nationality upon naturalisation elsewhere could not be regarded as a deprivation.[107]

In the 1915 United States Supreme Court case *MacKenzie v Hare*, the Court held that "Mrs. MacKenzie had voluntarily relinquished her citizenship because her marriage was voluntary, and she had notice of the consequences".[108] The case is no longer good law in the United States, but the International Law Association's Committee on Feminism and International Law points out that

---

[106] In Switzerland for example, prior to 1984 it was impossible to prevent such an extension of Swiss nationality upon marriage. Although renunciation of the newly acquired Swiss nationality was possible after the fact, for many women who had lost their original nationality because of the automatic (and involuntary according to the author's conception) acquisition of the new Swiss nationality, such renunciation would not however have restored their original nationality, but in fact made them stateless. Bigler-Eggenberger's essay on "Loss of nationality through marriage: a dark stain in recent Swiss legal history", which concentrates on the automatic loss of Swiss nationality by women upon marriage until 1953, briefly mentions the situation of foreign women who became Swiss automatically through marriage to a Swiss man, but ignores the problems some thereby encountered, treating the provision as one favouring them and their Swiss husbands. Margrith Bigler-Eggenberger, "Bürgerrechtsverlust durch Heirat: Ein dunkler Fleck in der jüngeren Schweizer Rechtsgeschichte", *Recht* , (1999) no. 2, 33–42. This was also the case in the USA, from 1907–1922. See Candice Lewis Bredbenner, *A nationality of her own – women, marriage, and the law of citizenship* (Berkeley: University of California Press, 1998), 3. Bredbenner points out that "the foreign born wives of Americans" were given "the ambiguous distinction of being the first and only group of adults to receive United States citizenship derivatively". Bredbenner, *A nationality of her own – women, marriage, and the law of citizenship*, 15. In relation to women and loss of nationality upon marriage, see generally International Law Association, Committee on Feminism and International Law, "Final report on women's equality and nationality in international law", presented at the Sixty-ninth Conference of the International Law Association (London: ILA, 2000), 272–76.

[107] Hailbronner, Renner, and Kreuzer, *Staatsangehörigkeitsrecht*, 157.

[108] David Weissbrodt, *Immigration law and procedure in a nutshell*, 2nd ed., (St. Paul: West Publishing Co., 1989), 262, citing *MacKenzie v. Hare*, 239 U.S. 299 (1915).

Although independent nationality for married women is now widely accepted, there are still states that maintain reservations or interpretive declarations to article 9(1) of the Women's Convention, which provides that women have equal rights with men to acquire, change or retain their nationality and, in particular, that neither marriage to an alien nor change of nationality by the husband during marriage shall automatically change the nationality of the wife, render her stateless or force upon her the nationality of the husband.[109]

For this reason, in order to incorporate an accurate assessment of the treatment of sex in relation to multiple nationality, the effects of marriage on the acquisition and loss of nationality must be included in the template, as well as when the acquisition or loss of nationality by one person is extended to other persons, in particular spouses and children.

Even when another nationality is acquired by voluntary naturalisation, or by voluntary conduct, in the writer's opinion this cannot be said to amount to voluntary loss or renunciation of the former nationality, as it is the state which withdraws it, not the individual who requests that it be withdrawn. Knowledge of the consequences of an act, or acquiescence in this sense, does not amount to authoring the consequences.

Weis disagrees, as does the municipal legislation of various countries:

Rules of municipal law inflicting loss of nationality on nationals on the ground of their actions or conduct, such as, for instance, loss in consequence of entry into foreign public service, absence over a prolonged period, etc., are based on the assumption that the national by his action or conduct tacitly expresses the will to sever the ties connecting him with his country of nationality. This may be called implied expatriation.[110]

While the author's position is not that states cannot denationalise their citizens on these and other grounds, arguments stemming from municipal and international human rights law that reason against acceptance of the tacit expression of will posited above seem persuasive.[111] The above-mentioned area of disagreement is, however, not

---

[109] International Law Association, "Final report on women's equality and nationality in international law", 263.

[110] Weis, *Nationality and statelessness in international law*, 117. This interpretation is a legislative presumption in some countries. In the USA, the Nationality Acts of 1940 and 1952 (Congress amended existing legislation in 1986 following Supreme Court rulings), listed "service in the military or government of a foreign state, voting in a political election in a foreign state, . . . court martial conviction and discharge from the armed services for desertion in wartime, and conviction of treason" as expatriating acts. A series of cases over 30 years gradually changed the relevance of the individual's own will vis-à-vis his or her American citizenship when the expatriating act was performed. This started with the position that subjective intent was irrelevant, arriving at today's standard that the performance of an expatriating act results in a loss of American nationality only if it is performed with the express intent of relinquishing US nationality. Weissbrodt, *Immigration law and procedure in a nutshell*, 260–68. See generally the exposition on United States nationality in the survey of state practice.

[111] Although authors disagree about the nature and ramifications of individual consent, and

vital for the template proposed, or the assessment of state practice. Weis's overall categorisation of loss of nationality is instructive:

> *Nationality may be lost by an act of the State or by an act of the national. In the first instance it is called deprivation of nationality or denationalisation.*[112]

The loss of nationality can be ascertained according to established criteria, regardless of whether the underlying act is attributed to the state, or to the individual. The issue is fundamentally one of underlying presumptions, and in many states, may not enter into consideration at all. The illustration cautions us, however, as far as the way in which states lay out their legislation and the assumptions that underlie this. For this reason, the author has chosen to avoid general categories, and instead to look to the underlying acts that provide for a loss of nationality, to capture the range of state practice. Common modes of loss are thus canvassed generally without categorising them into the general headings of "deprivation" and "renunciation".

Magnus lists: renunciation, emigration, residence outside national territory, voluntary naturalisation, marriage to a foreigner, legitimation, accepting foreign protection, entry into foreign state service without permission, non-fulfilment of military obligations, failing to return when obliged to do so, revocation of naturalisation, loss extended to wife and minor children, change of territory.[113] While we may suspect that some of these modes may be outdated, such as that relating to acceptance of foreign protection, they do in fact co-incide with most surveys of municipal legislation on nationaltiy, and form the basis for the template in this regard, although they are expanded somewhat.

It was pointed out that the laws reviewed will not relate to multiple nationality as such, but to the acquisition and loss of one nationality. There are some exceptions. States may have specific legislation in relation to multiple nationality, such as forced election upon attainment of a certain age, or instituted bilateral or multilateral treaty arrangements in relation to multiple nationality. These areas are canvassed under "policy", below.

---

national laws and standards vary greatly, a not irrelevant comparison is the study by Elias and Lim on the nature and requirements of individual state consent in international law, who conclude that consent in that context is fundamental on the plane of international law. See generally O. A. Elias and C. L. Lim, *The paradox of consensualism in international law*, vol. 31, *Developments in international law* (The Hague: Kluwer Law International, 1998).

[112] Weis, *Nationality and statelessness in international law*, 115.

[113] Magnus, ed., *Tabellen zum internationalen Recht. Zweites Heft. Staatsangehörigkeitsrecht.*

TEMPLATE FOR THE EXAMINATION OF MUNICIPAL LEGISLATION

Pursuant to these considerations, the examination of municipal legislation on nationality in the Appendix is based on the following, although the exact structure of analysis varies slightly due to space requirements.

I. Nationality category or status

    A. Description of the status and its legal parameters and consequences
    B. Attribution / acquisition of nationality

> *For each category it must be asked whether attribution is limited or conditioned in relation to possible multiple nationality, or whether the attribution is conditional upon renunciation/loss of other nationalities.*

    1. Birth
       a. Jus Soli: in national territory (define: overflying airspace, on national ship, in territorial waters, etc.)
          i. possible conditions attached
       b. Jus sanguinis: by parentage/descent
          i. Both parents possess nationality (possible conditions attached)
          ii. One parent possesses nationality (possible conditions attached)
          iii. Otherwise by descent (not naturalisation by virtue of descent)
    2. Naturalisation
          i. possible conditions attached
    3. Change in status provoked by relation to a national
       a. Adoption
       b. Legitimation
       c. Affiliation
       d. Marriage
       For each ask whether   i. automatic upon event / involuntary
                               ii. by registration / or voluntary act
                               iii. conditions attached
                               iv. right / entitlement to naturalisation
    4. Resumption of nationality / reintegration (possible conditions attached)
    5. Government / military / state service
       a. Automatic (not right / entitlement to naturalisation)
          i. possible conditions attached
    6. Acquisition of nationality extended to others (conditions attached)
       a. Spouse
       b. Children
    7. Other / special considerations

C. Withdrawal / loss of nationality

   1. Renunciation

      a. Voluntary

      b. No provisions for renunciation (permanent allegiance, or "semel civis, semper civis")

      c. "Election" between nationalities in case of multiple nationality

         i. consequences of no election

      d. Permission required for renunciation (some states express as permission required for foreign naturalisation)

   2. Naturalisation in foreign state

      a. Voluntary naturalisation (upon application)

      b. Where naturalisation automatic (no voluntary application)

         i. Akin to registration upon adoption, marriage

      c. Permission required for naturalisation in foreign state or other norm that blocks loss (fulfilment of obligations first)

   3. Marriage to foreign national

      a. Where foreign nationality granted automatically upon marriage

      b. Where marriage does not automatically result in grant of foreign nationality

   4. Service to a foreign state

      a. Military service

      b. Government service / political activity

      c. Other relationship to foreign state

   5. Adoption by parents of foreign nationality

      a. Where nationality automatically conferred

      b. Where nationality conferred upon naturalisation / application

   6. Attribution of nationality by foreign state (other than by naturalisation)

      a. Resumption of nationality / reintegration

      b. Other

   7. Loss of nationality by family member extended to others

      a. Children

      b. Spouses

   8. Other grounds for loss (deprivation) of nationality

      a. Punishment / pursuant to court ruling

      b. Emigration / absence, etc.

6. The analysis of policy

The survey of state practice examines only official government statements or documents that relate directly to the question of multiple nationality as evidence of policy, and excludes other sources. This approach warrants consideration, as there are arguably many areas of municipal law, and by extrapolation government policy, which are affected by multiple nationality in practical respects. Human rights concepts and obligations, national defence, taxation, and labour policy are all examples of areas where the multiple nationality of an individual can affect the state's ability to implement its will vis-à-vis its national, and conversely which may be affected by the state's position toward multiple nationality. Nationality brings with it rights and entitlement that vary greatly from state to state. For example, do states that provide universal health care to their citizens discourage multiple nationality more than states that leave health care to an individual's private means and discretion? Might such areas not warrant study in themselves in terms of their impact on governments' policies toward multiple nationality?

As in consideration of the factors that influence states regarding nationality generally, the author has rejected such an approach as both unworkable and unnecessarily broad. An examination of state policy toward each of these areas individually would arguably reveal little in terms of each area's influence on state practice toward multiple nationality beyond what is revealed through a direct examination. It is also to be expected that some or many of these areas of municipal legislation will be taken up as part of the formulation of policy toward multiple nationality, thus obviating the need to address them independently. While specific areas may be more or less influential in the practice of individual states, a cumulative analysis through examining only attitudes directly on point will not result in a partial or biased picture of the state's attitude. Nevertheless, some latitude in examining specific areas will be adopted, should it be deemed that a state's circumstances require this.

The starting point in the examination of policy is of course an examination of general statements of principle and evidence of practice, which can then be compared with the actual legislative provisions enacted on nationality. For example, a country that provides for automatic deprivation of nationality upon naturalisation elsewhere, but takes no steps to ascertain or implement the deprivation can be contrasted with countries that have the same legal standard, but conclude reciprocal treaties of notification of naturalisation. In terms of perceiving the spectrum of state practice outlined in chapter four, however, an even more detailed examination of policy is warranted. Such examination is especially relevant to discerning nuances in the practice of states that somehow recognise or incorporate multiple nationality into their legal order, but can even be useful in examining the situation of states that claim to disapprove of the status but whose actual practice may not reflect this.

It should be emphasised again that there are many possible avenues available to discern policy vis-à-vis multiple nationality, or to test the implementation of nationality legislation. Most go beyond the scope of what can be taken up here, as nationality itself is relevant to so many areas of law. Thus, based on the overview of municipal and international law related to nationality and multiple nationality in chapters three and four, it is proposed that the examination of policy cover, wherever possible (1) diplomatic protection of multiple nationals, and (2) recognition of foreign travel documents held by a national. These two areas, which are related, are directly on-point as far as revealing state practice, in practical, as opposed to theoretical terms, and provide evidence of some level of recognition (or lack thereof) of multiple nationality. This is especially useful in examining varying levels of tolerance of multiple nationality. An extreme example is the state that permits its own national to enter, remain and depart its territory on the basis of another state's travel document and nationality, even allowing that state a right of diplomatic protection in that case. Such policy evinces an attitude toward multiple nationality that might be labelled complete and systemic recognition related to the individual's choice of nationality. The middle-ground of tolerance might be reflected by states that recognise their nationals' multiple nationality as far as protection vis-à-vis third states, but view nationality combined with territorial presence as trumping any other relationship or right. A weak level of tolerance might be the state that never considers that its nationals have any other ties, while not depriving them of their nationality on the basis of such a tie (essentially, 'we don't care what other states think, we only care what we think').

The spectrum sketched above in relation to tolerance of multiple nationality might be expected to continue in the direction of "intolerance" of multiple nationality, and the question is posed how related nuances might be best discerned. To a certain extent this is illusory, as one might say that while there are various degrees of tolerance, intolerance is by definition exclusionary. It should be pointed out that in this sense behaviour which in and of itself results in loss of nationality, such as military service in foreign armed forces, will be reflected in the analysis of municipal legislation. It is not the loss of nationality as such that is important here, but only such loss as results from the acquisition or retention of another state's nationality. Thus, in the author's conception, state practice in terms of rejection of multiple nationality will be seen most clearly from the legislation reviewed, and administrative procedures adopted, to implement and enforce the loss of nationality. Whether such provisions indicate a view of multiple nationality however, is uncertain. It might be argued that they instead indicate a view of legal procedures and standards.

Along these lines it should be noted that any anecdotal evidence, or evidence of individual treatment that either does or does not accord with national legislation and policy has been strictly excluded. It should be remarked, however, that in practice there would seem to be many instances of special treatment accorded to individuals that do not accord with a state's legal provisions. Such discrepancies may be functions of a range of variables, from subjective decision-making powers accorded administrative officials, to corruption and nepotism. Likewise, there is evidence that individuals who have lost their nationality under a state's municipal laws, for example by being naturalised elsewhere, go to considerable lengths to retain benefits of nationality to which they are no longer entitled by law. This is usually done by not informing the state in question of the naturalisation. These issues are explored only in terms of the steps taken by states to implement their own rules in relation to nationality.

Two other areas of consideration could be proposed in terms of an examination of policy. In the author's opinion they are relevant, but strictly speaking ride the edges of this topic. The first is the identification of an objective standard of the loyalty that a state requires as a consequence of nationality. As presented in chapter three, this might be found in parts of states' legislation on national security and defence. When the same standards are used to judge nationals and non-nationals for crimes against the state (treason or equivalent crimes), an obligation of loyalty arguably does not attach to nationality as such. Such evidence of states' views of the relevance of nationality itself, combined with their specific legal provisions on nationality, might reveal nuances in policy and attitude. But it will be argued in chapter three, loyalty to the state is a consequence of duties under municipal law as opposed to international law. Within the constraints of international law, states may impose any standard they chose on their nationals.

Secondly, the exclusion from entitlements or rights on the basis of multiple nationality also evinces an attitude in terms of policy that could be taken into account. For example, whereas Australia arguably has a very tolerant approach to multiple nationality, its constitutional provision that the subject of a foreign power cannot be elected to Parliament, meaning the exclusion of all Australians who are multiple nationals, arguably provides a disincentive (albeit on a restricted level, recognising that most people do not entertain the idea of representing a constituency in Parliament) to retain foreign (multiple) nationality.

On the other hand, an examination of the fundamental obligations and rights related to a state's nationality as such, and its relation to other categories of relationship to the state, such as citizenship, permanent residence and alien status, is not proposed herein. While arguably relevant, such questions go beyond the scope of enquiry.

As access to treaty texts varies greatly from state to state, bilateral treaties (usually consular) are mentioned when relevant in relation to policy, but are not listed for each country for purposes of comparison.

TEMPLATE FOR THE EXAMINATION OF NATIONAL POLICY

Based on these considerations, the following issues will be considered in the examination of state policy related to multiple nationality.

1. General attitude toward multiple nationality.
   a. Statement of principle.
   b. Applicable municipal laws
   c. Practice – evidence of toleration or avoidance supporting or notwithstanding the statement of principle
      i. Steps taken to ascertain/implement loss of nationality
2. Recognition of Multiple Nationality
   a. Statement of principle
   b. Practice
      i. Recognition of foreign travel documents held by a national
         a. Entry onto / exit from national territory
      ii. Diplomatic / consular protection of multiple nationals

---

F. SIGNIFICANCE OF THE STUDY

It should be noted that the subject addressed is strictly in relation to natural persons; while the nationality of ships, aircraft and companies is certainly interesting and important, especially in an era of globalised services and products, it is not the subject of the current study. The fact that many private enterprises or organisations as legal persons can no longer be associated with a particular country or group of nationals, notwithstanding place of incorporation, headquarters, or listing on a particular stock exchange, must however provoke reflection given the subject matter dealt with.

The present study attempts to break new ground in several respects. It develops and adds to existing literature and research on multiple nationality (and nationality itself) in various ways: through the scope of its inquiry, its focus on international law divorced from policy and emotional preferences, an assumption that state practice toward multiple nationality is nuanced and cannot be categorised in black and white terms, and the proposition that the consequences and nature of nationality itself on the international plane can be discerned through an examination of state practice in relation to multiple nationality.

In relation to the scope of inquiry, it is hoped that placing current state practice within a larger historical context (not just the past one hundred years) will promote the drawing of conclusions that do not incorporate bias in relation to the desirability or not, of multiple nationality, in context. As regards the overview of state practice itself, while several studies have included such reviews, none have done so with the specific intent of discerning state practice *sensu largo*. Indeed, most reviews of municipal legislation on nationality encompass European, North American and a few other developed states. As such they pay short shrift to the fundamental principle in international law of the equality of states. The selection of states is specifically focused on obtaining a sample that is both generally representative of the international community, and specifically representative in terms of municipal legislation and policy on nationality and multiple nationality.

It is the author's hope that this study will contribute to the current understanding of the position of the individual in relation to the state in international law, within the overarching context of attitudes of states toward inclusion and exclusion, and the rights of individuals in relation to the state. Some elaboration on that context is warranted.

The Office of the United Nations High Commissioner for Refugees adopted a line from Euripides' play *The Medea*, first performed in 431 BC, in its campaign to promote understanding of the plight of refugees in the world today.

There is no greater sorrow on earth than the loss of one's native land.[114]

---

[114] Euripides, "The Medea", in *Refugees* (2000) vol. 3, no. 120, cover page.

Another translation reads, with surrounding text to illustrate the context:

> *She listens when she is given friendly advice.*
> *Except that sometimes she twists back her white neck and*
> *Moans to herself, calling out on her father's name,*
> *And her land, and her home betrayed when she came away with*
> *A man who now is determined to dishonor her.*
> *Poor creature, she has discovered by her sufferings*
> *What it means to one not to have lost one's own country.*[115]

In fact Medea was a jilted lover, who according to Greek legend chose to leave her native land willingly to follow Jason, betraying her family and murdering her own brother in the process of escaping.[116] Leaving the details of the story aside, it is clear that there are countless examples throughout history of individuals who have chosen to leave their native lands in varying circumstances, with or without residual emotional attachment.[117] The retention of ties to, and rights in, a place of origin where one is no longer physically present, however origin is defined and whatever the nature of the attachment, is clearly a practical issue for law and politics in an era where communication is increasingly easy, and movement common.[118] Dismissing for a moment her purported crimes against her own country (her father happened to be King), an issue taken up in chapter three in terms of notions of loyalty and allegiance in relation to nationality, why should Medea, or anyone else, not be allowed to return to her native land, or to keep her position within her own country, even if choosing to follow her heart or other inclination meant physical separation? Why should her children be denied a legal relationship to a country with which a she had a close connection?[119] Conversely, why should persons with a close connection to one country, for example permanent residence, be forced back to another, strictly on the basis of

---

[115] Euripides, "The Medea," in *Euripides I*, ed. David Greene and Richmond Lattimore (Chicago: University of Chicago Press, 1955), 60.

[116] Ibid. Greene and Lattimore note that the legend would have been well-known to Greek audiences when the play was first performed.

[117] The author in no way wishes to belittle the sentiment behind the UNHCR's use of Euripides' words. Moreover, the quotation used by the UNHCR accurately reflects the experience of the author's paternal grandparents, who had no choice but to leave the country of their birth. Notwithstanding the great personal hardship caused by the underlying events, and the great appreciation and admiration they felt for their adopted homeland, the separation was a matter of life-long sorrow.

[118] "More than 150 million people worldwide, from senior managers to refugees, are long-term residents in countries other than their own – a number that has doubled in the past 35 years – the International Organisation for Migration said". "Migration boom", *The Australian*, 3 November 2000, 8.

[119] There are many reasons why people wish to return home. Notwithstanding the demise of many Silicon Valley (California) businesses in late 2001, many Australians' decision to return to Australia reportedly had less to do with economics than with family and cultural issues. Georgie Raik-Allen, "They want to call Australia home again", *The Sydney Morning Herald*, 19 February 2002, 12.

their nationality?[120] But what is a "native" land, and what constitutes a "close con-nection"? States' perception of their interests and practice may vary greatly, but what is the situation under international law? State practice vis-à-vis multiple nationality clearly reflects attitudes towards these questions.

It is perhaps particularly apt to reflect on Medea's sex, as a woman who had left her country to marry a foreigner. As such (crossing most borders, cultures and legal orders) she would historically not have had the same ability to retain a legal, family, or cultural attachment to her native land. Issues of conservation of nationality upon marriage and transmission of nationality to children in the context of women's (equal) rights in relation to nationality generally will be discussed in chapter four, but the example of the abandoned and stranded Medea challenges us to examine multiple nationality within the broader context of human rights.

In addressing one aspect of the evolving and complicated relationship of the indi-vidual and the state, this study bears upon the practical context and significance of multiple nationality in the world we live in, a world in which the term "globalisa-tion" has become an issue in virtually all walks of life and areas of human inter-course.[121] Unlike for Medea, the consequences of leaving home are arguably not what they once were, due to advances in technology. At least in terms of physical capac-ity, it is today possible to remain in touch with friends and family by various means of telecommunications, even to receive almost instantaneous news of events in remote places. This is true even of people of relatively modest economic means. Emigration once meant life-long separation due to physical and technological factors, whereas it arguably no longer does today. Whether increased technological capacity influences motives for movement is a question not taken up herein. There is no doubt, however, that it is increasingly common for people to move between countries without neces-sarily wishing to abandon their country of origin, or assuming that leaving means never going back. In this sense globalisation seems to be changing the nature and reality of human association and migration.[122]

---

[120] Xiang Dong Wang, an Australian permanent resident who migrated with his family to Australia in 1985 at the age of 17 and then spent another 17 years in Australian prisons for convictions of serial rape, was to be deported to China on the order of the Administrative Appeals Tribunal, as a danger to the community, following his release from prison. The order was made notwithstanding considerations that he had no relatives in China (the family had migrated ostensibly to escape persecution because of Russian-Jewish heritage), spoke little Mandarin, and might even risk the death penalty under Chinese law for the crimes for which he was incarcerated in Australia. Leonie Lamont, "Deported rapist faces execution in China", *The Sydney Morning Herald*, 2 July 2003, 3.

[121] Ohmae (known as "Mr Strategy") argues that the world has in fact fundamentally changed due to technology, labeling the phenomenon a new continent, composed of a visible dimension, a drive for borderless commerce, communications/technological advances that change the habits of consumers and producers, and the magnitude of the combinations that ensue. Kenichi Ohmae, "A world no longer round. The new frontier is shifting fundamental life assumptions", *The Australian*, 26 July 2000, 36.

[122] The facility with which existing structures and associations are tested by developments

The author hopes that this book, while not taking a specific stand on the issue, will contribute toward placing the emotional debate over the desirability or not, of multiple nationality, into clearer perspective within its broader context. It does so only by addressing one specific area of that wider context, that of international public law. But it behoves us to reflect on just what the broader context is, of multiple nationality. There is no doubt that the topic is related to national and individual interest, to the inclusion of people within legal frameworks, to human rights, to the movements of persons between nations, and to the loyalty people feel, or are required to feel or act upon, toward the states of which they are nationals, and perhaps even those of which they are not. Multiple nationality has even been posited as a vehicle for peace in relation to settlement of disputes, or in the alternative, as a source of armed conflicts between states.[123] The topic is certainly related to statehood and the international system. But even that statement, in the author's opinion, does not go far enough.

The wider context of multiple nationality is in fact how we view, and provide for, the interests of the individual and the collective on a global scale. In an era when "250 million children between the ages of five and 14 work as slaves",[124] claims to

---

in communications' technology is demonstrated by a proposal for the "conservative evangelical" Anglican Archbishop of Sydney, Peter Jensen, to assume "alternative episcopal oversight" over various congregations of the Church of England, ostensibly to replace the oversight of the Archbishop of Canterbury. Jensen reportedly represents a beacon of hope for a minority of the British Church, as he decries the tolerance toward homosexuals espoused by the English Primate. Peter Fray and Kelly Burke, "Archbishop tongue-lashed for tilt at the London boss", *The Sydney Morning Herald*, 22 January 2003, 1 and 8. It is doubtful whether such an idea could have been entertained without technological advances. Opposition to immigration in the context of globalisation appears to be common. For a survey of issues in relation to migration, see Frances Cairncross, "The longest journey. A survey of migration", *The Economist*, 2 November 2002, insert. Another article in The Economist argues that competition for the brightest and facilitated migration for educated persons to developed countries means a loss of skilled workers and harms developing countries. It suggests that "One way to encourage a sense of participating in two cultures, rather than one, is to extend the availability of dual citizenship, something that developing countries have sometimes been reluctant to do". "Outward bound. Do developing countries gain or lose when their brightest talents go abroad?", *The Economist*, 28 September 2002, 24–26, 26. Yet The Economist's articles over time reflect the complexity of the issues related to migration and national interest.

[123] See the joint declaration in 1992 of the presidents of the Federal Republic of Yugoslavia and the Republic of Croatia. United Nations. General Assembly, "Letter dated 21 October 1992 from the Chargé d'affaires a.i. of the Permanent Mission of Yugoslavia to the United Nations addressed to the Secretary-General. Annex: Joint declaration made at Geneva on 20 October 1992 by the President of Croatia and the President of Yugoslavia", Forty-seventh session, A/47/572, 22 October 1992, 2. See also Dan Albert S. de Padua, "Ambiguous allegiance: multiple nationality in Asia", Philippine Law Journal (1985) vol. 60, no. 2, 239–267.

[124] According to the International Labour Organisation. "Slave-ships in the 21st century?", *The Economist*, 21 April 2001, 42.

an "end of history"[125] in this wider context are belied in the author's opinion by the continuing friction in balancing these interests. Caring for human beings remains the great test of politics, civil society, and our legal systems. The broad context of multiple nationality is in fact the myriad challenges facing humanity at the dawn of the third millennium, the many kinds of human suffering, disease, war, persecution, natural disasters, and poverty, that are not new tests in the history of the human race. In this sense, the fact that millions of individuals are considered by governments to belong to more than one national order, internally, and in external expression vis-à-vis other states, bears upon a greater human framework of how we live together and provide for the common good nationally and internationally.

---

[125] A claim made by Fukuyama in relation to ideology. See generally Francis Fukuyama, *The end of history and the last man* (New York: Free Press, 1992).

Chapter 2

Ties that Bind: Views of Nationality, Citizenship, Ethnicity and Identity

For almost a quarter century he was the conscience of Germany, and that this conscience resided on Swiss soil, in a republic and in a city that is a kind of polis, is surely no mere coincidence. He was born for the ways of a democratic republic, and he took the greatest of pleasure in human exchange that was conducted in that spirit. Nothing, in any case, pleased him so much in recent years as the conferring on him of Swiss citizenship. He used to say that for the first time he could be in agreement with a state. That was no rejection of Germany. He knew that citizenship and nationality did not need to coincide – for he was and remained a German – but he knew too that citizenship was not merely a formality either.

Hannah Arendt, public memorial service for Karl Jaspers, Universität Basel, 4 March 1969[1]

A. DEFINING NATIONALITY AND CITIZENSHIP

The terms *nationality* and *citizenship* are perhaps so often confused precisely because they are so closely connected. O'Leary warns that "their present legal significance

---

[1] Lotte Kohler and Hans Saner, eds., *Hannah Arendt Karl Jaspers Correspondence 1926–1969* (New York: Harcourt Brace Jovanovich, 1992), 685.

and content are of recent origin and are closely linked to a series of historical and political developments which have varied from place to place".[2] The words are often used interchangeably, depending on the language in which a text is written, an author's concept of the underlying relationship or status being described, and the legal system within which a particular commentator works.

Aside from their historical significance, Arendt's words are cited here as an illustration of popular usage of the terms nationality and citizenship which does not accord with their usage in international law.[3] Arendt uses the term "citizenship" to characterise Jaspers' connection to the Swiss state, and the term "nationality" to point to his ethnic German background and subjective identity. For the purposes of international law, the connection that links individuals to a particular state is labelled a link of "nationality", notwithstanding a particular individual's ethnic background or origin, or identity. The word "citizenship" on the other hand should not strictly be used to denote that an individual belongs to a state for the purposes of international law, but that an individual possesses particular rights under a state's municipal law. In this case, Jaspers had become, by virtue of his naturalisation in the City and Canton of Basle (Basel), a Swiss national for the purposes of international law, and a Swiss citizen for the purposes of Swiss law. Because Germany withdrew its nationality from Jaspers as a consequence of his naturalisation in Switzerland (in any case, Swiss law at the time required applicants for naturalisation to undertake to renounce any previous nationality), Jaspers ceased to be both a German national and a German citizen, while remaining German in ethnic terms.

Some authors writing on subjects related to international law use the word *citizenship* to denote the conceptual and practical status or relationship which has traditionally been labelled *nationality*.[4] In terms of municipal and international law, such usage is imprecise, and it behoves us to maintain a theoretical distinction because the practical legal consequences of these statuses can still be distinguished.[5] This is true

---

[2] Síofra O'Leary, *The evolving concept of community citizenship – from the free movement of persons to Union citizenship* (The Hague: Kluwer Law International, 1996), 12. Caporal implies that much confusion is due to the lack of precision in the terminology used over the last c. 200 years. Stéphane Caporal, "Citoyenneté et nationalité en droit public interne", paper presented at the conference: De la citoyenneté, Faculté de droit et des sciences politiques de Nantes, 3–5 November 1993, ed. Geneviève Koubi, (Nantes: Litec, 1993), 59–68, 59–60.

[3] The author in no way wishes to maintain or imply that her use of the terms is incorrect, simply that their use is not the same in international law.

[4] The reader is cautioned to take care when referring to texts cited herein, as authors may define these terms differently and in competing ways.

[5] In her comprehensive work on nationality in international law, Donner chooses to use the terms synonymously, stating that "nationality confers membership of the community, also called political status". Ruth Donner, *The regulation of nationality in international law*, 2nd ed. (Irvington-on-Hudson (USA): Transnational Publishers Inc., 1994), xv. O'Leary specifies that the tie of nationality reflects a *relationship* between the state and an individual, whereas citizenship is a specific status. O'Leary, *The evolving concept of community citizenship – from the*

notwithstanding the fact that under the municipal laws of many countries, nationality and citizenship seem to be the same thing.[6] Whether they are considered to be the same thing is influenced by views of the nature of the state, in addition to black letter law.[7]

This chapter outlines the relationships underpinning these and related categories and their legal consequences, and describes the importance of the issues raised in relation to the specific topic of multiple nationality in international law.

The presentation of these various categories and their attached notions of relationships and rights raises an important question: does state practice toward multiple nationality indicate a shift either in the categories themselves or their consequences in international law?[8] Or, would a trend for the categories to merge or diverge in practice mean that their respective and complementary consequences in international law have changed? These issues are taken up in the conclusions herein.

For purposes of clarity, an explanatory table is attached, summarising the main ways these terms have been, and are, used.

free movement of persons to Union citizenship, 10. Spiro does not distinguish between the two. Peter J. Spiro, "Dual nationality and the meaning of citizenship", *Emory Law Review* (1997) vol. 46, no. 4, 1412–1485. Oppenheim states that "[n]ationality of an individual is his quality of being a subject of a certain State, and therefore its citizen". L. Oppenheim, in *International law. A treatise*, ed. Hersch Lauterpacht (London: Longmans, Green & Co., 1948), 586. But he does arguably differentiate between the two, going on to clarify that "[f]or international purposes, all distinctions made by Municipal Laws between subjects and citizens, and between different kinds of subjects, have neither theoretical nor practical value, and the terms 'subject' and 'citizen' are, therefore, synonymous so far as International Law is concerned. Oppenheim, 587–88.

[6] "Unter den heutigen Bedingungen haben diese Unterschiede ihre praktische Bedeutung nahezu volständig verloren, sind aber konzeptionell von grosser Tragweite. In den meisten Ländern ist heute Nationalität gleichbedeutend mit Staatsbürgerschaft". (Author's translation: *In today's circumstances these differences have almost completely lost their practical significance; in theoretical terms such difference remains however of great import. In most countries today, nationality means the same thing as citizenship.*) Ulrich K. Preuss, "Probleme eines Konzepts europäischer Staatsbürgerschaft", in *Transnationale Staatsbürgerschaft*, ed. Heinz Kleger, *Theorie und Gesellschaft* (Frankfurt: Campus Verlag, 1997), 251.

[7] "The truth about citizenship is not only that it elevates statehood to displace nationhood, but that it also is the decisive condition for articulating the idea of a common good under modern sovereignty". William B. Allen, "The truth about citizenship: an outline", *Cardozo Journal of International and Comparative Law*, (1996) vol. 4, no. 2, 355–372, 371.

[8] Spiro postulates that the general trend toward the acceptance of multiple nationality will redefine citizenship itself, although he does not specifically distinguish between citizenship and nationality. Spiro, "Dual nationality and the meaning of citizenship".

TERM	USED HEREIN	OTHER USE 1	OTHER USE 2	OTHER USE 3
NATIONALITY	Legal status in, or relationship with, a state giving rise to personal jurisdiction over the individual, and standing vis-à-vis other states under international law	Belonging to an ethnic group, sometimes called a "race" or "nation", or an "historic-biological" idea of nationality	Legal subclass used to group persons in the municipal law of certain states, usually according to ethnic background	
MULTIPLE NATIONALITY	More than one state attributes its nationality to the same person	Belonging or identifying with more than one ethnic group or "nation"		
CITIZENSHIP	Possession of the highest category of political rights/ duties in municipal law	Nationality (as used herein)	Nationality as used herein, including rights of citizenship	Belonging to groups that exist outside the state
SUBJECT STATUS	Avoided	Nationality (as used herein)	Possession of nationality without any rights of citizenship	Owing personal obligations to a monarch or sovereign

B. HISTORICAL DEVELOPMENT

Writers disagree on the meaning and consequences of the terms nationality and citizenship. Both involve concepts of the relationship between the individual and the state (or wider community), or the status of the individual within the state. It is clear that the specific relationships and statuses have changed over time, as political relations and systems of governance have changed and developed. As already indicated, the terms are not synonymous in international law, but have largely converged in modern times because the people who are nationals of a state most often also make up its citizens. O'Leary points out that this convergence in modern times is "a result of the democratization of the state, the development of the idea of one nation state, the development of an industrial and capitalist society and the consequent tendency to close off the nation state".[9]

---

[9] O'Leary, *The evolving concept of community citizenship – from the free movement of persons to Union citizenship*, 4.

1. The nature of Greek and Roman ideas of citizenship

Greek and Roman ideas of citizenship help us to understand how we got to where we are today, but are not direct predecessors of the "nationality" used at present in international law. This is because the modern concept of nationality is of recent origin, with feudal European roots, and essentially related to power over territory as well as natural persons. Nevertheless, Greek and Roman ideas of citizenship can be said to provide a foundation for today's notion of "nationality" and are directly relevant to current definitions of citizenship.

In ancient Greek cities (in the centuries around the third century BCE), concepts of citizenship revolved around political and economic rights at the local level,[10] in addition to religious privileges and duties.[11] Only in later times did the concept expand to rights within a wider community. O'Leary cites Koessler's definition of modern citizenship as "possession . . . of the highest or at least of a certain higher category of political rights and (or) duties, established by the nation's or state's constitution".[12] This definition of citizenship, adopted herein, reflects the ancient a Greek concept of citizenship, related to the rights of persons within a community, and the relationship among citizens as members of a "polis" or community.[13] In ancient Greece for example, the laws prohibiting marriage or cohabitation of Athenian male citizens or Athenian women, with foreigners, were based on principles against the usurpation of citizenship rights and the rights of offspring in the community.[14] The

---

[10] See Preuss, "Probleme eines Konzepts europäischer Staatsbürgerschaft," 253.

[11] Ilias Arnaoutoglou, *Ancient Greek laws. A sourcebook* (London: Routledge, 1998), xvi.

[12] O'Leary, *The evolving concept of community citizenship – from the free movement of persons to Union citizenship*, 5. quoting Maximilian Koessler, "'Subject,' 'Citizen,' 'National,' and 'Permanent Allegiance'", *Yale Law Journal*, (1946) vol. 56, 58–76, 61. The word *citizenship* is sometimes used outside the context of the nation-state, to denote individual belonging or identification with groups or associations that exist beyond or within the state. Political scientists analyse citizenship in the "broader context governed by power and identity". C. R. D. Halisi, Paul J. Kaiser, and Stephen N. Ndegwa, "Guest editors' introduction: the multiple meanings of citizenship – rights, identity, and social justice in Africa", *Africa Today*, (1998) vol. 45, no. 3–4, 337–350, 337. See generally Will Kymlicka, *Multicultural citizenship – a liberal theory of minority rights* (Oxford: Clarendon Press, 1995). For an African example, illustrating the mixture of identities and the exercise of rights in various contexts, using Tanzanian Ismailis and the Burundian diaspora as an example, see Rose M. Kadende-Kaiser and Paul J. Kaiser, "Identity, citizenship, and transnationalism: Ismailis in Tanzania and Burundians in the Diaspora", *Africa Today*, (1998) vol. 45, no. 3–4, 461–480. The authors use the term "dual citizenship" outside the context of the nation-state, to denote membership of trans-national communities of identity.

[13] See generally Arnaoutoglou, *Ancient Greek laws. A sourcebook*.

[14] Id., 17–18. This is also seen from a law in Gortyn (Crete) on the status of the offspring of 'mixed' marriages, meaning between free women and slaves, as the children's status depended on that of the mother. In Athens, a child's status depended on that of both parents. Id., 30.

prohibition was not related to any conflict that might arise between communities over the individuals in question. In this sense, citizenship does not seem to have had negative ramifications outside the polis, or in terms of the relationships among poleis. Multiple citizenship however, was indeed a possibility:

> In ancient Greek poleis the assembly of the citizens could grant citizenship to an individual or to citizens of other poleis in exceptional circumstances. [Accordingly] . . . the Thasians extend[ed] the right to Thasian citizenship to all those, men and women, born by Thasian women living in Neapolis, one of their colonies in the mainland, as part of the reorganization following the political upheavals of the late 5th century BC.[15]

Likewise, citizens of different poleis could receive reciprocal rights or privileges by agreement, for example in the context of colonisation. In the colonisation of Naupaktos by Lokris in 460–450 BC,

> The citizens of the colony los[t] some of their rights as citizens of Lokris but could participate in the sacrifices and other ceremonies of the mother-polis, as foreigners. In particular, arrangements were made for the property left behind and ateleia was granted, oath of allegiance and alliance was to be sworn, and the citizens of both mother-polis and colony would have judicial preference in courts.[16]

O'Leary remarks that the practice of conferring citizenship on allied poleis became common, which in turn reduced the value of citizenship in terms of its exclusivity.[17]

Roman concepts of citizenship also involved the rights of certain groups vis-à-vis other groups in society.[18] Patricians, who owned property, were citizens who "had certain public duties and responsibilities within the city-state".[19] Plebians, or landless tenants, did not. As in Greek city-states, "little by little the internal importance of the citizenship/non-citizenship distinction diminished until it finally disappeared around AD 212 when citizenship was granted to most of the Roman world".[20] The significance of Roman citizenship is best understood in terms of the application of Roman law.

---

[15] Id., 92–93.

[16] Id., 111–12.

[17] O'Leary, The evolving concept of community citizenship – from the free movement of persons to Union citizenship, 4. De Castro cites these instances in ancient Greece as the first example of what he calls dual nationality. F. de Castro, "La nationalité la double nationalité et la supra-nationalité", Recueil des cours (Académie de droit international), (1962) vol. 102, no. 1, 515–634, 589–590. He refers to three types: (1) simpoliteia, or political alliance between cities involving common citizenship, (2) isopoliteia, or reciprocal citizenship rights for individuals between poleis, and (3) concession of citizenship to individuals, not involving the loss of citizenship rights elsewhere. F. de Castro, 590–1.

[18] O'Leary, The evolving concept of community citizenship – from the free movement of persons to Union citizenship, 4–5.

[19] Id., 5.

[20] Ibid.

Roman (private) law was a personal, not a territorial, law. It controlled and was applicable to, not all persons within a certain district but, all Roman citizens, wherever they were. Originally law made by and for the citizens of Rome, it always had its chief seat in Rome and within a mile outside the walls. After the second Punic war, praefects were sent to the Campanian towns to administer Roman as well as other law. In the provinces the Governors administered it, though not to the exclusion of the Roman praetor. Further the Roman dominion was a complex of communities; and those which did not possess the citizenship of Rome, whether formally autonomous like the Latins, or federated peoples, or simply permitted to remain autonomous, maintained their own administration of justice, when neither party to a suit was a Roman citizen. If one was a Roman citizen, the Roman law usually applied. But the autonomy was sometimes broken by arbitrary interference on the part of Roman officials. Foreigners at Rome were apparently readily admitted to the Roman Courts . . .[21]

De Castro notes that dual citizenship was common in Rome for political reasons, and while it may have been unacceptable for a Roman citizen to be subjected to foreign authority, it was beneficial to Rome for foreigners to possess Roman citizenship.[22] He states that Cicero's well-known phrase, *ex nostro jure duarum civitatum nemo esse possit*, used to oppose multiple nationality in some cases in early modern Europe, cannot be cited for that purpose, as although Romans may have lost their Roman citizenship by for example performing certain political acts elsewhere, they only had to traverse Rome's borders to recuperate their rights and citizenship: *nisi post liminium recuperassent.*[23]

It is in this context that (Saint) Paul of Tarsus' well-known claim to Roman citizenship, which spared him torture and probable death, should be seen as a claim related to the law that should be applied to him, and not as an ancient-world version of a claim to diplomatic protection.[24]

---

[21] Henry John Roby, *Roman private law in the times of Cicero and of the Antonines*, vol. 1 (Cambridge: Cambridge University Press, 1902), 16.

[22] F. de Castro, "La nationalité la double nationalité et la supra-nationalité", 592. Thus, one could be both a Roman and a foreigner at the same time, having rights in both place of origin and in Rome. Ibid.

"A partir d'Auguste, les étrangers qui acquéraient la citoyenneté romaine, tout en conservant leur propre citoyenneté, devinrent de plus en plus nombreux. La citoyenneté romaine était considérée comme un privilège important et apprécié, de sorte que parmi les meilleures familles grecques des villes et parmi les propriétaires terriens les plus riches, rares étaient ceux qui ne possédaient pas la citoyenneté romaine en plus de leur propre citoyenneté. (Author's translation: *Starting with Augustus [Caesar] foreigners who acquired Roman citizenship while retaining their own citizenship became more and more numerous. Roman citizenship was considered to be an important and appreciated privilege, such that among the best families of the Greek cities and among the owners of the richest estates hardly anyone did not possess Roman citizenship in addition to his own.*). Id., 593.

[23] Id., 592.

[24] The text from Chapter 22 of the *Acts of the Apostles* states: *23 And as they were crying out and throwing off their cloaks and tossing dust into the air, 24 the commander ordered him*

The Roman classification of persons was, however, more complicated than simply citizen versus non-citizen. In terms of fundamental categories, the Roman world was divided into free persons and slaves, the latter having no legal rights, while free persons were not necessarily citizens, but divided into the categories of citizens, Latins, foreigners, or *dediticii* ("foreigners who had fought against the Romans and surrendered").[25]

Foreigners were

> *Freemen who were not either Roman citizens or Latins . . . not regarded by the Romans as having such full rights over their children as Romans had, . . . but certain rights of inter-marriage with Romans were recognized, with the effect that the children became in some cases Roman citizens or Latins. Business was transacted with them according to what the Romans called the law of the world (jus gentium).*[26]

---

to be brought into the barracks, stating that he should be examined by scourging so that he might find out the reason why they were shouting against him that way. 25 But when they stretched him out with thongs, Paul said to the centurion who was standing by, "Is it lawful for you to scourge a man who is a Roman and uncondemned?" 26 When the centurion heard this, he went to the commander and told him, saying, "What are you about to do? For this man is a Roman." 27 The commander came and said to him, "Tell me, are you a Roman?" And he said, "Yes." 28 The commander answered, "I acquired this citizenship with a large sum of money." And Paul said, "But I was actually born a citizen." 29 Therefore those who were about to examine him immediately let go of him; and the commander also was afraid when he found out that he was a Roman, and because he had put him in chains. And from Chapter 25: *7 After Paul arrived, the Jews who had come down from Jerusalem stood around him, bringing many and serious charges against him which they could not prove, 8 while Paul said in his own defense, "I have committed no offense either against the Law of the Jews or against the temple or against Caesar." 9 But Festus, wishing to do the Jews a favor, answered Paul and said, "Are you willing to go up to Jerusalem and stand trial before me on these charges?" 10 But Paul said, "I am standing before Caesar's tribunal, where I ought to be tried. I have done no wrong to the Jews, as you also very well know. 11 "If, then, I am a wrongdoer and have committed anything worthy of death, I do not refuse to die; but if none of those things is true of which these men accuse me, no one can hand me over to them. I appeal to Caesar." 12 Then when Festus had conferred with his council, he answered, "You have appealed to Caesar, to Caesar you shall go."* The Lockman Foundation, *New American Standard Bible, Acts of the Apostles, Chapters 22–25* (internet), http://www.biblegateway.com/passage/?search=Acts%2022–25;&version=49;, consulted 15 March 2006.

[25] See Roby, *Roman private law in the times of Cicero and of the Antonines*, 18–20. See also Ph. J. Thomas, *Introduction to Roman law* (Deventer: Kluwer Law and Taxation Publishers, 1986), 135–44.

[26] Roby, *Roman private law in the times of Cicero and of the Antonines*, 19. Jus gentium is thus sometimes cited as a kind of Roman international law, an inapt definition and comparison. As law applied according to personal status, jus gentium determined which personal law would be applied, and thus might be compared to current rules relating to conflicts of law, or "international private law". Vattel states that the Romans did recognise that law between nations existed, citing the existence of embassies, as well as *fetial law*. At the same time, he points out that the Romans confused what they called the law of nations, or *jus gentium*, with

Acquisition and loss of status could occur by various means, and as in the Greek provisions mentioned above, the status inherited by a child depended on the status of his or her parents. Roman citizenship could be acquired by birth, grant, manumission, and statute.[27] In this sense, although the nature of Roman citizenship was not the same as nationality in international law today, there are certain similarities in the form of the rules surrounding the acquisition and loss of Roman citizenship and rules on the acquisition and loss of nationality,[28] as well as parallels related to personal jurisdiction. The inherent differences between the two statuses should however, not be confused as a consequence.

2. The origin and definition of "nationality"

Although Koessler states that "'nationality' is a young word. Its matrix, the French *nationalité*, appeared for the first time in the 1835 edition of the Dictionnaire de l'Académie Française",[29] it does appear to have Roman origins. As opposed to political participation, rights, and applicable law, the Roman origin of ideas related to nationality involved belonging to a group of persons, the group, or *nation*, being determined either by lineage or geography.[30] The idea of a nation in this sense was not specifically linked to political or legal structures. This is what O'Leary, drawing on much preceding scholarship, defines as an "historic-biological" notion of "subjective corporate sentiment of unity of members of a specific group forming a "race" or "nation".[31] This is also the way Arendt, cited above, used the word "nationality" to characterise Jaspers' relationship to Germany, although in the terms of international law he had lost his German nationality.

---

the law of nature, demonstrating the gap between his concept of nations in terms of sovereign states, and the Roman one. Emmerich de Vattel, *The law of nations or the principles of natural law applied to the conduct and to the affairs of nations and of sovereigns*, trans. Charles G. Fenwick, 1758 ed., vol. 3 (Washington: The Carnegie Institution of Washington, 1916), 3a–4a.

[27] Roby, *Roman private law in the times of Cicero and of the Antonines*.

[28] For example, deprivation of nationality as a consequence of naturalisation elsewhere or other foreign involvement might be compared with Roman loss of citizenship in certain cases. There are, however, many differences. A Roman who had been captured in war became a slave to his captors, but resumed his previous rights and status upon return to Roman controlled lands, as long as he had no intention of returning to the enemy. A deserter on the other hand had no right of return. Id., 41–42.

[29] Maximilian Koessler, "'Subject,' 'Citizen,' 'National,' and 'Permanent Allegiance'", *Yale Law Journal*, (1947) vol. 56, 58–76, 61.

[30] O'Leary, *The evolving concept of community citizenship – from the free movement of persons to Union citizenship*, 6.

[31] Ibid. The "historico-biological approach regards nationality in the light of the historical, cultural and social ideal of the nation. The latter consists of an authentic, national and organic

In the Greek and Roman world the rights of citizenship outlined above reflected the fact that political interaction was seen as taking place within communities, as opposed to between them. This changed in Europe in the middle ages, when political life

> Tended to centre on the struggle for power between different political administrative enti-
> tles. Members enjoyed privileges and immunities and were subject to obligations on the
> basis of established social hierarchies and on the basis of their relationship of allegiance
> with the sovereign. They were treated as subjects rather than individuals.[32]

As in Roman times, the link that bound the individual to authority under Anglo-Saxon and feudal law had nothing to do with an idea of ethnic or national groups as such. In mediaeval Europe the link that bound the individual to authority was a territorial one, individuals being tied to the land, and subject to the sovereign who controlled it.[33] Today's definition of nationality in international law has evolved from these

---

community, formed on the basis of destiny, history and the cultural characteristics of its components. This historic-biological aspect of nationality is also sociologically determined and cannot, therefore, be qualified and constrained simply by positive law. It will not necessarily coincide with the positive legal definitions of nationality referred to above. A parallel distinction can be sketched between the nation and the state. The former is a cultural, historical and social concept, while the latter is generally a legal concept which refers to autonomous public institutions". Ibid. Oppenheim states "'nationality,' in the sense of citizenship of a certain State, must not be confused with 'nationality' meaning membership of a certain nation in the sense of a race. Thus, according to International Law, Englishmen, Scotsmen, and Irishmen are, despite their different nationality as regards their race, all of British nationality as regards their citizenship. Thus further, although all Polish individuals are of Polish nationality *qua* race, for many generations there were no Poles *qua* citizenship". Oppenheim, *International law. A treatise.*, 588. Koessler agrees. Koessler, "'Subject,' 'Citizen,' 'National,' and 'Permanent Allegiance'", 61. Weiss cites Vishniak (1933) as the source of the distinction. Peter Weis, *Nationality and statelessness in international law* (Alphen aan den Rijn: Sijthoff & Noordhoff, 1979), 3 n. 1. "Nation" in its "historic-biological" sense is often used as a synonym of the word "people". This is important, as under Articles 1(2) and 55 of the United Nations Charter and subsequent UN General Assembly resolutions and declarations, "peoples" enjoy a right of self-determination at international law. Peter Radan, *The break-up of Yugoslavia and international law*, *Routledge Studies in International Law* (London: Routledge, 2002), 9–11. United Nations Charter, United Nations, Charter of the United Nations (internet), http://www.un.org/aboutun/charter/, consulted on 1 March 2006. Radan outlines the two theories about what constitutes a "people" possessing a right to self-determination, the "classical" theory indicating the inhabitants of a defined territory, and the "romantic" theory stipulating a "nation" in "historic-biological" terms. He argues that "people" must also include "nations" in the romantic ("historic-biological") sense. Radan, 20.

[32] O'Leary, *The evolving concept of community citizenship – from the free movement of persons to Union citizenship*, 5.

[33] See generally Parry, Clive, ed. A British digest of international law. Vol. 5. London: Stevens & Sons, 1965.

feudal ties, linking individuals to territories. O'Leary labels this second concept of nationality a "politico-legal" notion of legal membership in the community (state, or nation), defined by law.[34]

The connection between the two aspects of the word "nation", and their evolution with respect to one another, is directly traceable to the emergence of the modern Westphalian system of sovereign states after 1648.[35] Throughout the 19th and early 20th centuries, the idea of the "nation-state" mostly corresponded to a "romantic" ideology of the state, according to which states were in fact made up of "nations" in the historic-biological sense.[36] Radan mentions German and Italian unification, the emergence of Albania, Bulgaria, Greece, Norway, Romania, Serbia, and Sweden, and the break-up of the Austro-Hungarian Empire, as examples. Illustrating that the idea is far from gone, he cites the (romantic) *national* pressures on the Federal Republic of Yugoslavia in the 1990s, and its subsequent break-up more-or-less along what were perceived as ethnic lines.[37] The romantic ("historic-biological") idea (or ideal) of the nation is thus still a major force in domestic and international relations.

Certain states, however, did not fit the romantic idea of the nation-state in reality or ideology. Exceptions to this ideology included the United States and France following their respective revolutions in 1776 and 1789. These states were instead defined by a "liberal national" ideal, according to which the focus of the individual's self-identification and loyalty was the state itself, as opposed to a (or "the") nation.[38] Radan labels this the "citizen-state" as opposed to the "nation-state". He argues that much semantic confusion stems from the appropriation of terminology relevant to the "nation-state" by the "citizen-state", such as when *states* which do not pretend to have "nations" as their fundamental basis continue to be referred to as "nations".[39] On the other hand, whether a state is itself a "nation" or made up of "nations" is a matter of controversy in many places, such as in Spain, where any hint of regional

---

[34] O'Leary, *The evolving concept of community citizenship – from the free movement of persons to Union citizenship*, 6.

[35] See generally Oppenheim, *International law. A treatise.*, 5. Prior to the Treaty of Westphalia, neither the Roman nor the feudal world held the idea of sovereign, equal states. This was arguably also the case in Asia and other parts of the world, where various kingdoms and political entities vied for power, but did not have theories about their political position vis-à-vis other such entities, and in any case rarely saw themselves as equals. The Chinese example is apt, whose world-view essentially consisted of China, and the barbarian hordes surrounding her, or lesser political entities that paid tribute.

[36] Whether this corresponded to reality is hotly debated. This is discussed below. See Radan, *The break-up of Yugoslavia and international law*, 12–15.

[37] Id., 15. He also points to the creation of the states of Bangladesh and Israel as examples of the power of "historic-biological" nationality in leading to the creation of states, but views them as exceptions, given and the many moves toward "national" self-determination which have not succeeded. Id., 18–19.

[38] Id., 12–15.

[39] Id., 14–15.

identity that might claim to be "national" was severely repressed under the dictatorship of Francisco Franco.[40]

Thus, since the emergence of the modern system of sovereign states within a system of international law and relations, both concepts of "nation" and "nationality" can be said to have reflected different views of the state. Both developed in tandem with the modern notion of the community of sovereign states, each the equal of the other in international law. But at some point, the political nation-state was divorced from romantic ideas of the nation-state, and the "politico-legal" notion of *nationality* as a tie that binds the individual to the sovereign (or state, as personal ties to monarchs were replaced by ties to republican governments or constitutional monarchies), clearly distinguished from ethnicity.[41] One might speculate that influences included ideological developments in relation to the equality of individuals within states, or perhaps it became clear that many states did not in fact have at their core a *nation* in the historic-biological sense. This is still an area of much heated controversy. What is important for the arguments herein, is that "politico-legal" nationality be distinguished from "historic-biological" nationality, as only the former gives rise to a juridical definitional link between the state and an individual in international law.

It should be mentioned that some states' practice seems to make the water even murkier, as they give some, albeit limited, legal effect to the "historic-biological" notion in their municipal law. Soviet policy was to recognise and categorise people in municipal law according to what was arguably the "historic-biological" notion of nationality described above, their Soviet "politico-legal" nationality as part of the state as a whole being a separate issue. Koessler provides other examples that demonstrate that "nationality, ethnologically, while essentially a sociological conception with

---

[40] Witness the heated debate in 2005 over whether Catalonia should be allowed to define itself as a "nation" within Spain, and whether Spain is a "nation" or state constituted of "nations". See Renwick McLean, *Spanish Parliament to weigh Catalan autonomy*, International Herald Tribune, 4 November 2005 (internet), http://www.iht.com/articles/2005/11/03/news/spain.php, consulted 19 December 2005. Discussion in the early 21st century in relation to "nation-building" in Afghanistan centres around the state in politico-legal terms, as opposed to the many ethnic groups or "nations" in Afghanistan. Due to the mixing of terminology, the "nation" of Afghanistan is often labelled a "multi-national" state, populated by Pashtuns, Tajiks, Uzbeks, Hazaras, and others. Thus, "nation-building" in a politico-legal sense may be seen to come at a cost to nations in the "historic-biological" sense. Native American tribes are recognized as "nations" in the United States, whose sovereignty vis-à-vis the US federal government is on par with that of the fifty states.

[41] It is impossible to delineate exactly when the "politico-legal" notion of state nationality emerged as distinct from the "historic-biological". Radan believes it is the Second World War. Id., 14. But already in 1758 Vattel's theory of sovereign states excluded nations that were not self-governing. Albert de Lapradelle, "Introduction," in Emmerich De Vattel, *The law of nations or the principles of natural law applied to the conduct and to the affairs of nations and of sovereigns*, (Washington: Carnegie Institution of Washington, 1916), xi.

political implications, may occasionally have a palpable legal effect".[42] Again, this is not the *nationality* in question here.

A clear illustration of confusion (and arguably abuse) in the delineation of people in relation to nationality, and an apt example of the issues that surround delimitation of groups along ethnic, state, identity, rights-based, and indeed even religious lines, was the attribution of nationality to Greeks and Turks in the aftermath of almost twenty years of conflict that resulted in a massive population exchange.[43] Rather than place of origin or residence, subjective identity, language, and certainly not according to the individual's will,

> *the only criterion used was religion. Over a million Christians (some of them monoglot Turkish speakers) were deported from Anatolia, and hundreds of thousands of Muslims (some of them Greek-only speakers) were dispatched from Greece to Turkey. By turning Greece into a country that was 97% Orthodox Christian, at least in name, the population swap made church and nation seem even more inseparable. To be Greek was to be Orthodox, most people thought, and the church hierarchy did nothing to discourage the idea.[44]*

---

[42] Koessler, "'Subject,' 'Citizen,' 'National,' and 'Permanent Allegiance'", 62. He cites the dissolution of the Austro-Hungarian monarchy, in which "the right of option . . . depended to a measurable extent upon the ethnological quality of the optant". Additional examples, in the context of forced population exchanges, are the attribution of German nationality/citizenship in 1939 to Czechoslovakian citizens of German ethnicity, and Hungary's acknowledgment of German claims of a right to protect ethnic Germans in that country. Id., 62. The Israeli "Law of Return" for Jewish persons wishing to migrate to Israel might be considered a relevant example, as is the provision in Article 116(1) of the German constitution or "Basic Law" that provided German nationality to migrants of ethnic German stock from East European countries. Whiteman mentions the Polish Nationality Act of 8 January 1951, which conditioned acquisition of Polish nationality on Polish ethnic origin, with some leeway. Whiteman, *Digest of international law*, 15 vols., vol. 8, (Washington: Department of State, 1968), 74–75.

[43] See generally Bruce Clark, "A survey of Greece. Roll out the welcome mat", *The Economist*, 12 October 2002, Supplement, 7.

[44] Ibid. The Turkish Ministry of Foreign Affairs has until recently claimed that discrimination against Greek citizens of Turkish ethnic origin is still an issue. "The Turkish Minority of Western Thrace constituted 65% of the population in Western Thrace in 1921 when it was ceded to Greece. Now, it only makes up 35% of the population, despite their high birth rate. In order to achieve its goal to eradicate the Turkish Minority as an ethnic, religious and cultural entity, Greece arbitrarily expelled thousands of Minority members from citizenship, through application of the former Article 19 of the Greek Citizenship Code. Article 19 was abrogated by the Greek Parliament in June 1998. Yet, inasmuch as the abrogation is not retroactive in nature, thousands of stateless minority members are still unable to regain their Greek citizenship unlawfully taken away by Greek authorities. Article 19 of the Greek Citizenship Code, reads as follows: 'A person of non-Greek ethnic origin leaving Greece without the intention of returning may be declared as having lost Greek nationality'. According to a document released in the local 'Hronos' newspaper on November 7, 1997, the number of

3. The convergence of nationality and citizenship in certain states

In many states, as citizenship (political, property and other) rights were extended to all sectors of a state's community over time, any distinction that may have existed between the concepts of nationality and citizenship began to disappear.[45] In terms of international law however, the two categories are arguably still distinguishable. This is expanded upon in the following section. Weil and Hansen note a convergence in the municipal legislation on nationality in European states, a parallel issue.[46] Nationality (in its "politico-legal" sense) can be

> regarded as an undetermined attribute which is used as a tool by municipal, inter-national and even [European] Community law to determine who belongs to what state. In other words, it identifies who enjoys what legal consequences, rather than which legal consequences they enjoy. The latter task is left to citizenship. Indeed, some authors have argued that nationality is a purely "formal frame" which gives rise to no fixed legal consequences.[47]

---

people deprived of their citizenship through the implementation of Article 19 is around 450,000. Republic of Turkey. Ministry of Foreign Affairs, *Deprivation of citizenship* (internet), http://www.mfs.gov.tr/grupa/ac/acd/acda/wt depriv.htm, consulted 27 January 2001. This text has since disappeared from the Ministry's website. Human Rights Watch claimed the number of persons deprived of citizenship under the provision was 60,000. Human Rights Watch, "Positive steps by the Greek State", 2004 (internet), http://www.hrw.org/reports/1999/greece/Greec991–05.htm, consulted 15 March 2006.

[45] O'Leary, *The evolving concept of community citizenship – from the free movement of per-sons to Union citizenship*, 7–9. The French Revolution brought with it debates about national membership and the rights of citizenship, with arguments that Jews, as members of a distinct *nation* to the French *nation*, should be excluded from the rights of citizens. These were swept aside by republican arguments. Caporal, "Citoyenneté et nationalité en droit public interne", 67. For another historical overview see Benoît Guiguet, "Citizenship and nationality: tracing the French roots of the distinction," in *European citizenship. An institutional challenge*, ed. Massimo La Torre, *European Forum* (The Hague: Kluwer Law International, 1998), 95–111.

[46] Patrick Weil and Randall Hansen, "Citoyenneté, immigration et nationalité: vers la con-vergence européenne", in *Nationalité et citoyenneté en Europe*, ed. Patrick Weil and Randall Hansen, *Collection "Recherches"* (Paris: Éditions La Découverte, 1999), 9–28.

[47] O'Leary, *The evolving concept of community citizenship – from the free movement of per-sons to Union citizenship*, 9. See Koessler, "'Subject,' 'Citizen,' 'National,' and 'Permanent Allegiance'", 70. Robert maintains that whereas nationality is a human right, evidenced by Article 15 of the Universal Declaration of Human Rights stating that everyone has a right to a nationality, citizenship is not a right. "La citoyenneté, par ailleurs, n'est pas un droit. C'est un ensemble de compétences politiques reconnues par un Etat à une personne qui vit sur son territoire et qui, en général, est déjà un « national »". (Author's translation: *Besides, citizenship is not a right. It is a collection of political competences recognized by a state vis-à-vis a per-son who lives on its territory and who in general is already a "national".*) Jacques Robert, "Préface", paper presented at the conference: De la citoyenneté, Faculté de droit et des sciences politiques de Nantes, 3–5 November 1993, ed. Geneviève Koubi (Nantes: Litec, 1993), i–v, i.

Whether or not nationality gives rise to fixed legal consequences is discussed in the following chapter.

C. THE MEANING OF NATIONALITY IN INTERNATIONAL LAW AS OPPOSED TO CITIZENSHIP

The "nationality" which is the subject of this book describes the specific, primary relationship between the state and an individual (a *national* of said state), which gives rise to particular rights and obligations in relation to that individual on the plane of the law of nations.[48] This status is sometimes described as *citizenship* precisely because citizens form the greatest part of a country's nationals, and writers thus tend to use the words interchangeably.[49] This is however incorrect in a pure sense, as the inverse is not true: not all of a given state's nationals are its citizens.[50]

> *On appelle en général citoyen le national investi de la plénitude des droits. Il ne faut pas confondre, comme on le fait trop souvent, ces deux termes. Tout national, en effet, n'est pas citoyen, si tout citoyen est national. En France, par exemple, les mineurs, les femmes mariées, les interdits ne sont pas citoyens, mais sont pourtant de nationalité française : ils sont privés des droits politiques et n'ont que la jouissance des droits civils. . . . Il ne sera question, bien entendu, ici, que de la nationalité nue, et nullement des droits qui en sont ordinairement la conséquence, mais qui, on le voit, n'ont pas avec elle un lien essentiel et nécessaire.*[51]

---

[48] This is also expressed as: "[n]ationality is the principal link between individuals and the benefits of the Law of Nations". Oppenheim, *International law. A treatise*, 588.

[49] Robert considers that citizens must by definition be nationals. Robert, "Préface", ii. Weis says such usage is frequent in republican states. "It is no mere coincidence that American writers are prone to use these two terms indiscriminately and frequently alternatively". Weis, *Nationality and statelessness in international law*, 4.

[50] Hammar, rather than dividing *nationality* into two senses, divides *citizenship* into two categories: the legal membership of the state, and political status. His definition of this legal membership, however, substantially matches the "politico-legal" sense of nationality described above. Tomas Hammar, "State, nation, and dual citizenship", in *Immigration and the politics of citizenship in Europe and North America*, ed. William Rogers Brubaker (Lanham: University Press of America, 1989), 81–95, 85.

[51] (Author's translation: *In general, nationals invested with full rights are called citizens. These two terms should not be confused, as is too often the case. All nationals are not in fact citizens, while all citizens are nationals. In France, for example, minors, married women and convicts are not citizens, but are of French nationality: they are excluded from political rights and do not enjoy civil rights. . . . We are here of course only speaking of nationality in a bare sense, and not of the rights which ordinarily ensue from it, but we can see that the latter are not essentially and necessarily tied to it.*) George Cogordan, *La nationalité au point de vue des rapports internationaux* (Paris: L. Larose, Libraire-Éditeur, 1879), 6–7.

There are many historical examples for this proposition, but notwithstanding changes
to notions of civil rights in many countries, for example the emancipation of women
and minorities, the characterisation of nationality holds true today. The convergence
of nationality and citizenship in many states' municipal legislation should not be
interpreted as a convergence of the nationality and citizenship on the plane of international law.[52] Furthermore, examples of non-citizen nationals still exist, especially in
the context of colonial territories, whose populations have sometimes been accorded
the nationality of the metropolitan state, without the rights of citizenship. This is the
case of British Nationals (Overseas) who possess British nationality due to their connection with Hong Kong when it was a Crown Colony of the United Kingdom. Their
position is discussed in chapter four.[53] Likewise, the legal category of United States
non-citizen National still exists, although it relates only to "persons born in or having ties with" American Samoa and Swains Island, as well as "certain inhabitants of
the Commonwealth of the Northern Mariana Islands".[54] These US nationals can obtain
the rights of US citizenship easily if they move to the United States.

---

[52] Koessler cites the 19th century French practice of providing for two types of naturalisation, *grande naturalisation* conferring citizenship and rights, and *petite naturalisation* making
the person French, without voting rights. He further cites the anti-Jewish Nuremberg laws,
which "established a gradation among those who were simply *Staatsangehörigen* or nationals,
and those who possessed the racial qualities which were required for the possession of the privileged status of *Reichsbürger*, or citizen. These laws substantially duplicated the sixteenth century Spanish enactments, instigated by the Inquisition, which made the possession of Christian
blood a requirement for the status of *civis pleni juris* or full citizenship". Koessler, "'Subject,'
'Citizen,' 'National,' and 'Permanent Allegiance'", 64–65. While such discriminatory categories
might be questioned today, Koessler (writing in 1947) does not state that they contradict international law per se, but notes that they would in effect bar the state from asserting a right of
protection over persons against whom the state so blatantly discriminates. Id., 71 note 80. Weis
goes further: "the thesis of the irrelevance in international law of differentiations between
nationals under municipal law requires a further qualification, namely, that if provisions of
municipal law concerning nationality amount to an infringement of essential elements of the
conception of nationality in international law, they do become relevant for international law.
[P]ersons belonging to the specific group of "German nationals" (*Staatsangehörige*) in the
meaning of the Reich Citizenship Law of 1935 were not to be regarded as nationals in the
meaning of international law". Weis, *Nationality and statelessness in international law*, 6.
National Socialist German treatment of certain categories of nationals is discussed in chapter
four, in relation to current German treatment of multiple nationality and redress for actions by
the National Socialist Government. Regarding the prohibition of racial discrimination in international law, see generally Roland Alfred Strauss, *Das Verbot der Rassendiskriminierung:
Völkerrecht, internationales Übereinkommen und schweizerische Rechtsordnung*, vol. 72,
Schweizerische Studien zum internationalen Recht (Zürich: Schulthess, 1991).
[53] See generally Johannes M. M. Chan, "Hong Kong: an analysis of the British nationality
proposals", *Immigration and nationality law and practice*, (1990) vol. 4, 57–62; Johannes
M. M. Chan, "The right to a nationality as a human right. The current trend towards recognition", *Human Rights Law Journal*, (1990) vol. 12, no. 1–2, 1–14.
[54] United States Department of State, *Certificates of Non-Citizen Nationality* (internet),

Caporal points out that non-citizen nationals still include persons deprived of political or other rights, or citizenship, who remain subjects of the state, or nationals.[55] Deprivation of citizenship rights does not necessarily mean deprivation of nationality, although it may.[56]

In his 1906 *Digest of International Law*, Moore presents another argument that the terms should not be used interchangeably, stating

---

http://travel.state.gov/law/citizenship/citizenship_781.html, consulted 15 March 2006. Koessler points out that at various points in United States' history, Filipinos (before the independence of the Philippines), Native Americans, and African-American were all denied the status of citizens, while considered "nationals" and accorded diplomatic protection. Koessler, "'Subject,' 'Citizen,' 'National,' and 'Permanent Allegiance'", 66–67.

[55] Caporal, "Citoyenneté et nationalité en droit public interne", 62.

[56] *See Trop v. Dulles, Secretary of State* 356 U.S. 86 (1958), cited in Whiteman, *Digest of international law*, vol. 8, 179.: "Citizenship [nationality] is not a license that expires upon misbehavior . . . citizenship [nationality] is not lost every time a duty of citizenship is shirked. And the deprivation of citizenship [nationality] is not a weapon that the government may use to express its displeasure at a citizen's conduct, however reprehensible the conduct may be". As opposed to deprivation of nationality, however, "[t]he United States stands virtually alone among democracies in having laws that continue to disenfranchise former prisoners even after they have paid their debts to society and finished parole or probation. A vast majority of the nearly five million U.S. citizens who were barred from voting in the last presidential election would have been free to vote in Australia, Britain, France and Canada. International Herald Tribune (New York Times), "Letting ex-prisoners vote", 30 August 2005 (internet), http://www.iht.com/articles/2005/08/29/opinion/edfelon.php, consulted 15 March 2006. Returning to deprivation of nationality, Israeli legal provisions do not appear to rise to the US standard. On 9 September 2002 the Interior Minister revoked the citizenship of Nahad Abu Kishaq pursuant to Article 11(b) of the Israel Citizenship Law, under which people whose actions violate the obligation of loyalty to the state can be stripped of their citizenship [nationality]. Abu Kishaq was accused (not convicted) of having been involved in suicide attacks and bombings as a central figure in 'Hamas'. A Ministry spokesman was quoted as saying Abu Kishaq would not become stateless as he possessed a Palestinian Authority identity card. Mazal Mualem and Jalal Bana, "Yishai revokes citizenship of Israeli Arab", *Ha'aretz*, 10 September 2002 (internet), http://www.haaretz.com, consulted 10 September 2002. The act provoked debate in the Israeli Knesset. Mazal Mualem, "I'm not Israeli, says Arab stripped of citizenship", *Ha'aretz*, English ed., 12 September 2002, 2. The issue of which acts threaten state security is a divisive one and opinions vary greatly. In May 1999 Merve Kavakci was stripped of her Turkish citizenship (nationality) and denied the parliamentary seat to which she had been elected, after wearing a headscarf to the swearing-in ceremony. The reason cited for the deprivation was her failure to inform Turkish civil and electoral authorities that she had become a United States citizen, a requirement, even though Turkey "allows" multiple nationality (naturalisation in another country does not provoke a loss of Turkish nationality). The speed with which her nationality was revoked however (two days), was cited as evidence of political motives for the decision. Gareth Jenkins, *Turkey threatened by a scarf*, Al-Ahram Weekly, 20–26 May 1999 (internet), http://www.ahram.org.eg/1999/430/re6.htm, consulted 15 March 2006; Stephen Kinzer, "Scarf MP loses citizenship", *Sydney Morning Herald*, 17 May 1999, 8.

National character, in legal and diplomatic discussion, usually is denoted by the term "citizenship". In most cases this is not misleading, since citizenship is the great source of national character. It is not, however, the only source. A temporary national character may be derived from service as a seaman, and also, in matters of belligerency, from domicil, so that there may exist between one's citizenship and his national character, for certain purposes, an actual diversity. For these reasons, on my work on International Arbitrations, I gave to the chapter in which citizenship is discussed the title "Nationality," in order that it might comprehend not only those who may be called "citizens," but all those who, whether they be citizens or not, may be called nationals.[57]

It will be argued in the following chapter that characterizing the above-mentioned situations as being of a "temporary national character" is misleading, absent an attribution of nationality. But Moore's view is still representative, as it sees nationality as reflecting relationships between the individual and the state. There are various views of the nature of nationality. Moore cites Chief Justice Waite in *Minor v. Happersett*,[58] who characterises *nationality* as the relationship of a political community, or nation, to its members. Members owe allegiance to the collective, and the collective in turn owes its members protection. These obligations are reciprocal, one compensating the other.[59] O'Leary sees weaker consequences. He also emphasises the nature of the juridical link of nationality as a *relationship* (as opposed to a status), but states that "rights and duties may flow from the primary legal (nationality) relationship between the individual and the state, but they are not the essence of that relationship.[60] Koessler goes further, seeing nationality as a formal status divorced from a specific right-duty relationship.[61]

The views are perhaps not as opposed as they might seem: the authors arguably agree that nationality does not give rise to *citizenship* rights, per se.[62] The issue of the consequences of nationality at international law will be covered in the following

---

[57] John Bassett Moore, *A digest of international law as embodied in diplomatic discussions, treaties and other international agreements, international awards, the decisions of municipal courts, and the writings of jurists, and especially in documents, published and unpublished, issued by Presidents and Secretaries of State of the United States, the opinions of the Attorneys-General, and the decisions of courts, Federal and State*, 8 vols., vol. 3 (Washington: Government Printing Office, 1906), 273.

[58] *Minor v. Happersett*, 88 U.S. 162, 21 Wall. 162 (1874).

[59] John Basset Moore, *A digest of international law*, 274.

[60] O'Leary, *The evolving concept of community citizenship – from the free movement of persons to Union citizenship*, 10.

[61] Koessler, "'Subject,' 'Citizen,' 'National,' and 'Permanent Allegiance'", 70–71.

[62] O'Leary cites authors critical of the view that nationality does not give rise to any formal consequences, who maintain that the right to a nationality found in Article 15 of the UN Declaration of Human Rights, and Article 24 of the International Covenant of Civil and Political Rights, shows that nationality is not a nominal category. O'Leary, *The evolving concept of community citizenship – from the free movement of persons to Union citizenship*, 9–10. See also Robert, "Préface".

chapters on nationality in international law, and the influence of human rights on attitudes toward multiple nationality.

O'Leary characterises *citizenship* as the "internal reflection of state membership", a status conferring political, social and economic rights, whereas *nationality* is the "external manifestation of state membership".[63] Moore seems to approve:

> *Citizenship, strictly speaking, is a term of municipal law, and denotes the possession within the particular state of full civil and political rights, subject to special disqualifications, such as minority or sex.*[64] *The conditions on which citizenship is acquired are regulated by municipal law.*[65]

Robert agrees with this definition of citizenship, but stipulates that citizens must be nationals.[66] If citizenship is indeed regulated by municipal law, this may be questioned. In this sense, the increasing provision of certain rights of citizenship to nonnationals, as in the rapidly evolving framework of agreements underpinning the free movement of persons, goods, and capital in the European Union, underscore the difference of nationality and citizenship. It would seem to be a matter of controversy whether *citizenship* as a status of municipal law produces consequences in international law.[67]

---

[63] O'Leary, *The evolving concept of community citizenship – from the free movement of persons to Union citizenship*, 10.

[64] It is to be remembered that when Moore was writing women in most countries had no, or only very restricted, civil and political rights. Moore's view that these issues were well outside the bounds of international law was generally accepted at the time. Should a state disenfranchise whole groups based on sex or race today, it is submitted that this would no longer be the case, although Charlesworth raises doubts in this regard in relation to the nature of the state. Hilary Charlesworth, "The sex of the state in international law", in *Sexing the subject of law*, ed. Ngaire Naffine and Rosemary J. Owens (Sydney: LBC, 1997), 265. See also Hilary Charlesworth and Christine Chinkin, *The boundaries of international law – a feminist analysis*, ed. Dominic McGoldrick, *Melland Schill Studies in International Law* (Manchester: Manchester University Press, 2000), and Natalie Kaufman Hevener, *International law and the status of women* (Boulder: Westview Press, 1983).

[65] Moore, *A digest of international law*, 273.

[66] "Le citoyen est simplement la personne qui, dans un Etat démocratique, participe – dans les conditions et selon les modalités prévues par la loi- à l'exercice de la souveraineté, soit dans la démocratie indirecte par l'élection des représentants, soit dans la démocratie semi-directe par l'assistance à l'Assemblée du peuple ou le référendum. Mais il est déjà et nécessairement un national". (Author's translation: *The citizen is simply the person who, in democratic states, participates in the exercise of sovereignty according to the conditions and modalities provided by law, either in indirect democracy through the election of representatives, or in semi-direct democracy through the people's assembly or referendum. But he is already and of necessity a national*) Robert, "Préface", ii.

[67] See Weis, *Nationality and statelessness in international law*, 6.

1. Nationality and citizenship in federal states

Regarding federal states, using the United States as an example, where the word "citizenship" is used at both the state (local) and the federal levels, Moore says that as conditions for state (local) citizenship vary greatly, some states (provinces) may consider people to be their "citizens" even though they remain non-citizens on the federal level, even allowing them to vote in elections. Only federal citizens can however, be considered U.S. nationals "on the grounds of citizenship".[68] Whether an individual is characterized as a "subject", an "inhabitant" or a "citizen", depends principally on the form of government, but these are categories of municipal law.[69]

Beaud discusses nationality in federal states in terms of the dual nature of citizenship in such states (citizenship on the local and federal levels), and the rights of individuals on both levels. He cites the effects of a federal nationality on the constituent parts, and in terms of the consequences for the federation itself. But he does not distinguish between nationality and citizenship as done herein.[70] Jackson does make the

---

[68] Moore, *A digest of international law*, 274. Motomura comments almost a century after Moore that non-citizens "generally may not vote in public elections" although not mentioning that they once could in many US states. Hiroshi Motomura, "Alienage classifications in a nation of immigrants: three models of "permanent" residence," in *Immigration and citizenship in the twenty-first century*, ed. Noah M. J. Pickus (Lanham: Rowman & Littlefield, 1998), 199–222, 201. Likewise commenting on moves to restrict entitlements and rights for permanent resident aliens in the United States, Tichenor states that this stands in contrast to the fact that the obligations of citizens and permanent residents were and remain, almost the same. He also remarks that "only such political tasks as voting stand out as special duties for citizens". Daniel J. Tichenor, "Membership and American social contracts: a response to Hiroshi Motomura," in *Immigration and citizenship in the twenty-first century*, ed. Noah M. J. Pickus (Lanham: Rowman & Littlefield, 1998), 223–227, 223 and note 1. Koessler notes that US courts resolved that the "alien-vote" did not constitute *citizenship*. Koessler, "'Subject,' 'Citizen,' 'National,' and 'Permanent Allegiance'", 63–64. For a discussion of nationality in federal or confederated states, see Weis, *Nationality and statelessness in international law*, 14.

[69] Moore, *A digest of international law*, 274, quoting *Minor v. Happersett*, 165–166. Koessler agrees that the term "subject", which had been used as a synonym of "citizen", even in the United States after the Declaration of Independence, was abandoned in favour of "citizen", as a vestige of feudal law. Koessler, "'Subject,' 'Citizen,' 'National,' and 'Permanent Allegiance'", 59. Bernier describes federalism and international law as having a "love-hate relationship". Whereas international law looks to state sovereignty, federalism by definition divides such sovereignty "in order to make room for more effective action". Ivan Bernier, *International legal aspects of federalism* (London: Longman Group Ltd., 1973), 269. He notes that in traditional international law participation was allowed to constituent parts of federal states, as long as the federal state itself did not object, but few federal states adopted this practice. Bernier, *International legal aspects of federalism*, 271. He views federalism as provoking changes in the rules and nature of international law.

[70] Olivier Beaud, "The question of nationality within a federation: a neglected issue in nationality law," in *Dual nationality, social rights and federal citizenship in the U.S. and*

distinction, suggesting that the experience of federal states provides an illustration of the issues and conflicts raised by competing legal hierarchies and loyalties in relation to multiple nationality. While essentially remaining neutral in relation to the desirability of multiple nationality, she argues that "the federal form provides a useful set of models for a gradual process of developing new legal regimes in which multiple citizenships are accommodated but not necessarily encouraged".[71]

D. THE IMPORTANCE OF THE MEANING AND CONTEXT OF CITIZENSHIP

Having distinguished between *nationality* and *citizenship*, note should be made of the specific ideas and context of citizenship itself. This is important not only because citizenship status is so closely related to nationality, but because it is possible to imagine that the two concepts may merge, or draw further apart, in the future. Likewise, state practice toward multiple nationality is clearly influenced by the perceived consequences of nationality, and as citizenship is most often one of these, it cannot simply be dismissed as not relevant to the present study.[72]

In most countries, attribution of nationality by the state means possession of citizenship and the rights attached, with notable exceptions, such as the United Kingdom.[73] Just as the attribution of nationality at international law is a matter left to states, so is the attribution of citizenship.[74] As presented above, the effects or

---

Europe. The reinvention of citizenship, ed. Randall Hansen and Patrick Weil (New York: Berghahn Books, 2002), 314–330.

[71] Vicki C. Jackson, "Citizenship and federalism", in *Citizenship today. Global perspectives and practices*, T. Alexander Aleinikoff and Kouglas Klusmeyer eds., (Washington: Carnegie Endowment for International Peace, 2001), 124–182, 129.

[72] O'Leary's definition of citizenship is instructive: "[citizenship is] comprised of a number of diverse elements. It is a juridical link implying membership, which once possessed, confers a status involving a number of rights, duties and entitlements. In particular, it confers civil and political rights of participation which emphasise a departure from hierarchical social structures to the participation of the individual in state sovereignty". O'Leary, *The evolving concept of community citizenship – from the free movement of persons to Union citizenship*, 15.

[73] The UK has various categories of nationality, divorced from rights of citizenship and rights of residence. See generally Laurie Fransman, *British nationality law* (London: Butterworths, 1998), and Laurie Fransman, "The case for reform of nationality law in the United Kingdom", in *Citizenship and nationality status in the new Europe*, ed. Síofra O'Leary and Teija Tiilikainen (London: Sweet & Maxwell, 1998), 123–147, 126–28.

[74] Brubaker postulates that the lack of harmonisation in municipal laws on nationality in the European Union is due to the weighty stakes states have in granting individuals the rights of citizenship, labelling it the "last bastion of sovereignty". Rogers Brubaker, *Citizenship and nationhood in France and Germany* (Cambridge (Massachusetts): Harvard University Press, 1992), 180.

consequences of nationality are not the same as the effects and consequences of citizenship. Some countries extend many of the rights usually associated with citizenship to non-nationals/citizens, usually permanent residents.[75] Possession of the status of citizen does however not necessarily mean that citizenship rights or entitlements can be exercised. For example, in many countries citizens resident overseas cannot exercise their franchise in their home countries.

On the other hand, citizen status, or even permanent resident status, can produce obligations that must be fulfilled, simply on the basis of that connection. In the United States, the obligation to file an income tax return applies not only to permanent residents of the country, a typical provision in tax laws, but to all citizens of the United States, regardless of their place of permanent residence. The obligation of military service is a similar category, although state practice would seem to be moving toward a more defined link based on age and residence, in addition to citizenship status or nationality.

As outlined in the preceding chapter, in order to present a picture of current state practice toward multiple nationality, in addition to a review of municipal legislation, state policy must be examined. It was outlined that the policy that would be addressed is only that which directly relates to multiple nationality, as opposed to the many areas of municipal law that are arguably affected by multiple nationality, considerations which can often be labeled as related to citizenship. In this sense the separation of the two areas seems more difficult. Because the two categories are so closely woven together in much municipal legislation, one is confronted with the issue whether in terms of policy they can in fact be separated. For example, where authors do not specifically differentiate between nationality and citizenship, their analysis must be considered to reflect the fact that some of the factors that states incorporate into their municipal laws on acquisition and loss of nationality arguably have to do with the exercise of rights and performance of duties belonging to *citizenship*, as opposed to *nationality*, yet the state labels them as the same thing.[76]

---

[75] Ideas of what kind of relationship to a state merits political participation have varied. In 1793 a French decree made Thomas Paine, Jeremy Bentham, A. Cloots, George Washington, Alexander Hamilton, James Madison and Friedrich Schiller, French citizens, noting *Considérant que, si cinq ans de domicile en France suffisent pour obtenir à un étranger le titre de citoyen français, ce titre est bien plus justement dû à ceux qui, quel que soit le sol qu'ils habitent, ont consacré leurs bras et leurs veilles à défendre la cause des peuples contre le despotisme des rois, à bannir les préjugés de la terre et à reculer les bornes des connaissances humaines.* (Author's translation: *Considering that five years' domicile in France are enough for a foreigner to obtain the title of French citizen, such title is much more appropriately due to those who, no matter where they live, have dedicated their power and efforts to the defence of the peoples' cause against the despotism of kings, to banish prejudice from the Earth, and to push against the limits of human knowledge.*) Caporal, "Citoyenneté et nationalité en droit public interne", 64. This is to be distinguished from grants of honorary citizenship. See Whiteman, *Digest of international law*, vol. 8, 14–17.

[76] See generally Spiro, "Dual nationality and the meaning of citizenship".

Thus when persons lose nationality by taking part in a foreign election, as was the case in the United States until the Supreme Court case of *Afroyim v. Rusk*,[77] or when naturalisation abroad results in a loss of the rights of citizenship,[78] the two categories are easily confused. If exercising the franchise is the exercise of the political rights of citizenship, which provokes a loss of nationality, it is unclear whether the policy involved is related to the nationality relationship, or the citizenship status or rights exercised. In those terms, citizenship as a factor in the production and elimination of multiple nationality should be taken into account in any study of multiple nationality, but given the lack of separation between the categories in most municipal legislation, this would seem difficult.

1. Classes of citizenship

Just as all classes of nationality must be included in the current study, where they exist, the question is posed whether the disparate treatment of citizens by a state in effect creates a different class of persons for the purpose of nationality. States do not typically create labels for such groups, as they do for classes of nationality, where the latter exist. For example, should a government program benefiting one group or part of society be considered as diminishing or changing the value of the citizenship that applies to those outside the group? Should "affirmative action" programs in the United States, special government funding to Aboriginal communities in Australia, or legal preferences and benefits extended to the *Bumiputra* (ethnic Malay or assimilated groups) majority in Malaysia be considered as affecting the nature or value of these groups' citizenship vis-à-vis other groups?[79]

Along these lines, Davis considers there to be two separate classes of Israeli citizenship, noting that

> over ninety-two per cent of the territory of the State of Israel is reserved by law only to persons recognized by the state to be 'Jews'. . . Thus, the Palestinian citizen of Israel has equal access (as the Jewish citizens) to the courts of law (civil rights) and equal access to the political process of voting and elections (political rights), but not to the welfare and educational resources of the state (social rights), nor to its land and water resources (economic rights). The distinction, thus, classifies two separate classes of Israeli citizenship segregating between nearly one million Palestinian citizens of Israel from four million Jewish citizens.[80]

---

[77] *Afroyim v. Rusk*, 387 U.S. 253 (1967).

[78] As under the French Consitution of 3 September 1791. Caporal, "Citoyenneté et nationalité en droit public interne".

[79] For a discussion of minority rights within the nation state and liberalism see generally Will Kymlicka, *Multicultural citizenship – a liberal theory of minority rights* (Oxford: Clarendon Press, 1995).

[80] Uri Davis, *Citizenship and the State – a comparative study of citizenship legislation in Israel, Jordan, Palestine, Syria and Lebanon* (Reading (UK): Garnet Publishers, 1997), 8–9.

For the purposes of this study, even if it is accepted that the quality of the citizen-ship rights is indeed affected, it is only necessary to enquire whether such classes of citizenship affect the relationship of nationality of such groups to the state. But it should be asked, in terms of multiple nationality, are such groups treated differently? Do any of the ingredients of state policy vis-à-vis multiple nationality reflect such classes of citizenship?[81]

E. MULTIPLE NATIONALITY AND/OR MULTIPLE CITIZENSHIP

Another question that should be canvassed is whether, although this essay examines state practice toward *multiple nationality*, the identifiable effects in international law would change if the issue were practice toward *multiple citizenship*? While this ques-tion seems beyond the scope of what is examined here, due to the inter-penetration of the two statuses, or insufficient definition of one status in relation to the other in municipal law, its context is certainly relevant. Robert's comment reflects a negative answer:

> . . . *les nationalités peuvent se juxtaposer: on parlera de double-nationaux. Les citoyen-netés, elles, ne peuvent éventuellement que se superposer. L'Union européenne, n'étant pas un Etat, ne peut accorder une nationalité! Mais elle peut créer une citoyenneté qui se superposera aux citoyennetés nationales en conférant à son titulaire plusieurs droits, par exemple la liberté de circulation sur l'Etat de l'Union, le droit de vote et l'éligibilité aux élections locales et européennes, la protection diplomatique et consulaire . . .*[82]

This statement clarifies that whether diplomatic and consular protection is a right of citizenship depends on municipal law. Under international law it is a state's right vis-à-vis other states pursuant to a link of nationality. This will be discussed in chap-ter three. It is arguable that should the European Union provide for a "right of citi-

---

Peled states that much of this differentiation results from Israeli Arabs not being subject to mil-itary service, which in Israel leads to social and other benefits. Yoav Peled, "Ethnische Demokratie und die rechtliche Konstruktion der Staatsbürgerschaft: Die arabischen Bürger des jüdischen Staates", in *Transnationale Staatsbürgerschaft*, ed. Heinz Kleger, *Theorie und Gesellschaft* (Frankfurt: Campus Verlag, 1997), 160–185, 161.

[81] If political views create such classes, the example of Merve Kavakci cited in note 56 above, is perhaps an illustration of multiple nationality being used as a pretext for implement-ing the Turkish state's secular views, but only in terms of enforcement of a policy that on its face applies equally to all.

[82] (Author's translation: . . . *nationalities may be juxtaposed: one may speak of dual nation-als. Citizenships may only be superimposed. The European Union, not being a state, may not attribute a nationality! But it may create a citizenship which is superimposed on national cit-izenships by conferring various rights on the recipient, for example the freedom of circulation within the Union, the right to vote, and eligibility to stand for local and European elections, diplomatic and consular protection* . . .). Robert, "Préface", ii.

zenship" which includes diplomatic and consular protection, this would in fact be no more than an international agreement giving rise to a *"protégé"* relationship, still based on a link of *nationality*.[83] Thus again, it is vital that the consequences of nationality in international law outlined in the next chapter be clearly defined and distinguished from the municipal law of citizenship.

It was argued at the outset of this chapter that nationality and citizenship are still recognisable categories for the purposes of municipal and international law, as their consequences are separable, and the individuals included in each category do not coincide in certain states (and do not have to). Should it become evident, however, that the categories' membership overlaps exactly in a large majority of states, this would create a need for an examination whether their consequences in international and municipal law have indeed merged.[84]

F. NATIONALITY, ETHNICITY AND GLOBALISATION

O'Leary's, Oppenheim's and Weis' presentations of issues surrounding the "historic-biological" aspect of nationality discussed above can be said to coincide with ideas of ethnicity. While the reader may by now appreciate that this is not the subject of the present study, analyses of ethnicity and nationalism gives pause for reflection in terms of the associated legal implications for the context in which multiple nationality is viewed and related norms have developed.

Friedman argues that the idea that nation states are made up of ethnic groups (or majorities) which have long perceived themselves as such, and which are united by commonalities, is both new, and false. Instead, most nation states are recent constructions,

---

[83] See Oppenheim, *International law. A treatise*, 589. Ruzié points out that such protection, as provided in the Maastricht Treaty, could be opposed by third states against whom a claim of protection of a non-national is brought. He salutes the fact that the European Commission did not adopt the European Parliament's proposal that diplomatic protection stem from the Union itself, for want of a legal personality. David Ruzié, "Citoyenneté et nationalité dans l'Union Européenne", in *Vorträge, Reden und Berichte aus dem Europa-Institut – Sektion Rechtswissenschaft*, ed. Georg Ress and Torsten Stein, vol. 313 (Saarbrücken: Europa-Institut Universität des Saarlandes, 1994), 3–19, 6–7. See European Union, "EU citizenship", 2006 (internet), http://europa.eu.int/youreurope/nav/en/citizens/factsheets/lu/rightsoutsideeu/consular protection/en.html, consulted 15 March 2006.

[84] There are signs that in practical terms, the categories do not co-incide, even when they seem to, as states continue to treat categories of citizens differently. An illustration is the debate over voting rights for citizens resident abroad, discussed in chapter four. Proponents of an argument that citizenship should be divorced from nationality in order to guarantee municipal law rights while fostering a sense of national identity cite the "historical demonization of dual citizenship" as confusing dual nationality with dual citizenship, only the former being justified due to the exclusivity of a relation of national allegiance. "The functionality of citizenship", *Harvard Law Review*, (1997) vol. 110, no. 8 , 1814–1831, 1827 note 90.

and cannot be said to coincide with individuals' historical self-definition, or their relationship to other groups of people. He postulates that "nationalism *creates* ethnicity,
it also creates majorities and minorities",[85] and that countries need to "create a sense
of ethnicity, even when there was none before".[86] He then relates these developments
to technological progress, arguing that affiliations that seem to be innate are in fact
often a matter of choice, and that "governments . . . have an interest in manipulating
these choices".[87] Friedman goes on to state that in the present context, technological
advancement is the primary factor in the movement of people from poor to rich countries ('traditional' notions of which countries produce emigrants and which countries
take immigrants no longer hold true), and the source of pressure on the laws of citizenship and immigration.[88]

McNeill agrees, but takes the argument further. He argues that "the wars of
1914–45 augured the eclipse of nationalism and of ethnic homogeneity within separate polities as clearly as the wars of 1702–1815 had announced the triumph of the
principle of nationality and of an assumed ethnic homogeneity within separate sovereign states".[89]

Miller takes the opposite view, arguing that an ethnic idea of nationality is, and
should be, deeply held. While recognising that "there is indeed something distinc-
tively modern about our idea of nationhood, even though it builds upon ideas about
the tribal division of the human species that can be traced much further back in
time", he maintains that nationality as identity, and politically expressed through the
nation state, is not only desirable, but here to stay. Attacks on the "historic-biological"
aspect of nationality by cosmopolitanism , multiculturalism, and the "homogenizing
cultural effects of the global market" will lead to the impoverishment of the group he
labels the "majority *non-élite*", and will be to the detriment of the common good.[90]

---

[85] Lawrence M. Friedman, "Ethnicity and citizenship", paper presented at the conference:
Citizenship and Immigration, University of Milano Law Faculty, 1996, Vincenzo Ferrari,
Thomas Heller and Elena de Tullio eds. (Milano: Dott. A. Giuffrè Editore, 1998), 65–78, 69.
McNeill agrees, postulating that polyethnicity has been a worldwide norm, with the exception
of north-western Europe in recent centuries. William H. McNeill, *Polyethnicity and national
unity in world history. The Donald G. Creighton lectures* (Toronto: University of Toronto Press,
1986), 34.

[86] Friedman, "Ethnicity and citizenship", 70. While the authors do not subscribe to
Friedman's thesis as such, in the context of the development of the Baltic states see generally
Gottfried Hanne, Eva-Clarita Onken, and Norbert Götz, "Ethnopolitik", in *Handbuch Baltikum
heute*, ed. Heike Graf and Manfred Kerner (Berlin: Berlin Verlag Arno Spitz GmbH, 1998),
299–334.

[87] Friedman, "Ethnicity and citizenship", 71–73.

[88] Id., 77–78.

[89] McNeill, *Polyethnicity and national unity in world history. The Donald G. Creighton lectures*, 34.

[90] David Miller, *On nationality*, *Oxford Political Theory* (Oxford: Clarendon Press, 1995),
184–87. Miller sees nation states and national institutions as best-suited to protect minority
rights in the form guaranteeing welfare projects, while at the same time arguably implying that

The argument that technological advancement caused individuals' perception of their relationship to the wider world to change from local to "national", and caused nation states to find ways to bind individuals to the state has clear implications for state practice regarding multiple nationality. Attempts to reduce or eliminate multiple nationality, canvassed in chapter four, seem to provide evidence for such views. But aside from adding to the discussion on why states make rules about nationality and multiple nationality, the argument raises the effects of the consequences of continued technological advance. Do current trends toward political and economic integration (or *globalisation*) stemming from (or resulting in) technological advancement continue to cause states to bind individuals more closely to themselves? If so, one would expect intolerance of multiple nationality in national legal frameworks to coincide with attempts to define state membership in exclusive terms. Conversely, does an increasing tolerance of multiple nationality indicate that technological advancement has reached a level requiring a supra-national need for mobile human capital, thus in fact breaking down the exclusivity of a relationship of nationality?

Even weightier questions are provoked by such ideas, however. If the "national" concept involving some form of ethnic or other created homogeneity was indeed an anomaly, does this portend the demise of the state as we know it, and the system of international law based on sovereignty? Although McNeill sees increasing resistance to polyethnic societies, and the "pretense of ethnic unity within sovereign national states for some time to come", he does not doubt that the trend is definite, and otherwise.[91] More importantly, drawing on historical models, he sees the "participatory equality" and political freedom of liberal national states as threatened by an ever more closely-linked world.

> *Modern national states of the liberal tradition accepted foreigners as at least potential citizens; and women, too, achieved political rights, though only in the twentieth century. Whether these principles will survive the impact of an interacting world in which vast differences of skills, culture, wealth, and physical appearance exist is one of the capital questions for the next century. Very likely things will muddle along for decades to come. . . . But social strains and frictions are almost sure to increase within nations playing host to different ethnic groups; and sporadic resort to riot and even to wholesale murder is likely. It is a high price to pay for open frontiers; yet the costs of artificial isolation and of maintaining ethnic purity by the exercise of force are even greater. Civilized peoples have confronted this awkward choice from the beginning of urban existence.[92]*

---

minorities should not exist as such in an ideal version of the nation state. "If a state houses a minority who for one reason or another do not feel themselves to be fully part of the national community, but who do not want or cannot realistically hope to form a nation-state of their own, then national identity must be transformed in such a way that they can be included". Miller, *On nationality*, 187–188.

[91] McNeill, *Polyethnicity and national unity in world history. The Donald G. Creighton lectures*, 81–82.

[92] Id., 83–84.

It is important to emphasise that this study is not directed at answering the fundamental questions surrounding these ideas, whether one approves of them or not.[93] Yet issues surrounding "globalisation" clearly affect the nature of states, and their relationship to individuals, whether nationals, citizens, residents, or aliens. Globalisation is clearly a factor influencing states, and thus the laws between them. An analysis of current state practice toward multiple nationality may allow for commentary on these and related trends, but arguably cannot provide, on its own, grounds for extrapolation to prove one world view or another.[94]

G. IDENTITY, OR THE PSYCHOLOGY OF NATIONALITY AND CITIZENSHIP

It would be remiss not to mention the connection between the specific legal regulations applicable to nationality (and citizenship), and individual and collective identity.[95] Here, nationality seems to enter the realm of emotion and conviction, but with palpable legal effect. The extent to which identity is, or should be an issue in conferring citizenship rights or nationality is a matter of controversy.

---

[93] There is disagreement with Friedman and McNeill that is perhaps more indirect in its distinctions than those drawn by Miller. "Those who herald the emerging postnational age are too hasty in condemning the nation-state to the dustbin of history. They underestimate the resilience, as well as the richness and complexity, of an institutional and normative tradition that, for better or worse, appears to have life in it yet". Brubaker, *Citizenship and nationhood in France and Germany*, 189. In a study of the incorporation of "guest workers" in Europe, Soysal sees changes in the groundings and practice of citizenship that are influenced by transnational developments, part of a developing international order "which, while insisting on the nation-state and its sovereignty, at the same time, legitimate a new form of membership that transcends the boundaries of the nation state". Yasemin Nuhoglu Soysal, *Limits of citizenship – migrants and postnational membership in Europe* (Chicago: The University of Chicago Press, 1994), 137. She finds however, that "the classical formal order of the nation-state and its membership is not in place. The state is no longer an autonomous and independent organization closed over a nationally defined population. Instead, we have a system of constitutionally interconnected states with a multiplicity of membership". Id., 163–64.

[94] Bosniak argues that "various practices and experiences that we conventionally associate with citizenship do, in some respects, exceed the boundaries and jurisdiction of the territorial nation-state". Linda Bosniak, "Denationalizing citizenship", in *Citizenship today. Global perspectives and practices*, ed. T. Alexander Aleinikoff and Douglas Klusmeyer (Washington: Carnegie Endowment for International Peace, 2001), 237–252, 241.

[95] Identity is a concept which can reflect a link to any group or collective, focusing on an individual's self–definition and relationships. Nationality (in either of its two senses) is one example of such associations. The term *citizenship* has also been used to denote general participation in a non-state group or collective, focusing on various aspects of identity that lead to or signify the relationship. See Kadende-Kaiser and Kaiser, "Identity, citizenship, and transnationalism: Ismailis in Tanzania and Burundians in the Diaspora".

In raising the "desacralization of citizenship", Brubaker highlights the fact that even nationality as a "politico-legal" relationship is seen or interpreted in two ways: (1) as purely instrumentalist or functional, versus (2) incorporating values of belonging divorced from juridical convenience, bringing with it obligations of sacrifice for the state.[96] Those advocating the latter view favour policies including restrictions on acquisition of nationality or dual nationality, which to Brubaker also reflects an assumption that certain immigrants are unassimilable.[97] Views of the role identity should play in the relationship of nationality and the status of citizenship thus have consequences in the legal realm. Even systems of attribution of nationality can be said to reflect world views of individual and collective identity: *jus soli* focuses on presence in designating a tie to the state, whereas *jus sanguinis* focuses on transmitted ideas or values.[98]

The transformation of immigrant into citizen (and national) can be seen as the source of much proposed nationality law reform, as well as specific rules adopted regarding nationality. Views of individual and national identity clearly influence how states respond to issues of integration and equality in the context of immigration.[99] In this sense Brubaker argues that debates about citizenship in France and Germany revolve around identity as opposed to interest,[100] and there is no reason to think that

---

[96] Brubaker, *Citizenship and nationhood in France and Germany*, 145–48. He cites the huge numbers of Franco-Algerian dual nationals as highlighting the friction, stating that many such persons feel an emotional tie to Algeria, choosing to perform military service there as opposed to in France, and regarding their French citizenship as a nationality of convenience. This attitude is rejected by "nationalists" who feel that French nationality (citizenship) must reflect an emotional commitment to the state. See also "The functionality of citizenship", 1817–18, noting that surveys of individuals naturalised in the Netherlands and the USA also indicate concern with obtaining legal rights and status, as opposed to an emotional affinity or bond.

[97] Brubaker, *Citizenship and nationhood in France and Germany*, 149.

[98] Id., 185–89.

[99] Brubaker, writing in 1992, mentions that "[I]f *jus soli à la française* is unimaginable in Germany, this results in part from the lack of a viable assimilationist tradition. Unilaterally to attribute German citizenship to immigrants – especially to those who, according to surveys, have remarkably little interest in acquiring it – is out of the question. Id., 177. See the following note for further discussion, as in 1999 Germany did adopt jus soli attribution of nationality.

[100] Id., 182–83. In another text, he cites Hailbronner's view that Germany "is not and cannot become a country of immigration in the North American sense", his rejection of *jus soli* for Germany as a consequence, and his position that "it would be illusory . . . to think of naturalization as a solution to the various problems of integration faced by foreigners in the Federal Republic of Germany". William Rogers Brubaker, "Introduction," in *Immigration and the politics of citizenship in Europe and North America*, ed. William Rogers Brubaker (Lanham: University Press of America, 1989), 1–27, 24. Whether Hailbronner is correct is another matter, but his opinion was not followed by the German government, with the adoption in 1999 of a new German nationality law specifically incorporating jus soli in order to encourage assimilation. In Brubaker's terms, did interest win out over identity? To see the development of his views, and on German nationality law generally, see Kay Hailbronner, Günter Renner, and Christine

such considerations should be limited to those two countries. Trans-national ties and identification also influence ideas of the state's role and its formal ties to other states, such as in the case of the developing European Union.[101]

Views of nationality's practical essence (instrumentalist versus obligations entailing sacrifice) are important as far as they may influence municipal legislation on nationality. The topic also raises the issue of the "allegiance" required of nationals, and prompts us to enquire whether this involves difficult-to-qualify trappings of identity, either in its definition or in its requirements, in terms of the state's right to represent a national vis-à-vis another state. In other words, does a subjective standard related to identity influence supposedly objective or black-letter legal norms in international law? This is discussed in the following chapter.

Identity is thus an issue for nationality in terms of the specific rules states make regarding acquisition and loss of nationality and practice in terms of multiple nation-

---

Kreuzer, *Staatsangehörigkeitsrecht*, 3rd ed., vol. 55, *Beck'sche Kurz-kommentare* (München: Verlag C. H. Beck, 2001). US policy arguably views naturalisation as fostering integration and community spirit, as does Australian policy. "The functionality of citizenship", 1816–18. See also, Department of Immigration & Multicultural & Indigenous Affairs (Australia), *Promoting Australian Citizenship* (internet), http://www.citizenship.gov.au, consulted on 15 March 2006. It is to be expected that naturalisation and assimilation will continue to be focal points surrounding government regulation of nationality. Thränhardt portrays European countries as "new" countries of immigration, whose lack of a capacity to recognise themselves as such could result in policies of inclusion and exclusion not based on practical realities, but on "pure" categories such as nationality, which increasingly do not include a good part of European states' populations. See generally Dietrich Thränhardt, "Entwicklungslinien der Zuwanderungspolitik in EG-Mitgliedsländern", in *Zuwanderungspolitik in Europa. Nationale Politiken- Gemeinsamkeiten und Unterschiede*, ed. Hubert Heinelt, *Gesellschaftspolitik und Staatstätigkeit* (Opladen: Leske & Budrich, 1994), 33–63. For a discussion of the German case, see Simon Green, "Citizenship policy in Germany: the case of ethnicity over residence", in *Towards a European nationality. Citizenship, immigration and nationality law in the EU*, ed. Randall Hansen and Patrick Weil (Houndmills: Palgrave, 2001), 24–51.

[101] See the volume introduced by Heinz Kleger, "Einleitung: Ist eine politische Mehrfachidentität möglich", in *Transnationale Staatsbürgerschaft*, ed. Heinz Kleger (Frankfurt: Campus Verlag, 1997), 9–20. French sociologist, historian and political commentator Aron defends a national ideal of citizenship and identity, seeing state sovereignty in the world order as dictating that the state remain the basis for national and international relations. He acknowledges separate identities within states, but draws the line at political independence. Raymond Aron, "Kann es eine multinationale Staatsbürgerschaft geben?", in *Transnationale Staatsbürgerschaft*, ed. Heinz Kleger (Frankfurt: Campus Verlag, 1997), 23–41, 39–41. Ruzié points to the qualms surrounding the creation of a citizenship of the European Union and its significance for member states, represented by Denmark's declarations that EU citizenship did not overlap with or lead to a right to national citizenship, however leaving the door open for possible evolution. Ruzié, "Citoyenneté et nationalité dans l'Union Européenne", 13–14. See also Gerard-René de Groot, "The relationship between the nationality legislation of the member states of the European Union and European citizenship", in *European citizenshp. An institutional challenge*, ed. Massimo La Torre, *European Forum* (The Hague: Kluwer Law International, 1998), 115–147.

ality, and the nature of the relationship that catapults the state's link to an individual onto the international level. It also bears on the legal consequences of nationality in municipal law, in terms of a given state's framework of the rights of citizenship.[102]

H. NOTE ON CITIZENSHIP AND THEORIES OF THE STATE

Just as the term *nationality* is used to denote various ideas, the term *citizenship* is also used in a broad sociological context and in relation to theories of the state, encompassing ideological views of politics and morals. *Citizenship* as a national legal status which confers rights and/or entitlements under municipal law, to which *nationality* as used in this essay has been compared, must be distinguished from such broader usage.

In this sense, "Max Weber distinguished three distinct meanings for citizenship in social history: classes that share a specific communal or economic interest; membership determined by rights within the state; and strata defined by standard of living or social prestige".[103] The second of these meanings is that which is usually confused with, compared to, or equated with the "politico-legal" aspect of *nationality*. The broader spectrum within which this aspect of citizenship is placed involves discussions about the essence and workings of the state and society. Much recent comment and scholarship in this field stems from the work of T. H. Marshall, who divided citizenship into three progressive stages or types: legal, political, and social.[104]

---

[102] Arguments that questions of identity linked to nationality-status should be de-coupled from the rights of citizenship arguably do not take the ramifications for international law into account. They underplay the fact that the two statuses are different, even when municipal law treats them the same. See "The functionality of citizenship". The author argues that municipal law should distinguish between citizenship and nationality.

[103] Halisi, Kaiser, and Ndegwa, "Guest editors' introduction: the multiple meanings of citizenship – rights, identity, and social justice in Africa", 339. Max Weber, "On the concept of citizenship", in *Max Weber on charisma and institution building*, ed. Shmuel N. Eisenstadt (Chicago: University of Chicago Press, 1968), 239.

[104] For a discussion of Marshall's ideas and their relevance today, see Anthony M. Rees, "T. H. Marshall and the progress of citizenship", in *Citizenship today. The contemporary relevance of T. H. Marshall*, ed. Anthony M. Rees and Martin Bulmer (London: UCL Press Ltd., 1996), 1–23. For counter-theses and arguments which revolve around the extrapolability of Marshall's ideas to a non-British context, see Michael Mann, "Ruling class strategies and citizenship", in *Citizenship today. The contemporary relevance of T. H. Marshall*, ed. Martin Bulmer and Anthony M. Rees (London: UCL Press Ltd., 1996), 125–144. For a general discussion of theories of citizenship (*sensu largu*) see J. M. Barbalet, *Citizenship. Rights, struggle and class inequality*, ed. Frank Parkin, *Concepts in the social sciences* (Stony Stratford (UK): Open University Press, 1988). Regarding citizenship and competing views of the state, see Preuss, "Probleme eines Konzepts europäischer Staatsbürgerschaft", 255–61.

In practical terms, the issues surrounding these broader parameters and ramifications of citizenship are well illustrated by the way governments view them.[105] In its
inquiry about establishing a system of national indicators and benchmarks on citizenship, the Australian Senate Standing Committee on Legal and Constitutional Affairs
sought to measure "at regular intervals the extent to which the legal, economic, social
and cultural rights and responsibilities of Australian citizens are implemented.[106]
Kashyap sees Indian citizenship in terms of both legal status, and broader values.[107]

I. OTHER CLASSIFICATIONS/TERMS OF NOTE

1. Ressortissant

It is a matter of debate whether the French term *ressortissant* is synonymous with
national in international law, or whether it is broader, encompassing non-nationals
who are nevertheless under a state's protection. This is mainly due to non-uniform
usage in treaty texts. Weis mentions the debate, but seems to side with the latter view,
citing French and international tribunals which held that *ressortissant* includes non-
national members of the armed forces (who are assimilated to nationals), as well as
nationals of states which were under foreign protection. Thus Tunisian nationals were
French ressortissants while Tunisia was under French protection and Egyptian nationals were British ressortissants while Egypt was under British protection. *Protégés* and

---

[105] Rubinstein notes government enquiries in the USA, Canada, the United Kingdom, the
European Union, in addition to Australia. Kim Rubenstein, "Citizenship in Australia: unscrambling its meaning", *Melbourne University Law Review*, (1995) vol. 20, 503–527, 503 note 3.

[106] Senate Legal and Constitutional References Committee (Australia), *Discussion paper on
a system of national citizenship indicators* (Canberra: Parliament of the Commonwealth of Australia,
1995), 5. Illustrating the confusion the term *citizenship* can cause due to its various meanings
and contexts, the Committee's discussion paper sought essentially to clarify its use of the term
citizenship, which had clearly been misunderstood by a good portion of respondents who had
made submissions until that time. Senate Legal and Constitutional References Committee (Australia),
Discussion paper on a system of national citizenship indicators, 1. Rubinstein notes this lack
of understanding of the various ways in which the term *citizenship* is used in Australia, arguing that the legal status of citizenship (and in Australia, nationality) does not match the "social
and economic membership rights" of the individual members of the Australian community. She
argues that certain rights should be extended to "citizens in the common cause of humanity"
rather than attaching to the specific status of Australian citizenship. Rubenstein, "Citizenship in
Australia: unscrambling its meaning", 527.

[107] Subhash C. Kashyap, *Citizens and the Constitution. (Citizenship values under the
Constitution)*, (New Delhi: Publications Division, Ministry of Information and Broadcasting,
Government of India, 1997), 1–22. See also Derek Heater, "Citizenship: a remarkable case of
sudden interest", *Parliamentary Affairs*, (1991) vol. 44, 140–156.

protected persons can be considered ressortissants, while stateless persons cannot.[108] Whiteman characterises the Mixed Arbitral Tribunals' interpretation of the term as "liberal", citing a case where a line was drawn nevertheless: a Turkish subject who had been an Italian Consular Agent in Turkey, was held not to be a *ressortissant*.[109]

Ruzié states that *ressortissant* applied to categories of foreigners and points to the term's use by the European Union. The term *ressortissant*

> *servait à désigner parmi les étrangers, des personnes relevant d'un régime plus avantageux que l'ensemble de la catégorie des "étrangers", distingués des "nationaux". Ainsi, depuis la mise en place progressive de la C.E.E. et notamment dans le cadre de la consécration de la liberté de circulation, en arrivait-on à utiliser l'expression de "ressortissants des pays membres de la C.E.E.". Désormais, le contenu de la situation juridique de ces "ressortissants" s'enrichira, en quelque sorte, non seulement d'un droit de vote et d'éligibilité pour certaines élections, limitativement énumérées par le traité de Maastricht mais également d'un droit à une protection diplomatique de la part d'un autre Etat membre.*[110]

2. Protected person

Protected persons are those who, while not considered nationals, may enjoy a state's diplomatic protection on the basis of a link of responsibility to the state or territory of which they are inhabitants or nationals. Such persons have been held to be *ressortissants* of the power granting protection. The status was used to a great extent by Great Britain, to describe the inhabitants of British protectorates and mandated and trusteeship territories.[111] Whiteman maintains that the right of the protecting state to

---

[108]   Weis, *Nationality and statelessness in international law*, 8–9.

[109]   Whiteman, *Digest of international law*, vol. 8, 27.

[110]   (Author's translation: *served to designate among foreigners, persons benefiting from a more advantageous regime than the rest of the category of "foreigners", distinguished from "nationals". Thus, since the progressive establishment of the European Economic Community [EEC] and notably in function of the right to free movement, the expression "ressortissants of EEC member states" has come into use. Henceforth the content of these "ressortissants'" legal situation was in some sense expanded, not only by a right to vote and eligibility [to stand] in certain elections as set out in the Treaty of Maastricht, but also by a right of diplomatic protection by other member states.*) Ruzié, "Citoyenneté et nationalité dans l'Union Européenne", 14–15.

[111]   Clive Parry, ed., *A British digest of international law*, vol. 5 (London: Stevens & Sons, 1965), 3–9. See Whiteman, *Digest of international law*, vol. 8, 22–24. In the case of the United Kingdom, "[t]he territories are those in which Her Majesty exercises jurisdiction but which do not belong to the Queen's dominions". Weis, *Nationality and statelessness in international law*, 19. Weis cites the case of *Pablo Najera* before the Franco-Mexican Claims Commission as evidence that subjects of a mandated territory are protected persons (or *protégés*). Weis, *Nationality and statelessness in international law*, 25.

represent such persons is trumped only if the individual in question is the national of another state.[112]

3. Protégés (*de facto subjects*/nationals)

Whiteman notes two meanings. The first, probably obsolete, meaning nationals of states in the service of another state, as *de facto subjects* of the latter. The second meaning encompasses nationals being protected by diplomatic or consular representatives of another state, in countries where their own state has no representation, under an agreement between the two states. This category includes 'protecting powers' as used in the laws of armed conflict.[113]

4. *Denizens*

Koessler defines *denizen* as "the status of alien-born individuals who had been naturalized by letters-patent of the King. They were English subjects *ex donatione regis*, or *donaisons*, hence 'denizen'". He mentions that in the United States prior to independence from Great Britain the words "subject" and "denizen" were frequently used terms for which "citizen" would be used today.[114] Weis' definition substantially agrees, but follows Blackstone, as he stipulates that denizens "have somewhat inferior rights to those enjoyed by other subjects – a distinction which is irrelevant from the viewpoint of international law".[115] Oppenheim states that *denization* is a particular form of

---

[112] Whiteman, *Digest of international law*, vol. 8, 23.

[113] Id., 26–27. See also Weis, *Nationality and statelessness in international law*, 39, and Oppenheim, *International law. A treatise*, 589–90.

[114] Koessler, "'Subject,' 'Citizen,' 'National,' and 'Permanent Allegiance'", 58–59 and note 2. Whiteman quotes Blackstone's *Commentaries on the Laws of England*: "A denizen is an alien born, but who has obtained *ex donatione legis* letters patent to make him an English subject. He occupied formerly, a kind of a middle state, between an alien and natural-born subject, and partook of both of them. He might take lands by purchase or devise, which an alien could not, until the law was altered. But a denizen could not take by inheritance: for his parent, through whom he must have claimed, being an alien, had no inheritable blood and therefore could convey none to the son. And, upon a like defect of hereditary blood, the issue of a denizen, born *before* denization, could not inherit to him; but his issue born *after* [denization] might. No denizen 'could or can – for the right of the Crown to grant letters of denization is still preserved' – be of the privy council, or either house of parliament, or have any office of trust, civil or military, or be capable of any grant of lands, &c., from the crown". Whiteman, *Digest of international law*, vol. 8, 10.

[115] Weis, *Nationality and statelessness in international law*, 7. See *United States ex rel. Zdunic v. Uhl, District Director of Immigration, etc., et al.*, 137 F.2d 858, 861 (2d. Cir. 1943), which concluded that the status must include some form of allegiance.

naturalisation in the United Kingdom, making an alien a British subject, but "which has not been used for many years and seems not likely to be resorted to. It is not referred to in the British Nationality Acts of 1948 or 1981".[116]

Hammar decides to use this "old English word" to designate

> *the growing category of privileged noncitizens, in between ordinary foreigners – lacking work, residence, and welfare rights – and citizens. . . . Denizens are foreign citizens who have a secure permanent residence status, and who are connected to the state by an extensive array of rights and duties. They have their legal domicile or effective residence in the host country . . . In countries that do not confer citizenship automatically on persons born in their territory, the descendants of immigrants could conceivably remain outside the community of citizens over several generations.*[117]

5. Subjects

As seen above, the term "subject" has been used as a synonym of both "national" and "citizen", depending on the context. In terms of the former category, Weis points to the case of Romanian Jews who were considered 'subjects' but not 'citizens' until 1918, as were Jews in the Papal State.[118] It should be regarded today as a term of municipal law, unless clearly defined otherwise.

It is also used to denote the relationship of personal allegiance due, or at one time the personal jurisdiction of, a monarch or sovereign. As set out in the first chapter, in the case of the Commonwealth of Nations and countries where Elizabeth II is Head of State, it is doubtful whether such personal obligations persist in the absence of specific statutory provisions. Subject status has been abolished as a term of nationality law in both Australia and the United Kingdom.

6. Indigenat; Heimatrecht; Vecinidad; Unterthan

Weis points to the first three terms (the first used up to 1919 in Germany, the second in Austria, the third in Spain) as examples of statuses that have been confused with the term *nationality*, but that instead refer to a local (municipal) territorial relationship.

The German word "Unterthan" may also be translated as "subject", with a local connotation, harking back to the feudal rights of personal sovereignty over inhabitants of a particular territory.

---

[116] Robert Jennings and Arthur Watts, "Oppenheim's International Law", (London: Longman, 1992), 875 note 2.

[117] Hammar, "State, nation, and dual citizenship", 84.

[118] Weis, *Nationality and statelessness in international law*, 5.

7. "United Nations Nationals"

The term does not denote a *nationality* of the United Nations, but was defined in the Treaty of Peace between Italy and the United States as encompassing persons possessing the nationality of any United Nations member state.[119]

---

[119] Whiteman, *Digest of international law*, vol. 8, 11.

Chapter 3

Nationality in Municipal and International Law

This chapter summarises the significance and consequences of nationality in municipal and international law in order to allow conclusions to be drawn about the consequences of current state practice related to multiple-nationality. Specific issues related to multiple nationality as a phenomenon are largely dealt with in the following chapter. As multiple nationality is not a thing in itself, but in fact the juxtaposition of two or more separate statuses or relationships which exist independently of the other, the underlying *nationality* must be understood on its own, in order for conclusions to be drawn about its consequences and the consequences of multiple nationality. One aspect of the questions raised here is whether state practice toward multiple nationality has implications for the meaning and consequences of the underlying nationality itself, both on the municipal and the international level. The following summary cannot be seen as providing an exhaustive précis of nationality in international law, but is submitted as a thorough overview of the issues raised by the topic relevant in the current context.

The chapter is divided into a separate examination of nationality in international law, and nationality in municipal law. It will be seen that there are important differences between nationality in municipal law and in international law. For municipal and international law, both the definition of, and rules in relation to, nationality, as well as the consequences of nationality, must be considered.

A. INTRODUCTION AND OVERVIEW

Differing views about the nature of nationality and its relationship to issues of rights and duties lead to different opinions as to the definition of nationality and its consequences in *municipal law*. While commentators agree that nationality is an important basis for aspects of both municipal and international law, they cannot agree whether it is a status or a relationship. In fact both ideas seem applicable.[1]

Santulli remarks that a relationship with the state is not a component of nationality, but a condition of such nationality.

> *En effet le lien de fait est une condition de la nationalité mais pas une composante de celle-ci. Le droit interne choisit des « faits » qu'il utilise comme éléments de* rattachment (Anknüpfung) *pour opérer attribution de la nationalité. Mais, parce que le droit interne les utilise comme conditions de fait pour l'attribution de la nationalité, celle-ci se distingue logiquement de ceux-là ; si bien que, si on les retient dans la définition de la nationalité, c'est parce qu'ils sont nécessaires à son attribution et non parce qu'ils en seraient un élément constitutif.*[2]

Weis states the general rule, with which all experts seem to agree: "nationality as a term of municipal law is defined by municipal law".[3] Used in this way, each state can have its own definition of nationality, and dictate its consequences.[4] Weis then proposes a general characterisation of nationality on the municipal level as a "specific relationship between individual and State conferring mutual rights and duties".[5] Here however, Randelzhofer disagrees, noting that nationality may be a condition for such rights and duties, but is not their source. He points to the fact that municipal legislation on nationality is confined to the attribution of nationality to human beings, and does not deal with consequential rights and duties.[6] Weis thus sees the status/

---

[1] Albrecht Randelzhofer, "Nationality", in *Encyclopedia of Public International Law*, ed. Rudolf Bernhardt and Max Planck Institute for Comparative Public Law and International Law, vol. 8 (Amsterdam: Elsevier, 1985), 416–424, 417. For a detailed discussion, see Peter Weis, *Nationality and statelessness in international law* (Alphen aan den Rijn: Sijthoff & Noordhoff, 1979), 29–32.

[2] (Author's translation: *In fact the real link is a condition of nationality but not a component of nationality. Municipal law chooses "facts" that it uses as elements of rattachment ("Anknüpfung") to operate attribution of nationality. However, as municipal law uses them as actual conditions for the attribution of nationality, such "facts" are logically to be distinguished from nationality itself. If we retain them as part of the definition of nationality it is because they are necessary for its attribution and not because they are a constitutive element thereof.*) Carlo Santulli, *Irrégularités internes et efficacité internationale de la nationalité* (Paris: Université Panthéon-Assas Paris-2, 1995), 3.

[3] See Weis, *Nationality and statelessness in international law*, 29.

[4] Ibid.

[5] Ibid.

[6] Randelzhofer, "Nationality", 417.

relationship of nationality in municipal law as involving reciprocal substantive rights and duties depending on the state, whereas Randelzhofer sees it simply as a categorisation which may lead to such rights and duties.

The latter view seems to underscore arguments herein that nationality and citizenship are discrete things, and that maintaining the distinction is important for the weighing of the effects of state practice vis-à-vis multiple nationality. It is interesting to note that Oppenheim's ninth edition begins the section on nationality by stating: "Nationality of an individual is his quality of being a subject of a certain state",[7] whereas the seventh edition read: "Nationality of an individual is his quality of being a subject of a certain State, and therefore its citizen".[8] The abandonment of the link to citizenship is arguably a reflection of the detailed discussions of the nature of citizenship that have taken place over the past years, outlined in the previous chapter, as well as the view that nationality must be analysed on its own.

According to Randelzhofer's view, nationality's effects on the municipal plane seem to be restricted to determining who is included in the class of nationals. As discussed in the previous chapter, one may speculate as to potential future changes, depending on the parameters of nationality and citizenship. Weis is however correct to point out that whether nationality itself has direct consequences in municipal law depends on municipal law, not on international law, and in many states this does involve rights and duties directly, especially where nationality and citizenship are indistinguishable as legal categories, or when municipal law provides a right to claim diplomatic protection or to enter the state. Diplomatic protection and admission to territory are both usually considered consequences of nationality on the international plane, in terms of inter-state relations. This is discussed below.

As to the definition of nationality at *international law*, Weis says that nationality "is a technical term denoting the allocation of individuals, termed nationals, to a specific State – the State of nationality – as members of that State, a relationship which confers upon the State of nationality . . . rights and duties in relation to other states".[9] It should be emphasised that it is the state that possesses these rights and duties, not the individual, and that they apply in relation to other states. Weis lists these rights and duties, discussed at length below, as the duties of allowing nationals residence and admission, and the right of exercising protection vis-à-vis other states.

Usually, a person's nationality is the same under municipal law and international law. There may however be instances where international law gives the effect of nationality of a particular state to persons who may not have that status under a state's municipal law.

---

[7] Robert Jennings and Arthur Watts, "Oppenheim's International Law", (London: Longman, 1992), 851.

[8] L. Oppenheim, in *International law. A treatise*, ed. Hersch Lauterpacht (London: Longmans, Green & Co., 1948), 585–86.

[9] Weis, *Nationality and statelessness in international law*, 59.

Persons may be regarded as nationals in the usage of international law who, for some reason or other, are not deemed to be nationals under the municipal law of the State concerned as long as that State is under a duty of international law to grant them a right of sojourn on a territory under its sovereignty and to admit them to such territory, and as long as its right of protection is recognised by international custom.[10]

An example is the state that denationalises nationals while they are abroad, without them acquiring or having acquired another nationality. The former state has a duty to admit them should other states not tolerate their presence.[11] This is discussed below.

On the other hand, there are also instances when although a state attributes its nationality to an individual under its municipal laws, international law does not recognise that nationality for its purposes. That is to say, other states are not required to recognise such nationality for the purposes of international law. In the author's view this is best described as the issue of recognition of (municipal) nationality at international law, as opposed to saying that an individual lacks a particular nationality on the international plane, an expression favoured by some writers.[12] This issue is especially relevant in terms of multiple nationality, which is discussed below.

B. NATIONALITY IN INTERNATIONAL LAW

The introductory comment to the draft convention on the law of nationality proposed by a committee of the Harvard Law School in 1929 stated

Nationality has no positive, immutable meaning. On the contrary its meaning and import have changed with the changing character of states. Thus nationality in the feudal period differed essentially from nationality, or what corresponded to it, in earlier times before states had become established within definite territorial limits, and it differs now from what it was in the feudal period. It may acquire a new meaning in the future as the result of further changes in the character of human society and developments in international organization. Nationality always connotes, however, membership of some kind in the society of a state or nation.[13]

This premise that the nature of nationality under international law is not immutable is an important point of departure for any enquiry about the consequences of current state practice toward multiple nationality. There would seem to be few hard and fast

---

[10] Id., 59–60.

[11] Randelzhofer, "Nationality", 422.

[12] It should be noted that much confusion results from the word "nationality" being used in various ways by different authors.

[13] Manley O. Hudson and Richard W. Flournoy Jr., "Nationality – Responsibility of states – Territorial waters, drafts of conventions prepared in anticipation of the first conference on the codification of international law, The Hague 1930", *The American Journal of International Law*, (1929) vol. 23, April, Supplement, 21.

rules of international law that dictate the contours of nationality in international law. It will be explained below that this is because rules of nationality are still considered largely to be within the domain reserved to states' municipal law. The analysis of state practice herein asks to what extent that balance between international law and the reserved domain is modified, if at all, by current state practice toward multiple nationality. In order to guide the reader, the following categories of possible rules of *international law* related to nationality are proposed: (1) rules relating to the attribution/acquisition or deprivation/loss of nationality, (2) rules relating to the recognition of nationality by other states, and (3) rules relating to the consequences of nationality. The issue of statelessness is discussed in relation to attribution and deprivation of nationality.

1. Attribution/acquisition and deprivation/loss of nationality

It is a generally accepted principle of international law that it is up to each state to determine who its nationals are, subject to obligations due to other states.[14] Attribution of nationality is thus a matter of municipal law, although the state may enter into international agreements that affect its ability to legislate in any manner it chooses. Whether such nationality must be recognised on the international plane is another

---

[14] Jennings and Watts, "Oppenheim's International Law," 852. The Permanent Court of International Justice held in its Advisory Opinion in the *Nationality Decrees in Tunis and Morocco* case that nationality is generally within the domain reserved to states, as far as international law is concerned. As to whether international law considers that a matter is within the domain reserved to state jurisdiction, the Court held that this is fluid, and a function of international relations. Jennings and Watts, "Oppenheim's International Law", 852. For a discussion of the case see Nathaniel Berman, "The Nationality Decrees Case, or, of intimacy and consent", *Leiden Journal of International Law*, (2000) vol. 13, no. 1, 265–295. See also Wolfgang Benedek, "Nationality decrees in Tunis and Morocco (Advisory Opinion)", in *Encyclopedia of Public International Law*, ed. Rudolf Bernhardt and Max Planck Institute for Comparative Public Law and International Law, vol. 3 (Amsterdam: Elsevier, 1981), 510–511; *Nationality Decrees Issued in Tunis and Morocco (Advisory Opinion)*, PCIJ, (1923) Series B, No. 4. Juss decries the consequences of the reserved domain in relation to nationality: "Nationality has long been a concept in international law. It is high time that it was recognized that as such it is too important, especially in the changing conditions of the modern world, to be left to the mercy of nation States where today, in many cases, nation States themselves are undergoing fundamental change". Satvinder S. Juss, "Nationality law, sovereignty, and the doctrine of exclusive domestic jurisdiction", *Florida Journal of International Law*, (1994) vol. 9, no. 2, 219–240, 222. He argues that in the context of the United Kingdom's change of the nationality status of Hong Kong British nationals that states in fact do not, or at least should not, have exclusive domestic jurisdiction in international law in relation to the rules of nationality. Zilbershats also postulates that "global justice" requires a rule of international law requiring states to attribute nationality to residents. Yaffa Zilbershats, "Reconsidering the concept of citizenship", *Texas International Law Journal*, vol. 36, no. 4, 689–734.

matter that is discussed below. According to Randelzhofer, the only limitation in international law on this freedom is that "a State can regulate only its own nationality and not that of another state".[15]

Oppenheim comments that municipal laws that distinguish between categories of nationals or citizens are of no importance to international law, as it is nationality in the wider sense, as opposed to specific rights of citizenship, which is relevant internationally.[16]

The general notion of attribution of nationality should be divided into rules related to the granting of nationality (or from the individual's standpoint, its acquisition), and rules related to withdrawal (or loss, by the individual) of nationality. This is because it would seem that international law may constrain states more in terms of when they can withdraw their nationality from an individual, than when they may grant it. This is discussed below.

1.1 Acquisition/Grant

While international law arguably provides a right to a nationality, the norm seems unenforceable, which is also evidenced by the prevalence of statelessness and the lack of success in combating it. This must be seen as a reflection of the general principle that states have basically unfettered freedom in determining whom they consider a national.[17]

---

[15] Randelzhofer, "Nationality", 417.

[16] Jennings and Watts, "Oppenheim's International Law", 856–57.

[17] The Universal Declaration of Human Rights states in article 15(1) that "everyone has the right to a nationality". United Nations, Universal Declaration of Human Rights, adopted and proclaimed by General Assembly resolution 217 A (III) of 10 December 1948 (internet), http://www.un.org/Overview/rights.html, consulted on 15 March 2006. The American Declaration on the Rights and Duties of Man states in article 19 that "Every person has the right to the nationality to which he is entitled by law and to change it, if he so wishes, for the nationality of any other country that is willing to grant it to him". University of Minnesota Human Rights Library, American Declaration of the Rights and Duties of Man, O.A.S. Res. XXX, adopted by the Ninth International Conference of American States, 1948, (internet), http://www1.umn.edu/ humanrts/oasinstr/zoas2dec.htm, consulted on 15 March 2006. This seems to be a weaker statement. The American Convention on Human Rights goes further in extending real rights. It states in article 20 that (1) Every person has the right to a nationality. (2) Every person has the right to the nationality of the state in whose territory he was born if he does not have the right to any other nationality. (3) No one shall be arbitrarily deprived of his nationality or of the right to change it. University of Minnesota Human Rights Library, American Convention on Human Rights, O.A.S. Treaty Series No. 36, 1144 U.N.T.S. 123, entered into force July 18, 1978 (internet), http://www1.umn.edu/humanrts/oasinstr/zoas3con.htm, consulted on 15 March 2006. The African Charter on Human and People's Rights does not mention a right to nationality, providing in article 12(1) "every individual shall have the right to freedom of movement and residence within the borders of a State provided he abides by the

A corollary of that general principle is that there are no specific rules of international law regarding the criteria for acquisition of nationality, just common modes thereof.[18] Although these might be categorised differently, for discussion herein the following major modes are proposed: (1) birth in national territory, known as *jus soli*, (2) birth to parents one or both of whom possess a state's nationality, known as *jus sanguinis*, (3) naturalisation, (4) resumption, and (5) by transfer of territory.[19]

---

law". In Henry J. Steiner and Philip Alston, *International human rights in context – law politics morals*, Second ed. (Oxford: Oxford University Press, 2000), 1451.

[18] Jennings and Watts, "Oppenheim's International Law", 869. Randelzhofer notes that although all states use jus soli and jus sanguinis, or a combination thereof, they are not prescribed by customary international law. Randelzhofer, "Nationality", 418. Weis labels jus soli and jus sanguinis "predominant modes" but argues that because "concordance of municipal law does not yet create customary international law, a universal consensus of opinion of states is equally necessary", examining modes of acquisition of nationality cannot demonstrate a general principle of law. Weis, *Nationality and statelessness in international law*, 96. Brownlie states that Weis "is thought to underestimate the significance of legislation as evidence of the opinion of states". Ian Brownlie, *Principles of public international law*, Fifth ed. (Oxford: Clarendon Press, 1998), 397.

[19] Commentators see or label such categories differently, including as to when a specific form of attribution fits into one or the other. Oppenheim sees birth as a category, and only speaks of *jus soli* and *jus sanguinis* within that category. What is called "resumption" here, he labels "reintegration", and "transfer of territory" he calls "annexation and cession". Randelzhofer lists the following criteria and extrapolations therefrom for grants of nationality (see Randelzhofer, "Nationality", 418–19) recognised, or not, by customary international law:

(1) *Jus soli*, or birth within national territory:

(1a) Children born in a *jus soli* country to parents who enjoy diplomatic or consular immunity do not receive the nationality of the country of their birth. It is assumed that they will receive their parents' nationality (or perhaps nationalities) via *jus sanguinis*. See Article 12 Convention on Certain Questions Relating to the Conflict of Nationality Laws, 12 April 1930, 179 LNTS 89, no. 4137, (entry into force: 1 July 1937); Vienna convention on diplomatic relations, 18 April 1961, 500 UNTS 95, no. 7310 (entry into force: 24 April 1964); Optional protocol to the Vienna convention on diplomatic relations concerning acquisition of nationality, 18 April 1961, 500 UNTS 223, no. 7311 (entry into force: 24 April 1964); Optional protocol to the Vienna convention on consular relations concerning acquisition of nationality, 24 April 1963, 596 UNTS 469, no. 8639 (entry into force: 19 March 1967).

(1b) Birth on a vessel travelling on the high seas or on an aircraft is deemed to take place within the territory of the vessel's flag state. Countries that follow *jus soli* are thus able to confer nationality through birth on such vessel.

(2) *Jus sanguinis*, or descent from a national.

(3) "Acquisition of domicile with the intention of establishing a permanent residence (*animo manendi*)". He notes that this can even be against the individual's will. Even temporary residence *animo manendi* is sufficient, as long as the individual consents.

(3b) Settlement of aliens pursuant to a treaty means that such individuals cannot be granted nationality against their will.

(4) Service to the state, usually military.

Depending on the circumstances of the state, there may be other modes or extrapolations from modes.[20]

Modes of attribution that have been held invalid for international purposes, notwithstanding that they may be valid municipally, include purchase of real estate, and naturalisation without a genuine connection to the state.[21] This is discussed below in terms of *recognition* of nationality. Oppenheim distinguishes forced naturalisation, stating that it has in some cases been held as contrary to international law itself. He thus seems to go beyond the question as to whether a nationality validly attributed municipally must be recognised by other states. If supported, this constitutes a direct constraint on states' freedom in terms of bestowal of nationality.[22] On the other hand,

---

(5) Changes in civil status provoked through a relationship to a national, such as adoption, legitimation, affiliation, or marriage (automatically, conditionally, or upon application or naturalisation based on such a link). This is discussed in relation to marriage and the development of women's rights in chapter four. Randelzhofer notes that there is today a "strong tendency to replace the principle of family unity by the principle of sexual equality" in treaty law, but maintains that automatic conferral of nationality upon marriage, even against the will of the individual concerned, is a valid prerogative of the state at international law. On the other hand, the ILA's Committee on Feminism and International Law points out that "the principle that the nationality of the wife follows that of the husband was not a principle of international law". International Law Association, Committee on Feminism and International Law, "Final report on women's equality and nationality in international law", presented at the Sixty-ninth Conference of the International Law Association (London: ILA, 2000), 272. But while demonstrating that the practice is biased against women and thus discriminatory and arguably flawed, the Committee's report does not maintain it is contrary to customary law.

(6) Voluntary naturalisation. He adds that the conditions usually attached, such as long-time residence, are not required by international law, neither is consent by the state of original nationality. Individual will expressed through an application is as powerful a link as any. A corollary must be that withdrawal of nationality upon naturalisation elsewhere is also not required by international law except, according to Weis, where a discharge of former nationality is sought. Weis, *Nationality and statelessness in international law*, 133. Nor is it a requirement of international law that an individual seek to divest herself or himself of an existing nationality upon naturalisation elsewhere. See generally Weis, *Nationality and statelessness in international law*, 127–34.

[20] For example the Vatican State, which uses residence combined with the holding of an office. Randelzhofer, "Nationality", 418. See generally Yves De La Brière, "La condition juridique de la Cité du Vatican," in *Recueil des Cours*, vol. 33 (Paris: Librairie du Recueil Sirey, 1930), 114–163.

[21] Randelzhofer, "Nationality", 419. Weis distinguishes between compulsory acquisition of nationality and naturalisation and disagrees with statements that certain modes are invalid as such. "It appears difficult to deduce from these instances of State practice and official opinions and from the few arbitral awards on this problem, a general rule of international law concerning the conditions on which States may or may not confer their nationality, which goes beyond the rule already mentioned, namely, that the acquisition of a new nationality must contain an element of voluntariness on the part of the individual acquiring it, that it must not be conferred against the will of the individual". Weis, *Nationality and statelessness in international law*, 110.

[22] "The question whether the forced naturalisation is contrary to international law is distinct

whether such a grant is valid municipally would seem to be purely a matter for municipal law. In this sense the matter remains one of recognition on the international plane.[23] To this extent, a grant of nationality seems to be unreservedly within the purview of each state's municipal law, until such nationality is raised to the international level.

1.2 Loss

As in the grant of nationality, the grounds upon which individuals lose their nationality are basically left to the state's discretion.[24] Common modes of withdrawal used by states include (1) release or renunciation, (2) deprivation, and (3) expiration.[25]

---

from the question whether the nationality thus purportedly accorded will be acknowledged in other states". Jennings and Watts, "Oppenheim's International Law", 874–75. Randelzhofer seems to disagree generally. He maintains that aside from the fundamental limitation that one state cannot regulate another state's nationality, limitations in international law are only expressed in terms of the duty to recognise a nationality on the international plane. This is discussed below. "The validity of the conferment of nationality in municipal law is in no way limited by international law". Randelzhofer, "Nationality", 417. See also David Renton, "The genuine link concept and the nationality of physical and legal persons, ships and aircraft", dissertation presented at Universität Köln (Köln: Hohe Rechtswissenschaftliche Fakultät, 1975). Oppenheim seems to add another exception to the general rule, namely that once a state has deprived someone of his or her nationality, it cannot unilaterally impose it again without the individual's consent while he or she resides outside the country. This would however seem to lead to a right not to recognise such nationality under international law, as opposed to the invalidity of the nationality under municipal law. Jennings and Watts, "Oppenheim's International Law", 853 note 8. Judge Guggenheim's remark in dissent in Nottebohm, cited by Oppenheim, actually seems to support the latter view. *Nottebohm Case (second phase), Judgment of April 6th, 1955*, I.C.J. Reports (1955), 4, 54.

[23] In his dissent in the Nottebohm case, Judge Guggenheim differentiates between a right to refuse diplomatic protection and a right to refuse to recognise nationality, or a change in nationality, generally. Id., 65.

[24] These have varied greatly over time. An illustration is the response from the British Foreign Office to an enquiry by the British Consul General in Egypt in 1853 as to whether a Briton who had abjured Christianity in favour of Islam was still a British subject. McNair (Lord), *International law opinions*, vol. 2 (Cambridge: Cambridge University Press, 1956), 28–29. The fact that a Consul entertained the possibility that religious conversion could entail a loss of nationality might seem remarkable today, but it should be remembered that freedom of religion as currently interpreted is a very recent phenomenon in western states, and that it still does not exist either in practice or theory in many states. In the Kingdom of Saudi Arabia all citizens must be Muslims. Conversion to another religion would not result in the loss of nationality or citizenship, but instead constitute the crime of apostasy, punishable by death unless the perpetrator recants. See United States Department of State, *Saudi Arabia. International religious freedom report 2005*, (internet), http://www.state.gov/g/drl/rls/irf/2005/51609.htm, consulted 15 March 2006.

[25] Ivan A. Shearer, *Starke's international law*, 11th ed. (London: Butterworths, 1994), 311.

While expiration (loss of nationality provoked by prolonged residence abroad) seems to be rare today (as demonstrated in the Appendix), Weis distinguishes between loss of nationality by act of the state (deprivation or denationalisation) and loss of nationality by act of the individual (expatriation) and notes that both categories do "not necessarily coincide with the distinction between voluntary and involuntary loss".[26] This was discussed in the first chapter.

Some authors interpret the freedom of discretion enjoyed by states as limited to some extent by international law. Oppenheim appears to add a caveat to his formulation of the general principle of state discretion in relation to loss by remarking that "the matter is of direct importance for international law".[27] Although subtle, this addition is important, as it may signal a degree of difference in the freedom states have in granting nationality, versus the freedom they have in withdrawing it. Randelzhofer, on the other hand, sees no difference in states' freedom.[28]

Should such a difference in fact exist, it might arguably be a reflection of the fact that the primary practical relevance of a grant of nationality is on the municipal level, through attached citizenship rights or when the statuses overlap. Should a grant of nationality overstep the boundaries of international law, it does not have to be recognised on the international plane by other states, but in national terms the grantee enjoys the consequences of the status. In contrast, withdrawal of nationality by a state provides very different practical consequences on the international plane. While the former national may suffer hardship by being excluded on the municipal level, withdrawal of nationality by a state means that the individual in question is, for lack of a better phrase, "someone else's problem" on the international plane. The individual is left without the consequences of nationality, discussed below. Whether international law or sovereignty is viewed as the foundation of a system of state responsibility for individual human beings, one may speculate that there is much greater incentive for states to promote the development of international norms that prevent states from rejecting or abandoning their nationals in a way that has negative repercussions on other states. This is to say that a unilateral act by a state that causes an individual to be stateless, amounts to that state shirking its responsibilities vis-à-vis other states, or foisting what amounts to a problem on the international community at large.

Statelessness may be considered one such problem, as it results from no state attributing its nationality to an individual. When statelessness results from the withdrawal of an existing nationality, this is akin to a state unilaterally presenting the

---

[26] Weis, *Nationality and statelessness in international law*, 115–17.

[27] Jennings and Watts, "Oppenheim's International Law", 877. Shearer confirms that in terms of recognition of loss "so far as both international law and municipal law are concerned, there is a presumption against the loss of one nationality that has been held for some time, and a heavy onus of proof must be discharged". Shearer, *Starke's international law*, 311.

[28] Randelzhofer, "Nationality", 420. Except he points out that states cannot shirk their duty of admission of nationals if they are denationalised abroad without acquisition of another nationality. Id., 422.

international community with a problem, which could have been avoided.[29] While there may be disagreement as to the desirability or not of multiple nationality, issues canvassed in the following chapter, there is uniform agreement that statelessness is undesirable for states and individuals.[30]

A claim that there exists an obligation to avoid statelessness may overstep the requirements of international law; however its unwelcome effects do seem to cause a certain greater hesitation in terms of states' discretion to withdraw nationality.[31] The norms are unclear, and given the serious lacuna in international law created by statelessness certainly not as firm as they should arguably be. But while this discussion may involve shades of grey as opposed to distinct colours, it is nonetheless important in terms of the rules examined.

The various means by which states withdraw their nationality were considered in the first chapter. Whether the general principle that states have freedom in these matters may be limited (to some extent) only by a possible obligation to avoid statelessness, or by other considerations, is also open to question. There are many grounds upon which states deprive individuals of their nationality. Oppenheim cites "entering into foreign civil or military service without permission of his national state, voting

---

[29] In the opinion of the author, statelessness caused by a lack of a grant of nationality can be differentiated from statelessness caused by withdrawal of nationality: in the latter case it comes about due to the actions of a state that formerly had a link to the individual in question, whereas in the former case, no state had a link. It is arguably easier to recall an existing prior obligation or link, than to argue about which states should create such a link in the first place. Weis supports this idea: "In practice, investigations into the question of the admissibility of measures of municipal law resulting in loss of nationality have been confined almost exclusively to denationalisation. The reasons for this are obvious: while deprivation of nationality by the State may result in statelessness and the refusal to take back former nationals, and may thus lead to disputes between States, voluntary abandonment of nationality will, as a rule, only take place upon acquisition of another nationality and is not likely to lead to international friction". Weis, *Nationality and statelessness in international law*, 117.

[30] Shearer recalls not only the practical problems for states and individuals caused by statelessness, but says it "involves the existence of a serious gap in the application of international law". Shearer, *Starke's international law*, 312. Likewise, Jennings and Watts, "Oppenheim's International Law", 887. Oppenheim does not say that a deprivation of nationality resulting in statelessness is contrary to international law, but calls it "retrogressive" and remarks that "no vital national interest requires it". Id., 880.

[31] In the Convention on the Reduction of Statelessness states party agree generally that deprivation of nationality should not result in statelessness, but allow for exceptions in relation to naturalised persons and those born outside the state's territory that obviate the general principle. See articles 7 and 8. Convention on the reduction of statelessness, 30 August 1961, 989 UNTS 175, no. 14458 (entry into force: 13 December 1975). See also generally Convention relating to the status of stateless persons, 28 September 1954, 360 UNTS 130, no. 5158 (entry into force: 6 June 1960). In relation to the problems faced by women, see International Law Association, Committee on Feminism and International Law, "Final report on women's equality and nationality in international law", 266.

in political elections in a foreign state, committing acts of treason against the state or desertion from its armed forces, making false statements in applying for naturalisation, and prolonged residence abroad (particularly if in order to evade public service obligations), and becoming naturalised in a foreign state",[32] noting that "there would not seem to be anything contrary to international law in a state depriving its nationals of their nationality on such grounds".[33] An important corollary is that international law also does not require deprivation on such grounds.[34]

Oppenheim notes however that examples of large scale deprivations of nationality on the basis of uninterrupted residence abroad, or for political or racial reasons, "raise more difficult questions [as to] their compatibility with international law and the extent to which they should be recognised by other states". However he then cites examples for the proposition that there is a tendency to regard such denationalisation as effective on the international plane.[35]

As opposed to deprivation of nationality by the state, authors disagree as to whether individuals possess a right of *expatriation* at international law, or an inherent right to renounce effectively an existing nationality in favour of another. Oppenheim maintains it "has not yet become part of the general practice", citing many states' insistence on obtaining consent, or the fulfilment of conditions such as military service.[36] The 1930 Hague Convention provides no unconditional right to expatriation,[37] although the Harvard Research draft convention had incorporated a right of expatriation in the context of naturalisation elsewhere, without the consent of the previous state of nationality.[38] This probably reflects the United States' long-standing insistence that expatriation is a fundamental right of the individual.[39] This stand had

---

[32] Jennings and Watts, "Oppenheim's International Law", 878. Weis sees such acts as stemming from the individual's conduct, and thus puts them under the heading "expatriation" rather than "deprivation". Weis, *Nationality and statelessness in international law*, 117.

[33] Jennings and Watts, "Oppenheim's International Law", 878.

[34] Id., 881. Oppenheim points out in particular that "substitution", meaning naturalisation abroad provokes a loss of the original nationality under a state's municipal law, is not a requirement of international law, but of municipal law. Id., 881.

[35] Jennings and Watts, "Oppenheim's International Law", 879. In relation to the denationalisation of German Jews resident abroad by the National Socialist government of Germany in 1941, and the reaction of governments and courts, see Weis, *Nationality and statelessness in international law*, 121–23.

[36] Jennings and Watts, "Oppenheim's International Law", 867–68.

[37] Article 7, Convention on Certain Questions Relating to the Conflict of Nationality Laws, 179. Even multiple nationals require authorisation to surrender nationality. Article 6.

[38] Hudson and Flournoy Jr., "Nationality – Responsibility of states – Territorial waters, drafts of conventions prepared in anticipation of the first conference on the codification of international law, The Hague 1930", 45. In the Harvard draft although expatriation was to be automatic upon naturalisation in another state, existing obligations to the first state, such as military service, remained valid.

[39] John Bassett Moore, *A digest of international law as embodied in diplomatic discussions, treaties and other international agreements, international awards, the decisions of municipal*

resulted in 1870 in the United Kingdom dropping the common law doctrine of perpetual allegiance, according to which a subject could never divest him- or herself of nationality and the corresponding duty of allegiance.[40] Weis states that while consistent treaty practice "is not sufficient to establish the principle of automatic loss of nationality by acquisition of a new nationality as a principle of international law, the practice has, it is believed, restricted the right of States to refuse release from their nationality on acquisition of a new nationality".[41]

1.3   Note on transfer of territory / state succession

Randelzhofer states that "the transfer of territory does not cause an automatic change of nationality, but it is recognised that the successor State has the right to confer its nationality on the population domiciled in the transferred territory, under the condition that the acquisition of territory is lawful".[42] He adds that the relevant right is not a duty. Brownlie disagrees, stating that it is a rule that state succession automatically results in the population losing one nationality, and acquiring another.[43]

---

courts, and the writings of jurists, and especially in documents, published and unpublished, issued by Presidents and Secretaries of State of the United States, the opinions of the Attorneys-General, and the decisions of courts, Federal and State, 8 vols., vol. 6 (Washington: Government Printing Office, 1906), 99.

[40] For a treatise which influenced the United Kingdom's move away from the doctrine of perpetual allegiance, see Alexander Cockburn, Nationality: or the law relating to subjects and aliens, considered with a view to future legislation (London: William Ridgway, 1869). "The conflict between the law of England and that of so many of the leading nations of the world as to the origin of nationality, and the inconvenience to which such conflict may give rise, as well as the inconsistency of our rule as to the immutability of allegiance, at a time when emigration from this country to America is annually taking place on so large a scale, are now so sensibly felt, that an alteration of the law has become inevitable". Cockburn, Nationality: or the law relating to subjects and aliens, considered with a view to future legislation, 3. In 1895 Lawrence remarked that "most states hover between the old doctrine of inalienable allegiance, set forth in the maxim "Nemo potest exuere patriam," and the "right of expatriation" which has been asserted by the Congress of the United States in a statute of 1868 to be 'a natural and inherent right of all people'". T. J. Lawrence, The principles of international law, ed. Percy H. Winfield, 7th ed. (London: Macmillan & Co., 1895), 204.

[41] Weis, Nationality and statelessness in international law, 133.

[42] Randelzhofer, "Nationality", 420.

[43] Brownlie, Principles of public international law, 564. In relation to the option of nationality in treaties and generally from the Second World War until the 1960s related to both change of territory and state succession, see Karl Matthias Meessen, Die Option der Staatsangehörigkeit, vol. 38, Schriften zum Öffentlichem Recht (Berlin: Duncker & Humblot, 1966). In relation to nationality and state succession, see generally Jeffrey L. Blackman, "State successions and statelessness: the emerging right to an effective nationality under international law", Michigan Journal of International Law, (1998) vol. 19, 1141–1194; Tanja Gerwien, "The citizenship problems of the Baltic states in the light of public international law", mémoire presented at the Université de Genève Institut Universitaire de Hautes Etudes Internationales, 1996;

The practice of the United Kingdom vis-à-vis Hong Kong and Portugal vis-à-vis Macao, in relation to the resumption of the exercise of sovereignty by the People's Republic of China over those territories in 1997 and 1999, respectively, is described in chapter four. Whereas Portugal refused to denationalise its citizens by virtue of a connection to Macao, the United Kingdom has left the vast majority of its former Hong Kong citizens with a status it labels "nationality", but that does not provide a right of entry or abode in the United Kingdom.

At its fifty-first session, the International Law Commission (ILC) adopted a preamble and set of draft articles on "Nationality in relation to the succession of States" and recommended that these be adopted by the United Nations' General Assembly as a declaration.[44] The draft articles reflect an overriding concern as far as avoiding statelessness, while arguably leaving considerable leeway to the states concerned in terms of the attribution and withdrawal of their respective nationalities. A primary focal point is a real and effective connection to the territory concerned. In relation to multiple nationality, the articles may be characterised as neutral. In fact, the Commission went out of its way to characterise them as such in the commentary to article 9.

> *(2) It is not for the Commission to suggest which policy states should pursue on the matter of dual or multiple nationality. Accordingly, the draft articles are neutral in this respect. The Commission is nevertheless concerned with the risk of statelessness.*[45]

Article 9 provides that renunciation of nationality may be a condition of attribution of the successor state's nationality, as long as no statelessness ensues, even temporarily. Likewise, article 10 provides that states concerned may deprive individuals of their nationality should they choose to retain or acquire another in relation to the state succession. Under article 11 respect for the individual will is paramount, but this does not automatically extend multiple nationality to individuals should they desire this outcome. Article 12 exhorts the states concerned to "take all appropriate mea-

---

Hansjörg Jellinek, *Der automatische Erwerb und Verlust der Staatsangehörigkeit durch völkerrechtliche Vorgänge, zugleich ein Beitrag zur Lehre von der Staaten sukzession*, ed. Carl Bilfinger, vol. 27, *Beiträge zum ausländischen öffentlichen Recht und Völkerrecht* (Berlin: Carl Heymanns Verlag, 1951); Christine Kreuzer, *Staatsangehörigkeit und Staatensukzession*, vol. 132, *Schriften zum Völkerrecht* (Berlin: Duncker & Humblot, 1998); Alenka Mesojedec-Prvinsek and Slavko Debelak, "Citizenship and legal continuity after the declaration of independence of the Republic of Slovenia", *Croatian Critical Law Review*, (1998) vol. 3, no. 1–2, 191–214; Jelena Pejic, "The international legal aspects of citizenship", *Croatian Critical Law Review*, (1998) vol. 3, no. 3, 303–336; United Nations High Commissioner for Refugees (UNHCR), *Citizenship in the context of the dissolution of Czechoslovakia*, vol. 2, no. 4, *European Series* (Geneva: UNHCR Regional Bureau for Europe, 1996); European Commission for Democracy through Law, *Consequences of state succession for nationality, Report by the Venice Commission*, Council of Europe, 1996, (Strasbourg: Council of Europe, 1998).

[44] International Law Commission, *Report of the Commission to the General Assembly on the work of its fifty-first session* 1999, (internet), http://www.un.org/law/ilc/sessions/51/51sess.htm, consulted 1 April 2003.

[45] Id.

sures to allow [a] family to remain together or to be reunited", which in terms of practice might in some cases best be served by multiple nationality,[46] but it is clear that there is no obligation in that sense.

2. Recognition of nationality

It has been shown that states are free to attribute their nationality to whomever they choose on the basis of various modes, with no, or perhaps very few, exceptions. It is an accepted general principle of law that determinations of nationality are, for the purposes of international law, within the domain reserved to each state's municipal law, basically a reflection of state sovereignty within the system of international law and relations. The wide freedom accorded to states, if unfettered, could obviously lead to anomalous and dangerous results, should states begin to abuse this power. Thus, rather than obliging states not to legislate in a certain way with respect to attribution of nationality, international law dictates that when the consequences of such attribution are felt on the international level, it is up to international law whether a bestowal or removal of nationality must be recognised by other states. These are issues related to *recognition* of nationality. It should be remembered that the basic consequences of nationality at international law are the state's right to diplomatic protection of its nationals, and obligation to allow entry and residence of its nationals.

What constitutes an abuse of state power in this regard is a matter that may be considered controversial. For example, the offer by Spain to attribute Spanish nationality to the grandchildren of Spaniards directly, upon one year's residence, has led to estimates that over one million people, 400,000 from Argentina alone, will move to Spain pursuant to the offer.[47] Spanish generosity in relation to attribution of its nationality was also extended to the survivors of the "Abraham Lincoln Brigade" in 1996 (approximately 90 remaining men), who had travelled from the United States to fight the forces of Francisco Franco in the 1930s.[48] While Spain may validly consider these groups its nationals, to what extent are Argentina and the United States bound to do so?

---

[46] See generally Karen Knop, "Relational nationality: on gender and nationality in international law", in *Citizenship today. Global perspectives and practices*, ed. T. Alexander Aleinikoff and Douglas Klusmeyer (Washington: Carnegie Endowment for International Peace, 2001), 89–124.

[47] David Sharrock, "Spanish welcome migrants", *The Australian*, 15 January 2003, 9; Terra, *Cambió legislación ibérica. Unos 400.000 argentinos podrán ser ciudadanos españoles*, 8 January 2003 (internet), http://www.terra.com.ar/canales/informaciongeneral/60/60672.html, consulted 15 March 2006. In relation to the reasons underpinning the program, see Isambard Wilkinson, "Job, house, plane trip – just the ticket to viva España", *The Sydney Morning Herald*, 4–5 January 2003, 8.

[48] "An earlier foreign war. They fought Franco, in Abe's name", *The Economist*, 3 May 2003, 33.

The general rule in relation to attribution and recognition of nationality on the international plane is found in Article 1 of the 1930 Hague Convention:

> *It is for each State to determine under its own law who are its nationals. This law shall be recognised by other States in so far as it is consistent with international conventions, international custom, and the principles of law generally recognised with regard to nationality.*[49]

International law thus seems to view nationality through a different lens than municipal law. It may recognise attribution of nationality or not, and as already stated, it may even find nationality where a state does not attribute it under its municipal legislation, although to label it as such causes semantic confusion.[50]

A related issue is when states agree among themselves to treat their own nationals as aliens, in certain circumstances, when they are dual or multiple nationals. For example, Australia entered into a Consular Treaty with Hungary that was accompanied by an Exchange of Notes according to which Hungarian-Australian dual nationals will be regarded as Australians by Hungary if they enter that country on Australian passports with visas for temporary visits, and vice-versa.[51]

2.1   General bases for non-recognition of nationality under international law

Although a nationality may be valid municipally, international law provides that states are not obliged to recognise such nationality (and may thus deny the state claiming

---

[49] Convention on Certain Questions Relating to the Conflict of Nationality Laws, 179. Randelzhofer states that it is the common view that the article reflects of rule of customary international law. Randelzhofer, "Nationality", 417.

[50] Jennings and Watts, "Oppenheim's International Law", 853 note 10. See generally Hans Jürgen Sonnenberger, "Anerkennung der Staatsangehörigkeit und effektive Staatsangehörigkeit natürlicher Personen im Völkerrecht und im Internationalen Privatrecht", paper presented at the 20. Tagung der Deutschen Gesellschaft für Völkerrecht, Tübingen, 1987, in *Berichte der deutschen Gesellschaft für Völkerrecht*, vol. 29 (Heidelberg: C.F. Müller Juristischer Verlag, 1988), 9–36; Hans von Mangoldt, "Anerkennung der Staatsangehörigkeit und effektive Staatsangehörigkeit natürlicher Personen im Völkerrecht und im Internationalen Privatrecht", paper presented at the 20. Tagung der Deutschen Gesellschaft für Völkerrecht, Tübingen, 1987, in *Berichte der deutschen Gesellschaft für Völkerrecht*, vol. 29 (Heidelberg: C.F. Müller Juristischer Verlag, 1988), 37–97.

[51] Ryszard W. Piotrowicz, "The Australian-Hungarian Consular Treaty of 1988 and the regulation of dual nationality", *The Sydney Law Review*, (1990) vol. 12, no. 2/3, 569–583. Although Piotrowicz points out that the provisions of the agreement are not watertight in terms of the guarantees provided (see Id., 572–576) he states that "the agreement is capable of being construed as a reflection of the dominant nationality rule", and that while not unique as far as state practice, represents new juridical ground for Australia. Id., 583. The agreement must in some sense have been uncomfortable as far as fitting into the Hungarian legal framework, as its 1957 Citizenship Law did not recognise the effects of foreign nationality for its citizens. Id., 578–579.

the nationality the usual right of diplomatic protection) when the nationality in question has not been attributed in accordance with international law. Aside from the possible categories already discussed, examples include instances where the connection between the individual and the state is not deemed sufficient to warrant the state's claim to protect an individual vis-à-vis other states. Thus:

(1) Naturalisation of nationals of other states who are unconnected to either the territory or the nationals of a State is not required to be recognised,[52]
(2) naturalisation of all persons of a given religious faith or political persuasion, speaking a given language, or being of a given race is not required to be recognised,[53]
(3) acquisition of real estate as a basis for a grant of nationality is questionable,[54]
(4) inhabitants of mandated and trust territories are not considered nationals of the administering State,[55]
(5) inhabitants of occupied territories can not be considered nationals of the occupying State,[56]
(6) automatic attribution of nationality upon marriage is cited by the ILC.[57]

In the example cited above, Spain decided to attribute its nationality to descendants of Spaniards upon their application and only after a period of residence, thus arguably reinforcing a claim to have validly attributed its nationality.

2.2   Considerations in relation to multiple nationals

While multiple nationality is not contrary to international law, the phenomenon has led to the production of specific rules related to the diplomatic protection of multiple nationals. Randelzhofer, while not stating they are customary, says they have found considerable support in international tribunals.[58] These are discussed below under *diplomatic protection*, and in the following chapter.

---

[52] Randelzhofer, "Nationality", 419.

[53] Ibid.

[54] Ibid. Randelzhofer states that "It is incompatible with international law to confer nationality automatically by subsequent legislation to aliens who have acquired real estate prior to this legislation. To provide that in future cases the acquisition of real estate has the consequence of acquisition of territory [sic. nationality] is, however, compatible with international law". Ibid.

[55] Ibid.

[56] Ibid.

[57] International Law Commission, *Report of the International Law Commission to the General Assembly, Fifty-fourth session*, Official Records, Fifty-seventh session, Supplement no. 10, A/57/10, (New York: United Nations, 2002), 174–75. It is interesting to note the ILC's inclusion of this category, as few authors mention it, probably given the fact that it reflected commonly accepted until very recent times. In that sense, what seems to be the almost complete abandonment of the practice may have dictated its inclusion here.

[58] Randelzhofer, "Nationality", 423.

2.3 Other considerations of recognition of nationality and the "Nottebohm" case

The *Nottebohm Case (Liechtenstein v Guatemala)*[59] is often cited (or confused) as dealing with issues of multiple nationality or conferment of nationality generally. This is arguably because the International Court of Justice (ICJ) applied a test of *effective nationality* to the case, a test which is commonly used by governments and courts in cases involving multiple nationality (discussed below). In fact, it is uncontroverted that Mr Nottebohm was never a multiple national according to the municipal laws of the countries in question. Rather, his case involved the right of a state not to recognise another state's attribution of nationality, and thus to exclude the second state from exercising a right of diplomatic protection. Some authors draw its relevance even more narrowly, in relation to the prerogative not to recognise a nationality attributed by naturalisation in certain circumstances.[60] The case has precipitated much comment and controversy.[61]

Mr Nottebohm had lived in Guatemala as a German national for 34 years, when during a trip to Europe before the outbreak of the Second World War, he acquired the nationality of the Principality of Liechtenstein by naturalisation, on what might be considered flimsy grounds (payment of a substantial fee and an annual tax, and the swearing of an oath of allegiance). It was uncontroverted that he thereby lost his German nationality.[62] Nottebohm returned to Guatemala on a Liechtenstein passport. His property was seized (as that of a German national or "enemy alien" during the Second World War) and he was interned in the United States pursuant to an agreement with the Government of Guatemala. Liechtenstein was neutral during the Second World War. It brought suit against Guatemala in the ICJ for the purportedly illegal confiscation of its national's property, and the treatment he suffered.

The ICJ held that Guatemala was not obliged to recognise Nottebohm's Liechtenstein nationality (i.e. to recognise Liechtenstein's claim on behalf of Nottebohm), as there was no genuine or effective link between the two, other than Nottebohm's naturalisation. It should be noted that the Court did not rule that Liechtenstein was not entitled to protect Nottebohm generally, just not vis-à-vis Guatemala. The Court also expressly avoided comment on the validity of Nottebohm's naturalisation under international law, Guatemala having urged it to declare the naturalisation itself invalid

---

[59] *Nottebohm Case (second phase), Judgment of April 6th, 1955.* For a summary of the facts, holdings and significance accompanied by interesting comments about the advocates, see Weis, *Nationality and statelessness in international law,* 176–81.

[60] Randelzhofer, "Nationality", 421.

[61] See Weis, *Nationality and statelessness in international law,* 178–80.

[62] Although Weis notes that before his acquisition of Liechtenstein's nationality, the German government had circulated a memorandum to its diplomatic and consular representatives stating that persons who acquired foreign nationality and thereby lost their German nationality could be assured that applications for resumption of nationality would receive "favourable consideration". Id., 179. It is to be assumed that this did not apply to Germans who were persecuted by the National Socialist regime.

under general principles of law. The issue was one of specific opposability. But the case seemed to extend the principle of the genuine or effective link from the context of multiple nationality (discussed below), to recognition, or opposability of nationality, generally.

Randelzhofer cites the 1958 Flegenheimer Claim before the United States-Italian Conciliation Commission as evidence to the contrary.[63] There, the Commission limited *Nottebohm* to its facts, holding that the effective link test should not be applied to persons possessing a single nationality.

> But when a person is vested with only one nationality, which is attributed to him or her either jure sanguinis or jure soli, or by a valid naturalization entailing the positive loss of the former nationality, the theory of effective nationality cannot be applied without the risk of causing confusion. It lacks a sufficiently positive basis to be applied to a nationality which finds support in a state law. There does not in fact exist any criterion of proven effectiveness for disclosing the effectiveness of a bond with a political collectivity, and the persons by the thousands who, because of the facility of travel in the modern world, possess the positive legal nationality of a State, but live in foreign States where they are domiciled and where their family and business center is located, would be exposed to non-recognition, at the international level, of the nationality with which they are undeniably vested by virtue of the laws of their national State, if this doctrine were to be generalized.[64]

Weis also maintains that the Nottebohm case cannot be cited as evidence for a generalisation of the genuine/effective link theory, and distinguishes the circumstances of the Nottebohm case as exceptional.[65] Moreover, applying a test of effective nationality to naturalised persons only, belies the fact that even native-born nationals may have no "effective link" to their state of nationality.[66]

Like the *Flegenheimer* Commission, Weis maintains that a generalisation of the ICJ's test in *Nottebohm* would lead to uncertainty in issues surrounding nationality of claims.[67] It is certainly correct to point out that questioning the lack of an effective link on the basis of naturalisation would distinguish naturalised persons from other nationals in a way that is hardly justifiable. Is it possible that *Nottebohm* may be limited to only certain kinds of naturalisations (although there is not even obiter dicta to

---

[63] Randelzhofer, "Nationality", 421.

[64] *Flegenheimer Claim, 20 September 1958 (Italian-United States Conciliation Commission)*, International Law Reports (1958) 91, 150.

[65] He notes that his opinion matches that of the three judges who dissented in the case, that the question of nationality should have been discussed with the merits of the case, that is the confiscation of Nottebohm's property, according to which the ICJ could arguably have found for Guatemala without going to the issue of Nottebohm's nationality. See discussion at Weis, *Nationality and statelessness in international law*, 180. See *Nottebohm Case (second phase), Judgment of April 6th, 1955*, 33, 49, 80.

[66] Weis, *Nationality and statelessness in international law*, 178–81; Randelzhofer, "Nationality", 421.

[67] Weis, *Nationality and statelessness in international law*, 180–81.

support this contention), those pursuant to what amounts to a purchase of nationality? No small number of states provide for what seems to be naturalisation in return
for investment.[68] Judge Guggenheim in dissent expressed the view that the Court
could go no further than to ask whether the naturalisation was "genuine" under the
laws of Liechtenstein, with the exception of fraudulent intent in acquisition, such as
in order to conceal enemy property in wartime.[69] "There was no question of a fictitious marriage between Liechtenstein and Nottebohm".[70]

In refusing to comment on the quality of Nottebohm's naturalisation in Liechtenstein, it would seem that the ICJ in fact did not limit the context of its holding to

---

[68] What for all intents and purposes amounts to outright purchase of nationality should
arguably be distinguished from national policies which encourage migration on the basis of an
investment, where nationality can subsequently be obtained by naturalisation on the usual bases
such as prolonged residence, local ties, language knowledge, understanding of the government,
and statement of loyalty or allegiance. Koslowski disagrees, linking the two. See Rey
Koslowski, "Challenges of international cooperation in a world of increasing dual nationality",
in *Rights and duties of dual nationals. Evolution and prospects*, ed. David A. Martin and Kay
Hailbronner (The Hague: Kluwer Law International, 2003), 157–182, 170–177. An example of
the former case includes Tonga, which between 1983 and 1991 it is reported "sold more than
5,000 passports, raising about $62 million". Barbie Dutter, "Tongans hunting a 'natural-born
fool' and $40m", *The Sun-Herald*, 7 October 2001, 56. The scheme "was to sell a special pass-
port which would have given holders a travel document but no right of abode in the Kingdom.
It was targeted at residents of the then Crown Colony of Hong Kong who were fearful of the
hand-over to China. But the scheme hit a hitch when Australia, Fiji and New Zealand, refused
to recognise the passports. To overcome this Tonga then sold citizenship and passports as a
package. Citizenship in Tonga comes with an entitlement to an allotment of land and to meet
this Tonga even designated an empty island – vacant because it was an active volcano – into
sections for the new citizens. . . . In the end the Tonga Supreme Court ruled the citizenship sale
illegal, so the noble and royal dominated assembly simply changed the constitution retrospec-
tively". Michael Field, "Jester fools island kingdom", *Fiji Times Weekend*, 20 October 2001, 8.
Regarding a similar scheme in Nauru, see Craig Skehan, "Nauru Inc: the scheme to privatise
a nation", *The Sydney Morning Herald*, 1–2 March 2003, 6. Such schemes are not the same
as the relaxation of residency requirements for citizenship that amount to breaches of municipal law. Allegations were made in 2002 that "quite a number of Asian recipients of Solomon
Island citizenship collected it after only two years residence, instead of the legally required
seven years". Robert Keith-Reid and Mere Tuqiri, "Whispers. Funny business", *Pacific*,
February 2002, vol. 28, no. 2, 9. Judge Guggenheim's dissent in *Nottebohm* cited above raises
the question whether the Solomon Islands' nationality referred to, fraudulently acquired, is valid
on the international plane. This would seem to turn entirely on the Solomon Islands' municipal law, as in any case two years' residence and voluntary acquisition seems to reflect a connection to the state for general purposes of international law. Such questions are the subject of
a study by Santulli, who concludes that absent a determination of valid nationality by the state
concerned, the nationality is invalid on the international plane. Santulli, *Irrégularités internes
et efficacité internationale de la nationalité*.

[69] *Nottebohm Case (second phase), Judgment of April 6th, 1955*, 57 and 65.

[70] Id., 57.

naturalisation, but applied the effective link test to test the opposability of Notte-bohm's Liechtenstein nationality (as any nationality) versus Guatemala. It appears that whether the test of effectivity can be applied to a single nationality, however acquired, is not clear, given the ICJ's holding. The dissenting judges certainly interpreted the judgment thus.[71] The case thus raises the issue of whether long-term or permanent residence in a state may be equated with nationality, or, in other terms, whether Nottebohm was in effect treated as a multiple national because of his long-term connection to Guatemala, as oposed to any possible link to Germany, or questionable link to Liechtenstein. Such a rule was not followed by the ILC in its draft rules on diplo-matic protection.

> *Moreover, the Commission was mindful of the fact that if the genuine link requirement proposed by* Nottebohm *was strictly applied it would exclude millions of persons from the benefit of diplomatic protection as in today's world of economic globalization and migra-tion there are millions of persons who have drifted away from their state of nationality and made their lives in states whose nationality they never acquire[,] or have [national-ity] acquired by birth or descent from states with which they have a tenuous connection.*[72]

3. Consequences of nationality

Once attributed, nationality has consequences on both the international and the munic-ipal planes of law. In terms of municipal law, certain rules (rights, entitlements, priv-ileges, obligations) are applicable to nationals but not to aliens. This is discussed in the next section. Weis points out that in order to distinguish the consequences of nationality at international law from the numerous rights and duties inherent in nationality under municipal law, one must extricate from the relationship between the state and its nationals those elements that "presuppose the co-existence of States, which confer rights or impose duties on the State in relation to other *subjects* of inter-national law" (i.e. states, not individuals).[73]

In the international context, Shearer[74] lists the "international importance" of nation-ality as: (1) entitlement to exercise diplomatic protection, (2) state responsibility for nationals, (3) [duty of] admission, (4) allegiance, (5) right to refuse extradition, (6) determination of enemy status in wartime, and (7) exercise of jurisdiction. In quali-fying these elements as being of "international importance", he indicates that they

---

[71] "The fact that the Judgment only applies to the particular case and that the *res judicata* is not binding on third States in no way detracts from the force of these considerations". Id., 60. Other commentators came to the same conclusions. Albrecht D. (Freiherr von) Dieckhoff, *Fehlerhaft erworbene Staatsangehörigkeit im Völkerrecht. (Fall Nottebohm)*, (Vaduz: Liechtensteiner Volksblatt, 1956).

[72] International Law Commission, *Report of the International Law Commission to the General Assembly, Fifty-fourth session*, 176.

[73] Weis, *Nationality and statelessness in international law*, 32.

[74] Shearer, *Starke's international law*, 309.

relate both to international law and to the general international context of nationality. For our purposes here, it is important to examine these areas in terms of whether they constitute consequences or functions of nationality in international or municipal law, or are linked to a wider perception or importance of nationality in international relations.

3.1 The state's right of diplomatic, consular or international protection, and international claims

Arguably the most important consequence (or function) of nationality on the international plane is that a state may protect, or intervene on behalf of its nationals, when they are harmed by other states.[75] This involves providing help or protection to nationals abroad by diplomatic or consular agents, or invoking a claim for compensation when another state has treated a national in violation of international law.[76] The right involved is one of customary international law, *of the state* of nationality, not the individual. It is unconditional and is unlimited in time, but while states may provide a right to diplomatic protection to their nationals in their municipal laws, in terms of international law its exercise is at the complete discretion of the state.[77]

---

[75] See generally Pierre Michel Blaser, "La nationalité et la protection juridique internationale de l'individu", dissertation presented at the Université de Neuchâtel (Lausanne: Imprimerie Rencontre, 1962). In relation to continuity of nationality, see Eric Wyler, "La règle dite de la continuité de la nationalité dans le contentieux international", doctoral thesis presented at the Université de Genève (Geneva: Institut Universitaire de Hautes Etudes Internationales, 1989). It has been seen that states sometimes protect persons other than their own nationals, such as British Protected Persons, protégés, and ressortissants. Whiteman states that the effect of this practice on the right of protection is "probably that international tribunals have jurisdiction to entertain claims by the protecting State on behalf of such persons provided that they are not nationals of any other State. This is so especially when the particular relationship of the protecting State to the territory in question has been internationally recognized. The same principle applies to diplomatic protection". Marjorie M. Whiteman, *Digest of international law*, 15 vols., vol. 8 (Washington: Department of State, 1968), 23–24. See note 78 below.

[76] Randelzhofer, "Nationality", 420–21. For an interesting survey of US-Mexican relations and the exercise of diplomatic protection between 1825 and the 1920s, see Frederick Sherwood Dunn, *The diplomatic protection of Americans in Mexico* (New York: Columbia University Press, 1933). In relation to diplomatic protection in the British Commonwealth, see Cuthbert Joseph, "Nationality and diplomatic protection", (Leyden: A. W. Sijthoff, 1969), originally presented as a doctoral thesis at the University of Geneva.

[77] See generally Weis, *Nationality and statelessness in international law*, 32–44. The jurisprudence of both the Permanent Court of International Justice and the International court of Justice supports the general rule. In the *Mavrommatis Concessions* case the PCIJ held that in exercising a right of diplomatic protection the state asserts its own rights as opposed to those of its national. *Mavrommatis Concessions Case, 20 August 1934*, Permanent Court of International Justice, (1924) Series A, no. 2, 12. The PCIJ held in the *Panevezys-Saldutiskis Railway Case* that it is the bond of nationality that gives right to the right of intervention by the state. *Panevezys-Saldutiskis Railway Case*, Permanent Court of International Justice, (1939) Series A/B, vol. 76, 16. This was confirmed by the ICJ in the *Nottebohm* case. *Nottebohm Case (sec-*

It would appear that sometimes states choose to subject their nationals to foreign jurisdiction.[78]

> [Diplomatic protection] *is an inherent element of the personal jurisdiction of States over their nationals, and its exercise has to be recognised by other States, who can only question it by denying the existence of that specific relationship between State and individual which it presupposes, or the existence of the situation for which redress is claimed by the protecting State, i.e., a breach of international law by another State in the person of the protected national or his rights.*[79]

As already mentioned, states may in some instances provide international protection to non-nationals.[80] The issue of protection of nationals and the use of force, or what

---

ond phase), Judgment of April 6th, 1955. The ICJ outlined rules surrounding diplomatic protection in *Reparation for injuries suffered in the service of the United Nations, 11 April 1949,* International Court of Justice, Annual Digest of Reports of Public International Law Cases, (1949) vol. 16, 318. Regarding withholding of international protection by states, Weis notes that persons deprived of international protection, such as refugees, are often considered as being in the same position as stateless persons, as "unprotected persons". Weis, *Nationality and statelessness in international law,* 44.

[78] An editorial in a leading Australian daily newspaper highlighted a case in which nationals were by default subjected to foreign jurisdiction well before any question of diplomatic or consular protection was raised. "Sydney women, Jane McKenzie and Deborah Spinner . . . are serving 50-year sentences in Bangkok's Klong Prem Prison while the masterminds of their 1996 drug run, who were arrested in Sydney, have already been released. The case is further clouded by the fact that it was Australian police who tipped off the Thais. The masterminds were allowed to travel on to Sydney, but the "mules" were arrested in Bangkok, resulting in sentences far harsher [sic. than] those allowed under Australian law". "Prisoner repatriation for humanity's sake", *The Sydney Morning Herald,* 4 October 2002, 10. Similarly, in 2006 four Australians brought a case against the Australian Federal Police for providing information to Indonesian police that could lead to their executions. As a result of the information provided they were arrested in Indonesia and accused of drug-smuggling, a capital offense. The Court dismissed the case, holding the police had not breached any applicable duty of care. *Rush v Commissioner of Police,* Federal Court of Australia (2006) FCA 12 (23 January 2006). Koessler, writing in 1946, notes that "a definite practice has been established that in certain typical situations diplomatic protection should normally be denied in spite of the American nationality of the applicant". Maximilian Koessler, "'Subject,' 'Citizen,' 'National,' and 'Permanent Allegiance'", *Yale Law Journal* (1947) vol. 56, 58–76, 68–69. The refusal to extend diplomatic protection to certain persons detained by the United States in Guantánamo Bay (on the island of Cuba) by their respective states of nationality has caused controversy in some circles. See for example Gay Alcorn, "Locked away in Guantanamo Bay", *The Age,* 22 May 2002 (internet), http://www.theage.com.au/articles/ 2002/05/21/1021882051530.html, consulted 15 March 2006: "Foreign Affairs Minister Alexander Downer has made it clear that the government is unconcerned at criticism that it has abandoned its citizens. People who 'muck about' with groups like al Qaeda were 'bound to get into trouble', he said". Ibid.

[79] Weis, *Nationality and statelessness in international law,* 43.

[80] Weis divides protection of non-nationals into two categories (1) temporary, local protection to persons who are still protected by their state of nationality, and (2) protection in lieu of protection by the state of nationality. In the context of European Union treaty arrangements,

has been termed "rescue" of nationals, as well as the issue of whether attacks on nationals abroad give rise to a right of self-defence, is discussed below, in section (3.6).

3.2 Diplomatic/consular protection of multiple nationals

As in issues surrounding recognition of nationality, the diplomatic protection of multiple nationals essentially involves questions of opposability of nationality against other states. It would seem, however, that an increasingly important area of practical concern to states is when their nationals, who are also nationals of a second state, are treated by third states as nationals of the second state, when this results in harm or detrimental treatment.[81]

Returning to opposability, a situation in which the issue often arises is that of international claims, the issue being whether a particular nationality should be notionally attributed to a particular individual vis-à-vis a particular state in relation to a particular claim, usually under a treaty. This issue of protection can be divided into situations where the individual to be protected possesses the nationality of the state against which protection is sought, and situations where a third state or a court is confronted with an individual who possesses more than one nationality.[82] The issue of opposability and recognition may or may not be seen as reflecting an idea of standing at international law.[83]

According to the *principle of equality*, found in Article 4 of the 1930 Hague Convention on Certain Questions Relating to the Conflict of Nationality Laws, "[a] State may not

---

see David Ruzié, "Citoyenneté et nationalité dans l'Union Européenne", in *Vorträge, Reden und Berichte aus dem Europa-Institut – Sektion Rechtswissenschaft*, ed. Georg Ress and Torsten Stein, vol. 313 (Saarbrücken: Europa-Institut Universität des Saarlandes, 1994), 3–19. See also the related discussion and rule proposed by the International Law Commission, International Law Commission, *Report of the International Law Commission to the General Assembly, Fifty-fourth session*, 130, 87–92; International Law Commission, *Report of the International Law Commission to the General Assembly, Fifty-second session*, General Assembly Official Records, Fifty-fifth session, Supplement no. 10, A/55/10 (New York: United Nations, 2000), 170–73.

[81] Canadian Prime Minister Jean Chrétien protested to the United States over the treatment of Canadian-Syrian dual national Maher Arar, who was deported to Syria from the United States rather than to Canada, on suspicion of having terrorist links. Arar alleged that while in Syria he was beaten, held in harsh conditions, and forced to sign a false confession. DeNeen L. Brown and Dana Priest, "Chretien protests deportation of Canadian", *The Washington Post*, 6 November 2003, A24.

[82] For a general discussion see Blaser, "La nationalité et la protection juridique internationale de l'individu", 54–64.

[83] In the *Salem Case* the court stated "the rule of international law [is] that in a case of dual nationality a third power is not entitled to contest the claim of one of the two powers whose national is interested in the case by referring to the nationality of the other power". *Salem Case, 8 June 1932 (United States Egypt Special Arbitral Tribunal)*, U.N. Reports (1932) vol. 2, 1161. Thus arguably, all states of nationality have in-principle standing to maintain a claim of protection.

afford diplomatic protection to one of its nationals against a State whose nationality such person also possesses".[84] According to the *principle of effective or dominant nationality* (or, genuine or effective link, mentioned above), applied only vis-à-vis third states in the 1930 Hague Convention, the multiple national is to be treated as only possessing one nationality, "either the nationality of the country in which he is habitually and principally resident, or the nationality of the country with which in the circumstances he appears to be in fact most closely connected".[85] The principle of effective nationality was applied by the International Court of Justice in the *Nottebohm Case*, discussed above, in the context of a single nationality. Australian courts also cited the principle in interpreting obligations under international refugee law with respect to East Timorese asylum-seekers from Indonesia who were Portuguese nationals, combining it with an idea of "effective protection".[86]

---

[84] Convention on Certain Questions Relating to the Conflict of Nationality Laws, 179. The principle was characterised as "the ordinary practice" by the ICJ in the *Reparation for Injuries* case. *Reparation for injuries suffered in the service of the United Nations*, 186. Rode labels this "non-responsibility of states for claims of dual nationals". He traces the doctrine to the claim of the Executors of R.S.C.A. Alexander, before the American-British Claims Commission, 3 Moore, International Arbitrations 2529 (1898). Zvonko R. Rode, "Dual nationals and the doctrine of dominant nationality", *The American Journal of International Law* (1959) vol. 53, 139–144, 140.

[85] Article 5, Convention on Certain Questions Relating to the Conflict of Nationality Laws, 179. The principle has been applied by the Iran-US Claims Tribunal on various occasions. See *Case No. A/18 concerning the question of jurisdiction over claims of persons with dual nationality*, International Legal Materials (1984) vol. 23, 489; Peter E. Mahoney, "The standing of dual-nationals before the Iran-United States Claims Tribunal", *Virginia Journal of Internaional Law* (1984) vol. 24, no. 3, 695–728. Rode cites use of the principle of effective/dominant nationality against the other state of nationality, not just vis-à-vis third states. He refers to the British Privy Council's holding in the case of James Louis Drummond, 2 Knapp, P.C. Rep. 295, 12 Eng. Rep. 492 (1834), as the first instance of the application of the doctrine of dominant or effective nationality in relation to multiple nationality. Rode, "Dual nationals and the doctrine of dominant nationality", 140. The Court held that Drummond did not have a claim as a British subject under the 1814 Treaty of Paris, which provided for settlement of claims of British subjects for the seizure of their property in France. Drummond was both a British and a French national, who lived in France and whose dominant nationality was held to be French. The Court held the seizure to have been one of the French government vis-à-vis its own national. Ibid. See also Anna Maria Del Vecchio, "La considerazione del principio di effettività nel vincolo di nazionalità e di cittadinanza doppia o plurima (e problematiche relative)", *Rivista internazionale dei diritti dell'uomo* (2000), vol. 13, no. 1, 11–31; Rolf Grawert, *Staat und Staatsangehörigkeit – Verfassungsgeschichtliche Untersuchung zur Entstehung der Staatsangehörigkeit*, vol. 17, *Schriften zur Verfassungsgeschichte* (Berlin: Duncker & Humblot, 1973), 232–46.

[86] See *Jong Kim Koe v. Minister for Immigration & Multicultural Affairs* [1997] 306 FCA (Federal Court of Australia); *Lay Kon Tji v. Minister for Immigration & Ethnic Affairs* [1998] 1380 FCA; *'SRRP' and Minister for Immigraiton and Multicultural Affairs* [2000] AATA 878 (Administrative Appeals Tribunal of Australia); Kerry Carrington, Stephen Sherlock and Nathan

Randelzhofer points out that it is doubtful whether the two principles can in fact be separated as provided for in the Hague Convention.[87] It has been seen that in the general context of international law, an insufficient connection to a state is grounds for non-recognition of its nationality by other states in certain situations. The principle of effective nationality arguably develops this rule, in the context of multiple nationality. The nationality to be recognised is that of the state to which the individual has the closest ties. An exception to this rule is *the principle of the unopposability of the nationality of a third State*, cited by the Commission in *Flegenheimer*, approving the holdings in the *Salem* and *Strunsky Mergé* cases.

> *The theory of effective or active nationality was nevertheless limited in its application by the principle of the unopposability of the nationality of a third State, which, in an international dispute caused by a person with multiple nationalities, permits the dismissal of the nationality of the third State, even when it should be considered as predominant in the light of the circumstances.*[88]

> *The [Mergé] Commission . . . pointed out that effective nationality does not allow a Respondent State to invoke, against the Plaintiff State that accords protection to one of its nationals, the fact that the latter is also in possession of the nationality of a third State.*[89]

The rule as espoused in the 1930 Convention does, however, not simply prioritise the nationalities in question: it eliminates one or more in favour of just one. The Convention may on the one hand be seen as providing a "solution" to the issue of how multiple nationals should be treated, but it can also be seen as providing a "solution" to multiple nationality, if seen as a problem, when it affects third states. It represents a policy decision that rather than allow two states to maintain rights with respect to one individual, it is preferable that only one be given standing on the international plane. It is an open question whether current international developments facilitating contacts to more than one state threaten the ability to characterise an individual as being more closely attached to one country or another. The successful and widespread use of the principle in issues of conflicts of law (or "private international law") would seem to negate such a contention.

Writing in 1959, Rode predicted that

Hancock, "The East Timorese asylum seekers: legal issues and policy implications ten years on", Current Issues Brief no. 17 2002–03, Parliament of Australia Parliamentary Library (internet), http://www.aph.gov.au/library/pubs/CIB/2002–03/03cib17.htm, consulted 7 May 2006.

[87] Randelzhofer, "Nationality", 423. In fact, the *Canevaro Case* (1912), cited by Weis as a "leading case" for the "principle of active or effective nationality", applied the principle to a situation where according to the 1930 Convention, the principle of equality would have prevented diplomatic protection. See Weis, *Nationality and statelessness in international law*, 170. *Canevaro Case*, 1 Scott, Reports 284–96 (1912).

[88] *Flegenheimer Claim*, 149.

[89] Id., 150. See *Mergé Claim*, International Law Reports (1955) vol. 22, 443.

The older doctrine of dominant nationality might again prevail in the future. The doctrine of non-responsibility of states in claims of dual nationals, more frequently used in the first half of this century, might gradually fall into disuse.[90]

He argued that in the context of Communist governments' flounting of fundamental judicial guarantees, the United States had an interest in asserting protection over its nationals, even against a state that also considered the individual in question to be its national. However, he went on to note that

If an individual was injured by the action of his original country, he generally was able to seek redress as a citizen of that country. Such a doctrine was justified in the 19th and in the beginning of the 20th century, when social conditions in most of the civilized countries were stabilized, and denial of justice was an exception rather than the rule. The situation is quite different today.[91]

Rode's argument that diplomatic protection should be related to the practical reality of judicial guarantees and procedures under municipal law is important. If states can rely on their nationals being treated fairly by other states, why indeed should they not defer to the reality or quality of the ties in question in cases of multiple nationality? Acceptance of the principle of effective nationality along these lines is linked to faith in the actions of other states.

The principle of equality as presented in the 1930 Convention is hard and fast; it involves no such appreciation of the quality of the tie involved between the state and the individual it claims as its national.[92] This must be considered to reflect the general rule that it is up to each state to determine who possesses its nationality, and the overriding principle of the sovereign equality of states vis-à-vis one another. For example, if one state were allowed to prevail over another in terms of the latter's treatment of its own nationals under its own municipal laws, because the first state had a closer tie to the individual in question, this would arguably constitute a direct diminution of the latter's sovereignty. In this sense the principle of equality can not be seen to challenge the idea behind the principle of effective nationality (that it is preferable for only one state to be seized of an individual's representation internationally), as it is applied only when one state seeks to espouse its rights against another state, when they are placed on equal footing with respect to an individual.

Yet the principle of equality ignores that states may in fact not be on equal footing with respect to a particular individual. The principle, in equating all relationships where states claim nationality, certainly leaves room for abuse should a state claim a

---

[90] Rode, "Dual nationals and the doctrine of dominant nationality", 143.

[91] Ibid.

[92] Loehr states that "dual nationals holding two passports may not invoke diplomatic protection of their national States against each other, except when overriding rules of humanitarian law are involved". Friedrich Loehr, "Passports," in *Encyclopedia of Public International Law*, ed. Rudolf Bernhardt and Max Planck Institute for Comparative Public Law and International Law (Amsterdam: Elsevier, 1985), 428–341, 429.

link of nationality without a real tie to underpin it. It has already been pointed out that the rules related to recognition of nationality under international law allow for leeway precisely because of such potential abuse by states under the principle of freedom of nationality. The principle of equality would in fact seem to permit such abuse, or at least to leave it unchecked. Is there not room for a test of an effective link even in these cases?

The Commission in the *Mergé Claim* recognised this, holding that

> The principle, based on the sovereign equality of States, which excludes diplomatic protection in the case of dual nationality, must yield before the principle of effective nationality whenever such nationality is that of the claiming State. But it must not yield when such predominance is not proved, because the first of these two principles is generally recognized and may constitute a criterion of practical application for the elimination of any possible uncertainty.[93]

Thus although the Commission held that both the principles of equality and effectivity are valid and in fact complementary, and emphasised that their application was not to exclude one nationality in favour of another, but to determine whether diplomatic protection can be exercised in a particular case, it essentially held that the principle of equality could be rebutted by proof of an effective link otherwise.[94]

There would seem to be variety in terms of practice.[95] The British rules applying to international claims state in Rule III that

> Where the claimant is a dual national, HMG may take up his claim (although in certain circumstances it may be appropriate for HMG to do so jointly with the other government entitled to do so). HMG will not normally take up his claim as a UK national if the respondent state is the state of his second nationality, but may do so if the respondent state has, in the circumstances which gave rise to the injury, treated the claimant as a U.K. national.[96]

In its forty-eighth session (1996), the International Law Commission (ILC) took up diplomatic protection as a subject for codification, appointing Mr Mohamed Bennouna as Special Rapporteur.[97] In 1999 Mr Christopher John R. Dugard assumed the position.[98] Far from dismissing diplomatic protection as less important than in the past, the Special Rapporteur declared that the basis for his proposed articles was that

---

[93] *Mergé Claim*, 455.

[94] Id., 454. Piotrowicz characterises the major weakness of the active link as the fact that it cannot be applied when states do not recognise multiple nationality, or when they give effect to the principle of equality. Piotrowicz, *The Australian-Hungarian Consular Treaty of 1988 and the regulation of dual nationality*, 582.

[95] Piotrowicz states that state practice is ambiguous. Ibid.

[96] Colin Warbrick, "Current legal developments", *International and Comparative Law Quarterly* (1988) vol. 37, no. 4, 983–1012, 1006–7.

[97] International Law Commission, *Report of the International Law Commission to the General Assembly, Fifty-second session*, 141.

[98] International Law Commission, *Report of the International Law Commission to the General Assembly, Fifty-fourth session*, 121.

as long as the State remained the dominant actor in international relations, the espousal of claims by States for violations of the rights of their nationals remained the most effective remedy for human rights protection.[99]

In 2004, the ILC adopted 19 draft articles on diplomatic protection, articles six and seven being directly relevant to multiple nationality.[100]

Article 6
Multiple nationality and claim against a third State

1. Any State of which a dual or multiple national is a national may exercise diplomatic protection in respect of that national against a State of which that individual is not a national.
2. Two or more States of nationality may jointly exercise diplomatic protection in respect of a dual or multiple national.

Article 7
Multiple nationality and claim against a State of nationality

A State of nationality may not exercise diplomatic protection in respect of a person against a State of which that person is also a national unless the nationality of the former State is predominant, both at the time of the injury and at the date of the official presentation of the claim.

Judge Guggenheim raised the issue of dividing diplomatic protection into its two aspects, consular and diplomatic protection on the one hand, and espousal of claims by the state on the other, in his dissenting opinion in *Nottebohm*.[101] Should the effective link principle attach in the same way to both? Might current state practice toward multiple nationality provide room for reflection in this regard?

---

[99] International Law Commission, *Report of the International Law Commission to the General Assembly, Fifty-second session*, 143.

[100] International Law Commission, *Report of the International Law Commission to the General Assembly, Fifty-sixth session*. New York: United Nations General Assembly Official Records, Fifty-ninth session, Supplement No. 10 (A/59/10), 2004, 38–44. See also the original submission of these articles in 2002: International Law Commission, *Report of the International Law Commission to the General Assembly, Fifty-fourth session*, 168. Article five is discussed in detail on pages 181–183 of the Report, and article six on pages 183–187. The ILC cited the views of the ILA with approval in its report. International Law Commission, *Report of the International Law Commission to the General Assembly, Fifty-fourth session*, 186. See International Law Association, Committee on Diplomatic Protection of Persons and Property, "First Report" presented at the 69th Conference of the ILA," (London: International Law Association, 2000), 604–630.

[101] "Even if it be admitted that nationality can be dissociated from diplomatic protection in the present case, there remains the question as to what are the consequences of the total or partial invalidity under international law of a nationality validly acquired under municipal law. Is the invalidity confined to the sphere of diplomatic protection, or does it extend to the other effects of nationality on the international level, for example, treaty rights enjoyed by the nationals of a particular State in regard to monetary exchange, establishment and access to

3.3 State responsibility to other states for acts of its nationals

Shearer states that "[t]he state of which a particular person is a national may become responsible to another state if it has failed in its duty of preventing certain wrongful acts committed by this person or of punishing the person after these wrongful acts are committed".[102]

Is it plausible that a state might argue that it is not responsible for the acts of one of its nationals, who is a multiple national, on the grounds that the other state of nationality should be held responsible, or even co-responsible?

The definition of state responsibility and the notion of imputability clarify that this cannot be the case. States are responsible to other states for "the breach of some duty which rests on a state at international law and which is not the breach of a purely contractual obligation".[103] But the internationally delinquent act must be imputable to the state itself, not just to its national generally.[104] For this reason, the commission of an internationally delinquent act by a multiple national raises no conflict in terms of attribution of such conduct to one state or another, as for the act to be raised to the international plane it has to be linked to a specific state itself. This includes failure in carrying out a duty of punishment of guilty persons who harmed the state's national in question. The multiple nationality of individuals thus appears to raise no difficulties in this context.

The ILC's Articles on State Responsibility also specifically refer to the ILC's work on diplomatic protection, cited above. Article 44(a) of the former states that any claim of state responsibility must be brought according to "any applicable rule relating to the nationality of claims", and Crawford's commentary to the articles notes that

> *Paragraph (a) does not attempt a detailed elaboration of the nationality of claims rule or of the exceptions to it. Rather, it makes it clear that the nationality of claims rule is not only relevant to questions of jurisdiction or the admissibility of claims before judicial bodies, but is also a general condition for the invocation of responsibility in those cases where it is applicable.*[105]

Likewise, should a multiple national be harmed by another state, the ILC's draft articles on diplomatic protection stipulate that the states of nationality may exercise diplomatic protection jointly.[106]

---

the municipal courts of a third State, etc.?" *Nottebohm Case (second phase), Judgment of April 6th, 1955,* 63.

[102] Shearer, *Starke's international law,* 309.

[103] Id., 275.

[104] See generally Id., 277–80. This is confirmed by articles 2 and 4–11 of the ILC's Articles on State Responsibility. James Crawford, *The International Law Commission's articles on state responsibility. Introduction, text and commentaries* (Cambridge: Cambridge University Press, 2002), 61–63.

[105] Crawford, *The International Law Commission's articles on state responsibility. Introduction, text and commentaries,* 264.

[106] International Law Commission, *Report of the International Law Commission to the General Assembly, Fifty-fourth session,* 168, article 5.

The existence of universal jurisdiction over some international crimes, for example grave breaches of the 1949 Geneva Conventions, or piracy, does not call these rules into question.[107] In fact, universal jurisdiction removes the necessity of either territorial or personal jurisdiction over an individual, essentially making the nationality of the offender an independent consideration.

3.4 The duty to admit nationals and to allow residence

A state must grant its nationals entry onto its territory and allow them to reside there, and is under an obligation not to expel them.[108] Weis considers a right to residence to be a matter for municipal law, pointing out that rights of the individual vis-à-vis his or her state of nationality only rise to the international plane when other states are drawn in. This is because it is "an accepted rule of international law that States are not – unless bound by treaty obligations – under an obligation to grant to aliens an unconditional and unlimited right of residence, though they may not expel them arbitrarily and without just cause".[109] Thus a state that refuses to admit its nationals, or expels them to a state unwilling to receive them, violates a fundamental duty of positive international law in relation to territorial supremacy.[110] This is the case, for

---

[107] See generally Shearer, *Starke's international law*, 212–13.

[108] Weis, *Nationality and statelessness in international law*, 45. Randelzhofer finds no right of the individual, just a duty of the state toward other states. Randelzhofer, "Nationality", 422. Oppenheim characterises the obligation as "that of receiving on its territory such of its nationals as are not allowed to remain on the territory of other states". Jennings and Watts, "Oppenheim's International Law," 857.

[109] Weis, *Nationality and statelessness in international law*, 45–46. See Marco Cuniberti, "Espulsione dello straniero e libertà constituzionali", *Diritto Pubblico* (2000) no. 1; Guy Goodwin-Gill, *International law and the movement of persons between states* (Oxford: Clarendon Press, 1978), 21; Christian Joppke, "The evolution of alien rights in the United States, Germany, and the European Union", in *Citizenship today. Global perspectives and practices*, ed. T. Alexander Aleinikoff and Douglas Klusmeyer (Washington: Carnegie Endowment for International Peace, 2001), 36–62; Matti Pellonpää, *Expulsion in international law. A study in international aliens law and human rights with special reference to Finland* (Helsinki: Suomalainen Tiedeakatemia, 1984); Rüdiger Wolfrum, "Völkerrechtliche Rahmenbedingungen für die Einwanderung", in *Einwanderungsrecht – national und international. Staatliches Recht, Europa- und Völkerrecht*, ed. Thomas Giegerich and Rüdiger Wolfrum (Opladen: Leske & Budrich, 2001), 23–25.

[110] Weis, *Nationality and statelessness in international law*, 47. As evidence for this duty, Weis cites the actions of the National Socialist Government of Germany in expelling certain categories of nationals. Even a Government widely regarded as criminal in nature did not openly expel its nationals, but "forced them to emigrate, usually under the cloak of voluntary emigration", or deported them to territories in eastern Europe under German occupation. When such Germans were returned to Germany by other states (Switzerland, for example), "Germany did not, as a rule, refuse readmission, but subjected the returned nationals to cruel measures of persecution, such as indefinite detention in concentration camps, which led, directly or indirectly, to their extermination". Weis, *Nationality and statelessness in international law*, 49.

example, of forced exile, when the receiving state has not consented.[111] The treatment of British Nationals (Overseas), and British Overseas Citizens, may thus be called into question, as members of both categories are denied the right of abode in the United Kingdom under immigration legislation.[112]

Regarding former nationals, Weis finds that "no rule of universal customary international law can be proved to exist which binds States to admit former nationals who have not acquired another nationality".[113] He does admit one exception to this rule, following general principles of international law, in cases that would constitute fraud, where a state denationalises individuals while overseas "solely for the purpose of denying them readmission or to prevent their return".[114] In other cases of denationalisation of an individual while abroad, he is willing only to say that there is "greater force" to the argument that the former state of nationality must readmit the individual. This is because the good faith of the state that admitted him on the basis of his former nationality would otherwise be betrayed.[115] In cases where an individual is

---

Oppenheim cites the United Kingdom's acceptance of "many thousands of persons of Asian origin expelled from Uganda in 1972", who had retained British nationality, and to whom all other states refused entry. Jennings and Watts, "Oppenheim's International Law", 859. In fact, the Court of Appeal determined that the relevant persons were British Protected Persons, not British nationals. See James Crawford, "Decisions of British Courts during 1974–1975. Case No. 7. R. v. Secretary of State for the Home Department, ex parte Thakrar", *The British Year Book of International Law* (1977) vol. 47, 352–356. In the 1970s the British government's refusal to admit its own nationals was challenged in the European Commission of Human Rights. "In 1970 certain citizens of the UK and colonies who had been resident in some East African countries but who had left in order to come to the UK instituted proceedings before the European Commission of Human Rights arising out of the refusal of the UK authorities to allow them to enter the UK. In 1973 the Commission found the applications admissible (*East African Asians v United Kingdom, 15 December 1973*, European Commission on Human Rights, (1973) 3 EHRR 76): the matter was eventually settled between the applicants and the UK Government". Jennings and Watts, "Oppenheim's International Law", 859 note 6. See Goodwin-Gill, *International law and the movement of persons between states*, 11–14.

[111] Pellonpää, *Expulsion in international law. A study in international aliens law and human rights with special reference to Finland*, 21. Pellonpää notes that denaturalisation and expulsion are common means of disposing of political dissidents. Id., 24–25.

[112] This will be discussed in the following chapter. As British Nationals (Overseas) have the right of abode in Hong Kong under Hong Kong (Chinese) law, it can be argued that the United Kingdom is not under an obligation under international law to admit them as long as Hong Kong (China) is. Yet this technicality around what Van Panhuys says is "so important a consequence of nationality that it is almost equated with it" seems to mean that this purported status of "British national" is one of limited value at international law vis-à-vis other states. H. F. van Panhuys, *The rôle of nationality in international law – an outline* (Leyden: A. W. Sythoff, 1959), 56. See Pellonpää, *Expulsion in international law. A study in international aliens law and human rights with special reference to Finland*, 19.

[113] Weis, *Nationality and statelessness in international law*, 57.

[114] Ibid.

[115] Id., 55. Randelzhofer maintains that the duty of admission persists in this situation due

deprived of her or his nationality within the country, for example as in the cases of punitive deprivation mentioned in chapter two, no international duties are called into question unless the state attempts to expel the individual.[116]

3.5 Jurisdiction

"Jurisdiction is an aspect of sovereignty and refers to judicial, legislative, and administrative competence. . . . The starting-point in this part of the law is the proposition that, at least as a presumption, jurisdiction is territorial".[117] This presumption is clear when enforcement of rules by states is contemplated. Without territorial presence of the person or *res* concerned, no enforcement of legal rules or obligations is possible. But it is clear that ability or power to enforce do not constitute jurisdiction. "Mere physical presence is not enough: the state must be able to show that it is exercising its enforcement power on a recognised basis of prescriptive jurisdiction".[118] Shearer labels these "the territorial principle, the nationality principle, the protection principle, the universality principle, the passive personality principle".[119]

Nationality is one of the key bases upon which states exercise jurisdiction over individuals, on a personal basis as opposed to a territorial one, jurisdiction which may be characterised as very broad. Already in 1895 Lawrence stated that modern international law adopts territorial jurisdiction

> as fundamental. But, inasmuch as it could not be applied at all in some cases, and in others its strict application would be attended with grave inconvenience, various exceptions have been introduced, based upon the alternative principle that a state has jurisdiction over its own subjects wherever they may be.[120]

The point of departure for considerations in relation to jurisdiction is state sovereignty.

> The notion of state sovereignty recognises the exclusive authority that a state has within its own borders over its own citizens, and over other persons present there, and it also presumes . . . that matters arising entirely within that state, or as between a state and its own citizens, are not subject to international law. . . . Exceptions are: the international law of state responsibility with respect to injury to aliens; the powers of the UN Security Council to act in the case of breaches of, or threats to, international peace and security

---

to what would otherwise amount to deception of the state which has allowed the individual to enter on the basis that she or he can be obliged to return to her or his state of nationality. Randelzhofer, "Nationality", 422.

[116] Weis, *Nationality and statelessness in international law*, 54–55.

[117] Brownlie, *Principles of public international law*, 301.

[118] Ivan A. Shearer, "Jurisdiction", in *Public international law. An Australian perspective*, ed. Sam Blay, Ryszard Piotrowicz, and B. Martin Tsamenyi (Melbourne: Oxford University Press, 1997), 161–192, 165.

[119] Id., 166.

[120] Lawrence, *The principles of international law*, 199.

(recent practice has tended to include also gross breaches of human rights occurring within state borders as constituting a threat to international peace and security); and the application of fundamental norms of human rights, which are no longer seen as lying behind an impermeable barrier of domestic jurisdiction.[121]

It is not necessary to delimit issues of territorial jurisdiction here, but to delve into the parameters of the personal jurisdiction created by a link of nationality, and when nationality is related to other prescriptive bases of jurisdiction. Conversely, whether other links to a state create some kind of personal jurisdiction must be considered.[122] While jurisdiction can mean competence in terms of subject matter, personal jurisdiction means competence in relation to individuals. Issues of jurisdiction are thus arguably essentially issues of power over individuals, and it is in this context that the subject is addressed herein.

Firstly, the upper and lower boundaries to the power of states over their nationals, and individuals generally, should be considered. It is well known that prior to the United Nations Charter and Universal Declaration of Human Rights few restrictions, if any, were conceived as attaching to how a state could treat its own nationals on its territory.[123] Today, it is clear that international human rights law does place limits on how states treat their own nationals. This arguably does not constitute interference in nationality as the primary link between the individual and international law, as international systems and ideas of human rights essentially place limits on states, rather than providing individuals with rights or entitlements, with notable exceptions.[124] International law affirms the state's broad rights in relation to its nationals, except for what might be termed the most fundamental humanitarian and human rights norms.

---

[121] Shearer, "Jurisdiction", 161–62.

[122] Lawrence states that the rules that have developed in relation foreigners who reside permanently in a state with an intention to remain are mostly rules of municipal law, and when raised to the international plane matters of conflicts of law, "but in so far as they bear on questions of belligerent capture at sea, and the liability of domiciled aliens to war burdens, both personal and pecuniary, they form part of the rules of warfare". Lawrence, *The principles of international law*, 206–07.

[123] Lauterpacht, in his seventh edition of Oppenheim's *International Law* of 1948, doubted whether international law guarantees rights to individuals. ". . . it is generally recognised that a State is entitled to treat both its own nationals and stateless persons at discretion and that the manner in which it treats them is not a matter with which International Law, as a rule, concerns itself". Oppenheim, *International law. A treatise*, 583. Even the precursor to part of what is today considered a "human right", namely the right of refugees who seek asylum not to be returned to persecution, attached to the foreign state receiving them. It did not prevent the state of nationality from treating its subject in any way it pleased once it got control over the individual. See generally Lawrence, *The principles of international law*, 228–32.

[124] Such as the Inter-American Convention of Human Rights and the European Convention of Human Rights. Lauterpacht recognised a fundamental shift in international law in 1948 in terms of it providing a source of individual human rights: "It is possible that the Charter of

Evidence for this proposition is reflected by other systems of protection established for the individual under international law (diplomatic protection being the norm). Among these are the protection of international humanitarian law in time of armed conflict, and international human rights treaties and systems.

In terms of protection of *civilians* in time of armed conflict, Article 4 of the Fourth Geneva Convention[125] provides:

> *Persons protected by the Convention are those who, at a given moment and in any manner whatsoever, find themselves, in case of a conflict or occupation, in the hands of a Party to the conflict or Occupying Power of which they are not nationals. Nationals of a State which is not bound by the Convention are not protected by it. Nationals of a neutral state who find themselves in the territory of a belligerent State, and nationals of a co-belligerent State, shall not be regarded as protected persons while the State of which they are nationals has normal diplomatic representation in the State in whose hands they are.*

Notwithstanding this provision, Article 13 of the treaty[126] stipulates that that the general protection provided by the Convention against the direst consequences of war apply irrespective of nationality. In fact, general principles of protection apply to all protected persons without any adverse distinction founded on nationality.[127]

The Convention thus excludes protection vis-à-vis an individual's own state of nationality, or if diplomatic protection is feasible, except for the most basic norms of humanity (or human rights) that are applicable at all times.[128] This might be contrasted to the provisions of the Third Geneva Convention (1949) related to prisoners of war, which does not use nationality as a point of reference.[129] It is not an unfair

---

the United Nations, with its repeated recognition of 'human rights and fundamental freedoms,' has inaugurated a new and decisive departure with regard to this abiding problem of law and government". Oppenheim, *International law. A treatise*, 585. He sees this is the context of the UN Charter, "though professing to be based on the principle of "the Sovereign equality of all its members,' constitutes a significant landmark in the gradual modification of the traditional doctrine of equality of States". Id., 247.

[125] *Geneva Convention (IV) relative to the protection of civilian persons in time of war*, 12 August 1949 (entry into force: 21 October 1950), (Geneva: International Committee of the Red Cross, 1991).

[126] Ibid.

[127] See Frits Kalshoven, *Constraints on the waging of war* (Geneva: International Committee of the Red Cross, 1991), 42.

[128] For a brief overview of the overlap between international humanitarian law and the international law of human rights, see Alfred Michael Boll, "The Asian values debate and its relevance to international humanitarian law", *International Review of the Red Cross* (2001) vol. 841, 45–58.

[129] The question whether a national detained by his own country after having fought in an international armed conflict for an enemy power has a right to prisoner of war status under the third Geneva Convention of 1949 is a matter of controversy, however consensus seems to be to approve of a right, notwithstanding the traditional deference of international humanitarian law to the relationship between states and their own nationals. Article 4 of the Convention does

extrapolation to cite these provisions as evidence for what might be termed a "default setting" or "common denominator" in international law that the relationship/status of nationality provides the greatest protection for the individual vis-à-vis other states, and only when it fails, cannot apply, or is unrelated to the context of the protection provided to the individual, do other systems of protection become relevant. The Fourth Convention excludes specific protection against nationals' own states, because it may be expected that it is not needed. The Third Convention provides it because fundamental standards of respect for human beings may require it.

In this sense international law sets minimum standards for states' conduct in relation to all persons, in addition to providing a right of diplomatic protection to states to protect their own nationals against other states. But as opposed to minimum standards and regimes that protect the individual both against other states and against his or her own state, is there an upper limit to what a state can require individuals to do? Requirements themselves are principally found in municipal law.[130] Some rules apply to individuals universally, others apply according to membership in various categories, one being nationality. Nationals may have special duties to their own state, and aliens can certainly have duties to states of which they are not nationals.

---

not mention nationality, and neither do articles 43 and 44 of the First Additional Protocol of 1977 to the Convention. United States law also seems to support such a conclusion. Levie, citing two US cases states "it is believed that the principle to be extracted from these two opinions expresses the proper rule of international law, and that any individual who falls into the power of a belligerent while serving in the enemy armed forces should be entitled to prisoner-of-war status no matter what his nationality may be, if he would be so entitled apart from any question of nationality". Howard S Levie, "Prisoners of war in international armed conflicts", *International Law Studies – US Naval War College* (c. 1977) vol. 59, 76. Importantly, however, such protection does not prevent him or her being tried for treason, an issue explored below, and in the following chapter. Following this line of argument, the International Criminal Tribunal for the Former Yugoslavia stated in the Tadic Case "while previously wars were primarily between well-established States, in modern inter-ethnic armed conflicts such as that in the former Yugoslavia, new States are often created during the conflict and ethnicity rather than nationality may become the grounds for allegiance. Or, put another way, ethnicity may become determinative of national allegiance. Under these conditions, the requirement of nationality is even less adequate to define protected persons. In such conflicts, not only the text and the drafting history of the Convention but also, and more importantly, the Convention's object and purpose suggest that allegiance to a Party to the conflict, and correspondingly, control by this Party over persons in a given territory, may be regarded as the crucial test". *Prosecutor v Dusko Tadic, 15 July 1999*, International Criminal Tribunal for the Former Yugoslavia, Appeals Chamber (internet), http://www.un.org/icty/tadic/appeal/judgement/index.htm, paragraph 166, consulted 15 March 2006. See also Bartram S. Brown, "Nationality and internationality in international humanitarian law", *Stanford Journal of International Law* (1998), vol. 34, no. 2, 347–406.

[130] There are of course exceptions: individual conduct is the subject of the grave breaches provisions of the 1949 Geneva Conventions which provide a regime of universal jurisdiction in terms of enforcement. See generally *Geneva Convention (IV) relative to the protection of civilian persons in time of war.*

There is no question that individuals can be subject to municipal laws irrespective of nationality, when the jurisdiction extended is based on a factor such as territorial presence. The criminal law applies equally within territorial jurisdictions, irrespective of nationality.[131] Likewise tax laws are generally supposed to apply equally to those who purchase goods or derive income from activities or investments within a jurisdiction, although many national tax systems apply different rules to individuals based on residence. Nationality may be used to extend the state's jurisdiction over its nationals outside its borders, but within its territory only its municipal laws and applicable international law limit its jurisdiction over all persons.

When jurisdiction is extended over nationals extra-territorially it is usually criminal, but not exclusively.[132] The United States' practice of taxation on the basis of nationality has already been mentioned. But as already noted, such jurisdiction "cannot as a rule be enforced unless the subjects in question come within the territorial or maritime jurisdiction of the state to which they belong".[133] Such prescriptive jurisdiction is known as the *principle of (active) nationality*. In the context of criminal jurisdiction, a state may initiate proceedings against its own nationals for conduct outside its territory, a corollary being that "no state is bound to extradite from its territory a national guilty of an offence committed abroad".[134] Arnell contends that current developments strengthen arguments for "the adoption of general nationality based criminal

---

[131] Although diplomatic or consular immunity of course usually coincides with foreign nationality.

[132] Lawrence mentions military service and "grave political offences" although the latter can also be considered criminal jurisdiction. Lawrence, *The principles of international law*, 213. Jurisdiction can be extended based on residence, as under the New South Wales *Crimes (Female Genital Mutilation) Amendment Act* 1994 (NSW), which applies to conduct outside New South Wales (Australia) "if the person mutilated is ordinarily there". David Lanham, *Cross-border criminal law* (Melbourne: FT Law & Tax Asia Pacific, 1997), 108. While this is an example of jurisdiction based on the residence of the victim, there are many examples of jurisdiction extended over the accused. In this case, Lanham notes "[i]t would no doubt be an unusual case where proceedings were brought in New South Wales against a foreign perpetrator, who carried out the practice abroad without any prior connection with New South Wales. In that unlikely event some defence, at least of ignorance of New South Wales law, should be available. But there is no need to hold the foreign participant liable. It is enough that the Australian residents be covered, either through the device of acting through an innocent agent or that of causing the harm prohibited". Lanham, *Cross-border criminal law*, 108.

[133] Lawrence, *The principles of international law*, 213.

[134] Shearer, "Jurisdiction", 169–70; Shearer, *Starke's international law*, 210. Extradition of nationals is discussed below. Brownlie remarks that in practice states often limit their use of the principle to serious offences "since the territorial and nationality principles and the incidence of dual nationality create parallel jurisdiction and possible double jeopardy". Brownlie, *Principles of public international law*, 306. But he points out that "in any event nationality provides a necessary criterion in such cases as the commission of criminal acts in locations such as Antarctica, where the 'territorial' criterion is inappropriate. Brownlie, *Principles of public international law*, 306. See also Lanham, *Cross-border criminal law*, 31–32. Lawrence, writing in 1895, mentions the 19th century British practice of "the establishment of a magistracy

jurisdiction"[135] in the United Kingdom, an argument that might be made more generally. He cites

> [i]ncreasingly frequent crime-specific reference to nationality based jurisdiction, the devel-
> opment of European Union law, the ever-greater mobility of nationals, the ability to com-
> mit crimes remotely, the incorporation of the European Convention of Human Rights and
> Fundamental Freedoms into United Kingdom law, an evolution in the citizen-state rela-
> tionship, and the increasing internationalisation of criminal law.[136]

According to the *passive personality principle*, or *principle of passive nationality*,
states whose nationals suffer injury or civil damage may claim jurisdiction in relation
to the harm done abroad.[137] It can be seen as an extension of diplomatic protection,
although the harm done might be seen as further removed from the state, as the principle's practical and theoretical basis is injury to the individual national, not to the
state.

> The justification, if any, for exercising jurisdiction on this principle is that each state has
> a perfect right to protect its citizens abroad, and if the territorial state of the locus delicti
> neglects or is unable to punish the persons causing the injury, the state of which the vic-
> tim is a national is entitled to do so if the persons responsible come within its power.[138]

---

in barbarous districts bordering on [a State's] possessions but neither owned nor protected by
any civilized power. . . . They are simply sent out into the wilderness to see that their fellow-
citizens behave with a reasonable amount of propriety. Their authority is an emanation from
the personal jurisdiction of the state over all its subjects wherever they may be; and it is capable of exercise in places outside the dominions or colonial protectorates of any civilized power,
because no territorial jurisdiction exists there to override it". Lawrence, *The principles of international law*, 213–14. This is not the same as the practice by European states (as well as Japan
and the United States) of forcing agreements on Asian and other states in the late 19th and
early 20th centuries that exempted nationals of the former from the jurisdiction of the latter,
and establishing their own "consular courts". This was done in the form of treaties (called
"capitulations") or "on the common law of nations" on the claimed basis of "the defective
character of much of the Oriental administration of justice, and the different views on the subject of trial and punishment entertained generally in Eastern and Western countries". Lawrence,
The principles of international law, 232. Lawrence mentions Western states' abolition of their
consular courts in Japan following Japan's demonstration of "her strength and her civilization"
in 1894 on the basis that "her native tribunals would afford sufficient security for the lives and
property of their subjects resident in her territory". Lawrence, *The principles of international
law*, 235. It might be imagined that Japan's victory over the Russian navy had in fact presented
a different practical reality to that of the position of weakness of many Asian states which had
allowed Western states to take such advantage and liberties.

[135] P. Arnell, "The case for nationality based jurisdiction", *International and Comparative
Law Quarterly* (2001) vol. 50, 955–962.

[136] Id., 955.

[137] See Shearer, "Jurisdiction", 174–5; Shearer, *Starke's international law*, 210–11.

[138] Shearer, *Starke's international law*, 211.

It would seem that although the principle is embodied in the municipal legislation of various countries, it is not universally accepted, and that states that do not accept it are not bound to acquiesce in proceedings against their nationals.[139]

Various treaties concerned with trans-national crimes of substantial magnitude accept the principle as a basis for jurisdiction either implicitly or explicitly.[140] Shearer cites the 1970 Hague Convention on the Suppression of Unlawful Seizure of Aircraft and the 1979 International Convention against the Taking of Hostages, noting in any case that those conventions establish "quasi-universality" of jurisdiction.[141]

Oeter cites the requests of various European states (Spain, Belgium, France and Switzerland) for the extradition of Chilean Senator (and former president) General Augusto Pinochet Ugarte, from the United Kingdom, as evidence of the principle's "widespread acceptance" today, even in cases of multiple nationality.[142]

> *The only real problem that has already arisen in practice – again in the Pinochet case – is the conflict which may evolve between the state where the acts were committed, and which is also the state of effective nationality of the victims holding dual nationality and the other state whose nationality the victims possessed. If the state where the crime was committed has decreed an amnesty, for any political reasons whatsoever it will protest against prosecution of the offender by a third state basing its jurisdiction on a purely formal or ineffective nationality. Personal jurisdiction based on passive personality tends to override in these cases the primary responsibility of the territorial state where offenders and victims resided and where the acts were committed.[143]*

It should be noted however, that in the case against General Pinochet, the Law Lords rejected jurisdiction and extradition to Spain on the basis of passive nationality, as "the United Kingdom does not recognize this principle with regard to its own nationals".[144] The charges against General Pinochet were thus maintained on the basis of

---

[139] Ibid. Shearer points to Judge Moore's assertion in the *Lotus Case* before the Permanent Court of International Justice, that "an article of the Turkish penal Code whereby jurisdiction was asserted over aliens committing offences abroad 'to the prejudice' of a Turkish subject was contrary to international law, but it is unclear to what extent other members of the court shared or differed from this view". Ibid. Brownlie separates this as the least justifiable principle for the exercise of criminal jurisdiction. Brownlie, *Principles of public international law*, 306. Lanham states that US courts appear to be reaching limited acceptance of the principle, citing cases in relation to hostage taking and terrorism, linked also to universal jurisdiction. Lanham, *Cross-border criminal law*, 34–35.

[140] Shearer, "Jurisdiction", 174.

[141] Id., 174–5.

[142] Stefan Oeter, "Effect of nationality and dual nationality on judicial cooperation, including treaty regimes such as extradition", in *Rights and duties of dual nationals. Evolution and prospects*, ed. David A. Martin and Kay Hailbronner (The Hague: Kluwer Law International, 2003), 55–77, 61.

[143] Id., 61–62.

[144] Michael Ratner, "The Lords' decision in Pinochet III", in *The Pinochet papers. The case of Augusto Pinochet in Spain and Britain*, ed. Reed Brody and Michael Ratner (The Hague:

universal jurisdiction, as opposed to the passive nationality principle.[145] But there is no question that the states that requested his extradition on the basis that he had ordered the murder or torture of their nationals did not see the alleged victims' concurrent Chilean nationality as constituting a bar to their jurisdiction.[146]

According to the *protective (or security) principle of jurisdiction*, "international law recognises that each state may exercise jurisdiction over crimes against its security and integrity or its vital economic interests".[147] Delineating the contours of this jurisdiction, and relating it to the underlying obligations is important as far as understanding the duties nationals and aliens owe states. But it seems difficult to circumscribe the norm, as it is left to each state to judge what is included. The category of 'acts that affect the state's security or vital economic interests' can be so widely interpreted that the standard seems close to being arbitrary.[148] Might it constitute a basis for Iran's notorious charge of heresy against British author Salman

---

Kluwer Law International, 2000), 33–51, 36. *See Regina v. Bartle and the Commissioner of Police for the Metropolis and Others, ex parte Pinochet; Regina v. Evans and another and the Commissioner of Police for the Metropolis and Others, ex parte Pinochet,* (1999) 2 W.L.R. 827.

[145] See also generally Madeleine Davis, *The Pinochet case* (London: Institute of Latin American Studies, 2000); Diana Woodhouse, ed., *The Pinochet case. A legal and constitutional analysis* (Oxford: Hart Publishing, 2000).

[146] BBC News, *Switzerland calls for Pinochet extradition*, 1998 (internet), http://www.bbc.co.uk/ 1/hi/uk/201994.stm, consulted 22 July 2003. At the outset of the Pinochet case, lawyers for the family of a Chilean-British dual national, William Beausire, allegedly "disappeared" by Chilean security forces in 1975, held out the possibility that should the case by Spain for extradition be unsuccessful, his "case could play a crucial role for those wanting to bring Gen Pinochet to justice". BBC News, *Briton William Beausire 'returns' to haunt Pinochet*, 1998 (internet), http://news.bbc.co.uk/1/hi/special_report/1998/10/98/ the_pinochet_file/201678.stm, consulted 15 March 2006.

[147] Shearer, "Jurisdiction", 170–1; Shearer, *Starke's international law*, 211. Lawrence, citing other 19th century authors, opposes jurisdiction on both the principle of passive nationality and the security principle, and denies a right of jurisdiction in such cases. He argues that "an occasional failure of justice is preferable to putting the subjects of every state at the mercy of the law and administration of its neighbors". Lawrence, *The principles of international law*, 222. But the security principle has old roots, arguably reflecting an idea expressed by Vattel. "A Nation or State has the right to whatever can assist it in warding off a threatening danger, or in keeping at a distance things that might bring about its ruin. The same reasons hold good here as for the right to whatever is necessary for self-preservation. Vattel, *The law of nations or the principles of natural law applied to the conduct and to the affairs of nations and of sovereigns*, 14.

[148] Shearer cites United States cases where aliens have been prosecuted under the protective principle in relation to immigration offences, sham marriages and fraudulent concealment of assets abroad. Shearer, *Starke's international law*, 211 note 10. An Australian example of this power is perhaps found in the *Passports Act* 1938 (Cth) that "extends to acts, matters and things outside Australia, and to everyone irrespective of nationality or citizenship". Lanham, *Cross-border criminal law*, 272.

Rushdie?[149] Importantly, the jurisdiction is "over aliens for acts done abroad".[150] Thus if aliens can be held liable for such acts, the standard applicable to nationals also seems to be a matter of importance to international law. Are nationals held to an even higher standard, as far as obligations of loyalty to the state?[151] Are there higher standards? This is discussed below.

According to the *principle of universal jurisdiction*, certain crimes are so heinous that any state may try them without reference to territory or nationality, such as piracy, war crimes, and genocide.[152] Treaties such as the 1949 Geneva Conventions and their 1977 Additional Protocols provide for such jurisdiction, but whether states choose to exercise it in their municipal laws would seem to be another matter altogether. Such attempts have been the cause of much controversy.[153]

3.6 Protection of nationals and the use of force

An altogether different issue is whether states have the right to use force to protect their own nationals abroad, when the the state in which they are present is either unwilling or unable to protect foreign nationals. Genoni remarks that the right to use force outside national territory to this end was generally accepted until the First World War,[154] but protection of nationals was sometimes used as a pretext to intervene in the political or economic affairs of other states. He cites examples such as the military intervention by France, Germany, the United Kingdom, Japan, the United States and others, during the "Boxer Rebellion" in China in 1900.[155]

---

[149] Shearer, "Jurisdiction", 170–1.

[150] Brownlie, *Principles of public international law*, 307. Lanham however, cites cases in relation to acts of nationals abroad, for this principle. Lanham, *Cross-border criminal law*, 35–36.

[151] Both Brownlie and Shearer point to the case of *Joyce v DPP* in which the House of Lords found that an alien could be tried for the crime of treason. But the case does not seem to give rise to a general rule: as the alien in question had been issued with a British passport, and had held himself out as a Briton, the Court found that he thus owed a certain duty of allegiance to the Crown. See Brownlie, *Principles of public international law*, 307, and note 225 in this chapter.

[152] Shearer, "Jurisdiction", 171–74. For example, Spain's Constitutional Court ruled in 2005 that crimes of genocide and human rights violations could be prosecuted in Spanish courts, even if no Spaniards were involved. M. Elkin, "Court gives Spanish judiciary right to try any foreign genocide", *El País (English edition with the International Herald Tribune)*, 6 October 2005, 1.

[153] Stefaan Smis and Kim Van der Borght, *Belgian Law concerning the Punishment of Grave Breaches of International Humanitarian Law: A contested law with uncontested objectives*, The American Society of International Law. ASIL Insights 2003 (internet), http://www.asil.org/insights/insigh112.htm, consulted 4 July 2003).

[154] Maurizio A. M. Genoni, *Die Notwehr im Völkerrecht*, vol. 48, *Schweizer Studien zum internationalen Recht* (Zürich: Schulthess Polygraphischer Verlag, 1987), 58–59.

[155] Id., 60–61.

Other writers posit that notwithstanding examples of what they label "highly dubious" justifications of use of force by states to protect their nationals in foreign territory, which instead constituted political intervention, such

> *Abuse of the right to use force to protect nationals in foreign territory does not amount to a denial that the right exists. The practice of states and their expressions of opinio juris indicate that states do believe in this right and will continue to practice it when they consider it necessary to do so.*[156]

A recent example is the ultimatum given by Thai Prime Minister Thaksin Shinawatra to Cambodian Prime Minister Hun Sen in January 2003, to restore order and protect Thai nationals, or face Thai commandos in Pnomh Penh. Thailand accused Cambodian officials of inciting mobs to violence, resulting in injuries to six Thai nationals, the looting of Thai-owned businesses, and the burning of the Thai Embassy. "The Thai Ambassador, Chatchawad Chartsuwan, forced to flee with his staff by scaling a back wall and jumping into a boat on the nearby river, said police and firefighters had stood by".[157]

In many instances injury to nationals does not lead to "rescue" or use of force, but to demands to be involved in the investigative process. An example is the involvement of the United States Federal Bureau of Investigation (FBI) in the murders of two US citizens in Indonesia, allegedly planned and carried out by members of the Indonesian military forces.[158]

Use of force is usually based on one of two arguments.[159] The first is that the right stems from a state's inherent right of self-defence under Article 51 of the United Nations' Charter, the attack, or threat thereof, amounting to an attack on the state itself. The second, that under customary law, the right exists alongside the UN Charter, and amounts to an exception to the ban on the use of force in Article 2(4).

Genoni takes the opposite view. Although acknowledging that there is no uniform opinion on the matter, he argues that Article 51 of the United Nations Charter does not include a right to use force for the protection of nationals in foreign territory. But perhaps in the spirit of *realpolitik* (he does not cite customary law) he remarks

---

[156] Timothy McCormack, "The use of force", in *Public international law. An Australian perspective*, ed. Sam Blay, Ryszard Piotrowicz, and B. Martin Tsamenyi (Melbourne: Oxford University Press, 1997), 238–270, 253. McCormack cites the United States' armed interventions in Grenada and Panama (1990) as such instances.

[157] Mark Baker, "Fiery tug-of-war over Angkor Wat", *The Sydney Morning Herald*, 31 January 2003, 7. Such incidents can lead to long-term adverse effects on bi-lateral relations. Thailand closed its border as a result of the riots, and "threatened to expel hundreds of thousands of [Cambodian] illegal immigrants". Ibid.

[158] Matthew Moore, "FBI joins inquiry into US murders in Papua", *The Sydney Morning Herald*, 17 January 2003, 9.

[159] See McCormack for the exposition of the two arguments. McCormack, "The use of force", 251–53.

Das Abweichen vom soeben dargelegten Grundsatz muss vernünftigerweise, wie Neuhold es postuliert, in Notsituationen in Kauf genommen werden. Unabdingbare Voraussetzung ist es jedoch, dass der zum Schutze seiner Staatsangehörigen eingreifende Staat sämtliche Mittel der friedlichen Streitbeilegung ausgenützt hat und dass der infolge des Eingriffs in seine territoriale Integrität verletzte Staat jede friedliche Streiterledigung verweigert und die grobe Menschenrechtsverletzung weiter aufrechterhält.[160]

Another basis for such use of force on behalf of nationals claimed by some authors is the doctrine of humanitarian intervention. Although what might be termed the classic concept of humanitarian intervention was based on notions of humanity, having developed from ecclesiastical justifications, and involved intervention by one state on behalf of persons in another state,[161] some authors include intervention on behalf of nationals within studies surrounding the doctrine and practice.[162]

Does a state have a right to use force against another state to protect its nationals, when the individuals in question also possess the nationality of the other state? If such right to use force is rejected generally, the point is of course moot. However, even if it is accepted that states have the right to use force to protect their nationals against other states, does multiple nationality change the equation? Extrapolating from the *principle of equality* in relation to the diplomatic protection of multiple nationals, it would seem that the right is weakened in relation to multiple nationals. The right to use force on behalf of nationals is claimed to exist when the second state is unable or unwilling to protect individuals *as foreigners*. Thus any intervention on the basis of the first state's nationality seems unjustified, as the *principle of equality* dictates that the second state may regard the individual solely as its national, and treat him or her accordingly. Even if the first state's nationality is the effective one, intervention only seems justified should the second state's treatment of the individual in

---

[160] Genoni, *Die Notwehr im Völkerrecht*, 187. (Author's translation: *Departure from the principle presented must sensibly be put up with, as postulated by Neuhold, in situations of need (distress). An absolute (inalienable) condition is however, that the state intervening to protect its nationals have used all means for the peaceful resolution of disputes and that the state whose territorial integrity is injured as a consequence of the intervention have refused all means of peaceful conflict resolution and maintained its coarse human rights abuses.*) He thus sees some legal justification for the Israeli operation in 1976 in Entebbe to free a group of hostages, including Israelis, but none for the United States' operation in relation to the taking of United States hostages in 1979 in Iran. Genoni, *Die Notwehr im Völkerrecht*, 194–95.

[161] Francis Kofi Abiew, *The evolution of the doctrine and practice of humanitarian intervention* (The Hague: Kluwer Law International, 1999), 30–59.

[162] Id., 32–33, note 39. Abiew argues that "Whether the right of protection of nationals flows from self-defence or not, the ultimate objective involved here is the protection of human rights. For purposes of this book humanitarian intervention will be taken to encompass intervention for protection of nationals". But he notes authors who disagree on the basis that protection of nationals abroad is a consequence of independence, and less controversial than 'humanitarian intervention'. Ibid. For an overview of current issues (2003) in relation to humanitarian intervention, see generally J. L. Holzgrefe, ed., *Humanitarian intervention. Ethical, legal and political dilemmas* (Cambridge: Cambridge University Press, 2003).

question be related to the first nationality, and not to its own. This is the substance of the British claims rules cited above in relation to diplomatic protection (not "rescue").

However, while there may indeed be no basis for intervention in favour of multiple nationals against the other state of nationality on grounds of protection of nationals, in cases where there is justification to intervene generally, assuming the legality of an humanitarian intervention, multiple nationality would certainly not constitute a bar. This is because the intervention is not predicated on, or related to, nationality, but based on grounds of humanity.

In this sense, it would seem that the legality of any such intervention on behalf of multiple nationals depends on the legal basis for such intervention. The question might, however, be taken one step further. If general humanitarian grounds for intervention exist irrespective of nationality, does any multiple nationality of the victims provide added weight to underpin the legality of such intervention, or does it amount only to what might be called political or social incentive? On its face, it would seem the question is more related to the nature and scope of humanitarian intervention than to questions related to nationality.

In the present context it should be emphasised that the use of force to protect nationals does not seem to have been applied in favour of just one individual. Along these lines, use of force to protect an individual or small group of individual nationals against a state whose nationality she, he or they also possess, would indeed seem to lack a legal foundation.

3.7   The right to refuse extradition and issues of judicial co-operation

3.7.1   Extradition

A "state has a general right, in the absence of a specific treaty binding it to do so, to refuse to extradite its own nationals to another state requesting surrender".[163] Shearer notes that most relevant treaty provisions either bar such extradition absolutely or provide that the states concerned "'shall be under no obligation' to surrender their own nationals".[164] He traces the origins of the practice to antiquity.[165]

It was mentioned above that this is a corollary to the principle of active nationality, which embodies what seems to be a preference in international law, that the state of nationality should prosecute its own nationals, or at least get the "first bite".[166]

---

[163] Shearer, *Starke's international law*, 309.

[164] Ivan A. Shearer, "Non-extradition of nationals", *The Adelaide Law Review* (1966) 273–309, 273.

[165] Id., 274.

[166] An example is the rule related to jurisdiction embodied in the Statute of the International Criminal Court, according to which either the state of nationality, or the state where the crime was allegedly committed, must consent to the Court's jurisdiction. See generally Rights & Democracy International Centre for Human Rights and Democratic Development and The

Shearer reasons that the provisions of municipal law affect state policy. The Anglo-American attitude of liberal consent to extradition of nationals reflects the fact that under the Common Law jurisdiction in criminal law was for many years based strictly on territoriality. Thus, non-extradition of a national would amount to sanctioning impunity.[167]

However, as the maxim *aut punire aut dedere* shows, on the basis of applicable treaties offenders must be punished or handed over.[168] Thus according to rules of state responsibility canvassed above, a state can be held liable should it fail to prosecute or punish its national for crimes in relation to foreign nationals or states.

In answer to the question whether multiple nationality might allow an alleged criminal to escape the jurisdiction of one state of nationality by fleeing to another, the response must be yes, and that a state's municipal law or policy may prevent the individual in question from being extradited. Although the second state might be held responsible at international law for not extraditing or trying the individual, this is far from certain. But Brownlie notes that "in general, states refuse to extradite nationals, but in some cases to do so without assuming responsibility for trying the suspect is an obvious abuse of power".[169] Depending on the particular circumstances, as in any question of extradition, it would seem that a refusal to extradite a national charged with a serious offence to another state of nationality, combined with a refusal or inability to prosecute such offence, might present a case of abuse of power. It would arguably be more egregious in cases where the effective nationality is that of the first state. Such a policy would in any case not be conducive toward friendly relations between states.

Oeter states that "questions of the dominant or effective nationality have never been raised internationally in cases of extradition, it seems", but concludes that rather than holding the problem out as an argument against multiple nationality, it is in fact related to the policy by some (mostly European) states not to extradite their nationals.[170] He points out that the underlying problem is in fact the same in relation to mono-nationals who live outside their countries of nationality, and proposes that the prohibition against extradition of nationals be abolished.[171]

Regarding extradition requests based on the principle of active nationality (discussed above under jurisdiction), and the possibility that various states of nationality might compete for the same individual, Oeter argues that "the principles governing

---

International Centre for Criminal Law Reform and Criminal Justice Policy, *International Criminal Court. Manual for the ratification and implementation of the Rome Statute* (Vancouver: Rights & Democracy International Centre for Human Rights and Democratic Development, The International Centre for Criminal Law Reform and Criminal Justice Policy, 2000), 84–86.

[167] Shearer, "Non-extradition of nationals", 297–98.

[168] Here, and generally in relation to extradition, Shearer, *Starke's international law*, 317.

[169] Brownlie, *Principles of public international law*, 319–20.

[170] Oeter, "Effect of nationality and dual nationality on judicial cooperation, including treaty regimes such as extradition", 58–59.

[171] Id., 59.

the decision by the executive to grant extradition are flexible enough . . . to cope with the resulting problems".[172] He reasons that such competing requests are routine, for example when one state requests extradition on the basis of territoriality, and another on the basis of nationality.[173] As to competing extradition requests on the basis of passive nationality, as in cases of application of the principle of active nationality, there are means for states to arrive at decisions, and they are left considerable leeway. In relation to the *Pinochet* scenario canvassed above, Oeter's argument that personal jurisdiction based on passive nationality can override territoriality and active nationality in certain egregious cases, has already been mentioned.[174] Although the ILC's draft articles on diplomatic protection canvassed above would exclude diplomatic protection in such cases, the exercise of jurisdiction for a harm done to a national that would otherwise not be addressed arguably falls into a different category of legal norm.

Although this study does not attempt to discern state practice with regard to the extradition of multiple nationals, it should be asked whether the state practice canvassed affects the rules of international law in this regard.

3.7.2   Other areas of judicial co-operation

Aside from extradition, various issues are related to judicial co-operation in criminal matters. Regarding the transfer of sentenced persons and the execution of foreign judgments, Oeter concludes that while the nationality of the individual in question is relevant, other criteria such as "questions of administrative and political propriety will probably dominate the decision-making" in practice.[175] In relation to co-operation in terms of evidence, service, and transmission of information, nationality is not a criterion, and a refusal to co-operate in cases of multiple nationality could only be premised on *ordre public* arguments, "but the requested state would then have to examine whether it should not prosecute the offender under its own criminal law".[176]

Regarding the execution of foreign judgments in civil matters however, Oeter states that "the effects of nationality may lead to serious problems in cases of dual nationality".[177] He discusses marriage and divorce, maintenance obligations, parental custody, and inheritance matters.[178] These issues are beyond the scope of the analysis here, as they are matters of municipal law, and conflicts of law. It may be noted however, that rather than seeing problems in this regard as reasons to prevent multiple nationality, Oeter instead calls for a "harmonization of substantive standards, or at least of the rules on conflict of laws", and "a system of coordinated competences con-

---

[172] Id., 60.
[173] Id., 61.
[174] Id., 61–62.
[175] Id., 63.
[176] Ibid.
[177] Id., 64.
[178] Id., 64–76.

cerning dual nationals [based on] . . . the criterion of effective nationality".[179] In over-all terms, he concludes that multiple nationality is not a source of major problems in the field of judicial co-operation.[180]

3.8 Determination of enemy status in wartime

Weis notes that nationality is sometimes used in municipal legislation as far as deter-mining "enemy character" in wartime, but emphasises the distinction between the two notions.[181] He notes that

> each belligerent State is free to apply – without prejudice to existing treaty obligations – its own laws for determining enemy character. . . . Moreover, nationals of a neutral State acquire enemy character if they have in some way, identified themselves by their conduct with the enemy, e.g., by joining his armed forces: they have become 'assimilated to enemy nationals'. This applies even to the belligerent's own subjects.[182]

Brownlie remarks that this amounts to a "functional approach to nationality" accord-ing to which aliens are not treated as nationals of their particular state of 'technical' nationality, but on other bases such as allegiance, residence, control, and so on.[183] Neff notes the difficulties states face in determining the nationality of persons and things in times of conflict, and separating "neutral" from "enemy" character. He remarks that the issue whether nationality of a neutral state automatically confers neu-tral status, remains unresolved.[184]

It is important to emphasise again that such determinations are matters for munic-ipal law. As demonstrated above, while nationality may become relevant in the appli-cation of the Fourth Geneva Convention of 1949 (relating to the protection of civilian persons in time of armed conflict and occupied territories) as far as specific protec-tion for those who are either not taking part in combat and not covered by diplomatic protection, the fundamental rules related to protection of victims of armed conflict are not affected by nationality.

3.9 Allegiance/Loyalty[185]

The question of whether nationals are held to a certain standard of loyalty or obliga-tion to the state under international law, posed above in the discussion on jurisdiction,

---

[179] Id., 75–77.

[180] Id., 76–77.

[181] Weis, *Nationality and statelessness in international law*, 9–12.

[182] Id., 11.

[183] Ian Brownlie, "The relations of nationality in public international law", *The British Yearbook of International Law* (1963) vol. 39, 284–364, 347.

[184] Stephen C. Neff, *The rights and duties of neutrals. A general history* (Manchester: Manchester University Press, 2000).

[185] Much of this section has been previously published in Alfred Boll, "Nationality and

was left unanswered. It is in this context that ideas and obligations of allegiance and loyalty must be clearly defined and set out, in particular because they are so often confused. Although allegiance and loyalty are distinct things for the purposes of international law, they are dealt with here together, because in a certain context allegiance means or implies loyalty, and in another context it means or implies nationality. The fact that loyalty is expected of nationals in legislative and emotional reality makes the ease with which commentators and legislators mix the terms easy to understand. For the purposes of international law, however, such mixing is imprecise and arguably incorrect.

Ideas of loyalty in an international context can be seen to move on two interconnecting planes. They are centered on the relationship between the individual and his or her own state, but go to the duty to defend it vis-à-vis other states. The notion thus seems to operate inwardly or internally, as well as outwardly or externally. This has important ramifications for the consequences and context of multiple nationality.

Although an obligation of loyalty by nationals to their states certainly appears to be international in nature, it will be argued that in terms of "black letter law" it is a concept and rule of municipal law, as opposed to international law. Loyalty can be said to be an important issue in terms of international relations, or in terms of states' expectations of their own nationals vis-à-vis other states, but the international context of loyalty, or allegiance as loyalty, should not be confused with the dictates of international law in relation to nationality. Likewise, emotional issues surrounding loyalty to the state must be separated from what the state can oblige persons to do, and the acts for which nationals and aliens can be held accountable by states. It will be demonstrated that because even non-nationals bear obligations to states generally, expressing these as an obligation of loyalty when a state's nationals are involved, arguably does little to delineate the relevant legal standards.[186]

---

obligations of loyalty in international and municipal law", *The Australian Year Book of International Law* (2004) vol. 24, 37–63.

[186] The emotionally charged nature of the subject cannot be ignored. The idea of an obligation of loyalty attaching to the national's relationship to his or her state seems to have its roots in the early days of modern international law and the establishment of nation states. The feudal relationship of allegiance, expanded on below, which incorporated rights and duties, is directly relevant in this sense. A difference can nonetheless be detected between the feudal norm and the "national" one; whereas the former was contractual, the latter is emotional. Vattel, writing in terms of the post-feudal nation-state, says "If every man is bound in conscience to love his country sincerely, and to procure its welfare as far as lies in his power, it is a shameful and detestable crime to do an injury to one's country. He who becomes guilty of it violates the most sacred of compacts and exhibits a base ingratitude; he disgraces himself by the blackest perfidy, since he abuses the confidence of his fellow-citizens and treats as enemies those who had reason to expect from him only his help and his services. We find traitors to their country only among men who are moved solely by base motives, who look to their own interest first, and whose hearts are incapable of any sentiment of affection for others. Therefore they are justly despised by all the world as the most infamous of all criminals". Vattel, *The law of nations or the principles of natural law applied to the conduct and to the*

Allegiance as a term of international law must first be defined, and its other meanings distinguished. Allegiance is

a term of English law, derived from feudal notions, and connoting the duty owed by the individual to his lord or sovereign as the correlative of his claim of protection upon such superior. Until displaced by the statutory scheme of nationality and citizenship introduced by the British Nationality Act 1948, the concept of permanent allegiance lay at the root of the status of a British subject – of British nationality. . . . As a common law term and concept, the notion of allegiance has of course passed into the law of the United States and of some other (particularly Commonwealth) States with common law roots. It may possibly belong naturally to other municipal systems with feudal origins. Its increasing use by Anglophone writers to describe the duty owed by any individual to any State, though natural, has little justification.[187]

---

affairs of nations and of sovereigns, 52. Gans points out that the relationship between citizen and country casts an "intimacy" over even the duty to obey the law in one's country, as opposed to the laws of other states. Chaim Gans, *Philosophical anarchism and political disobedience* (Cambridge: Cambridge University Press, 1992), 8. He maintains that even if not completely justified, duties to obey the law cannot easily be separated from the relationship to the surrounding political collective in which the individual lives. Id., 9–10.

[187] Clive Parry et al., eds., *Encyclopaedic dictionary of international law* (New York: Oceana Publications Inc., 1986), 16–17. See also Clive Parry, ed., *A British digest of international law*, vol. 5 (London: Stevens & Sons, 1965), 48. De Burlet labels the United Kingdom the exception in terms of adherence to allegiance as a source of nationality into modern times, indicating that the idea had ceased to be valid in most European states with the end of the absolute monarchies. "C'est à la suite d'une assez longue évolution que la notion féodale d'allégeance qui désignait primitivement la foi absolue et inconditionelle due au suzerain par le vassal et qui impliquait protection du vassal par le suzerain, est devenue une institution permettant de départager l'étranger du non'étranger. Il fallut pour cela que l'allégeance en arrive à ne plus désigner que la foi due au Roi par ses sujets, ce qui ne fut possible qu'à partir du moment où la féodalité ayant englobé tous les hommes dans une hiérarchie de vassaux et de suzerains, le Roi se trouva placé au sommet de cette hiérarchie avec cette conséquence qu'il devenait automatiquement le seul bénéficiaire de la féauté lige ou foi inconditionelle". (Author's translation: *It is following quite a long course of events that the feudal notion of allegiance which initially designated the absolute and unconditional loyalty due the suzerain by the vasssal and which involved the protection of the vassal by the suzerain, became an institution allowing for the separation of foreigners from non-foreigners. For this to happen, allegiance had to come to mean only the loyalty due the king by his subjects. This only became possible once the feudal world had engulfed all persons in a hierarchy of vassals and suzerains, the king finding himself placed at the summit of this hierarchy with the consequence that he automatically became the only beneficiary of lige feudalty or undconditional loyalty.*) Jacques de Burlet, *Nationalité des personnes physiques et décolonisation* (Bruxelles: Établissements Émile Bruylant, 1975), 17. The feudal roots of the term "allegiance" are illustrated by the lack of ideas of reciprocity underpinning obligation in Roman law. Yet obligation was clearly a consequence of membership in, or relationship to, the state, albeit not necessarily citizenship as such. See generally on treason and crimes against the state in Rome, O. F. Robinson, *The criminal law of ancient Rome* (London: Gerald Duckworth & Co. Ltd., 1995), 74–89.

Parry thus clarifies that the term "allegiance" is used to denote (1) a feudal legal relationship, (2) the present relationship/status of nationality, and (3) duties to the state. His criticism of its use in the latter sense is supported herein, but such use can also have palpable legal effect in some countries, for example in the United States.[188] It will be demonstrated that other states hold individuals to the same duty of obedience, without labelling this permanent or temporary "allegiance".

Koessler states that

> the term "allegiance" in itself has become archaic. In its feudal setting, "allegiance" denoted a reciprocal correlation of interconnected rights and duties. But in modern states the obligations of the national to the nation are unconditional, rather than contingent upon the state's compliance with corresponding duties.[189]

He thus concludes that the terms "nationality" and "permanent allegiance" must today mean the same thing.[190]

It is clear that the historical nature of the feudal relationship of allegiance as reciprocal rights and duties leads modern authors to imply duties to the state into the relationship/status of nationality, which supplanted feudal allegiance.[191] Parry's questioning of the use of the term "allegiance" to denote duties to the state, including loyalty in the abstract, should be examined more closely, especially in light of Koessler's statement that today, a national's obligations to his or her state are unconditional. A quick survey will illustrate that both Parry and Koessler are correct.

---

[188] "Treason, being in essence a breach of allegiance to the government, can be committed only by a person who owes either perpetual or temporary allegiance. The term allegiance is not synonymous with loyalty but refers to the duty of obedience which one owes to a sovereign power within whose jurisdiction he finds himself in return for the protection which he receives from that sovereign. Allegiance is owed to the United States not only by its citizens, whether citizenship was acquired by birth or naturalization, but also by aliens temporarily present within the country. The difference between the allegiance owed by citizens and that owed by aliens is that the duty of a citizen exists wherever he may be, while the duty of an alien exists only while he is physically present within the United States". Charles E. Torcia, *Wharton's criminal law*, vol. 4 (Rochester, NY: The Lawyers Co-operative Publishing Co., 1981), 499–500. Used in this sense, allegiance gives rise to a right to exercise jurisdiction territorially, and generally over nationals. The definition of "treason" however, does not match that of many countries' laws, an issue discussed below.

[189] Koessler, "'Subject,' 'Citizen,' 'National,' and 'Permanent Allegiance'", 68.

[190] "Deprived of one of the essential ingredients which went into its feudal meaning, namely of the subject's *right* to claim his lord's protection, and also *minus* the whole general background of the one-time feudal society, 'permanent allegiance,' referred to in a modern definition of nationality, cannot be more than a synonym for 'nationality'." Id., 69.

[191] De Burlet even links the feudal relationship of "allegiance" to the notion of effective nationality. "Il est possible que la notion de nationalité effective trouve sa source dans la réalité de l'allégeance, cette dernière ayant indéniablement influencé la notion moderne de nationalité". (Author's translation: *It is possible that the origin of the notion of effective nationality is to be found in the reality of allegiance, as it undeniably influenced the modern notion of nationality*.) de Burlet, *Nationalité des personnes physiques et décolonisation*, 19.

This issue seems all the more important because the overriding objection to persons possessing the nationality of more than one state has been seen in terms of conflicting loyalties and obligations to the states involved. These arguments are canvassed in the following chapter. The topic raises fundamental questions in relation to multiple nationality, as far as the multiple national's obligations when her or his states of nationality require acts that are in fundamental discord. The context of armed conflict between states is the most-cited example and reason for many commentators adopting the view that multiple nationality in itself is a calamity for the states and the individuals affected.[192] In fact, the notion of loyalty (or allegiance as loyalty) would seem to be universally perceived as attaching to the relationship/status of nationality, but not without certain limits.[193]

---

[192] For example, see generally Ludwig Bendix, *Fahnenflucht und Verletzung der Wehrpflicht durch Auswanderung*, ed. Georg Jellinek and Gerhard Anschütz, *Staats- und völkerrechtliche Abhandlungen* (Leipzig: Verlag von Duncker & Humblot, 1906); Ernst Otto Hörnig, "Die mehrfache Staatsangehörigkeit in Rechtsprechung, Verwaltung und Gesetzgebung. Eine rechtsvergleichende Studie", dissertation presented at the Eberhard-Karls-Universität zu Tübingen (Bleicherode am Harz, 1939); Hudson and Flournoy Jr., "Nationality – Responsibility of states – Territorial waters, drafts of conventions prepared in anticipation of the first conference on the codification of international law, The Hague 1930"; Georg Schulze, "Die Bedeutung des Militärdienstes für Verlust und Erwerbung der Staatsangehörigkeit" dissertation presented at the Königlichen Bayerischen Julius-Maximilians-Universität (Würzburg, 1910).

[193] "That we have some special obligation to our country is a view not confined to rabid nationalists but almost universally held. This appears particularly clearly in the case of war". Alfred Cyril Ewing, *The individual, the state, and world government* (New York: The Macmillan Company, 1947), 213. But Simmons writing on political obligation, concludes, "citizenship does not free a man from the burdens of moral reasoning. . . . Most of us have no special obligation of obedience. But second, even if we had such an obligation, the citizen's job would not be to blithely discharge it in his haste to avoid the responsibility of weighing it against competing moral claims on his action. For surely a nation composed of such "dutiful citizens" would be the cruellest sort of trap for the poor, the oppressed, and the alienated". A. John Simmons, *Moral principles and political obligations* (Princeton: Princeton University Press, 1979), 200–01. The question of loyalty is thus directly related to questions of political obligation, moral obligation, and obedience. Even Vattel sees limits to loyalty, albeit in terms of love of country as self-interest. "This love of one's country is natural to all men. The good and wise Author of nature has been careful to give them a sort of instinct which binds them to the place of their birth, and they love their Nation as a thing intimately connected with them. But that natural instinct is often weakened or destroyed by unfortunate circumstances. The injustice or severity of the government too easily destroys it in the hearts of the subjects. Can self-love bind an individual to the interests of a country in which everything is done in view of a single man? On the other hand, we find every free people filled with zeal for the glory and prosperity of their country. Let us call to mind the citizens of Rome in the prosperous days of the Republic, and let us look to-day at the English and the Swiss. Vattel, *The law of nations or the principles of natural law applied to the conduct and to the affairs of nations and of sovereigns*, 51. In classical Athens, a right of emigration without a loss of property was interpreted to mean that "if a person remains in Athens under these circumstances he signifies his approval of the regime and undertakes 'under no compulsion or misunderstanding' to live his life 'as a

The contours of a requirement of loyalty in the international context must thus be defined. Defining loyalty and its relationship to nationality would seem to be of paramount importance in terms of understanding nationality's nature and effects generally, and the implications of current state practice toward multiple nationality. It is here that the international context of loyalty, or allegiance as loyalty, must be separated from the requirements of international law, and Koessler's definition of "permanent allegiance" as overlapping with that of "nationality" in international law.

The consequences of nationality on the international plane enumerated so far all relate to the state and its relationship to other states: its right to exercise diplomatic protection and personal jurisdiction, its duty to admit nationals, the rights to refuse extradition and use force to protect nationals, and even the responsibility to other states for its nationals' acts. The loyalty of the individual or performance of duties to the state can clearly be separated from those considerations: the state may choose not to exercise its right of diplomatic protection on behalf of even the most ardently loyal citizen; the obligation to admit nationals seems to attach to the status as long as it exists, even to those who might be characterised as disloyal, and as has been seen may even attach to ex-nationals in certain circumstances. It is a duty toward other states, not a right of the individual concerned.

The individual's duties to the state thus seem to bear no relation to the consequences of nationality under international law enumerated thus far. Simply adding a duty of loyalty to the list of nationality's effects, balancing the consequences for the state with one binding the individual might be tempting, but is incorrect. International law itself does not define either what constitutes loyalty or allegiance in that sense.[194] The details of what loyalty (and allegiance, used in that sense) entails for the individual can only be found in municipal, as opposed to international law, and importantly, can extend both to nationals and categories of aliens.

> It seems desirable to eliminate "allegiance" from any technical use and redefine "nationality" in plain words meaning the status of belonging to a state for certain purposes of international law.[195]

---

citizen in obedience to us'". Richard E. Flathman, *Political obligation*, ed. Michael Walzer, *Studies in political theory* (New York: Atheneum, 1972), 293.

[194] "Most people have a working knowledge of the meaning of 'nationality,' but even scholars are at a loss to explain 'allegiance.' Characteristically, the Harvard Research on Nationality suggests defining nationality as 'the status of a natural person who is attached to the state by the tie of allegiance,' and then muddies the picture by saying 'No attempt is made in this draft to define the meaning of allegiance. It may be observed, however, that the 'tie of allegiance' is a term in general use to denote the sum of the obligations of a natural person to the state to which he belongs'. The draft itself does not spell out these obligations, since they are quite different in different societies". Koessler, "'Subject,' 'Citizen,' 'National,' and 'Permanent Allegiance'": 69.

[195] Ibid. An example of mixing of these ideas is found in a United States Government statement on dual nationality. "The country where a dual national is located generally has a stronger claim to that person's allegiance. However, dual nationals owe allegiance to both the United

In pointing out that the meaning of "allegiance" does not coincide with duties to the state generally, Parry simply reinforces Koessler's contention that "allegiance" means "nationality" in terms of belonging to a state for the purposes of international law. The duties of the national to his or her state would indeed seem to be unconditional, but are found and defined in *municipal law*. The word "allegiance" may be used in

---

States and the foreign country. They are required to obey the laws of both countries. Either country has the right to enforce its laws, particularly if the person later travels there". United States Department of State, *Dual nationality*, 2002 (internet), http://travel.state.gov/dualnationality.html, consulted 28 October 2002. It is submitted that the meaning of "allegiance" is unclear from this statement. The first sentence seems to use "allegiance" in the context of loyalty or obligation, whereas the next sentences seem to describe the status/relationship of nationality at international law. By injecting what seems to be an emotional notion that presence implies a stronger obligation of loyalty, the statement arguably does not reflect that United States laws place obligations on all United States citizens/nationals without distinction based on multiple nationality. This statement seems largely unchanged from a State Department administrative ruling referred to by the United States Supreme Court in *Kawakita v United States* (1952) 434 US 717, 734. The US Supreme Court seems to have approved of the view adopted in the government statement on dual nationality, although the Court's holding can be distinguished as it seems to recognise duties not based on foreign nationality as such, but on residence and general obligation, which might apply to any person: "That is a far cry from a ruling that a citizen in that position owes no allegiance to the United States. Of course, an American citizen who is also a Japanese national living in Japan has obligations to Japan necessitated by his residence there. There might conceivably be cases where the mere nonperformance of the acts complained of would be a breach of Japanese law. He may have employment which requires him to perform certain acts. The compulsion may come from the fact that he is drafted for the job or that his conduct is demanded by the laws of Japan. He may be coerced by his employer or supervisor or by the force of circumstances to do things which he has no desire or heart to do. That was one of petitioner's defenses in this case. Such acts – if done voluntarily and wilfully – might be treasonable. But if done under the compulsion of the job or the law or some other influence, those acts would not rise to the gravity of that offense. The trial judge recognized the distinction in his charge when he instructed the jury to acquit petitioner if he did not do the acts willingly or voluntarily 'but so acted only because performance of the duties of his employment required him to do so or because of other coercion or compulsion.' In short, petitioner was held accountable by the jury only for performing acts of hostility toward this country which he was not required by Japan to perform". *Kawakita v United States* (1952) 434 US 717 at 734. Does the US government statement imply a policy in relation to the diplomatic protection of multiple nationals and the principle of equality? An American columnist's charge regarding the allegedly feeble protest lodged by the United States at the conviction in Egypt of Saad Eddin Ibrahim, a dual United States-Egyptian national, to seven years "hard labor for promoting democracy" may provide support for the idea. Thomas Friedman, "Fear for the voice of democracy when power speaks louder", *The Sydney Morning Herald*, 5 August 2002, 13. However the USA apparently did take action according to "The Economist", albeit in that journal's view not mainly for the protection of its national. "Foreign aid, when not strictly humanitarian, is a political instrument, to be given or withheld for reasons of enlightened self-interest. America, having failed by other means to persuade Egypt to reconsider the unjust punishment of an American citizen, has said it will not be giving the

various ways by systems of municipal law, usually to denote an obligation of loyalty to the state, but such obligation does not stem from international law. Another use of the word "allegiance" in the United States illustrates such a national obligation of loyalty. In the Adjudicative Guidelines for Determining Eligibility for Access to Classified Information, allegiance is defined as

> *the duty a citizen owes to his or her government. If allegiance is in doubt, an individual's willingness to safeguard classified information is also in doubt. Criticism of the U.S. Government is protected by freedom of speech. Expression of unpopular or antigovernment beliefs does not show lack of allegiance. An allegiance issue arises only when a person acts or prepares to act on those beliefs in a manner that violates the law.*[196]

But whereas international law may not require or define loyalty, it does not seem to prohibit states from defining or requiring it either. The question is thus posed whether international law places an upper limit on what states may require of their nationals, in terms of loyalty or otherwise.

It has already been mentioned that prior to the United Nations Charter and the Universal Declaration of Human Rights it was possible for states to maintain that while they might be responsible to other states for ill treatment of foreign nationals, they had unfettered power over their own nationals. The classical approach of international law to the state-individual relationship was one of basically unconstrained power of the state. This is no longer the case. The Universal Declaration of Human Rights and universal and regional systems of international human rights treaties have limited states' power in a way that would have been inconceivable prior to 1945. While the regime of diplomatic protection allows states to protect their nationals (and certain other persons enumerated above) against other states, international human rights law protects persons even against their own states.

Thus in broad terms, a state's own municipal laws or constitutional framework, its international obligations, and international law itself, limit its discretion in how it treats its own nationals. In terms of minimum standards of treatment, international limitations might be found in international human rights treaties to which the state has become party, such as the International Covenant on Civil and Political Rights (ICCPR). But that said, the state still enjoys great freedom with respect to its own

---

Egyptians some extra money they had asked for. A generous price for a man, perhaps, but perfectly proper. But is this all it was? It could, perhaps, turn out to be the start of something important: America using aid and influence to encourage an opening up of the closed Arab world". "Slapping Egypt's wrist", *The Economist*, 24 August 2002, 11.

[196] Defense Security Service (USA), *Allegiance test*, 1997 (internet), http://www.dss.mil/nf/adr/alleg/allegT.htm, and *Adjudicative guidelines for determining eligibility for access to classified information*, 1997 (internet), http://www.dss.mil.nf/adr/adjguid/adjguidT.htm, consulted 7 July 2003. For the current (modified) text see: http://www.dss.mil/search-dir/training/csg/security/S3stndrd/Adjudica.htm, consulted 15 March 2006. Under the Guidelines, multiple nationality is not an issue in relation to "allegiance" as defined, but in relation to possible foreign influence and foreign preference. This is discussed in chapter 4.

nationals, if not the freedom of pre-United Nations Charter regimes' ability to claim that how they treated their own nationals was of no concern to other states. In fact, the development of international human rights law and the greater standing of the individual on the plane of international law have created a more nuanced spectrum of the rights and duties that might define the relationship between the individual and his/her state of nationality.

Additional areas of protection for the individual in international law do not, however, prevent the state from requiring loyalty from its nationals. International humanitarian law provides ample evidence of this: while the Geneva Conventions and their Additional Protocols provide a system of fundamental protection and respect for the individual irrespective of nationality, as demonstrated above they do not attempt to replace the system of diplomatic protection of nationals where it can be implemented, and they do not provide protection from charges of treason by states against their own nationals.[197]

It would seem that any limitations provided under international law as to what a state can require of its nationals, including loyalty, is the same upper limit as applies to issues generally. Should a state's requirement of loyalty (or definition of allegiance) demand that an individual participate in a breach of international law, the relevant rule would arguably be void on the international plane. These issues may thus be seen within the context of general limitations placed on states' conduct. But another way to reflect on the issue is to ask what a state can require of non-nationals, and whether nationals can be subjected to higher levels of obligation. International law does provide standards for the treatment of aliens vis-à-vis nationals. It will be argued that the standard of duty or obligation that can be imposed on aliens under international law is so high, that the only practical difference in terms of the loyalty or obligation a state can require of its nationals is a duty of general military service, participation in armed conflict outside national territory, and to refrain from participation in international armed conflicts against the state.

These contentions are presented in the next section in relation to nationality in municipal law. But the crucial point is that obligations of loyalty are issues for municipal, not international, law. As opposed to setting standards of obligation for nationals, international law sets limits on the way states may treat *aliens*, because of their duties to other *states*, in addition to limiting how they treat their own nationals.

From a state's perspective, multiple nationality is one of many possible ties individuals can have to a foreign state. There are many examples of an individual's loyalty being questioned on the basis of a foreign tie, whether real or perceived.[198] Some

---

[197] See also generally Kalshoven, *Constraints on the waging of war*, 40–60. This argument is presented below.

[198] Such as Mr Gladstone's questioning, as British Prime Minister in the early 1870s, whether Catholics could be trustworthy subjects of the state, not only on grounds of influence held by the Holy See which could influence their civil responsibilities, but on grounds of the sway even the national Catholic church could have over its members. See the spirited public response that seeks to explain the Church's doctrine of papal infallibility in theological terms,

of these issues may lead states to regulate their municipal laws on nationality in one way or another, influence their positions on multiple nationality, or have ramifications for law and policy in specific areas, but the details are issues for municipal law.[199] The term allegiance may be used to denote the loyalty required of individuals, but loyalty or duties to the state are not consequences of nationality under international law or on the international plane, but may be consequences of nationality under municipal law. Use of the term "allegiance" to denote loyalty, duty or nationality should be abandoned, especially in relation to the international plane, as Koessler aptly suggested over fifty years ago.

---

as opposed to political, repudiating Gladstone's stand. John Henry Newman, *A letter addressed to his Grace the Duke of Norfolk on occasion of Mr. Gladstone's recent expostulation* (London: B. M. Pickering, 1875). "The English people are sufficiently sensitive of the claims of the Pope . . . Those claims most certainly I am not going to deny; . . . And I uphold them as heartily as I recognize my duty of loyalty to the constitution, the laws, and the government of England. I see no inconsistency in my being at once a good Catholic and a good Englishman". Newman, *A letter addressed to his Grace the Duke of Norfolk on occasion of Mr. Gladstone's recent expostulation*, 4. In terms of divided allegiance, Newman argues that the allegiance owed to the Pope is separable from that owed to the temporal power, but that even when there are competing claims on loyalty, individuals can separate their obligations appropriately. "When, then, Mr. Gladstone asks Catholics how they can obey the Queen and yet obey the Pope, since it may happen that the commands of the two authorities may clash, I answer, that it is my *rule*, both to obey the one and to obey the other, but that there is no rule in this world without exceptions, and if either the Pope or the Queen demanded of me an 'Absolute Obedience,' he or she would be transgressing the laws of human nature and human society. I give an absolute obedience to neither. Further, if ever this double allegiance pulled me in contrary ways, which in this age of the world I think it never will, then I should decide according to the particular case, which is beyond all rule, and must be decided on its own merits". Newman, *A letter addressed to his Grace the Duke of Norfolk on occasion of Mr. Gladstone's recent expostulation*, 53. Pressing the argument in case of a direct conflict, "Again, were I actually a soldier or sailor in her Majesty's service, and sent to take part in a war which I could not in my conscience see to be unjust, and should the Pope suddenly bid all Catholic soldiers and sailors to retire from the service, here again, taking the advice of others, as best I could, I should not obey him". Newman, *A letter addressed to his Grace the Duke of Norfolk on occasion of Mr. Gladstone's recent expostulation*, 52.

[199] The Argentine military government that ruled between 1976 and 1983 basically reversed Argentine policy that had been in effect since the Constitution of 1853, not favouring the naturalisation of foreigners. A legal difference was instituted between nationality, which could be obtained after two years of residence, and citizenship, which could only be obtained after three more years of residence; candidates for naturalisation were obliged to divest themselves of foreign nationality and swear an oath of loyalty to this effect; numerous grounds for naturalised citizens to be denaturalised were established; and for the first time grounds were instituted for the revocation of the Argentine nationality of the native-born, namely treason, and naturalisation abroad. Dionisio Petriella, *El Convenio de Doble Ciudadanía entre la Argentina e Italia*, vol. 30 (Buenos Aires: Asociación Dante Alighieri, 1988), 15–16. These provisions and their specific effects were reversed by the subsequent civilian government.

4. Nationality in bilateral and multilateral treaties and relations

Nationality may be used as a category of reference in international agreements in order to identify groups of individuals regardless of the subject matter involved. Nationality (or often "citizenship") is also used in international agreements to identify or categorise individuals with respect to certain topics of importance to states. This is because municipal law uses nationality as a means to categorise individuals in terms of providing privileges and entitlements, or imposing obligations, which is reflected when states make agreements with one another. Thus, whether or not nationality is used to delineate persons in international agreements essentially depends on the subject matter and how municipal law deals with the issue. Most bilateral taxation agreements are not centred on nationality, as the group of persons that both states wish to tax is either broader or narrower than their respective (or mutual) nationals. However United States tax treaties must deal to some extent with US nationals as a category, as the United States attempts to tax its nationals' worldwide income irrespective of residence. In other treaties, such as agreements relating to military service, nationality is the single focus of identifying the objects of the treaty, as states that impose such an obligation commonly use nationality or citizenship as the criteria for defining the group affected.

The treaty norms of the European Union, which provide for equal treatment for all nationals of EU member states in many areas of law, and prohibit discrimination on the basis of nationality generally, illustrate the subject matter for which nationality has been used to discriminate among groups of persons.[200] The prohibition against discrimination based on nationality has been interpreted in terms of the basic freedoms established by EU states, namely the freedom of movement, and the freedom of establishment,[201] harking back to 19th century freedom of commerce and navigation treaties.

Whether nationality as a relational factor or means of categorisation is either gaining or losing importance in municipal law or international relations is unclear. In anecdotal terms this is, however, the place where issues of globalisation perhaps become most relevant to the topic of multiple nationality. If movement and contact across borders by individuals is indeed increasingly easy and frequent, it might be expected that states would not choose nationality as a fundamental means of categorising the rights, entitlements and obligations of individuals, but factors such as residence or employment. In Australia, all citizens have a right to participate in the national medical scheme, Medicare, but only those citizens resident in Australia and thus subject to taxation, and similarly-situated permanent residents, are entitled to receive benefits under the scheme. Where national funds are concerned, states clearly

---

[200] See generally Brita Sundberg-Weitman, *Discrimination on grounds of nationality. Free movement of workers and freedom of establishment under the EEC treaty* (Amsterdam: North-Holland Publishing Company, 1977).

[201] Id., 14.

have an interest in avoiding financial benefits accruing to the same individual from multiple states, simply on the basis of a formal status. There is evidence to suggest that states are increasingly aware of such issues, but also of the hardship that can be caused to individuals in this regard.[202] Aleinikoff and Klusmeyer recommend for example, that "citizenship status not be the gatekeeper to access to social benefits and the labor market".[203] On the other hand, nationality is a convenient way to delineate whole categories of people should this result be desired. As in issues surrounding state policy toward inclusion and exclusion, it may be expected that the desirability of nationality as an *Anknüpfungspunkt* may vary over time, and according to subject matter.

C. NATIONALITY IN MUNICIPAL LAW

1. Generally

Rules relating to the attribution or determination of nationality in municipal law have been covered above. Rules relating to the international recognition of nationality are relevant in international terms, as discussed above, but not on the level of municipal law in relation to determinations of who falls within the category of nationals. That is of course left to municipal law. Recognition of nationality in municipal law is however relevant when municipal law expressly regulates when multiple nationality will or will not be recognised, and when such policies have effects in municipal law.

---

[202] Treaties and agreements in relation to social security/insurance are a case in point, such as when national pension funds allow for a person with an entitlement in one country, to draw the financial benefit in another, in many cases pooling the years worked in both countries as far as calculating the benefit. An honest pensioner who drew pensions in two different countries, one related to each nationality, quickly found the overall payment to him reduced when he informed the government of the link. George Cochrane, "Honesty the best policy", *The Sun-Herald*, 3 November 2002, Investor, 8. But the point of reference in allowing the pensioner to receive his British pension in Australia is the fact that he is an Australian resident, and he receives the pension because he has worked in Britain, not because he is of British nationality.

[203] T. Alexander Aleinikoff and Douglas Klusmeyer, *Citizenship policies for an age of migration* (Washington, DC: Carnegie Endowment for International Peace, 2002), 63. See generally pp. 62–77 and pp. 79–99 in relation to social benefits for nationals and certain categories of foreigners in Germany, Austria, the Netherlands, Canada, the USA, France, the United Kingdom, Australia, and Israel. In relation to the USA, see also Michael Jones Correa, "Seeking shelter: immigrants and the divergence of social rights and citizenship in the United States", in *Dual nationality, social rights and federal citizenship in the U.S. and Europe. The reinvention of citizenship*, ed. Randall Hansen and Patrick Weil (New York: Berghahn Books, 2002), 233–263; Susan Martin, "The attack on social rights: U.S. citizenship devalued," in *Dual nationality, social rights and federal citizenship in the U.S. and Europe. The reinvention of citizenship*, ed. Randall Hansen and Patrick Weil (New York: Berghahn Books, 2002), 215–232.

It was argued that the consequences of nationality in municipal law depend solely on municipal law, and thus vary from state to state. If one follows Weis and other authors, nationality is a relationship or status that confers mutual rights and duties. If one follows Randelzhofer, nationality is never a source for rights and duties, just a condition for their extension.

Fundamental consequences of nationality at international law that at first glance seem to provide benefits to the individual, the state's right of diplomatic protection, and the duty to allow nationals entry, may be the subject of a state's municipal law, but this seems seldom to be the case, as many states do not express either norm as a right or entitlement capable of being claimed by their nationals.[204]

2. Nationals and aliens

Classifying human beings in municipal law using nationality as a lens should allow one to discern its significance as a category in municipal law. This means dividing municipal law's scope as it relates to human beings according to the basic categories of nationals and aliens. Those categories can of course be divided further. Sundberg-Weitman presents four categories according to which states treat individuals: (1) aliens to whom prohibitions and restrictions apply, (2) aliens who are accorded preferences, (3) nationals who are subject to certain limitations, and (4) nationals to whom favours are extended by law.[205]

It has already been seen that some countries have categories of nationals to whom different laws apply: China has at least three categories (avoiding the sensitive question of the "Chinese" nationality of people on Taiwan), being related to "mainland" China, Hong Kong and Macau.[206] In most countries the category of nationals overlaps with the category of citizens.

There are a few exceptions however, where individuals cannot be classified into basic categories of "national" and "alien". An example is that of the Cook Islands, whose municipal legislation does not create a category of nationals or citizens at all. It establishes a category of persons with the rights of permanent residency, but all Cook Islanders are New Zealand citizens and nationals. It is submitted that this does not necessarily mean that for the purposes of international law there are no nationals

---

[204] Many passports contain annotations requesting that the bearer be allowed to pass, and be afforded assistance by foreign authorities should she or he require it, but no mention related to diplomatic protection or a right of entry. An exception is the Swiss passport, which contains no request for unhindered passage or assistance, but reads "The holder of this passport is a Swiss citizen and is entitled to return to Switzerland at any time".

[205] Sundberg-Weitman, *Discrimination on grounds of nationality. Free movement of workers and freedom of establishment under the EEC treaty.*

[206] They are arguably categories of nationality and not of citizenship, because the territory to which individuals would be returned by other states is not all of China, but the relevant administrative region. This proposition may, however, be questioned.

of the Cook Islands, just that the country's municipal legislation has not identified who they are, and that their protection has been delegated to New Zealand by agreement.[207] Perhaps the more important question regards the international legal personality of both the Cook Islands (and Niue, as another state associated with New Zealand), given that all persons over whom those countries might claim nationality-based jurisdiction are uncontrovertibly New Zealand nationals/citizens. Yet the Cook Islands is party to bilateral and multi-lateral agreements in its own right, and maintains accredited diplomatic representatives in Wellington.[208] It would seem that for the purposes of Cook Islands' municipal law, nationality is irrelevant, and one can not divide persons into Cook Island nationals, and aliens. Permanent residents and non-residents are subject to the Cook Islands' territorial jurisdiction alike, but the state does not extend personal jurisdiction either inside or outside its borders in relation to the category of people who would normally constitute its nationals, as such. That is left to New Zealand.

In the typical case, however, there is only one category of nationals, over whom the state can exercise jurisdiction wherever they reside. As discussed above, the principles of equality and the effective/genuine link may limit the opposability of nationality in relation to multiple nationals on the international plane, but not in terms of a state's treatment of its own nationals, even when abroad. Regardless of residence,

---

[207] Upon "decolonisation" many newly independent states existed for some time before they enacted laws on nationality. In the context of former French territories in Africa, see Günter Breunig, *Staatsangehörigkeit und Entkolonisierung. Die Abgrenzung des Staatsvolkes bei der Verselbständigung der frankophonen Staaten Schwarzafrikas unter völkerrechtlichen Gesichtspunkten, Schriften zum Völkerrecht* (Berlin: Duncker & Humblot, 1974).

[208] The New Zealand Ministry of Foreign Affairs and Trade states that "The Cook Islands is a self-governing state in free association with New Zealand. The key features of the free association relationship are provided for in the Cook Islands Constitution Act 1965. . . . In May 1973 the Prime Minister of New Zealand, Rt Hon Norman Kirk, and the Premier of the Cook Islands Hon Albert Henry exchanged letters in which they clarified aspects of the relationship of free association. The exchange emphasised that there were no legal fetters on the freedom of the Cook Islands and the relationship was a voluntary one of partnership turning on the wish of Cook Islanders to remain New Zealand citizens. The exchange emphasised that shared citizenship created an expectation that the Cook Islands would uphold in its laws and policies a standard of values generally acceptable to New Zealanders. In June 2001, to mark the Centenary of formal relations between the two countries, a new statement was signed by the Prime Ministers of the Cook Islands and New Zealand. The 'Joint Centenary Declaration of the Principles of the Relationship between New Zealand and the Cook Islands' updates the Kirk/Henry Exchange". New Zealand Ministry of Foreign Affairs and Trade, *Cook Islands Country Paper March 2006, Relations with New Zealand*, 2006 (internet), http://www.mfat. govt.nz/foreign/regions/pacific/country/cookislands paper.html, consulted on 19 March 2006. See also Cook Islands Government (2002), *Special Relationship with New Zealand* (internet), http://www.ck/govt.htm#nz, consulted on 19 March 2006. Juss, citing Crawford for the principle, says "a State is not sovereign if it does not have exclusive competence in respect to its own internal affairs and nationality is one of those affairs". Juss, "Nationality law, sovereignty, and the doctrine of exclusive domestic jurisdiction", 222.

nationals can be obliged to declare worldwide income and pay taxes on it, as in the case of the USA,[209] be obliged to vote in national elections,[210] and to perform military service.[211] These issues are discussed in chapter four, in the context of multiple nationality. But there are also clearly privileges of nationality or citizenship in many countries that distinguish nationals from aliens or permanent residents (usually the most preferentially treated class of aliens under municipal law).[212] The treatment accorded depends on municipal law; in theory a state could extend the benefits of nationality/citizenship to all persons regardless of nationality.[213]

---

[209] "Every U.S. citizen or resident must file a U.S. income tax return unless total income without regard to the foreign earned income exclusion is below an amount based on filing status". Internal Revenue Service, United States Department of the Treasury, *Publication 54*, 2005 (internet), http://www.irs.gov/publications/p54/ar02.html, consulted on 19 March 2006. Taxation of worldwide income on the basis of nationality seems infrequent.

[210] Although voting is compulsory for citizens residing in Australia, they can be removed from the electoral roll if they reside abroad. If they are on the roll however and do not vote, even if abroad, the obligation persists and they must tender reasons for not having voted. See generally Australian Electoral Commission, *"Going overseas? – frequently Asked* Questions, 2006 (internet), http://www.aec.gov.au/_content/What/enrolment/faq_os.htm, consulted on 19 March 2006. To the author's knowledge, no state obliges nationals or citizens permanently resident overseas to vote in elections, however it is increasingly common for states to facilitate voting from abroad.

[211] This is discussed below and in chapter four in relation to multiple nationality, as a duty of military service would seem to be the primary objection of many commentators to individuals possessing more than one nationality, or put differently, states attributing their nationality to the same individual. In any case, for much of the twentieth century it was uncontroverted that states could oblige their nationals to perform military service, even those resident abroad, which led to hardship for multiple nationals. In practice, bilateral agreements were drawn up between many states to deal with this issue as it affected individuals who were nationals of both, and well as multilateral frameworks. See for example Council of Europe, *Explanatory report on the Additional protocol to the Convention of 6 May 1963 on the reduction of cases of multiple nationality and military obligations in cases of multiple nationality* (Strasbourg: Council of Europe, 1978); Council of Europe, *Explanatory report on the protocol amending the Convention of 6 May 1963 on the reduction of cases of multiple nationality and military obligations in cases of multiple nationality* (Strasbourg: Council of Europe, 1978).

[212] For an excellent overview of these issues, see the various studies in Atsushi Kondo, ed., *Citizenship in a global world. Comparing citizenship rights for aliens* (Houndmills (UK): Palgrave, 2001).

[213] While such an idea may seem absurd, as far as it devalues the national vis-à-vis the alien on the municipal plane, states that facilitated entry and naturalisation, typical of 19th century states in the Americas, arguably came close to this. In Argentina, basically open immigration was combined with easy naturalisation, and no obligation to divest oneself of a previous nationality. A 1869 law delineating the constitutional norm stated "son ciudadanos por naturalización los extranjeros mayores de dieciocho años que residieran en la República dos años continuos y manifiesten ante los Jueces Federales de sección su voluntad de serlo". Petriella, *El Convenio de Doble Ciudadanía entre la Argentina e Italia*, 14 and generally 13–17. (Author's

An attempt to delineate the obligations, rights, entitlements and privileges of nationality found in municipal law cannot be comprehensively undertaken here.[214] The general areas themselves can be discerned however, from how states regulate their conduct vis-à-vis aliens, either as a purely internal matter, or under agreements with other states. Non-discrimination is the overall issue, thus the existence of discrimination arguably indicates areas where nationality is relevant, even adopting the view that nationality itself does not necessarily give rise to rights and entitlements itself, as it is still a precondition for those things. These areas include: civil and political rights, the right to contract, religious freedom, freedom of speech and publication, access to eduction, access to the courts and judicial guarantees, employment, membership in professions, the right to apply for licenses and to enter into fiduciary relationships, entitlements to participation in social insurance or pension schemes, rights of inheritance, rights in relation to real and personal property, treatment in terms of taxation, and an obligation of military or other service to the state.[215]

Juxtaposed to nationals as a category is the category of aliens, which can in turn be subdivided into more specific categories of persons according to each state's municipal law. Permanent resident non-nationals seem to be the most privileged group: they may in some cases vote, they are generally allowed to work and travel freely, to purchase real estate, to exercise most professions, and to return to, and reside in, the state. But they may also be obliged to fulfil some of the duties that apply to nationals, such as paying taxes. It would seem that the only difference in their treatment, stemming from international law, is that they are exempt from compulsory military service, with certain exceptions.[216] This is discussed below, in terms of loyalty and obligation. But both privileges and obligations are extended to them

---

translation: *naturalised citizens are foreigners over the age of 18 who have resided in the Republic for two years continuously and have expressed their will to be such before a federal judge.*)

[214] These come in all forms: Swiss nationality is one of the prerequisites for applying to serve in the Papal Guard. Patricia Messerli, "Swiss Guard at Swiss Abroad Day", *Swiss Review* (2002) vol. 4, 12–13, 13. Sometimes the benefits of nationality are material, demonstrated by Afghans contemplating returning to their native land in 2002. "For those comfortably settled in the United States, Australia or France, however, the choice is harder. It could mean losing the prospect of asylum or foreign citizenship, as well as leaving behind western salaries, comfortable apartments and running water". "Returning Afghans. No place like home", *The Economist*, 23 February 2002, 37. Normally, Canadian nationality entails visa-free entry into the United States. But "Canada has urged any of its citizens born in some Middle Eastern countries to think carefully before entering the United States in view of tough new US anti-terrorism laws". "Canada warns on tough new US law", *The Sydney Morning Herald*, 1 November 2002, 9.

[215] In the context of the United States, see generally Whiteman, *Digest of international law*, vol. 8, 376–696, in relation to the treatment of aliens under municipal and international law in these and other areas. See also Kondo, ed., *Citizenship in a global world. Comparing citizenship rights for aliens.*

[216] See Shearer, *Starke's international law*, 315.

on the basis of their territorial link to the state, as opposed to a personal link. There seems to be no barrier in international law however, to the revocation of privileges extended to resident non-nationals under municipal law, with the exception of vested rights, which applies to all persons regardless of alienage.[217]

This is a reflection of the broad discretion with which states can treat aliens on their own territory. Should they abuse or ill-treat aliens (including "grossly unfair discrimination or outright arbitrary confiscation of the alien's property"),[218] their states of nationality can exercise diplomatic protection or assert a claim for compensation.[219] But there is no specific duty to admit aliens, and no duty not to expel or deport them.[220] And once they have been admitted, there is also no obligation to accord them national treatment.[221] Shearer notes that

---

[217] Id., 316. According to Weil and Hansen this demonstrates the continued significance of nationality as a legal relationship or status. See Patrick Weil and Randall Hansen, "Citoyenneté, immigration et nationalité: vers la convergence européenne", in *Nationalité et citoyenneté en Europe*, ed. Patrick Weil and Randall Hansen, *Collection "Recherches"* (Paris: Éditions La Découverte, 1999), 9–28.

[218] Shearer, *Starke's international law*, 315–16. For arguments challenging claims of states' general right to exclude aliens from their territory with the exception of treaty obligations, see James A. R. Nafziger, "The general admission of aliens under international law", *American Journal of International Law* (1983) vol. 77, no. 4, 804–847. Nafziger argues "for a qualified duty to admit aliens when they pose no danger to the public safety, security, general welfare, or essential institutions of a recipient state". Id., 805. Regarding the fundamental limitations of international human rights law on how states treat aliens see Declaration on the human rights of individuals who are not nationals of the country in which they live, 13 December 1985, United Nations General Assembly Resolution 40/144, UN Document Series: ST/DPI (New York: United Nations, 1985).

[219] There are numerous examples of states intervening on behalf of their nationals in various contexts, many limited to enquiring about a specific government policy or action, such as Indonesia's request for Australia to explain the context of the search of homes and property belonging to Indonesian nationals permanently resident in Australia, purportedly in relation to terrorism. See Matthew Moore, Linda Morris, and Deborah Cameron, "Don't keep us in dark, says angry Jakarta", *The Sydney Morning Herald*, 1 November 2002, 1. Indonesian officials subsequently requested Indonesian nationals in Australia to report "violations of their human rights in raids aimed at investigating terrorism" directly to the Indonesian authorities. "Jakarta warns citizens", *The Sydney Morning Herald*, 2–3 November 2002, 13.

[220] See generally Shearer, *Starke's international law*, 314–16. Shearer points out however, that the right to deport does not give rise to unfettered discretion in the manner of expulsion, which must be reasonable, and not such as to contravene human rights norms or place individuals in danger. Shearer, *Starke's international law*, 316.

[221] In the *Oscar Chinn Case* the Permanent Court of International Justice held that general treaty provisions relating to freedom of trade in the Treaty of Saint-Germain of 10 September 1919 did not prevent the Belgian government from making rules which in fact favoured Belgian companies over foreign-owned ones as far as making it more commercially attractive to do business with the former. Commercial equality based on nationality did not give rise to vested rights. The requirement in question did not prevent the foreign business from operating,

A number of states, including the Afro-Asian group, hold that the national standard of treatment should apply, inasmuch as aliens entering impliedly submit to that standard, otherwise they could elect not to enter.[222]

It could also be argued that aliens are, or should be aware, that when they enter national territory they are in some respects a legally disadvantaged group. Were they not, diplomatic protection might seem superfluous and indeed to some extent unjustified. While international law may not define the contours of nationals' loyalty to their own states, it does put limits on the way states may treat aliens.

3. Loyalty and obligation

It was argued above that loyalty or obligation to the state is fundamentally a concept of municipal law, as opposed to a concept of international law. Related laws must be separated from emotions or opinions surrounding nationality and loyalty and the trappings thereof. It must be recognised however, that questions of nationality and multiple nationality are imbued with emotion in terms of the individual's link to the state. In the United Kingdom, an oath of allegiance as part of the naturalisation process was only introduced in 2002, for emotional as opposed to legal reasons.[223]

---

it just made its operations less attractive. *The Oscar Chinn Case*, World Court Reports (1934) vol. 3, 416. See also *Chinn Case*, 1933 and 1934 Annual Digest and Reports of Public International Law Cases (1934) 312. The 1951 Convention relating to the status of refugees prohibits certain discrimination against resident aliens who have been accorded refugee status, but these norms seem very basic. National treatment is provided under article 4 in terms of religious practice and religious education of children, under article 14 regarding artistic rights and industrial property, and article 16 for access to the courts. Article 7 provides that they should be treated at least as well as aliens are generally. Convention relating to the status of refugees, 28 July 1951, 189 UNTS 150 (entry into force: 22 April 1954), United Nations High Commissioner for Refugees, (internet), http://www.unhcr.org/cgibin/texis/vtx/protect?id=3c0762ea4, consulted on 19 March 2006.

[222] Shearer, *Starke's international law*, 316.

[223] "Britain said yesterday asylum seekers would have to swear allegiance to their newly adopted country, as well as pass a 'Brit test' of basic English language and customs, if they wanted to be granted citizenship. Immigrants would take the oath in an initiation ceremony designed to give arrivals the feeling becoming a Briton was 'something to celebrate'". "Asylum seekers to swear allegiance", *The Age*, 8 February 2002, 9. In Australia, a popular daily newspaper decried a dearth of public expressions of patriotism: "Keeping loyalties and passions private has been a useful trait in a multicultural nation since it helps people with different beliefs live harmoniously. If patriotism can be diffident, that is the Australian brand, and it keeps us out of trouble. But diffidence can also be taken too far if it means we are unwilling to publicly acknowledge some sort of national allegiance outside sporting events. It might be nice to stand up for Australia for a change. Miranda Devine, "We should stand up for our country", *The Sun-Herald*, 13 October 2002, 15. And there is no reason to think that geographical or cultural difference dictates different views: "In his anniversary address on July 1, [2002, Chinese

The view adopted regarding whether nationality is a reciprocal relationship between an individual and the state, or just a condition for such a relationship, dictates in turn how the notion of loyalty is viewed within municipal law. Following Weis (nationality as reciprocal rights and duties), its definition and parameters vary according to the municipal law of each state. Following Randelzhofer however, it would seem that loyalty proves to be an exception to his statement that nationality itself does not involve rights and duties on the municipal level, if one accepts that a duty of loyalty, however defined, attaches directly to the status/relationship of nationality. For our purposes, either view can be adopted.

If an obligation of loyalty (i.e. allegiance as loyalty) does attach to nationality as such in municipal law, it might be characterised as part of what the state requires and has a right to expect from its nationals, as opposed to aliens. Yet it is clear that a state can also impose various degrees of obligation on non-nationals, or categories thereof. Within a state's territory, aliens are subject to most laws on the same basis as nationals. In relation to acts outside a state's territory, it has already been mentioned that states maintain jurisdiction over acts of aliens committed abroad that affect the security or financial interests of the state, under the principle of protective or security jurisdiction. Non-nationals can thus be held to a very high standard of accountability to any state generally, even if the state has no specific basis for territorial or personal jurisdiction over the relevant individual. Implementation of this notion is of course contingent on the state being able to seize the individual in question and thereby enforce its laws. But the practical modalities of enforcement do not influence the underlying norm.

Thus it must be asked, how is the level of obligation imposed on those with a relationship to the state, either personal or territorial, higher? Shearer states that "[r]esident aliens owe temporary allegiance or obedience to their state of residence, sufficient at any rate to support a charge of treason".[224] The proposition that residence implies a higher level of obligation to the state is important, and is explored below. But the definition of "treason" depends on municipal law, and in many states can be committed by anyone. Shearer's statement, while certainly correct, could be extended further: even non-resident aliens can be charged with treason or the equivalent, if a state's municipal law so provides.[225] The Inter-American Court of Human Rights confirmed

---

President] Jiang [Zemin] reminded Hong Kong's 7 million people that their prime responsibility was now to their motherland and that the return to Chinese rule was a 'test' of their loyalty. 'They should, therefore, keep enhancing their sense of the country and of the nation, make conscious efforts to safeguard the security and unification of the motherland and endeavour to defend its overall interests', Jiang said. For good measure, Jiang also called on the Hong Kong government to 'do a better job,' an implied criticism of lawmakers and the courts". David Lague, "Hong Kong. Interim report. After five years of mainland sovereignty, Beijing signals that it wants a more hands-on role", *Far Eastern Economic Review*, 11 July 2002, 20.

[224] Shearer, *Starke's international law*, 316.

[225] It should be noted that "treason" in terms of the Common Law, related to levying war

this when it held that Peru's prosecution of Chilean nationals for treason did not violate the Inter-American Convention on Human Rights' provisions on the right to nationality.

----

against the sovereign, "levying war" encompassing "to use force to prevent the government from the free exercise of any of its lawful powers", cited in *The State v Ratu Timoci Silatolu and Josefa Nata, 26 March 2002*, High Court of Fiji 2002, (internet), http://www.humanrights.org.fj/rightFair/SilaFHRC.htm, consulted 4 August 2003. In the Silatolu case, the Fijian High Court summarised the law of treason in Fiji, stemming from the law of England, and held that "Treason is an offence against the King or Sovereign (His Majesty's Person or against the Government, and I think that it may be committed by 'any person or persons' whether allegiance is owed or not". *The State v Ratu Timoci Silatolu and Josefa Nata*, 19. Thus while treason can only be committed by someone owing "allegiance" under the laws of the USA (see note 188 above), the Court held that it could be committed by anyone under the laws of England and Fiji. The holding in Silatolu arguably reflects the fact that "treason" as defined by Fijian law is simply one expression in municipal law of an obligation of loyalty to the state, irrespective of nationality or territorial presence. This kind of obligation may be expressed differently in different states, but it is not uncommon for it to attach to anyone, perhaps reflecting the security principle of jurisdiction. The famous British prosecution of William Joyce for treason (known as "Lord Haw-Haw" and his pro-Nazi wartime radio broadcasts to Britain) is a counter-example, as the prosecution was based on an argument of constructive allegiance. Joyce was not a British national, but had obtained a British passport under false pretences. The Court held that Joyce's use of the passport brought with it a duty of loyalty to Britain and he could thus be prosecuted for treason. See Nigel Farndale, "Haw-Haw: The tragedy of William and Margaret Joyce", Houndmills: Macmillan, 2005. Before 1997 crimes endangering state security were known as "counterrevolutionary" crimes in the People's Republic of China. Lawyers Committee for Human Rights, *Wrongs and rights. A human rights analysis of China's revised Criminal Law* (New York: Lawyers Committee for Human Rights, 1998), 41. This is not to say that the substance of what is criminalised under current Chinese law, notwithstanding what is to many a more palatable label, accords with international rules and standards of human rights. See Lawyers Committee for Human Rights, *Wrongs and rights. A human rights analysis of China's revised Criminal Law*, 41–46. Mittlebeeler points out that in much of South African society, the traditional African notion of treason "embraced many elements which would not in a Western system constitute treason. The crime of treason was any action that might be considered antagonistic to the welfare of the Ndebele king or the Shona chief. This included injuries to his person or household, as well as seditious plots . . . misuse of his cattle could, in some cases, be considered treason, as well as the invocation of magic against him". Emmet V. Mittlebeeler, *African custom and western law. The development of the Rhodesian Criminal Law for Africans* (New York: Africana Publishing Company, 1976), 24. There are countless examples. In Sweden any person regardless of nationality or residence can commit treason (högmålsbrott) and crimes against state security. The Swedish Penal Code, 21 December 1962 (entry into force: 1 January 1965), Chapters 19 and 22, as of 1 May 1999, Government Offices of Sweden (internet), http://www.sweden.gov.se/content/1/c6/02/77/77/cb79a8a3.pdf, consulted 19 March 2006. Under Romania's Communist government, offences against state security were broadly defined. Treason could only be committed by a Romanian citizen or stateless person residing in Romania, but exactly the same acts committed by foreigners or stateless persons were punishable by penalties including death. Simone-Marie

Whatever the consequences of nationality in law, they exist solely with respect to Chile and not Peru, and are not altered by the fact that the criminal behavior in question is classified as treason. "Treason" is simply the nomem iuris *that the State uses in its laws and does not mean that the defendants somehow acquired the duties of nationality that Peruvians owe.*[226]

Obligations of the individual to the state can be related to two different considerations, one relating to obedience generally, the other to residence or closer personal connection.[227] On the one hand, all persons present in the territory of a state can be made subject to generally applicable laws such as those related to public order. Being a tourist does not arrest the application of criminal laws. But it would be highly unusual for a state to attempt to tax the income earned abroad by tourists based simply on their temporary presence. It is unclear whether such a municipal law would contravene international law, but in any case it would arguably be very bad for tourism in the state concerned. On the other hand, taxing the foreign-earned income of resident aliens is quite common, based on their residence.

This is simply a reflection of the fact that in practical terms, municipal law can impose greater duties on persons with a territorial, but not necessarily personal, tie to the state. It is thus natural that residence may (and arguably should) entail an obligation of loyalty beyond simple obedience of the law generally. But if international law provides no grounds for opposing the prosecution of non-resident aliens for treason or equivalent crimes against the state, one must ask just what constitutes the

---

Vrabiescu Kleckner, ed., *The Penal Code of the Romanian Socialist Republic* (London: Sweet & Maxwell, 1976). In Nigeria, following England, treason and sedition were general crimes, not related to a link of nationality. C. O. Okonkwo, *Okonkwo and Naish on criminal law in Nigeria* (London: Sweet & Maxwell, 1980), 337–48. For an historical survey of treason in feudal France, see S. H. Cuttler, *The law of treason and treason trials in later medieval France* (Cambridge: Cambridge University Press, 1981).

[226] *Castillo Petruzzi et al. Case*, Judgment of 30 May 1999, para. 102, Inter-American Court of Human Rights, (internet), http://www.corteidh.or.cr/seriec_52_ing.doc, consulted 19 March 2006. The Court held, however, the Peru had violated numerous other provisions of the Convention. In *Caso Lori Berenson Mejía vs. Perú*, Sentencia de 25 de noviembre de 2004, the Inter-American Court found that Peru had violated the Convention's provisions on judicial guarantees by trying Berenson (accused of treason) in a military court, but restated the position that the state had the right and obligation to guarantee its own security, doing this within the law and such as to preserve fundamental rights. Inter-American Court of Human Rights, (internet), http://www.corteidh.or.cr/seriec_119_esp.doc, para. 91, consulted 19 March 2006. The Court did find a breach of the Convention's right to nationality in *Baruch Ivcher Bronstein vs. Peru*, Judgment of 6 February 2001, Inter-American Court of Human Rights, (internet), http://www.corteidh.or.cr/seriec_ing/seriec_74__ing.doc, consulted 19 March 2006.

[227] The designation "temporary allegiance" is used by some authors to signify the former, and by others to signify the latter. Given the argument herein that loyalty to the state is not a consequence of nationality under international law, just important to the context of nationality, use of the designation "temporary allegiance" is confusing and should be avoided. See section 3.2 on temporary allegiance, below.

"loyalty" or obligation that attaches to residence or nationality (either directly or as a consequence). It would seem that it can only be related to military service, or an obligation to physically defend the interests of the state vis-à-vis other states in the context of armed conflict. This was argued, although not in relation to an issue of loyalty, by the Conservative MP Enoch Powell in 1981 in relation to revision of the United Kingdom's Nationality Act: "Nationality, in the last resort, is tested by fighting. A man's nation is the nation for which he will fight".[228] It might be noted however, that

> national patriotism is a relatively modern basis for [military] service. It requires a sense of one's country as an entity that can legitimately demand contributions and to which loyalty should be given. Principled refusal to comply on the grounds of dissatisfaction with government is also relatively modern; such a basis of refusal depends on a belief that there are reciprocal obligations between citizens and their governments.[229]

But even resident aliens can be obliged to perform compulsory military service to maintain public order or in case of a sudden invasion.[230]

---

[228] International Law Association Committee on Feminism and International Law, "Final report on women's equality and nationality in international law", 265. The MP made the statement while opposing transmission of British nationality by mothers to their children by jus sanguinis. "[T]his law was for some bound up with a stereotype of women as devoted to 'the preservation and care of life' and therefore incapable of demonstrating the love of country that would entitle them to pass its nationality on to their children.... Ayelet Shachar argues that even now, the Israeli paradigm of the citizen as soldier means that women are, to some degree, lesser citizens of Israel because although both men and women are obliged to perform military service, women can be exempted if they are wives or mothers". Ibid.

[229] Margaret Levi, *Consent, dissent, and patriotism* (Cambridge: Cambridge University Press, 1997), 42–43. "Throughout the eighteenth century (and into the nineteenth) a single shilling pressed into the hand of a drunken man in a public house by a recruiting sergeant constituted the enlistment of a soldier in the British army. In France, the dreaded *milice royale* relied on a lottery to choose which peasants would be forced into the King's service. The army was not a popular institution, at least not for those who had to serve in its rank and file. Some joined because they liked the life, but most did so because they were coerced or needed the work or were fleeing from something worse. Those who refused did so because being in the army was inconvenient or actively repugnant.... It was only with the American and French revolutions that national patriotic feeling began to take root, but it took root very slowly". Levi, *Consent, dissent, and patriotism*, 42–43. The notorious reputation of press gangs lives on today.

[230] Shearer, *Starke's international law*, 315. In *Polites v The Commonwealth*, the High Court of Australia unanimously held that an Act of Parliament obliged aliens to serve in the armed forces, notwithstanding any possible rule of international law to the country. The Court accepted that there was a general rule of international law "which prevented the imposition upon resident aliens of an obligation to serve in the armed forces of the country in which they resided, unless the State to which they belonged consented to waive this ordinarily recognized exemption. This rule, however does not prevent compulsory service in a local police force, or, apparently, compulsory service for the purpose of maintaining public order or repelling a sudden invasion.... [T]he distinction is drawn between the use of military force for ordinary

It would seem that the quality or nature of the service imposed is important in this sense. Karamanoukian cites the quasi-unanimous opinion of writers that military service cannot be imposed on resident aliens in peacetime,[231] and a similar prohibition in time of war.[232] He remarks however, that state practice "n'est pas conforme à cette conception . . . et certains Etats poussent l'illégalité jusqu'à l'incorporation des nationaux des pays occupés".[233] Although he states that no legal justification can be found to compel aliens either temporarily or permanently resident to do military service in wartime,[234]

---

national or political objects and police action to preserve social order or to protect the population against an invasion by savages". *Polites v The Commonwealth*, (1945) 70 CLR 60, 70. It held that regulations requiring aliens to serve in the Pacific region were valid, notwithstanding the rule. While several justices held that such service during the Second World War did not contravene the rule, Chief Justice Latham held that Parliament knew what it was doing and the legislation was valid under the Australian Constitution and thus valid. "It is not for a court to express an opinion upon the political propriety of this action. It is for the Government of the Commonwealth to consider its political significance, taking in to account the obvious risk of the Commonwealth having no ground for objection if Australians who happen to be in foreign countries are conscripted for military service there. Parliament has, in my opinion, placed upon the Executive the responsibility of making agreements with other countries which will remove international difficulties or of accepting the risk of such difficulties being created". *Polites v The Commonwealth*, 73. "During the Second World War most belligerent states compelled resident aliens to perform some kind of service connected with the war effort, even to the extent of making voluntary service in the armed forces an alternative to the performance of compulsory civilian duties". Shearer, *Starke's international law*, 315. "In the US, aliens can be called up for service, but have the right to opt out, in which event: (a) if they subsequently leave the US, they cannot return; and (b) if they stay, they will not be granted US citizenship. The position as to alien migrants, as distinct from temporarily resident aliens, is at least open to doubt. In 1966 the Australian Government purported to make alien migrants subject to compulsory service, formal protests being received from the USSR, Italy, Spain, and other countries". Shearer, *Starke's international law*, 315 note 13. For historical examples of the liability of aliens to military service see McNair (Lord), *International law opinions*, 113–37. It would seem that the further removed the alien is from the state, the smaller his or her duty is to it. In the context of political obligation, Simmons points out that physical presence does not lead to moral bonds, as the political obligations of citizens are not the same as those of visiting aliens. As evidence, he says "This again seems clearest in the event of war, where visiting aliens are not supposed by anyone to be bound to participate in the country's military efforts. In fact, this intuition is given voice in the principle of international law which specifies that aliens have no specifically 'political' duties toward their host countries, but are bound only to conform to the 'social order' of those countries". Simmons, *Moral principles and political obligations*, 34 note h.

[231] Aram Karamanoukian, *Les étrangers et le service militaire* (Paris: Editions A. Pedone, 1978), 163–68.

[232] Id., 219–23.

[233] (Author's translation: *does not conform to this idea . . . and certain states push the breach of the law as far as the enlistment of nationals of occupied countries*.) Id., 219.

[234] "Une personne vivant à l'étranger ne rompt pas ses liens juridiques avec sa patrie jusqu'à

Quant à l'incorporation d'office des étrangers résidants, elle semble prendre de plus en plus d'extension ; de grandes puissances comme de petites s'en rendent coupables. Une telle pratique est désapprouvée par la doctrine, et le droit international positif, coutumier et conventionnel, l'interdit. Mais le comportement continu des Etats apportant des atteintes au statut des étrangers dans le domaine pourrait conduire à la neutralisation de la coutume actuellement existante.[235]

Such practice, even if incompatible with international law, illustrates the limits inherent in Shearer's qualification of the imposition (to be approved of in terms of international law), of an obligation on the restricted category of resident aliens, to assist in the maintenance of public order, and in the event of a "sudden invasion".

If this is accepted, the national's duty of loyalty cannot be distinguished by an obligation to defend national territory as such, as resident aliens can be obliged to do so as well when the nation's territory itself is at risk. Obligation or a duty of loyalty as a consequence of nationality must thus relate to military service in terms of a system of conscription, and in relation to conflicts fought outside national territory, which aliens, even permanent residents, can clearly not be obliged to undertake.[236] It might be reduced to an obligation to take part physically in the "long-term" protection of the state, should municipal law require this. Prior to the United Nations Charter, which outlawed war with certain exceptions, it might have been labelled an obligation to take part physically in an element of the outward expression of the state's foreign policy. The limitations on the use of force contained in the Charter arguably serve to restrict the significance of such obligations in practical terms, at least in terms of recent practice.

---

ce qu'elle perde sa nationalité par une manifestation expresse de sa volonté, ou par une décision de l'Etat don't elle est la ressortissante. Donc elle continue à être soumise à la compétence personnelle de son pays d'origine qui limite, dans le cas d'imposition du service militaire, la compétence territoriale de l'Etat de résidence. La souveraineté territoriale ne peut aller jusqu'au rejet des « droits que chaque Etat peut réclamer pour ses nationaux en territoire étranger » ; elle ne peut imposer le service militaire aux personnes qui ne sont pas ses sujets sans le consentement de leur propre Etat". (Author's translation: *Someone living overseas does not break legal ties to his or her country until he or she loses his or her nationality through an expression of free will, or by a decision of his or her state of nationality. He or she therefore remains subject to the personal competence of his/her country of origin, which in the case of imposition of military service, limits the territorial competence of the state of residence. Territorial sovereignty does not go as far as to permit the rejection of the 'rights that each state can claim for its nationals in foreign territory', and does not allow for the imposition of military service on non-nationals without the consent of their own state.*) Id., 264–65.

[235] (Author's translation: *The conscription of resident aliens seems to be a more and more widespread practice, of which great as well as small powers are guilty. Doctrine disapproves of such practice and positive, customary and conventional international law forbids it. However continuous state practice infringing upon foreigners' status in this field could lead to the neutralization of current custom.*) Id., 264.

[236] For a study on the history of military service in Australia, Canada, France, Great Britain, New Zealand and the USA in terms of the general issue of why citizens do or do not consent to actions by the state, see Levi, *Consent, dissent, and patriotism.*

Issues of obligation or loyalty however, not only go to what the state can require individuals to undertake, but what it can prevent them from doing. This is essentially the basis for the security principle of jurisdiction. In terms of participation in armed conflict, international humanitarian law does not prevent the attribution of (privileged) combatant status, and thus the potential to become a prisoner of war, on the basis of nationality.[237] Membership in the armed forces of a party to the conflict brings with it the privilege to engage in hostilities and not be prosecuted simply on that basis, although serious breaches of humanitarian law of course attract sanction and universal jurisdiction. Thus, within the framework of the laws of armed conflict, a national could join enemy armed forces, and assuming she or he is not a mercenary or a spy, be entitled to immunity from prosecution for having taken part in hostilities as such. But such immunity does not entail exemption from prosecution for treason or similar crimes under municipal law.

> Any individual who falls into the power of a belligerent while serving in the enemy armed forces should be entitled to prisoner-of-war status no matter what his nationality may be, if he would be so entitled apart from any question of nationality ; subject to the right of the Detaining Power to charge him with treason, or a similar type of offense, under its municipal law and to try him in accordance with the guarantees contained in the relevant provisions of the Convention.[238]

The case of deserters who join the opposing side is similar, although they do not seem to benefit from the protections of the Geneva Conventions if captured by their (original) side.

> If such persons are captured by members of their own forces, they are entitled to receive from the soldiers capturing them the same treatment as any other captive, even though their national authority may decide, in accordance with national law, that they are not to be treated as enemy combatants and prisoners of war, but as members of its own forces liable to trial for treason. They may also be tried for treason after the termination of hostilities and their repatriation to their home country.[239]

But without the nationality of the state in question, it is hard to see how the same obligation related to loyalty could be imposed on aliens who are combatants under international law. This is especially so, given that the privilege to partake in hostilities as a combatant is a cornerstone of the modern law of armed conflict. Of course the

---

[237] See Article 43(2) of the Protocol additional to the Geneva Conventions of 12 August 1949, and relating to the protection of victims of international armed conflicts (Protocol I), of 8 June 1977 (entry into force: 7 December 1978). See Levie, "Prisoners of war in international armed conflicts", 74–76.

[238] Id.: 76.

[239] L. C. Green, *The contemporary law of armed conflict* (Manchester: Manchester University Press, 1993), 115–16. Levie distinguishes between deserters and defectors, noting that both become prisoners of war while in the power of the opposing side and that both may be tried for treason, but that defectors are not entitled to prisoner of war status. Levie, "Prisoners of war in international armed conflicts", 76–81.

same cannot be said for non-international armed conflicts, where humanitarian law contains no notion of privilege and the status of combatant does not exist. In those situations nationals and non-nationals alike may be held to the same standard of obligation or loyalty to the state, and be equally prosecuted for taking part in hostilities.

Along these lines, it may be argued that a higher standard of obligation or loyalty can be imposed against nationals, in terms of not taking up arms against the state in situations of international armed conflict, even when other persons could not be held responsible for the same conduct. But it would seem that states' municipal legislation has not always concurred with this delineation of an obligation of loyalty: a 19th century French statute held ex-French nationals to the same standard of obligation and loyalty as nationals, punishing them with death should they ever take up arms against their former country.[240] Today, Colombia's Constitution stipulates that former nationals who act against the national interest in an international war may be tried and sentenced for treason.[241]

Oppenheim remarks that naturalised persons might be seen as owing a greater duty of allegiance than the native born, pointing to the fact that states often apply deprivation of nationality as a penalty only to naturalised persons (in the form of denaturalisation).[242] But this is not the case everywhere. In September 2002 the Israeli government revoked the citizenship (nationality) of a native-born Israeli (Arab), Nahad Abu Kishaq, for allegedly having been involved in suicide bombings, with further cases for revocation pending.[243] Abu Kishaq had not been convicted of any crime, but was stripped of his citizenship under "Article 11(b) of the citizenship law, which grants

---

[240] George Cogordan, *La nationalité au point de vue des rapports internationaux* (Paris: L. Larose, Librairie-Éditeur, 1879), 246–47. Cogordan approves of the provision.

[241] *Constitución Política de la República de Colombia de 1991* (as amended until 2005) Article 97, Base de Datos Políticos de las Américas (internet), http://pdba.georgetown.edu/Constitutions/Colombia/col91.html, consulted 15 May 2006. The provision also states that Colombians by naturalisation and foreigners domiciled in Colombia may not be obliged to take up arms against their country of origin; Colombians naturalised abroad may not be obliged to fight against their "new" country of nationality. Ibid.

[242] Jennings and Watts, "Oppenheim's International Law", 887 note 3. Carter points out that "in the United States, a willed allegiance is required only of immigrants seeking to become citizens. . . . Even if one concedes that a national community is in fact desirable, our history teaches us to be suspicious of the loyalty oath, and our recent constitutional jurisprudence, for better or worse, teaches that an oath cannot be imposed". Stephen L. Carter, *The dissent of the governed. A meditation on law, religion, and loyalty* (Cambridge, Massachusetts: Harvard University Press, 1998), 13.

[243] Mazal Mualem and Jalal Bana, "Yishai revokes citizenship of Israeli Arab", *Ha'aretz*, 10 September 2002 (internet), http://www.haaretz.com, consulted 10 September 2002. See also Ross Dunn, "Citizenship Israel's new weapon in war against suicide bombers", *The Sydney Morning Herald* 2002, 10; Mazal Mualem, "I'm not Israeli, says Arab stripped of citizenship", *Ha'aretz*, 12 September 2002, 2.

the interior minister the authority to revoke the citizenship of anyone whose actions violate his obligation of loyalty to the state".[244]

Loyalty or obligation to the state thus arguably falls into three basic categories: (1) all persons can be held accountable to a state for acts against its security or financial interests; (2) resident aliens can be held to an even higher duty of loyalty in terms of being obliged to defend the state physically during an invasion. They cannot be forced to perform general military service; and (3) nationals are bound by all of the above, and in addition can be obliged to perform general military service, to fight for their state of nationality outside its borders, and may be obliged to avoid partaking in international hostilities against the state. While international law provides this basic framework, it is municipal law that defines the details of each of the three categories. And while states may place special obligations on their nationals in municipal law, by a special category of offence applicable only to their nationals and related to loyalty to the state, as demonstrated, this seems largely emotional in character, as states can and do criminalize the same conduct by non-resident aliens. The special context of a national's acts is illustrated by the judge's comment in sentencing Ana Montes for treason against the United States, upon her a conviction of spying for Cuba. "If you cannot love your country, . . . you should at least do it no harm".[245]

States may in fact choose to exempt foreign nationals from charges of treason and similar offences in order to boost confidence or perhaps make themselves more attractive as a place to live or do business. In 2003 the Hong Kong government reportedly amended its draft anti-subversion bill

> to exempt foreign nationals from treason charges, a move to reassure several hundred thousand affluent residents who have obtained citizenship elsewhere, most often Britain or Canada, as a precaution against a clampdown by Beijing.[246]

Because the definition of what constitutes loyalty or obligation in municipal law varies from state to state, it can be said to be related to the concept embodied in each state's municipal law of the appropriate relationship between the individual and the state. This might be termed a national concept of human rights. At any given point in time, it must also reflect social norms, including ideas of patriotism.[247] For

---

[244] Mualem and Bana, "Yishai revokes citizenship of Israeli Arab".

[245] Tim Golden, "Unapologetic American who spied for Cuba gets 25 years' jail", *The Sydney Morning Herald*, 18 October 2002, 12.

[246] Tyler Marshall, "HK subversion bill sparks alarm on human rights", *The Sydney Morning Herald*, 15–16 February 2003, 21.

[247] For a discussion of moral duties and legal obligations, including the duties of citizenship, see Simmons, *Moral principles and political obligations*, 16. Simmons relates political obligation to citizenship, and distinguishes this from moral obligations. Id., 32. Gans raises the connection made by many authors between the duty to obey the law and political obligation, or "the 'good citizen' concept, that of the citizen who plays his or her part in the support and defence of his country and its institutions". Gans, *Philosophical anarchism and political disobedience*, 8.

example, stating an opinion critical of a government official may be uncontroversial in one state, protected in another, judged defamatory in a third, held to be seditious in a fourth, and in a fifth constitute a violation of an obligation of loyalty such that the orator's nationality might be revoked.[248] Notions of loyalty (or "allegiance" in that sense) and obligation in municipal law thus depend on the state's own national concept of democratic rights or entitlements, and the individual's position vis-à-vis the state.[249]

On the other hand, a state's municipal legislation does not have to have a concept of, or rules regarding, loyalty (or "allegiance" in that sense). Instead, loyalty may be seen as a natural part of every person's emotional existence within the state. Vattel saw reason and individual interest dictating such emotion:

> *The love and affection of a man for the State of which he is a member is a necessary result of the wise and rational love which he owes to himself, since his own happiness is bound up with that of his country, a sentiment which should also follow from the contract which he has made with the social body. He promised to procure its welfare and safety as far as should be in his power. How, then, can he serve it zealously, faithfully, and courageously if he has no real love for it?*[250]

Whether multiple nationality affects this balance of interests and emotions is an important question, but one which is arguably divorced from the specific legal obligations, or potential legal obligations, attached to nationality.

---

[248] It was only in 2005 that the People's Republic of China declared that the number of victims of natural disasters would no longer be considered a state secret. China Daily, "Natural disaster toll no longer state secret, 12 September 2005 (internet), http://www.chinadaily.com.cn/english/doc/2005–09/12/content_477 122.htm, consulted 19 March 2005.

[249] In most states these ideas have changed markedly over time, most recently in relation to concepts of fundamental human rights, and their international context.

[250] Vattel, *The law of nations or the principles of natural law applied to the conduct and to the affairs of nations and of sovereigns*, 51. Carter points out that the American Revolution announced by the Declaration of Independence was "an act of disallegiance, the breaking of the tie of presumptive obligation that we describe as loyalty". Carter, *The dissent of the governed. A meditation on law, religion, and loyalty*, 4. He postulates that the Declaration's famous idea that governments must be based on the consent of the governed belies the real justification behind the American colonists' breaking the tie of allegiance to George III, namely the lack of capacity for dissent. He emphasises that what "should perhaps be treated as the heart of the Declaration [are the words]: 'In every stage of these Oppressions We have Petitioned for Redress in the most humble terms: Our repeated Petitions have been answered only by repeated injury. A Prince, whose character is thus marked by every act which may define a Tyrant, is unfit to be the ruler of a free people'". Carter, *The dissent of the governed. A meditation on law, religion, and loyalty*, 5.

3.1 Morality and duties to the state on the basis of nationality, and the essence of nationality

Having considered the legal characterisation and essence of obligation toward the state in terms of nationality in both international and municipal law, note should be made of arguments as to the moral underpinning of such obligations. Of course the topic can in no way be dealt with exhaustively here. It will be seen that the reasoning posited by various authors (the views of Goodin and Miller are taken as examples here[251]) bears upon the essence of nationality, and whether it embodies a relationship between the state and the individual, or whether it amounts to a status of the individual vis-à-vis the state, which can be compared to the analysis submitted herein in relation to municipal and international law.

Goodin asks "what is so special about our fellow countrymen", and concludes that "in the present world system, it is often – perhaps ordinarily – wrong to give priority to the claims of our compatriots".[252] What might seem to be a relatively confronting conclusion to many is reasoned along the following lines:[253] individuals feel (or are seen to owe) special duties toward persons and groups to whom they are linked by a special relationship, which implies that they should treat them well, or better than others. This does not hold true for compatriots however, as under international law, governments may (or must) often treat aliens better than their own nationals. This might be premised on

> *nation-states [being] . . . conceptualized as ongoing mutual-benefit societies . . . [in which] imposing harms is always permissible – but only on the condition that some positive good comes of it, and only on condition that those suffering the harm are in some sense party to the society in question.*[254]

But Goodin reasons that the "mutual benefit" model cannot constitute the moral underpinning of the nation-state as, bearing resident aliens in mind, "formal status is only imperfectly and contingently related to who is actually generating and receiving the benefits".[255] He thus concludes that along moral lines, the special duties we owe to countrymen must in fact be a function of the duties we owe other human beings generally, according to what he terms an "assigned responsibility model".

---

[251] See also for example Friderik Klampfer, "Does membership in a nation as such generate any special duties?", in *Nationalism and ethnic conflict. Philosophical perspectives*, ed. Nenad Miscevic (Chicago: Open Court Publishing Company, 2000), 219–238; Daniel Weinstock, "National partiality: confronting the intuitions", in *Nationalism and ethnic conflict. Philosophical perspectives*, ed. Nenad Miscevic (Chicago: Open Court Publishing Company, 2000), 133–155.

[252] Robert E. Goodin, "What is so special about our countrymen?", *Ethics* (1988) vol. 98, no. 4, 663–686, 663 and 686.

[253] See generally Ibid.

[254] Id., 675.

[255] Id., 676.

National boundaries simply visit upon those particular state agents special responsibility
for discharging those general obligations vis-à-vis those individuals who happen to be
their own citizen. . . . [W]e have been assigned responsibility for compatriots, in a way
that we have not been assigned any responsibility for foreigners. . . . What justifies states
in pressing the particular claims of their own citizens is, on my account, the presumption
that everyone has been assigned an advocate/protector.[256]

In terms of the moral underpinning of the relationship between the individual and the
state, Goodin's proposal seems to view the nature of the reciprocal obligations
involved along the same lines that have been used herein to describe nationality: the
allocation of individuals to particular states for purposes of international law. According to his view, morality dictates that nationality can be no more than a status that
permits human beings to organise themselves on the international level. It might be
added that the fact that states use the quality of their ties to individuals to decide who
has priority among them in relation to a particular individual does not seem to detract
from this reasoning. Effective nationality is only an issue when states compete with
each other in relation to an individual, and does not bear on the quality of the individual's relationship or ties to the states in question on the municipal level.

Yet accepting Goodin's reasoning also means accepting his view of morality and
the nature of the state. His fundamental premise is that

there are some "general duties" that we have toward other people, merely because they
are people. Over and above those, there are also some "special duties" that we have
toward particular individuals because they stand in some special relation to us.[257]

His reasoning might for example be questioned by maintaining that there are no such
general duties, or that what he calls "special treatment" is not really "special" but
normal. As long as the state is devoid of an ethnic, biological, or even emotional
notion of the nation, as it is purported to be in international law, Goodin's argument
seems hard to assail. But if the state is conceived of as more than that, as it often is,
is it perhaps simply easier to note that the state is not based on moral considerations
as he defines them?[258]

---

[256] Id., 682–84. He highlights two crucial differences in terms of effect between his model,
and the mutual-benefit-model: if society is conceived in terms of mutual-benefit, the helpless
or unproductive may be cast out, whereas if states' responsibilities stem from a general duty
to mankind, "casting off useless members of society would simply amount to shirking their
assigned responsibility". Goodin, "What is so special about our countrymen?", 683. Secondly,
he reasons that mutual-benefit dictates intercourse among states only on the basis of self-
interest, whereas assignment would dictate that "sufficient resources ought to have been given
to every such state agent to allow for the effective discharge of those responsibilities. . . . If
some states prove incapable of discharging their responsibilities effectively, then they should
either be reconstituted or assisted". Goodin, "What is so special about our countrymen?", 685.
[257] Goodin, "What is so special about our countrymen?", 663.
[258] Goodin challenges this by stating that "[n]othing in this argument claims that one's

Miller rejects the view that "attribut[ing] deeper significance to boundaries is to be explained as some sort of moral error", arguing that "once we see why national boundaries make a difference, we shall be in a position to see what space they leave for duties that transcend those limits".[259]

> *[I]f we start out with selves already heavily laden with particularist commitments, including national loyalties, we may be able to rationalize those commitments from a universalist perspective. Whether we should seek to do so is another matter, and it depends on how successfully we can resist the pull of a universalism which . . . is so prominent a feature of contemporary ethical culture.*[260]

Although he initially adopts an historic-biological view of nationality, his later use of the term does largely seem to coincide with the state. He argues that loyalty to co-nationals can in fact be based on both universalist and particularist perspectives. In particularist terms, although both nationality and ethnicity may be based on fraudulent assumptions and beliefs, the fact that such constitutive beliefs are held in fact, means that more than just borders separate states. He thus concludes that the nation (or here, the state) is "potentially a worthy object of allegiance".[261]

> *Some nations are just not viable, either for internal or for external reasons; but where nationality works, so to speak, members of the nation can exercise at the collective level the equivalent of autonomy at the individual level; that is, they can shape their future (including their own future character) by conscious decision, on the basis of a self-understanding informed by a common past.*[262]

But he also sees a universalist argument for sentiment or obligation to co-nationals, based on the contention that ideas of obligation to human beings generally must be practical, and related to consensus in terms of the relationship between the individual and the wider collective.

> *We do not yet have a global community in the sense that is relevant to justice as distribution according to need. There is no consensus that the needs of other human beings considered merely as such make demands of justice on me, nor is there sufficient agreement about what is to count as a need. It is therefore unrealistic to suppose that the choice lies between distributive justice worldwide and distributive justice within national societies. . . . The universalist case for nationality, therefore, is that it creates communities with the widest*

---

nationality is a matter of indifference. There are all sorts of reasons for wishing national boundaries to be drawn in such a way that you are lumped together with others 'of your own kind'. . . . My only point is that those are all considerations that bear on the drawing and redrawing of boundaries; they are not, in and of themselves, the source of special responsibilities toward people with those shared characteristics". Id., 682.

[259] David Miller, "The ethical significance of nationality", *Ethics* (1988) vol. 98, no. 4, 647–662, 647 and 48.

[260] Id., 662.

[261] Id., 659.

[262] Ibid.

feasible membership, and therefore with the greatest scope for redistribution in favor of the needy.[263]

By adopting existing commitments and emotions as a point of departure, Miller arguably sees the morality underpinning nationality in terms of the real, existing relationship in practical terms, thereby deriving justifications for the obligations that ensue. Or, obligations to the world at large, if not backed up by a consensus that such duties exist, and which may (more egregiously) be unimplementable, cannot be said to be dictated by morality.

It is interesting to note that while Goodin's universalist concept of the morality underpinning loyalty and obligation seems to conform to notion (and consequences) of nationality on the international plane, making nationality a status, or means for allocation of individuals, Miller's argument would seem to see a moral basis for the relationship of nationality on the municipal level. In any case, whether nationality is a status or a relationship, and the moral grounds for the obligations involved, clearly depends on views of the nature of the state.

3.2 Note on "Temporary Allegiance"

"Temporary allegiance, equally, characterized and comprised the duty of the non-subject or alien present within the State or otherwise constructively a subject towards the latter".[264]

It is clear that 'temporary allegiance' means neither "nationality" nor "loyalty":

> *It is not disputed in this case that a citizen in enemy country owes temporary allegiance to the alien government, must obey its laws and may not plot or act against it . . . 'This defendant, while residing in the German Reich, owed qualified allegiance to it. She was obliged to obey its laws, and she was equally amenable to punishment with citizens of that country if she did not do so. At the same time, the defendant, while residing in Germany during the period stated in the indictment, owed to her Government, that is, the United States Government, full, complete and true allegiance.*[265]

The use of the terms "temporary national character" or "temporary allegiance" seems both inapt and out of place in current usage, as far as representing the status or obligation to which they refer. Such useage is unhelpful as it causes confusion. As has been seen, a strong case is presented by authors for the term "allegiance" to be defined as a synonym of "nationality" in international law, as the common connotation of "allegiance" implies a specific duty of loyalty that should be distinguished. In addition, both "nationality" and "allegiance" relate traditionally to the personal jurisdiction a state exercises over its nationals, whereas what is referred to here is the territorial jurisdiction a state exercises over non-nationals. But the status, obligations,

---

[263] Id., 661.

[264] Parry et al., eds., *Encyclopaedic dictionary of international law*, 17.

[265] Gillars v United States, 182 F.2d 962 at 980 (DDC 1950) cited in Whiteman, *Digest of international law*, vol. 8, 4.

and rights of people who do fall into this category vary greatly from place to place. Persons who are "permanent residents", "residents", "nationals", or "tourists" may possess varying degrees of rights, entitlements and obligations under municipal law, but the basic standard of obedience or respect for municipal law to which they are subject should not be confused either with loyalty or nationality.

D. THE IMPORTANCE OF NATIONALITY

It should be clear from the summary presented in this chapter of the rules related to nationality in municipal and international law, and the consequences of nationality in those areas, that nationality is still relevant in very practical terms for both individuals and states. Whether multiple nationality as such is relevant, and to what extent, is arguably another question, to be addressed in the following chapter.

Arguments surrounding the importance of nationality in a macro or political context have already been mentioned in chapter one, and related to issues of globalisation and movements toward, or away from, political and economic integration, the movement of people, the rights of individuals, and the needs of states. On the one hand, state practice toward multiple nationality may have effects that make such trends more or less possible or desirable, or conversely, such trends may influence state practice toward multiple nationality.

Lauterpacht characterised the context and importance of nationality in 1948 as follows:

> It is through the medium of their nationality that individuals can normally enjoy benefits from the existence of the Law of Nations. This is a fact which has consequences over the whole area of International Law. Such individuals as do not possess any nationality enjoy no protection whatever, and if they are aggrieved by a State they have no way of redress, since there is no State which would be competent to take their case in hand. As far as the Law of Nations is concerned, there is, apart from restraints of morality or obligations expressly laid down by treaty, no restriction whatever to cause a State to abstain from maltreating to any extent such stateless individuals. On the other hand, if individuals who possess nationality are wronged abroad, it is, as a rule, their home State only and exclusively which has a right to ask for redress, and these individuals themselves have no such right. It is for this reason that the question of nationality is very important for the Law of Nations.[266]

In contrast to Lauterpacht's characterisation, it has been argued that international law does today place restrictions on states' treatment of individuals, whether nationals, aliens, or stateless persons, albeit restricted to basic or fundamental rules of humanity or human rights. In terms of the characterisation of the value of nationality, does current state practice toward multiple nationality influence the extent to

---

[266] Oppenheim, *International law. A treatise*, 583.

which nationality is still the major link between the individual and the benefits of international law? But Lauterpacht's point of departure in viewing the importance of nationality in terms of protection of the individual cannot be abandoned glibly. This is because the real challenge to the concept of nationality within the international community of sovereign states and international law, as he indicated, remains the position of stateless persons, who receive no benefit from nationality at whatsoever.

Chapter 4

Views and Treatment of Multiple Nationality in Historical Perspective and the Influence of Human Rights

I rather believe with Faulkner, "The past is never dead, it is not even past," and this for the simple reason that the world we live in at any moment is the world of the past; it consists of the monuments and the relics of what has been done by men for better or worse; its facts are always what has become.... In other words, it is quite true that the past haunts us; it is the past's function to haunt us who are present and wish to live in the world as it really is, that is, has become what it is now.[1]

Hannah Arendt

The concept of multiple nationality and debates in relation to it have followed, and evolved with, fundamental changes in the structure of society, and the emergence of the nation-state and the consequent development of international law. Views and treatment of multiple nationality cannot be separated from views and treatment of nationality itself, and its consequences, reflecting the central issues of the power of states over their nationals, and in relation to each other in their mutual dealings. Such

---

[1] Hannah Arendt, "Home to Roost: A Bicentennial Address", *New York Review of Books* (1975) 26 June 1975, 3–6, 6.

debate continues of necessity today, and can be expected to continue in the future. It reflects the reality that the relationship between the individual and the state, or the powers of one in relation to the other, does not remain static in perception or deed in the course of human government and affairs. Likewise, it can be assumed that international relations between states will continue to evolve, such that states' treatment of multiple nationality will also continue to change. This is not to argue however, that the trend toward degrees of tolerance or acceptance of multiple nationality noted herein will of necessity continue, and no predictions on the future of the phenomenon commonly referred to as globalisation and its effects are offered.

This chapter sketches historical considerations and developments in relation to the treatment of multiple nationality, and presents in greater detail more recent arguments on its nature, effects, and relative desirability.

A. THE DELIMITATION OF NATIONALITY IN RELATION TO MULTIPLE NATIONALITY

One of the primary, albeit perhaps almost unnoticed, consequences for individuals of the birth of the international community of sovereign states in the 17th century was the emergence of the modern relationship or status of nationality.[2] The ties between the individual and various levels of sovereigns in feudal Europe were complicated, and related to what de Castro classifies as several horizontal and vertical personal and territorial relationships.[3] With the emergence of the nation state, the territorial link between individual and sovereign (state) replaced, or took precedence over, personal links. "Allegiance", which in England had been conceived of as part of such personal links, emerged as one of the consequences of the territorial connection.[4] But today, even in countries such as the United Kingdom, where the Sovereign still exists in the form of a natural person, it is highly doubtful whether remnants of obligations of personal allegiance to her persist in the absence of specific legal provisions to that effect. What is perhaps remarkable is that "allegiance" continued to be a source of British nationality until 1948, as opposed to the consequence of nationality that it is conceived of by most authors today.[5]

---

[2] Although the French Revolution in 1789 is often cited as the birth of the nation-state. John Torpey, *The invention of the passport – surveillance, citizenship and the state* (Cambridge: Cambridge University Press, 2000), 2.

[3] F. de Castro, "La nationalité la double nationalité et la supra-nationalité", *Recueil des cours (Académie de droit international)*, (1961) vol. 102, no. 1, 515–634, 543. For a summary of the development of nationality, from its feudal roots until modern times, see generally Castro, "La nationalité la double nationalité et la supra-nationalité", 526–87.

[4] Nissim Bar-Yaacov, *Dual nationality*, (London: Stevens & Sons Ltd., 1961).

[5] See S. K. Agrawala and M. Koteswara Rao, "Nationality and international law in Indian perspective", in *Nationality and international law in Asian perspective*, ed. Ko Swan Sik (Dordrecht:

Even before Grotius and the development of the modern nation-state and international law, the notion of one individual having ties, even reciprocal rights and obligations, to more than one sovereign, was not unknown in feudal Europe. Indeed, Parry cites a source for the existence "of true dual allegiance during the Norman and Angevin times (as distinct from the duality of lesser feudal ties)".[6] Questions surrounding personal ties to more than one sovereign thus seem to have emerged even before the nation-state took its current form, as long as the relationship between sovereign and subject has been a matter of legal definition, and as long as different systems for the attribution of nationality, or similar subject status, have been used. As already mentioned in chapter two, it would be inapt however to extend nationality's specific roots too far into history, and Greek and Roman systems of legal status for the individual do not, for example, provide useful analogies to the present situation. This is expanded upon below. Sucharitkul points out that

> the concept of nationality in contemporary international law is a product of recent developments in international relations. Nationality did not occupy a prominent place in primitive international law either as applied in Asia or elsewhere. Accordingly, in Thai legislation, as in the legislation of other States, the regulation of nationality is of comparatively recent growth.[7]

Returning to the feudal origins of European ideas of nationality, Parry rejects claims that a "rule of Europe", or tacit agreement that sovereigns would attribute nationality according to place of birth, or jus soli, exclusively, existed until the *Code Napoléon*.[8]

Martinus Nijhoff Publishers, 1990), 65–123, 67, who points out that India "had decided to continue to be a Commonwealth country and by virtue of that all its citizens were to be regarded as 'British subjects' or Commonwealth citizens' entitled to enjoy all privileges and benefits to which they had been used to in the pre-republic days under the laws of the United Kingdom. This position was somewhat anomalous, since the basis of the British nationality law was the common law doctrine of allegiance to the British Crown, while after independence neither India nor Indians could owe any such allegiance to the British Crown". Regarding the divisibility of the Crown, see D. P. O'Connell, "The Crown in the British Commonwealth", *The International and Comparative Law Quarterly* (1957) vol. 6, no. 1, 103–125.

[6] Clive Parry, ed., *A British digest of international law*, vol. 5 (London: Stevens & Sons, 1965), 11. See also Castro, "La nationalité la double nationalité et la supra-nationalité", 527–41.

[7] Sompong Sucharitkul, "Thai nationality in international perspective", in *Nationality and international law in Asian perspective*, ed. Ko Swan Sik (Dordrecht: Martinus Nijhoff Publishers, 1990), 453–491,453. Recalling the difference between ideas of nationality and citizenship, Castro points out that while examples from Greece and Rome are not apt to analysis of the origin of modern nationality, they did influence nationality as it currently relates to ideas of citizenship rights. Castro, "La nationalité la double nationalité et la supra-nationalité", 527.

[8] A claim made, for example, by Baty. Théodore Baty, "La double nationalité est-elle possible?", *Revue de droit international et de législation comparée* (1926) vol. 7, 622–632, 623. Arguments about the nature and relative desirability of jus soli versus jus sanguinis attribution of nationality have not subsided. Responding to a reporter's statement that jus soli has a reputation as being progressive whereas jus sanguinis is seen as reactionary, Weil states that

He states that in England, jus sanguinis became established in addition to the pre-existing jus soli at least in the fourteenth century.[9] The effect of the concurrent operation of the two main systems of attribution of nationality is of course to produce a greater number of instances of multiple nationality, hence the significance of this assertion. He also makes clear that the practice of the United Kingdom for most of its history demonstrates both explicit and implicit admission of the existence of multiple nationality, which did not however mean that the foreign nationality was necessarily given any effect in British law. Thus, a dual allegiance might exist, but the quality of the tie between the national and his or her state might not be affected by such other nationality.

In Europe, increased freedom of movement produced by the elimination of feudal ties made the early 19th century the "golden age of the codification of citizenship laws, a process directly motivated by the need to establish who did and who did not have a right to the benefits of membership in these states".[10] Torpey agrees with

---

"C'est, en effet, le code civil de Napoléon qui, en 1803, donne très officiellement droit de cité au *jus sanguinis* – "est français l'enfant né d'un père français" – mais il ne faut pas y voir la connotation ethnique, voire ethniciste, qu'on lui applique à notre époque. Il s'agit là, en réalité, d'un progrès, car nous assistons à l'émergence d'un droit de la personne, en opposition au droit féodal qui prévalait avant la Révolution, et selon lequel tout individu résidant sur le territoire du royaume appartenait à son souverain maître, le roi en l'occurrence. Lorsque l'on quittait le territoire, on perdait *ipso facto* tous les droits afférents à la condition de sujet du roi, notamment celui de succession. L'Ancien Régime était donc soumis au *jus soli*, que nous considérons aujourd'hui comme le plus égalitaire mais que la Révolution battit en brèche au motif qu'il légitimait un droit d'allégeance. (Author's translation: *It was in fact Napoleon's 1803 Civil Code that officially provided citizenship rights according to* jus sanguinis – *"the child born of a French father is French" – but we should not see in this the ethnic, or rather ethnicist, connotation applied in our times. In reality, this represented a step forward, as we see here the emergence of personal rights as opposed to the feudal law which prevailed before the revolution, according to which all individuals residing in the kingdom belonged to their sovereign lord, in this case the king. When one departed the territory one lost,* ipso facto, *all rights related to the status of being the king's subject, notably the right of inheritance. The Ancien Régime was based on jus soli, which we consider today the most egalitarian system, but which the revolution rejected on grounds that it legitimated feudal obligations of allegiance.*) Daniel Bermond, "La nationalité française: und histoire à rebondissements (interview with Patrick Weil)", *Label France* (Janvier-Mars 2003) vol. 49, 34–36, 34–35. Weil states that France reinstated the *jus soli* principle in 1889 in response to strong immigration to France and Algeria. Bermond, "La nationalité française: und histoire à rebondissements (interview with Patrick Weil)", 36. In practical terms, Torpey links the adoption of both major systems of attribution of nationality (*jus soli* and *jus sanguinis*) to states' interests in "holding onto" people. Whereas *jus soli* is ideal in a world where people do not move around, *jus sanguinis* is ideally suited to a migratory world. He labels jus soli "sedentary mercantilism", and jus sanguinis "migratory mercantilism". John Torpey, *The invention of the passport – surveillance, citizenship and the state* (Cambridge: Cambridge University Press, 2000), 72.

[9] Parry, ed., *A British digest of international law*, 10 and 92.

[10] Torpey, *The invention of the passport – surveillance, citizenship and the state*, 59 and 71 and generally 57–92.

Brubaker that the dynamics of international relations affected the legal delimitation of nationality in European states, but argues that

> *the distinction between "internal" and "external" – remained in many respects inchoate at this time. . . . [U]nlike the situation in post-revolutionary France, many German towns during the first half of the nineteenth century retained rights to define membership and exclude non-members that were incompatible with citizenship systems conceived on the model of the internally unified nation-state, in which all were putatively equal before the central government.[11]*

Relative levels of centralization of government can thus also be cited in the delimitation of nationals, and it should be remembered that in many European states, until the early 19th century, people from neighbouring provinces were "foreigners" on the same terms as people from other countries.[12]

It should be noted that the author's citation of developments in Europe is not intended to dismiss or ignore the situation of other states. It is the author's intent to engage in an analysis from a global perspective, but as Ko points out, eurocentrism in international law may be "sad rather than reproachful", as far as it reflects a practical reality of European and American factual contexts and accessibility to historical records, as opposed to political bias.[13] But it may rightly be inquired why the regulation of nationality and discussion of issues related to multiple nationality seems to have begun in European and American states. In this sense the development of the modern nation-state in Europe within a context of many states in relatively close geographical proximity, significant population movements between areas, overlapping and disputed historical claims to both persons and territory, and finally colonisation of other parts of the world, is certainly relevant.[14] If Europe provides fertile ground to examine the beginnings of modern concepts of nationality and multiple nationality, it is in this context.

---

[11] Id., 72.

[12] Id., 9. Torpey remarks that in France the concept of "foreigner" moved away from the local level in the late medieval period. Torpey, *The invention of the passport – surveillance, citizenship and the state*, 20.

[13] Ko Swan Sik, ed., *Nationality and International Law in Asian Perspective* (Dordrecht: Martinus Nijhoff Publishers, 1990), xliii. de Padua, writing in 1985, states that in relation to regulation of multiple nationality, "Asia, however, lags behind. Except for a handful of bilateral treaties dealing primarily with overseas Chinese, there has been little discussion, much less action, on the topic of multiple nationality in the region. Yet the potential for conflict in Asia remains great, what with Indochinese refugees accumulating on Thai and Philippine soil – population movements similar to those in the wake of world wars which gave rise to innumerable cases of dual nationality. Moreover, the Chinese are on the move again, this time fleeing the impending reversion of Hongkong to Chinese territory. Dan Albert S. de Padua, "Ambiguous allegiance: multiple nationality in Asia", *Philippine Law Journal* (1985) vol. 60, no. 2, 239–267, 241.

[14] Torpey goes further, predicating his study on the idea that "the dominance of Western states in the period examined has been relatively clear-cut, and . . . the imposition of Western ways on most of the rest of the world has been one of the most remarkable features of the

This argument finds support from historical developments related to the regulation of nationality in other parts of the world. Chiu points out for example for example that imperial China under the Manchu government (Qing Dynasty) saw no need to enact a nationality law as long as its official policy of isolation was in effect, banning the immigration of foreigners and the emigration of Chinese. Another version of the Celestial Empire's position is perhaps less flattering:

> *Chinese who were so unwise and disloyal as to prefer living among barbarians to remaining in China to tend the ancestral tombs and share the benefits of civilisation were unworthy of the protection of the imperial government.*[15]

Changes in the policy of isolation, as well as pressures from foreign governments, led of necessity to the adoption of a nationality law in 1909. In 1907 the Dutch in the Netherlands Indies attempted to force Chinese living in Java to become Netherlands subjects, arguing that as China had no law on nationality, it had no right to claim any jurisdiction over ethnic Chinese living in Java, and no right to protect them.[16]

Hosokawa states that until the 19th century there were no international factors that might have influenced Japanese laws or views on nationality: from the eighth century on the population had stabilised into a homogenous group; there was little inward flow from, or outward flow to, foreign countries; there were no overseas territories; and ties with foreign nations were limited.[17] These factors were reinforced by the closure of Japan to virtually all outside contacts by the Tokugawa Shogunate from the 17th century until the restoration of imperial Japan by the Meiji Emperor in 1868. It is thus noteworthy that Japan's opening to the foreign world was matched just three

---

era.... This should not be taken to imply any denigration of non-Western cultures, but only the recognition that those societies have not been sufficiently powerful to impose their ways upon the world". Torpey, *The invention of the passport – surveillance, citizenship and the state*, 2–3.

[15] Jerome Alan Cohen and Hungdah Chiu, *People's China and international law. A documentary study*, vol. 1 (Princeton, NJ: Princeton University Press, 1973), 746. de Padua cites a Chinese Imperial Edict of 1709: "Once a Chinese – always a Chinese". de Padua, "Ambiguous allegiance: multiple nationality in Asia", 258.

[16] Hungdah Chiu, "Nationality and international law in Chinese perspective – with special reference to the period before 1950 and the practice of the administration in Taipei", in *Nationality and international law in Asian perspective*, ed. Ko Swan Sik (Dordrecht: Martinus Nijhoff Publishers, 1990), 27–64, 63. and Cohen and Chiu, *People's China and international law. A documentary study*, 748. See also generally Hellmuth Hecker, "Die Staatsangehörigkeit von Chinesen, die vor 1900 nach Niederländisch-Indien eingewandert sind, und ihrer Nachkommen", in *Gutachten zum internationalen Recht*, ed. Hellmuth Hecker, *Werkhefte des Instituts für Internationale Angelegenheiten der Universität Hamburg* (Hamburg, Frankfurt: Alfred Metzner Verlag GmbH, 1975).

[17] Kiyoshi Hosokawa, "Japanese nationality in international perspective," in *Nationality and international law in Asian perspective*, ed. Ko Swan Sik (Dordrecht: Martinus Nijhoff Publishers, 1990), 177–253, 179–81.

years later in 1871 by a family registration law, and in 1873 by the first legislation on nationality.[18]

Likewise, the case of Thailand seems to indicate that movement of people and contact with foreign nations was a determinative factor in developments related to the delimitation of nationals. Sucharitkul asserts that although Thailand experienced both conflict over territory, and significant movements of people, policies of non-discrimination and assimilation from 1293 onwards meant that there was no particular need for a specific determination of nationality, as all people were accorded national treatment. It was only the regime of extra-territoriality insisted upon by European powers in the 19th and 20th centuries that led indirectly to the first modern nationality enactment in 1913.[19]

For many states, colonisation and political status as opposed to migration seem to have been the determinative factors as far as the genesis of treatment of nationality generally, and views on multiple nationality. Sucharitkul maintains that

> with the exception of Thailand and a handful of other States, the Asian nations are newly independent States with new nationalities. Each of these States has followed a different historical path in its legal development, undergoing changes as necessary consequences of the process of colonization and decolonization.[20]

The situation of both Indonesia and the Philippines, the former ruled by the Netherlands, the latter by Spain and then the United States, demonstrates that attitudes toward nationality evinced by newly independent states emerging from colonisation are affected by the specifics of the colonial and post-colonial experience.[21]

B. VIEWS OF THE RELEVANCE OF MULTIPLE NATIONALITY

It is not the author's purpose to chronicle the extent to which each state historically rejected, recognised, or incorporated considerations related to multiple nationality into its municipal legal order. It is important however, to discern when such concerns began to be raised on the plane of international law itself.[22] Historically, views and

---

[18] Id., 190–91.

[19] Sucharitkul, "Thai nationality in international perspective", 462–63.

[20] Id., 454.

[21] See Irene R. Cortes and Raphael Perpetuo M. Lotilla, "Nationality and international law from the Philippine perspective", in *Nationality and international law in Asian perspective*, ed. Ko Swan Sik (Dordrecht: Martinus Nijhoff Publishers, 1990), 335–422, 339, 342–8, and Ko Swan Sik and Teuku Moh. Rhadie, "Nationality and international law in Indonesian perspective", in *Nationality and international law in Asian perspective*, ed. Ko Swan Sik (Dordrecht: Martinus Nijhoff Publishers, 1990), 125–176, 133 and 141.

[22] Spiro notes that the term "dual nationality" was not used to describe the phenomenon of an attachment by the individual to more than one state until the turn of the 20th century, and

practice in relation to multiple nationality seem to fall into two principal categories, those that regard the attribution of another nationality as irrelevant to the individual's relationship to the state, and those that regard it as relevant. Over time, a variation on the latter view seems to have taken hold in the late 19th, or early 20th century in the form of disapproval of multiple nationality and its effects, such that efforts at its elimination became a preoccupation of international law and relations.

Views that multiple nationality is irrelevant to the individual's relationship to the state might go so far as to take the form of a denial of its existence, or even an opinion that multiple nationality is a legal impossibility under municipal law. But even such seemingly unrealistic views demonstrate practice that still falls within a spectrum of levels of recognition of foreign nationality and its effects on a country's municipal laws. In this instance, the state that denies the existence of an individual's other nationality simply maintains in effect that it will not recognise a foreign state's relationship to a person it considers to be its national. It is in some ways ironic that this approach actually seems closer to tacit approval of multiple nationality, when compared to the state that withdraws its nationality on grounds of opposition to multiple nationality.

The latter case is an example of state practice that regards multiple nationality as relevant to its relations to natural persons and to other states, in what might be characterised as an intolerant or disapproving attitude. The relevance and intolerance are reflected by the fact that the state deems it necessary to eliminate the status itself by unilateral withdrawal of its own nationality.[23] An example of state practice that deems multiple nationality relevant in a tolerant or perhaps even approving sense is the state that does not withdraw its nationality on the basis of multiple nationality, but instead deals with some of the effects or consequences of multiple nationality.

It should be noted that the characterisation of such practice as "tolerant" or in some cases even "approving" is only in relation to multiple nationality as such, as the related state practice may or may not facilitate the lives of the individuals affected. For example, states that do not afford consular or diplomatic protection to their citizens in countries that also consider them nationals, by definition do not assist their (multiple) nationals in certain cases.[24] In its consideration of the application of the principle of effective nationality in the case of multiple nationals, the International Law Commission pointed out that

---

that it was seen before that as an issue principally related to conflicts of law. Peter J. Spiro, "Dual nationality and the meaning of citizenship", *Emory Law Review* (1997) vol. 46, no. 4, 1412–1485, 1431. While the this proposition is supported by the author's arguments, certain state practice outlined below, for example that of Spain, dates the use of the term in the modern context earlier.

[23] Spiro notes the prevalence of two doctrines that states adopt in order to promote an exclusive relationship between themselves and their nationals, expatriation upon naturalization, and forced election between nationalities held. Id., 1432.

[24] This is not the same as when states refuse consular or diplomatic protection to their nationals generally. Piotrowicz points out that a refusal to provide such protection to trafficked

in addition, dual nationality conferred a number of advantages on those who held two nationalities and the question was raised why they should not suffer disadvantages as well.[25]

On the other hand, states also conclude treaties dealing with the military service of multiple nationals, which arguably facilitates their lives.

C. THE ORIGINS OF STATE PRACTICE TOWARD MULTIPLE NATIONALITY: SEMEL CIVIS, SEMPER CIVIS

It is impossible to point to a specific point in time when issues of multiple nationality as such can be said to have emerged into the consciousness of states in terms of their international relations, and rights vis-à-vis one another. Certainly Spiro's assessment that "dual nationality has for several centuries been held in almost reflexive distaste" is overstated and too broad a proposition in terms of state practice generally, although it reflects the preoccupation of the United States in the early to mid 19th century to ensure a right of expatriation from European countries of naturalised US citizens, and the opinion of later writers on nationality.[26] Likewise, characterisations

---

women amounts to a denial of effective nationality, and in the case of such victims, de facto statelessness, as opposed to the simple exercise of a state's discretion in matters of international protection of its nationals. Ryszard Piotrowicz, "Victims of trafficking and de facto statelessness", *Refugee Survey Quarterly* (2002) vol. 21, Special Issue, 50–59, 54. Already in 1954 the International Law Commission's Special Rapporteur pointed out that in proposals to eliminate or reduce statelessness "the Commission is not only obligated to deal with juridical statelessness, but is also under the solemn obligation to provide juridical solutions for the situation of thousands of human beings who are in a much worse position than those who only are *de jure* stateless. . . . *de facto* statelessness is much worse than *de jure* statelessness not only quantitatively but also qualitatively". Roberto Córdova, "Third report on the elimination or reduction of statelessness", *Yearbook of the International Law Commission* (1960) vol. 1954, no. II, 26–42, 30.

[25] International Law Commission, *Report of the International Law Commission to the General Assembly, Fifty-second session*, United Nations General Assembly Official Records, Fifty-fifth session, Supplement no. 10, A/55/10 (New York: United Nations, 2000), 167.

[26] Spiro, "Dual nationality and the meaning of citizenship", 1415. The article traces historical attitudes toward multiple nationality in the United States, and argues in favour of acceptance of multiple nationality. Dzialoszynski criticises the US position in the mid 19th century as hypocritical, maintaining that until 1868 the United States essentially held fast to a principle of perpetual allegiance for its own nationals, while rejecting other states' refusal to recognise their nationals' expatriation upon emigration, or naturalisation elsewhere. He seems to contradict himself however, in pointing out that until 1859 at least with respect to Prussia, the policy of the United States was to treat Prussians who had emigrated and been naturalised in the United States as Prussians once they returned to that country. He chronicles the events and related

such as Hailbronner's of "older" state practice as demonstrating a tendency to avoid multiple nationality, or at least to reduce problems associated with it, is imprecise, as such practice would seem to have become more pronounced only in the late 19th century and the first decades of the 20th century, and was even then far from uniform.[27]

Vattel already recognised a right of expatriation, which could however not be exercised if to do so would amount to abandoning one's country in time of need,[28] as well as that laws relating to the free movement of persons varied from state to state.[29] He mentions that states have a right to exile or banish citizens temporarily or permanently, but also that this may infringe upon other states' rights to control who enters their territory.[30] But he does not mention the possible overlap of nationalities, or potential conflicts of law, interest, or emotion that might thereby ensue, either as an impossibility, or in favourable or unfavourable terms. His commentary in relation to emigration and expatriation is best seen in the context of his views of personal liberty, and the rights of the sovereign and outdated notions of feudal rights over individuals in Europe.

---

change in US policy that led to the so-called Bancroft Treaties in 1868. Salo Dzialoszynski, "Die Bancroft-Verträge", dissertation presented at the Königlichen Friedrich-Wilhelms-Universität zu Breslau, (Breslau, 1913), 5–9. Spiro confirms that "although the United States never professed the doctrine of perpetual allegiance, it appeared at some points to have permitted substantial qualification of the right of voluntary expatriation". Spiro, "Dual nationality and the meaning of citizenship", 1426. Scott and Maúrtua refer to the *Williams Case*, Wharton's State Trials, 652, of 1799, in which Chief Justice Ellsworth of the Circuit Court of the United States stated, "In countries so crowded with inhabitants that the means of subsistence are difficult to be obtained, it is reason and policy to permit emigration. But our policy is different, for our country is but sparsely settled, and we have no inhabitants to spare". James Brown Scott and Victor M Maúrtua, *Observations on nationality* (New York: Oxford University Press, 1930), 6. But they cite the 1779 Act of the Legislature of Virginia, attributing it to Thomas Jefferson (then Governor), which contained a right of expatriation, as a precursor to the 1868 legislation by the US Congress. Scott and Maúrtua, *Observations on nationality*, 6.

[27] Kay Hailbronner, "Doppelte Staatsangehörigkeit", paper presented at the Hohenheimer Tage zum Ausländerrecht 1999 und 5. Migrationspolitisches Forum, Hohenheim, ed. Klaus Barwig, Gisbert Brinkmann, Kay Hailbronner, Bertold Huber, Christine Kreuzer, Klaus Lörcher, Christoph Schuhmacher, (Nomos Verlagsgesellschaft, 1999), 97–114, 100.

[28] Emmerich de Vattel, *The law of nations or the principles of natural law applied to the conduct and to the affairs of nations and of sovereigns*, trans. Charles G. Fenwick, 1758 ed., vol. 3 (Washington: The Carnegie Institution of Washington, 1916), 51 and 89. This issue seems to have become a central one between countries from which people emigrated and the countries to which they immigrated, for example Germany and the United States. See generally Ludwig Bendix, *Fahnenflucht und Verletzung der Wehrpflicht durch Auswanderung*, ed. Georg Jellinek and Gerhard Anschütz, *Staats- und völkerrechtliche Abhandlungen* (Leipzig: Verlag von Duncker & Humblot, 1906).

[29] Vattel, *The law of nations or the principles of natural law applied to the conduct and to the affairs of nations and of sovereigns*, 90–91.

[30] Emmerich de Vattel, *Le droit des gens ou principes de la loi naturelle*, 1758 ed., vol. 1 (Washington: The Carnegie Institution of Washington, 1916), 208–10.

Il paroit . . . que le Droit des Gens établi par la Coûtume dans ces pays-là, il y a quelques siécles, ne permettoit pas à un Etat de recevoir au nombre de ses Citoyens les sujets d'un autre Etat. Cet article d'une Coûtume vicieuse, navoit d'autre fondement que l'esclavage dans lequel les peuples étoient alors réduits. Un Prince, un Seigneur, comptoit ses sujets dans le rang de ses biens propres ; il en calculoit le nombre, comme celui de ses troupeaux : Et, à la honte de l'humanité, cet étrange abus n'est pas encore détruit par tout.

Si le Souverain entreprend de troubler ceux qui ont le droit d'émigration, il leur fait injure ; & ces gens-là peuvent légitimement implorer la protection de la Puissance qui voudra les recevoir. C'est ainsi que l'on a vû le Roi de Prusse FRIDERIC-GUILLAUME accorder sa protection aux Protestans émigrans de Saltzbourg.[31]

The quote should arguably not be read as either citation of a prohibition on multiple nationality at the time Vattel labels "a few centuries ago", or as his approval or disapproval of multiple nationality, but commentary in relation to emigration and the right of one sovereign to protect certain persons against another. He does not comment, for example, on the rights of the individual or sovereign should the former return to his native land. Multiple nationality was simply not conceived as an issue as such by Vattel and early writers on the law of nations.[32] De Castro does refer, how-

---

[31] (Author's translation: *It would seem . . . that international law established by custom in those countries a few centuries ago did not allow one State to include among its citizens the subjects of another State. This aspect of a vicious custom had no other basis than the slavery to which peoples were reduced. A prince, a sovereign, counted his subjects among his personal goods; he calculated their numbers, as he did his troops. And to humanity's disgrace, such abuses have not yet been eliminated everywhere. Should the sovereign try to trouble and thereby injure those who have the right of emigration, such people may legitimately seek the protection of the power that receives them. It was thus that King Frederick-William of Prussia accorded his protection to the Protestant emigrants from Salzburg.*) Id., 207–08.

[32] Orfield points out that Vattel did propose that a child's nationality should be that of his father, unless the latter has moved to another state, in which case she or he receives that state's nationality. While this may demonstrate an opinion that a child should not receive two nationalities at birth, this is unclear. Lester B. Orfield, "The legal effects of dual nationality", *The George Washington Law Review* (1949) vol. 17, no. 4, 427'445, 443. In any case, Orfield characterisation of Vattel's formula as a "compromise solution" cannot be taken to mean that Vattel saw multiple nationality as a problem – this is unclear from his writings. Orfield, "The legal effects of dual nationality", 443. See Vattel, *Le droit des gens ou principes de la loi naturelle*, 199. For example, in relation to naturalisation, Vattel states only that states may naturalise foreigners, not that the effect of such naturalisation is loss of nationality elsewhere. Vattel, *Le droit des gens ou principes de la loi naturelle*, 198–99. For the views of early writers in the 17th century on these subjects, see for example Hugo Grotius, *De jure belli ac pacis libri tres (The three books on the law of war and peace)*, trans. Francis W. Kelsey, 1646 ed., vol. 2 (Oxford: Clarendon Press, 1925), 200–05, 232–35, 252–55; Samuel von Pufendorf, *De jure naturae et gentium libri octo*, trans. C. H. Oldfather and W. A. Oldfather, 1688 ed., vol. 2 (Oxford: Clarendon Press, 1934), 1348–59; Samuel von Pufendorf, *De officio hominis et civis juxta legem naturalem libri duo (The two books on the duty of man and citizen according to the natural law)*, trans. Frank Gardner Moore, 1682 ed., vol. 2 (New York: Oxford University

ever, to the citation in the early 18th century of feudal customs permitting vasselage to more than one lord, to answer the question whether one could be the subject of one sovereign and the ambassador of another.[33] He cites a statement of the Dutch jurist Cornelius Van Bynkershoek that

> « Un seul sujet peut rendre hommage, tributs, et bonne foi à chacun de ses deux princes. Que voulons-nous de plus ? » En effet, continue-t-il, une seul personne peut être au service de plusieurs princes et prêter serment de fidélité à chacun d'entre eux du moment que leurs exigences ne sont pas contraires ou bien sous réserve de ne pas les servir pour ce qui pourrait les opposer.[34]

In this sense, he says that the beginnings of views on multiple nationality from the Middle Ages until modern times depended on the status of, and relationships between, individuals, that predominated in each country.[35] Thus he cites cases favourable to multiple links in Holland, Germany, Italy and various Swiss cantons. He attributes the "modern" rejection of multiple nationality to France, citing 16th century cases and the development of the doctrine of state sovereignty.[36]

It would seem that in general terms, certain state practice can be cited for the proposition that emigration from Europe to the Americas, combined with the independence of large numbers of South and North American states in the late 18th and 19th centuries, led to the crystallisation of issues surrounding the overlap of claims to personal jurisdiction by states over individuals. The point of departure was however not disapproval of multiple nationality as such, but in fact just the opposite (pointed to by Vattel and others): an unwillingness by many states to relinquish personal jurisdiction over emigrants.[37]

Lauterpacht cites British insistence on the common law doctrine of permanent allegiance (nemo potest exuere patriam – no man may abjure his country)[38] and the consequent impressment of Britons naturalised in the United States as one of the causes

---

Press, 1927), 144–46. Stülken, writing in 1934, notes that multiple nationality was "formerly" not viewed as detrimental, but as nationality "in our times" means more than ties to the state, it is increasingly seen as a source of serious conflicts among states. Gustav Stülken, "Die mehrfache Staatsangehörigkeit", dissertation presented at the Universität zu Göttingen, (Quakenbrück, 1934), 41.

[33] Spiro, "Dual nationality and the meaning of citizenship", 1420.

[34] (Author's translation: "A single subject may render homage, tribute and loyalty to each of his two princes. What should we want more?" In effect, he continues, a single person may serve several princes and swear loyalty to each among them as long as their requirements are not contrary to each other, or under reservation not to serve them in fields where they might be opposed.) Ibid.

[35] Id., 593.

[36] Id., 595–98.

[37] See generally the excellent study by Aurelia Álvarez Rodríguez, Nacionalidad y emigración (Madrid: La Ley, 1990). See also Spiro, "Dual nationality and the meaning of citizenship".

[38] Spiro, "Dual nationality and the meaning of citizenship", 1420.

of the war of 1812, as well as disputes between the United States and Prussia over the right of expatriation that carried on into the late 19th century.[39] The latter led to the so-called "Bancroft Treaties" regarding mutual recognition of naturalisation and consequent expatriation, as well as resumption of nationality in certain cases.[40]

The Bancroft Treaties provide an early example that contradicts popular wisdom and some academic writings that Germany has always been opposed to multiple nationality.[41] Dzialoszynski, writing in 1913, laments the position of the German

---

[39] L. Oppenheim, in *International law. A treatise*, ed. Hersch Lauterpacht (London: Longmans, Green & Co., 1948), 608–9 note 3. See also Spiro, "Dual nationality and the meaning of citizenship", 1421–24. See also the treatise by the Lord Chief Justice of England, advocating revision to the United Kingdom's nationality laws such as to provide for an end to the doctrine of permanent allegiance to the British Crown upon naturalisation elsewhere, with an exception should this amount to an avoidance of duties owed, and a concurrent recommendation that naturalised Britons be accorded full civil and political rights, and diplomatic protection abroad, which had not been the case. Alexander Cockburn, *Nationality: or the law relating to subjects and aliens, considered with a view to future legislation* (London: William Ridgway, 1869), 201 and 209.

[40] The treaties are best known as 1868 conventions between the United States and the German States of the North German Confederation, Bavaria, Baden, Württemberg, and Hesse prior to the unification of Germany in 1871, relating to military service, expatriation, resumption of nationality, and the effect of naturalisation. Such conventions, also known as "Bancroft Treaties", after the American diplomat and historian George Bancroft who was the US diplomatic envoy in Berlin from 1867–1874, were however also negotiated by the United States with 20 other countries, including Mexico, China, Belgium, Sweden and Norway, the United Kingdom, Ecuador, Denmark, and Haiti. Hellmuth Hecker, "Doppelstaatigkeit, Bancroft-Verträge und Osteuropa", *WGO Monatshefte für Osteuropäisches Recht* (2000), 409–430, 410–11. Hecker notes that of the 25 treaties only that with Bulgaria (1923) is still in force, those with German states and Austria-Hungary having ceased to be in force with the entry of the United States in the First World War, the United Kingdom having abrogated the relevant treaty in 1954, and the USA having withdrawn from those with Belgium, Costa Rica, Haiti, Honduras, Portugal, El Salvador, Uruguay, Sweden, Norway, Denmark, Nicaragua and Peru in October 1981. Hecker, "Doppelstaatigkeit, Bancroft-Verträge und Osteuropa", 411. Hecker argues that the Bancroft Treaties provide an example of how problems related to multiple nationality can be addressed through agreements, as opposed to attempting to achieve some concordance among states' municipal laws. See also Bendix, *Fahnenflucht und Verletzung der Wehrpflicht durch Auswanderung.*, who argues that the treaties with south German States were invalid at international law. Dzialoszynski provides an historical overview of the treaties' negotiation and substance in relation to German states. Dzialoszynski, *Die Bancroft-Verträge.*

[41] For example, Kreuzer's statement that "Dual nationality had always been considered as being inconsistent with the concept of loyalty and attachment to Germany" lacks historical perspective. Christine Kreuzer, "Double and multiple nationality in Germany after the Citizenship Reform Act of 1999", in *Rights and duties of dual nationals. Evolution and prospects*, ed. David A. Martin and Kay Hailbronner (The Hague: Kluwer Law International, 2003), 347–359, 348. Likewise, Kay Hailbronner, "Germany's citizenship law under immigration pressure", in *Dual nationality, social rights and federal citizenship in the U.S. and Europe. The reinvention of citizenship*, ed. Randall Hansen and Patrick Weil (New York: Berghahn Books, 2002), 123.

Empire and other countries, as far as maintaining that naturalisation by their subjects elsewhere had no effect on their existing nationality. The new nationality law, or *Lex Delbrück*, adopted that same year seemed to implement Dzialoszynski's advice, providing for automatic loss of German nationality upon naturalisation elsewhere. But Álvarez Rodríguez points out that the German Empire's new law on nationality specifically provided that Germans could request authorisation to retain German nationality to counteract the provision, amounting to an express incorporation of dual nationality into German law. This was declared by Delbrück himself to be a function of concrete state interests in economic and political terms.[42] The incorporation of multiple nationality into the German legal order was heavily criticised on doctrinal bases, and rejected specifically by article 278 of the Treaty of Versailles.[43] The provision remains a part of German law.[44]

Returning to the discussion in the previous chapter, it is interesting to note that Mr Nottebohm lost his German nationality upon naturalisation in Liechtenstein, not having applied to retain it. But one of the arguments that may have swayed the Inter-

---

Although some German states' nationality laws contained provisions for "expiration" of nationality, these could be avoided by consular inscription abroad.

[42] Álvarez Rodríguez, *Nacionalidad y emigración*, 36–37.

[43] Id., 37. Article 278 reads : *Germany undertakes to recognise any new nationality which has been or may be acquired by her nationals under the laws of the Allied and Associated Powers and in accordance with the decisions of the competent authorities of these Powers pursuant to naturalisation laws or under treaty stipulations, and to regard such persons as having, in consequence of the acquisition of such new nationality, in all respects severed their allegiance to their country of origin.* Marjorie M. Whiteman, *Digest of international law*, 15 vols., vol. 8 (Washington: Department of State, 1968), 82. Cordóva's first report as Special Rapporteur for the International Law Commission even labelled the law's provision for possible retention of German nationality upon naturalisation elsewhere as an example of "not legal" municipal legislation: "There are cases in which international law considers that a certain national legislation is not legal because it comes into conflict with the broader interests of the international community. Such was the case, for instance, with the so-called Delbrück Law, enacted by Germany, under which a German citizen could be nationalized in a foreign country without losing his original German nationality". Roberto Córdova, "Report on the elimination or reduction of statelessness", *Yearbook of the International Law Commission* (1959) vol. 1953, no. II, 167–195, 169.

[44] Contained in section 25 of the *Staatsangehörigkeitsgesetz* (2000). Masing characterises the provision's contents (in its current form in the nationality law that took effect on 1 January 2000) as discriminatory, in favouring Germans who emigrate (and thus more likely to be of ethnic German stock) over those who were naturalised in Germany and who would like to resume their former nationality. Johannes Masing, *Wandel im Staatsangehörigkeitsrecht vor den Herausforderungen moderner Migration* (Tübingen: Mohr Siebeck, 2001), 16–18. The provision was cited by the German Constitutional Court (*Bundesverfassungsgericht*) in 1990 as one of the reasons for its decision not to regard loss of German nationality upon naturalisation elsewhere as a deprivation of nationality. Kay Hailbronner, Günter Renner, and Christine Kreuzer, *Staatsangehörigkeitsrecht*, 3rd ed., vol. 55, *Beck'sche Kurz-kommentare* (München: Verlag C. H. Beck, 2001), 157.

national Court of Justice in its decision not to allow Liechtenstein to protect Mr Nottebohm against Guatemala, cited by Weis, was the liberal practice of National Socialist German authorities in allowing Germans (albeit not German Jews or their families or others who had been forced to emigrate) to retain their nationality upon naturalisation or providing them with an opportunity to resume it later.

The majority of the Court may have been impressed by a Circular letter of the German Foreign Office of July 4, 1939 submitted by Guatemala to German representatives in Latin America in which it was said that 'a preponderant German interest may call for the acquisition of a foreign citizenship by German nationals. In this case, if the granting of approval for the retention of German nationality is not compatible with the law of the respective foreign State and does not need to be considered, there are no objections to accommodating the person involved for the purpose of acquisition of foreign citizenship by granting him an assurance that a possible future application for renaturalization in Germany will receive favourable consideration'. The Lex Delbrück was also frequently mentioned in the pleadings. Professor Henri Rolin's allusions, in his eloquent pleadings as Counsel for Guatemala, that Nottebohm . . . had been a member of the Nazi party . . . may also have left an impression.[45]

Spain's practice related to her former colonies mirrors an attitude that might be compared to permanent allegiance until 1836, albeit not expressed as such, and for political, as opposed to legal or doctrinal reasons. Furthermore, Fernández Marcane's summary indicates that from 1836, when Spain finally recognised the independence of her former colonies in the Americas, until the early twentieth century, its practice regarding nationality seems generally to have been directed at maintaining a link to (and for) Spanish emigrants and their descendents to Spain, via enactments and treaties on nationality.[46] Álvarez Rodríguez clarifies however, that retention of Spanish nationality during this period was dependant on registration abroad, that nationality was automatically lost by naturalisation elsewhere, and that reinstatement of nationality involved returning to Spain, a declaration of intent, and renunciation of foreign nationality.[47] Nevertheless, the maintenance of ties to Spain involved a system of dual nationality.

---

[45] Peter Weis, *Nationality and statelessness in international law* (Alphen aan den Rijn: Sijthoff & Noordhoff, 1979), 179.

[46] See generally Luis Fernández Marcane, *Contribución al estudio de la doble nacionalidad de los hijos de Españoles nacidos en América* (La Habana: Imprente "El Siglo XX", 1924). See also Álvarez Rodríguez, *Nacionalidad y emigración*, 119–25. In addition to practice from 1836–1863, the law of 20 June 1864 obliged Spanish Governments entering into treaties with other states in relation to nationality to provide the offspring of Spaniards with a right to recover Spanish nationality, should conservation of nationality not have been possible in the first place. Fernández Marcane, *Contribución al estudio de la doble nacionalidad de los hijos de Españoles nacidos en América*, 57. But Dzialoszynski's dissertation, presented in Breslau eleven years before Fernández Marcane's wrote his treatise, cites Spain approvingly as one of the countries having adopted what he calls the "French Principle", that foreign naturalisation automatically results in loss of nationality. Dzialoszynski, "Die Bancroft-Verträge", 3–4.

[47] Álvarez Rodríguez, *Nacionalidad y emigración*, 47–58. But the Constitution of 1931

The Spanish Constitution of 1837 defined as Spaniards all those born in Spanish dominions, as well as children of a Spanish father or mother born outside of Spain. The latter provision was later qualified: Spaniards were those born in Spain; certain foreigners present in Spain would be provided with an option and right to Spanish nationality based on descent should they choose this, but Spanish nationality or attached obligations would in no way be imposed upon them.[48] Starting in 1840, Spain embarked on a systematic conclusion of treaties in relation to nationality with her former colonies, which after 1863 incorporated a system of dual nationality, centred around application of the *lex fori* to minors possessing both nationalities.[49] This system was not abandoned in the 19th century, having resulted from American states' insistence on *jus soli* attribution of nationality, and Spain's maintenance of *jus sanguinis*. Domicile as opposed to nationality, was thus affirmed as the primary criterion for exercise of personal jurisdiction in the Hispano-American conferences of 1888, 1889, 1900, and 1923.[50] Although it dealt directly with issues of conflicts of law, the system cannot be dismissed as unrelated to nationality on the international plane simply because it excluded a right to diplomatic protection.

From 1958 onwards Spain adopted a new system of direct incorporation of dual nationality by treaty with respect to certain countries, concluding treaties with Chile, Peru, Paraguay, Guatemala, Nicaragua, Bolivia, Ecuador, Costa Rica, Honduras, the Dominican Republic, and Argentina. Likewise, conventions regulating the effects of dual nationality were adopted with France, Portugal, Argentina, and Venezuela.[51] Aznar Sánchez cites different justifications and principles found in the conventions as far as the reasons for dealing with, and favouring with respect to certain countries, multiple nationality, both practical and emotional. Article four of the convention with Chile (1958) states in practical terms:

---

specifically excluded naturalisation in Latin American countries as provoking loss of Spanish nationality. Álvarez Rodríguez, *Nacionalidad y emigración*, 67. García Haro notes the movement of Spaniards resident in Argentina founded in 1913, advocating the establishment of a political district for the Spanish Senate (in Argentina), and the automatic attribution of Argentine nationality, such that emigrant Spaniards might possess the two nationalities. Ramón García Haro, *La nacionalidad en América Hispana*, vol. 29, *Biblioteca de la "Revista general de Legislación y Jurisprudencia"* (Madrid: Editorial Reus, 1922), 16.

[48] Fernández Marcane, *Contribución al estudio de la doble nacionalidad de los hijos de Españoles nacidos en América*, 41–42.

[49] Id., 43–57.

[50] Id., 72–85, 111–16.

[51] Juan Aznar Sánchez, *La doble nacionalidad* (Madrid: Editorial Montecorvo, 1977), 28–29. See this text generally for a complete description of the treaty system. In relation to current Spanish practice vis-à-vis multiple nationality, see Aurelia Álvarez Rodríguez, *Guía de la nacionalidad española* (Madrid: Ministerio de Trabajo y Asuntos Sociales, 1996), 119–38, and for Spanish legislation on nationality generally, including treaty the texts, María Teresa Echezarreta Ferrer, ed., *Legislación sobre nacionalidad*, 3rd ed. (Madrid: Tecnos, 1999). See also Castro, "La nationalité la double nationalité et la supra-nationalité", 611–32.

Que no hay ninguna objeción jurídica para que una persona pueda tener dos nacionalidades, a condición de que sólo una de ellas tenga plena eficacia, origine la dependencia política e indique la legislación a que está sujeta,[52]

whereas the Preamble to the convention with Argentina (1969) appeals only to emotion:

En el deseo de estrechar los vínculos que unen a los dos países y de ofrecer mayores facilidades para que sus nacionales lleguen a ser, respectivamente, argentinos o españoles, conservando su nacionalidad de origen, rindiendo con ello tributo al linaje histórico y a la existencia de un sustrato comunitario entre España y la República Argentina . . .[53]

This system of dual nationality by treaty is built around the principle that acquisition of one country's nationality does not entail loss of the original nationality, involving at any given time an active, and a passive or latent, nationality. It covers the exercise of political rights; military service; diplomatic protection; and civil, social and work-related rights.[54] Spain also concluded treaties with Latin American countries that did not wish to accept dual nationality for their citizens, for example with Colombia, providing for facilitated naturalisation and resumption of nationality upon acquisition

---

[52] (Author's translation: *That there is no legal objection as far as one person being able to possess two nationalities, on the condition that only one of them have full effect, give rise to political dependence and the legislation to which the person is subject.*) Convenio de doble nacionalidad con Chile de 24 de mayo de 1958, Echezarreta Ferrer, ed., *Legislación sobre nacionalidad*, 213. See Aznar Sánchez, *La doble nacionalidad*, 31. It should be noted that the first and second articles of the Convention do appeal to emotion, stating that Spaniards and Chileans form part of the same community in terms of sharing tradition, culture and language, and that they do not feel foreign in each other's country. Echezarreta Ferrer, ed., *Legislación sobre nacionalidad*, 213.

[53] (Author's translation: *In the desire to tighten the bonds that unite the two countries and to offer better opportunities for their nationals to be, respectively, Argentines or Spaniards, conserving their nationality of origin, thereby paying tribute to the historical lineage and to the existence of an underlying community between Spain and the Argentine Republic . . .*) Convenio de doble nacionalidad con Argentina de 14 de abril de 1969, Echezarreta Ferrer, ed., *Legislación sobre nacionalidad*, 252. See Aznar Sánchez, *La doble nacionalidad*, 31. García Haro also invoked what he termed a common "patriotism to the Spanish language" as far as the "romantic movement" between Spain and the American republics, calling their peoples "of one language and one race". García Haro, *La nacionalidad en América Hispana*, 15.

[54] Prieto Castro proposes that the Ibero-American treaty system evolve to constitute a system of "supranationality", which might involve multiple nationality in the form of a dominant and a latent nationality, but which in any case would entail privileged naturalisation, and the integration of nationality and citizenship rights and status for Ibero-American states. Fermin Prieto-Castro y Roumier, *La nacionalidad múltiple* (Madrid: Consejo Superior de Investigaciones Cientificas Instituto "Francisco de Vitoria", 1962), 179–186. In this sense, it might be seen as the political expression of privileged inclusion, and management of personal / civil status within a system of conflicts of law. See also Castro, "La nationalité la double nationalité et la supra-nationalité", 611–632.

of domicile.[55] The treaty with Colombia was modified by an Additional Protocol in
1998 to reflect Colombia's change in policy, accepting multiple nationality for its
citizens.[56]

Evidence of the link between emigration and the emergence of competing claims
of personal jurisdiction in terms of nationality, as well as a reluctance to abandon personal jurisdiction (thereby at least tolerating the possible production of multiple
nationality), is not only provided by European and American examples. Qing Dynasty
attempts to strengthen its position domestically involved efforts to secure the support
of overseas Chinese, calling on their "unswerving loyalty to their native country".[57]
China in fact claimed the allegiance of all overseas Chinese, but was criticised for
lacking a law on nationality.[58] When an Imperial Chinese nationality law was enacted
in 1909 it contained a stipulation that permission had to be obtained in order to
secure release from Chinese nationality before naturalisation abroad.[59] The effect of
this provision would not be to negate the foreign naturalisation, but to treat the individuals in question as Chinese nationals if permission had not been obtained prior to
naturalisation. The first Japanese proclamation on nationality of 1873 contained no

---

[55] *Decreto 3541, reglamenta la ley N° 71 de 1979 que aprobo el Convenio de Nacionalidad
entre Colombia y España*, 26 December 1980, Centro de Información Migratoria para América
Latina (internet), http://www.cimal.cl/cimal/interior/legislacion_migratoria/colombia/decretos/
d_3541_80.htm, consulted 15 May 2006.

[56] *Ley 638 de 2001, por medio de la cual se aprueban el "Protocolo adicional entre la
República de Colombia y el Reino de España, modificando en Convenio de Nacionalidad del
27 de junio de 1979*, 4 January 2001, Secretaria del Senado de Colombia (internet),
http://www.secretariasenado.gov.co/leyes/L0638001.htm, consulted 15 May 2005.

[57] Cohen and Chiu, *People's China and international law. A documentary study*, 747.

[58] Id., 747–48.

[59] Chiu, "Nationality and international law in Chinese perspective – with special reference
to the period before 1950 and the practice of the administration in Taipei", 34. See de Padua,
"Ambiguous allegiance: multiple nationality in Asia", 257. de Padua remarks that "[i]n practice, the necessary permission seems to have been rarely granted, if at all sought". de Padua,
"Ambiguous allegiance: multiple nationality in Asia", 257. Restrictions on emigration were not
unique to China. Permission to be naturalised in a foreign state might be compared to permission to emigrate, a requirement in various German States in the 19th century, for example.
Until the mid-19th century, German states taxed emigrants in order to discourage departure.
Torpey cites the desire for a "safety-valve" for social unrest in response to the 1848 revolution
as well as the liberalism related to the Frankfurt Parliament, as sources of relaxation in the
restrictions. Torpey, *The invention of the passport – surveillance, citizenship and the state*, 75.
In the context of Germany and the Bancroft Treaties surrounding military service, Bendix cites
the "Zirkularerlass an sämtliche Königliche Regierungen und an das Königliche Oberpräsidium
Hannover, betreffend das strafrechtliche Verfahren bei unerlaubter Auswanderung eines Bundes-
angehörigen nach den Vereinigten Staaten von Nordamerika vom 6. Juli 1868". (Author's translation: *Circular decree to all Royal Governments and to the Royal Presidium in Hannover, regarding
criminal proceedings in relation to emigration without permission to the United States of North
America of a citizen of the Confederation, of 6 July 1868.*) Bendix, *Fahnenflucht und Verletzung der Wehrpflicht durch Auswanderung*, 440.

provision on expatriation, except for women upon marriage. This was only changed in 1890.[60]

In fact, the seemingly straightforward assumption that while states from which people emigrated in the 19th century might have favoured some continuation of legal ties to emigrants, states to which people immigrated uniformly saw an interest in a right to expatriation, does not hold true. Dzialoszynski's argument that the United States did not abrogate the doctrine of perpetual allegiance contained in the British-inherited Commom Law until 1868, while still advocating that states from which naturalised Americans had emigrated be obliged to cut ties, has already been mentioned.[61] Álvarez Rodríguez notes that other states that received immigrants in the Americas also held to the maxim *semel civis, semper civis*, in order to increase the number of their nationals. She cites the Venezuelan Constitution of 1864 as an example, in force until 1891, which provided that the acquisition of foreign domicile or nationality had no effect on Venezuelan nationality.[62] Likewise she states that loss of nationality in many American states was ambiguous rather than effective, as laws referred to loss of citizenship as opposed to nationality.[63]

D. DISAPPROVAL OF MULTIPLE NATIONALITY AND THE DEVELOPMENT OF TREATY REGIMES

From these examples of the historical practice of various countries in relation to multiple nationality, it is evident that generalisations as to the early and universal rejection, or disapproval of, multiple nationality, are either amiss, or oversimplified. By the early 20th century, however, many commentators such as Baty, cited in chapter one,

---

[60] Hosokawa, "Japanese nationality in international perspective", 182–3. The change did not benefit women in terms of providing them with an independent nationality unaffected by marriage, but provided generally for expatriation upon naturalisation abroad.

[61] Dzialoszynski, "Die Bancroft-Verträge", 5–9. See also Scott and Maúrtua, *Observations on nationality*, 4–8. Koessler points out that the loss of nationality upon naturalisation in another state is claimed as a principle of international law according to the "American doctrine of voluntary expatriation". Doctrine or not, it was not followed at the 1930 Hague Codification Conference, although it was proposed in the draft convention. Maximilian Koessler, "'Subject,' 'Citizen,' 'National,' and 'Permanent Allegiance'", *Yale Law Journal* (1947) vol. 56, 58–76, 68. See *Convention on Certain Questions Relating to the Conflict of Nationality Laws, 12 April 1930*, (1937) 179 LNTS 89, no. 4137 (entry into force: 1 July 1937), and article 13 of Manley O. Hudson and Richard W. Flournoy Jr., "Nationality – Responsibility of states – Territorial waters, drafts of conventions prepared in anticipation of the first conference on the codification of international law, The Hague 1930", *The American Journal of International Law* (1929) vol. 23 Supplement, 45–46.

[62] Álvarez Rodríguez, *Nacionalidad y emigración*, 24.

[63] Id., 24 note 51. García Haro agrees. García Haro, *La nacionalidad en América Hispana*, 42.

seemed to agree that multiple nationality was undesirable. This is discussed below in greater detail in relation to more recent arguments against, and for, multiple nationality and related issues. A typical comment is that of Dzialoszynski in 1913:

> *Unseres vollen Beifalls kann v. Martitz sicher sein, wenn er in seinen ausgezeichneten Ausführungen es für eine sittliche Forderung erklärt, dass keine Rechtsordnung eine doppelte Staatsangehörigkeit zulasse. Es erscheint in der Tat unmöglich, dass eine Person zwei souveränen Staaten in gleicher Weise angehöre, ohne in bestimmten Fällen in den schärfsten Widerstreit der Pflichten zu geraten.*[64]

Not all practice followed such opinion, and as noted above, the German government did not follow the proposition when it adopted a new law on nationality that same year (the *Lex Delbrück*). In contrast to Dzialoszynski, García Haro writing in 1922 heaps praise on legislation allowing for what he calls "conditional nationality", citing the *Lex Delbrück*, and the provisions then in force in France and Belgium, meaning

> *legislaciones que toleran a sus súbditos la adopción de otra ciudadanía, mientras la utilidad, ya para el Estado, ya para el individuo, no reclame la eficacia del vínculo originario, pues en tal caso reaparece ipso facto aquella nacionalidad, cuyo ejercicio quedó suspendido. Indudablemente esta orientación marca un gran progreso en la vida internacional.*[65]

But even the beginnings of the rejection of multiple nationality involved confusion in terms of practice, as opposed to opinion. Italy's 1912 law on nationality/citizenship, which excluded multiple nationality, probably in deference to the United States, held that the effect of naturalisation elsewhere was expatriation in Italy, but that military service obligations persisted nonetheless when in Italy.[66] Torpey points to the problematic essence: "one of the principal reasons states might have for denying recogni-

---

[64] (Author's translation: *Von Martitz can count on our complete approval in terms of the characterisation in his excellent discourse, as a moral obligation, that no legal system admit dual nationality. It in fact seems impossible, that one person belong in the same fashion to two sovereign States, without falling in some situations into the worst kinds of conflict over obligations.*) Dzialoszynski, "Die Bancroft-Verträge", 3. Characterising multiple nationality as a problem was not uncommon. Kaspar Müller, "Das Problem der mehrfachen Staatsangehörigkeit", dissertation presented at the Universität Köln, (Köln: Hohen Rechtswissenschaftlichen Fakultät, 1927).

[65] (Author's translation: *legislation that tolerates the acquisition of another citizenship, while the utility for both the individual and the state of the effectiveness of original nationality is not necessary, then when it is, the former nationality whose exercise had been suspended reappears ipso facto. Without a doubt this position represents great progress in international life.*) García Haro, *La nacionalidad en América Hispana*, 16–17. Another example of a system of regulated multiple nationality cited with approval by García Haro is that in Central America, whereby Guatemala, Nicaragua and Honduras treated nationals of all Central American countries as their own, should they desire this, including those of Costa Rica and El Salvador, notwithstanding the lack of reciprocity in those two countries. García Haro, *La nacionalidad en América Hispana*, 27–28.

[66] Torpey, *The invention of the passport – surveillance, citizenship and the state*, 105.

tion of dual citizenship [is] the possibility of conflicting military loyalties and obligations".[67] Although it might be argued that the law did no more than seize the principle that obligations had to be fulfilled before expatriation would be recognised, it
arguably sowed confusion in terms of the nature of expatriation, creating obligations
for the individual at the same time as the notional corresponding rights and obligations of the state had been withdrawn.

A far more egregious example of continuing obligations following expatriation is
provided by Article 5 of the French Imperial Decree of 1811, altering the *Code
Civil*,[68] which had nothing to do with fulfilment of existing obligations, but created a
life-long obligation for former nationals, without any related benefits of nationality.
Following the Decree, a Frenchman who had lost his French nationality pursuant to
naturalisation in a foreign country (with the permission of the French government)
could nevertheless be charged under Article 75 of the Penal Code

> *qui punit de mort le Français prenant les armes contre la France. On a discuté beaucoup
> sur le point de savoir si cette disposition était contraire ou non au droit des gens.
> Certains pensent, comme Martens, que quand l'État a consenti à la dénationalisation, tous
> les liens sont rompus : mais nous croyons, avec Bello, que la loi française, bien qu'il-
> logique est juste. On permet au Français de perdre cette qualité, mais nullement de servir
> dans les armées d'un souverain étranger contre la France, ce qui est absolument différent.
> Outre ce qu'il y a de choquant et de blessant à voir un individu prendre les armes con-
> tre le pays où il est né, où il a vécu, où réside le plus souvent sa famille, il y a aussi la
> crainte parfaitement légitime que, par sa connaissance des lieux, de la langue, des gens,
> il ne fournisse des renseignements utiles.*[69]

Lauterpacht dates the tide of sentiment against multiple nationality to the period
immediately after the First World War, stating that

> *The inconveniences and hardships resulting from double nationality became particularly
> prominent in consequence of the changes of nationality arising out of the Peace Treaties
> of 1919, and this was probably one of the reasons why the Hague Codification Conference
> of 1930 reached agreement on certain aspects of the matter.*[70]

---

[67] Ibid. He says "the law facilitated the rapid resumption of citizenship by expatriates".

[68] George Cogordan, *La nationalité au point de vue des rapports internationaux* (Paris:
L. Larose, Libraire-Éditeur, 1879), 246–48.

[69] (Author's translation: *which punishes with death the Frenchman who takes up arms
against France. Whether this provision went against international law was much discussed.
There are those, such as Martens, who think that when the State has consented to denationalisation all ties are broken. But we believe, following Bello, that the French law, although illogical, is correct. A Frenchman is permitted to lose that status, but never to serve in the armies of
a foreign sovereign against France, which is completely different. In addition to the shock and
hurt provoked by seeing someone take up arms against the country of his birth, where he lived,
where his family usually lives, there is also the perfectly legitimate concern that through his
knowledge of places, the language, and the people, he not provide useful information.*) Id., 247.
A similar provision in the current Colombian Constitution's was mentioned in chapter 3 at note
241.

[70] Oppenheim, *International law. A treatise*, 608–9.

He does however, not state in any detail what those "inconveniences and hardships" were.[71] Arendt's comment that in the aftermath of the First World War the "nation had conquered the state",[72] in the context of the collapsed multi-national European and Eastern empires, recalls that the hardening of opinion against multiple nationality took place within an atmosphere directed by convictions that peace in Europe would be achieved by delimitation of (contrived) ethnic-national boundaries as political boundaries.[73] It is in this sense not at all surprising that this was accompanied by views rejecting any latitude in the legal delimitation of individuals as well, vis-à-vis the state. Torpey argues that although freedom of movement in Europe from the late 19th century to the First World War was unprecedented, it was matched by a proliferation of identity documents that allowed for the honing in practical terms of the distinction between national and non-national.[74]

The 1930 Hague Convention,[75] with three Protocols and eight associated resolutions, which entered into force on 1 July 1937, is the only universal multilateral treaty to deal with multiple nationality as such.[76] Its provisions have been mentioned in the previous chapter. The treaty's preamble states that it is directed at "the abolition of all cases both of statelessness and of double nationality", and that it is to be seen "as a first step toward this great achievement", while recognising that it is "not possible

---

[71] Lauterpacht characterises the position of "sujets mixtes" as "awkward on account of the fact that two different States claim them as subjects, and therefore claim their allegiance. In case a serious dispute arises between these two States which leads to war, an irreconcilable conflict of duties is created for these unfortunate individuals". Id., 608.

[72] Hannah Arendt, *The origins of totalitarianism* (New York: Harcourt, Brace & Company, 1973), 274–75. cited in Torpey, *The invention of the passport – surveillance, citizenship and the state*, 127.

[73] See Torpey, *The invention of the passport – surveillance, citizenship and the state*, 122–27.

[74] Id., 93.

[75] *Convention on Certain Questions Relating to the Conflict of Nationality Law*, 179.

[76] Hecker, "Doppelstaatigkeit, Bancroft-Verträge und Osteuropa", 409. The three Protocols are: *Protocol relating to a certain case of statelessness, 12 April 1930*, (1937) 179 LNTS 115, no. 4138 (entry into force: 1 July 1937); *Protocol relating to military obligations in certain cases of double nationality, 12 April 1930*, (1937) 178 LNTS 229, no. 4117 (entry into force: 25 May 1937); *Special protocol concerning statelessness, 12 April 1930*, (not yet in force). The protocol on military service and multiple nationality, has been ratified/acceded to by 26 states, and signed by another 14. See United Nations, Multilateral treaties deposited with the Secretary-General (internet), http://untreaty.un.org, consulted on 25 March 2006. The Protocol exempts multiple nationals from military service in countries of their nationality if they reside in another country in which they are nationals, and are most closely connected to that country (article one). The Protocol does not prevent the production of multiple nationality. In relation to the "right of option" under international conventions in cases of multiple nationality, see Alexandre N. Makarov, "Le droit d'option en cas de double nationalité dans les conventions internationales", *Nederlands Tijdschrift voor Internationaal Recht*, (1959) vol. VI, Special issue: July 1959, 194–202.

to reach immediately a uniform solution". In fact, the Convention arguably does little to prevent the production of multiple nationality, while being of more significance in relation to statelessness.[77]

More importantly however, it enunciates general rules in relation to nationality, and sets down rules in relation to how states should deal with multiple nationals. Article three confirms that a multiple national may be regarded as a national by each relevant state, and article four states that "a state may not afford diplomatic protection to one of its nationals against a State whose nationality such person also possesses". Article six provides a qualified right to renunciation, while article five says that third states shall treat multiple nationals as possessing only one nationality, that of principal residence or closest connection. The Convention attempts to prevent the occurrence of multiple nationality only in relation to married women, in a clearly discriminatory fashion (articles 8–11), while establishing rules that would prevent a married woman's statelessness. In contrast, the 1957 Convention on the Nationality of Married Women does not contain provisions that would frustrate multiple nationality in married women.[78]

The 1930 Hague Convention has been ratified/acceded to by 22 states, signed by 27 others, and was denounced by Canada in 1996.[79] All ratifications/accessions took place in the 1930s, except for succession by one state in 1953, two states in the 1960s, two states in the 1970s (plus accession by Swaziland), and Kiribati in 1983. Only two states became party relatively recently, Zimbabwe having declared itself a successor in 1998, and Liberia acceding in 2005. Its indicative value as far as state practice vis-à-vis multiple nationality is thus severely limited. As will be seen, many of the signatory states, as well as some of those that ratified the treaty, evince

---

[77] In relation to statelessness, see *Convention relating to the status of stateless persons, 28 September 1954*, (1960) 360 UNTS 130, no. 5158 (entry into force: 6 June 1960). The Convention is of greater significance, having 59 parties, and 22 additional signatories. See United Nations, Multilateral treaties deposited with the Secretary-General (internet), http://untreaty.un.org, consulted on 25 March 2006. See also *Convention on the reduction of statelessness, 30 August 1961*, 989 UNTS 175, no. 14458, (entry into force: 13 December 1975), with 31 parties and five additional signatories. United Nations, Multilateral treaties deposited with the Secretary-General (internet), http://untreaty.un.org, consulted on 25 March 2006.

[78] *Convention on the nationality of married women, 20 February 1957*, (1958) 309 UNTS 66, no. 4468 (entry into force: 11 August 1958). The Convention does not provide for equal treatment between women and men, but stipulates that neither marriage, nor change of nationality by a husband, should affect the wife's nationality (article one). In fact, the stipulation in article two that "neither the voluntary acquisition of the nationality of another State nor the renunciation of its nationality by one of its nationals shall prevent the retention of its nationality by the wife of such national" arguably constitutes a level of tolerance of multiple nationality. The treaty has 77 parties, and 29 additional signatories. United Nations, Multilateral treaties deposited with the Secretary-General (internet), http://untreaty.un.org, consulted on 25 March 2006.

[79] United Nations, Multilateral treaties deposited with the Secretary-General (internet), http://untreaty.un.org, consulted on 1 April 2003.

practice demonstrating considerable tolerance of multiple nationality. Its limited value in this regard is confirmed by the Harvard Law School project that prepared the draft convention for the 1930 Codification Conference. The draft convention contained many provisions that would have reduced the incidence of multiple nationality, which were omitted in the 1930 Convention. These included restrictions on *jus sanguinis* attribution at birth (article four), retention of only one nationality beyond the age of 23 (article 12), loss of nationality upon naturalisation (article 13), loss of nationality upon resumption of former nationality (article 16), and state succession leading to only one nationality (article 18).[80]

Three years later the Seventh International Conference of American States concluded two multilateral conventions related to nationality, the first being the "Convention of the Nationality of Women", the first treaty to prohibit all sex-based discrimination regarding nationality,[81] and the second a "Convention on Nationality." In relation to multiple nationality, the latter stipulates that naturalisation provokes a loss of previous nationality (article one), and provides that naturalising states have an obligation to communicate news of such naturalisation to the state of former nationality (article two).[82] Whiteman notes that few states have become parties.[83]

---

[80] Hudson and Flournoy Jr., "Nationality – Responsibility of states – Territorial waters, drafts of conventions prepared in anticipation of the first conference on the codification of international law, The Hague 1930", 13–16. The 1930 Convention did essentially incorporate the draft convention's articles five and six providing that that *jus soli* attribution of nationality could not attach to children born to persons enjoying diplomatic immunity, and that children of foreign officials or consuls might divest themselves of such nationality (article 12) provided that they possessed their parents' nationality. The provision in relation to diplomatic agents was confirmed in article two of the *Optional protocol to the Vienna convention on diplomatic relations concerning acquisition of nationality, 18 April 1961*, (1964) 500 UNTS 223, no. 7311 (entry into force: 24 April 1964), and also applied in the *Optional protocol to the Vienna convention on consular relations concerning acquisition of nationality, 24 April 1963*, (1967) 596 UNTS 469, no. 8639 (entry into force: 19 March 1967). The former Optional Protocol has 51 parties and 18 signatories, the latter 39 parties and 18 signatories. United Nations, Multilateral treaties deposited with the Secretary-General (internet), http://untreaty.un.org, consulted on 25 March 2006. Bredbenner documents the negotiations before, during, and after the Hague Conference in relation to women's nationality. Although the result did not favour women's equality, the negotiations were a precursor to changes in the treatment of women's nationality in the United States and other countries. Candice Lewis Bredbenner, *A nationality of her own – women, marriage, and the law of citizenship* (Berkeley: University of California Press, 1998), 195–242.

[81] "Final Act, Seventh International Conference of American States, Montevideo, Uruguay, 3–26 December 1933", *American Journal of International Law*, (1933) vol. 28 Supplement (Concord (USA): The Rumford Press, 1933), 52–64, 61–62. The provisions thus stand in stark contrast to the 1930 Hague Convention. For a brief history of women's rights in the Inter-American system, see (in Spanish), Lomellin, Carmen, Breve Historia de la Protección de los Derechos Humanos de las Mujeres en el Sistema Interamericano (internet), http://palestra.pucp. edu.pe/pal_int/?file=derechos/lomellin.htm, consulted on 25 March 2006.

[82] *Final Act, Seventh International Conference of American States, Montevideo, Uruguay,*

Whiteman mentions the articles adopted as model rules by the Asian-African Legal Consultative Committee in 1964, in consideration of "dual nationality".[84] They basically repeat the provisions found in previous conventions regarding nationality generally (right of state to determine its nationals, obligation to recognise nationality only if the attribution is consistent with international law, and so on) and multiple nationality (treatment of multiple nationals by third states, military obligations, right of renunciation). Article seven would however seem to be innovative:

> A person who knows that he possesses two nationalities acquired without any voluntary act on his part should renounce one of them in accordance with the law of the State whose nationality he desires to renounce, within twelve months of his knowing that fact or within twelve months of attaining his majority age, whichever time is the latter [later].[85]

It is noteworthy that the Committee did not advocate (or perhaps could not agree upon) denationalisation in cases of multiple nationality, but placed an obligation on the individual concerned, albeit not a binding one, to exercise her or his free will in order to eliminate the incident multiple nationality. No corresponding obligation is placed on the state to provide a mechanism for this process, and no corresponding exhortation urges the state to defer to the individual along practical lines, such as by considering that the elimination of multiple nationality should take precedence over the fulfillment of military service obligations in such cases.

The principal regional treaty regime dealing with multiple nationality is that established under the auspices of the Council of Europe (COE), although the treaties are open to accession by non-COE member states. While creating a regional web of ties, the above-mentioned treaties entered into by Spain in relation to multiple nationality do not constitute a regional system (although Hecker qualifies them as such),[86] but really amount to a series of bilateral treaties between Spain and various countries. A true web of bilateral treaties classified as a regional system by Hecker is constituted by 34 treaties between (former) Communist (or Eastern-block) states, many of which are still in force, which concentrate on the prevention, elimination and limitation of

---

3–26 December 1933, 63. The notification provision found in article two is mirrored by the Commission internationale de l'état civil, *Convention concernant l'échange d'informations en matière d'acquisition de nationalité, 1964* (internet), http://perso.wanadoo.fr/ciec-sg/Liste Conventions.html, consulted 25 March 2006, which has been signed and ratified by eight European states. See Commission internationale de l'état civil (internet), http://perso. wanadoo.fr/ciec-sg/SignatRatifConv.pdf, consulted 25 March 2006.

[83] Whiteman, *Digest of international law*, vol. 8, 82., verified by the successor to the Pan American Union, the Organization of American States (OAS): six states signed the treaty, of which five ratified/acceded to it, plus Brazil, which subsequently denounced it in 1951. Organisation of American States, *Inter-American treaties and conventions: signatures, ratifications, and deposits with explanatory notes*, (Washington: OAS General Secretariat, 1993).

[84] Whiteman, *Digest of international law*, vol. 8, 82.

[85] Id.

[86] Hecker, "Doppelstaatigkeit, Bancroft-Verträge und Osteuropa", 410.

multiple nationality (as opposed to the Spanish model).[87] Nevertheless, four of the treaties allow for the possibility of multiple nationality.[88] Hecker states that in 1992, 21 of these treaties were in force,[89] and questions whether a multi-lateral treaty between the states concerned would not have been a more apt vehicle.[90]

It should be noted that efforts at regulating multiple nationality may involve more than formal agreements. The sensitive issue of multiple nationality in relation to large ethnic Chinese communities in south-east Asia was addressed by the People's Republic with mixed success, although joint declarations with several concerned states, and bilateral agreements with Indonesia (later abrogated) and Nepal, were negotiated.[91] A different case is the system established by Nordic countries in the

---

[87] Ibid. For a detailed explanation of the treaty system see Hellmuth Hecker, "Die Doppel-staaterverträge des Ostblocks", *WGO Monatshefte für Osteuropäisches Recht* (1986) 273–283. What in some respects might be seen as predicating the Eastern Block treaty network relating to multiple nationality is treaty practice in relation to option of nationality, which "played an important rôle in the international law and diplomacy of the second half of the nineteenth century and the first quarter of the twentieth". George Ginsburgs, "Option of nationality in Soviet treaty practice, 1917–1924", *The American Journal of International Law*, (1961) vol. 55, 919–946, 919. In relation to option of nationality generally, and state practice from the Second World War until the mid-1960s, see Karl Matthias Meessen, *Die Option der Staatsange-hörigkeit*, vol. 38, *Schriften zum Öffentlichem Recht* (Berlin: Duncker & Humblot, 1966).

[88] Hecker, "Die Doppelstaaterverträge des Ostblocks", 281–82. Regarding the situation in "post-Communist states" see generally André Liebich, "Plural citizenship in post-Communist states", *International Journal of Refugee Law*, (2000) vol. 12, no. 1, 97–107.

[89] Hellmuth Hecker, "Staatsangehörigkeitsfragen in völkerrechtlichen Verträgen osteuro-päischer Staaten", *Archiv des Völkerrechts* (1992) vol. 30, no. 3, 326–354, 327–28. See this text for a complete list, including participation by the states concerned in other multilateral and bilateral treaties related to nationality, extradition, and judicial assistance.

[90] Hecker, "Die Doppelstaaterverträge des Ostblocks", 275.

[91] See *Treaty between the People's Republic of China and the Republic of Indonesia con-cerning the question of dual nationality, April 22, 1955* (in force 20 January 1960, unilaterally abrogated by Indonesia on 10 April 1969), in Shao-Chuan Leng and Hungdah Chiu, eds., *Law in Chinese foreign policy: Communist China and selected problems of international law* (Dobbs Ferry, NY: Oceana Publications, Inc., 1972), 301–05. The treaty provided for election between the two nationalities, and for automatic determination where no election had taken place. See also Sasmojo, ed., *Menjelesaikan masalah dwikewarganegaraan RI-RRT* (Jakarta: Penerbit Djambatan, 1959). In relation to Nepal, the text can be found in Cohen and Chiu, *People's China and international law. A documentary study*, 769. The text only relates to Tibet. Joint communiqués were issued by the People's Republic and Malaysia (31 May 1974), the Philippines (9 June 1975) and Thailand (1 July 1975) stating that the two states did not recog-nise dual nationality, and that acquisition of nationality in one state resulted in automatic expa-triation in the other. Yu Sheng, "China's nationality law and the principles of international law", in *Selected articles from the Chinese Yearbook of International Law*, ed. Chinese Society of International Law (Beijing: China Translation and Publishing Corp., 1983), 213. The text in relation to Thailand is reproduced in Tung-Pi Chen, "The nationality law of the People's Republic of China and the overseas Chinese in Hong Kong, Macao and South-east Asia", *New*

1950s (Denmark, Finland, Iceland, Norway and Sweden) which also excludes multiple nationality, but provides for a system of free movement of persons and facilitated acquisition of nationality.[92]

The evolution in the provisions of the five COE treaties indicates a definite trend away from disapproving attitudes vis-à-vis multiple nationality over time, which is also demonstrated by a fundamental change in the premise and outlook of the treaties. Likewise, this series of developments in the COE treaties clearly demonstrates the influence of notions and provisions of human rights and standards of treatment of the individual, such as the principle of non-discrimination. The preambles to the first convention in 1963, and the last, of 1997, best illustrate this shift. The aim of the *Convention on Reduction of Cases of Multiple Nationality and Military Obligations in Cases of Multiple Nationality* (1963) is to "reduce as far as possible the number of cases of multiple nationality". In contrast, the *European Convention on Nationality* (1997) begins by recognising that both individuals and states have interests related to nationality and that states have various approaches regarding multiple nationality. It concentrates "on the desirability of finding appropriate solutions to consequences of multiple nationality and in particular as regards the rights and duties of multiple nationals". It seeks only to avoid discrimination, and statelessness.[93]

York Law School Journal of International and Comparative Law, (1984) vol. 5, 281–325, 306. Statements by Premier Chou En-lai were also made in relation to Singapore, Burma and Cambodia in 1956. Cohen and Chiu, *People's China and international law. A documentary study*, 769–70. China's policy was one of advocating individual choice of nationality. It thus condemned South Vietnam's acts to force ethnic Chinese to become Vietnamese nationals, and participated in heated disputes in 1959 with India over the nationality of certain persons in Tibet, and with the Soviet Union in 1960. George Ginsburgs, "The 1980 nationality law of the People's Republic of China", *American Journal of Comparative Law*, (1982) vol. 30, 459–498, 468–70. In relation to a Chinese Nationalist (or Kuomintang-Taiwan) perspective, see Bincun Qiu, *Hua qiao shuang chong guoji zhi zhi ben zhenli* (Taibei: Xin sheng chu ban she, 1957). A Filipino author writing about multiple nationality in Asia claims that overseas Chinese still "present actual problems of multiple nationality in the Asian setting", dramatically (and perhaps showing related bias) beginning a section on the regulation of nationality in China with the words "China. Mother to millions, threat to millions of others". de Padua, "Ambiguous allegiance: multiple nationality in Asia", 256.

[92] For example, national legislation in Denmark, Norway and Sweden in 1951 provided that birth and residence until the age of 12 in one country would be considered the equivalent in any of the others. Regarding reciprocal social rights as agreed by treaty in 1955 for citizens of Denmark, Finland, Iceland, Norway and Sweden and their implementation in each country, see Tredje Udgave, *Nordiske Statsborgeres sociale Rettigheder under ophold i andet nordisk land* (København: Den nordiske socialpolitiske Komité efter henstilling fra Nordisk Råd, 1963). The Economist noted that in 2002, however, notwithstanding the Oresund rail-and-car bridge between southern Sweden and Denmark, and cheaper housing prices in Sweden, few Danes chose to move there due to tax and social security rules. Adam Roberts, "A survey of the Nordic region", *The Economist*, vol. 367, no. 8328, 14–20 June 2003, survey, 6.

[93] *Convention on reduction of cases of multiple nationality and military obligations in cases of multiple nationality, 6 May 1963*, (1968) 634 UNTS 221, no. 9065 (entry into force: 28

The 1963 Convention, which has been ratified/acceded to by 13 countries, de-nounced by one of these, and signed by two other states,[94] contains significant pro-visions in its first chapter in terms of its aim to reduce cases of multiple nationality, while its second chapter deals with military obligations in cases of multiple national-ity.[95] States wishing to accede could choose between accepting both chapters, or only chapter II (provided in article 7).[96]

The treaty was amended in 1977, in order to clarify the position of multiple nation-als of one state with compulsory military service and another without, to enable states to accept chapter one only, and most significantly, to amend the provision in article 2(2) cited in note 95, to eliminate the restrictive conditions on renunciation and require only ordinary residence outside the state whose nationality is to be re-nounced.[97] It is perhaps in some respects ironic that while the amending protocol in no way questioned the 1963 Convention's purpose of reducing the instances of mul-tiple nationality, the drafters recognised that "national legislation has instituted many more cases of automatic multiple nationality . . . and more attention is being paid to the individual's desire to choose freely which of the nationalities he possesses auto-matically he will retain".[98] The latter amendment was thus specifically predicated on

March 1968), and *European convention on nationality, 6 November 1997*, ETS 166, Council of Europe, (entry into force: 1 March 2000).

[94] Council of Europe, Chart of signatures and ratifications (internet), http://conventions. coe.int, consulted on 25 March 2006.

[95] Article one provides that naturalisation in another contracting state results in loss of nationality in the other contracting state, with certain stipulations related to minor children. Article 2(2) provides a right of renunciation of "nationality a person of full age possesses *ipso jure*, provided that the said person has, for the past ten years, had his ordinary residence out-side the territory of that Party and also provided that he has his ordinary residence in the ter-ritory of the Party whose nationality he intends to retain", and article three states that no "special tax" may be levied for such renunciation. *Convention on reduction of cases of multi-ple nationality and military obligations in cases of multiple nationality*, 634. However the treaty does not prevent multiple nationality that results from attribution at birth, and the options for reservations provided in annex to the convention (that nationality could be retained if the state granting the new nationality consented, for example) amount to loopholes that would in fact admit multiple nationality.

[96] Killerlby notes that the option was included such that states favouring multiple national-ity might take part in relation to military service. Margaret Killerby, "Steps taken by the Council of Europe to promote the modernization of the nationality laws of European states", in *Citizenship and nationality status in the new Europe*, ed. Síofra O'Leary and Teija Tiilikainen (London: Sweet & Maxwell, 1998), 21, 29.

[97] *Protocol amending the Convention on the reduction of cases of multiple nationality and military obligations in cases of multiple nationality, 24 November 1977*, ETS 95, Council of Europe (entry into force: 8 September 1978). The amending protocol has been ratified/acceded to by eight states and signed by three more. See Council of Europe, Chart of signatures and ratifications (internet), http://conventions.coe.int, consulted 25 March 2006.

[98] Council of Europe, *Explanatory report on the protocol amending the Convention of 6 May*

an idea of individual human rights. At the same time an additional protocol was opened for signature to require notification of relevant state parties of acquisitions of nationality, modelled on the International Commission on Civil Status's (CIEC) *Convention concernant l'échange d'informations en matière d'acquisition de nationalité*.[99] Killerby notes that the Additional Protocol is "not extensively used".[100]

In contrast to the first amendment to the 1963 Convention in 1977, the second amendment in 1993 represents a sea change in approach, although the relevant treaty has only been ratified by three states.[101] The Second Protocol (1993) amending the 1963 Convention specifically allows for multiple nationality such that certain second-generation immigrants (only those from other states party) might be naturalised in their countries of residence without losing their original nationality, to allow spouses

---

1963 on the reduction of cases of multiple nationality and military obligations in cases of multiple nationality (Strasbourg: Council of Europe, 1978), 5. The reference to increased cases of automatic multiple nationality is a reflection of attempts to treat men and women equally in terms of ability to transmit nationality to children. Gerard-René de Groot, "The European Convention on Nationality: a step towards a ius commune in the field of nationality law", *Maastricht Journal of European and Comparative Law*, (2000) vol. 7, no. 2, 117–157, 118. de Groot notes that "the fact that, on the one hand, multiple nationality was placed on the blacklist as something to be avoided as often as possible, but that, on the other hand, multiple nationality was accepted . . . as a consequence of mixed marriages . . . was one reason for initiating new discussions on the desirability of avoiding cases of multiple nationality". de Groot, "The European Convention on Nationality: a step towards a ius commune in the field of nationality law", 118.

[99] *Additional protocol to the Convention on the reduction of cases of multiple nationality and military obligations in cases of multiple nationality, 24 November 1977*, ETS 96, Council of Europe (entry into force: 17 October 1983). See Council of Europe, *Explanatory report on the Additional protocol to the Convention of 6 May 1963 on the reduction of cases of multiple nationality and military obligations in cases of multiple nationality* (Strasbourg: Council of Europe, 1978), and Commission internationale de l'état civil, *Convention concernant l'échange d'informations en matière d'acquisition de nationalité*.

[100] Killerby, "Steps taken by the Council of Europe to promote the modernization of the nationality laws of European states", 30. The Additional Protocol has been signed by six states of which four have ratified. Council of Europe, Chart of signatures and ratifications (internet), http://conventions.coe.int/Treaty, consulted on 25 March 2006. At the time of the first amendment to the Convention there were already indications that governments were giving greater weight to factors that contributed to incidences of multiple nationality. de Groot points to two resolutions by the Council of Europe's Committee of Ministers in 1977, and its Recommendation in 1988 that "it was desirable for each of the spouses of a mixed marriage to have the right to acquire the nationality of the other without losing the nationality of origin. de Groot, "The European Convention on Nationality: a step towards a ius commune in the field of nationality law", 117–18.

[101] *Second protocol amending the Convention on the reduction of cases of multiple nationality and military obligations in cases of multiple nationality, 2 February 1993*, ETS 149, Council of Europe (entry into force: 24 March 1995). For signatures/ratifications see Council of Europe, Chart of signatures and ratifications (internet), http://conventions.coe.int/Treaty, consulted 25 March 2006.

to acquire each other's nationalities, and to allow children to acquire the nationality of their parents. The Convention's preamble states that its leitmotifs are interests in integration of migrants, unity of nationality within the same family, and conservation of nationality of origin.[102] Killerby cites this as evidence of "a growing trend, at least in certain states, to allow multiple nationality in a greater number of cases".[103]

The 1993 amendment was but a harbinger of further fundamental change, namely the provisions and approach of the 1997 *European Convention on Nationality*.[104] Not only does the European Convention not seek to reduce or eliminate multiple nationality, it in fact contains provisions in article 14 that support the continuation of multiple nationality: states must allow the retention of nationalities acquired at birth, and nationality acquired automatically upon marriage. Aside form this provision the Convention may be characterized as neutral toward multiple nationality,[105] although the provision in article eight that a renunciation requirement for naturalization cannot be maintained where unreasonable or impossible might be seen as favouring multiple nationality. On the other hand, the rules relating to acquisition of nationality in article six favour automatic attribution of nationality *jus sanguinis*, meaning a systemic change that would reduce the numbers of automatic multiple nationals due to the avoidance of *jus soli* attribution.

The Convention seems to concentrate on the practical considerations that give rise to real ties between states and individuals, demonstrated by the categories of people for whom states party are obliged to facilitate the acquisition of nationality: spouses of nationals; children of nationals; children one of whose parents acquires/has acquired nationality; adopted children; persons born in a state and lawfully and habitually there resident; persons lawfully and habitually resident for a certain time before the age of 18; stateless persons and recognized refugees lawfully and habitually resident.[106] Aside from the provisions in articles 14 and 16 already mentioned that favour the existence of multiple nationality, the Convention provides in article 15 that it is up to each state to determine whether acquisition or possession of another nationality results in the loss of its nationality, and whether the "acquisition or retention of its nationality is subject to the renunciation or loss of another nationality". This leads Killerby to characterize the Convention as "acceptable both to those states which wish to allow multiple nationality in many cases or without restriction and to those

---

[102] Ibid.

[103] Killerby, "Steps taken by the Council of Europe to promote the modernization of the nationality laws of European states", 31. See also de Groot, "The European Convention on Nationality: a step towards a ius commune in the field of nationality law", 118–19.

[104] *European convention on nationality*. The treaty has been adhered to by 15 states and signed by 11 others. It is open to accession by all states. Council of Europe, Chart of signatures and ratifications (internet), http://conventions.coe.int/Treaty, consulted on 25 March 2006.

[105] de Groot, "The European Convention on Nationality: a step towards a ius commune in the field of nationality law", 120. He notes that "the Convention neither incorporates the approach of the 1963 Convention nor the exceptions made by the Second Protocol of 1993".

[106] *European convention on nationality*.

states which wish to restrict, as far as possible, the number of cases of multiple nationality".[107]

Importantly, the European Convention deals with consequences of multiple nationality, adopting the same provisions in the 1963 Convention (as amended) in relation to military service, and including civil service (articles 21 and 22), and providing that the possession of another state's nationality does not affect the rights and duties of nationals in their state of nationality (article 17). De Groot points out that its real significance is however not in relation to multiple nationality, but its enunciation of general principles in relation to nationality, its prioritization of the avoidance of statelessness, and its provisions relating to the legal position of resident aliens.[108] Along these lines he draws attention to the provisions of the explanatory report to the Convention in relation to article 17(2), which provide that the Convention does not affect the rules of international law relating to diplomatic or consular protection of multiple nationals. The explanatory report first refers to the provision of the 1930 Hague Convention on Nationality that "a State may not afford diplomatic protection to one of its nationals against a State whose nationality such a person also possesses", and adds

> *However, owing to the developments that have taken place in this area of public international law since 1930, in exceptional individual circumstances and while respecting the rules of international law, a State Party may offer diplomatic or consular assistance or protection in favour of one of its nationals who simultaneously possesses another nationality, for example in certain cases of child abduction.*[109]

---

[107] Killerby, "Steps taken by the Council of Europe to promote the modernization of the nationality laws of European states", 32. De Groot basically agrees. de Groot, "The European Convention on Nationality: a step towards a ius commune in the field of nationality law", 150.

[108] de Groot, "The European Convention on Nationality: a step towards a ius commune in the field of nationality law", 119–20. Regarding statelessness, the Convention is near watertight in terms of preventing it. Article 7(3) read with article 7(1)(b) provides that loss of nationality may not be allowed to provoke statelessness, with one exception: nationality acquired "by means of fraudulent conduct, false information or concealment of any relevant fact attributable to the applicant". Regarding equal treatment of women and men, de Groot draws attention to the fact that the European Convention only contains the provision provided in the second sentence of Article 9(1) of the Convention on the elimination of all forms of discrimination against women of 18 December 1979, and not the idea provided in the first sentence. The first sentence of article 9(1) of said convention states "States Parties shall grant women equal rights with men to acquire, change or retain their nationality". De Groot laments the omission, labeling the provision "particularly useful in cases of indirect discrimination against women in nationality law". de Groot, "The European Convention on Nationality: a step towards a ius commune in the field of nationality law", 127–28. He also indicates that the omission of Article 9(2) of the Women's Convention, providing "States Parties shall grant women equal rights with men with respect to the nationality of their children" is most likely due to the fact that the European Convention allows for such discrimination, albeit against men: its article 6(1)(a) allows states to prevent fathers from transmitting their nationality to children born out of wedlock. de Groot, "The European Convention on Nationality: a step towards a ius commune in the field of nationality law", 128.

[109] Council of Europe, Explanatory report to the European Convention on Nationality ETS

1. Treaties as evidence of state practice

It would appear that the impact of multilateral and regional treaties in relation to nationality and multiple nationality is limited both in terms of the treaties as evidence of state practice, and their effect on state practice. Above all paucity in ratification, but also lack of agreement on scope, limitation to specific regions, cultural or political contexts, and fundamental changes in approach over time, indicate that no clear consensus evidenced by consistent treaty practice can be cited as evidence of either a particularly tolerant or intolerant attitude by even a relatively small number of states vis-à-vis multiple nationality.

Hecker points out that in addition to the principal treaties, there are today countless bilateral treaties that touch on multiple nationality in one way or another.[110] This is arguably because nationality itself is of such fundamental importance in municipal law, and how states deal with individuals on both the municipal and international planes. The importance of nationality in practice was emphasised by the rejection by the International Law Commission's Special Rapporteur of a proposal that the problem of statelessness be addressed by attributing an "international nationality" to such persons. Nationality, it is clear, is relevant principally in municipal law, and cannot be imported into (or imposed on) municipal law from the international plane.

> *At the present stage of the political and juridical organization of the world, it is not feasible to grant to stateless persons in relation to the United Nations, rights similar to those bestowed by the various States upon their nationals.*[111]

2. The work of the International Law Commission

The work of the International Law Commission (ILC) in fact touched on nationality and multiple nationality at its first session in 1949, when "nationality, including state-

---

no. 166 (internet), http://conventions.coe.int, consulted 25 March 2006. See de Groot, "The European Convention on Nationality: a step towards a ius commune in the field of nationality law", 152. Very usefully, de Groot also mentions that a previous draft of article 17(2) of the European Convention read "a State Party may afford diplomatic protection to one of its nationals, for humanitarian or similar purposes, against a State whose nationality the person concerned also possesses". de Groot, "The European Convention on Nationality: a step towards a ius commune in the field of nationality law", 152.

[110] Hecker, "Doppelstaatigkeit, Bancroft-Verträge und Osteuropa", 410.

[111] Córdova, "Third report on the elimination or reduction of statelessness", 29. This comment is significant because it comes at the end of what has been called the "Nansen passport system" whereby an international body, the League of Nations, determined the juridical status of certain individuals. Individuals rejected by a growingly strict state-system were nevertheless recognized by international agreement. This has been cited as the precursor to modern international refugee law. Torpey, *The invention of the passport – surveillance, citizenship and the state*, 129.

lessness" was selected as a topic for codification. The topic of statelessness was subsequently taken up, and draft conventions on the elimination of future statelessness, and the reduction of future statelessness adopted.[112] The Commission's report on International Responsibility in 1956 is likewise of interest,[113] culminating in its Articles on State Responsibility issued over forty years later.[114]

In his consideration of "nationality, including statelessness", the ILC's Special Rapporteur decided to address the topic of multiple nationality in a report presented to the Commission in April of 1954, which was to constitute a working paper as a basis for discussion.[115] The report was a "continuation of the work already done" by the United Nations Secretariat in its "Survey of the problem of multiple nationality".[116] These documents are also mentioned below in relation to ideas surrounding the desirability and essence of multiple nationality. Just two months after considering the topic, the Commission voted unanimously (with four abstentions) to defer all questions relating to multiple nationality (and nationality), with the exception of statelessness.[117] The topic of multiple nationality as such has not been taken up since by

---

[112] International Law Commission, "Report of the International Law Commission to the General Assembly", *Yearbook of the International Law Commission*, (1960) vol. 1954, no. II, 140–149. For a discussion of the provisions and their development, see Córdova, "Report on the elimination or reduction of statelessness", and as follows: *A protocol on the elimination of present statelessness*, and a *Convention on certain measures for the reduction of present statelessness* were proposed in the Special Rapporteur's Second Report, Roberto Córdova, "Second report on the elimination or reduction of statelessness", *Yearbook of the International Law Commission* (1959) vol. 1953, no. II, 196–199. The former was revised in his third report, and the latter modified to be a Protocol, or in the alternative, a Convention on the elimination of present statelessness, and a Convention on the reduction of present statelessness. Córdova, "Third report on the elimination or reduction of statelessness". See also International Law Commission, "Report of the International Law Commission to the General Assembly", *Yearbook of the International Law Commission*, (1959) vol. 1953, no. II, 219–230.

[113] F. V. García Amador, "International responsibility", *Yearbook of the International Law Commission*, (1957) vol. 1956, no. II.

[114] See James Crawford, *The International Law Commission's articles on state responsibility. Introduction, text and commentaries* (Cambridge: Cambridge University Press, 2002). Article 44 states that "the responsibility of a State may not be invoked if: (a) the claim is not brought in accordance with any applicable rule relating to the nationality of claims", the Commentary referring such questions to the ILC's work on diplomatic protection. Crawford, *The International Law Commission's articles on state responsibility. Introduction, text and commentaries*, 264 note 722.

[115] Roberto Córdova, "Report on multiple nationality", *Yearbook of the International Law Commission*, (1960) vol. 1954, no. II, 42–52, 43.

[116] Ibid. See United Nations Secretariat, "Survey of the problem of multiple nationality prepared by the Secretariat", *Yearbook of the International Law Commission*, (1960) vol. 1954, no. II, 52–111.

[117] International Law Commission, "252nd meeting. Nationality, including statelessness (item 5 of the agenda)" A/CN.4/83, A/CN.4/84, *Yearbook of the International Law Commission*, (1954) no. I, 52–57, 57.

the ILC, although it has dealt with multiple nationality in the context of diplomatic protection and the succession of states.[118]

Córdova chose to deal with multiple nationality "immediately after the study of statelessness" and "excluding other aspects of the problem as a whole, especially that

---

[118] For the text of the draft articles on nationality of natural persons in relation to the succession of States provisionally adopted by the Commission on first reading, and commentary, see International Law Commission, "Report of the Commission to the General Assemby on the work of its forty-ninth session", *Yearbook of the International Law Commission*, (2000) vol. 1997, no. II Part 2, 14–43. The Commission reiterated its request to governments for comments on the draft articles in 1998, International Law Commission, "Report of the Commission to the General Assembly on the work of its fiftieth session", *Yearbook of the International Law Commission*, (2001) vol. 1998, no. II Part 2, 18, and adopted the draft preamble and 26 articles on second reading, recommending that the United Nations General Assembly adopt these as a declaration. International Law Commission, *Report of the Commission to the General Assembly on the work of its fifty-first session, 1999* (internet), http://untreaty.un.org/ilc/ilcsessions.htm, consulted 25 March 2006. For the full text of the ILC's recommendation, including draft articles and commentary, see International Law Commission, *Report of the Commission to the General Assembly on the work of its fifty-first session*. In relation to multiple nationality, in the Commentary to Article 9, the Commission withheld judgment on the relative desirability of multiple nationality: "It is not for the Commission to suggest which policy States should pursue on the matter of dual or multiple nationality. Accordingly, the draft articles are neutral in this respect. The Commission is nevertheless concerned with the risk of statelessness related to the above requirement of prior renunciation of another nationality". International Law Commission, *Report of the Commission to the General Assembly on the work of its fifty-first session*. Although the articles pay some attention to individual will (article 11), as long as persons affected by state succession do not become stateless, it is the states in question that determine whether related multiple nationality will be permitted (articles 9 and 10). The ILC established a working group on diplomatic protection in 1997. For its first development of the topic, see International Law Commission, "Report of the Commission to the General Assemby on the work of its forty-ninth session", 60–63. In 1998 the Commission discussed the legal nature of diplomatic protection, the rights involved, the topic's relationship to human rights, the preconditions for its exercise, and the relationship to the topic of state responsibility. The Commission concluded that the nature of diplomatic protection is related to a state's own rights as well as the rights of its nationals. International Law Commission, "Report of the Commission to the General Assembly on the work of its fiftieth session", 43–49. The Special Rapporteur's first report and first eight draft articles were considered in 2000. International Law Commission, *Report of the International Law Commission to the General Assembly, Fifty-second session*, 141–75. Draft articles 9–11 were considered in 2001. International Law Commission, *Report of the International Law Commission to the General Assembly, Fifty-third session*, United Nations General Assembly, Official Records, Fifty-sixth session, Supplement no. 10, A/56/10, (New York: United Nations, 2001), 507–21. Draft articles 12–16, as well as the issue of denial of justice, were considered in 2002, as well as draft articles 1–7, which had been provisionally adopted by the Commission. International Law Commission, *Report of the International Law Commission to the General Assembly, Fifty-fourth session*, United Nations General Assembly, Official Records, Fifty-seventh session, Supplement no. 10, A/57/10, (New York: United Nations, 2002), 120–92. Their contents were taken up in chapter three.

of the nationality of married persons".[119] The basis for this decision was his recognition that:

> There exists, of course, a certain inter-relation between the three problems; statelessness, multiple nationality, and nationality of married persons, and in dealing with the first two problems, care was taken to include provisions with regard to marriage and dissolution of marriage, with a view to preventing such changes in the personal status from producing statelessness or multiple nationality.[120]

Córdova's report relates to the elimination and reduction of multiple nationality, and specifically excludes issues relating to the diplomatic protection of multiple nationals, or "the obligations and rights derived from nationality".[121]

> The rights derived from nationality are, from the point of view of the State, those of requiring the services, whether military or otherwise, of its nationals, the collection of taxes, etc. and the obligations are those of protecting its nationals abroad, and, when they reside in national territory, of providing them with elementary education, courts of justice, sanitation, etc. The problem of avoiding multiple nationality evidently does not include the enumeration of the rights and duties either of the State towards its nationals or of the nationals towards the State.[122]

Córdova's decision to deal with multiple nationality before problems related to marriage and nationality, and to define multiple nationality as a problem, as opposed to its consequences constituting problems for states and individuals, is significant. It reflects a view that the relationship between the individual and the state must be exclusive and subordinates the practical and real problems faced by individuals in relation to multiple nationality to this view. The rejection of this approach by the Commission in turn suggests a changing view of human rights in terms of the weight given to the individual's will, and a recognition of the gravity of the forced breaking of legal ties by states against an individual's will.

In its discussion of the report, the Commission's members could not only not agree on the way in which multiple nationality might be eliminated, but on whether the Commission should recommend that it be eliminated at all.[123] The argument put forward by Mr Pal is illustrative:

> Multiple nationality only gave rise to really serious difficulty in war time, and it was not the Commission's function to help nations to prepare for war. Multiple nationality was the

---

[119] Córdova, "Report on multiple nationality", 45.

[120] Id., 45–46.

[121] Id., 46.

[122] Id.

[123] The Special Rapporteur had put forth a proposal that *jus soli* should be applied over *jus sanguinis*. Various members felt that this was not a practical solution, and that no country would easily give up its usual system of attribution of nationality at birth. Various members cited this as a reason instead to concentrate on questions such as diplomatic protection and military service of multiple nationals, as opposed to the elimination of multiple nationality. International Law Commission, "252nd meeting. Nationality, including statelessness (item 5 of the agenda)".

almost unavoidable result of modern freedom of movement coupled with the rigidity of the several systems of nationality legislation.[124]

In the end, the Commission seems to have been swayed by arguments that

it should concentrate on topics with respect to which it could reasonably expect States to surrender some of their prerogatives. . . . The topic of nationality as a whole would probably not be ripe for discussion by the Commission for many years.[125]

In fact, just the opposite of the approach, and substance, proposed by Córdova seems to have taken place over the medium-term, reflecting the consensus reached by the ILC in 1956 not to pursue his project. Marriage in relation to nationality was taken up as a treaty topic by states, and international efforts in relation to multiple nationality have concentrated on addressing some of its consequences (such as in relation to military service and diplomatic protection), as opposed to its elimination. This is a reflection of what the Commission's Secretary, Mr Liang, labelled certain states' desire to "preserve the person's freedom of will",[126] or a sign of an evolving standard of human rights that dictates that the individual's relationship to the state should not be easily or summarily dismissed, for example on the basis that the individual possesses the nationality of another state. This is discussed below.

E. ARGUMENTS SURROUNDING THE RELATIVE DESIRABILITY OF MULTIPLE NATIONALITY

Views on the nature and relative desirability of multiple nationality have been posited in various ways and argued along diverse lines.[127] While few authors see it as an unmitigated good, few authors go as far as de Padua in characterising it as the pos-

---

[124] Id., 54. There was fundamental disagreement about the relative undesirability and nature of multiple nationality. While Pal argued that stateless persons suffered real and profound hardship whereas multiple nationals were in a completely different situation, Córdova stated that "if statelessness was a tragic human problem it did not give rise to disputes between States, whereas dual or multiple nationality might". Lauterpacht discerned a trend toward acceptance of multiple nationality, and argued against efforts by the Commission to eliminate it. International Law Commission, "252nd meeting. Nationality, including statelessness (item 5 of the agenda)", 54–55.

[125] International Law Commission, "252nd meeting. Nationality, including statelessness (item 5 of the agenda)", 56, as proposed by Mr Scelle.

[126] Id., 54.

[127] For various assessments see for example T. Alexander Aleinikoff and Douglas Klusmeyer, *Citizenship policies for an age of migration* (Washington, DC: Carnegie Endowment for International Peace, 2002); Bar-Yaacov, *Dual nationality*; Karl Doehring, "Mehrfache Staatsangehörigkeit im Völkerrecht, Europarecht und Verfassungsrecht", in *Staat-Souveränität-Verfassung. Festschrift für Helmut Quaritsch zum 70. Geburtstag*, ed. Dietrich Murswiek, Ulrich Storost, and Heinrich A. Wolff (Berlin: Duncker & Humblot, 2000), 255–264; Randall Hansen and Patrick Weil, eds.,

sible source of "at least two armed conflicts in Asia".[128] As introduced in chapter one, arguments against multiple nationality have often been centred around views of the state's interest, versus the interest of the individual. But even this assertion must be qualified, as interest is often a subjective issue. This section will outline and discuss such views generally. Views related to the work of the International Law Commission have been addressed above and are not covered here.

At the outset, it may prove useful to point to what seem to be views at opposite ends of the spectrum in terms of the relative desirability of multiple nationality, in order to sketch the issues and gradations of opinions involved. Bar-Yaacov will be cited here as a principal source for disapproval of multiple nationality: "the status of dual nationality is undesirable and should be abolished".[129] His conclusions in 1961 went so far as to propose a system for the systematic elimination of the status by states working together to legislate to that effect.[130] His suggested solution involves applying what he terms a "development of the doctrine of effective nationality", but in fact seems to amount to a rejection of multiple nationality as such, as opposed to some level of recognition.[131]

Specifically, he proposes that only one mode of attribution of nationality at birth be used, neither *jus soli* nor *jus sanguinis*, as neither is guaranteed to reflect the actual tie of the individual to the state whose nationality is attributed, but "the nationality

---

Dual nationality, social rights and federal citizenship in the U.S. and Europe (New York: Berghahn Books, 2002); Karin Kammann, *Probleme mehrfacher Staatsangehörigkeit unter besonderer Berücksichtigung des Völkerrechts*, vol. 398, *Europäische Hochschulschriften (European University Studies) – Series II* (Frankfurt am Main: Peter Lang, 1984), 227–37; Hakkı Keskin, "Staatsbürgerschaft im Exil", paper presented at the conference: *Doppelte Staatsbürgerschaft – ein europäischer Normalfall?*, ed. Ulrich Büschelmann (Berlin: Senatsverwaltung für Gesundheit und Soziales, 1989); Wolfgang Löwer, "Doppelte Staatsbürgerschaft als Gefahr für die Rechtssicherheit", paper presented at the conference: *Doppelte Staatsbürgerschaft – ein europäischer Normalfall?*, ed. Ulrich Büschelmann (Berlin: Senatsverwaltung für Gesundheit und Soziales, 1989); David A. Martin and Kay Hailbronner, eds., *Rights and duties of dual nationals. Evolution and prospects* (The Hague: Kluwer Law International, 2003); Stanley A. Renshon, *Dual citizens in America. An issue of vast proportions and broad significance*, Center for Immigration Studies, 2000 (internet), http://www.cis.org/articles/2000/back700.html, consulted 25 March 2006); Peter H. Schuck, *Citizens, strangers, and in-betweens – essays on immigration and citizenship* (Boulder: Westview Press, 1998), 229–42; Spiro, "Dual nationality and the meaning of citizenship"; Patrick Weil and Randall Hansen, eds., *Nationalité et citoyenneté en Europe* (Paris: Éditions La Découverte et Syros, 1999).

[128] de Padua, "Ambiguous allegiance: multiple nationality in Asia", 266.

[129] Bar-Yaacov, *Dual nationality*, 266. As already illustrated, Bar-Yaacov is far from being alone.

[130] Hecker, writing more recently, agrees that multiple nationality is undesirable, but proposes that treaty regimes are the only means of dealing with the "problem" as "Unterschiede im innerstaatlichen Recht nie aufhören werden". (Author's translation: *differences in municipal laws will never cease to exist.*) Hecker, "Doppelstaatigkeit, Bancroft-Verträge und Osteuropa", 409.

[131] Bar-Yaacov, *Dual nationality*, 272.

of the country in which their parents have established their permanent residence".[132]
To regulate nationality upon marriage, Bar-Yaacov applauds the provision of the
Convention on the Nationality of Married Women whereby women do not automatically acquire the nationality of the husband. He decries however what he regards as
a loophole, that should a woman nevertheless opt to acquire her husband's nationality, loss of her original nationality is not automatic.[133] He proposes that voluntary naturalisation provoke an automatic loss of the original nationality.[134] In cases of transfer
of territory, Bar-Yaacov sees voluntary transfer of territory leading to automatic transfer of personal jurisdiction, and a refusal to relinquish such jurisdiction as amounting
to a burden on the new sovereign. He says that "in these circumstances, third States
would be entitled to recognise exclusively the new nationality".[135] Such an approach
raises issues in relation to international standards of human rights and respect for the
individual. This is taken up below in relation to Hong Kong and Macao and the treatment of their inhabitants by the United Kingdom, Portugal and China. While the
United Kingdom essentially deprived its former Hong Kong citizens of rights usually
associated with nationality, Portugal did not.

An opposing view is that of Spiro, who argues that

> *acceptance of dual nationality is . . . not only consistent with but demanded by republi-*
> *canism, communitarian, and liberal conceptions of citizenship. Maintaining additional national*
> *attachments becomes an expression of individual identity, both a reflection of and a con-*
> *tributor to community ties, and a mechanism for undertaking civic participation in that*
> *sphere; and the facilitation of these virtues will, I argue, ultimately benefit society as well*
> *as the individual. Dual nationality should not be merely tolerated; it should now be*
> *embraced, and citizenship law should be amended to eliminate the renunciation of foreign*
> *allegiances long required in the citizenship oath.*[136]

---

[132] Id., 271. This would of course have the effect that parents and children would not necessarily possess the same nationality.

[133] Id., 269. See articles 1 and 2 in *Convention on the nationality of married women.* As of
25 March 2006 there are 73 states parties. United Nations, Multilateral treaties deposited with
the Secretary-General (internet), http://untreaty.un.org, consulted 25 March 2006.

[134] Bar-Yaacov, *Dual nationality,* 267.

[135] Ibid. Aleinikoff and Klusmeyer differentiate between instances of state succession and
cession of territory. In instances of state succession they cite a presumption that successor state
will confer its nationality on residents, but the imposition of nationality "must be construed as
an offer that must be accepted to be valid . . . In cases of territorial cession, the ceding state is
obligated to remove its nationality from those persons who receive the nationality of the acquiring state and to respect the municipal law of the acquiring state. (This obligation is grounded
on the premise that a ceding state's refusal to withdraw nationality is tantamount to a state
imposing nationality on a foreign national residing outside its territory . . .). Should the ceding
state not fulfill this obligation, third-party states have a duty to recognize only the nationality
of the acquiring state". T. Alexander Aleinikoff and Douglas Klusmeyer, "Plural nationality:
facing the future in a migratory world," in *Citizenship today. Global perspectives and practices,* ed. T. Alexander Aleinikoff and Douglas Klusmeyer (Washington: Carnegie Endowment
for International Peace, 2001), 63–88, 64–65 note 1.

[136] Spiro, "Dual nationality and the meaning of citizenship", 1416. The reference is to the
oath of renunciation upon naturalisation in the United States.

These views and related issues are discussed below under the general headings (1) the rejection of multiple nationality and (2) the embrace of multiple nationality. Because many of the issues are cited by partisans of various aspects of the arguments, they are mainly addressed in either one section or the other, but arguments both for and against multiple nationality can be found in both sections.

1. The rejection of multiple nationality

Bar-Yaacov's arguments against multiple nationality essentially fall into three main categories, those related to (1) the essence of nationality, (2) identity and the emotional attachment of the individual to the state, and (3) legal obligations and rights as a consequence of nationality, as well as what amount to arguments that are a mixture of the three categories. Likewise, he discusses the significance of state practice that tolerates or recognises multiple nationality. These categories are discussed separately hereafter.

1.1 The essence of nationality

Aleinikoff and Klusmeyer recall that opposition to multiple nationality is premised both on specific questions that might arise between states in cases of multiple nationality ("allegiance", international protection, intervention), and the structure of the present international regime.[137]

> For reasons of administrative order and international peace, a regime of nation-states needs to know where individuals belong. Belonging means membership or citizenship. The fundamental rule of the international regime is that states should look after their own, and only their own. To do more is to interfere in the affairs of other states.... [P]ersons with two or more state memberships might be seen as causing headaches for states.[138]

Bar-Yaacov's argument that the value of nationality is reduced in cases when states decline to exercise diplomatic protection of their nationals who reside permanently abroad follows these lines in terms of its perception of the essence of nationality. From this he extrapolates that "it may be questioned whether there is any justification in the possession of such 'qualified nationality' which does not bring the individual the benefits usually enjoyed by nationals".[139] It should be noted, however, that mere residence abroad does not amount to possession of another nationality, and that declining to protect nationals on the basis of residency, as opposed to multiple nationality, cannot reflect the value of nationality, just residence.

Spiro points out that the refusal to protect multiple nationals against their other state of nationality was directed at avoiding international disputes, and preventing

---

[137] Aleinikoff and Klusmeyer, "Plural nationality: facing the future in a migratory world", 79.

[138] Ibid. Aleinikoff and Klusmeyer do not argue this, but hold this argument out as a theoretical one.

[139] Bar-Yaacov, Dual nationality, 268.

individuals from taking unfair advantage of states. He cites US President Grant's 1874 annual message to Congress, complaining of

> person[s] claiming the benefit of citizenship, while living in a foreign country, contributing in no manner to the performance of the duties of a citizen of the United States, and without intention at any time to return and undertake those duties, to use the claims to citizenship of the United States simply as a shield from the performance of the obligations of a citizen elsewhere.[140]

Grant's complaint refers principally to the benefits of nationality, and its related obligations, on the municipal plane. It is implicit in his statement that persons contemplating returning to the United States, and performing duties of citizenship, will and should be protected by the United States. Schuck's comparison of the relationship of nationality to marriage likewise seems restricted to the municipal plane.[141] Bar-Yaacov's attribution of value to nationality here however, is restricted solely to the international plane.

Spiro's sweeping comment cited at note 136 above in favour of multiple nationality, which views its value in terms of identity, community ties and participation, also challenges Bar-Yaacov's characterization of the essence of nationality. Even restricting consideration to the international plane alone, Medea of Colchis, whose emotional predicament (albeit not her legal predicament, as it may be surmised that had she returned to Colchis she would have been tried for murder) was mentioned in chapter one, may be alluded to for the proposition that the right to return to a country and permanently reside there is of tangible value to the individual, even without diplomatic protection.

1.2 Emotion and identity

Issues and arguments related to identity and emotion vis-à-vis nationality have been addressed in previous chapters.[142] Here, it behooves us to examine such arguments specifically in relation to multiple nationality. An overarching theme of Bar-Yaacov's argument is that nationality is more than simply a formal legal category, but an

---

[140] Spiro, "Dual nationality and the meaning of citizenship", 1432–33. He states that the United States' practice was to take a case-by-case approach to protection of multiple nationals against their other country of nationality, and argues that "diplomatic protection is no longer so much a function of nationality, in which states take care of their own, as it is covered by the umbrella of international human rights, in which the international community protects the abused regardless of nationality. The intersection of diplomatic protection and dual nationality was far more uncomfortable in a world in which states could treat their own nationals as they pleased". Spiro, "Dual nationality and the meaning of citizenship", 1433 and 1462.

[141] Schuck, Citizens, strangers, and in-betweens – essays on immigration and citizenship, 240–41. Schuck contemplates the relative desirability of multiple nationality from the standpoint of its effects on society, as opposed to its effects in international law.

[142] See generally David Miller, On nationality, Oxford Political Theory (Oxford: Clarendon Press, 1995). In relation to changes in national identity and the development of the European

expression of the relationship between the individual and the state, or "'sociological reality', involving the identification of the individual with a particular country and the continuous exercise on his part of certain rights and obligations", that demands exclusivity. As such, he believes "the conclusion that the status of dual nationality is inherently self-contradictory would seem obvious".[143] Arguments against multiple nationality along these lines can on the one hand be predicated on emotion or identity, or on the other, see the consequences of multiple nationality as having a negative impact on emotion and identity. A case can be made that the choices made by the independent Baltic states in relation to multiple nationality are definitely related to issues of identity, in particular ethnicity.[144]

But emotion and identity as ingredients and products of nationality are also cited by various authors in favour of multiple nationality. The example of Spain's treaties in the 19th and 20th centuries with various mostly Latin American countries already cited is relevant in this regard. The 1969 Spanish-Argentine Convention cited above in note 53 refers to emotion and identity as creating an interest in multiple nationality, as well as multiple nationality providing a mechanism for the propagation of the underlying identity and emotion. No less than Winston Churchill is reported to have

---

Union, see Soledad García, "European Union identity and citizenship", in *European citizenship and social exclusion*, ed. Maurice Roche and Rik van Berkel (Aldershot: Ashgate, 1997), 201–212; Heinz Kleger, "Einleitung: Ist eine politische Mehrfachidentität möglich", in *Transnationale Staatsbürgerschaft*, ed. Heinz Kleger (Frankfurt: Campus Verlag, 1997), 9–20. Likewise, identity and emotion are often unrelated to the nation state as such, among the various groups that constitute a country. Kadende-Kaiser and Kaiser present a case that expatriate Burundians and Tanzanian Ismailis have used "various communication media to forge transnational identities", arguing that "traditional liberal notions of citizenship that are exclusively limited to the "nation-state" level are not sufficient to explain the relationship between the individual and his or her community, because many communities in sub-Saharan Africa are not coterminous with national boundaries. Rose M. Kadende-Kaiser and Paul J. Kaiser, "Identity, citizenship, and transnationalism: Ismailis in Tanzania and Burundians in the Diaspora", *Africa Today*, (1998) vol. 45, no. 3–4, 461–480, 463 and 474. Regarding identity and membership of the state in Africa, see generally C. R. D. Halisi, Paul J. Kaiser, and Stephen N. Ndegwa, "Guest editors' introduction: the multiple meanings of citizenship – rights, identity, and social justice in Africa", *Africa Today*, (1998) vol. 45, no. 3–4, 337–350. Regarding different levels of rights and identity in relation to the state, see Francis Delpérée, "La citoyenneté multiple", *Annales de droit de Louvain*, (1996) no. 1, 261–273.

[143] Bar-Yaacov, *Dual nationality*, 257.

[144] Barrington documents that whereas Estonia initially prohibited multiple nationality, a change in 1995 allowed only ethnic Estonians who were already foreign citizens to retain multiple nationality.Lowell W. Barrington, "The making of citizenship policy in the Baltic states", *Georgetown Immigration Law Journal*, (1999) vol. 13, no. 2, 159–199, 180. Virtually the same developments took place in Lithuania. Barrington, "The making of citizenship policy in the Baltic states", 169–71. In any case, Barrington documents that policies toward inclusion of ethnic Russians who had migrated to the Baltic states during the Soviet period and their descendants, were driven by an "ethnic definition of the nation" and related perceptions of vulnerability. Barrington, "The making of citizenship policy in the Baltic states", 187–91.

proposed the creation of a common Franco-British nationality to symbolise the commitment of the two nations to each other during the Second World War, as well as a
common British-American nationality that would continue to unite Anglo-Saxon peoples even after the war ended.[145]

Keskin argues that multiple nationality is the only way to reflect the emotional
attachments of immigrants, in addition to assisting them in dealing with the practical
realities that surround moving from one country to another, and fostering assimilation.[146] Renshon on the other hand, although his legal analysis may be questioned,
opposes multiple nationality claiming to approach the subject matter in terms of its
"psychological implications and political consequences".[147] He concludes that most immigrants to the United States come from countries which "allow" multiple nationality
to varying degrees, and that this constitutes a barrier to assimilation, especially in the
context of what he labels the United States' current situation of "immigrants entering
a country whose cultural assumptions are fluid and 'contested'".[148] Schuck takes the

---

[145] Castro, "La nationalité la double nationalité et la supra-nationalité", 608–09.

[146] Keskin, "Staatsbürgerschaft im Exil", 48–49.

[147] Renshon, *Dual citizens in America. An issue of vast proportions and broad significance*.
Renshon states he is a Professor of Political Science at the City University of New York, and
a certified psychoanalyst. He criticizes scholarship advocating multiple nationality as "ordinarily based on narrow legal analysis wherein anything permitted is acceptable, or on the 'post-
modern' advocate's highly abstract theoretical musings, wherein anything permitted is suitable".
His style is polemical, but the basic errors contained in his text are not related to his conclusion that multiple nationality of current immigrants to the United States poses a challenge to
assimilation: "[Ask] . . . how many countries would allow a citizen to do all of the following:
take out one or more other citizenships, swear allegiance to a foreign state, vote in foreign
elections, hold high office in another country, and/or fight in another country's army even if
that country were hostile to the interests of the 'home' country. Chances are the looks you
receive will change from puzzlement to disbelief. . . . Then, to complete the experiment, ask if
they are aware that the United States is the only country in the world (so far as I can establish) to allow its citizens, natural or naturalized, to do all of these things. If their disbelief has
not broadened to astonishment, further inform them that a number of academic, legal, and ethnic activists welcome these developments, and are critical only of the fact that the United
States hasn't gone farther, faster to reduce and loosen the ties that bind Americans to their
country, instead of helping them to develop identifications and emotional ties to larger and, in
their view, more democratic 'world communities'". Renshon, *Dual citizens in America. An
issue of vast proportions and broad significance*. As demonstrated in the survey of state practice, the view of United States practice presented is incorrect, and there are many countries that
not only permit all the acts decried by Renshon, but can even be seen to go beyond them.
Likewise, Renshon misrepresents the duty of loyalty required of citizens under United States
law generally.

[148] Renshon, *Dual citizens in America. An issue of vast proportions and broad significance*.
Pickus also postulates that "the nature and legitimacy of the nation is being challenged internally by multiculturalism and alienation and externally by the globalization of markets and the
movement of people". Noah M. J. Pickus, "To make natural: creating citizens for the twenty-
first century," in *Immigration and citizenship in the twenty-first century*, ed. Noah M. J. Pickus

opposite view: "Citizenship probably facilitates (as well as reflects) the assimilation of newcomers by imparting a sense of welcome and belonging, reinforcing their attachment to American values and improving their English language skills".[149]

1.3 Legal obligations and rights

To the idea that nationality requires exclusivity of identification and emotion, and vice versa, Bar-Yaacov links practical concerns related to "the physical impossibility of performing simultaneously the rights and duties of citizenship in different geographical locations".[150] He cites conflicts over personal jurisdiction between states, as well as the paramount obligations of allegiance, stating "it is difficult to maintain that a status which is inherently incompatible with the obligations of a person in time of war could be admissible in time of peace".[151]

Bar-Yaacov's view of allegiance in relation to nationality brings together issues he regards as practical, and emotional.

> *States conceive nationality as a status involving the identification of the individual with his State, as well as active exercise of the responsibilities of citizenship. Thus, nationality is considered to imply not only strictly defined legal obligations, such as the performance of military service, but also the loyalty and devotion of the individual. This being so, it is difficult to imagine how an individual could possess the qualifications required for the possession of the nationality of two different States.*[152]

(Lanham: Rowman & Littlefield, 1998), 107–133, 109. He proposes a process for both native and naturalised citizens that "generates a sense of mutual commitment". Pickus, "To make natural: creating citizens for the twenty-first century", 108.

[149] Schuck, *Citizens, strangers, and in-betweens – essays on immigration and citizenship*, 231. In the French context, see Jacqueline Costa-Lascoux, "'Devenir français aujourd'hui...' Réflexion sur la sociologie des naturalisations", paper presented at the conference: *Être français aujourd'hui... Premier bilan de la mise en oeuvre du nouveau droit de la nationalité*, ed. Hugues Fulchiron (Lyon: Presses Universitaires de Lyon, 1995), 137–159. It would appear in any case that the specific situation of both country of departure and country of reception must be taken into account. Manuh documents Asante Ghanaian migration to Canada, lobbying for Ghana to admit multiple nationality, and the related effects on the group's cultural identity and relationship to both Ghana and Canada. Takyiwaa Manuh, "Ghanaians, Ghanaian Canadians, and Asantes: citizenship and identity among migrants in Toronto", *Africa Today*, (1998) vol. 45, no. 3–4, 481–494. He states that Ghana's "recognition" in 1996 of multiple nationality restricted multiple nationals from holding elective office and other participation in public life, caveats resented by male emigrants. Women emigrants however, viewed simple presence in Canada as "offering them financial autonomy and a full complement of rights" and did not contemplate return. Manuh, "Ghanaians, Ghanaian Canadians, and Asantes: citizenship and identity among migrants in Toronto", 489.

[150] Bar-Yaacov, *Dual nationality*, 265.

[151] Ibid.

[152] Id., 263. Bar-Yaacov cites Louis-Lucas, who taught a course on *Les conflits de nationalités* at the Hague Academy in 1938, for this proposition. His argument is that as nationality

It is noteworthy that Bar-Yaacov does not argue that individuals cannot identify with, or feel emotion for, more than one state, simply that in legal terms there is an overriding interest in giving effect to only one set of these feelings. Embodied in this argument is the question of divided loyalties. "In a world divided between competitive and mutually exclusive nation-states, we need ultimately to know which side everyone is on".[153] Spiro notes that the development of the United States' approach to multiple nationality has been driven in many respects by concerns related to the loyalty of the individual. In outlining the relaxation in the 1960s of the laws that withdrew American nationality on the basis of the performance of certain expatriating acts that might indicate a foreign attachment (other than mere possession of foreign nationality), he makes a case that the risks associated with "sharing nationals" were reduced as the implausibility of armed conflict grew. Likewise, persons formerly held in the Soviet political embrace

> could be trusted to transfer both paper and sentimental loyalties, at the same time that those who might have in fact entertained allegiances to our adversary were not likely to advertise them with formal affiliations.[154]

In terms of Bar-Yaacov's argument that practical aspects (obligations owed by the individual to more than one state) militate against multiple nationality, he does not discuss in detail the possibility that such issues might be regulated by treaty or agreement among states, as is in fact often the case, such as in relation to military service. Likewise, he does not explore the essence of emotional attachment in terms of any practical obligations that might cause real difficulties for the individual and the state concerned, except for military service and the possibility of war between states, issues addressed in the previous chapter.

---

obliges the individual to go as far as to sacrifice his or her life for the state, and obliges the state to provide the individual with aid and protection, multiple nationality is aberrant and illogical. Bar-Yaacov also cites Flournoy, writing in 1925: "Why is dual nationality anomalous? I think that is almost answered when you realise that nationality involves also allegiance. Dual allegiance at least is a permanent condition and certainly seems anomalous. Allegiance relates not merely to a technical condition and status, but also involves the feelings and wishes and intentions of the individual . . . the military obligations are not the only obligations of a citizen . . . a citizen is expected to contribute his part to the State, either in a material or in a spiritual way". Cited in Bar-Yaacov, *Dual nationality*, 263 note 33.

[153] Aleinikoff and Klusmeyer, "Plural nationality: facing the future in a migratory world", 83. The authors reject arguments that nationality must be an exclusive relationship, or that oppose multiple nationality on the basis of divided loyalties. Aleinikoff and Klusmeyer, "Plural nationality: facing the future in a migratory world", 82–84. Klusmeyer points out that the actual value of nationality to multiple nationals may have little to do with the issues raised by commentators in relation to multiple nationality. Douglas Klusmeyer, "Introduction", in *Citizenship today. Global perspectives and practices*, ed. T. Alexander Aleinikoff and Douglas Klusmeyer (Washington: Carnegie Endowment for International Peace, 2001), 1–14, 5.

[154] Spiro, "Dual nationality and the meaning of citizenship", 1452. An example of the incorporation of considerations related to multiple nationality in a state security assessment is provided below.

1.3.1 Obligations of military service

Issues related to multiple nationality and obligations of compulsory military service are not necessarily the same as considerations related to the prospect of armed conflict between states, which is discussed separately below.[155] In relation to military service generally, service in the armed forces of a foreign state has been common practice, and history is replete with examples of men going to war, or practically being impressed into such, on behalf of sovereigns not their own.[156] Vattel held that enlistment in a foreign army was subject to express approval of an individual's sovereign, and foreigners could not be compelled to enlist; enlistment of foreigners without their sovereign's permission constituted the crime of *"Plagiat, ou vol d'homme"*.[157]

In this sense it is perhaps apt to consider the current policies of France and Spain relating to their respective foreign legions, as examples of diverging practice. It is an express requirement that candidates for the Spanish *Legión* be either Spanish nationals or permanent residents,[158] and if of foreign nationality, from a country that shares historical, cultural and linguistic bonds with Spain, whose national legislation does not contain a prohibition against such enlistment, and does not deprive the candidate of his or her nationality on this basis.[159] In contrast, no nationality or residence requirement attaches to enlistment in the French *Légion étrangère*.[160] Instead, French nationality might be characterised as a consequence or reward of service, should it be desired.[161]

Objections to multiple nationality on the basis of obligations of military service may be predicated on the notion that any foreign military service is generally incompatible with state interests.[162] Furthermore, should military service be compulsory, and

---

[155] For a comparison of compulsory military service obligations in NATO and other countries in Europe, see ODIN. Ministry of Defence (Norway), *Norwegian Defence Facts and Figures 2002. G. Military Service. 1. Compulsory Service*, 2002 (internet), http://odin.dep.no/fd/english/publ/veiledninger/010011–120027/ index-hov007–b-n-a.html, consulted 25 March 2006.

[156] See generally Aram Karamanoukian, *Les étrangers et le service militaire* (Paris: Editions A. Pedone, 1978), 10–162.

[157] Vattel, *Le droit des gens ou principes de la loi naturelle*, 14.

[158] La Legión, *Los requisitos para alistarse en La Legión*, 2006 (internet), http://www.lalegion.com/ser/ requisitos.htm, consulted 25 March 2006.

[159] La Legión, *Ley 32–2002, de 5 de julio, de modificación de la Ley 17/1999, de 18 de mayo, de Régimen del Personal de las Fuerzas Armadas, al objeto de permitir el acceso de extranjeros a la condición de militar profesional de tropa y marinería*, 2006 (internet), http://www.lalegion.com/ser/ley_32_2002.htm, consulted 25 March 2006.

[160] Embassy of France (USA), *French Foreign Legion. Enlistment requirements*, 2001 (internet), http://www.info-france-usa.org/atoz/legion/enlist.asp, consulted 25 March 2006.

[161] "After three years of service, a legionnaire can ask for the French nationality and may also be entitled to a French resident permit if he has obtained a certificate of satisfactory military service. The resident permit is valid for ten years and is renewable. At the end of his career the legionnaire is assisted in his return to civilian life". Embassy of France (USA), *French Foreign Legion. Miscellaneous*, 2003 (internet), http://www.info-france-usa.org/atoz/legion/misc.asp, consulted 25 March 2006.

[162] de Groot mentions the Austrian reservation to Article 7(1)(c) of the 1997 European Convention

foreign military service prohibited, a multiple national would be faced with mutually incompatible obligations, in effect sailing between Scylla and Charybdis. Spiro points out that "treason, of course, could be undertaken by those without other national attachments, but the fact of formal dual allegiances made disloyal conduct far more likely, in some instances inevitable, even for an honorable individual".[163] This would however, not seem to be the case at the present time, although practice could of course change. Compulsory military service is increasingly uncommon,[164] and authors do not note penalties other than denationalisation for such service. In that sense, Legomsky notes that "no treaties of which I am aware *require* states parties to denationalize individuals who perform foreign military service", but he characterises most treaties as "imprecise and ambiguous on this crucial issue",[165] and notes that "[a]ctual state practices vary".[166]

Should service in foreign military forces be permitted, however, the conflict in terms of the individual's obligations vanishes, regardless of whether military service is compulsory or not. But even if military service as such is not an obstacle, multiple nationals subject to military service in their countries of nationality are without doubt exposed to hardship, should they have to serve in more than one country. While noting that state practice varies, and finding only a qualified right of the individual to renounce his or her nationality, Legomsky argues that "subject to certain quali-

on Nationality, and paragraph 32 of the Austrian Nationality Act according to which an Austrian may be deprived of nationality by voluntarily serving in foreign military forces. de Groot, "The European Convention on Nationality: a step towards a ius commune in the field of nationality law", 141.

[163] Spiro, "Dual nationality and the meaning of citizenship", 1443. Although he states that he is not in a position to state whether such provisions apply in current municipal law, Reermann notes that in the past, aside from deprivation of nationality, multiple nationals who did not fulfil military service obligations could suffer penalties such as imprisonment and confiscation of their assets, and upon fulfilment of military service obligations in one state of nationality, might suffer such penalties in the other. Olaf Reermann, "Dual nationality and military service", in *Rights and duties of dual nationals. Evolution and prospects*, ed. David A. Martin and Kay Hailbronner (The Hague: Kluwer Law International, 2003), 127–134, 127–28.

[164] Many authors note a trend toward the elimination of conscription in Europe and North America, and that many states never instituted it in the first place. See Aleinikoff and Klusmeyer, *Citizenship policies for an age of migration*, 34; Stephen H. Legomsky, "Dual nationality and military service: strategy number two", in *Rights and duties of dual nationals. Evolution and prospects*, ed. David A. Martin and Kay Hailbronner (The Hague: Kluwer Law International, 2003), 79–126, 89–91; Reermann, "Dual nationality and military service", 127.

[165] Legomsky, "Dual nationality and military service: strategy number two", 115.

[166] Id., 116. See pp. 114–119. Another issue is whether multiple nationals are permitted to serve in the armed forces of their own countries, simply because they are multiple nationals. Legomsky cites no state practice with the exception of a Mexican decree of 1998 that "requires members of the Mexican armed forces to be Mexican citizens by birth in Mexico who have not acquired any foreign nationality". Legomsky, "Dual nationality and military service: strategy number two", 87.

fications ... dual nationals should be free to renounce one of their nationalities even while otherwise liable to military conscription".[167]

In terms of the actual conscription of multiple nationals, notwithstanding any possible reduction in the practice,

> *Even today, some naturalized citizens fear conscription in the event they visit certain countries of origin, including Turkey, Greece, and Iran, which might not recognize the renunciations of their original nationalities prior to fulfillment of military service.*[168]

This embodies the long-standing controversy over military service and nationality, which did not involve rejection of multiple nationality as such, but arguments that states could insist on the performance of all obligations owed, including military service, before being obligated to "release" individuals from their nationality, or recognise expatriation upon naturalisation elsewhere.[169] This is clearly still the case in some states today,[170] and in others, even recognised loss of nationality may not entail the end of military obligations.[171]

In relation to the conscription of multiple nationals, Legomsky cites and discusses "a complex network of worldwide, regional, and bilateral agreements, all superimposed on a shifting foundation of nonuniform domestic laws and policies".[172] He

---

[167] Legomsky, "Dual nationality and military service: strategy number two", 114, and generally 109–114.

[168] Id., 89.

[169] See for example Bendix, *Fahnenflucht und Verletzung der Wehrpflicht durch Auswanderung*, and Georg Schulze, "Die Bedeutung des Militärdienstes für Verlust und Erwerbung der Staatsangehörigkeit", dissertation presented at the Königlichen Bayerischen Julius-Maximilians-Universität (Würzburg: 1910).

[170] In Germany, "for persons liable to military service, giving up their nationality requires the consent of the Federal Minister of Defense. This goes back to the basic conviction that such persons – as Legomsky puts it – should not be allowed to 'eat their dinner and then flee the restaurant when the bill arrives,' an expression which aptly illustrates the attitude of states proceeding in the same manner as Germany". Reermann, "Dual nationality and military service", 131. The Republic of Korea in 2005 amended its legislation such that dual nationals could not give up their Korean nationality to avoid military service. "The soldier's tale", *The Economist*, 16 July 2005, 50.

[171] According to the United States Department of State, "persons considering renunciation should also be aware of the fact that the fact that they have renounced U.S. nationality may have no effect whatsoever on their U.S. tax or military service obligations". United States Department of State, *Renunciation of U.S. citizenship by persons claiming a right of residence in the United States*, 2006 (internet), http://travel.state.gov/law/ citizenship/citizenship_777.html, consulted 25 March 2006. Legomsky states only that "[t]he United States, in contrast, allows renunciation whenever the person commits any of several specified acts with the intent to relinquish citizenship; the law does not disqualify persons liable to conscription. Legomsky, "Dual nationality and military service: strategy number two", 111.

[172] Legomsky, "Dual nationality and military service: strategy number two", 98 and generally 91–109.

argues that no new multilateral instrument is called for, and that unilateral action and bilateral agreements are the most efficient way to deal with the issues raised.[173] Bilateral treaties dealing with compulsory military service obligations are common among states.[174]

Aleinikoff and Klusmeyer state that "[c]oncern about conflicting military obligations no longer provides a convincing rationale for rigid rules absolutely barring dual citizenship", but contend that due to the possibility of colliding interests "some mechanism for voluntary expatriation, with only minimal qualifications, should be preserved".[175] Legomsky characterises military service as one of several "smaller issues that require positive policy prescriptions".[176]

1.3.2   Exercise of functions involving the public trust
Schuck points to the fact that military service obligations are a separate issue from questions of war, the need for states to ensure the loyalty of their citizens, and the exercise of functions involving the public trust. He states that

> Our world is one in which hostilities may take the form not only of formal military campaigns but also of clandestine acts of terrorism or theft of valuable technologies undertaken on behalf of undemocratic regimes that nevertheless can claim the fervent political and religious loyalty of their people. Although legal or illegal aliens can also engage in such conduct, citizens probably have somewhat greater opportunities at the margin to do so. . . . The fact that few dual nationals pose any greater danger of disloyalty than those with only one nationality does not preclude the risk that the dual citizenship of those few may place them in a better position to wreak immense damage.[177]

The potential for multiple nationality to lead to bias or susceptibility to influence does not always mean it is a barrier to assuming very sensitive positions. Franck states that the head of the Estonian Army from 1991–1995 was an American citizen, as were the Foreign Ministers of Armenia and Bosnia-Herzegovina.[178] There are also many examples of individuals who possess a right to a second nationality under a state's municipal legislation playing important roles: when Czech President Vaclav Havel openly suggested that then serving US Secretary of State succeed him as president of the

---

[173] Id., 98–109.

[174] See the sample list of treaties in Id., 125–26.

[175] Aleinikoff and Klusmeyer, *Citizenship policies for an age of migration*, 35.

[176] Legomsky, "Dual nationality and military service: strategy number two", 79. See also generally Löwer, "Doppelte Staatsbürgerschaft als Gefahr für die Rechtssicherheit", 160–62.

[177] Schuck, *Citizens, strangers, and in-betweens – essays on immigration and citizenship*, 239.

[178] Thomas M. Franck, "Multiple citizenship: autres temps, autres moeurs", in *Mélanges en l'honneur de Nicolas Valticos*, ed. René-Jean Dupuy (Paris: Éditions A. Pedone, 1999), 149–158, 153–4. Aleinikoff and Klusmeyer recommend that multiple nationals not be placed in high-level policymaking positions. Aleinikoff and Klusmeyer, *Citizenship policies for an age of migration*, 41.

Czech Republic there was no indication that Albright actually possessed Czech nationality, but certainly the expectation that she could easily obtain it.[179]

There is ample evidence, however, that in areas of defence-related or other security concerns, governments do take multiple nationality into account. In New South Wales, Australia, for example, defence contractor Boeing won the right to exclude Australian multiple nationals from work on certain projects, if the second nationality raised security concerns.[180] Access to classified government information by United States dual nationals is surveyed below. But it would seem that in the private sector dual nationality is often seen as a benefit to companies, when it allows employees additional flexibility in terms of travel and access to labor markets.

There are also examples of opposition to the multiple nationality of specific individuals not on the basis of specific security concerns or national obligations, but simply along the lines of propriety. News reports that Brazilian President Lula da Silva's wife and children had applied for and been granted Italian nationality led to public criticism that such things could happen only in "third-class republics" and served as a symbol of the confidence the first family had in the President and of what they expected for the nation's future.[181]

1.3.3   Political participation and other issues

Participation in political life is rarely an obligatory consequence of citizenship or nationality. The Australian exception in this regard was mentioned in chapter three. Objections on the basis that political involvement by multiple nationals could embarrass states, lead to conflicts, or prove to be a threat to state security, are discussed below under the heading "democratic values and the rights of citizenship". Issues related to economic and social costs, benefits and rights, conflicts of law, and the facilitation of criminality, are also discussed under the "embrace" of multiple nationality, because most authors argue that these areas do not constitute grounds for opposition to multiple nationality as such.

1.4   The significance of tolerance/incorporation of multiple nationality in law

Bar-Yaacov dismisses the attitude of states whose practice demonstrates tolerance of the existence of multiple nationality by arguing that they only accept it to the extent that it is in their narrow interests to do so, and that such acceptance is qualified in essence.

---

[179] "Albright tipped for Czech Presidency", BBC News, 28 February 2000 (internet), http://news.bbc.co.uk/1/hi/world/europe/659215.stm, consulted 29 March 2006.

[180] Leonie Lamont, "State clears Boeing for discrimination pass", *The Sydney Morning Herald*, 1 April 2005 (internet), http://www.smh.com.au/news/National/State-clears-Boeing-for-discrimination-pass/2005/ 03/31/1111862537239.html?oneclick=true, consulted 25 March 2006.

[181] Cândido Prunes, Opinião e Notícia, "O resgate da cidadania (italiana)", 9 December 2005 (internet), http://www.opiniaoenoticia.com.br/interna.php?mat=1814, consulted 27 March 2005.

*The United Kingdom, which has shown, in its recent legislation, that it does not regard dual nationality as especially undesirable, is an exception which proves the rule. To quote M. Jones: '. . . many persons of **unimpeachable British association** (as was proved in the two world wars) became naturalised in foreign countries for **purely business reasons**, and it was no longer felt justifiable to cause them to lose their nationality automatically in such circumstances.' It is obvious that what is required from a British national is loyalty and readiness to serve his country. It is hardly probable that the United Kingdom would grant British nationality to a person who would like to avail himself of that nationality for 'purely business reasons', while possessing an 'unimpeachable association' with a foreign state.*[182]

It is to be wondered whether the foreign states that naturalised the Britons referred to by Bar-Yaacov would be amenable to such a view and related insinuation that their nationality is strictly "business" while the tie to Britain should be "unimpeachable". Indeed, Bar-Yaacov takes only one aspect of the situation into account, and in the author's opinion thus fundamentally misinterprets the consequences of British practice. Even if his proposal that the United Kingdom would never naturalise persons with "unimpeachable associations" to foreign states is taken as true (a proposition not asked, and tested only indirectly herein – as will be seen, naturalisation in the United Kingdom is not conditional on divesting oneself of a previous nationality), the very fact that the United Kingdom acquiesced as far as such other states possessing the right to require their nationals (also UK nationals) to be 'loyal and ready to serve the country', reflects a view that the relationship of nationality must not of necessity be an exclusive one in terms of state interests.

Bar-Yaacov's criticism of multiple nationality here is unrelated to practice by various states amounting to the selling of nationality, absent any substantive or real ties to the state concerned. Aleinikoff and Klusmeyer argue that "the selling of nationality unquestionably cheapens its value as a form of allegiance",[183] and oppose the practice on the basis that

the emerging consensus in international law reflected in the Nottebohm case suggests that a substantial connection should tie the individual to the state of which he or she is a national. Nationality should not become a commodity that individuals can purchase to further their business or personal interests.[184]

---

[182] Bar-Yaacov, *Dual nationality*, 263–4 (emphasis added).

[183] Aleinikoff and Klusmeyer, "Plural nationality: facing the future in a migratory world", 84.

[184] Ibid. Seealso Rey Koslowski, "Challenges of international cooperation in a world of increasing dual nationality," in *Rights and duties of dual nationals. Evolution and prospects*, ed. David A. Martin and Kay Hailbronner (The Hague: Kluwer Law International, 2003), 157–182, 170–79.

2. The embrace of multiple nationality

A considerable amount of recent scholarship argues that a clear trend toward tolerance of multiple nationality can be observed. Aleinikoff and Klusmeyer contend that
"the limited state reaction to dual nationality can be explained primarily by the
paucity of actual adverse consequences".[185] They predict that although there will be
periodic, localised backlashes, "in all likelihood, dual nationality will continue to increase
owing to high levels of immigration, changes in state policies, and the continuation
of both *jus sanguinis* and *jus soli* citizenship norms".[186]

Whereas Aleinikoff and Klusmeyer note the increase in multiple nationals, the likelihood that conditions will not change, and the innocuousness of the phenomenon,
Spiro argues for the systematic embrace of multiple nationality. Although categorised
according to the "citizenship frames" of "republicanism", "communitarianism" and
"liberalism", Spiro's arguments that there are specific state interests in embracing
multiple nationality are essentially related to: (1) the naturalisation of resident aliens,
and (2) the nature of the democratic state and process.[187] They are premised on the
idea that conditioning naturalisation upon expatriation elsewhere will discourage residents from doing so, and that the naturalisation of immigrants is fundamentally beneficial
to the state.[188] He argues against mere tolerance of multiple nationality by the United
States, but for its complete "acceptance", and the elimination of even a notional
requirement of renunciation of previous nationality as a condition of naturalization.[189]

---

[185] Aleinikoff and Klusmeyer, "Plural nationality: facing the future in a migratory world",
86. Their analysis has been canvassed above in relation to the arguments posited by Bar-
Yaacov. They conclude that "the practice of citizenship tends to be local"; "it is difficult to
identify situations around the world where tensions approaching hostility exist between nations
with significant numbers of shared dual nationals"; "the number of dual nationals is dwarfed
by the number of cross-border migrants and refugees"; and "dual nationality appears to be
more an individual than a group phenomenon". Aleinikoff and Klusmeyer, "Plural nationality:
facing the future in a migratory world", 85. Groenendijk also states that in light of large numbers of multiple nationals in the Netherlands, there are few actual problems that stem from the
situation. Kees Groenendijk, "Doppelte Staatsangehörigkeit und Einbürgerung in den Niederlanden:
Pragmatismus und soziale Stabilität", paper presented at the conference: *Hohenheimer Tage
zum Ausländerrecht 1999 und 5. Migrationspolitisches Forum*, ed. Klaus Barwig, Gisbert
Brinkmann, Kay Hailbronner, Bertold Huber, Christine Kreuzer, Klaus Lörcher, Christoph
Schuhmacher (Nomos Verlagsgesellschaft, 1999), 189–197, 197.

[186] Aleinikoff and Klusmeyer, "Plural nationality: facing the future in a migratory world",
86–87.

[187] Spiro, "Dual nationality and the meaning of citizenship", 1461–79.

[188] Id., 1479.

[189] Id., 1460–61 and 66. The oath sworn upon naturalisation in the United States requires
the renunciation of allegiance to any foreign state or sovereign, but it is not enforced in terms
of a requirement that the individual actually demonstrate effective renunciation of foreign
nationality. Karin Scherner-Kim, "The role of the oath of renunciation in current U.S. nationality policy – to enforce, to omit, or maybe to change?", *The Georgetown Law Journal*, (2000)

Inherent in Spiro's arguments, outlined below, is the idea that "acceptance" of multiple nationality goes beyond simply permitting the status to exist, to varying levels of tolerance. Spiro not only argues that multiple nationality is inoffensive to state interests, but that multiple nationals should not be treated differently from other nationals. Whether this reflects state practice is a question posed herein. Schuck essentially adopts very similar views, but believes that even in tolerating multiple nationality "we must still decide . . . which kinds of continuing commitments to other polities are deemed consistent with . . . loyalty".[190]

2.1 Armed conflict and multiple nationality

Spiro reasons that opposition to multiple nationality has revolved around the prospect of war between states, and that the increasing implausibility of armed conflict renders the reasoning essentially moot. Even the quality of many armed conflicts at the present time, complemented by arguments that democratic states resolve disputes otherwise than by recourse to armed force, indicates that states should not be threatened by multiple nationality.[191]

> *Lightning wars conducted by volunteer armies present few opportunities for shadowy fifth columns. That was the case with the Persian Gulf "war" (and could perhaps also be said*

---

vol. 88, no. 2, 329–379, 329. In relation to the oath of allegiance to the United States generally, see David Weissbrodt, *Immigration law and procedure in a nutshell*, 2nd ed., (St. Paul: West Publishing Co., 1989), 237. Scherner-Kim argues that the effect of the chasm between oath and reality is detrimental to the United States, and that expatriation should be a requirement of naturalisation, in order to "ensure that naturalization decisions include elements of allegiance to and appreciation of the political and legal values forming the basis of the nation that the naturalizing individual is about to join". Scherner-Kim, "The role of the oath of renunciation in current U.S. nationaltiy policy – to enforce, to omit, or maybe to change?", 332–33. For arguments that would in turn set a low threshold for naturalisation in relation to the rights of citizenship, see Joseph H. Carens, "Why naturalization should be easy: a response to Noah Pickus", in *Immigration and citizenship in the twenty-first century*, ed. Noah M. J. Pickus (Lanham: Rowman & Littlefield, 1998), 141–146.

[190] Schuck, *Citizens, strangers, and in-betweens – essays on immigration and citizenship*, 242. He doubts arguments that multiple nationality "is now acquired too easily and/or for the wrong reasons" but posits that such concerns could be addressed, although "any effort to create distinct classes of citizens – particularly with respect to their legal rights – would raise constitutional difficulties". Schuck, *Citizens, strangers, and in-betweens – essays on immigration and citizenship*, 242–43. Rather, he argues that the American naturalisation oath be modified to require naturalised American citizens to proffer the interests of the United States over other countries, and forswear the holding of any high public office. He disagrees with Spiro's contention that the renunciation requirement contained in the oath be eliminated, calling this "a colossal, even tragic political blunder . . . [which] would arouse intense, widespread political opposition and animus, which would be directed against immigrants". Schuck, *Citizens, strangers, and in-betweens – essays on immigration and citizenship*, 243–47.

[191] Spiro, "Dual nationality and the meaning of citizenship", 1461.

of the lengthier theater conflicts in Korea and Vietnam). If for some now unfathomable reason we end up at arms with Mexico, it won't be accompanied by the sorts of vulnerabilities (real or perceived) associated with World War II or the Cold War. Finally, assuming the truth of the democratic peace, those regimes with which we do find ourselves in conflict will be by their nature (that is, anti-democratic) unrepresentative of their citizens and thus less likely to instill the real loyalties of dual nationals even where they command their formal ones. Who is to say that dual Iraqi-Americans sided with Saddam Hussein during that engagement? Indeed, those U.S. residents (citizens or not) native-born to countries involved in recent U.S. military operations seem to have been at a premium with American commanders. The very son of Somali warlord Mohammed Aidid (practically, if not formally, an enemy of the United States and United Nations forces) was put on active duty in the U.S. Marines during the peacekeeping operation in that country and has since returned to Somalia to take his dead father's place.[192]

Schuck's caveat to this proposition has been mentioned.[193] Likewise, it may be questioned whether real (as opposed to perceived) vulnerabilities have indeed changed in any fundamental sense since the Cold War.

Aside from the general issue as to whether the prospect or reality of conflict between states should militate against the possession of multiple nationality, Legomsky states that

[o]n one point the law is settled: International law forbids states from compelling any persons – whether dual nationals or mononationals – to take up arms against their other states of nationality. This principle was first codified in article 23 of the Annex to the 1907 Hague Convention Respecting the Laws and Customs of War on Land. Although not all the world's nations have ratified it, the Convention appears to have attained the status of customary international law.[194]

This contention is dubious, and may be questioned. In fact it seems unlikely that the treaty provision was intended to relate to multiple nationals, and Legomsky cites no primary or secondary sources in support of his proposition. Such a rule would not seem to exist in international law, and it actually seems quite certain that the opposite is true: nationals may be compelled to participate in armed conflicts even against another state of nationality, at their own peril in terms of their obligations under the municipal laws of the other state.

Article 23 of the 1907 Regulations is not contained in the section on belligerents, but in the section on (the conduct of) hostilities. It is one of seven articles in a chapter entitled "Means of Injuring the Enemy, Sieges, and Bombardments", and thus arguably meant to be a constitutive norm in relation to the means and methods of warfare, as opposed to rules relating to protected persons. The relevant section (h) was not contained in the 1899 version of the rules.[195] It reads (in relevant part):

---

[192] Id., 1461–62.

[193] See text and note at note 177 above.

[194] Legomsky, "Dual nationality and military service: strategy number two", 119.

[195] To compare the 1899 and 1907 provisions, see Dietrich Schindler and Jiří Toman, eds.,

Art. 23. In addition to the prohibitions provided by special Conventions, it is especially forbidden –
  (h) To declare abolished, suspended, or inadmissible in a court of law the rights and actions of the nationals of the hostile party.
  A belligerent is likewise forbidden to compel the nationals of the hostile party to take part in the operations of war directed against their own country, even if they were in the belligerent's service before the commencement of the war.[196]

While the Convention and its attached regulations have indeed been characterised as customary norms,[197] a general or customary rule of international law prohibiting states from employing persons they regard as their nationals, in an armed conflict against another state of nationality, is not cited by other writers on the subject. On its face, the provision does not state that it applies to multiple nationals.

It may be remarked at the outset that the general context of the development of norms in relation to multiple nationality argues against Legomsky's interpretation, including multilateral and bilateral treaty practice in relation to military service generally. Such a rule would (in 1907) have entailed the express recognition of multiple nationality, at a time in history when, as has been seen, some version of indelible allegiance or nationality was still in the minds of legislators and commentators, and as opposed to giving effect to foreign nationality, much state practice and comment favoured forcible expatriation upon attribution of another nationality on the basis of conflicting obligations. It seems more apt to qualify practice as 'in denial' as far as even the existence of multiple nationality, and certainly unfavourable to obliging states to give effect to another nationality in such a constraining fashion. The obligation to fight for one's country if so required was unquestionable and ineffaceable, and the primary reason for opposition to the existence of multiple nationality in the first place. The 1930 Hague Convention discussed above contains no such rule, and no treaties dealing with nationality or military service can be cited for the proposition.

Moreoever, not only the position of the article within the Regulations, but the development of international humanitarian law generally, calls Legomsky's reading of the 1907 Regulations into question. The 1899 and 1907 Peace Conferences codified much of the customary law of war, complementing the Geneva Conventions of 1864 and 1906. Rules relating to specific attribution of what today would be called combatant status, and that of protected person, were still basic in nature. The rule espoused in Article 23(h) was arguably intended as such a basic or fundamental norm,

---

The laws of armed conflicts. A collection of conventions, resolutions, and other documents, 3rd ed. (Dordrecht: Martinus Nijhoff Publishers, 1988), 83.

[196] "Convention (IV) Respecting the Laws and Customs of War on Land, signed at The Hague, 18 October 1907. Annex to the Convention. Regulations Respecting the Laws and Customs of War on Land," in *The laws of armed conflicts. A collection of conventions, resolutions and other documents*, ed. Dietrich Schindler and Jirí Toman (Dordrecht: Martinus Nijhoff Publishers, 1988), 69–98.

[197] Schindler and Toman, eds., *The laws of armed conflicts. A collection of conventions, resolutions, and other documents*, 63.

to prevent states from forcing nationals to fight against their own countries, for example because they were permanently resident, or in the context of occupied territories. To maintain that states extended this rule in 1907 to persons they deemed to be their own nationals, is unfounded, as it is at the present time.

The well-known *Kawakita* case may be cited as an illustration in this regard.[198] Although Kawakita, a dual United States-Japanese national, had not fought in the Japanese military against the United States, he was convicted of treason for mistreating American prisoners in his work as an interpreter in Japan during the Second World War. Holding that American dual nationals are subject to obligations that are unconditional, the Court stated that a defence to charges of treason is compulsion, but cited no obligation on the part of the other state of nationality not to use the national against his own (other) country. That military service against another state of nationality in wartime should be an exception seems an unwarranted extrapolation.

> *Circumstances may compel one who has a dual nationality to do acts which otherwise would not be compatible with the obligations of American citizenship. An American with a dual nationality who is charged with playing the role of the traitor may defend by showing that force or coercion compelled such conduct.*[199]

Importantly, the Court cites with approval an excerpt from an article by Orfield, which can be said to entail the rule, in addition to reflecting reality:

> *In time of war if he supports neither belligerent, both may be aggrieved. If he supports one belligerent, the other may be aggrieved. One state may be suspicious of his loyalty to it and subject him to the disabilities of an enemy alien, including sequestration of his property, while the other holds his conduct treasonable.*[200]

---

[198] *Tomoya Kawakita v. United States*, 343 U.S. 717, 72 S. Ct. 950 (1952).

[199] *Tomoya Kawakita v. United States*, 72 S. Ct. 950, 962 (1952). At another point the Court stated "Of course, an American citizen who is also a Japanese national living in Japan has obligations to Japan necessitated by his residence there. There might conceivably be cases where the mere nonperformance of the acts complained of would be a breach of Japanese law. He may have employment which requires him to perform certain acts. The compulsion may come from the fact that he is drafted for the job or that his conduct is demanded by the laws of Japan. He may be coerced by his employer or supervisor or by the force of circumstances to do things which he has no desire or heart to do. That was one of petitioner's defenses in this case. Such acts – if done voluntarily and willfully – might be treasonable. But if done under the compulsion of the job or the law or some other influence, those acts would not rise to the gravity of that offense. The trial judge recognized the distinction in his charge when he instructed the jury to acquit petitioner if he did not do the acts willingly or voluntarily 'but so acted only because performance of the duties of his employment required him to do so or because of other coercion or compulsion'. In short, petitioner was held accountable by the jury only for performing acts of hostility toward this country which he was not required by Japan to perform". *Tomoya Kawakita v. United States*, 961.

[200] Ibid. See generally Orfield, "The legal effects of dual nationality".

As regards the **voluntary** taking up of arms by a multiple national on behalf of one state of nationality against another, Legomsky states that state practice varies as to whether such conduct results in denaturalisation.[201] He notes virtually unanimous practice as far as criminalising such behaviour however, with no exception for multiple nationals.[202] It was argued in the previous chapter that this is a function of states' municipal laws, and that states have wide latitude in prescribing the standard of loyalty expected of their nationals. Rather than punishing dual nationals for such conduct, Legomsky argues that states should instead regard such participation as either a "voluntary decision to expatriate" or grounds for denationalisation.[203] Aleinikoff and Klusmeyer only call for a facilitated ability to ensure expatriation by the individual.[204] Whereas Legomsky (erroneously, it would seem) regards the issue as a matter of choice due to his interpretation of the 1907 Hague Regulations, Aleinikoff and Klusmeyer relate the issues to "a broader point: Dual nationality is not invariably in the interest of the persons holding such a status".[205]

2.2   The incorporation of resident aliens into the body politic

Spiro agrees with Schuck's arguments that republicanism demands inclusion: residents should be citizens, such that their exercise of the franchise will ensure governmental accountability, and realistic policies that respond to actual needs. A requirement of renunciation of previous nationality bears no relation to these interests, whereas other conditions for naturalisation, such as adherence to the political system and language knowledge, can be justified.[206]

2.3   Democratic values and the rights of citizenship

The US case of *Perez v. Brownell* held that from the standpoint of the state voluntary political participation by a dual national might implicate and embarrass the other state of nationality, leading to disputes.[207] On this basis the Court held that a provision expatriating citizens upon the exercise of the franchise abroad was valid. US

---

[201] Legomsky, "Dual nationality and military service: strategy number two", 120.

[202] Ibid. See pp. 120–122.

[203] Id., 122.

[204] Aleinikoff and Klusmeyer, *Citizenship policies for an age of migration*, 35.

[205] Ibid.

[206] Spiro, "Dual nationality and the meaning of citizenship", 1466–68. In terms of communitarianism, he argues that inclusion in the category of nationals goes to more than just the individual's relationship with the state, but to the community at large. Barriers to naturalisation thus prevent effective assimilation. "In Schuck's terms, permitting the retention of prior nationality would 'lower the price' of citizenship but might also lower its value". Spiro, "Dual nationality and the meaning of citizenship", 1473.

[207] *Perez v. Brownell*, 356 U.S. 44 (1958), and Spiro, "Dual nationality and the meaning of citizenship", 1446.

practice has changed completely in the intervening years. Today, even Americans exercising high foreign political office may retain their American nationality from the US standpoint.[208] Spiro dismisses the arguments in *Perez*, asserting that individual conduct (including voting) is not held to reflect that of the state of nationality, and the state is not held accountable for the acts of its citizens.[209]

There are many instances of states encouraging their nationals abroad, many of them multiple nationals, to vote. In 2004 Mexico implemented a law allowing for the approximately ten million Mexican citizens in the United States to vote in presidential elections.[210] The Premier of the Spanish province (*Comunidad Autónoma*) of Galicia traveled to Buenos Aires and Montevideo in 2005 to campaign for regional elections, correctly judging that election results would turn on the 12% of voters who live outside Spain (he lost).[211] Italy goes further by allowing non-resident citizens to stand for Parliament: it reserves 18 seats (of more than 900) for them in overseas constituencies.[212]

To arguments that political participation by multiple nationals might open the way for foreign governments to influence other countries' political processes, Spiro responds that this is unlikely, and that in any case, any inclination to vote according to the interests of a foreign state, or under pressure from a foreign state, can take place without any foreign nationality.[213]

---

[208] Spiro, "Dual nationality and the meaning of citizenship", 1455. Although loss of US citizenship is possible depending on the individual's subjective intent. The US Department of State treats seeking public office in a foreign state differently from other acts, but "the Department does not normally consider such service alone, as sufficient to sustain the burden of showing loss of U.S. citizenship by a preponderance of the evidence when the individual has explicitly expressed a contrary intent". United States Department of State, *Advice about possible loss of U.S. citizenship and seeking public office in a foreign state*, 2006 (internet), http://travel.state.gov/law/citizenship/citizenship_779.html, consulted 27 March 2006.

[209] Spiro, "Dual nationality and the meaning of citizenship", 1464. The Australian (dual) nationality of a British hedge fund millionaire who was revealed to be the largest secret backer of the British Conservative Party was reported in the Australian press, but did provoke criticism. James Button, "Secret Tory lender is Australian", *The Sydney Morning Herald*, 28 March 2006 (internet), http://www.smh.com.au/articles/ 2006/03/27/1143441083323.html, consulted 28 March 2006.

[210] "Vote, sweet vote", *The Economist*, 26 June 2004, 58.

[211] P. Marcos and X. Hermida, "Galician premier takes election bandwagon to Buenos Aires", *El País (English supplement to the International Herald Tribune)*, 10 May 2005, 3; Nuno Ribeiro, "Eleições na Galiza serão decididas por 36 mil votos de emigrantes", *Público* (Lisbon), 28 June 2005, 16.

[212] Catherine Munro, "Playing on the right for Italy", *The Sydney Morning Herald*, 2 April 2006 (internet), http://www.smh.com.au/news/world/on-the-right-wing/2006/04/01/1143441378366. html#, consulted 2 April 2006. The article reports that 10 of the 17 candidates for Italy's "electorate" of 190,000 persons covering Australia, Asia, Africa and Antarctica, are Australian, one of whom is a former high-profile Chairman of Soccer Australia with ties to the Australian Labor Party, now running for Italian office as a "neo-fascist". Ibid.

[213] Spiro, "Dual nationality and the meaning of citizenship", 1469–72. Keskin points out that

Americans have long voted their ethnic affiliation, even where they have not maintained their original nationality. They have in the process sometimes been accused of acting for "unpatriotic reasons". So long as the interests of the United States and the other nation are not unalterably opposed – and at present there are few relationships or issues in which that is the case – it is not clear why those motivations should deform the process.[214]

Aleinikoff and Klusmeyer agree, stating that there is no empirical evidence for the proposition that multiple nationals may heed the interests of one state while voting in elections elsewhere, and that in any case "the problem of divided loyalty reflected in the franchise is not peculiar to dual nationals. Rather it appears to be the price a society pays for accepting immigration".[215] Along similar lines, they reject arguments that multiple nationality provides an unfair advantage as far as an "exit option", or that multiple nationality reduces commitment to the state of residence.[216] Aleinikoff and Klusmeyer also reject arguments that oppose voting in more than one country (on the basis that such voting allows individuals to have a say in the political process without having to bear the consequences, or that this distracts from political participation elsewhere) as "more symbolic than real . . . If, under ideas as old as Aristotle, we believe that participation in politics is a primary goal of citizenship, then it is not clear on what basis we should condemn such conduct".[217]

As regards positions that entail the public trust, Aleinikoff and Klusmeyer also reject arguments that office-holding by multiple nationals should give rise to objections.

In cases where officeholders are open about their dual national status, both states are put on notice about potential conflicts of interest and may act accordingly to minimize the possible risks. If dual nationals are permitted to occupy influential positions in large multinational corporations with business enterprises in the same states of which they are nationals, it seems unclear why they should be prohibited fom doing likewise in most areas of government service.[218]

---

loyalty and emotional attachment to a state cannot be achieved by simply promulgating laws, but have to do with overall treatment in society. Keskin, "Staatsbürgerschaft im Exil", 52.

[214] Spiro, "Dual nationality and the meaning of citizenship", 1471.

[215] Aleinikoff and Klusmeyer, "Plural nationality: facing the future in a migratory world", 81. Contentions related to voting in more than one country's elections are discussed below, in relation to arguments favouring multiple nationality.

[216] Id., 82.

[217] Id., 80. In the German context, see Keskin, "Staatsbürgerschaft im Exil", 43–44. For other arguments in this regard, see generally Aleinikoff and Klusmeyer, *Citizenship policies for an age of migration*; Hansen and Weil, eds., *Dual nationality, social rights and federal citizenship in the U.S. and Europe*; Martin and Hailbronner, eds., *Rights and duties of dual nationals. Evolution and prospects*; Weil and Hansen, eds., *Nationalité et citoyenneté en Europe*.

[218] Aleinikoff and Klusmeyer, "Plural nationality: facing the future in a migratory world", 82. In another text they specifically recommend that multiple nationals should not hold what they call "high-level policy and security-sensitive responsibilities" in national governments. Aleinikoff and Klusmeyer, *Citizenship policies for an age of migration*, 41.

While governments may not seek to take inappropriate or unfair advantage of their nationals who hold public office overseas, some do appear to be keen to preserve or deepen ties to such individuals: In 2005 the Portuguese government created a forum to bring together all Portuguese public office holders overseas.[219]

2.4 Economic and social rights, costs and benefits, and the facilitation of criminality

There are many instances of individuals changing their nationality for business or social reasons, often to comply with national requirements in owning assets. Such changes may or may not involve multiple nationality, depending on municipal legislation. When media magnate Rupert Murdoch became a US citizen in 1985 to meet the terms of US media ownership laws he automatically lost his Australian nationality under Australian law. Should Emilio Azcárraga Jean, CEO of Mexico's Televisa become an American in order to push into the US market, he would not automatically lose his Mexican nationality under Mexican law.[220]

Schuck argues that multiple nationality benefits US business, as far as their employees' ability to travel and work abroad, as well as the specific language and trans-national skills likely to accompany multiple nationality. He also cites economic advantages such as tax revenues generated by multiple nationals. In an overall sense, he contends that

> *Just as genuinely free trade among nations tends to benefit all participants, so too does the international flow of human, financial, and technological capital that dual citizenship facilitates.*[221]

On the other hand citizenship usually means a right to social welfare benefits. Both Motomura and Tichenor cite legislative moves in the mid 1990s in the United States to remove social welfare benefits and other rights from non-citizens, including permanent residents. While Motomura argues that legal permanent residence is a transition to citizenship and should thus give rise to benefits and rights, Tichenor states that the same transition model can be cited to justify giving benefits and rights only to those who actually follow-through.[222] In either case, Schuck points out that a policy

---

[219] "Comunidades Fórum de luso-eleitos", *Correio da Manhã* (Lisbon), 6 April 2005, 33.

[220] Andrew Walker, "Rupert Murdoch: Bigger than Kane", *BBC News*, 31 July 2002 (internet), http://news.bbc.co.uk/1/hi/uk/2162658.stm, consulted 28 March 2006. "Reunited", *The Economist*, 18 February 2006, 61.

[221] Schuck, *Citizens, strangers, and in-betweens – essays on immigration and citizenship*, 231.

[222] Hiroshi Motomura, "Alienage classifications in a nation of immigrants: three models of 'permanent' residence", in *Immigration and citizenship in the twenty-first century*, ed. Noah M. J. Pickus (Lanham: Rowman & Littlefield, 1998), 199–222; Daniel J. Tichenor, "Membership and American social contracts: a response to Hiroshi Motomura", in *Immigration and citizenship in the twenty-first century*, ed. Noah M. J. Pickus (Lanham: Rowman & Littlefield, 1998), 223–227. See generally James F. Hollifield, *Immigrants, markets, and states – the political economy of postwar Europe* (Cambridge (USA): Harvard University Press, 1992).

such as encouraging naturalisation by allowing multiple nationality creates costs for government that would not exist should the persons in question have remained aliens.[223]

It is interesting to note that while several authors discuss social rights and benefits in relation to citizens, residents, and aliens,[224] there is little evidence of opposition to multiple nationality on the basis of an individual potentially receiving social rights and benefits in more than one country,[225] because he or she is a multiple national. This may be because in practical terms, although nationality (or citizenship) may be a prerequisite for such benefits or rights, so is residence, thus making the incident multiple nationality essentially irrelevant. Were it not, state practice regarding taxation of income might be expected to follow nationality, as opposed to residence.[226] Most claims by multiple nationals probably involve a real link beyond the simple possession of the nationality of the state from which the benefit is claimed. One such case may be the East Timorese soldiers who had been part of the Portuguese colonial military, attempting to secure pensions from Portugal,[227] even as there was speculation in Portugal that the government wished to limit the number of Portuguese-Timorese dual nationals.[228]

This is different to issues of tax evasion. Koslowski states that multiple nationality can be used to facilitate crime:

> *If wealthy business people, however, can use dual nationality to conceal their international movements, hide their assets from tax authorities, and elude border controls, so can those who engage in terrorism and illegal economic activities like drug smuggling, money laundering, and human smuggling. The growth of transnational crime is keeping pace with*

---

[223] Schuck, *Citizens, strangers, and in-betweens – essays on immigration and citizenship*, 233. Bommes argues that welfare states that encourage migration also thereby reduce the value of nationality. Michaèl Bommes, "Migration and ethnicity in the national welfare-state," in *Migration, citizenship and ethno-national identities in the European Union*, ed. Marco Martiniello (Aldershot: Avebury, 1995), 120, 124–29.

[224] Aleinikoff and Klusmeyer, *Citizenship policies for an age of migration*, 62–77; Michael Jones Correa, "Seeking shelter: immigrants and the divergence of social rights and citizenship in the United States", in *Dual nationality, social rights and federal citizenship in the U.S. and Europe. The reinvention of citizenship*, ed. Randall Hansen and Patrick Weil (New York: Berghahn Books, 2002), 233–263.

[225] Although Aleinikoff and Klusmeyer do state that multiple nationals should receive entitlements according to their principal place of residence. Aleinikoff and Klusmeyer, *Citizenship policies for an age of migration*, 40.

[226] The exception of the United States in this regard has already been mentioned. See Koslowski, "Challenges of international cooperation in a world of increasing dual nationality", 171–2.

[227] "Fate for former Portuguese soldiers unclear", *Dili Suara Timor Lorosae*, 16 March 2005 (author's translation from Indonesian).

[228] "Timorenses perdem dupla nacionalidade", *Diário de Notícias* (Lisbon), 16 February 2004, 1, 20.

economic globalization, and transnational criminal organizations are becoming increasingly sophisticated.[229]

Koslowski does not argue for the elimination of multiple nationality, however, but for the elimination of economic citizenship programs, and in any case for the sharing of information between states in relation to their multiple nationals, which would reduce the potential for abuse.[230] On the other hand, speculation in the United States that children of immigrants might pose a risk of terrorism has not focused on any possible multiple nationality, but specifically on their American nationality and consequent ability to travel on US passports.[231] Perhaps because of this, US authorities reportedly "quietly stepped up their scrutiny of all incoming travelers of Pakistani descent, including US citizens".[232]

There are, however, certainly cases where multiple nationals have used one nationality to avoid prosecution in their other country of nationality. Depending on the viewpoint adopted, former Peruvian President Alberto Fujimori's (dual) Japanese nationality either allowed him to avoid prosecution in Peru, or escape unfair treatment by political opponents. A local mayor in Portugal, Fátima Felgueiras, became nationally known for fleeing to Brazil to avoid corruption charges, using her status as a native-born Brazilian (dual) national to avoid extradition. Claiming her innocence, she eventually returned to Portugal voluntarily, and was re-elected with charges still pending.[233]

Aleinikoff and Klusmeyer recall the difficulties multiple nationals face when their states base municipal law determinations on nationality, but argue that conflicts' and treaty regimes are adequate to deal with the problems.[234]

---

[229] Koslowski, "Challenges of international cooperation in a world of increasing dual nationality", 174.

[230] Id., 177 and 179. In relation to sharing information between countries, see also generally Heike Hagedorn, "Administrative systems and dual nationality: the information gap", in *Rights and duties of dual nationals. Evolution and prospects*, ed. David A. Martin and Kay Hailbronner (The Hague: Kluwer Law International, 2003), 183–200.

[231] Josh Meyer, "Fear over US-born extremists is brewing", *Los Angeles Times*, 1 August 2005 (internet), http://www.hvk.org/articles/0805/1.html, consulted 28 March 2006.

[232] Id.

[233] José Augusto Moreira, "Fátima Felgueiras acusada de 28 crimes", *Público* (Lisbon), 30 April 2004, 2; Paulo de Vasconcellos, "Fátima Felgueiras 'vive uma vida normal e já não fala mais em voltar'", *Público* (Lisbon), 6 May 2005, 18; "Câmara delega 31 competências em Fátima Felgueiras", *Diário de Notícias* (Lisbon), 24 November 2005 (internet), http://dn.sapo.pt/2005/11/24/nacional/camara_delega_ competencias_fatima_fe.html, consulted 28 March 2006.

[234] Aleinikoff and Klusmeyer, *Citizenship policies for an age of migration*, 35–36. Löwer points out that regarding taxation, as long as nationality can be used as a point of connection, multiple taxation of multiple nationals is possible. Löwer, "Doppelte Staatsbürgerschaft als Gefahr für die Rechtssicherheit", 156–60. In relation to conflicts of law generally, see pp. 164–169.

2.5 Multiple nationality as international protection

Several international bodies cite multiple nationality in various contexts as a possible mechanism in favour of protection of the individual. At its 17th meeting, in August 2000, the United Nations Sub-Commission on the Promotion and Protection of Human Rights suggested that the World Conference against Racism, Racial Discrimination Xenophobia and Related Intolerance, held in August- September 2001, investigate "the role that can be played by recognition of dual citizenship" in eliminating such phenomena.[235] Likewise, the United Nations Sub-Commission on Prevention of Discrimination and Protection of Minorities, at its 25th meeting, in August 1997

> *Appeal[ed] to the States concerned by immigration to study the possibility of granting migrant workers dual nationality which would constitute a positive factor for integration, with due respect for cultural identity, and also protection against the evils of racial discrimination.*[236]

The same Sub-Commission in 1998 requested that a working paper be prepared on the rights of non-citizens in their countries of residence in relation to racial discrimination.[237]

F. THE MANAGEMENT OF MULTIPLE NATIONALITY: THE PRACTICE OF INTERNATIONAL ORGANISATIONS

On the international, as opposed to the municipal plane, there are other areas that can be cited as evidence of how states deal with the potential for conflicts of obligation and loyalty vis-à-vis one another in terms of multiple nationality. Inter-governmental international organizations such as the United Nations and its agencies take account of nationality in terms of employment, due to national quota requirements. UN policy is not to take account of multiple nationality as such for competitive examinations, but to allow multiple nationals to apply for positions as long as one of their

---

[235] United Nations. Sub-Commission on the Promotion and Protection of Human Rights, "World Conference against Racism, Racial Discrimination, Xenophobia and Related Intolerance", 17th meeting, 11 August 2000, E/CN.4/2001/2, E/CN.4/Sub.2/2000/46 (Geneva: United Nations, 2000), 19, and 24 at no. 17(n).

[236] United Nations. Sub-Commission on the Prevention of Discrimination and Protection of Minorities, "Situation of migrant workers and members of their families", 25th meeting, 21 August 1997, E/CN.4/1998/2, E/CN.4/Sub.2/1997/50 (Geneva: United Nations, 1997), 19 and 20 no. 7.

[237] United Nations, Commission on Human Rights, "The rights of non-citizens", Subcommission on Prevention of Discrimination and Protection of Minorities, 50th session, Geneva, 3–28 August 1998, E/C.4/1999/4–E/CN.4/Sub.2/1998/45.-30 Sept. 1998 (Geneva: United Nations, 1998), 79.

countries of nationality is on the list of eligible nations.[238] Practice by the International Committee of the Red Cross (ICRC), an international organization *sui generis*,[239] is just the opposite. The ICRC's delegates may be of any (multiple) nationality, but any nationality is a vital issue in terms of practical perceptions of the organisation's neutrality. As for the UN, multiple nationality itself is not at issue, but as opposed to the UN example cited above, any nationality of a delegate that could call the ICRC's neutrality into question in a particular operational context would serve as a bar to work in such situation, notwithstanding the possession of another, contextually uncontroversial nationality. In operational contexts, however, there is evidence that the UN acts similarly, such as when the UN commander in Cyprus refused to deploy a Dutch-Turkish dual national soldier, citing the soldier's safety.[240]

Perhaps the most obvious presence of nationality in the world today in the international sphere, one which certainly involves emotion, identity, duty, competition, and conflict, is participation in international sporting events, in particular the Olympic Games. Following the spirit of Bar-Yaacov's arguments outlined above, a multiple national who chooses to play for one of her or his countries of nationality might well be considered to have chosen one over the other, and thus of having violated an ingredient of public obligation. She or he might even be accused of having divided loyalties. This does not seem to be the case in practice. As opposed to prohibiting multiple

---

[238] United Nations, *United Nations national competitive recruitment examination. NCRE Frequently asked questions*, 2006 (internet), http://www.un.org/Depts/OHRM/examin/exam.htm, consulted 28 March 2006.

[239] Regarding the unique legal nature of the ICRC as an international organization independent of governments, but whose mandate is conferred by the international community in the 1949 Geneva Conventions, their 1977 Additional Protocols, and the Statutes of the International Red Cross and Red Crescent Movement, see Christian Dominicé, "La personnalité juridique internationale du CICR", in *Etudes et essais sur le droit internationale humanitaire et sur les principes de la Croix-Rouge en l'honneur de Jean Pictet. Studies and essays on international humanitarian law and Red Cross principles in honour of Jean Pictet*, ed. Christophe Swinarski (Genève: Comité international de la Croix-Rouge, Martinus Nijhoff Publishers, 1984), 663–673; Paul Reuter, "La personnalité juridique internationale du Comité international de la Croix-Rouge", in *Etudes et essais sur le droit internationale humanitaire et sur les principes de la Croix-Rouge en l'honneur de Jean Pictet. Studies and essays on international humanitarian law and Red Cross principles in honour of Jean Pictet*, ed. Christophe Swinarski (Genève: Comité international de la Croix-Rouge, Martinus Nijhoff Publishers, 1984), 783–791; and Christophe Swinarski, "La notion d'un organisme neutre et le droit international", in *Etudes et essais sur le droit internationale humanitaire et sur les principes de la Croix-Rouge en l'honneur de Jean Pictet. Studies and essays on international humanitarian law and Red Cross principles in honour of Jean Pictet*, ed. Christophe Swinarski (Genève: Comité international de la Croix-Rouge, Martinus Nijhoff Publishers, 1984), 819–835.

[240] "Argentinean commander refuses to accept the service of a Dutch soldier", 7 July 1998, Hellenic Resources Network (internet), http://www.hri.org/news/Cyprus/tcpr/1998/98-07-08.tcpr.html, consulted 25 May 2006.

nationals from competition, or forcing them to choose between nationalities once and for all, the Olympic Charter specifically addresses multiple nationality in the Bye-law to Article 42, which sets down the fundamental principle that multiple nationals may elect which country they will represent in the Olympics. Once they have represented a country in certain international sporting events however, they must wait three years before being allowed to represent another state, although exceptions can be made if all parties agree.[241] Article 42 of the Olympic Charter rules only that competitors must be nationals of the national olympic committee entering them, and that any disputes be resolved by the International Olympic Committee (IOC) Executive Board.[242] The IOC thus defers to the state in terms of attribution of nationality, and the Olympic Charter is devoid of further provisions regarding the quality or nature of a state's attribution of nationality, only recognizing that this may be an area of controversy that may require its involvement.

Similar provisions for dealing with multiple nationality can be found elsewhere, and while nationality seems to be an important criterion in relation to team participation and representation, it is not an exclusive one. The right of representation in World Air Sports Federation events operates along similar lines to the Olympic Charter, with a three year minimum interval required before changing representation, although residents may also represent countries.[243] Rules for participation in World Chess Federation individual and team competitions provide that players may be qualified by citizenship or naturalisation, in addition to residence.[244] Multiple nationals or persons qualified to represent more than one team may represent another team after a hiatus of one to five years.[245]

As far as notions of loyalty and obligation are concerned, it would seem that sportspeople frequently choose to switch countries entirely, adopting another nationality altogether without necessarily becoming multiple nationals, purely on the basis of subjective self-interest. Such interest may be related to training facilities offered by countries, financial or pecuniary incentives, the potential for winning, or even the chance to be put forward by a country to compete in the international arena. The world of international tennis has been cited for this proposition.[246] In comparison, a

---

[241] International Olympic Committee, *Olympic Charter, in force as from 1 September 2004*, 2006 (internet), http://multimedia.olympic.org/pdf/en_report_122.pdf, consulted 28 March 2006. Paragraph 3 states that in cases of new states, competitors may elect one time only whether they will continue to represent their former state, or the new state.

[242] Ibid. Paragraph 4 of the Bye-law reiterates the IOC Executive Board's competence in relation to all questions related to "nationality, citizenship, domicile or residence" of the competitors. Ibid.

[243] World Air Sports Federation, *Sporting Code. Chapter 8. Licences*, 2004 (internet), http://www.fai.org/sporting_code/scg_c8.asp, consulted 28 March 2006.

[244] World Chess Federation, *FIDE Handbook. C. General rules and recommendations for tournaments. 5. General rules for participation in FIDE events*, (internet), http://www.fide.com/official, consulted 28 March 2006.

[245] Ibid.

[246] Chip Le Grand, "Pragmatism takes hold in nationality stakes. Adopting a new country

multiple national's choice to represent one country as opposed to another, especially when the nationalities might all be considered "effective", that is nationality that is substantiated by a real or substantive link to a country, does not seem as flagrant or even remarkable.

Of course comparing multiple nationals' competition in international sporting events to their participation in armed conflicts is inapt as far as the relative magnitude of the events for both states and individuals, and the potential penalties imposed on individual multiple nationals for such participation (notwithstanding the fact that people may place greater value on sporting competitions than on the potential for their respective countries to become involved in an armed conflict). In this sense, it must be asked whether the ban on the "threat or use of force against the territorial integrity or political independence of any state" contained in Article 2(4) of the United Nations Charter[247] has fundamentally changed the nature of the political context of armed conflict, with implications for the participation of individuals.

G. THE MANAGEMENT OF MULTIPLE NATIONALITY: AN EXAMPLE OF GOVERNMENT PRACTICE IN RELATION TO LOYALTY AND SECURITY

Another example of the treatment of multiple nationality in practice, in relation to loyalty and state security, is provided by the United States Defense Security Service's Adjudicative Guidelines, which are used by US government departments in determinations of eligibility for access to classified information. The adjudicative process is an

> overall common sense determination based upon careful consideration of the following, each of which is to be evaluated in the context of the whole person . . . a. Allegiance to the United States, b. Foreign influence, c. Foreign preference, d. Sexual behavior, e. Personal conduct, f. Financial considerations, g. Alcohol consumption, h. Drug involvement, j. Criminal conduct, k. Security violations, l. Outside activities, m. Misuse of information technology systems.[248]

Multiple nationality is taken into consideration principally in relation to (c) foreign preference, but also (b) foreign influence and possibly (l) outside activities. The Guidelines state that "it is emphasized that dual citizenship, by itself, is not automatically a

---

is a common occurrence in world tennis", *The Weekend Australian*, 20–21 January 2001, Sports, 34.

[247] United Nations, *United Nations Charter* (internet), http://www.un.org/aboutun/charter/index.html, consulted on 28 March 2006.

[248] Defense Security Service (USA), *Adjudicative guidelines for determining elegibility for access to classified information*, 1997 (internet), http://www.dss.mil.nf/adr/adjguid/adjguidT.htm, consulted 7 July 2003.

concern . . . [it] is an issue only if the subject has actively maintained or exercised the other citizenship or if the subject travels to a country that still claims the subject as a citizen".[249]

> *A person with dual citizenship is generally interviewed to explore the circumstances that have led to dual citizenship, relationships with the other country, past and potential future travel to the other country, and the individual's attitudes toward allegiance to the United States under various circumstances that could prompt a conflict of interest. Dual citizenship is a Foreign Preference issue when a U.S. citizen or U.S. national has, within the past 10 years or so, taken any steps to maintain or exercise the benefits of another country's citizenship. Such circumstances need to be examined carefully to identify a subject's primary loyalty and weigh the potential for conflicting loyalties. Possible indicators of foreign preference include:*
>
> • *Maintaining a foreign passport.*
> • *Using a foreign passport in preference to a U.S. passport to travel to any foreign country.*
> • *Registering for military service or serving in the military forces of a foreign country. (Service in a foreign military involves swearing allegiance to that country.)*
> • *Accepting or exercising benefits (including the right to vote, or educational, employment, retirement, medical or social welfare benefits) provided to citizens of a foreign country.*
> • *Registering with a foreign consulate or embassy to obtain such benefits.*
> • *Traveling to or residing in a foreign country for the purpose of fulfilling citizenship requirements or obligations.*
> • *Maintaining dual citizenship to protect financial interests or gain financial benefits. (In many countries, the laws pertaining to property ownership, taxes, business licenses, and inheritance are different for citizens and non-citizens.)*[250]

Under the category "foreign influence" multiple nationality is only enumerated as a concern in terms of an individual's vulnerability to influence by a foreign state, such as "when a dual national travels to another country that does not recognize the subject's renunciation of its citizenship, i.e., a country that believes it has a legal right to exercise jurisdiction over the subject".[251] The guideline is much more concerned with susceptibility to influence, but notes that a disproportionate number of Americans convicted of espionage were either naturalised citizens, or had foreign relatives.[252] Along these lines, guideline (l) relating to outside activities specifies that work or service for a foreign entity or interest generally, may present a security

---

[249] Defense Security Service (USA), *Foreign preference test*, 1997 (internet), http://www.dss.mil/nf/adr/forpref/forprefT.htm, consulted 7 July 2003.

[250] Ibid.

[251] Defense Security Service (USA), *Foreign influence test*, 1997 (internet), http://www.dss.mil/nf/adr/forinfl/forinflT.htm, consulted 7 July 2003.

[252] Ibid.

concern.[253] It is to be assumed that not all countries are viewed as presenting the same security concerns, issues that one may surmise may change according to the United States' international relations at any given point in time.

By not excluding multiple nationals automatically from access to classified information, but delving into the context of the incident multiple nationality, the Guidelines treat multiple nationality only as one concern out of many in the overall context of foreign connections, which are of paramount concern in terms of security. In this sense, they seem to embody a view that nationality itself may be related to security, but that even mono-nationals present security risks. The example is not submitted as evidence of state practice generally, but is evidence of what seems to be a practical response that deals with the consequences and effects of multiple nationality. The Guidelines accept its existence, and treat it as a reality that can be managed along practical lines.

H. AN "ALLEGIANCE TO HUMANITY"?

A different perspective is provided by Rotblat (1995 Nobel Peace Prize Winner). In calling for an "allegiance to humanity", he does not advocate "us becoming formally subjects of a world government, with passports and the other trappings associated with a central administrative regime", but links the avoidance of war to ideas of common responsibility and solidarity among human beings.[254] "Just as in the course of history we have acquired a loyalty to our family, and then to our nation, we must now take the next step and develop an allegiance to humanity".[255]

I. HUMAN RIGHTS AND MULTIPLE NATIONALITY

When Bar-Yaacov wrote his treatise over forty years ago, his recommendation that multiple nationality be abolished by means of complementary municipal legislation may have seemed a realistic possibility. It reflected the proposals made in 1929 and the spirit of the 1930 and 1963 Conventions mentioned above.[256] In fact, just the

---

[253] Defense Security Service (USA), *Adjudicative guidelines for determining elegibility for access to classified information.*

[254] Joseph Rotblat, "Preface", in *World citizenship: allegiance to humanity*, ed. Joseph Rotblat (London: Macmillan Press Ltd., 1997), ix and xi.

[255] Id., x.

[256] *Convention on Certain Questions Relating to the Conflict of Nationality Laws*, 179. Hudson and Flournoy Jr., "Nationality – Responsibility of states – Territorial waters, drafts of conventions prepared in anticipation of the first conference on the codification of international law, The Hague 1930".

opposite would seem to have occurred, or at least, as demonstrated hereafter, current state practice tolerates and even contributes to the existence of multiple nationality in significant ways. As we are not specifically concerned here with why states choose to adopt one policy or another vis-à-vis multiple nationality, we might do no more than note in passing the rejection, in terms of application, of Bar-Yaacov's and others' recommendations. To do so would be, however, to ignore important developments in international law and standards already alluded to that may affect (or clarify) the definition or concept of nationality used by Bar-Yaacov and even the International Court of Justice in the *Nottebohm* case.

The evolution in concepts and standards of human rights since the adoption of the United Nations Charter has affected not only how states treat their own nationals, but how states treat aliens, and human beings generally. Perhaps surprisingly, an historical starting point is not necessarily the clear disability of aliens. In mercantilist European states, foreigners typically enjoyed the same treatment as subjects, but were privileged as far as being allowed to emigrate, whereas controls on the movement of subjects within their own state could be strict.[257] In England, the Magna Carta of 1215 allowed foreign merchants to enter and depart at will, except those from countries at war with England, with an exemption should English subjects be well-treated in said state.[258] In this sense foreigners were often exempt from restrictions placed on subjects.

The establishment in 1792 of civil status, or *l'état civil*, took place at the same time as fundamental changes were occurring in the delimitation of "foreign" versus "national" in France.[259] The same period saw the introduction of the visa, previously unknown, allowing authorities in a destination country to vet and control the entry and travel of foreigners, on the same terms as they did their own subjects/citizens.[260] But privileges and exemptions for foreigners that gave way to equal treatment, quickly turned to disability. In such a world, diplomatic protection of nationals who were unprivileged in terms of rights and benefits while abroad, and defined by their exclusion from the group of nationals, would become an increasingly important means of securing individual rights, at least potentially, through the state of nationality. By setting limits on how states treat categories of persons, as nationals, aliens, or simply human beings, modern developments in the international law of human rights have significantly altered this balance of considerations.

Whether international law provides a right to nationality is unclear, but there is a clear trend toward recognition of such a right, certainly as a complement to the hardening of the principle against the avoidance of statelessness.[261] Neither tendency,

---

[257] Torpey, *The invention of the passport – surveillance, citizenship and the state*, 42.

[258] Id., 69.

[259] Id., 43–44.

[260] Id., 52–56. This was the case in France. In German states, which until the mid-19th century refused to issue passports to subjects wishing to depart, in particular Prussia, unless it could be shown they would be guaranteed entry, the issuance of a visa amounted to a condition-precedent for being allowed to leave, not enter. Torpey, *The invention of the passport – surveillance, citizenship and the state*, 66.

[261] Chan traces the development of ideas of nationality as a human right, and argues that

either taken alone or together, can however be said to contribute to the existence of multiple nationality. Balancing the state's prerogative to attribute and withdraw its nationality with a right to nationality, Chan states that

> *the position is accurately stated by the Inter-American Court of Human Rights: while the regulation of nationality falls primarily within the domestic jurisdiction of a State, the powers of the State are circumscribed by their obligations to ensure the full protection of human rights. International supervision is concerned only with the compatibility of the exercise of these powers with recognized international human rights standards, and must carefully balance all conflicting interests.*[262]

"there is a clear trend in international law towards a gradual recognition of an individual's right to nationality . . . As long as nationality remains the key to the enjoyment of fundamental political rights in domestic law, recognition of a right to nationality will be an inevitable and necessary consequence. This right to nationality, though not yet firmly secured in international law, includes three distinct aspects: the right to have a nationality, or in the negative form, the right to be protected from statelessness, the right to change one's nationality, and the right not to be arbitrarily deprived of one's nationality". Johannes M. M. Chan, "The right to a nationality as a human right. The current trend towards recognition", *Human Rights Law Journal*, (1991) vol. 12, no. 1–2, 1–14, 13. He points out that the right to nationality found in Article 15 of the Universal Declaration of Human Rights is of little practical value, as no state is obliged to attribute its nationality to particular individuals. "Unfortunately, not only did these ambiguities remain unclarified in the subsequent transposition of the Declaration into binding legal instruments, but the right to nationality was further watered down in the International Covenant on Civil and Political Rights" (ICCPR). Chan, "The right to a nationality as a human right. The current trend towards recognition", 3. Article 12 of the ICCPR states that people are free to leave any country, including their own, but then creates a huge caveat, subjecting the provision to ill-defined limits based on national security, public order and public health or morals, in addition to other categories. The article provides that "[n]o one shall be arbitrarily deprived of the right to enter his own country", but the use of the word "arbitrary" also arguably creates a black hole in legal terms for potential abuse. Likewise, "own country" is not defined. Article 24(3) of the ICCPR states that "[e]very child has the right to acquire a nationality", but places no obligations on states as far as attributing their nationality to children. See United Nations, *International Covenant on Civil and Political Rights*, 1966 (internet), http://www.hrweb.org/legal/cpr.html, consulted 1 August 2003. Chan cites the Inter-American Convention on Human Rights as "the only internationally binding instrument which contains a general right to a nationality", remarking that "the failure of the European countries to agree on a new Protocol on a right to nationality is a major step backward in the promotion of human rights". Chan, "The right to a nationality as a human right. The current trend towards recognition", 5 and 14. Such a right was subsequently provided in Article 4 of the 1997 European Convention on Nationality. *European convention on nationality.* de Groot disputes the character of a right to nationality, labelling it a "dubious" human right and not as essential as other human rights contained in the Universal Declaration, as it is not necessarily linked to defined rights or obligations in either municipal or international law. Gerard-René de Groot, *Staatsangehörigkeitsrecht im Wandel – eine rechtsvergleichende Studie über Erwerbs- und Verlustgründe der Staatsangehörigkeit* (Köln: Carl Heymanns Verlag KG, 1989), 15.

[262] Chan, "The right to a nationality as a human right. The current trend towards recognition", 14. See Inter-American Court of Human Rights, *Advisory opinion OC-4/84 of January*

Although the 'international supervision' referred to by Chan relates to political reluctance by European states to submit individual claims to nationality to the European Court of Human Rights, international supervision of claims to nationality by individuals can be compared and contrasted to claims by states vis-à-vis one another as a consequence of nationality, and the issue of effective nationality. If human rights standards constrict states with regard to the attribution and withdrawal of nationality, it may be asked whether they also play a role in determining the effectivity of one state's attribution of its nationality vis-à-vis another state, in particular in relation to multiple nationals. This question was mentioned above in relation to the 1997 *European Convention on Nationality*.[263] The proposition may be tested by the survey of state practice herein.

While there may be a right to a nationality, there is clearly no right to multiple nationality as such. However developments in individual rights in relation to nationality have in and of themselves contributed to the existence of multiple nationality. Changes related to the equal legal treatment of women and standards applied to deprivation of nationality can be cited in this regard. The former is outlined below, the latter in the conclusions herein, considering the overview of state practice. An example of contrary state practice is also provided, illustrating how a principle of avoidance of multiple nationality can be prioritised above other state-defined interests related to human rights.

1. The equal treatment of women

A specific example of how ideas and standards of human rights, in terms of the fundamental equality of human beings, have contributed to the production of multiple nationality is found in the (as yet partial) implementation of legal equality between women and men. Although there were notable exceptions, such as Spain's attribution of nationality in the 19th century through both the maternal and paternal lines, most states in the 19th and 20th centuries clearly discriminated against women in relation to nationality, and some continue to do so to varying degrees.[264]

19, 1984. Proposed amendments to the naturalization provision of the Constitution of Costa Rica. Requested by the Government of Costa Rica., 1984 (internet), http://www.corteidh.or.cr/seriea_ing/seriea_04_ing.doc, paragraphs 32–33, consulted 28 March 2006.

[263] See text and note at note 109 in relation to diplomatic and consular protection.

[264] The review here is not comprehensive as far as the treatment of women in relation to nationality, but concentrates on the issues raised in relation to multiple nationality. In relation to women's nationality, see Karen Knop and Christine Chinkin, "Remembering Chrystal Macmillan: Women's equality and nationality in international law", *Michigan Journal of International Law*, (2001) vol. 22, no. 4, 523–585. The authors also discuss the ramifications of equal rights and nationality law, related rights, and children's rights, at pp. 570–582. For a comprehensive illustration of the movement toward, and process whereby women's nationality was made independent of the marriage relationship in the United States, see Bredbenner, *A nationality of her own – women, marriage, and the law of citizenship*.

Knop and Chinkin divide such issues into those related to the effects of marriage on a woman's nationality, and inequality in treatment of men and women (and as spouses) in relation to nationality.[265] Marriage to a foreigner usually resulted in automatic deprivation of a woman's nationality, and involuntary attribution of the husband's nationality. It is estimated that in 1930 only one half of the world's women were able to maintain an independent nationality upon marriage, a great improvement compared to previous practice in terms of a woman's independent nationality.[266] Lack of complementarity among municipal legal systems was a major problem for women: divorce did not necessarily give rise to a right to resumption of the woman's previous nationality, while it could entail automatic loss of the husband's nationality acquired upon marriage, and thus statelessness.[267] Hegi pointed to the effects on women in the extreme case of Uruguay, whose laws provided that nationality could only be acquired by birth in Uruguay. "Car l'étrangère qui, selon la loi de son pays, perd sa nationalité lors de son mariage avec un étranger, devient apatride si elle épouse un Uruguayen".[268] Even when marriage did not result in loss of nationality, women were generally legally incapacitated as far as transmitting nationality to their children. The exclusion of a legal relationship between the mother's state of nationality and her child can be said to amount to a policy decision by that state to abandon a right of standing on the international plane vis-à-vis the parental relationship.[269]

---

[265] Knop and Chinkin, "Remembering Chrystal Macmillan: Women's equality and nationality in international law", 544.

[266] Bredbenner, *A nationality of her own – women, marriage, and the law of citizenship*, 195.

[267] Knop and Chinkin, "Remembering Chrystal Macmillan: Women's equality and nationality in international law", 544–50 and 61–64. See also International Law Association, Committee on Feminism and International Law, "Final report on women's equality and nationality in international law", in *Sixty-ninth Conference of the International Law Association*, ed. A. H. A. Soons and Christopher Ward (London: International Law Association, 2000)248–304.

[268] (Author's translation: *A woman who according to her country's laws loses her nationality upon marriage to a foreigner, becomes stateless if she marries a Uruguayan.*) René Hegi, "La nationalité de la femme mariée", thesis presented at the Université de Lausanne, Faculté de droit (Lausanne: Imprimerie La Concorde, 1954), 37. He also points to the effects on women of laws that precluded naturalisation, and where marriage had no effect on nationality, as was the case in Morocco and Tunisia. "La nationalité marocaine ne peut s'acquérir par le mariage. Ainsi, la femme étrangère qui épouse un Marocain devient apatride si elle ne conserve pas sa nationalité antérieure, aucune disposition locale ne permettant l'acquisition de la nationalité. En outre, la nationalité marocaine ne peut s'acquérir par naturalisation, le procédé de la naturalisation étant inconnu de la loi marocaine". (Author's translation: *Moroccan nationality cannot be obtained by marriage. Thus, the foreign woman who marries a Moroccan becomes stateless if she does not retain her former nationality, there being no local provision permitting the acquisition of [Moroccan] nationality. Moreover, Moroccan nationality cannot be acquired by naturalisation, this procedure being unknown to Moroccan law.*) Hegi, "La nationalité de la femme mariée", 38.

[269] See Knop and Chinkin, "Remembering Chrystal Macmillan: Women's equality and nationality in international law", 546–48. For an overview of the legislative treatment of

None of the principles mentioned above are rules of international law, but amounted only to provisions of municipal law. Views that women should lose their nationality upon marriage and that only fathers should transmit nationality to children were not only based on arguments of family unity of nationality, but also specifically predicated on the idea of the undesirability of multiple nationality.[270] Knop and Chinkin identify states' opposition to multiple nationality as an obstacle to women's equal rights, and to the protection of the family.[271] They note that "ridding nationality law of its patriarchal foundation has come at some cost to the unity of the family".[272] It can also be maintained that movement toward implementing equality between the sexes has contributed to tolerance of multiple nationality, and to changing the idea that elimination of multiple nationality is a priority to which equal rights of the individual should be subordinated, at least the equal rights of women.[273]

---

women's nationality in relation to marriage that illustrates the range of state practice in the mid-20th century, from what amounts to dependence on the husband's nationality to complete independence, see United Nations Département des affaires économiques et sociales, "Nationalité de la femme mariée", (New York: United Nations, 1963). The series covering municipal laws on women's nationality upon marriage edited by Bernard Dutoit and various collaborators over time is particularly useful in remarking changes in legislative practice, and the emergence of a woman's nationality independent from that of her husband. Three volumes and supplements cover (1) Europe, (2) Africa, and (3) the Americas, Asia and Oceania. Bernard Dutoit and Simon Affolter, *La nationalité de la femme mariée*, vol. 1: Europe de l'Est et pays de l'ex-URSS, Supplément 1989–1997 (Genève: Librairie Droz, 1998); Bernard Dutoit and Catherine Blackie, *La nationalité de la femme mariée*, vol. 3: Amérique, Asie, Océanie, Supplément 1980–1992 (Genève: Librairie Droz, 1993); Bernard Dutoit et al., *La nationalité de la femme mariée*, vol. 2: Afrique (Genève: Librairie Droz, 1976); Bernard Dutoit, Daniel Gay, and Terrence Vandeveld, *La nationalité de la femme mariée*, vol. 3: Amérique, Asie, Océanie (Genève: Librairie Droz, 1980); Bernard Dutoit and Denis Masmejan, *La nationalité de la femme mariée*, vol. 2: Afrique, Supplément 1976–1990 (Genève: Librairie Droz, 1991); Bernard Dutoit and Christine Sattiva Spring, *La nationalité de la femme mariée*, vol. 1: Europe – supplément 1973–1989 (Genève: Librairie Droz, 1990).

[270] As was the case in Japan. Hosokawa, "Japanese nationality in international perspective", 187. See Knop and Chinkin, "Remembering Chrystal Macmillan: Women's equality and nationality in international law", 565–69. The potential for divided loyalties and conflicts between states were cited as undesirable products of marriage between people of different nationalities. Knop and Chinkin, "Remembering Chrystal Macmillan: Women's equality and nationality in international law", 558–59. Rather than admit multiple nationality (recalling the views espoused by Bar-Yaacov) states followed arguments that called for married persons to share only one nationality, that of the husband, and consequently for children to receive only one nationality.

[271] Knop and Chinkin, "Remembering Chrystal Macmillan: Women's equality and nationality in international law", 566.

[272] Id., 550. In discussing what they call "third-generation issues of equality", Knop and Chinkin recall that family unity of nationality is still a vital issue in human rights' terms. This is discussed below. Knop and Chinkin, "Remembering Chrystal Macmillan: Women's equality and nationality in international law", 550–56.

[273] de Groot, "The European Convention on Nationality: a step towards a ius commune in

While discrimination according to sex is odious according to international rules and standards of human rights, it is arguably the invidious practical effects of such discrimination that has called the greatest attention to the injustice of the underlying situation. But whether it is the principle of non-discrimination on the basis of sex, or a rejection of the infelicitous practical effects of such discrimination, that has brought about change in the treatment and position of women in relation to nationality, this is not to argue that the same has occurred in relation to underlying issues of gender, for women or men.[274] The exception in the 1997 European Convention allowing for discrimination against unwed fathers in transmission of nationality to their children is perhaps a case in point.[275]

Among the most serious charges that can be levied against a state is that it has abandoned its nationals to their fate, rather than attempting to protect them against arbitrary or illegal treatment by other states. Bigler-Eggenberger argues that the policy of automatic loss of Swiss nationality by women upon marriage to a foreigner in force until 1952 was not only clearly discriminatory, but in the context of Swiss women married to non-Swiss Jews, amounted to abandoning them to the German National Socialist concentration camps.

> *Wenn wir bedenken, dass – abgesehen von der Frauen-, Fremden- und vor allem Judenfeindlichkeit – vordergründig für die Härte der Verwaltung die Furcht massgebend war, einer mit einem Ausländer verheirateten Schweizerin im Ausland diplomatischen und konsularischen Schutz gewähren oder eventuell gar finanzielle Aufwendungen im Falle materieller Not solcher Frauen erbringen zu müssen, so zeigt sich die ganze Erbärmlichkeit der Verlustpraxis jenes schlimmen Jahrzehnts. . . .*
>
> *Hätten die in Konzentrationslager verschleppten Ehefrauen von deutschen, französischen, ungarischen, österreichischen, polnischen Juden ihr Schweizerbürgerrecht behalten können, so hätte die Schweiz über ihre diplomatischen Vertretungen Menschenleben vor der sicheren und grausamen Vernichtung retten können. Zumindest aber hätte unser Land die Grenzen in den Jahren von 1938/39 bis 1945 nicht auch noch gegenüber rückkehrwilligen oder zur Flucht gezwungenen ehemaligen Schweizerbürgerinnen und deren Angehörigen schliessen dürfen oder können.[276]*

---

the field of nationality law", 118. Knop and Chinkin might take issue with this proposition: "Although there are some indications that states are becoming more tolerant of dual nationality, this is not a universal trend". Knop and Chinkin, "Remembering Chrystal Macmillan: Women's equality and nationality in international law", 564.

[274] See generally Karen Knop, "Relational nationality: on gender and nationality in international law," in *Citizenship today. Global perspectives and practices*, ed. T. Alexander Aleinikoff and Douglas Klusmeyer (Washington: Carnegie Endowment for International Peace, 2001), 89–124. Knop and Chinkin raise issues of gender and sex in relation to nationality, whereas the analysis in the ILA's report is centered more around issues related to sex than gender roles. Knop and Chinkin, "Remembering Chrystal Macmillan: Women's equality and nationality in international law", 528–32. and generally International Law Association, "Final report on women's equality and nationality in international law".

[275] See note 108 above.

[276] (Author's translation: *If we reflect that – aside from the hostility toward women,*

As far as the policy of denationalisation of women upon marriage was ostensibly based on a notion of family unity favouring the husband's nationality, the change in Swiss law in 1953 to allow women to retain their nationality upon marriage to a foreigner and regardless of any ensuing multiple nationality might be seen as representing a fundamental shift in concepts of women's human rights. This change did not provide equal treatment for women and men in terms of Swiss nationality however, as until 1984 only Swiss men could transmit nationality to their children. Knop and Chinkin label the issues of women's nationality in relation to marriage "first generation issues of equality", and the question of transmission of nationality "second generation issues".[277] This is particularly apt, noting that previous studies on women's nationality concentrated on marriage, often ignoring completely issues of equal treatment related to transmission of nationality to children.[278]

There are similar examples from various countries of the movement toward equal treatment of women and men in the same period. In 1950 the Japanese nationality law was likewise amended to eliminate automatic changes in nationality upon marriage, recognition and adoption, and rules that the wife's nationality had to conform to the husband's were abolished. Complete equality was not achieved however until legislative amendments in 1984, in preparation for ratification of the Convention on the Elimination of All forms of Discrimination against Women.[279] It would appear that women and men are today treated equally by most states in terms of the direct effects of marriage on nationality, and transmission of nationality to children.[280] Knop and

---

foreigners, and especially Jews– the decisive factor in the Administration's severity was fear that it would have to provide Swiss women married to foreigners with diplomatic and consular protection abroad or even financial assistance in cases of material need, the whole wretchedness of the policy of loss of nationality of that horrible decade is exposed. Had the wives of German, French, Hungarian, Austrian and Polish Jews who were dragged away to concentration camps been able to keep their Swiss citizenship, Switzerland, via its diplomatic posts, would have been able to save lives from certain and gruesome extermination. Our country would at least not have been allowed, or able, to close its borders to former Swiss female citizens with their families who wished to return, or who were forced to flee, between the years of 1938–39 and 1945.) Margrith Bigler-Eggenberger, "Bürgerrechtsverlust durch Heirat: Ein dunkler Fleck in der jüngeren Schweizer Rechtsgeschichte", Recht, (1999) vol. 2, 33–42, 42.

[277] Knop and Chinkin, "Remembering Chrystal Macmillan: Women's equality and nationality in international law", 544–50.

[278] The author does not wish to intimate criticism of Dutoit in this regard, as he clearly restricts his study to the effects of marriage on women's nationality.

[279] Hosokawa, "Japanese nationality in international perspective", 186–87.

[280] Although there are notable exceptions. Resistance to equal rights as far as transmission of nationality is not always on the basis of sex, however. "Should Jordanian women have equal rights with men to pass on their citizenship? Yes, ruled Jordan's government this week – unless they happen to be Palestinian. In the battle to keep their supremacy, Jordan's indigenous minority of East Bankers have launched a successful counter-attack against last month's decree by Rania, their Palestinian-born queen, that mothers as well as fathers can pass their nationality on to their children. Newspapers run by East Bankers accused the queen of using the cover of

Chinkin point out that in many related areas, such as naturalisation of spouses and residency rights, there is still much discrimination on the basis of sex. These areas are not addressed herein as they do not relate (admittedly narrowly) to multiple nationality as such.

In discussing what they call "third-generation issues of equality", Knop and Chinkin recall that family unity of nationality is still a vital issue in terms of family members' ability to live together and support one another. Implementing equality of the sexes in terms of nationality can cause hardship to families, as non-national spouses and children may be treated as aliens, and thus lack even basic rights in relation to one another and their respective states. They propose multiple nationality as a vehicle to guarantee family unity, and cite various court cases that link the practical ramifications of such unity, such as the right to live together, to basic human dignity.[281]

The shift in the treatment of women's nationality in the 20th century must be contemplated in relation to the more general changes in notions of human rights relating not only to women, but to the individual generally.[282] Arguments favouring the avoidance of multiple nationality appear to have given way in many countries to the equality and choices of individuals. This proposition may be tested by a survey of state practice. But in any case, there is no doubt that equal treatment of women has led to a greater number of multiple nationals in countries where nationality is transmitted according to jus sanguinis.[283] This holds true, notwithstanding exceptions such as in the case of Japan, where transmission of nationality by both men and women to their children does not produce multiple nationality over the long-term, pursuant to a policy of forced election. But these changes in the treatment of women constitute the clearest example of how practical considerations related to equality, fairness, and human rights have directly and indirectly affected state practice vis-à-vis multiple nationality.[284]

---

sex equality to naturalise hundreds of thousands of her Palestinian kinsmen in Jordan, and convert their homeland into Hashemite Palestine. If we do not stop the queen, they cried, we will be swamped". "Jordan and its Palestinians. The queen outmatched", *The Economist*, 7 December 2002, 46.

[281] Knop and Chinkin, "Remembering Chrystal Macmillan: Women's equality and nationality in international law", 550–56. They note that the *Second Protocol to the 1963 European Convention* made mixed marriges an exception to eliminating multiple nationality, and that the 1997 European Convention's approach is based only on fundamental equality and avoidance of statelessness. Knop and Chinkin, "Remembering Chrystal Macmillan: Women's equality and nationality in international law", 567–68.

[282] For a comprehensive overview (in Portuguese) see Antônio Augusto Cançado Trindade, *Tratado de direito internacional dos direitos humanos*, vol. 1 (Porto Alegre: Sergio Antonio Fabris Editor, 1997); Antônio Augusto Cançado Trindade, *Tratado de direito internacional dos direitos humanos*, vol. 2 (Porto Alegre: Sergio Antonio Fabris Editor, 1999).

[283] de Groot, "The European Convention on Nationality: a step towards a ius commune in the field of nationality law", 118.

[284] Even considerable efforts by some states fell victim to other states' preference against

The relative nature of concepts of human rights and their implementation is however all too clear from states' behaviour. At the same time as provisions on nationality affecting Japanese women were being modified in order to give some effect to principles of legal equality of the sexes, in 1952 Japan denationalised en masse most of its ethnic Korean residents, who had been considered nationals until that time. Chang argues that this act was in and of itself a violation of Japanese municipal law, international law, and basic international human rights standards and law.[285]

2. Prioritising avoidance of multiple nationality over redress for human rights abuses: a German case

Likewise in terms of the relativity of notions and standards of human rights, certain state practice can be cited as placing such great weight on the avoidance of multiple nationality, that it overrides other state-defined priorities related to human rights. This would seem to be the case of the Federal Republic of Germany, in the context of providing redress for National Socialist withdrawal of German nationality from certain citizens between 1933 and 1945, and the treatment of their families.[286]

---

their nationals possessing multiple nationality. When Switzerland gave women the ability to transmit Swiss nationality on equal terms with men in 1985 according to *jus sanguinis*, the state resorted to legal fiction, providing that children of Swiss mothers born prior to 1985 received Swiss nationality retroactively with effect from birth, according to an application procedure that was not labeled or considered "naturalisation" but "recognition". Thus children in this category are considered to have been Swiss at birth, although their Swiss nationality was not recognised by Switzerland until their application, and they may have lived in Switzerland for years as foreigners. This was done such that the attribution of Swiss nationality would be considered to have been automatic at birth, and thus not cause other states to withdraw their nationality on the basis that Swiss nationality had not been conferred automatically, or by naturalisation. See generally F. Sturm and G. Sturm, "Erwerb des Schweizer Buergerrechts durch Kinder einer Schweizer Mutter", *Das Standesmt*, (1986) vol. 39, no. 2, 29–34; Evelyn Beatrice Wiederkehr, "Erwerb und Verlust des Schweizer Bürgerrechts von Gesetzes wegen", dissertation presented at the Universität Zürich, Rechts- und staatswissenschaftliche Fakultät (Zürich: Schulthess Polygraphischer Verlag, 1983); *Botschaft zur Änderung des Bundesgesetzes über Erwerb und Verlust des Schweizer Bürgerrehcts, 18 April 1984, 84.037*, Bundesgesetzblatt (1984) vol. II, 211; *Botschaft zur Änderung des Bürgerrehctsgesetzes, 26 August 1987, 87.055*, Bundesblatt (1987) vol. III, 293. Germany did not interpret it thus, and expatriated citizens who applied for Swiss nationality under the provision, if they lived outside Germany. Hans-Konrad Ress, *Deutsche Rechtsprechung in völkerrechtlichen Fragen 1994. IV. Staatsangehörigkeit. 2. Mehrfache Staatsangehörigkeit*, Max-Planck-Institut für ausländisches öffentliches Recht und Völkerrecht 1994 (internet), http://www.virtual-institute.de/en/rspr94/ersp94_8.cfm, consulted 10 May 2003.

[285] Hyo Sang Chang, "Nationality in divided countries: a Korean perspective" in *Nationality and international law in Asian perspective*, ed. Ko Swan Sik (Dordrecht: Martinus Nijhoff Publishers, 1990), 255–308, 297–303.

[286] German disapproval of multiple nationality has usually been cited and illustrated in relation to the acquisition of German nationality by descendants of long-term foreign residents

It has already been mentioned that naturalisation elsewhere did not provoke an automatic loss of German nationality until the 1913 *Lex Delbrück*, which nonetheless contained a provision that still stands, for retention of German nationality notwithstanding such naturalisation, upon approval by German authorities.[287] What might be as seen recent limited acceptance of multiple nationality aside (see the Appendix in relation to Germany), Germany has held itself out as steadfastly opposed to multiple nationality for much of the 20th century. Notwithstanding, in 1993 there were an estimated 1.84 Million German multiple nationals.[288] The *Bundesverfassungsgericht* (Federal Constitutional Court) stated in 1974 that:

> It is accurate to say that dual or multiple nationality is regarded, both domestically and internationally, as an evil that should be avoided or eliminated in the interests of states as well as in the interests of the affected citizen. . . . States seek to achieve exclusivity of their respective nationalities in order to set clear boundaries for their sovereignty over persons; they want to be secure in the duty of loyalty of their citizens – which extends if necessary as far as risking one's life – and do not want to see it endangered by possible conflicts with a loyalty to a foreign state.[289]

---

born in Germany. See generally Keskin, "Staatsbürgerschaft im Exil". In relation to proposals for recent changes to German nationality law, see Rainer Hofmann, "German citizenship law and European citizenship: towards a special kind of dual nationality?", in *European citizenship. An institutional challenge*, ed. Massimo La Torre, *European Forum* (The Hague: Kluwer Law International, 1998), 149–165; Martin A. Klein, *Zu einer Reform des deutschen Staatsangehörigkeitsrechts – eine kritische Betrachtung under Einbeziehung Frankreichs* (Frankfurt am Main: Peter Lang, 1999); Günter Renner, "Erste Anmerkungen zur Reform des Staatsangehörigkeitsrechts", paper presented at the conference: *Hohenheimer Tage zum Ausländerrecht 1999 und 5. Migrationspolitisches Forum*, ed. Klaus Barwig, Gisbert Brinkmann, Kay Hailbronner, Bertold Huber, Christine Kreuzer, Klaus Lörcher, Christoph Schuhmacher (Hohenheim: Nomos Verlagsgesellschaft, 1999), 8–95; Günter Renner, "Mehr integration durch option gegen Mehrstaatigkeit?", paper presented at the conference: *Hohenheimer Tage zum Ausländerrecht 1999 und 5. Migrationspolitisches Forum*, ed. Klaus Barwig, Gisbert Brinkmann, Kay Hailbronner, Bertold Huber, Christine Kreuzer, Klaus Lörcher, Christoph Schuhmacher (Hohenheim: Nomos Verlagsgesellschaft, 1999); Andreas Zimmermann, "Staats- und völkerrechtliche Fragen der Reform des deutschen Staatsangehörigkeitsrechts", *IPRax Praxis des Internationalen Privat- und Verfahrensrechts* (2000) no. 3, 180–185. Regarding multiple nationality under German law in light of changes to legislation in 1999 and 2001, see Kreuzer, "Double and multiple nationality in Germany after the Citizenship Reform Act of 1999"; Marianne Wiedemann, "Development of dual nationality under German law", in *Rights and duties of dual nationals. Evolution and prospects*, ed. David A. Martin and Kay Hailbronner (The Hague: Kluwer Law International, 2003), 335–345.

[287] See text and notes at notes 39–45.

[288] Klein, *Zu einer Reform des deutschen Staatsangehörigkeitsrechts – eine kritische Betrachtung under Einbeziehung Frankreichs*, 225.

[289] *Opinion of the German Federal Constitutional Court, 21 May 1974*, cited in Aleinikoff and Klusmeyer, "Plural nationality: facing the future in a migratory world", 70–71.

On 25 November 1941 Germany summarily expatriated all nationals it defined as Jewish who resided outside Germany, under the Eleventh Supplementary Decree to the (1935) Reich Citizenship Law, or approximately 240,000 people.[290] From the very beginning to the last moments of the Nazi regime however, deprivation of nationality was applied (also as a criminal penalty) to political opponents and categories of people labelled "undesirable", allowing for confiscation of property, and in the case of the 1941 decree, constituted the formal legal basis for the "Final Solution", or mass murder, of German Jews.[291]

After the Second World War the re-established democratic (West) German government undertook to provide redress for the deprivations as part of a state-defined priority of *Wiedergutmachung*, meaning reparation or amends, literally, "to make good again". Accordingly, the German constitution, or Basic Law, provides in article 116(2) that

> *Frühere deutsche Staatsangehörige, denen zwischen dem 30. Januar 1933 und dem 8. Mai 1945 die Staatsangehörigkeit aus politischen, rassischen oder religiösen Gründen entzogen worden ist, und ihre Abkömmlinge sind auf Antrag wieder einzubürgern. Sie gelten als nicht ausgebürgert, sofern sie nach dem 8. Mai 1945 ihren Wohnsitz in Deutschland genommen haben und nicht einen entgegengesetzten Willen zum Ausdruck gebracht haben.*[292]

---

[290] Michael Hepp, "Wer Deutscher ist, bestimmen wir . . .", in *Die Ausbürgerung deutscher Staatsangehöriger 1933–45 nach den im Reichsanzeiger veröffentlichen Listen*, ed. Michael Hepp, vol. 1 (München: K. G. Saur, 1985), xxv–xl, xxxlv. For the text of the Decree in English translation, see Karl A. Schleunes, ed., *Legislating the Holocaust. The Bernhard Loesener memoirs and supporting documents* (Boulder: Westview Press, 2001), 170–71.

[291] Hans Georg Lehmann, "Acht und Ächtung politischer Gegner im Dritten Reich. Die Ausbürgerung deutscher Emigranten 1933–45", in *Die Ausbürgerung deutscher Staatsangehöriger 1933–45 nach den im Reichsanzeiger veröffentlichen Listen*, ed. Michael Hepp, vol. 1 (München: K. G. Saur, 1985), ix/xxiii, xi and xiv–xv. According to official lists, between 25 August 1933 and 7 April 1945, 39,006 Germans were individually deprived of nationality. Lehmann, "Acht und Ächtung politischer Gegner im Dritten Reich. Die Ausbürgerung deutscher Emigranten 1933–45", xiv.

[292] (Official Translation: *Former German citizens who, between 30 January 1933 and 8 May 1945, were deprived of their citizenship on political, racial, or religious grounds, and their descendants, shall be regranted German citizenship on application. They shall be considered as not having been deprived of their German citizenship if they have established their domicile (Wohnsitz) in Germany after 8 May 1945 and have not expressed a contrary intention. Basic Law of the Federal Republic of Germany (23 May 1949)*, Wiesbaden: Press and Information Office of the Federal Republic of Germany, 1977, 83.) "Grundgesetz für die Bundesrepublik Deutschland vom 23 Mai 1949," in *Verfassung des Landes Hessen und Grundgesetz für die Bundesrepublik Deutschland mit einer Einführung und Karten von Hessen und Deutschland* (Bad Homburg: Verlag Dr. Max Gehlen, 1963), 157. Lehmann states that it is often difficult to distinguish between persecution on the basis of race versus on the basis of political views or activity, as many political refugees were also Jewish. Lehmann, "Acht und Ächtung politischer Gegner im Dritten Reich. Die Ausbürgerung deutscher Emigranten 1933–45", ix.

German practice is to reinstate the nationality of those citizens (mostly Germans of Jewish religion or origin as defined in the First Decree to the 1935 Nationality Act or *Reichsbürgergesetz*)[293] who were deprived of their nationality for political, racial, or religious reasons between 1933 and 1945, and to attribute nationality to the group of their descendants, including grandchildren,[294] who would have had German nationality, but for the withdrawal, should they desire it. It does this regardless of any ensuing multiple nationality. But the group of people allowed to seek German nationality of right is as narrowly drawn as possible, notwithstanding the Constitutional provision that on its face seems to read otherwise. Many of those excluded have been denied German nationality on the basis of avoidance of multiple nationality, over and above considerations related to *Wiedergutmachung* or family unity of nationality.[295]

Article 116(2) has been interpreted by German courts to apply only to those persons who were affected by the withdrawal of nationality in strict legal terms.[296] The definition of "descendant", while extended to grandchildren, does in fact not include all descendants of persons who suffered deprivation of nationality, but only those descendants who under German law would have been German nationals, but for the deprivation.[297] Therefore, no matter how families suffered as a consequence of Nazi rule, the right to German nationality is provided only to a restricted group of "descendants" of persons deprived of nationality. This restrictive interpretation does not seem to be commonly known, including in specialised legal circles,[298] and even by German diplomatic missions overseas.[299]

---

[293] *Erste Verordnung zum Reichsbürgergesetz. Vom 14. November 1935*, Reichsgesetzblatt (RGBl.) (1935) I, 1333. For the German text see also "Reichsbürgergesetz. Vom 15. September 1935 (Reichsgesetzblatt (RGBl.) I (1935): 1146", in *Der Nationalsozialismus. Dokumente 1933–1945*, ed. Walther Hofer (Frankfurt am Main: Fischer Bücherei, 1957), 284. For an English translation see Schleunes, ed., *Legislating the Holocaust. The Bernhard Loesener memoirs and supporting documents*, 154–57.

[294] Christiane E. Philipp, *Deutsche Rechtsprechung in völkerrechtlichen Fragen 1993, IV. Staatsangehörigkeit, 1. Erwerb*, Max-Planck-Institut für internationales öffentliches Recht und Völkerrecht (internet), http://www.mpil.de/publ/en/rspr93/r93_7.cfm, consulted 29 March 2006.

[295] In relation to *Wiedergutmachung* and German nationality generally, see Fritz Sturm and Gudrun Sturm, *Das deutsche Staatsangehörigkeitsrecht. Grundriss und Quellen* (Frankfurt am Main: Verlag für Standesamtswesen, 2001), 30, although the authors do not mention the issues raised herein in relation to the restricted definition of "descendant" for the purpose of Article 116(2) of the Basic Law.

[296] Hans von Mangoldt, "The right of return in German nationality law", *Tel Aviv University Studies in Law*, (1997) vol. 13, 29–52, 34.

[297] von Mangoldt states that this interpretation "has given rise to much controversy and (perhaps deliberate) misunderstanding", labelling this "misplaced". von Mangoldt, "The right of return in German nationality law", 42.

[298] For example, although they address the issue of *Wiedergutmachung* in relation to nationality under current German law, the authors of a new manual on nationality state incorrectly that descendants of those deprived of nationality, including children and grandchildren, are extended an automatic right to naturalisation. Sturm and Sturm, *Das deutsche Staatsangehörigkeitsrecht.*

Thus, the children of German mothers deprived of their nationality by the National Socialists are not held to fall within the Article, as German mothers could not transmit nationality at that time, evidence of persecution is irrelevant, and the reinstatement of the mother's nationality has no automatic effect on her children.[300] Likewise, the effect of the interpretation is that children of German fathers who were deprived of their nationality are not included, if the offspring are of marriages between people of mixed religion, and born prior to the deprivation. The line of argument is that as the offspring themselves were not technically deprived of German nationality, as "*Mischlinge*" (or people of "mixed-race") under Article 5 of the First Decree to the 1935 *Reichsbürgergesetz*,[301] they are thus not "descendants" for the purpose of Article 116(2) of the Basic Law.[302] Germans who fled the Nazi regime, whether Jewish or

---

Grundriss und Quellen, 30. The restrictive interpretation is not mentioned by authors on multiple nationality, for example Kreuzer, "Double and multiple nationality in Germany after the Citizenship Reform Act of 1999"; Wiedemann, "Development of dual nationality under German law". The same is true for manuals of public international law that make specific reference to the provision. Georg Dahm, Jost Delbrück, and Rüdiger Wolfrum, "Kapitel 14: Der einzelne in seinem Verhältnis zum Staat: Die Staatsangehörigkeit," in *Völkerrecht. I: Die Grundlagen. Die Völkerrechtssubujekte. Teilband 2* (Berlin: Walter de Gruyter, 2002), 103. The Article 116 provisions are often cited as a right to naturalisation that is not discretionary, without further analysis. See for example Peter Friedrich Bultmann, "Dual nationality and naturalisation policies in the German Länder", in *Dual nationality, social rights and federal citizenship in the U.S. and Europe. The reinvention of citizenship*, ed. Randall Hansen and Patrick Weil (New York: Berghahn Books, 2002), 136–157. The author refers to "ethnic Germans" but cites Article 116 generally, not distinguishing between paragraphs (1) and (2).

[299] The German Embassy in Santiago in its information on nationality states "La Constitución Alemana (Grundgesetz) pos-guerra en su artículo 116 p. 2 otorgó y sigue otorgando a cualquier persona afectada por esta medida y sus descendientes (hijos, nietos) el derecho de recuperar la nacionalidad alemana, de (re)naturalizarse". (Author's translation: *Article 116(2) of the post-war German Constitution (Grundgesetz) granted and continues to grant to any person affected by this measure and his or her descendants (children, grandchildren) the right to regain German nationality, to be (re)naturalised.*) "Hoja informativa sobre la nacionalidad alemana", Deutsche Botschaft-Embajada Alemana Santiago (internet), http://www.santiago.diplo.de/es/04/Konsularischer__Service/Merkblatt__Staatsangeh_C3_B6rigkeit.html, consulted 30 May 2006.

[300] *Urteil vom 27. März 1990 – BVerwG 1 C 5.87*, Das Standesamt (1990) no. 11, 337.

[301] *Erste Verordnung zum Reichsbürgergesetz. Vom 14. November 1935*, and Schleunes, ed., *Legislating the Holocaust. The Bernhard Loesener memoirs and supporting documents*, 156.

[302] *Urteil vom 4. April 1996 – OVG 5 B 60.93 (Land Berlin gegen Alfred M. Boll)*, unreported case (1996), available from the *Oberverwaltungsgericht Berlin* Court Registry. The children of mixed Jewish-Christian marriages, following the 1935 Reichsbürgergesetz and the 1941 Nazi decree that deprived Jewish Germans of their nationality if they resided abroad, were not considered Jewish (and thus not themselves technically deprived of German nationality) unless they had been raised in the Jewish religion. In the incident case, the Court of Appeal, overturning the lower court's holding, held that while the father may have been deprived of his German nationality in 1941, his son (and presumably his Christian wife) had not, and thus had

not, who were naturalised abroad, are held to have acquired their new nationality of their own free will, thereby automatically losing their German nationality, regardless of the persecution they would have faced in Germany.[303]

It is to be wondered whether non-Jewish spouses and *Mischlinge* were really unaffected by their legal retention of German nationality.[304] Hepp documents the efforts of the German Embassy in Paris to deprive non-Jewish wives of German Jews and other "undesirables" and *Mischlinge* of their German nationality in 1941 and afterwards, due to breaches of the "obligation of racial loyalty". It was argued that such women were irredeemable, either due to their refusal to leave their husbands and children, or to the moral decrepitude that had set in after living for many years with the "Arab" (Jew).[305]

---

lost their German nationality pursuant to the exercise of their "free will" (*freien Willensentschluss*) through naturalisation in the United States in 1943. While the son had a right to seek naturalisation under other laws, Paragraph 12 of the Staatsangehörigkeitsgesetz (though not under the constitutional provision), according to which multiple nationality is no barrier to the attribution of German nationality, his childrens' entitlement under Paragraph 12 had expired on 31 December 1970, and no state interest in reparation with respect to the grandson could be cited to override the principle of avoidance of multiple nationality. The principle of family unity of nationality was not addressed, although the Court had been made aware that the father had been granted German nationality under Paragraph 12. Weis' citation of the liberal practice of National Socialist authorities in allowing Germans (albeit it may be supposed not German Jews or their families) to retain their nationality upon naturalisation or providing them with an opportunity to resume nationality later mentioned above at note 45 above might be recalled here. Weis, *Nationality and statelessness in international law*, 179.

[303] *Urteil vom 4. April 1996 – OVG 5 B 60.93 (Land Berlin gegen Alfred M. Boll).*

[304] Regarding the circumstances of German Jews, *"Mischlinge"*, and their families, their emigration/flight from Germany, and National Socialist Government policies of forcing emigration through terror, see generally Marion A. Kaplan, *Between dignity and despair. Jewish life in Nazi Germany* (New York, Oxford: Oxford University Press, 1998). Regarding forced emigration in relation to National Socialist extermination of German Jews and their families, see generally Hannah Arendt, *A report on the banality of evil. Eichmann in Jerusalem* (New York: Penguin Books, 1964), and Saul Friedländer, *Nazi Germany and the Jews. Volume I: The years of persecution: 1933–1939* (New York: HarperCollins Publishers, 1997). A dissertation on multiple nationality published in 1938 at the University of Rostock, and written according to "National Socialist Organic Thought" concluded that such thought should dictate that multiple nationality be an impossibility, but given its existence, that effective nationality should have nothing to do with subjective declarations by the concerned individual, but should be determined according to objective characteristics related to national (and racial) descent. Walter Ruthe, "Die organische Auffassung vom Staat und der Staatsangehörigkeit und die Frage der doppelten Staatsangehörigkeit", dissertation presented at the Universität Rostock (Düsseldorf, 1938), 1–7 and 52–54. For a contemporary dissertation, see Ernst Otto Hörnig, "Die mehrfache Staatsangehörigkeit in Rechtsprechung, Verwaltung und Gesetzgebung. Eine rechtsvergleichende Studie", dissertation presented at the Eberhard-Karls-Universität zu Tübingen (Bleicherode am Harz, 1939).

[305] Hepp, "Wer Deutscher ist, bestimmen wir . . .", xxxiii.

Various authors and indeed court decisions argue that the constitutional provision in Article 116(2) should, and could easily have been interpreted as covering all descendants of those deprived of nationality on political, racial and religious grounds, into the second generation. Silagi points out that any interpretation of the word "descendant" in Article 116(2) is problematic, and rejects the argument that the provision must be read restrictively, in terms of the provision's language, meaning and effect.[306]

> *Dem Zweck, Folgen nationalsozialistischer Unrechtsmassnahmen auf dem Gebiet der Staatsangehörigkeit zu beseitigen, und dem Gedanken einer sinnvollen "Wiedergutmachung" wird nämlich Art. 116 Abs. 2 GG durchaus gerecht, wenn man ihn im Sinne des aufgehobenen Urteils des VG Berlin auslegt.*[307]

In relation to providing a right of return to German Jews and their (sometimes non-Jewish) families, and to provide a measure of reparation for their expulsion, the (overturned) decision of the lower court held:

> *Die Betrachtungsweise . . . wird aber auch dem Sinn und Zweck des Art. 116 Abs. 2 Satz 1 GG nicht gerecht. Indem sie allein darauf abhebt, wie sich das (vorgestellte) Unterbleiben der Ausbürgerung des jeweiligen Elternteils staatsangehörigkeitsrechtlich auf die Abkömmlinge ausgewirkt hätte, greift sie lediglich einen Aspekt des Verfolgungsschicksals der von der Art. 116 Abs. 2 Satz 1 GG begünstigten Personen heraus. Dabei bleibt ausser Betracht, dass am Anfang dieser Schicksale in der Regel eine – durch die nationalsozialistische Willkürherrschaft erzwungene – Auswanderung oder Flucht stand. . . . Dieser Umstand kann bei einer am Wiedergutmachungsgedanken orientierten Auslegung des Art. 116 Abs. 2 Satz 1 GG nicht unberücksichtigt bleiben. Durch das erzwungene Verlassen Deutschlands wurde das Leben der Betroffenen allerdings derartig tiefgreifend verändert, dass es ausgeschlossen erscheint, nachträglich festzustellen, wie es ohne den nationalsozialistischen Rassenwahn verlaufen wäre. . . . Dies spricht für ein grosszügiges Verständnis des Art. 116 Abs. 2 Satz 1 GG im Sinne einer Wiedergutmachungsregelung für die staatsangehörigkeitsrechtlichen Folgen von Flucht bzw. Auswanderung und Ausbürgerung; dies kann nur ein Verständnis sein, das von problematischen hypothetischen Betrachtungen absieht und allein an den Status als Abkömmling eines Ausgebürgerten anknüpft.*[308]

---

[306] Michael Silagi, "Anmerkung (BVerwG, Urteil vom 27. März 1990 – BVerwG 1 C 5.87)", *Das Standesamt*, (1990) no. 11, 340–343, 341, and approving of the lower court's holding, Michael Silagi, "Anmerkung (VG Berlin, Urteil vom 27. Oktober 1986 – VG 2 A 39.85)", *Das Standesamt*, (1987) no. 5, 144–146, 145.

[307] (Author's translation: *The aim of eliminating the consequences of National Socialist injustices relating to nationality, and of (providing a) meaningful idea of reparation ("Wiedergutmachung"), is entirely realised by Article 116(2) if it is interpreted as in the overturned decision of the Berlin Administrative Court.*) Silagi, "Anmerkung (BVerwG, Urteil vom 27. März 1990 – BVerwG 1 C 5.87)", 343.

[308] (Author's translation: *Nor does this view . . . do justice to the meaning and purpose of the first sentence of Article 116(2) of the Basic Law. By only taking into account how the (imagined) non-existence of the respective parent's expatriation would have affected the descendant's nationality, it seizes only <u>one</u> aspect of the persecution and fate of the beneficiaries of Article*

Lehmann states that National Socialist propaganda systematically attempted to discredit emigrants who fled the regime, which in turn left what he terms 'indelible traces' after 1945: Many Germans continued to believe after the War that emigrants had been involved in anti-German or treasonous activities.[309] He documents that although the framers of the German constitution (Basic Law) treated the National Socialist deprivations as a nullity, administrative interpretation and practice followed positivist bureaucratic legal traditions that regarded them as effective. Minor officials especially, applied restrictive interpretations such as to frustrate those seeking to regain their German nationality.[310] He quotes a letter of complaint to the German authorities from a Dr A. F. sent from La Paz, Bolivia, who, upon application for restoration of his nationality, had been asked to submit answers to irrelevant questions such as in which regiment his grandfather had served.

Ich habe den peinlichen Eindruck, dass – ähnlich wie in der Weimarer Republik – der freiheitliche und demokratiche Geist der Verfassung auch heute wieder von den Behörden nach Kräften in seiner Auswirkung gehindert wird und dass die reaktionären Kräfte in den Ämtern dem guten Willen der Regierung und des Parlaments mit Erfolg entgegenarbeiten. Ich bin fest davon überzeugt, dass der Herr Bundespräsident und der Herr Bundeskanzler die Rechte der von Hitler Vertriebenen von Herzen anerkennen und ihre Wiederein-bürgerung raschestens und ohne Schwierigkeiten durchgeführt zu sehen wünschen; aber

---

116(2). Thereby left out of account is that this fate usually began with emigration or flight, forced by National Socialist despotism . . . These circumstances cannot be disregarded in any interpretation of the first sentence of Article 116(2), oriented toward thoughts of reparation. The lives of the affected persons were so fundamentally changed through the forced leaving of Germany that it would seem out of the question to determine after the fact, what would have happened without the National Socialist racial mania. This speaks for a generous understanding of the first sentence of Article 116(2) in terms of a provision of reparation for the consequences of flight, respectively emigration and expatriation. Such an understanding can only be one that disregards problematic hypothetical considerations, and only refers to status as a descendant of someone deprived of nationality.) VG Berlin, Urteil vom 27. Oktober 1986 – VG 2 A 39.85, 1987, Das Standesamt (1987) no. 5, 142, 144. In relation to the policy of providing reparation for the incident deprivation of nationality only in the strictest terms, it may be apt to reflect on the leeway the National Socialist regime left itself in matters of citizenship, or political rights. Citizenship rights were restricted not only to "Aryans", but to those people who obeyed. "Reichsbürger ist nur der Staatsangehörige deutschen oder artverwandten Blutes, der durch sein Verhalten beweist, dass er gewillt und geeignet ist, in Treue dem Deutschen Volk und Reich zu dienen". "Reichsbürgergesetz. Vom 15. September 1935 (Reichsgesetzblatt (RGBl.) I (1935) 1146", 284 (article 2(1)). Translation: *A "citizen of the Reich" [Reichsbürger] is only that subject who is of German or related blood and who, by his conduct, demonstrates that he is both willing and suited to serve faithfully the German people and Reich.* Schleunes, ed., *Legislating the Holocaust. The Bernhard Loesener memoirs and supporting documents*, 155.

[309] Lehmann, "Acht und Ächtung politischer Gegner im Dritten Reich. Die Ausbürgerung deutscher Emigranten 1933–45", x–xi.

[310] Id., xix–xx.

was nützt das, wenn der jeweilige Herr Sachbearbeiter, der vielleicht weniger von Sympathie für die jüdischen und politischen Emigranten erfüllt ist, diese Wieder-einbürgerung durch völlig überflässige und – gestatten Sir mir den Ausdruck – schikanöse Forderungen erschwert und dazu noch deutlich zu erkennen gibt, dass er sich auch dann noch, entgegen den Wortlaut der Verfassung, in seiner Entscheidung frei fühlt?[311]

It was only in 1968 that the German Constitutional Court held expressly that the Nazi deprivations of nationality had been legally ineffective, with an exception for those persons who no longer wished to be Germans, a decision that reportedly unleashed consternation among the German legal community at the time.[312]

The deprivation of nationality was not the first in post World War One Europe. In 1922 the Soviet government "denationalized the vast majority of Russian refugees, rendering them stateless".[313] In fact, the 1941 deprivation of nationality was not the first for German Jews. One of the National Socialists' initial acts in power was the "Law on the Retraction of Naturalizations and the Derecognition of German Citizen-ship" of 14 July 1933, adopted on Bastille Day, perhaps to signify (so Torpey sur-mises) their hated Weimar Republic, and aimed at East European Jews.[314] It allowed the regime to strip citizens naturalised between the end of the First World War and Hitler's nomination as Chancellor, of nationality.[315] It is perhaps in some ways remarkable that the regime waited until 1941 to forcibly expatriate German Jews, and then restrained itself to limit the denationalization to those resident (or deported) abroad. But what can only be described as a criminal and lawless regime did not reject denationalisation of its own nationals on its own territory due to standards of international law. The reality was that for German Jews in Germany in 1941, it did

---

[311] (Author's translation: *I have the unfortunate impression that, similar to the situation in the Weimar Republic, the free and democratic spirit of the Constitution is also today being pre-vented from being put into effect by officials, and that reactionary powers in official positions are successfully working against the goodwill of the government and the Parliament. I am com-pletely convinced that the Federal President and Chancellor genuinely recognise the rights of those who were expelled by Hitler, and that they wish to see their naturalisation effected as soon as possible and without difficulties. But what does that matter, if the respective case-worker, who is perhaps less imbued with sympathy for the Jewish and political emigrants, makes the naturalisation all the more difficult through completely superfluous and, permit me the expression, harassing demands, in addition to sending the clear message, even against the very words of the Constitution, that he gives himself full latitude in his decision.) Id., XX.*

[312] Ibid.

[313] Torpey, *The invention of the passport – surveillance, citizenship and the state,* 124.

[314] Id., 132. For the text in German, see "Gesetz über den Widerruf von Einbürgerungen und die Aberkennung der deutschen Staatsangehörigkeit. Vom 14. Juli 1933. Verordnung zur Durchführung des Gesetzes über den Widerruf von Einbürgerungen und die Aberkennung der deutschen Staatsangehörigkeit. Vom 26. Juli 1933", in *Die Ausbürgerung deutscher Staatsangehöriger 1933–45 nach den im Reichsanzeiger veröffentlichen Listen,* ed. Michael Hepp, vol. 1 (München: K G Saur, 1985), xli–xliii.

[315] Torpey, *The invention of the passport – surveillance, citizenship and the state,* 132.

not matter: Hitler had declined such proposals on the basis that after the War there would not be any Jews in Germany anyway.[316]

Regardless of whether or not the restrictive interpretation of the rule (or guarantee) regarding German nationality contained in Article 116(2) is approved of, for families affected by the National Socialist crimes in relation to nationality, the state-defined interests in *Wiedergutmachung* and family unity of nationality, are overridden by a clear preference in favour of the avoidance of multiple nationality.[317] For this group of people, this policy calls into question in a larger sense any *Wiedergutmachung* related to nationality, in terms of redress for their families' treatment by the National Socialist authorities.[318]

---

[316] Hepp, "Wer Deutscher ist, bestimmen wir...", xxxv.

[317] *Urteil vom 4. April 1996 – OVG 5 B 60.93 (Land Berlin gegen Alfred M. Boll)* and *Urteil vom 27. März 1990 – BVerwG 1 C 5.87.*

[318] This is not the same as the recent migration of Jews from the former Soviet Union to Germany, which has also been billed as *Wiedergutmachung* by some commentators. Eichhofer states that a consequence of the former German Democratic Republic's (GDR) declaration of regret to the victims of National Socialism in 1990, something the state had steadfastly refused to do as it did not consider itself to be a successor state to the German Empire (Deutsches Reich), was to begin a program of promoting Jewish immigration to the GDR from the former Soviet Union, with "*Wiedergutmachung*", as its stated purpose. André Eichhofer, *Die Aufnahme jüdischer Emigranten aus der ehemaligen Sowjetunion als Kontingentflüchtlinge (mit Berücksichtigung des Zuwanderungsgesetzes)*, paper presented at the Universität Trier Institut für Rechtspolitik, 2002 (internet), http://www.irp.uni-trier.de/13_Eichhofer.pdf, consulted 29 March 2006. Biehler notes that the continuation of the program by the Federal Republic of Germany after the union of the two states was at the behest of the leadership of Germany's Jewish community, who justified it as contributing to rebuilding Germany's decimated Jewish communities, and providing amends for National Socialist crimes. As of 2000, over 100,000 people had benefitted from the program. Gernot Biehler, "Ausländerrecht und jüdische Emigration aus der früheren Sowjetunion", in *Staat – Souveränität – Verfassung. Festschrift für Helmut Quaritsch zum 70. Geburtstag*, ed. Dietrich Murswiek, Ulrich Storost, and Heinrich A. Wolff (Berlin: Duncker & Humblot, 2000), 265–283, 267. Biehler and Eichhofer question whether the program was in fact compensatory, or part of an idea of "Wiedergutmachung", as the Jews who benefited had not been victims of the National Socialists. Biehler, "Ausländerrecht und jüdische Emigration aus der früheren Sowjetunion", 267; Eichhofer, *Die Aufnahme jüdischer Emigranten aus der ehemaligen Sowjetunion als Kontingentflüchtlinge (mit Berücksichtigung des Zuwanderungsgesetzes)*. Persons accepted included those with at least one Jewish parent, plus spouses and minor children. Only baptised Jews were excluded. Biehler, "Ausländerrecht und jüdische Emigration aus der früheren Sowjetunion", 268–69. See also Ruth Rubio-Marín, *Immigration as a democratic challenge – citizenship and inclusion in Germany and the United States* (Cambridge: Cambridge University Press, 2000), 226 note 93. This group of persons is allowed to retain multiple nationality under the provisions of the 2001 Federal Administrative Provision. Kreuzer, "Double and multiple nationality in Germany after the Citizenship Reform Act of 1999", 356–57. In relation to the definition of "former Germans" generally and in relation to the naturalisation privilege contained in Article 116(1) of the Basic Law with respect to ethnic Germans in Eastern European countries, see Michael Silagi, "Das Einbürgerungsprivileg des

Descendants of those deprived of nationality by the Nazis in 1941, or otherwise, who are not "descendants" for the purpose of Article 116(2) can apply for German naturalisation on the same terms as any other descendant of a German national.[319] In such cases, the German government and German courts have rejected arguments that the hardship faced by families through forced emigration/flight should override the principle of avoidance of multiple nationality. For the principle of *Wiedergutmachung* to override the principle of avoidance of multiple nationality it is necessary to prove that the consequences of the expulsion from Germany persist in relation to the specific descendant.[320]

The example is a stark one in terms of the weight placed on avoidance of multiple nationality over other state-defined interests, especially in light of the general conduct of the Federal Republic of Germany to provide reparations for National Socialist crimes, redress that is often held to be generous.[321] In this light, it is per-

§ 13 StAG", *Zeitschrift für Ausländerrecht und Ausländerpolitik*, (2001) vol. 21, no. 3 (2001), 104–111.

[319] *VG Berlin, Urteil vom 27. Oktober 1986 – VG 2 A 39.85.* The separate, more favourable statutory provision for those descendants who are judged to have been themselves persecuted on political, racial or religious grounds, who are held to have lost their German nationality automatically through naturalisation elsewhere (§ 12 Abs. 1 des 1. StAngRegG), has already been mentioned. Sturm and Sturm, *Das deutsche Staatsangehörigkeitsrecht. Grundriss und Quellen*, 82. This is applied to German Jews whose "voluntary naturalisation" abroad took place before the 1941 denationalisation decree. It excludes descendants who were not personally directly persecuted, such as family members of those granted German nationality under these provisions. The latter group had possessed a statutory right to German nationality until 31 December 1970.

[320] *Urteil vom 4. April 1996 – OVG 5 B 60.93 (Land Berlin gegen Alfred M. Boll).* The criteria used to judge when multiple nationality will be accepted in relation to specific applications for German nationality are not made public by the German Administration, but were taken up by the Court in the case cited. For aplications from within Germany, the relevant general provision is Paragraph 85 of the *Ausländergesetz*, for applications from outside Germany the relevant sections of the *Staatsangehörigkeitsgesetz* and the *Staatsangehörigkeitsregelungsgesetz*.

[321] Regarding financial compensation for victims of National Socialist Germany as *Wiedergutmachung* see Bundesministerium der Finanzen (German Ministry of Finance), "Leistungen der öffentlichen Hand auf dem Gebiet der Wiedergutmachung – Stand 31. Dezember 2004", 2004 (internet), http://www.bundesfinanz ministerium.de/cln_04/nn_3792/DE/Finanz__und__ Wirtschaftspolitik/Vermoegensrecht__und__Entschaedigungen/Kriegsfolgen__und__Wiedergutmac hung/8391.html, consulted 29 March 2006. The German government's efforts to combat anti-Semitism might also be mentioned in this context, which were praised in 1996 by the United Nations' Special Rapporteur on Contemporary forms of Racism, Racial Discrimination, Xenophobia and related Intolerance. United Nations. Economic and Social Council. Commission on Human Rights, "Implementation of the Programme of Action for the Second Decade to Combat Racism and Racial Discrimination. Report by Mr. Maurice Glélé-Ahanhanzo, Special Rapporteur on contemporary forms of racism, racial discrimination, xenophobia and related intolerance, submitted pursuant to Commission on Human Rights resolutions 1993/20 and 1995/12", Fifty-second session, E-CN.4–1996–72, 15 February 1996 (Geneva: United Nations, 1996), 6.

haps particularly ironic that amendments to German nationality law and administrative provisions in 1999 and 2001 provide an express exception to the retained principle against multiple nationality, for victims of political persecution or persons treated as refugees,[322] as the provision does not apply to family members of victims of German persecution, only to victims of non-German persecution.

As in relation to the restrictive interpretation of Article 116(2) generally, no mention is made by authors of the fact that multiple nationality (that is, the desire to retain their previous nationality) is used by German authorities as an underlying reason for rejecting applications for German nationality by the descendants of those forcibly expatriated by the National Socialists. It does not seem to be generally known in specific legal circles, and is not well documented. Klein states (quite correctly) for example

> Von grösserer praktischer Bedeutung als Quelle von Doppelstaatigkeit sind jodoch Rechtsansprüche auf Erwerb der deutschen Staatsangehörigkeit, ohne dass der Gesetzgeber den Verlust oder die Aufgabe der bisherigen Staatsangehörigkeit zur Voraussetzung gemacht hätte. Hierbei kommen zum einen die Ansprüche ehemals politisch verfolgter früherer deutscher Staatsangehöriger auf Wiedererlangung der deutschen Staatsangehörigkeit in Betracht (Art. 116 Abs. 2 GG).[323]

3. Human rights and the transfer of territory: the cases of Hong Kong and Macao

Bar-Yaacov's argument that voluntary transfer of territory leads to automatic transfer of personal jurisdiction, and Aleinikoff and Klusmeyer's differentiation between instances of state succession and cession of territory, were mentioned above at note 135. The policies of the United Kingdom and Portugal with regard to the populations of the former Crown Colony of Hong Kong, and Macao, respectively, shed an interesting perspective on this issue. The transfers of territory were widely cited as involving human rights issues, and neither state used the voting process to consult local populations directly as to the desirability of the respective handovers. Interestingly, both the United Kingdom and Portugal used their citizens' multiple nationality (China considered most of each territory's population to possess its nationality already) in addressing the handovers, albeit in opposing ways.

---

[322] Kreuzer, "Double and multiple nationality in Germany after the Citizenship Reform Act of 1999", 356–57; Wiedemann, "Development of dual nationality under German law", 341.

[323] (Author's translation: Of (even) greater practical significance as a source of dual nationality are, however, the legal rights to acquisition of German nationality for which the legislator did not make loss or surrender of previous nationality a condition. In this regard the rights of formerly politically persecuted former German nationals to regain German nationality are relevant (Article 116(2) Basic Law)). Hailbronner, "Mehrfache Staatsangehörigkeit und Einbürgerung in der Bundesrepublik Deutschland", 396.

Although the United Kingdom did not formally deprive its Hong Kong nationals of their British nationality when it departed Hong Kong in 1997, it left them with a status that does not give them the right of abode or residence in the United Kingdom. Britain maintains that these "British Nationals (Overseas)" (BNO) are its nationals, and that it is entitled to protect them vis-à-vis other states and assert related rights. Depriving nationals of a right of residence is exceedingly rare today, although there is evidence that states do contemplate it in certain circumstances: in 2005 the Dutch government announced plans to "deport 'underprivileged and problematic' young people" from the Netherlands Antilles, thereby apparently divorcing a right of residence in the Netherlands from possession of Netherlands' nationality for this group.[324]

Returning to Hong Kong and Macao, Portugal did not follow Britain, and Portuguese nationals in Macao retain full rights of citizenship in Portugal. This is especially noteworthy, because for the last years of its rule Portugal claimed only to be an administering power, not territorial sovereign, of Macao, notwithstanding previous assertions to sovereignty.[325] The United Kingdom on the other hand, claimed territorial sovereignty over Hong Kong Island and the Kowloon Peninsula pursuant to 19th century treaties labeled "unequal" by the People's Republic of China. China recognizes neither nationality with respect to its Hong Kong and Macau citizens, but tolerates their possession of UK and Portuguese passports.[326]

It might be argued that the United Kingdom did no more than follow the rule cited by Aleinikoff and Klusmeyer that a state ceding territory is obligated to remove its nationality from those persons who receive the nationality of the acquiring state. But this is arguably not the case: Britain did not in fact denationalize its Hong Kong citizens for the purposes of international law, but does deprive this cohort of persons of rights usually associated with nationality under municipal law. Similarly, as this group already possessed Chinese nationality, there was arguably no question of the imposition of an "old" nationality over a "new" one.

---

[324] "Deportations planned", *International Herald Tribune*, 14–15 May 2005, 6.

[325] See Rui Manuel Moura Ramos, "La déclaration commune Sino-Portugaise dans la perspective du droit international", in *Mélanges en hommage Michel Waelbroeck*, ed. Marianne Dony vol. 1 (Bruxelles: Bruylant, 1999), 97–109, 98. Macao's interesting history in relation to sovereignty claims is detailed in Austin Coates, *A Macao Narrative* (Hong Kong: Oxford University Press, 1978), 84–107.

[326] In April 2005 China arrested Ching Cheong, the chief China correspondent of Singapore's *The Straits Times,* on charges of spying for Taiwan. Ching is a China-born British BNO national who was raised in Hong Kong. The British Consulate in Hong Kong said China had denied it access to him. Keith Bradsher, "China formally arrests Hong Kong reporter as spy", *International Herald Tribune*, 6–7 August 2005, 2. Regarding Hong Kong Government assistance to Hong Kong residents in mainland China and abroad, see Hong Kong Special Administrative Region Government, Home Affairs Bureau, "Second report on the Hong Kong Special Administrative Region of the People's Republic of China in the light of the International Covenant on Civil and Political Rights", Hong Kong: Government Logistics Department, No. 2256256, 2005, paragraphs 141–143.

For argument's sake, even assuming that these instances of territorial cession required the withdrawal of nationality, in an age of respect for the individual according to fundamental norms of human rights, one might surmise that states would provide individuals in such a situation with the choice of retaining their original nationality, perhaps even if this meant leaving the territory in question. Such a choice might be considered all the more important in situations where territorial transfer was not made pursuant to an act of popular will. Portugal gave its Macao-based nationals the option to choose for themselves by not withdrawing its nationality and not creating a status of nationality without rights of citizenship. It could do so because China's attribution of its nationality to most Macanese meant that they did not have to opt between two nationalities they already possessed. Britain on the other hand arguably used its Hong Kong citizens' dual Anglo-Chinese nationality as a means to deprive them of the right of abode in Britain: as they can be returned to Hong Kong as *Chinese* nationals, Britain does in fact not have to accept them on its territory pursuant to international obligations to third states. But no matter how discriminatory and questionable Britain's treatment of its Hong Kong nationals may be, this is so on the plane of British municipal law.

White argues that no blame should attach to Britain for transferring the 3.5 million Hong Kong British citizens "to the control of another state, without requiring their consent", but he also suggests that an issue of human rights is raised.[327]

> *Bitterness was felt towards the United Kingdom for having agreed to strip millions of people of their nationality. This bitterness partly reflected concern at the lack of an escape route, such as entry to the United Kingdom, and partly reflected a sense of betrayal.*[328]

Roberti claims that reforms to the UK's nationality legislation in 1981 were "blatantly racist and discriminatory" and "clearly aimed at Hong Kong".

> *A person born in South Africa, for example, who had never lived in Britain and whose parents had never lived in Britain, was considered more British than someone born on British territory in Hong Kong, who had grown up under a British administration, attended British schools, pledged their loyalty to the Queen, and possibly even served in the military.*[329]

He also claims that senior civil servants and members of the Hong Kong Executive and Legislative Councils were assured that they would be provided with British citizenship (and the related right of abode in Britain) should there be a crisis. "Thus, the people in a position to fight for the rights of Hong Kong residents had no further incentive to do so".[330] Chan effectively argues that the United Kingdom is in violation

---

[327] Robin M. White, "Nationality aspects of the Hong Kong settlement", *Case Western Reserve Journal of International Law*, (1988) vol. 20, 225–251, 251.

[328] White, "Nationality aspects of the Hong Kong settlement", 248–49.

[329] Mark Roberti, *The fall of Hong Kong. China's triumph & Britain's betrayal*. (New York: John Wiley & Sons, Inc., 1996), 30.

[330] Roberti, *The fall of Hong Kong. China's triumph & Britain's betrayal*, 31.

of basic standards of human rights by not providing former Hong Kong British citizens whose status is now that of British Nationals (Overseas) with the right to enter and live in the United Kingdom. He proposed that the Anglo-Chinese citizens of Hong Kong be given an option to choose between the two nationalities prior to 1 July 1997.[331] The British Nationality (Hong Kong) Act 1990 allowed the Governor of Hong Kong to register 50,000 heads of households and their families as British citizens with the right of abode in the United Kingdom, "undoubtedly aimed at the more educated and wealthier class... The scheme was severely condemned by the PRC Government, which indicated that it would not recognize those British passports issued under the scheme".[332]

Fransman also argues that "nationality should incorporate the right of abode in the country of nationality" and points out that in relation to the United Kingdom "politically this may become a more realistic option following the return of Hong Kong (the most populated colony) to China on 1 July 1997".[333] It is unclear whether Fransman is arguing that Hong Kong British Nationals (Overseas) should be provided with undifferentiated British nationality, or that their exclusion after 1 July 1997 would make it politically palatable to give the right of abode to other British nationals, citizens of the remaining British colonies. The latter scenario is in fact what has taken place. In a Command Paper on the future of the UK's overseas territories published less than two years after Hong Kong's return to China, the British government recommended that all overseas territories citizens be granted British Citizenship, entailing a right of abode in the United Kingdom, citing the principle of "self-determination" given to each overseas territory as one of the bases for the respective political relationships. This was carried out in the *British Overseas Territories Act 2002*.[334]

While both White and Chan cite political issues as the origin of Britain's refusal to provide her former Hong Kong citizens with undifferentiated British nationality after 1 July 1997, Chang notes that Portugal's government would have been hurt politically had the same been done to Luso-Chinese in Macao.[335] Ironically, as Portuguese citizens the Luso-Chinese in Macao have the right of abode in the United

---

[331] Johannes Chan, "Nationality", in *Human Rights in Hong Kong*, ed. Raymond Wacks (Hong Kong: Oxford University Press, 1992), 470–508, 496–97.

[332] Andrew Byrnes and Johannes Chan, "The British Nationality (Hong Kong) Act 1990", in *Public Law and Human Rights. A Hong Kong Sourcebook*, ed. Andrew Byrnes and Johannes Chan (Hong Kong: Butterworths, 1993), 74–80, 74–75.

[333] Laurie Fransman, "The case for reform of nationality law in the United Kingdom", in *Citizenship and nationality status in the new Europe*, ed. Síofra O'Leary and Teija Tiilikainen (London: Sweet & Maxwell, 1998), 123–147, 135 and 139.

[334] *British Overseas Territories Act 2002*, Office of Public Sector Information, 2006 (internet), http://www.opsi.gov.uk/ACTS/acts2002/20020008.htm, consulted 29 March 2006.

[335] Jaw-ling Joanne Chang, "Settlement of the Macao issue: distinctive features of Beijing's negotiating behavior", *Case Western Reserve Journal of International Law*, (1988) vol. 20, 253–278, 265. See Moura Ramos, "La déclaration commune Sino-Portugaise dans la perspective du droit international", 102–04.

Kingdom via European Union treaty arrangements, while their Hong Kong neighbours with British BNO passports do not.[336]

J. SUMMARY

The outline provided in this chapter illustrates that views of, and practice toward, multiple nationality have been a function of the political and legal nature of the state, political and legal interests in delimitation of nationals especially in light of migration and the possibility and legitimacy of war between states, as well as perceptions of national and individual interest and their relative value in relation to one another.

This view is supported by Torpey's study of the development of documentary controls in relation to movement and identification of individuals in Western states. He demonstrates how delimitation of states' nationals in relation to foreigners developed over time, and was affected by the changing nature of the state as well as the particular interests of both the state and natural persons.[337] He argues that

> the emergence of passport and related controls on movement is an essential aspect of the "state-ness" of states, and it therefore seemed to be putting the cart before the horse to presume to compare states as if they were "hard," "really-existing" entities of a type that were more nearly approximated after the First World War". Moreover, what is remarkable about the contemporary system of passport controls is that it bears witness to a cooperating "international society" as well as to an overarching set of norms and prescriptions to which individual states must respond. This does not mean, as some seem to think, that there is no such thing as "sovereignty," but only that this is a claim states make in an environment not of their own making. To paraphrase Marx, states make their own policy, "but they do not make it just as they please; they do not make it under circumstances chosen by themselves, but under circumstances directly found, given, and transmitted from the outside".[338]

A clear trend in opinion can be observed that multiple nationality is an unavoidable product of differences among states and their inherent right to define their group of nationals. International efforts at elimination of multiple nationality following the First World War have been eclipsed by a return to policies favouring maintaining ties to nationals, if individuals so choose. Whereas such a view had formerly been predicated upon ideas of permanent allegiance essentially ignoring multiple nationality as an issue, today states seem to maintain a legal link that amounts to taking multiple

---

[336] See also Johannes M. M. Chan, "Hong Kong: an analysis of the British nationality proposals", *Immigration and nationality law and practice*, (1990) vol. 4, 57–62; Frank Ching, "Chinese nationality in the Basic Law", in *The Basic Law and Hong Kong's future*, ed. Peter Wesley-Smith and Albert H. Y. Chen (Hong Kong: Butterworths, 1988).

[337] Torpey, *The invention of the passport – surveillance, citizenship and the state*, 1–3.

[338] Id., 3.

nationality into account on some level. The overview of state practice in the Appendix is designed to examine the contours of such attitudes. As for permanent allegiance, current views may see expatriation as a basic right of the individual, however still potentially qualified by duties owed, and barring statelessness. This state of affairs reflects the influence of concepts of human rights that give individuals unprecedented, but not unlimited, standing vis-à-vis both their own, and other states.[339]

Whether this trend is definite or definitive cannot be answered here. It depends on international relations and states' definition of themselves as political and legal units and the legal paradigm they create for their nationals both internally and in their mutual relations. That international relations change in function of human interaction is no surprise, but such interaction even influences the extent to which the nation will continue to be the basic definitional unit for areas such as commerce, investment, employment, and so on. Economic studies that see the increasing internationalization of private sector companies leading to a decoupling of corporate and national prosperity give pause for thought.[340] Perhaps the current trend is no more than the swing of a pendulum, which at any time may change course, perhaps following predictions of the demise of globalisation. On the other hand, tolerance and even acceptance of multiple nationality in theory and practice may in fact herald or be a consequence of a new age of liberation for human beings as individuals vis-à-vis the state, perhaps reflecting what has been called "post-national membership".[341] Franck argues that increasing tolerance of multiple nationality is an indicator of changes in the way identity is perceived and expressed, and respect for individuals' choices.[342]

---

[339] Spiro points out that a refusal by states to automatically expatriate individuals upon naturalisation elsewhere might be seen as a new form of perpetual allegiance, albeit to the benefit of the individual (in terms of the rights of citizenship). Peter J. Spiro, *Embracing dual nationality* (Washington: Carnegie Endowment for International Peace, 1998), 17. He points out that this would force states either not to naturalise the person in question, should they insist on expatriation as a condition of naturalisation (which he characterises as unlikely in the United States), or accept multiple nationality. Ibid. As has been seen, this is already the case in states that require expatriation as a condition of naturalisation: Germany's laws create an exception for persons from states that do not permit expatriation or make it exceedingly difficult, for example. See Hessisches Ministerium des Innern und für Sport, "Rundschreiben vom 23.10.2000–II A 11–04–20", *Informationsbrief Ausländerrecht*, (2001) no. 1, 43.

[340] "Decoupled. Companies' and countries' prosperity", *The Economist*, 25 February 2006, 67. The authors argue that "the old relationship between corporate and national prosperity has broken down ... companies are no longer tied to the economic conditions and policies of the countries in which they are listed ... [and] the success of companies no longer guarantees the prosperity of domestic economies or, more particularly, of domestic workers". Id. "'What's good for General Motors is good for America', no longer rings true: over one-third of GM's employees work outside the group's home country". Id.

[341] Torpey, *The invention of the passport – surveillance, citizenship and the state*, 2, citing Rogers Brubaker, *Citizenship and nationhood in France and Germany* (Cambridge (Massachusetts): Harvard University Press, 1992), chapter 1.

[342] See generally Franck, "Multiple citizenship: autres temps, autres moeurs".

It is the author's opinion that neither view can constitute a difinitive statement as to the essence of nationality, or states' and individuals' interests in multiple nationality. The principal underlying interests of both states and individuals are in fact not related to multiple nationality as such, but to nationality, and the delimitation of which persons are provided with rights and benefits on the municipal level vis-à-vis the state and each other in the first place. Were this not the case, efforts at eliminating multiple nationality or otherwise regulating it on the international plane would probably have been more successful. If 16th and 17th century issues of freedom of movement in Europe depended on

> (1) how the economic advantages available in a particular area were to be divided up, whether these involved access to work or to poor relief; and
> (2) who would be required to perform military service, and how they would be constrained to do so,[343]

the sketch of opinion surrounding the relative desirability of multiple nationality presented above demonstrates that there seems to be little that sets the 21st century apart.

---

[343] Torpey, *The invention of the passport – surveillance, citizenship and the state*, 19.

Chapter 5

Principles of International Law that Govern Nationality and Areas of International Law Influenced by Multiple Nationality

Until they know the outcome of the succession in China and Indonesia, overseas Chinese want to remain highly mobile intermediaries, whose personal wealth stays safely salted away, earning high interest. . . . They shed no tears for nationalism. Mobility is everything. . . . 'When you reach this stage,' one said, 'craving US citizenship becomes pointless. I spend so little time in any one place that citizenship no longer matters.' To them nationalism is a vanity and a prejudice, like racism, which they cannot afford.[1]

Seagrave's characterization of the importance of nationality for a number of overseas Chinese may indeed reflect a certain reality. It does not seem representative, however, in terms of the value of nationality to the individual and the state, issues explored in the following chapters. It illustrates, however, that the value of nationality is a subjective issue. Any legal study in relation to it must thus attempt to divorce issues of

---

[1] Sterling Seagrave, *Lords of the rim. The invisible empire of the Overseas Chinese* (London: Transworld Publishers, 1995), 366.

'vanity and prejudice' from its parameters, or deal with them in a way that does not prejudice the outcome.

Drawing conclusions as to the effects of state practice on rules of international law may be seen as a precarious affair. In this sense the author has taken into account, but was not discouraged by, the admonition contained in the preface to a survey of US-Mexican relations in relation to diplomatic protection from 1825 until the 1920s:

> *Single diplomatic statements or arbitral awards may suggest the existence of an orderly, purely logical system. Viewed collectively, however, over the course of a century, they seem to indicate that one cannot divorce the reign of law from the reign of man.*[2]

While this caution can easily be distinguished from the present study, it is apt to recall here that current state practice toward multiple nationality cannot be divorced from the historical development of nationality, and the historical treatment of multiple nationality. Both are important in order to draw conclusions.

A. OUTLINE OF CONCLUSIONS IN THIS AND THE FOLLOWING CHAPTER

Other than canvassing related opinion, this study has avoided assumptions as to the relative desirability of multiple nationality. This and the following chapter outline conclusions drawn from the survey contained in the Appendix. It is argued that current state practice in many respects favours multiple nationality, in the sense that states' legislation contributes to its production, and evinces in most cases a direct acceptance of its existence. Although these general results may be expressed in terms that states "accept" or "contribute to" the "existence" or "production" of multiple nationality, or "tolerate" it, what is meant is really that multiple nationality is not viewed as an anomaly, and that it can be regarded as a "normal" function of international relations and law in state practice. Importantly, however, the "acceptance" in terms of tolerance of multiple nationality by states does not amount to an incorporation of multiple nationality as such into international law. These two general conclusions in turn have particular consequences for international law. The results of the survey of state practice herein are summarised below. As a consequence of the general conclusion that multiple nationality is not only a reality, but accepted in practice, it might be tempting to conclude that states themselves view multiple nationality as a desirable thing. This is neither an argument submitted by the author, nor a conclusion that can be drawn from the underlying enquiry.

As illustrated from the survey in the foregoing chapters, possessing the nationality of more than one state may indeed be a desirable status for those individuals for

---

[2] Parker Thomas Moon, "Preface", in *The Diplomatic Protection of Americans in Mexico*, ed. Frederick Sherwood Dunn (New York: Columbia University Press, 1933), vi.

whom the reality of life means a decision to maintain legal ties, usually also emotional ties and to do with identity, to more than one state. As long as emigration and immigration remain a reality, as long as families can be constituted by people from different states, and as long as states make up the fundamental component of an international system of human interaction, multiple nationality can be expected to exist in state practice.[3]

It is perhaps a characteristic of multiple nationality today that individuals can be said largely to have a choice as far as whether to maintain the status or not. It was also illustrated, however, that the practical reality of maintaining such ties implies the subjection of the individual to two or more legal orders, whose claims on the individual are equally valid on their respective municipal planes. This can no doubt cause hardship to the individual concerned, in terms of duties imposed, when nationality is the relevant criterion used to ascribe them. Multiple nationals may be subject to competing claims, certainly claims related to ideas and standards of loyalty, under states' municipal laws, which may in fact be mutually incompatible in certain situations. That bearing such risk, or accepting the onus of managing related administrative challenges, is left to the individual concerned, can be seen as a consequence of the legal position of the individual on both the municipal and international planes, and development of notions and standards of human rights and respect for the individual.

But in contrast to previous opinion unfavourable to multiple nationality as such, most current writers do not regard the possible conflicts related to multiple nationality as overly burdensome on states. In fact, most discussion seems directed at addressing the consequences of multiple nationality in practical terms, and few authors argue along the lines of Bar-Yaacov that multiple nationality itself must be eliminated. Although such reasoning is not an ingredient of the current study, it may be said to reflect what might be characterised as a symptom of the first conclusion of the analysis herein, the answer to Baty's question, posed on page one: multiple nationality is indeed not only possible, but today amounts to an accepted and practical reality of international law and international relations. The notion that there is a principle of avoidance of multiple nationality in international law, referred to by some writers, is belied by state practice: either such principle does not exist, or the majority of states do not respect it. It is submitted that international law contains no such principle. To refer to multiple nationality and statelessness as twin problems, so often done in the past, is to misrepresent fundamentally the issues involved, both for states and for individuals.

---

[3] Van Panhuys states that "[t]he function of nationality in international law is closely connected with the position of the sovereign State in the society of nations. If ever the day should dawn when the sovereignty of States yields to the rule of a universally recognized World Government, nationality will either be reduced to the level of residence in a municipality or a province under municipal law or, more probably still, it will lose its independent significance altogether". H. F. van Panhuys, *The rôle of nationality in international law – an outline* (Leyden: A. W. Sythoff, 1959), 219.

This is the starting point of analysis for the conclusions in this and the following chapter. It is argued that the effect of current state practice is largely to reinforce existing rules of international law related to nationality, while clarifying the scope of such rules or presumptions. While this chapter discusses the consequences of the existence of multiple nationality in relation to many of the specific issues raised in chapters one to four, the following chapter takes up the larger question of the definition or essence of nationality, and concludes that the existence of multiple nationality in state practice is relevant to understanding its nature, at least in its present form. The analysis returns to the idea that it behoves governments to understand nationality's essence and consequences on the international plane in context, and manage their mutual relations accordingly. Concerns related to international standards of protection for the human being also dictate that nationality's contours be properly understood. State practice toward multiple nationality illustrates the importance of nationality, as well as its inherent limitations in providing protection for the individual. In this sense, states could amend their municipal legislation in several respects in order better to serve their citizens.

B. GENERAL CONCLUSIONS PROPOSED AND DEVELOPED IN THIS AND THE FOLLOWING CHAPTER

As the analysis in the present chapter is in many ways predicated on more general conclusions related to the nature of nationality discussed in the following chapter, certain basic conclusions are enumerated here in order to guide the reader.

It is argued that the existence of multiple nationality and its practical incorporation in inter-state relations, notwithstanding certain state practice that rejects it:

(1) indicates that the nature or essence of nationality does not in and of itself demand or require exclusivity;
(2) reinforces the value or relevance of nationality as such in international law, while clarifying its scope on the international plane;
(3) reflects the essence of present international law in terms of state sovereignty and equality, and the rules of the United Nations Charter as to the use of force by states, perhaps even indicating a certain underlying trust built into the inter-state system and international law;
(4) cannot be seen outside the context of wider issues and norms related to minimum standards of treatment for human beings generally, and international systems of protection for the human being.

C. SURVEY OF STATE PRACTICE

As seen from the contents of the Appendix, it is clear that the analysis presented herein discerns nuances in state practice in various ways, revealing that the variety in state practice is indeed impressive.[4] Due to the changing nature of municipal regulations related to nationality, as well as the inherent difficulty in obtaining and verifying appropriate and reliable sources, it cannot be taken as a definitive statement of current law in each country, nonetheless, it is submitted as an accurate representation of state practice for the purposes of this study.

1. General positions on multiple nationality

Four general positions as to the <u>production</u> of multiple nationality are proposed: acceptance of multiple nationality without any reservation or restriction; acceptance of multiple nationality with conditions; discouragement of its production but no across-the-board prevention in all cases; attempts to eliminate it in all cases. In terms of the last category, it should be noted that no state in the survey herein makes acquisition of its nationality at birth conditional on not possessing another nationality at birth; the furthest states go in this sense would seem to be forcing an exercise of option upon majority (or a specified age) that is backed by deprivation in practice if the other nationality is retained.

The purpose of the following reflections is generalisation about state practice, which in a sense does not do justice to what is revealed by the overview of state practice in the Appendix. But such is the nature of generalisation. It is also clear that one may take issue with the generalisations submitted in the form of the following tables, as far as the inclusion of particular countries in particular categories. For example Brazil is included among the states that "accepts multiple nationality largely without reservation", which according to the criteria for inclusion should mean that production of multiple nationality at birth is not conditional, and loss of nationality is neither a consequence nor a condition of naturalisation. Yet according to its legislation, naturalisation elsewhere does provoke loss of Brazilian nationality, unless the individual would not be allowed permanent residence or the exercise of civil rights without it. As the latter is almost invariably the case, the condition seems to obviate the rule, thus Brazil is included in the first, as opposed to the second category of general positions. The reader may take issue with the author's separation of states along

---

[4] This is not to contract the conclusions made by Weil and Hansen that nationality law provisions in European countries are converging in various respects. See "Towards a European nationality. Citizenship, immigration and nationality law in the EU". Randall Hansen and Patrick Weil, eds. (Houndmills: Palgrave, 2001).

these lines, but it is submitted that the following considerations are accurate general-isations, and particularly apt as such for drawing the conclusions herein. Although a more detailed analysis of state practice is possible from the survey contained in the Appendix (indeed it is recommended to the reader), it is not believed that it is nec-essary beyond what is presented in this section for the conclusions drawn herein.

POSITION	CRITERIA	STATES
Accept largely without reservation (17)	*Production at birth is generally not restricted or conditional; Actual loss is not a condition of naturalisation; Actual loss is not a consequence of naturalisation elsewhere*	Argentina, Australia, Brazil, Canada, Cook Islands (New Zealand), Egypt, France, Hungary, Iran, Morocco, Portugal, Romania, Switzerland, Syria, United Kingdom, United States, Venezuela
Accept with conditions (16)	*Production at birth is generally not restricted or conditional; Either loss is not a condition of naturalisation, or loss is not a consequence of naturalisation elsewhere for all persons*	Hong Kong (China), India, Ireland, Israel, Italy, Ivory Coast, Latvia, Mexico, Nigeria, Russia, South Africa, Spain, Taiwan, Thailand, Turkey, Uruguay
States that discourage (8)	*Production at birth is generally not conditional: no forced election in all cases Possible restriction in relation to use of benefits of foreign nationality*	China, Germany, Indonesia, Korea, Malaysia, Netherlands, Philippines, Singapore
States that attempt to eliminate (4)	*Nationality attributed at birth is withdrawn later in life if no loss of foreign nationality*	Fiji, Japan, Kenya, Zimbabwe

2. Levels of tolerance and intolerance in municipal legislation

2.1 Acquisition of nationality at birth

Acquisition of nationality at birth is not conditioned in any way by multiple nation-ality in the vast majority of states examined herein, although the parameters of state practice certainly vary at the margins. It may be noted that of the states that may be said to force an election of nationality at some point in a person's life, there are con-siderable variations in practice. Whereas Japan forces an election, electing Japanese nationality does not seem to require loss of the other nationality in practice. The elec-tion to be forced on some Germans (only those by virtue of their birth in Germany to a permanent resident parent) is conditioned by so many exceptions that it also can-not be regarded as a very strong norm.

2.2 Subsequent acquisition of nationality

2.2.1 Loss of nationality as a condition of naturalisation

Taking loss of nationality as a condition of naturalisation as an indicator, of the 45 jurisdictions studied, even including in the "restrictive" category states where the condition is far from what might be called watertight, 20 have some norm requiring loss of nationality as a condition of naturalisation, whereas 25 impose no condition at all. Of the twenty "restrictive" states, one half can be said to have strict requirements preventing ensuing multiple nationality, whereas the other half admit exceptions to the rule.

2.3 Loss of nationality in relation to multiple nationality

2.3.1 Loss of nationality as a consequence of naturalisation

Again taking naturalisation as an example, naturalisation elsewhere resulted in deprivation of nationality in 23 of the 45 jurisdictions analysed, again reckoning according to strict legal provisions. But if possible legislative and discretionary exceptions are taken into account, the number drops to only seven countries. It would seem that stripping persons of nationality in relation to multiple nationality is increasingly out of fashion. Likewise, the number of states that take steps to ascertain such loss of nationality is small, and anecdotal evidence suggests that in practice there is wide latitude in administrative discretion and that persons affected are often able to perpetrate what amounts to fraud on the governments concerned by concealing such loss of nationality.[5]

3. Recognition of multiple nationality

Although most states have specific rules that require nationals to enter and depart their territory on national travel documents, specific provisions in no fewer than ten of the 45 jurisdictions encompassed herein were found to allow nationals to enter and depart their own countries on foreign travel documents. But only in a few cases did this lead to treatment as a foreigner. As far as international or consular protection of

---

[5] The author takes the liberty of mentioning what amounts to anecdotal evidence because it relates to practice, but it is of course neither to be considered evidence of state practice, nor submitted as such. A typical example known to the author is the prominent London physician who upon becoming naturalised in the United Kingdom went to the consulate of his (former) country of nationality, according to whose laws he was no longer a citizen due to his naturalisation abroad, and whose government takes pride in combating corruption, to surrender his passport. He was told that he should keep his passport and that he was the kind of person the country hoped would return home one day.

multiple nationals, little if any evidence was found that states view multiple nationality as an in-principle barrier to the exercise of such protection, even against another state of nationality, although state practice seems to admit that such protection may be prevented in practical terms, and legitimately so.

4. Summary

Factors behind the production of multiple nationality are widespread, and its existence seems unavoidable under most states' current municipal legislation. In terms of both legislation and policy, multiple nationality is essentially accepted as a reality, notwithstanding incidences of state practice that go against this generalisation. The positions of states are generally related to views of individual choice. The permanent allegiance of the 18th and 19th centuries seems to be a thing of the past, at least for the time being, although the practice of several states demonstrates that it still exists in varying forms.[6] Renunciation of nationality, barring statelessness, seems to be an option in the vast majority of states, but a significant number still place conditions on expatriation as far as obligations owed the state. Relatively few efforts to eliminate multiple nationality completely and effectively on a national level (Fiji, Kenya, Zimbabwe), and none on the international level, or directed at combating it as the "evil" proposed by Bar-Yaacov, can be noted. Although mentioned in the summary of "policy" in relation to the countries concerned, evidence of possible future changes in policy and legislation in both India and the People's Republic of China allowing wider latitude for their citizens to possess multiple nationality is of course not incorporated into the survey of legislative practice. Such harbingers should give rise to reflection, however, given the size of those countries' populations, and their important overseas communities.

D. THE ESSENCE OR QUALITY OF THE CURRENT "ACCEPTANCE" OF MULTIPLE NATIONALITY

Does the existence of multiple nationality indicate that states are not binding individuals as closely to themselves as they once did, or that identity plays less of a role in nationality on the municipal plane? This does not seem to be the case, as the vast majority of states would seem to attribute nationality only to persons who can in fact be said to have a genuine link or connection to the state. The fact that multiple nationality is not excluded by many states indicates respect for the individual who has existing ties to the state, as well as a view that state interests do not preclude

---

[6] It might be noted that "pure" perpetual allegiance seems to go against the provisions of Article 9A of the Universal Declaration of Human Rights, in terms of the right to change one's nationality.

other ties of nationality. This might be characterised as a decision by states to foster ties and links of identity to individuals who might previously have been excluded from the legal aspect of such links.[7]

The rejection of multiple nationality in the past in and of itself meant that the state excluded people who might otherwise well have been viewed as having a relationship to it. The systemic acceptance of multiple nationality can in the same sense be expected to have the effect of fostering the recognition of existing ties which were previously not given legal effect.

While it might be presumed that the existence of multiple nationality somehow indicates an interest in sharing nationals that exceeds the municipal plane, this is doubtful. Acceptance by states seems more related to their own specific needs and interests, as in the past, as opposed to wider or international interests, as long as they maintain that they can require the same obligations of multiple nationals that they can require of mono-nationals. Although the existence of numerous agreements related to military service and conscription of multiple nationals would seem to contradict this assertion, if these are seen as a means to regulate a sphere where legitimate state jurisdiction overlaps, it becomes clear that they do not indicate that multiple nationals are treated as a category apart, but military service as such is being regulated. Such agreements regulate military service, not nationality or the state's right to obligate its nationals to do military service, just as a double taxation agreement regulates taxation, not a state's right to tax, and tax whom it will. Likewise, rejection of multiple nationality also seems related to specific municipal considerations, as opposed to a wider view that multiple nationality undermines the international legal system.

This observation goes to the essence or quality of states' current acceptance of multiple nationality: it does not seem inherently to reflect an acceptance of a separate status for multiple nationals,[8] but seems instead to be premised on a practical conclusion that inter-state relations are not substantially negatively affected by multiple nationality. Acceptance of multiple nationality seems to have more to do with states' specific underlying reasons for maintaining links of nationality, as opposed to a view that multiple nationality in and of itself is a good thing. Specific cases in which countries agree to what amount to political ties related to nationality, as in the

---

[7] Immigration, inclusion and identity seem inseparable issues in many cases. The Economist reported that feelings of Dutch Muslims that "if we're going to be rejected anyway, however hard we try to be Dutch", led to an increase in women choosing to wear headscarves. "Immigrants in the Netherlands. Fortuynism without Fortuyn", *The Economist*, 30 November 2002, 46.

[8] For example, when possession of what one state deems an "innocuous" nationality in one context does not override possession of a nationality the state deems suspect. Australians who also possessed the nationality of countries the United States considered "hostile" were warned in 2002 by the Australian Department of Foreign Affairs and Trade that they could be subject to security measures due to their other nationality. "US visitors may be fingerprinted", *The Sydney Morning Herald*, 27 August 2002, 3.

case of Spain and many Latin American countries, do not contradict this proposal.[9] Such underlying reasons for maintaining links to categories of individuals by means of an attribution of nationality may in fact change from time to time, depending on the politics and policies of the day, just as political or other reasons for bilateral agreements binding nations together may change over time.[10] This is not to comment on the nature of such policies, which may be seen as good or bad, inclusive or exclusive. But it does not seem to be the essence of nationality itself that leads states to adopt one attitude or another.[11]

The conclusion that relative levels of acceptance of multiple nationality are largely linked to an idea that multiple nationals will not be treated differently from other citizens, that is to say that their obligations to the state are in no way reduced, is supported by evidence from areas where states might be expected to take multiple

---

[9] The political "supra-nationality" proposed by de Castro in 1962 and discussed in chapter four has, however, not become a reality beyond the countries that had already adopted this approach, and can probably be seen to have weakened in the case of the British Commonwealth, although the rights of citizenship in the European Union may of course be compared to the idea. See generally F. de Castro, "La nationalité la double nationalité et la supra-nationalité", *Recueil des cours (Académie de droit international)* (1962) vol. 102 (1961) no. 1, 515–634.

[10] Change over time may be rapid. A case in point that has been discussed at length is Germany, which in 1913 specifically allowed multiple nationality in function of its national interest, while it is not uncommon for authors today to mention that "[d]ual nationality had always been considered as being inconsistent with the concept of loyalty and attachment to Germany". Christine Kreuzer, "Double and multiple nationality in Germany after the Citizenship Reform Act of 1999", in *Rights and duties of dual nationals. Evolution and prospects*, ed. David A. Martin and Kay Hailbronner (The Hague: Kluwer Law International, 2003), 347–359, 348. See Randall Hansen and Patrick Weil, "Introduction. Dual citizenship in a changed world: immigration, gender and social rights", in *Dual nationality, social rights and federal citizenship in the U.S. and Europe. The reinvention of citizenship*, ed. Randall Hansen and Patrick Weil (New York: Berghahn Books, 2002), 1–23, 3.

[11] There is evidence that states will continue to legislate according to their needs, and perhaps their underlying values. The United Kingdom, for example, has introduced visa rules that are aimed at tempting young Australian professionals to settle in Britain. Michelle Gilchrist and Stefanie Balogh, "Visa rules lure young to Britain", *The Weekend Australian*, 21–22 June 2003, 2. In terms of exclusion, in August 2003 the Israeli Knesset legislated to prevent Palestinians "who marry Israelis from becoming Israeli citizens or residents", labelled "a way to preserve Israel's Jewish majority" by proponents, and "a racist measure that threatens to divide thousands of families or force them out of Israel", by critics. James Bennet, International Herald Tribune, *Israel's fresh limit on Palestinians*, 2003 (internet), http://www.iht.com/articles/104091.htm, consulted 1 August 2003. On the other hand, some arguably negative consequences of multiple nationality itself will probably not provoke any changes in legislation, such as some initial difficulty in identifying the number of people murdered at the World Trade Center in New York on 11 September 2001, due to multiple nationality. See Mark Riley and Kelly Burke, "Casualty count. Dual citizenship sows confusion as death toll tops 6,000", *The Sydney Morning Herald*, 22–23 September 2001, 2.

nationality into account, but choose not to.[12] Asking what state practice could be is of course a completely different question to asking what it is, but it should stimulate reflection in terms of whether this trend will continue, or in turn be influenced either by an increase in multiple nationals, or by underlying political reasons that affect international relations. This is a question taken up in the following chapter.

As long as states are free to determine in their municipal legislation the cohort of individuals to whom they accord their nationality, the factors influencing such attribution will not remain static. If historical evidence is taken as a guide, such factors will continue to change over time, and states as political units will find reasons to include or exclude individuals from among their nationals. Thus the temptation to conclude that the relative acceptance of multiple nationality noted herein is a function of globalisation and the ease and speed with which people move around the globe in comparison to previous generations, should be resisted. While this may indeed be true, it is not a conclusion that can be drawn from the work presented herein. Likewise, this study cannot be cited for the proposition that the state as an entity is in decline,[13] in fact its conclusions indicate that the state is in good health indeed, at least in terms of international law.

It might be recalled from the discussion in chapter four, that the development of nationality in municipal law was not the same in all countries, as ideas of belonging, and the internal and external consequences thereof, differed from place to place. The era of exclusivity in relation to nationality, if there ever was one, was short-lived, and efforts to eliminate multiple nationality met with failure. Instead, what might be called an underlying consensus that multiple nationality is an acceptable choice for states to adopt in their mutual relations seems to indicate a confirmation in some sense of an idea of nationality on the international plane. This is explored in the following chapter.

E. THE RESERVED DOMAIN: STATE DISCRETION IN THE ATTRIBUTION AND WITHDRAWAL OF NATIONALITY

Any enquiry into the effects of state practice on rules of international law related to nationality must start with what must be the most basic or fundamental principle of

---

[12] A United States Congressional Committee hearing in 1991 noted that there were over three million American citizens estimated to be living outside the United States, and discussed legislative changes that would facilitate their lives, and connection to the United States, without mentioning their possible multiple nationality at all. United States Congress, "Hearing before the Subcommittee on International Relations of the Committee on Foreign Affairs House of Representatives One Hundred Second Congress, First Session, June 25, 1991", (Washington: U.S. Government Printing Office, 1991).

[13] As posited by van Creveld. See generally Martin van Creveld, *The rise and decline of the State* (Cambridge: Cambridge University Press, 1999).

this area of law, the principle that questions of nationality fall within the domestic jurisdiction of each state. Here we should recall Article 1 of the 1930 Hague Convention, which is characterised as a customary rule of international law:[14]

> It is for each State to determine under its own law who are its nationals. This law shall be recognised by other States in so far as it is consistent with international conventions, international custom, and the principles of law generally recognised with regard to nationality.[15]

It was set out in chapter one that the International Court of Justice (ICJ) did not set limits on states' discretion in the attribution of nationality in the *Nottebohm* case, but characterised such limitation as issues of recognition on the international plane.

Brownlie contends that government pronouncements as to the doctrine of the freedom of states in matters of nationality are called into question by the divergence between a state's discretion in determining its nationals and the duty of other states to recognise such municipal determination, in that such divergence would seem to put an obligation on states not to legislate on nationality in a way which infringes upon the rights of other states.[16] Yet he notes that states have been loath to express the obligation in those terms.[17] This is perhaps what Brownlie labels a "structural defect in certain types of doctrine related to nationality".[18]

Whether or not such divergence is seen as a "structural defect", an important consequence of current state practice toward multiple nationality is arguably to strengthen and confirm the reserved domain in terms of states' discretion in matters of attribution and withdrawal of nationality in their municipal law. This point is vital for the arguments developed herein. State practice that tolerates widespread multiple nationality reinforces the reserved domain by indicating that attribution of nationality is indeed purely a question of municipal law, and that the nature and consequences of nationality in international law are indeed a function of the reserved domain. Such practice reinforces the distinction between nationality on the municipal and international planes and its separate consequences on those planes. Whereas Bar-Yaacov's principal argument against multiple nationality was a structural one in terms of the constitutive elements and consequences of nationality internationally, that it contravenes the "essence" of what nationality must be, current state practice demonstrates exactly the opposite, and clarifies that the "essence" of nationality is in fact that described by Weis. Importantly, the implication that the reserved domain as far as the attribution of nationality, is in fact reserved to states, has several consequences for

---

[14] Albrecht Randelzhofer, "Nationality", in *Encyclopedia of Public International Law*, ed. Rudolf Bernhardt and Max Planck Institute for Comparative Public Law and International Law (Amsterdam: Elsevier, 1985), 416–424, 417.

[15] *Convention on Certain Questions Relating to the Conflict of Nationality Laws*, 12 April 1930, (1937) 179 LNTS 89, no. 4137 (entry into force: 1 July 1937).

[16] Ian Brownlie, *Principles of public international law*, Fifth ed. (Oxford: Clarendon Press, 1998), 388–389.

[17] Ibid.

[18] Brownlie, *Principles of public international law*, 69.

the rules related to nationality discussed in chapters one to four herein. It elucidates areas that may have seemed unclear as far as states' obligations toward one another. That said, it would also seem to highlight the lack of a clear and universally accepted standard in relation to the opposability of nationality in cases of multiple nationality, while at the same time showing that the lack of clear norms is in no way fundamentally detrimental to international relations.

Unfortunately, confirmation of the strength of the reserved domain would also seem to support contentions that any "right" to a nationality provided under international law or treaties does in fact depend on the specific provisions of municipal law, notwithstanding how clear it is that nationality is vitally important to the individual.[19] Rather than emphasising the nature of the right, state practice toward multiple nationality illustrates that without obligations on states either in their municipal laws or by international agreement, it is a toothless norm that can neither be seized by individuals, nor by other states, in order to secure nationality or its legal consequences for individuals.

Another aspect of the reserved domain is the rule that one state may not regulate another state's nationality. The widespread tolerance of multiple nationality underscores the principle that <u>attribution</u> of a state's <u>own</u> nationality does not amount to interference in other states' reserved domains. Interference on the international plane in this sense can only come into play where the rights and duties of states vis-à-vis one another are brought into the equation.

State practice accepting the existence of multiple nationality emphasises the ICJ's holding in *Nottebohm* as far as separating nationality on the municipal and international planes, but indicates that the test of effectivity applied by the ICJ in *Nottebohm* to a single nationality should not be applied to such situations today. The prevalence of multiple nationality demonstrates that effectivity, or perhaps equality or another test, is vitally important as far as evaluating the competing claims of states with respect to multiple nationals. By indicating, however, that states continue to view their rights of attribution and withdrawal of nationality in their municipal laws as reserved, and effective on the municipal plane, state practice also emphasises the status of nationality itself, when it is attributed, and when it is not. It is the <u>attribution</u> of nationality as such, that is significant. Thus, a nationality attributed by a state is valid as such, until held against another nationality, when a test of effectivity or equality may be applied. Although it would be tempting to distinguish the holding in *Nottebohm*, it would seem that if municipal attribution of nationality is the crucial factor predicating its value in international law, there can be no de-facto, or virtual, nationality, as the Court seemed to create for Mr Nottebohm, in essentially holding that Guatemala could treat him as a *Guatemalteco*, and that his state of nationality had no means to protect him. Nationality, without a doubt, provides <u>standing</u> on the international plane.

---

[19] See for example Jim Jenkins, "My time in the long lens of the Syrian security police", *The Australian*, 10 February 2003, 15. The article demonstrates that without nationality, an individual enjoys few benefits under either municipal or international law.

While this conclusion may be seen as positive or not, in terms of the ability to predict standing related to nationality in international law, it also means, probably unfortunately, that it becomes more difficult to argue that states that "sell" their nationality may not do so because of a rule of international law. Such nationality may not be effective on the international plane in cases of multiple nationality, but if current state practice reinforces the reserved domain, such nationality must be seen as effective for the purposes of international law, if it is the only one possessed by an individual. If such attribution is deemed undesirable, treaty norms may be proposed to combat the practice.

1. Rules related to attribution and deprivation of nationality

The question is thus rightly posed, how far this slippery slope can go. May states impose their nationality on anyone they choose? The answer is clearly no, and is not just evidenced by the opinions of states,[20] but by their current practice as well. The acceptance or tolerance of multiple nationality noted herein has been accompanied by what seems to be the quasi-elimination of the automatic attribution of nationality, except at birth. In only two of the states covered in this study, for example, does marriage apparently result in an automatic attribution of nationality without some application for its attribution.[21] State practice clearly reflects what must be an underlying principle related to nationality, that there can be no attribution of nationality without an expression of individual will, or consent, as provided by Weis.[22] In exceptional situations, such as transfer of territory, one may speak of tacit consent. But if there were no such rule, the incidence of multiple nationality would at the very least indicate the need for such a rule. This is especially so due to the unclear standards, as argued below, related to the opposability of nationality in cases of multiple nationality, on the international plane. There is an absolute need for a minimum stopgap to prevent abuses by states in the attribution of their nationality to individuals. The state practice set out herein indicates that the production of multiple nationality in states' municipal laws is a reflection of an underlying norm that states may not attribute their nationality without the express or tacit consent of the <u>individual</u>. This would in turn indicate that the divergence noted by Brownlie is a confirmation of certain underlying principles, one of which can be discerned here.

Another related consequence of the general conclusion that state practice toward multiple nationality reinforces the reserved domain, is that naturalisation does not cre-

---

[20] See Brownlie, *Principles of public international law*, 388–389.

[21] See Peter J. Spiro, "Embracing dual nationality", in *Dual nationality, social rights and federal citizenship in the U.S. and Europe. The reinvention of citizenship*, ed. Randall Hansen and Patrick Weil (New York: Berghahn Books, 2002), 19–33, 20.

[22] See chapter three, note and text at note 21. Weis notes that no modes of attribution of nationality are invalid as such, except any attribution of nationality that might contradict the individual's will.

ate a different quality of nationality on the international plane, although it may in terms of municipal law.

From the argument above, it follows that the common modes states use to attribute their nationality to, and withdraw nationality from, individuals, should be seen as matters reserved to states. It should be noted, however, that modes that have been held invalid for international purposes do not seem to be used in practice by states, and thus rules of international law clarifying the status of such or other norms as invalid may have developed. This was not tested in the present study, and no opinion is offered. State practice that tolerates multiple nationality does not clearly indicate that states can not attribute their nationality in any way they see fit, but emphasises the holding in *Nottebohm* that the issue is one of recognition of nationality vis-à-vis other states, on the international plane.

Current state practice does confirm, however, that international law does not dictate a rule in relation to "substitution" of nationality. Multiple nationality is a reality that states may, and do, choose to accept for their own nationals.

Perhaps the most crucial question in terms of attribution and withdrawal of nationality is related to deprivation of nationality, when it results in statelessness. In reinforcing the ambit of the reserved domain, does current state practice toward multiple nationality in some sense facilitate the state's ability to deprive individuals of nationality? In specific terms, a reinforced reserved domain would indeed seem to make states' discretion in withdrawal of nationality purely an internal matter. It has always been relatively easy for states to denationalise individuals, and current state practice would not seem to modify this state of affairs. In 2001 there were an estimated 350,000 Iraqi Shia Muslim refugees in Iran who had been stripped of their Iraqi nationality by Saddam Hussein as part of a "nationality correction policy".[23]

But such a view would amount to viewing the significance of the reserved domain in isolation, which is incorrect: current state practice not only emphasises the distinction between nationality in municipal and international law, but its relevance and importance on those planes as well. By reinforcing the value of an attribution of nationality in municipal law, on the international plane, acceptance of multiple nationality by states in fact militates against statelessness. Such practice emphasises Shearer's qualification, mentioned in chapter three, that "no state interest requires it", and his enumeration of the strong presumption on the international plane that a nationality is not easily lost. In other words, states' obligations to other states clearly persist on the international plane when a deprivation of nationality, even as a consequence of individual choice, results in statelessness. At the same time, as in the case of claims of a "right" to nationality, it is clear that statelessness cannot be combated without the direct involvement of states, and their assumption of responsibility for individuals.

---

[23] Christopher Kremmer, "Nowhere to run", *The Sydney Morning Herald*, 16–17 June 2001, 31.

Of course state practice that incorporates multiple nationality, while in no way changing the obligations nationals owe their states, means that a "right of expatriation" becomes more important to multiple nationals, should they wish to avoid potential clashes. Such a right is clearly important for the purposes of municipal law however, not international law. Likewise, current state practice cannot be cited for the proposition that individuals possess such a right, barring specific provisions of municipal law to that effect. In fact, the acceptance or tolerance of multiple nationality in international relations would seem to dictate the conclusion that states may validly continue to consider individuals their nationals, as long as they wish to. Permanent allegiance may well be a thing of the past, but it is in no way made an invalid choice for states, unless there really is a right to change one's nationality. International norms for the voluntary expatriation of individuals, under defined circumstances, are arguably called for, and states would be advised to take steps in this regard. But it will be argued below that widespread acceptance of multiple nationality illustrates that once nationality is lost, or when it is not attributed in the first place, states may not treat the individuals in question as their nationals, absent their consent (meaning naturalisation in most cases). But likewise, if an international obligation in relation to nationality persists, it does so with or without nationality.

F. RECOGNITION OF NATIONALITY ON THE INTERNATIONAL PLANE

The starting point for consideration of obligations of recognition of nationality on the international plane is perhaps the observation that the current state practice noted herein indicates that there is no obligation on states to "recognise" any multiple nationality of their own nationals, for the purposes of municipal law. The state may of course choose to do so. This in turn indicates that on the international plane, there is no corresponding obligation to recognise a national's foreign nationality as effective, simply because it is possessed. At the same time the existence of multiple nationality clearly emphasises the need for rules and norms as to recognition, the clear need for a prioritisation of nationalities in that sense on the international plane in terms of states' rights, and that related norms do in fact exist.

But current state practice as analysed herein does not clearly indicate the rule to be applied in this sense by states. The relevant norms are of course the principles of equality, and of effectivity. The 2004 ILC draft articles on diplomatic protection canvassed in chapter three[24] adopt the principle of equality, unless overridden effectivity. Rode's argument, also mentioned in that chapter, was that the principle of effective or dominant nationality, which he characterised as the older doctrine, might prevail over the long-term, especially in a world characterised by trust among states. It is beyond the scope of this study to speculate on the factors that influence the devel-

---

[24] See chapter three, text and note at note 99.

opment of principles along these lines, although arguments that they include considerations of political relations among states and the practical needs related to the protection of individuals seem persuasive. The salient point to be made here is that issues related to the recognition of nationality on the international plane are only relevant when the consequences of nationality on that plane are taken into account: a right of protection, a duty of admission, and a duty to treat aliens as such, and two or more nationalities are held up to each other.

The need for a standard is clear, and it may be supposed that states would not accept multiple nationality in their mutual relations if one did not exist, but the overview of state practice herein does not seem to indicate that states clearly support the principle of equality or the principle of effective or dominant nationality. This is discussed below in relation to the consequences of nationality, where the contours of such a rule are taken up in light of current practice, and a case is made that a flexible standard may be expected to continue to evolve over time, as a function of international relations and the needs of states.

G. THE CONSEQUENCES OF NATIONALITY ON THE MUNICIPAL AND INTERNATIONAL PLANES

It has been argued that by emphasising the reserved domain in terms of attribution and withdrawal of nationality, and the consequent stress placed on the need for methods of recognition of states' rights on the international plane vis-à-vis each other in relation to multiple nationals, state practice toward multiple nationality also emphasises the distinction between nationality on the municipal and international planes. Weis' proposal, mentioned in chapter three, may be recalled here, that in order to distinguish the consequences of nationality that relate to municipal law from those in international law, one must extricate from the relationship between the state and its nationals those elements "that presuppose the co-existence of States, which confer rights or impose duties on the State in relation to other *subjects* of international law".[25]

It is clear that the existence of multiple nationality does not change Weis' conclusion that nationality on the international plane relates to a right of international protection vis-à-vis other states, and a duty to admit nationals. State practice emphasises these international consequences of nationality, confirms the delineation of their scope, and illustrates their inherent limitations in terms of protecting the individual. They are limited in these terms because international protection is clearly a prerogative of the state, and a duty to admit nationals does not constitute a right of entry, or residence, as such, possessed by the individual. These are perhaps strange conclusions

---

[25] Peter Weis, *Nationality and statelessness in international law* (Alphen aan den Rijn: Sijthoff & Noordhoff, 1979), 32.

for an era that many see as providing individuals with unprecedented rights vis-à-vis their own and other states, but state practice toward multiple nationality illustrates that in terms of their mutual relations, states have in fact ceded little, if any, power to their citizens in an overall sense. Likewise, whereas states' <u>rights</u> with respect to nationals in terms of the scope of protection they may exercise vis-à-vis each other are not clarified by this study, state practice towards multiple nationality elucidates the parameters of their obligations, and also makes clear that states' obligations to each other include treating <u>aliens</u> as such, in considering the obligations of individuals to the state.

Although the consequences of current state practice on the municipal and international planes are discussed separately in the sections that follow, it should be remembered that they are not always conceptually as separable as might be desired, as issues on the municipal plane involve the international context, and vice-versa. That said, multiple nationality clearly indicates that they are separate.

1. Consequences and nature of nationality on the international plane

1.1 International protection

In terms of exercising protection vis-à-vis other states on the basis of nationality, it was argued above that the emphasis placed on the reserved domain by systemic multiple nationality, meaning that the latter is in no way claimed to be an anomaly, dictates the relevance of the attribution of nationality as such. This strengthens arguments that there can thus be no "de-facto" or "virtual" nationality on the international plane, without municipal nationality. But in cases of multiple nationality, the need for a standard to judge states' claims vis-à-vis each other in cases of multiple nationality, is clear. It was also set out above that the state practice surveyed herein does not clearly indicate that states currently follow a rule of dominant or effective nationality, or equality. This statement should be qualified.

Cases of protection by one state of nationality against another state of nationality, and protection vis-à-vis third states, must be distinguished. In the latter case, it would seem that multiple nationality's reinforcement of the value of nationality in municipal law, and an underlying view in international law that such nationalities are of equal value for municipal purposes, means that states of nationality are in fact free to protect their national collectively should they so choose; in cases of competing claims, the principle of dominant or effective nationality should be applied, as the principle of equality is not relevant. Judge Guggenheim's proposal in his dissenting opinion in *Nottebohm*, and taken up in chapter three, to separate international claims from international protection, might be remembered here. While the principle of effective nationality is important for the former, it is not necessarily so for the latter, in which case it is the protection as such that is fundamentally important, as opposed to the rights of the state of nationality.

The situation in terms of protection by one state of nationality against another, is more complicated, and state practice seems mixed. On the one hand there is evidence that states are in certain circumstances willing to treat their own nationals as foreigners, in cases of multiple nationality, sometimes allowing them to use foreign travel documents to enter their territory, and even making agreements that allow for their diplomatic and consular protection against themselves, although such treatment does not amount to a reduction in obligations owed the state. However, notwithstanding general pronouncements that states may not be able to protect their nationals in another state of nationality, the caveat is often added that cases will be judged individually, and on their merits, and that protection may be attempted. Fundamental considerations of human rights have been cited as cause for states to exercise such protection.[26]

If the question posed is whether states may protect their nationals in these circumstances, the emphasis on municipal nationality in international law highlighted by state practice serves to stress the equality of such nationalities on the international plane, meaning that in terms of standing for the purposes of international protection, states would seem to be on equal footing. But the tendency for states to judge cases on their merits, indicates that states not only reserve standing to themselves, but that they feel they may prevail in these circumstances as well. Equality may be a point of departure, but it is arguably no more than that. Here again, it might be considered that protection of the individual is qualitatively different from protection of property, although priorities might be drawn along other lines as well.

The ILC's draft articles on diplomatic protection mentioned in chapter three, hold that while there may be a presumption that states will not protect their nationals against other states of nationality, they may do so when their nationality is effective or dominant. The survey of state practice noted herein seems to support this as a general approach. It does not, however, seem to be a rule, and some state practice seems still to support a rule of equality.[27] But by allowing leeway for the adjudication of each case individually and on its merits, states would seem to have, on some level, rejected both equality and effectivity for certain purposes. Although it is not always expressed as such, it is clear that when fundamental issues are at stake, such as human life or basic standards of respect for the human being, the need for states of nationality to protect their nationals, notwithstanding that such protection is claimed against even a state of effective nationality, is clear. In these cases, while nationality as such may provide states with standing, the principle of humanity, well known to

---

[26] See chapter four, text and note at note 109.

[27] Aleinikoff and Klusmeyer argue that in terms of rights, entitlements and obligations, residence should take precedence over nationality, and that the rule of "dominant and effective nationality, even as against other states of the person's nationality, should replace the old rule that disallowed diplomatic action in such circumstances". T. Alexander Aleinikoff and Douglas Klusmeyer, *Citizenship policies for an age of migration* (Washington, DC: Carnegie Endowment for International Peace, 2002), 40.

other areas of traditional international law, might be said to trump both effectivity and equality in relation to protection of nationals.

The question is thus posed whether current state practice affects the other legal relationships that states can have with individuals, which have consequences in external expression vis-à-vis other states. Does the accentuation of "nationality" provoked by state practice toward multiple nationality eliminate, for example, the categories of "ressortissant" and "protected person"? It was mentioned above that agreements between states with respect to diplomatic and consular protection seem to remain popular in practice, and no emphasis on the attribution of nationality in municipal law, and its effects on the international plane, would seem to argue against the effectiveness of such contracts. As to other statuses, it might first be noted that although the words "or ressortissant" still follow the word "national" in many countries' passports, the end of most colonial arrangements seems to have terminated much of the category's practical significance. That is not to say that such categories could not re-emerge.

Does the state practice noted herein influence the quality or characterisation of the tie between the state and an individual that catapults the state's rights onto the plane of international law? It is submitted that it does not, and that this remains a function of the state's attached obligation, to admit its nationals, and allow them residence. It would seem that as long as the state accepts this obligation with respect to other states, it retains its rights on the international plane, however the category of persons is labelled. State practice that accepts multiple nationality does not change this combination of rights and obligations, and in fact clarifies the rather limited scope of the obligation of admission in international law.

1.2 Duty to admit nationals and allow residence

Weis' statement that the duty to admit nationals and allow residence does not amount to a right of the individual, but is only relevant when duties to other states are drawn in, should be recalled here. It is perhaps sad that the limitations of states' obligations to allow their nationals entry and residence are best illustrated by the current and rare example outlined in chapter four in relation to British nationality and Hong Kong.[28] But in this example, the state's obligation can be avoided only because the persons in question are in fact multiple nationals.

It should be made clear at the outset that state practice is overwhelmingly and almost without exception, to allow nationals entry and residence, so much so that the obligation on the state in international law might be conceived as a right of the individual in international law. It has not been seen to be such a right however.[29] No opinion is offered here as to the effects of such overwhelming practice on customary

---

[28] See chapter four, pp. 229–232.

[29] Weis states that "[a]s between national and State of nationality the question of the right of sojourn is not a question of international law. It may, however, become a question bearing on the relations between States". Weis, *Nationality and statelessness in international law*, 45.

rules of international law, which may in fact dictate a higher standard than that applied by the United Kingdom with respect to its British Nationals (Overseas).[30] The state practice cited herein in no way contradicts such more stringent requirements. But by reinforcing nationality's consequences on the international plane as involving the rights and duties of states vis-à-vis one another, state practice toward multiple nationality arguably supports what can only be called low standards of international law in this respect, and demonstrates nationality's limited value to the individual in terms of a right of entry and residence. Because most states' municipal legislation does not distinguish between national and citizen, it is hard to tell whether rights of entry under municipal law adhere to the former or the latter category. But in any case, it seems that such a right is a function of municipal law.[31] Thus Bigler-Eggenberger's assertion, noted in chapter four, that had Swiss women not been deprived of their nationality upon marriage to aliens, Switzerland would have been able (or obliged) to protect them and their families during the Second World War, is true, but only because Switzerland's municipal law provides that Swiss nationals have a right of admission and residence, and protection in most cases.

There are today few countries that maintain categories of nationality, and none, it would seem, with the notable exception of the United Kingdom, that exclude their nationals from an unqualified right of admission and residence. The situation of British Nationals (Overseas), the cohort of former Citizens of the British Crown Colony of Hong Kong, has already been mentioned. As Hong Kong ceased to be a Dependent Territory of the United Kingdom at midnight on 30 June 1997, the United Kingdom could of course no longer guarantee to other states that British nationals could be returned to Hong Kong, as only the People's Republic of China could make such decisions with respect to its territory from that date onward. But rather than provide its nationals with a right of entry into the United Kingdom, as Portugal did for Macanese, or for that matter a choice of nationality, as Australia did in the case of Papua New Guinea, Britain maintains that the status of British National (Overseas), while not requiring a visa or entry certificate for admission to the United Kingdom, brings with it no right of residence.

---

[30] See Article 13(2) of the *Universal Declaration of Human Rights*, General Assembly Resolution 217 A (III), 10 December 1948 (internet), http://www.un.org/rights/50/decla.htm, consulted 2 April 2006. "Everyone has the right to leave any country, including his own, and to return to his country"; Article 12(4) of the *International Covenant on Civil and Political Rights*, Annex to United Nations General Assembly Resolution 2200 XXI, 16 December 1966 (internet), http://www.hrweb.org/legal/cpr.html, consulted 2 April 2006. "No one shall be arbitrarily deprived of the right to enter his own country"; Article 5(d)(ii) of the *International Convention on the Elimination of All Forms of Racial Discrimination*, United Nations General Assembly Resolution 2106 (XX), 21 December 1965 (internet), http://www.unhchr.ch/html/menu3/b/d_icerd.htm, consulted 2 April 2006, also provides that individuals have a right to return to their own country.

[31] For examples of states that provide such a right in their municipal laws, see Weis, *Nationality and statelessness in international law*, 45 n. 106.

It might rightly be asked whether this is nationality at all. But no matter how discriminatory and questionable such provisions may be according to fundamental standards of equality, they are so on the municipal plane, on which it is Britain's prerogative to provide its nationals with rights, or not. On the international plane, as long as the individual in question can be returned to a territory, provisions that exclude even entry and residence do not contravene the state's obligations vis-à-vis other states. Thus the crucial caveat that allows the United Kingdom this latitude is the fact that British Nationals (Overseas) are considered to be Chinese nationals by the People's Republic of China, and thus can in fact be sent back to Hong Kong, on that basis. Only this peculiar example of multiple nationality allows the United Kingdom to pretend that its British Nationals (Overseas) are British nationals at all, without any attached rights (it may be remembered that diplomatic protection is a matter of state discretion). It might be supposed that as states realise this, the value of BN(O) passports will decrease, and those of the Hong Kong Special Administrative Region will increase, as the latter represent a real connection to the territory.[32]

It is to be wondered whether the United Kingdom would in fact allow its "nationals" entry and residence, should China expatriate them. Even if there is a rule against the production of statelessness, which as canvassed in chapter three, is highly likely but unclear, it would seem that should Hong Kong Chinese-BN(O) dual nationals lose their Hong Kong Chinese nationality, they could not become stateless due to their British nationality. In this case, the United Kingdom would have a clear duty to allows its British Nationals (Overseas) admission and residence, at least as long as no other state would accept them. Although illustrating the inherent limitations in a "right of entry and residence" attached to nationality in international law, by highlighting that nationality on the international plane is related to the rights and obligations of states, it also emphasises the nature of the reserved domain's effects on the international plane. Thus, the fact that Britain attributes its nationality to many of its former Hong Kong citizens, is in and of itself significant. The duty of admission vis-à-vis nationals may be discretionary, but the duty of admission vis-à-vis other states is highlighted even more.

The example is certainly atypical, but illustrates that the link between territory and nationality remains the decisive factor in states' mutual relations in terms of their obligations related to the nationality of individuals. Without a territory to which persons can be guaranteed return by a state, there can be no nationality, and thus no rights of the state on the international plane. The example may rightly be seen as a twenty-first century left-over from a nineteenth century colonial world, and a sad

---

[32] The *Economist* notes: "How much is a British passport worth? Not much, if you are from Hong Kong. The 3.3m people there who hold a British national overseas (BNO) passport know their document does not entitle them to live in, well, Britain. They know it does not afford them consular protection in China, which tolerates the use of BNO passports as mere travel documents for Hong Kong Chinese, but nothing more. Now, with the recent case of one Wu Man, Hong Kongers have reason to believe other countries are also dismissive of the BNO passport's protection. "Chinese law. A very long arm", The Economist, 27 November 1999, 29.

example at that, but it illustrates that whatever the status is called, states' rights and obligations on the international plane with respect to persons have not fundamentally changed. The absence of nationality means the capacity to be deported, in real and practical terms.[33] But according to the traditional rules of international law, emphasised by current state practice in relation to multiple nationality, if another state will accept an individual, there is no obligation on the state of nationality to do so.

The conclusion thus seems inevitable that, barring more stringent obligations from other areas of international law such as the law of international human rights, the abandoned penalty of banishment is not negated by principles of international law related to nationality, as long as another state accepts the individual so treated. But while the penalty may be defunct today, the temptation to resort to such measures should perhaps not be underestimated. In 2005 the French Minister of the Interior, Nicolas Sarkozy, publicly reflected on withdrawing French nationality from radical clerics involved in promoting terrorism.[34] The *Economist* noted that "it is far from clear where such non-citizens might then be sent".[35] Similar laws have been proposed in the United Kingdom for naturalised citizens, and for those with dual citizenship in the Netherlands.[36]

Whether there is a duty to admit former nationals is a matter of controversy, and Weis' opinion that customary international law does not dictate such admission, barring fraud by the denationalising state, was mentioned in chapter three. Here however, current state practice that emphasises the separation and value of nationality on the municipal and international planes, indicates that denationalisation of individuals while they are abroad, unrelated to the acquisition of another nationality, cannot terminate a duty of admission. Thus, legislation, now apparently largely defunct, that dictates the "expiration" of nationality after a prescribed period of residence abroad without registration with diplomatic or consular authorities, would seem to be ineffective in these terms. Nationality may be lost, but states' obligations vis-à-vis each other can persist.

The case where nationality is lost prior to entering a foreign territory might be viewed as different, and any obligation of readmission arguably related to the

---

[33] In Hong Kong, over 5,000 people risk transfer to China, notwithstanding the fact that they have Hong Kong citizen (resident) parents. See Lynne O'Donnell, "Family fears knock of deportation", *The Weekend Australian*, 4–5 May 2002, 13.

[34] "The French lesson", *The Economist*, 13 August 2005, 25–26.

[35] Id., 26.

[36] Ian Bickerton, "Dutch murders result in tighter terrorism laws", *Financial Times*, 15 July 2005, 2; "Dealing with traitors", *The Economist*, 13 August 2005, 12–13. The Economist argued that "[t]hreatening naturalised citizens with deportation if they flirt with extremism, as the government intends, will create two classes of citizen: the British-born and the rest. That will do incalculable harm to race relations and undermine the inclusive British identity that Labour has tried to nurture". Id., 13. But when an attempted coup d'etat rocked Fiji in 2000, the publication had argued that the short-term solution to the crisis was to expel the (apparent) coup leader, George Speight. "Fiji's terrorists. Allow them to succeed, and it could destroy the country", The Economist, 3 June 2000, 16.

conditions in which the individual was permitted to enter the foreign territory. If a state has knowledge that someone entering has been deprived of, or has lost, his or her nationality, and nevertheless allows entry, it might be argued that it is estopped from maintaining that the state of former nationality has a duty of admission. But the ease with which such a rule could be abused is readily apparent. States admit categories of persons persecuted by their own states, as refugees, on the express basis that they can be returned to their countries when it is safe to do so. It thus seems that it is not when nationality is lost that is the turning point for an obligation of admission on the international plane, but the circumstances of the deprivation.

1.3 Jurisdiction in relation to nationality

Although Arnell's argument mentioned in chapter three that there is currently greater need for (active) nationality-based jurisdiction, seems valid, state practice that incorporates multiple nationality on the international plane arguably reinforces the presumption that jurisdiction is first and foremost territorial. If nationality were the primary basis for the exercise of jurisdiction over persons, not only might its nature and consequences on the international plane be expected to be different, but one could expect many more problems from instances of multiple nationality. By reinforcing or clarifying the nature of nationality, state practice also demonstrates the importance of territory in the international system.

This however, does not necessarily detract from the bases of jurisdiction in relation to nationality discussed in previous chapters. That such bases exist and are not a cause of major problems between states indicates the continuing importance of territory in jurisdiction, but may also be seen as consequences of a state system that puts much faith in other states. This would seem to be a fluid factor in international law and relations, and may change with political and legal developments.

It was argued that in terms of recognition of nationality on the international plane, and the diplomatic protection of multiple nationals, standards are required for the treatment of multiple nationality. In this sense, the fact that while the specific contours of such standards are arguably unclear, the fact that, as mentioned in chapter three, the passive personality/nationality principle has been characterised as gaining adherents, at the same time as states have moved toward an acceptance of multiple nationality in their mutual relations, is a further argument for the contention that state practice should be characterised as "accepting" multiple nationality, as opposed to "incorporating" it in a larger sense.

While widespread multiple nationality might be seen as arguing against application of the passive-nationality principle of jurisdiction, as long as states are free to treat their nationals as their own, and to choose whether or not they will recognise the effects of foreign nationality, the principle should rather be seen as a natural part of the state system, and political realities. States can still refuse to extradite their nationals (even mono-nationals), and choose when they will act on the requests of other states. The Pinochet case taken up in chapter three provides a good example: Spain, Switzerland, France and other countries that requested the General's extradition on the passive personality principle indeed have standing to do so, as their nationals were harmed. The fact that the harm was egregious and related to murder and torture, makes such claims on the basis of nationality important in practical terms. Chile, on the other hand, may validly reject such requests on the basis that the harm was done to Chileans (restricting the discussion to the passivity principle only, as Chile could also refuse to extradite its nationals, "*full stop*"). Third states must balance issues of politics, humanity and justice, if they accept the principle (which the United Kingdom did not), and it seems unclear whether effectivity, equality, humanity, or the interests of justice control one way or another. The state practice noted herein seems only to emphasise that while nationality may provide standing, territory and effective control make for the decision.

As opposed to jurisdiction over nationals, the question is raised as to jurisdiction over aliens. It will be argued that the state practice noted herein does not reduce the distinction between nationals and aliens outlined in chapters one to four, but in fact reinforces it in terms of municipal and international law. This is discussed in terms of duties to the state.

1.4 Duties to states and the international context of loyalty

It was argued in chapters three and four that obligations to the state in relation to nationality (in international context) can only relate specifically to military service or conscription, to physically take part in armed conflict on behalf of the state outside the its borders, and not to take part in international armed conflicts against the state. Resident aliens may be obliged to defend the state in cases of invasion, and even non-resident aliens can be held to a very high standard of loyalty in terms of not harming the state. Does current state practice accepting multiple nationality change this? It arguably does not. Moreover, the acceptance of multiple nationality noted herein might be characterised as a function of this basic framework.

In this respect, state practice toward multiple nationality cannot be considered without taking the wider context of the obligations of individuals to the state into account. It was argued that given the security principle of jurisdiction, the obligations of aliens to any state are very high, and states can hold individuals responsible for a broad range of acts that threaten the state. The vast majority of individuals' obligations to states do not correspond to, or follow, nationality, but accrue to all persons. This reflects the primacy of the territorial jurisdiction and power of the state. But specific or higher obligations related to nationality attach to the possession of nationality under municipal law alone.

The Permanent Court of International Justice (PCIJ) foreshadowed this conclusion in its Advisory Opinion on the Acquisition of Polish Nationality (1923), in which it recognised that the political allegiance of minorities might not in fact be to their state of nationality.[37] Although the case dealt more with an obligation to attribute

---

[37] *Acquisition of Polish nationality, Advisory Opinion no. 7*, September 15, 1923, Permanent Court of International Justice, Series B, No. 7, 6–26", in *World Court Reports*, ed. Manley O. Hudson (Dobbs Ferry, New York: Oceana Publications, Inc., 1969), 244.

nationality, and rights in municipal law as a consequence of nationality, by not addressing obligations to the state, the Court indicated that obligations of the individual are conceptually matters of municipal law.[38] But the prevalence of multiple nationality today also confirms that the absence of nationality, that is being an alien, is on some level significant. That aliens may not be obliged to fight in international wars on state's behalf is a function of their nationality of another state, and its rights vis-à-vis the first state. That aliens may be obliged to defend a state being attacked is a function of their territorial presence. By reinforcing the reserved domain, and the significance of the difference between nationality municipally and internationally, multiple nationality again illustrates the significance of nationality, and its limitations internationally in terms of only relating to states' rights and obligations vis-à-vis each other.

The author's argument thus far can be seen as portraying a world of international law related to nationality in which states have huge amounts of power over individuals, and individuals are provided with few rights vis-à-vis the state. In this sense, nationality as a means of protection of the individual is limited by its nature. But nationality as a means of protection cannot be contemplated without taking into consideration other international legal systems of protection for the individual, which is done in the following chapter.

2. Consequences of nationality on the municipal plane

2.1 Nationality and citizenship

Although multiple nationality may not be related to questions of nationality and citizenship, it is submitted that current state practice does have effects in this regard.

Can the practical legal consequences of nationality and citizenship still be distinguished, even when municipal legal orders do not do so? It has been argued that one of the effects of the systematic existence of multiple nationality is to reinforce the significance and consequences of nationality on the international plane, diplomatic protection, admission, and not imposing certain obligations on aliens. Thus, notwithstanding possible non-differentiation with citizenship rights on the municipal plane, multiple nationality in fact illustrates that the consequences of citizenship and nationality in municipal law have by no means merged for the purposes of international law. Thus, European Union agreements stipulating that one member state should provide diplomatic protection to the nationals of other member states amount to no more than protégé agreements (Ruzié's argument along these lines was mentioned in chapter four), illustrated by the stipulation that the Council of Ministers' Decision in 1995 to that effect would be reviewed "in five years". While both citizenship rights and nationality can transcend state boundaries, nationality, as far as its international essence and

---

[38] Ibid.

consequences, is of necessity linked to one state and its relations to other states, because of its particular use on the international plane.

2.2 Extradition

No argument that state practice changes the prerogative of states not to extradite their nationals is offered, especially if an overall effect of multiple nationality is to reinforce the reserved domain of nationality in municipal law. Other international obligations may come into play, and as Oeter argues (discussed in chapter four) it may be wise for states to abandon the practice for many reasons, including multiple nationality.

2.3 Loyalty

The acceptance of multiple nationality noted herein, as opposed to some greater level of incorporation of multiple nationality on the international plane, is related to, but also in part based on, the observation that multiple nationality does not lead to any reduction in the loyalty a state can expect from its nationals, whether they are multiple nationals or otherwise. Minimum standards of respect for the individual in international law apply to all persons, but nationality still means certain obligations that can go beyond what aliens can be required to do by the state. So while states can compel nationals to fight, they may not compel aliens to do so, except in immediate defence of the state. This makes provisions for renunciation of nationality all the more important, should individuals wish to avoid potential or actual conflicts. Claims that multiple nationals cannot be required to fight against one state of nationality by another must be rejected, reflecting a reality that can mean hard consequences for multiple nationals in extreme cases.

But states' tolerance of multiple nationality demonstrates that that this scenario is not an underlying assumption of the state system today, that these cases hardly exist, and when they do, that states are fully capable of managing them. The tolerance of multiple nationality supports Koessler's contention that a national's obligations to his or her state(s) are unconditional, but we might add, they exist within the boundaries of applicable international law. Nationality and allegiance are the same thing, and while multiple nationality does mean multiple obligations of loyalty, when such obligations are set out, they are circumscribed by both fundamental standards of treatment of the human being (the law of human rights), and the fact that states can require even aliens to respect high standards of obligation. The reality of multiple nationality emphasises that it is the individual who has to beware of being subject to the requirements of more than one state. Should more states decide to tax their nationals' income on the basis of nationality, for example, one might imagine that many multiple nationals would choose to renounce multiple nationality in favour of single nationality. In comparison, it may be supposed that the prospect of war between states today does not amount to a consideration that causes individuals to contemplate taking such a drastic step.

Chapter 6

Conclusion: The Relevance and Role of Nationality in International Law

Any conclusions as to the effects of state practice on rules of international law related to nationality as such must take first and foremost into account that, as stated in 1929,

> *Nationality has no positive, immutable meaning. On the contrary its meaning and import have changed with the changing character of states. . . . It may acquire a new meaning in the future as the result of further changes in the character of human society, and developments in international organization. Nationality always connotes, however, membership of some kind in the society of a state or nation.*[1]

Even if, for argument's sake only, this statement's context is restricted to nationality on the municipal plane, although this is doubtful, it is clear that the effects of nationality on the international plane are also a function of the same considerations. Thus, if nationality has no immutable meaning, but is a consequence of human society and international organisation, as long as there is a need for nationality to play a role in international relations and law, it will be a relevant category on the international plane.

---

[1] Manley O. Hudson and Richard W. Flournoy Jr., "Nationality – responsibility of states – territorial waters, drafts of conventions prepared in anticipation of the First Conference on the Codification of International Law, The Hague 1930", *The American Journal of International Law* (1929) vol. 23 Supplement, 21.

The question as to nationality's current meaning is thus posed, its relevance in international law, and how current state practice towards multiple nationality assists in discerning its role. Can it be seen as a means of protection for the individual in terms of international law, which is often seen as its primary purpose? On the international plane, it was seen that nationality is a means for states to protect individuals vis-à-vis other states and that it also has the effect of limiting the way states treat aliens, by preventing the imposition of all the obligations states impose on their nationals, on aliens.

Divorcing for these particular purposes questions of emotion and identity, it is clear that such obligations do not have to do with the loyalty of the individual, but with states' rights vis-à-vis each other with respect to a particular individual. The obligations and benefits, either direct or indirect, that accrue to individuals from nationality, fall on the municipal plane. While multiple nationality reinforces the relevance of nationality as a means of protection for the individual on the international plane, it also illustrates that it is a limited means, as the individual only receives benefits through the state, at its discretion. As opposed to weakening traditional rules, state practice that accepts multiple nationality reinforces them, and demonstrates that the primary function of nationality in international law is as a means of allocating individuals to states for states' purposes, as opposed to the rights or protection of individuals. Protection internationally, as obligation municipally, may be a consequence of nationality, but it cannot be its essence.

A. THE NATURE OR ESSENCE OF NATIONALITY

As a starting point for reflection, it is clear that the International Court of Justice's (ICJ) comment regarding naturalisation and allegiance in the *Nottebohm* case cannot involve standards of international law, as state practice towards multiple nationality clearly demonstrates that obligations are a consequence of nationality, notwithstanding multiple nationality.

> *Naturalization is not a matter to be taken lightly. To seek and to obtain it is not something that happens frequently in the life of a human being. It involves his breaking a bond of allegiance and his establishment of a new bond of allegiance.*[2]

State practice toward multiple nationality demonstrates that this clearly cannot be the case, dictating the separation, as proposed by Koessler fifty years ago, of issues of loyalty and allegiance, from the definition of nationality on the international plane. Loyalty and "allegiance" in that sense are properly issues of municipal law. Naturalisation

---

[2] *Nottebohm case (second phase)*, 6 April 1955, International Court of Justice (1955) I.C.J. Reports vol. 4, 24.

may create obligations to the new state of nationality, depending on its municipal laws, but there is no evidence that states view this as diminishing obligations to other states of nationality under their municipal laws, as long as the status persists. In this sense, there is no evidence that multiple nationality changes the quality of the personal link to the state that is announced by nationality.

It is thus clear that the ICJ's definition of nationality in *Nottebohm* must be related to the opposability of nationality on the international plane, as argued by Randelzhofer (canvassed in chapter three). The oft-cited quote states that nationality is

> ... *a legal bond having as its basis a social fact of attachment, a genuine connection of existence, interests and sentiments, together with the existence of reciprocal rights and duties. It may be said to constitute the juridical expression of the fact that the individual upon whom it is conferred, either directly by the law or as the result of an act of the authorities, is in fact more closely connected with the population of the State conferring nationality than with that of any other State.*[3]

It is submitted that given the existence of multiple nationality, this statement can today not amount to a general definition of nationality, but might constitute a definition of nationality under municipal law. States naturalise individuals, for example, on the premise that the individual in question is in fact more closely connected to them, than to other states. In essence, this may be seen as a function of the reserved domain, as any state of nationality has grounds to view itself as the state with the closest connection to the individual. Such connection may be by reason of place of birth, of blood ties, or of the declaration of individual will or consent that constitutes naturalisation. Along these lines, there is no evidence that nationality that is ineffective in terms of its opposability to other states of nationality under international law, is not to be considered nationality, either for the purposes of municipal law or generally. This was part of the Court's holding in *Nottebohm*, which is reinforced by current state practice toward multiple nationality. Opposability vis-à-vis other states, as opposed to questions of attribution, is clearly *the* crucial issue in terms of nationality on the international plane.

Along parallel lines, it is clear that state practice demonstrates that nationality is not by definition an exclusive relationship or status. It is submitted that Weis' definition of nationality in international law as

> *a technical term denoting the allocation of individuals, termed nationals, to a specific state – the state of nationality – as members of that State, a relationship which confers upon the State of nationality . . . rights and duties in relation to other states,*[4]

is underscored by the existence of multiple nationality in systemic terms. Bar-Yaacov's characterisation of nationality may be contrasted here:

---

[3] Id., 23.

[4] Peter Weis, *Nationality and statelessness in international law* (Alphen aan den Rijn: Sijthoff & Noordhoff, 1979), 59.

Nationality is a legal and political tie which binds individuals to a State and renders them subject to its personal jurisdiction. The present meaning of nationality is associated with the establishment of sovereign States, and denotes the sum of obligations – or allegiance – which an individual owes to a State.[5]

The prevalence of multiple nationality, as well as considerations related to the nature of obligations attached, demonstrates that Bar-Yaacov's characterisation of nationality mixes the consequences of nationality on the municipal and international planes. Far from being the sum of obligations that an individual owes a state under international law, nationality may be said to give rise to obligations under states' municipal laws, but on the international plane, as opposed to placing obligations on individuals, places obligations on states not to treat *aliens* in certain ways. For example, aliens cannot be obliged to take part in armed conflict on a state's behalf, except as already mentioned, in immediate defence of the state. At the very least, it gives states of nationality the right to protect their nationals vis-à-vis other states, as far as the latter states' treatment of persons as *aliens*.

Multiple nationality reinforces the fundamental consequences of nationality on the international plane, international protection and a duty of admission. Both have to do with obligations vis-à-vis other states. Multiple nationality emphasises this limited sphere for nationality on the international plane, indeed, if other obligations were attached on that level, one would expect to see many more problems related to multiple nationality, and probably opposition. This shows that these are problems of municipal law. The consequences of nationality on the international plane are still not reciprocal for the state and the individual, and in that sense cannot be seen to provide benefits to the individual. Multiple nationality even reinforces states' prerogatives concerning the nature and consequences of nationality in municipal law. Thus, arguments that when states do not exercise diplomatic protection on behalf of their nationals, they destroy the value of citizenship, may be completely correct, but they highlight that benefits conceived of on the municipal plane are not necessarily consequences on the international plane. For this to be so, the state would have to legislate to that effect, which some do. It would seem that a major step forward in terms of enhancing fundamental standards of respect for the human being would be the adoption in states' municipal legislation of a statutory right to diplomatic protection, in defined circumstances. Such rules would eliminate concerns related to government favoritism, and abandonment of unpopular or unwanted individuals. Such municipal law provisions would not cause problems with other states in cases of multiple nationality, as has been seen, nationality provides only standing in international law.

The question is posed whether the state practice noted herein influences the essence of nationality in municipal law. Is nationality the nexus between the individual and the state? Three views on the subject were presented in the preceding chapters: that nationality amounts to rights and duties, that it reflects rights and duties which are

---

[5] N. Bar-Yaacov, *Dual nationality*, ed. George W. Keeton and Georg Schwarzenberger (London: Stevens & Sons Ltd., 1961), 1.

nonetheless not the essence of the relationship, and that it is a formal status divorced from rights duties. The latter is certainly true for nationality in international law. At this point, Santulli's contention, mentioned in chapter three, that a relationship to the state is a characteristic of nationality, but not a component thereof, might be recalled. This is certainly the case in terms of opposition of nationality on the international plane. On the municipal plane, however, this is less clear.

The acceptance of multiple nationality in state practice highlights the distinction between nationality on the municipal and international planes, but arguably says little about its nature in municipal law. It emphasises Weis' statement that

> *nationality as a term of municipal law is defined by municipal law*,[6]

meaning that its municipal content is defined by municipal law. In fact, it might be supposed that states accept multiple nationality on the basis that it does not affect the municipal content and context of nationality.

But if municipal law determines the content of nationality, can higher degrees of obligation or loyalty persist with respect to former nationals, as under the French decree of 1811 mentioned in chapter four, and certain current state practice that seems close to holding the same? Put another way, the question really seems to be whether aliens can be held to a higher standard of loyalty to a state on the basis of previously having possessed that state's nationality. Although it might be tempting to argue that the ex-national might be held to such a standard, especially given the contention that states can define the loyalty required of nationals and the breadth of the obligations they can impose even on aliens, here, it would seem that a systematic incorporation of multiple nationality by states emphasises the importance of the *absence* of an attribution of nationality in municipal law. If, as was argued in chapter four, a national can be tried for taking up arms in an international armed conflict against his or her country of nationality, notwithstanding any "privilege" or status of "combatant" under legal norms, while an alien could not, this provides additional evidence for the argument that an absence of nationality, or being an alien, has the consequence of limiting states' treatment of individuals. Thus, rules that make expatriation conditional upon the fulfilment of obligations owed pose no problem in practice, but arguments that any higher obligations persist, notwithstanding a loss of nationality in municipal law, are dubious. That is to say, not obligations of municipal law such as paying taxes, but obligations related to states' rights vis-à-vis one another, admission, protection, and treatment as an alien for certain purposes. Again, multiple nationality highlights the significance of nationality in municipal law, here in terms of the absence of nationality, or being an alien, in terms of the obligations of states to each other in terms of nationality.

---

[6] Weis, *Nationality and statelessness in international law*, 29.

B. RELEVANCE TO THE NATURE OF THE STATE, SOVEREIGNTY, AND INTERNATIONAL LAW

Before proceeding, it may be noted that the widespread acceptance of multiple nationality supports Crawford's argument, discussed in chapter one, that nationality is dependent on statehood, not the reverse. If this were not so, the tolerance of multiple nationality would mean that statehood itself is akin to a shared phenomenon, in terms of the implication of human beings, something which seems highly doubtful.

In terms of sovereignty, because states' acceptance of multiple nationality for their own nationals is arguably not on the basis that their power over individuals is diminished, the existence of multiple nationality can be said to reinforce territory as the focus of sovereignty and jurisdiction. This recalls Baty's argument, cited at the outset of this thesis, that only nationality attributed *jure soli* should give rise to international rights and duties. While nothing in the arguments herein supports that specific contention (*jus sanguinis* is alive and well), the spirit of his argument, that territory must be the basis for states' rights and obligations vis-à-vis each other, rings true. At the same time, it does not necessarily mean that the extension of jurisdiction or power over individuals on the basis of nationality is of necessity weakened due to possible multiple links.

1. Trust in the inter-state system and international law

It was argued in the preceding chapters that multiple nationality could not lead to abuses in terms of claimed rights of intervention or the use of force to rescue nationals, as such rights are related to the abuse of individuals as foreigners, not of a state's own nationals. In the latter case a right of intervention may exist related to the larger interests of humanity, but not on the basis of protection of nationals. Multiple nationality neither constitutes a bar, nor a justification for intervention. But aside from applicable legal norms, it was mentioned that multiple nationality might be seen as providing "political" or "social" incentive to intervene in the affairs of other states. Is this not a reality in an age when the state is still fundamentally concerned with its rights? Criticism by one state of another is usually swept aside with ripostes based on sovereignty and internal affairs. Does the sharing of natural persons in terms of power and jurisdiction beyond the borders of the state not threaten the clarity needed for harmonious relations between states? It clearly does not seem to, at least as reflected by current state practice.

One may speculate about the reasons behind the current dearth of practice opposed to multiple nationality. We have seen that in the context of international armed conflict, multiple nationals can be forced into compromising situations with respect to their states of nationality, when such states' interests diverge, in addition to what may not constitute legal obligations, but acute levels of discomfort on the planes of emotion, identity, and loyalty in that sense, when states otherwise are at odds with each other.

It was demonstrated that as far as legal standards, only international armed conflict presents a direct potential difficulty in this sense. It is thus relatively easy to speculate that the general ban on the "threat or use of force against the territorial integrity or political independence of any state" contained in Article 2(4) of the United Nations Charter has fundamentally altered the parameters of what might be called fundamental rights of states vis-à-vis each other.[7] That greater levels of tolerance of multiple nationality seem to have developed with or followed the notion that armed conflict is to be an exception in international relations, taking place only under prescribed conditions, perhaps augurs well for the effectiveness and relevance of the international legal system of security established after the Second World War.

C. NATIONALITY AND INTERNATIONAL LEGAL STANDARDS FOR THE PROTECTION OF HUMAN BEINGS

One of the principal notions of the relevance of nationality was, recalling Lauterpacht's words cited in chapter three, that it constitutes the major link between the individual and the benefits of international law. Current state practice confirms that the question is in fact different. Nationality does not provide the benefits of international law, but allows the state to provide some benefit to the individual when it chooses to, or has a related obligation to other states, in addition to other benefits that may accrue to the individual by treaty. Thus protection against other states as a consequence of nationality should arguably not be conceived of as a "benefit" for the individual, as long as states are free to withhold it. States should provide a right to diplomatic protection to their nationals in their municipal laws, in defined circumstances, specifying, for example, policies of protection in relation to multiple nationals.

In fact, the relevance of nationality as a system of protection for individuals cannot be seen outside the context of wider issues and norms related to minimum standards of treatment for human beings generally, and international systems of protection for the human being. Multiple nationality has become a reality in international practice, if not in international relations, in a world where individuals are protected by various international systems of minimum guarantees, such as international humanitarian customary and treaty norms, and international and regional human rights treaties and systems. While states can require high standards of loyalty from all persons, even holding aliens to the same high standards of duty to the state as nationals under the "security principle", there are other "default settings" in international law that prevent them from abusing this same group of all persons in the most egregious ways. In this sense, one might not observe particular effects of multiple nationality on this system, but instead see the incidence of multiple nationality as a reflection of this system. In a world in which all persons must be treated by their own and other

---

[7] *Charter of the United Nations*, 26 June 1945 (internet), http://www.un.org/aboutun/charter/index.html, consulted 4 April 2006 (entry into force: 24 October 1945).

governments according to fundamental standards of respect for the human being, the role of any particular state is a general one, and nationality comes into play only in terms of a particular state being responsible for a particular individual on the international plane, when the latter suffers at the hands of another state. Already in 1959 Van Panhuys remarked on "[t]he waning significance of nationality in rules concerning the protection of human rights",[8] but concluded that

> the general concept of nationality – reflecting as it does the pattern of international (and largely inter-State) relations – should not, in the absence of a fully developed protection of individuals in their capacity of members of the international community, be lightly relinquished.[9]

Is the additional protection provided by nationality still needed? Even in these fundamental terms, individuals arguably still require states to represent their interests vis-à-vis other states. It has been argued that any current level of acceptance of multiple nationality depends first and foremost on perceptions of states' needs, and the individuals for whom they consider themselves responsible, or over whom they wish to exercise power. Spiro identifies opposition to multiple nationality as linked to the need for diplomatic protection.[10] The greater the need for states to protect their nationals against other states, the more multiple nationality can amount to a practical problem.

While it might be concluded that current state practice that tolerates multiple nationality indicates that diplomatic protection is no longer a crucial issue, this is doubtful. It is true only as long as nationality is not used to the detriment of aliens, and especially with respect to fundamental standards of treatment of the human being, such as the right to a fair trial.[11] The same considerations are illustrated by a dia-

---

[8] H. F. van Panhuys, *The rôle of nationality in international law – an outline* (Leyden: A. W. Sythoff, 1959), 219.

[9] Id., 238.

[10] Peter J. Spiro, "Embracing dual nationality," in *Dual nationality, social rights and federal citizenship in the U.S. and Europe. The reinvention of citizenship*, ed. Randall Hansen and Patrick Weil (New York: Berghahn Books, 2002), 22–26.

[11] Allegations that "[t]he American government's decision to apply double standards in its treatment of those suspected of terrorism – keeping jury trial and other legal rights for American citizens but introducing summary trial by military tribunal for non-Americans – contravenes the fundamental principle of common law, reflected in every code of human rights in the world, that the same rights to a fair trial apply to everyone within the national jurisdiction regardless of race or nationality", are linked to a questioning of fundamental treatment of aliens, and calls for diplomatic protection. Clifford Longley, "American justice on trial", *The Tablet* (5 January 2002), 2. The piece goes on to state "[n]o longer is the United States a place where one is safe from arbitrary arrest and imprisonment, when it ought to be the safest place in the world". Ibid. The American Ambassador to Australia justified the difference in approach to aliens and United States' citizens on the basis that only U.S. citizens are subject to treason. "'An American citizen is subject to the charge of treason,' he said. 'Obviously an Australian cannot commit treason against the US'". News.com.au, *Hicks 'significant Al-Qaeda links'*, 2003 (internet), http://www.news.com.au/n/printpage/ 0,6093,6730709,00.html, consulted 27 July

metrically opposed example, for instance when states subject their nationals willingly to other states' jurisdiction, such as Argentina's recent decision to allow former officials charged with murder and torture to be tried in Spain.[12] While this may be regarded as a decision more related to Argentine politics, without the guarantees of a fair trial, that is to say a trial in Spain on par with the guarantees provided to Spaniards, such extradition would in normal circumstances not be contemplated.

The significance of nationality in terms of its international consequences of diplomatic protection and admission is evident when aliens, as opposed to nationals, are treated badly by states.[13] While current practice may indeed demonstrate respect for aliens generally, there is no guarantee that states will continue to treat individuals relatively well, or on par with their nationals, even in terms of fundamental respect for the human being.[14] There is much evidence, however, that the real issues in this regard are again increasingly related to the treatment of individuals by their own countries, as opposed to the abuse of aliens.[15] But while nationality in international law may have the effect of preventing states from treating aliens in certain limited ways, its primary significance is diplomatic protection of nationals.

Even if one approves of Fukuyama's views that history has "ended", in the sense that ideologically all states are on their way to becoming free market-driven democracies which will lead to peaceful relations among states,[16] such ideas are countered by considerations that such developments will most likely take a considerable amount of time, and

> [i]n the long period ahead during which democracies and non-democracies are still living alongside each other they will sometimes get into fights, and some of these fights could be severe enough to disrupt the geopolitical pattern in unexpected ways.[17]

2003. As has been demonstrated, while true, this is a function of U.S. law, not international law, and nothing in international law prevents the United States from charging aliens with treason or similar crimes.

[12] Cesar Illiano, "Argentina orders arrest of 46 over war crimes", *The Sydney Morning Herald*, 26–27 July 2003, 15.

[13] For example, in relation to expropriation of property, where international standards can often dictate better treatment because of the state behind the individual. See Matthew Kalman, "How Jews were swindled of Haider estate", *The Sydney Morning Herald*, 11 February 2000, 10.

[14] Of course such questions are relative, but any holding that "[t]his court has firmly and repeatedly endorsed the proposition that Congress may make rules as to aliens that would be unacceptable if applied to citizens", makes clear that the issue can never be dismissed as long as there is a difference between national and alien. *Demore v. Kim*, United States Supreme Court, No. 01–1491, quoted in David G. Savage, "Holding pattern. High Court limits immigrants' detention rights, setting stage for terrorism cases", *ABA Journal* (2003) July, 22.

[15] Such as the lamentable position and treatment of displaced persons. See generally "Displaced people. When is a refugee not a refugee?", *The Economist*, 3 March 2001, 21.

[16] The author expresses no opinion in this regard, except as noted in chapter one.

[17] Brian Beedham, "A survey of the new geopolitics. The road to 2050. False heaven", *The Economist*, 31 July 1999, 4–7, 6.

More disconcertingly, Beedham goes on to argue that wars are often not about ideology, politics, or even economics, but about position, chauvinism, and a sense of
inclusion and exclusion, "we" versus "them".[18] These arguments indicate that diplomatic protection is and will remain a vital mechanism for *individuals* in practical
terms, as far as their treatment as *aliens*, by states.

A final note is required regarding the protection of multiple nationals. Rules and
arguments related to the effective link and states' rights vis-à-vis one other in terms
of their "shared" nationals were canvassed at length in previous chapters. As regards
third states, however, widespread tolerance of multiple nationality would seem to
reinforce the rule that third states may treat a multiple national as a national of either
state of nationality, if no specific law, agreement or entitlement otherwise applies.
This means that states that wish to ensure that third states treat individuals with reference to them, as opposed to the other state of nationality, have an interest in entering into consular or other agreements that contain relevant stipulations. Thus, in a
deportation case, such an agreement could oblige a state to deport an individual to
one state of nationality (assuming of course his or her consent) or at least engage in
consultations before deportation to the other state of nationality. States with significant numbers of citizens who also possess the nationality of states where they
might be subjected to ill-treatment certainly have an interest in such agreements.

D. THOUGHTS REGARDING FUTURE DEVELOPMENTS AND NEEDS

Although the author has attempted to avoid taking a position on the relative desirability of multiple nationality, it is appropriate again to turn to the reasons that may
underlie current state practice, in order to discern the factors that guide states' and
individuals' interests and choices with respect to multiple nationality, in relation to
future developments and needs.

Chapter four cited Torpey's analysis that 16th and 17th century issues of freedom
of movement in Europe depended on

*(1) how the economic advantages available in a particular area were to be divided
up, whether these involved access to work or to poor relief; and*
*(2) who would be required to perform military service, and how they would be con-
strained to do so,*[19]

and argued that these issues seem as relevant today as they did five hundred years ago,
and today might be cited as influences on state practice toward multiple nationality.

---

[18] Id., 7.
[19] John Torpey, *The invention of the passport – surveillance, citizenship and the state* (Cambridge:
Cambridge University Press, 2000), 19.

Many of Bar-Yaacov's arguments as far as the essence of nationality, and the legal ramifications of how states value or categorise identity and emotional attachment, may have been technically incorrect, or are at least rebutted by current state practice, but his opposition to multiple nationality as such on the basis of potentially conflicting obligations required by states of their nationals, is not an invalid position due to the dictates of international law.[20] It may not necessarily be an attractive position for individuals should it be used to force them to choose between countries to which they have important ties, and it may not represent how states currently manage their interests on the international plane, but it reflects issues that seem to depend on overall state relationships.

In light of the changing nature of human society, the legal rights and obligations as a consequence of nationality under municipal law may be expected to continue to evolve. Thus, the subjective underpinning of standards of loyalty in municipal law may also be expected to change over time, and therefore also the objective requirements of municipal laws. This may be the case in any society or political order. These considerations may be expected to continue to influence the latitude states provide their nationals, related to nationality, or to any association with a foreign state,[21] such as representing another country at a sporting event, and thereby helping them to win.[22] States' own behavior may change over time.[23]

---

[20] In this sense, Dzialoszynski's characterization of the difficulties related to multiple nationality cited in chapter four are closer to the mark, which Bar-Yaacov clearly oversteps.

[21] Even today individuals balance questions of emotion, identity, and practical considerations, and may choose one over the other. The multi-millionaire Sir J. Paul Getty II, chose to maintain his American nationality for decades for tax reasons, notwithstanding residence in, and close emotional connections to, the United Kingdom. Emotion seems finally to have won the day, and he became a Briton in 1997, receiving a knighthood the following year. Although under United States law he could have retained his U.S. nationality, it seems he did not, but his obituary does not mention whether this was for tax or other reasons. Suzy (ed.) Baldwin, "Getty fortune brought grief, then grace. Sir J. Paul Getty II, philanthropist", *The Sydney Morning Herald*, 24 April 2003, 38. The artist Pablo Picasso is known for his fervent Spanish patriotism, but was revealed to have applied for French nationality in 1940 for practical reasons of protection. He was turned down as an "anarchist sympathiser". Philip Delves Broughton, "Picasso not the patriot he painted", *The Sydney Morning Herald*, 19 May 2003, 10.

[22] Such as the win by the Swiss yacht "Alinghi", "led by Kiwi defector Russell Coutts". The non-Swiss members of the team were characterised as "a band of New Zealand and Australian mercenaries", reportedly causing "distress" and "fury" in Auckland. "Traitors ahoy, and it's driving the Kiwis cuckoo", *The Sydney Morning Herald*, 19 February 2003, 1.

[23] But such practical considerations often have less to do with possession of more than one nationality, than with simple residence outside a country of nationality, and resulting discriminatory treatment, for example in the case of pensions paid overseas, and benefits for work performed. The United Kingdom reportedly refuses to index pensions for citizens who live abroad, leading the Australian government to "top up" the pensions of resident Britons, costing the Australian taxpayer 450 million Australian Dollars per year. Tony Koch, "Fleeced by UK over pensions," *The Courier-Mail*, 21 June 2003, 25. The European Court of Human Rights held

But while sporting competitions may cause tempers to flare, state practice that tolerates multiple nationality as opposed to recognizing or incorporating it directly, indicates that acceptance is related to perceived levels of threat, along the same lines as
any foreign tie or connection that can be perceived as a threat by states.[24] Thus,
whether states are more or less disposed to exempt multiple nationals from obligations of military service may have less to do with multiple nationality, than with the
perceived needs of the state.[25] Recognition that "interests and policies can change
rather quickly" leads Aleinikoff and Klusmeyer to recommend that multiple nationals
not assume high-level policy-making positions in government.[26]

It has been argued that state practice toward multiple nationality in an overall sense
has less to do with multiple nationality as such, than with nationality itself, and
states' interests.[27] A few of the recommendations to governments found in recent surveys that relate to multiple nationality should be analysed in this light, when they
regard multiple nationality as an independent consideration, as opposed to nationality
itself, and the rights attached.[28] No predictions are offered here, but it is unclear

---

that nationality could not be used to discriminate against workers in terms of unemployment
insurance. *Gaygusuz v. Austria*, 1996, European Court of Human Rights (internet), http://
cmiskp.echr.coe.int/tkp197/view.asp?item=1&portal=hbkm&action=html&highlight=Gaygusuz%20
%7C%20Austria&sessionid=6516400&skin=hudoc-en, consulted 4 April 2006. But absent the
ECHR's holding in this case, no general protection exists to counter such discrimination by
states on the basis of nationality.

[24] Such as American and Indian "suspicions about the Chinese loyalties of the powerful
Hong Kong business family headed by Li Ka-shing . . . In 1962 India was defeated by China
in a border war. It still regards its larger neighbour as a long-term military threat, and without
doubt, as an espionage risk". "Fear of China. China crisis," *The Economist*, 7 June 2003, 59.
See also "Keeping out Li Ka-Shing", *The Economist*, 3 May 2003, 54.

[25] The Australian Department of Foreign Affairs and Trade continues to warn Australians that
they may be faced with obligations of military service if they go to a country that considers
them its national, although it notes that "[i]n most instances dual nationals can be provided
with a letter of exclusion from military service". Hilary Doling, "Shock for dual nationals",
The Sun-Herald, 20 January 2002, 6 (Travel).

[26] T. Alexander Aleinikoff and Douglas Klusmeyer, *Citizenship policies for an age of migration* (Washington, DC: Carnegie Endowment for International Peace, 2002), 41. Martin agrees.
David A. Martin, "New rules for dual nationality", in *Dual nationality, social rights and federal citizenship in the U.S. and Europe. The reinvention of citizenship*, ed. Randall Hansen and
Patrick Weil (New York: Berghahn Books, 2002), 55. See also German Marshall Fund Project
on Dual Nationality, "Recommendations of the German Marshall Fund Project on Dual Nationality",
in *rights and duties of Dual nationals. Evolution and prospects*, ed. David A. Martin and Kay
Hailbronner (The Hague: Kluwer Law International, 2003), 387, no. 7.

[27] Such as ensuring that tax is collected. For arguments that do not mention multiple nationality, but that the movement of people, "tax competition", or "[g]lobalisation, accelerated by
the Internet, is exposing serious flaws in the world's tax systems", see Matthew Bishop,
"Globalisation and tax. The mystery of the vanishing taxpayer," *The Economist*, 29 January
2000, Survey 1–18.

[28] Martin states for example that "[a] dual national should vote only in the state of residence,

whether an increase in multiple nationals will provoke states to treat this category of persons differently from other nationals, or to "recognise" multiple nationality in that sense. There is evidence to suggest that the consideration of multiple nationality as an issue may be at odds with consideration of issues related to the treatment of citizens resident abroad, many of whom may be expected to make up a state's category of multiple nationals. States may in fact see an interest in maintaining a relationship to these people, as opposed to limiting it on the basis of their other ties.[29]

The proposition that current state practice toward multiple nationality reinforces and clarifies the traditional notion of nationality in international law also has the effect of elucidating various principles within this area of international law. Some of these might be seen as enhancing the status of the individual within international law, or at least clarifying that even in relation to the reserved domain and the effects of nationality internationally, the individual cannot be dismissed, and must be the final beneficiary of states' interests. But the results of this survey also clearly point to the fact that because nationality on the international plane relates to states' rights and

and rapid changes of residence should not be recognised for purposes of qualifying to exercise the franchise". Martin, "New rules for dual nationality", 52. The recommendations by the German Marshall Fund Project state "[i]n service of the values of solidarity and equality (and also to promote an informed and responsible vote), dual nationals should focus their political activities in the state of residence, and generally should vote only there. States may validly limit the voting rights of dual nationals in accordance with this approach, particularly if such limitations will facilitate the wider acceptance of dual nationality status". German Marshall Fund Project on Dual Nationality, "Recommendations of the German Marshall Fund Project on Dual Nationality", 387, no. 6.

[29] For example when states consider how to maintain ties to citizens resident abroad, without considering their possible multiple nationality at all. United States Congress, "Hearing before the Subcommittee on International Relations of the Committee on Foreign Affairs House of Representatives One Hundred Second Congress, First Session, June 25, 1991", (Washington: U.S. Government Printing Office, 1991). The Economist argues that the pervasive and accessible nature of the internet will provoke an increase in demands for direct democracy, even across borders. David Manasian, "Digital dilemmas. A survey of the internet society. Power to the people", *The Economist*, 25 January 2003, Survey 13–15. There are also indications that states are searching for ways to foster voting and political rights from overseas, not conditioning these on multiple nationality, but on real ties to the state concerned. Elizabeth Olson, International Herald Tribune, *U.S. to test expat cybervoting*, 2003 (internet), http://www.iht.com/articles/104098.html, consulted 26 June 2003; Isabelle Schmidt-Duvoisin, "Ten years of postal voting for Swiss Abroad. Interview with OSA President Georg Stucky", *Swiss Review* (2002) no. 3 (July), 9. See also Michael Jones-Correa, "Under two flags: dual nationality in Latin America and its consequences for naturalization in the United States", in *Rights and duties of dual nationals. Evolution and prospects*, ed. David A. Martin and Kay Hailbronner (The Hague: Kluwer Law International, 2003), 303–333; Peggy Levitt, "Variations in transnational belonging: lessons from Brazil and the Dominican Republic", in *Dual nationality, social rights and federal citizenship in the U.S. and Europe. The reinvention of citizenship*, ed. Randall Hansen and Patrick Weil (New York: Berghahn Books, 2002), 264–289.

obligations to each other, nationality can not always be cited as the source of rights and protection that it might be. To blame international law and relations would be to ignore that this predicament is a consequence of international law and relations. But to say no more would be to admit tacitly that no more need, or can, be done in this sense.

In relation to claims that some rules of international law are not binding on certain states because they do not embody universal standards, Judge Jessup of the ICJ cited W. Friedman for the proposition that

> [t]he problems that arise in the relations of nations, are not posed by the general principles as such, but by the discrepancy between the theory of international law and the practice of nations.[30]

While the incidence of multiple nationality seems to be a reflection of both the interests of states and of individuals, in terms of identity, emotion and the legal rights and position of millions worldwide, as well as an indicator of the basically healthy relationship of states in their mutual relations, current state practice reveals a lamentable discrepancy between theory and practice in the areas related to nationality that matter the most. As long as the right to nationality remains unenforceable by those who should benefit from it,[31] as long as a right of entry and abode in one's own state of nationality remains a matter that may be contracted away in the most crass of fashions, and as long as protection vis-à-vis other states is essentially a whim of the Government or Administration of the day, no state can claim to have built an international system of fundamental respect for the human being that goes beyond its own particular narrow and changing interests. There is room for much work to be done, but such efforts do not require the reduction or elimination of multiple nationality for the purposes of international law.

---

[30] W. Friedman, The Changing Structure of International Law (1964), cited in Philip C. Jessup, "Non-Universal International Law", *Columbia Journal of Transnational Law* (1973) vol. 12, no. 1.

[31] An estimate characterized as conservative cites about 11 million stateless persons currently. Maureen Lynch, "The people who have no country . . .", *International Herald Tribune*, 18 February 2005.

Appendix

Overview of state practice*

The following tables outline various state practice toward multiple nationality. Countries marked with an asterisk (*) constitute part of the state sample for the analysis in the foregoing chapters. Source material for each country is cited in the footnotes to this chapter, not in the bibliography. Much relevant national legislation is directly and publicly accessible through the website of the Office of the United Nations High Commissioner for Refugees (UNHCR), in its section entitled "Research and Evaluation" under the option "Country of Origin and Legal Information", found at <http://www.unhcr.org/cgi-bin/texis/vtx/rsd>. Unless otherwise stated, documents cited as UNHCR (internet) come from the above-mentioned reference, consulted as of 1 April 2006.

The reader is cautioned that the following information is aimed at providing an overview of state practice toward multiple nationality, and that the form of presentation of various details surrounding attribution and withdrawal of nationality may not agree with official national or judicial legal interpretations. The following tables should serve as an outline of the law and policy of the states covered, but are of course not a definitive, complete or necessarily correct statement of the law. They are also not directed at questions related to immigration. The caution "conditions" has been added in places to warn the reader that further research is particularly advisable in an area of legislation or policy.

---

* *This information should not be relied upon for the determination of a particular status or related rights, or permissible conduct, which can only be done by consultation with the appropriate national authorities or upon competent legal advice in the country concerned.*

While care has been taken to ensure the information provided below is accurate (as of early 2006), changes to national legislation and practice regarding nationality are in many states frequent and not well-publicized, and authorities' implementation and interpretation of legal norms can change quickly. Likewise, information for acquisition and loss of nationality provided is as current as possible, meaning that different rules may apply for acquisition and loss of nationality in the past, for example, birth in 1977, or adoption by a non-national in 1995.

*Argentina[1]

Nationality category or status

Only one. The military decrees of the 1970s that divided nationals into "nativos" and "naturalizados" and attempted to eliminate or severely restrict multiple nationality were voided in 1984. Citizenship (political rights) is distinguished from nationality (the former can be lost, the latter not), and nationals become citizens at 18.

Attribution/acquisition of nationality

Event	Law	Condition is renunciation/ loss of other nationality
Birth	All born in Argentina (*except* to parents who are foreign functionaries) including territorial waters, airspace, diplomatic legations, warships, on Argentine flagged vessels.	NO
	Abroad to Argentine parent(s) serving the state,	
	Abroad to Argentine parent(s) who petitions within 18 years of birth, or child may petition thereafter in Argentina	
Naturalisation	Upon fulfilment of legal requirements	NO
Adoption	Not automatic	NO
Legitimation	(see birth)	NO
Marriage	Not automatic	
Resumption	(no need for provision)	
State service	Under certain conditions	NO
Parent acquires nationality	Under certain conditions	NO
Spouse acquires nationality	Not automatic	
Registration		

---

[1] ARGENTINA: *Ley 25.327 Ciudadanía y naturalización*, 9 November 2000; *Decreto 231/95*, 2 August 1995; *Ley 23.059 Ciudadanía y naturalización*, 22 March 1984; *Decreto nacional 3.213/84, Reglamentación de la Ley 23.059*, 28 September 1984; *Ley 346, Ciudadanía y naturalización*, 1 October 1869; *Constitución de la Nación Argentina*, 22 August 1994; *Ley*

Withdrawal/loss of nationality

Event	Law	Consequence of event is loss of nationality
Renunciation	No provision	NO
Attribution at birth conditional	No provision (see birth overseas)	NO
Naturalisation elsewhere	*(however loss of citizenship possible)*	NO
Adoption by a foreigner		NO
Marriage to a foreigner		NO
Spouse acquires other nationality		NO
Parent acquires other nationality		NO
Resumption of previous nationality		NO
Service to foreign state	By naturlised citizen leads to loss of political rights (citizenship) if without permission from Congress	NO

N° 21.795 Ley de Nacionalidad y Ciudadanía – Derogación de la Ley 346, 22 July 1978 ; *Ley N° 17.692 Nacionalidad Argentina de los Hijos de Argentinos que Prestan Servicio en Organizaciones Internacionales*, 22 May 1975; *Ley N° 16.569 Nacionalidad de los Hijos de Argentinos Nacidos en el Extranjero Durante el Exilio de sus Padres*, 29 October 1964, **UNHCR (internet)**; *Temas Consulares*, Ministerio de Relaciones Exteriores Comercio Internacional y Culto (internet), http://www.cancilleria.gov.ar, consulted 7 April 2006; *Países con los cuales exite Convenio de Doble Nacionalidad*, Ministerio del Interior, Dirección Nacional de Migraciones (internet), http://www.mininterior.gov.ar/migraciones/convenio.asp, consulted 7 April 2006; *Consular Information Sheet, Artentina*, 31 March 2006, United States Department of State (internet), http://travel.state.gov/travel/cis_pa_tw/cis/cis_1130.html, consulted 7 April 2006; Dennis Campbell and Susan Meek, eds., *International immigration and nationality law*, vol. 1 (The Hague: Kluwer Law International, 2001); María Teresa Echezarreta Ferrer, ed., *Legislación sobre nacionalidad*, Third ed. (Madrid: Tecnos, 1999); Michael Jones-Correa, *Under two flags: dual nationality in Latin America and its consequences for the United States, 2003* (internet), http://www.fas.harvard.edu/~drclas/publications/papers.html#, consulted 7 April 2006; Juan A. Lessing, *Problemas del derecho de nacionalidad. (Proposiciones de reforma)*, (Buenos Aires: Tipografica Editora Argentina, 1946); Dionisio Petriella, *El Convenio de Doble Ciudadanía entre la Argentina e Italia*, (Buenos Aires: Asociación Dante Alighieri, 1988).

Event	Law	**Consequence of event is loss of nationality**
Other attribution of nationality		NO
(Punitive) deprivation	Only of citizenship rights of naturalised citizens for fraud or certain crimes	NO
Special considerations		NO

General attitude toward multiple nationality
Argentina accepts multiple nationality for its citizens and recognises it in certain situations. No distinction is drawn among citizens on the basis of multiple nationality, although naturalised citizens can occupy certain government offices only after a period of years.

Recognition of Multiple Nationality
Argentine multiple nationals are permitted to enter/depart Argentina on a foreign passport, but must leave using an Argentine passport if they have been in the country more than 60 days, except when specific bilateral treaty provisions apply. Argentines naturalised in Israel have 180 days. For countries with which there are conventions on dual nationality, entry on a foreign passport is possible as a tourist, for up to three months. Argentina has entered into various treaties in relation to multiple nationals, including: Protocol to the Convention of Rio de Janeiro (1906): Chile, Colombia, Ecuador, El Salvador, Honduras, Nicaragua, Panamá; and conventions on dual nationality with: Spain, Italy, Sweden, Norway.

*Australia[2]

Nationality category or status

Only one, and the law does not distinguish between citizenship and nationality.

---

[2] AUSTRALIA: *Australian Citizenship Act*, 1948 (as amended); *Australian Citizenship Regulations*, as of 24 November 1998, **UNHCR (internet)**; *Consular Services Charter*, Department of Foreign Affairs and Trade (internet), http://www.dfat.gov.au/consular/consular_charter/section4.html, consulted 7 April 2006; *Changes to citizenship laws*, Department of Immigration and Multicultural and Indigenous Affairs (internet), http://www.citizenship.gov.au/media/change.htm, consulted 1 April 2006; *Return documents for Australian citizens and permanent residents*, Form 968I, Department of Immigration and Multicultural and Indigenous Affairs (internet), http://www.immi.gov.au/allforms/pdf/968i.pdf, consulted 1 April 2006; "Expats find their voice", The Weekend Australian, 11–12 August 2001, 1, 8. Lane, Bernard, "Dual citizenship benefits trade", The Australian, 6 August 2001, 1, 12. Stevenson, Andrew, "Citizenship plan welcomes back all our expatriates", The Sydney Morning Herald, 19 February 2000, 4. Este, Jonathan, "Citizenship for new century", The Weekend Australian, 19–20 February 2000, 3. Haslem, Benjamin, "Australia to accept dual citizenship", The Australian, 4–5 August 2001. Campbell and Meek, eds., *International immigration and nationality law;* John Chesterman and Brian Galligan, *Citizens without rights. Aborigines and Australian citizenship* (Cambridge, United Kingdom: Cambridge University Press, 1997); John Chesterman and Brian Galligan, eds., *Defining Australian citizenship – selected documents* (Carlton South (Victoria): Melbourne University Press, 1999); *Loss of Australian citizenship on acquisition of another citizenship. Discussion paper on Section 17 of the Australian Citizenship Act 1948*, Department of Immigration & Multicultural & Indigenous Affairs (Australia), June 2001 (internet), http://www.citizenship.gov.au/0601paper/index.htm, consulted 7 April 2006; Brian Galligan and John Chesterman, "Aborigines, citizenship and the Australian Constitution: did the Constitution exclude Aboriginal people from citizenship?", *Public Law Review* (1997) vol. 8, no. 1, 45–61; John Goldlust, *Understanding citizenship in Australia*, ed. Heather Kelly, *Understanding series* (Canberra: Australian Government Publishing Service, 1996); Joint Committee on Foreign Affairs and Defence (Australia), "Dual nationality (Report from the Committee)", (Canberra: Parliament of Australia, 1976); *Dual citizenship in Australia. Current issues brief 2000–01*, Parliamentary Library, Parliament of Australia (internet), http://www.aph.gov.au/library/pubs/cib/2000–01/01cib05.htm, consulted 7 April 2006; Georgie Raik-Allen, "They want to call Australia home again", *The Sydney Morning Herald*, 19 February 2002, 12; Kim Rubenstein, "Citizenship and the Constitutional Convention debates: a mere legal inference", *Federal Law Review* (1997) vol. 25, no. 2, 295–316; Kim Rubenstein, "Citizenship in Australia: unscrambling its meaning", *Melbourne University Law Review* (1995) vol. 20, 503–527; Greg Taylor, "Citizenship rights and the Australian Constitution", *Public Law Review* (2001) vol. 12, no. 3, 205–229; *Travel information for dual* nationals, Department of Foreign Affairs and Trade (internet), http://www.smartraveller.gov.au/tips/dualnat.html, consulted 7 April 2006. Gianni Zappalà and Stephen Castles, "Citizenship and immigration in Australia", *Georgetown Immigration Law Journal* (1999) vol. 13, no. 2, 273–316.

Attribution/acquisition of nationality

Event	Law	Condition is renunciation/ loss of other nationality
Birth	In Australia to at least one parent citizen or permanent resident,	NO
	In Australia to foreign parents and 10 years continuous residence,	
	In Australia and otherwise stateless, and not entitled to other nationality	
	Overseas to Australian parent citizen by birth, or to parent citizen by descent who has lived in Australia for at least two years, and for both, registration prior to age 25	
Naturalisation	Upon fulfilment of legal requirements	NO
Adoption	Of a minor by a citizen in Australia	NO
Legitimation	(see birth)	
Marriage	Not automatic	
Resumption	Possible in certain cases	NO
State service		
Parent acquires nationality	Where parent resumes Australian nationality, possible for minor children	NO
Spouse acquires nationality	Not automatic	
Registration	For citizenship by descent of person who did not register prior to age 25 (see birth)	NO
Special considerations	No attribution at birth if a parent was an enemy alien and birth in territory occupied by the enemy	

Withdrawal/loss of nationality

Event	Law	Consequence of event is loss of nationality
Renunciation	Possible if over 18 and multiple national or in order to acquire foreign nationality. Possible refusal in wartime or if against national interest.	YES

Event	Law	Consequence of event is loss of nationality
Attribution at birth conditional	No provision (see birth overseas and registration provision)	
Naturalisation elsewhere		NO
Adoption by a foreigner	(*Unless thereby lose parental relationship to Australian citizen*)	NO (*exception*)
Marriage to a foreigner		NO
Spouse acquires other nationality		NO
Parent acquires other nationality	(*No direct effect, but if parent loses Aus. citizenship child loses provided other parent not Aus. citizen, and not stateless*)	NO (*exception*)
Resumption of previous nationality		NO
Service to foreign state	(*Automatic deprivation if multiple national who serves in armed forces of country at war with Australia*)	NO (*exception*)
Other attribution of nationality		NO
(Punitive) deprivation	Revocation of citizenship by naturalisation if obtained by fraud, or if "contrary to the public interest for the person to continue to be an Australian citizen"	POSSIBLE

General attitude toward multiple nationality

Parliamentary discussion that led to the repeal of Section 17 of the Citizenship Act, effective 4 April 2002, thus allowing Australians to acquire another nationality without automatic deprivation of Australian nationality agreed that Australia's policy should be "inclusive" toward issues of citizenship, and accept multiple nationality. The repeal was directly related to advocacy by various groups, especially Australians resident overseas. A 1976 Parliamentary Committee recommended that Australians hold only one nationality, but did not conclude that requiring renunciation of a foreign nationality should be a prerequisite to naturalisation. Another such inquiry in 1994 rejected arguments that multiple nationality called the loyalty or allegiance of Australians into question. One Constitutional provision discriminates against multiple nationals directly, holding that citizens of a "foreign power" may not be members of Parliament.

Recognition of Multiple Nationality

Australian citizens are advised to use an Australian passport to enter and depart Australia as proof of citizenship – no visas will be placed in foreign passports held by Australian nationals. The Department of Foreign Affairs and Trade states it will always endeavour to assist all Australian citizens to the greatest extent possible, but may not be allowed to in countries where the person in question is also considered a national. As mentioned in chapter four, Australia has entered into various consular treaties according to which rights of protection are determined by which passport a dual national uses to enter and depart one of the two countries.

Austria[3]

Nationality category or status

Only one, and no distinction between nationality and citizenship.

---

[3] AUSTRIA: *Bundesgesetz mit dem das Staatsbürgerschaftsgesetz 1985 (StbG), das Tilgungsgesetz 1972 und das Gebührengesetz 1957 geändert werden (Staatsbürgerschaftsrechts-Nouvelle 2005)*, in force 23 March 2006, Bundesministerium für auswärtige Angelegenheiten (internet), https://cms.bmaa.gv.at/up-media/2106_staatsbuergerschaftsrechts_novelle_2005.pdf, consulted 7 May 2006; *Bundesgesetz über die österreichische Staatsbürgerschaft*, 1985, Bundesministerium für Inneres (internet), http://www.bmi.gv.at/downloadarea/Kunsttexte/ Staatsbuergerschaftsgesetz.pdf, consulted 6 May 2006; *Federal law concerning the Austrian nationality, 1985, Austria: whether a person with Austrian citizenship loses that citizenship by serving in another country's armed forces*, Immigration and Refugee Board of Canada, December 2004, **UNHCR (internet)**; *Staatsbürgerschaft*, Bundesministerium für auswärtige Angelegenheiten (internet), http://www.bmaa.gv.at/view.php3?r_id=1174&LNG=de&version=, consulted 7 May 2006; *Erwerb der österreichischen Staatsbürgerschaft*, Bundesministerium für auswärtige Angelegenheiten (internet), http://www.bmaa.gv.at/view.php3?f_id=3497&LNG= de&version=, consulted 7 May 2006; *Wiedererwerb der österreichischen Staatsbürgerschaft*, Bundesministerium für auswärtige Angelegenheiten (internet), http://www.bmaa.gv.at/view.php3?f_ id=3498&LNG=de&version=, consulted 7 May 2006; *Verlust der österreichischen Staatsbürgerschaft*, Bundesministerium für auswärtige Angelegenheiten (internet), http://www.bmaa.gv.at/ view.php3?f_id=3499&LNG=de&version=, consulted 7 May 2006; *Beibehaltung der österreichischen Staatsbürgerschaft*, Bundesministerium für auswärtige Angelegenheiten (internet), http://www.bmaa.gv.at/view.php3?f_id=3501&LNG=de&version=, consulted 7 May 2006; *Information für Anträge auf Bewilligung um Beibehaltung der österreichischen Staatsbürgerschaft für den beabsichtigten Erwerb einer fremden Staatsangehörigkeit gemäß § 28 StbG i.d.g.F.*, Bundesministerium für auswärtige Angelegenheiten (internet), http://www. bmaa.gv.at/view.php3?f_id=3502&LNG=de&version=, consulted 7 May 2006; *Muster-Antrag auf Bewilligung der Beibehaltung der österreichischen Staatsbürgerschaft durch Abstammung erworben*, Bundesministerium für auswärtige Angelegenheiten (internet), http://www.bmaa.gv.at/up-media/311_musterantrag_a_html.htm, consulted 7 May 2006; *Muster-Antrag auf Bewilligung der Beibehaltung der österreichischen Staatsbürgerschaft nicht durch Abstammung erworben*, Bundesministerium für auswärtige Angelegenheiten (internet), http://www.bmaa.gv.at/up-media/312_musterantrag_n_html.htm, consulted 7 May 2006; *Österreichischer Militärdienst für Doppelbürger*, Bundesministerium für auswärtige Angelegenheiten (internet), http://cms. bmaa.gv.at/up-media/1677__sterreichischer_milit_rdienst_f_r_doppelb_rger.doc, consulted 7 May 2006; *Passport Information*, Austrian Press and Information Service (internet), http://www. austria.org/visa_reg.shtml#austrian, consulted 7 May 2006; *Erfolg der AuslandsösterreicherInnen-Internet-Umfrage: hohe Teilnahme, viele Ideen, grosse Zufriedenheit*, Bundesministerium für auswärtige Angelegenheiten (internet), http://www.bmaa.gv.at/view.php3?f_id=10088&LNG=de& version=, consulted 7 May 2006.

Attribution/acquisition of nationality

Event	Law	Condition is renunciation/ loss of other nationality
Birth / (Descent)	To an Austrian in wedlock (including posthumous children)	NO
	To an Austrian mother out of wedlock	
	Foundling under six months presumed national by descent	
	Birth in Austria in wedlock to a parent also born in Austria, or out of wedlock to a mother also born in Austria	
Naturalisation	Upon fulfillment of conditions	YES (*exception*)
	(*exception for loss of nationality in connection with National Socialist German persecution; certain former citizens, if cannot renounce, if conditions for renunciation unreasonable* – conditions)	
Adoption		
Legitimation	Of an unmarried minor, with child's and representative's consent if over 14 (conditions) – extends to children born out of wedlock to legitimated woman (conditions)	NO
Marriage	Facilitated naturalisation possible (conditions)	YES
Resumption	Possible if loss other than by deprivation – naturalisation (conditions)	YES
State service	If granting of nationality is in the interest of Austria for actual or expected outstanding achievements (conditions)	NO
Parent acquires nationality	Parent's naturalisation extended to children (and if the latter are female, also to their children born out of wedlock): born in wedlock, born out of wedlock to a woman, born out of wedlock to a man and paternity established and has custody, adopted minor unmarried children (conditions)	YES

	Event	**Law**	**Condition is renunciation/ loss of other nationality**
	Spouse acquires nationality	Spouse may be naturalised at same time if fulfills conditions (conditions)	YES
	Registration		
	Special considerations	A non-EU national (or similar) person who takes up the post of university or college professor receives an automatic grant of nationality	NO
		The spouse and minor children of a professor who receives Austrian nationality receive nationality upon their declaration and fulfillment of conditions, at the professor's installation (conditions)	
		When between age 18–20, a person born in Austria and stateleless since birth with principal domicile at least ten years in Austria of which not less than five continuous years preceding the application, may apply for naturalisation (conditions)	

Withdrawal/loss of nationality

Event	**Law**	**Consequence of event is loss of nationality**
Renunciation	Possible if possess foreign nationality and not subject to sentence or subject to military service obligations (conditions)	YES
Attribution at birth conditional	No provision	
Naturalisation elsewhere	*(nationals may apply in advance of acquisition of foreign nationality to retain Austrian nationality – must be in national interest)*	YES *(exceptions)*
Adoption by a foreigner	Any voluntary acquisition of foreign nationality including when initiated by minor's legal representative, except if over age 14 must consent	YES
Marriage to a foreigner		NO

Event	Law	Consequence of event is loss of nationality
Spouse acquires other nationality		NO
Parent acquires other nationality	Parent's loss of nationality upon voluntary acquisition of foreign nationality is extended to most children (conditions)	YES
Resumption of previous nationality	Any voluntary acquisition of foreign nationality	YES
Service to foreign state	Any voluntary foreign military service	YES
	Any service to foreign government that severely damages Austria's interests or reputation	
Other attribution of nationality	Any voluntary acquisition of foreign nationality	YES
(Punitive) deprivation	For failure to divest oneself of foreign nationality when required to do so	YES

Special considerations

General attitude toward multiple nationality
Austria maintains a principle of avoidance of multiple nationality, although multiple nationality may be produced at birth, and pursuant to certain exceptions. An 2005 Austrian government study on nationality-related questions among Austrians abroad found that their main areas of concern related to retention of Austrian nationality, transmission of nationality to children, and permission to possess dual nationality. Changes to Austrian nationality law in 2005 that eased conditions for retaining Austrian nationality upon naturalisation abroad and facilitated resumption of citizenship were billed as improving the situation of Austrians resident abroad. Naturalisation abroad results in automatic deprivation of Austrian nationality, however an application may be made within two years before any foreign naturalisation to retain Austrian nationality. Austrians by descent or birth must set out grounds why it is in Austria's national interest for them to retain nationality, or special personal or family-related reasons; reasons for acquisition of foreign nationality are not considered. Austrians other than by descent or birth must set out their already accomplished and to-be-expected achievements as Austrians or the special national interest that might argue for retention of nationality. In order to ascertain whether Austrians resident abroad have obtained foreign nationality (and thereby lost Austrian nationality) applicants for passports overseas are required to submit a copy of their foreign residence visa or a certification from foreign immigration authorities that foreign nationality has not been acquired. Austria has entered into bilateral treaties with Switzerland and Argentina regulating military service and dual nationality.

Recognition of Multiple Nationality
Austria does not recognise multiple nationality.

Barbados[4]

Nationality category or status
Only one, and no distinction between nationality and citizenship.

Attribution/acquisition of nationality

Event	Law	Condition is renunciation/ loss of other nationality
Birth	In Barbados (unless parent diplomat – conditions) – includes birth abroad to Barbadian parent in diplomatic/consular service	NO
	Overseas to a Barbadian father in wedlock born in Barbados (conditions)	
	Overseas to a Barbadian mother out of wedlock born in Barbados (conditions)	
	Foundling deemed born in Barbados	
Naturalisation	Upon fulfillment of conditions	NO
Adoption	Upon adoption by Barbadian married father, or unmarried mother	NO
Legitimation	Parents' marriage leads to treatment as if legitimate at birth	
Marriage	By registration (conditions)	
Resumption		
State service		
Parent acquires nationality	Minor children of citizens may be registered (conditions)	
Spouse acquires nationality	No automatic effect	
Registration	Possible for various categories upon fulfillment of conditions	NO
Special considerations		

---

[4] BARBADOS: *Barbados Constitution*, Government of Barbados Information Service (internet), http://www.barbados.gov.bb/bdsconst.htm, consulted 3 May 2006; *Barbados Citizenship Act*, Cap. 186, last amended 1982, **UNHCR (internet)**.

Withdrawal/loss of nationality

Event	Law	Consequence of event is loss of nationality
Renunciation	Possible at age 21 if multiple national or about to acquire foreign nationality (possible limitation in wartime) – norm includes provivions to prevent statelessness	YES
Attribution at birth conditional	No provision	
Naturalisation elsewhere		NO
Adoption by a foreigner		NO
Marriage to a foreigner		NO
Spouse acquires other nationality		NO
Parent acquires other nationality		NO
Resumption of previous nationality		NO
Service to foreign state		NO
Other attribution of nationality		NO
(Punitive) deprivation	Not possible for citizens by birth. Possible for registration or naturalisation by fraud or misrepresentation, treason, certain crimes, disloyal/disaffected toward Barbados, unlawful ties or assistance to enemy in wartime, prejudicial activities to law and public order (conditions)	POSSIBLE
	Naturalised citizen who is deprived the citizenship of certain other countries (Commonwealth, Ireland) for a reason substantially similar to list above, may also be deprived of Barbadian citizenship (conditions)	

Special considerations

General attitude toward multiple nationality

Barbados has accepted multiple nationality for its citizens since independence from the United Kingdom in 1966. The Constitution specifies that Parliament may not deprive Barbadians who were born in Barbados, or who are citizens by virtue of birth overseas to a Barbadian, of their citizenship. The Citizenship Act's paragraph entitled "renunciation of citizenship by reason of dual citizenship or nationality" makes clear that loss of Barbadian citizenship is up to the individual, and must be the result of a specific declaration of renunciation of citizenship.

Belarus[5]

Nationality category or status
Only one, and no technical distinction between nationality and citizenship.

Attribution/acquisition of nationality

Event	Law	Condition is renunciation/ loss of other nationality
Birth	To Belarusian parents or single parent	NO
	To a Belarusian parent and other parent is stateless or unknown	
	To a Belarusian and a foreign parent, upon joint request unless child otherwise stateless	
	In Belarus to stateless permanent resident parents or parent	
	In Belarus to permanent resident foreign parent or parents and no other country confers nationality	
	Foundling	
Naturalisation	Upon fulfillment of requirements	YES *(exception)*
	(unless impracticable or cannot be obtained)	
Adoption	By Belarusian (conditions)	NO
Legitimation		
Marriage	No automatic effect	NO
Resumption	Facilitated naturalisation possible	
State service	Facilitated naturalisation possible	
Parent acquires nationality	Child acquires with parent by naturalisation or registration, upon parents' joint request if one parent	

---

[5] BELARUS: *Law of 1 August 2002 no. 136-3 on Citizenship of Belarus*, 1 August 2002, **UNHCR (internet)**; *Law on Citizenship*, 18 October 1991 (internet), http://www.legislationline. org/legislation.php?tid=11&lid=3176, consulted 25 May 2006; *Consular information sheet – Belarus*, 6 April 2006, United States Department of State (internet), http://travel.state.gov/ travel/cis_pa_tw/cis/cis_1033.html, consulted 25 May 2006.

		Condition is renunciation/
Event	**Law**	**loss of other nationality**
	remains foreign/stateless; if other parent stateless child acquires if stateless (conditions)	
Spouse acquires nationality		
Registration	Possible for certain groups (citizens of former USSR who were born or lived in Belarus before 1991, their spouses and descendants; children of Belarusian parent upon joint application by parents; certain abandoned children – conditions)	NO
Special considerations	Facilitated naturalisation for certain Belarusians and descendants, those who possessed citizenship or had a right thereto, previous citizens	

Withdrawal/loss of nationality

		Consequence of event is
Event	**Law**	**loss of nationality**
Renunciation	Possible if multiple national or about to acquire foreign nationality, unless under accusation or court sentence, or subject to tax or other governments debts	YES
Attribution at birth conditional	No provision	
Naturalisation elsewhere		NO
Adoption by a foreigner	*(adoptive parents may request renunciation of child's citizenship at age 16)*	NO *(exception)*
Marriage to a foreigner		NO
Spouse acquires other nationality		NO
Parent acquires other nationality	If parents renounce nationality, children or foster children under 14 lose, children or foster children	DEPENDS

Event	Law	Consequence of event is loss of nationality
	between 14–18 and adopted children must give written consent, parent(s) may request that children under 16 retain nationality even if they renounce (conditions, and special conditions for children under custody and guardianship)	
	If only one parent renounces and other parent retains, child may be allowed to renounce only on parents' joint request (conditions)	
Resumption of previous nationality		NO
Service to foreign state	Possible loss for enlistment in foreign military, police, security, justice or other public agency, unless under accusation or court sentence, or subject to tax or other governments debts, but not if thereby stateless	POSSIBLE
Other attribution of nationality		NO
(Punitive) deprivation	For fraud in acquisition within seven years	POSSIBLE
Special considerations		

General attitude toward multiple nationality
Belarus amended its Law on Citizenship in 2002 such that naturalisation abroad no longer provokes loss of Belarusian nationality. Effective renunciation (unless not possible) is still a condition of naturalisation. The Citizenship Act provides that "Citizens of the Republic of Belarus who also have other citizenships, may not for that reason be limited in rights or evade duties or be exempt from liability ensuing [from] the citizenship of the Republic of Belarus".

Recognition of Multiple Nationality
The Citizenship Act provides that "[f]oreign citizenship of a citizen of the Republic of Belarus shall not be recognised unless international treaties provide otherwise" and that the state shall guarantee its protection to all citizens when outside Belarus. Belarusian multiple nationals must use Belarusian documents to enter and depart the country.

Belgium[6]

Nationality category or status
Only one, and no distinction between nationality and citizenship.

Attribution/acquisition of nationality

Event	Law	Condition is renunciation/ loss of other nationality
Birth	In Belgium to a Belgian parent	NO
	Abroad to a Belgian parent born in Belgium or in Belgian Congo before 30 June 1960 or in Rwanda or Burundi before 1 July 1962	*(but see conditional attribution)*
	Abroad to a Belgian parent born abroad, who makes declaration on acquisition of nationality within 5 years of birth (conditions)	
	Abroad to a Belgian parent born abroad, and no other nationality attributed before age 18 – *lost if another nationality is attributed before age 18*	
	In Belgium and stateless (Foundling presumed born in Belgium)	
	In Belgium and lose only other nationality before age 18	
	In Belgium to foreign parent born in Belgium who lived in Belgium for 5 of 10 years preceding birth (conditions)	
Naturalization	Upon fulfillment of conditions	YES

---

[6] BELGIUM: *Code de la nationalité belge* (entry into force 22 July 1984), *20 juillet 2000 – Circulaire complétant la circulaire du 25 avril 2000 concernant la loi du 1ᵉʳ mars 2000 modifiant certaines dispositions relatives à la nationalité belge* (entry into force 27 July 2000), *25 avril 2000 – Circulaire concernant la loi du 1ᵉʳ mars 2000 modifiant certaines dispositions relatives à la nationalité belge* (entry into force 6 May 2000), *Circulaire du 14 juin 1999 concernant la modification du Code de la nationalié belge* (entry into force September 1999), **UNHCR (internet)**; *General information on acquiring Belgian nationality*, Belgian Foreign Ministry (internet), http://www.diplomatie.be/en/services/nationalitydetail.asp?TEXTID=42487, consulted 2 May 2006.

Event	Law	Condition is renunciation/ loss of other nationality
Adoption	Of child born in Belgium by Belgian parent	POSSIBLE
	Of child born abroad by Belgian born in Belgium, Belgian Congo before 30 June 1960 or Rwanda/Burundi before 1 July 1962	
	Of child born abroad by Belgian born abroad who makes declaration within 5 years of adoption (conditions)	
	Of child born abroad adopted by Belgian born abroad and no other nationality attributed before age 18 – *lost if another nationality is attributed before age 18*	
	Of child born in Belgium by foreign parent born in Belgium had main residence in Belgium for 5 of 10 years preceding adoption (conditions)	
Legitimation	If parentage acknowledged before age 18, see birth	NO
Marriage	No automatic effect – facilitated acquisition by declaration (conditions)	
Resumption	Possible by declaration (conditions)	YES
State service		
Parent acquires nationality	Automatic for children under 18 of parent or adoptive parent who holds parental authority	YES
Spouse acquires nationality	No automatic effect	
Registration (Declaration)	Possible for various categories (conditions)	DEPENDS
	Child born in Belgium to foreign parents or adoptive parents born abroad and request before age 12 (conditions)	
Special considerations	If nationality attributed erroneously possible to submit declaration of option	

Withdrawal/loss of nationality

Event	Law	Consequence of event is loss of nationality
Renunciation	Possible at age 18 if multiple national or about to acquire nationality	YES
Attribution at birth conditional	Automatic loss of Belgian nationality for multiple national at age 28 if born abroad after 1 January 1967 and main place of residence between ages 18–28 was not in Belgium, *unless* declaration to retain between ages 18–28 and once every 10 years thereafter	POSSIBLE
	Child born abroad to Belgian parent born abroad loses nationality if another nationality attributed before age 18	
	Nationality attributed upon adoption of child born abroad by Belgian parent born abroad is lost if another nationality attributed before 18	
Naturalisation elsewhere	Any voluntary obtention of a foreign nationality after age 18	YES
Adoption by a foreigner	Of child under 18 who receives foreign nationality upon adoption, unless parent spouse of adoptive parent is Belgian	YES
Marriage to a foreigner		NO
Spouse acquires other nationality		NO
Parent acquires other nationality	Loss of nationality extended to minor children unless other parent Belgian or child thereby stateless	YES
Resumption of previous nationality	(Any voluntary obtention of a foreign nationality after age 18)	YES
Service to foreign state		
Other attribution of nationality	(Any voluntary obtention of a foreign nationality after age 18)	YES
(Punitive) deprivation	Nationality obtained other than through Belgian parentage at birth upon serious breach of obligations as citizen (however children retain)	
Special considerations		

General attitude toward multiple nationality
Belgium tolerates multiple nationality only when it is obtained automatically without any voluntary action, such as attribution at birth. Any voluntary obtention of another nationality results in automatic deprivation of Belgian nationality, and renunciation is a condition of obtention of Belgian nationality. Increasing demands by expatriate Belgians for retention of Belgian nationality upon naturalisation elsewhere have led to various parliamentary discussions of the issue. The norm that dictates automatic loss of Belgian nationality for multiple nationals at age 28 if they were born abroad after 1 January 1967 and whose main place of residence between ages 18–28 was not in Belgium, can be avoided by submission of a declaration of desire to retain Belgian nationality made between the ages of 18–28, and once every 10 years thereafter. The norm that dictates automatic loss of Belgian nationality by a child born abroad to a Belgian parent who was also born abroad if another nationality is attributed to the child before age 18, cannot be circumvented.

Recognition of Multiple Nationality
Belgium does not recognise multiple nationality, and considers its multiple nationals as Belgians only.

*Brazil[7]

Nationality category or status
Only one, and no technical distinction between nationality and citizenship.

Attribution/acquisition of nationality

Event	Law	Condition is renunciation/ loss of other nationality
Birth	In Brazil (unless parents aliens in service of foreign state)	NO
	Overseas to Brazilian parent serving the state	
	Overseas to Brazilian parent, upon residence in Brazil and option for nationality, at any time	
Naturalisation	Upon fulfillment of requirements	NO
Adoption		
Legitimation	(see birth)	
Marriage	Not automatic	
Resumption	Possible for those who were deprived of nationality for having acquired foreign nationality previously	NO

---

[7] BRAZIL: *Constituição da República Federativa do Brasil*, 1988 (as amended), **UNHCR (internet)**; *Assistência e Proteção a Brasileiros*, Brazilian Embassy in Washington (internet), http://www.brasilemb.org/portugues/portuguese1.shtml, consulted 7 April 2006; *Manual de Servicio Consular e Jurídico* and *Perguntas Frequentes*, Ministério das Relações Exteriores, Serviço Consular, Brasileiros no Exterior (internet), http://www.mre.gov.br/portugues/servico_consular/brasileiros/assistencia/index.asp consulted 7 April 2006; Campbell and Meek, eds., *International immigration and nationality law*; Convenção sôbre dupla nacionalidade entre o Brasil e Portugal, in *Tratado sôbre nacionalidade*, ed. Ilmar Penna Marinho (Rio de Janeiro: Departamento de Imprensa Nacional, 1961); Anacleto de Magalhães Fernandes, *O direito da igualdade entre Portugal e Brasil* (São Paulo: Editôra Juriscrédi Ltda., 1972); Peggy Levitt, "Variations in transnational belonging: lessons from Brazil and the Dominican Republic", in *Dual nationality, social rights and federal citizenship in the U.S. and Europe. The reinvention of citizenship*, ed. Randall Hansen and Patrick Weil, 264–289, (New York: Berghahn Books, 2002); Ilmar Penna Marinho, *Tratado sôbre a nacionalidade*, 4 vols., vol. 4 (Rio de Janeiro: Departamento de Imprensa Nacional, 1961); Rui Manuel Moura Ramos, "La double nationalité et les liens spéciaux avec d'autres pays. Les développements et les perspectives au Portugal", *Revista de direito e economia* (1990–1993) vols. 16–19, 577–605.

Event	Law	Condition is renunciation/ loss of other nationality
State service	(naturalisation)	
Parent acquires nationality	No direct effect – may be naturalised concurrently	
Spouse acquires nationality	No direct effect	
Registration		
Special considerations		

Withdrawal/loss of nationality

Event	Law	Consequence of event is loss of nationality
Renunciation	No provision, unless upon naturalisation elsewhere (conditions)	
Attribution at birth conditional	No provision (see birth overseas and exercise of option)	
Naturalisation elsewhere	(*Provided that without naturalisation the Brasilian resident overseas would not be allowed permanent residence or the exercise of civil rights. This is interpreted according to will of the individual as to possession of Brazilian nationality*)	NO (*conditional*)
Adoption by a foreigner	No direct effect, although if leads to naturalisation, see above	NO
Marriage to a foreigner		NO
Spouse acquires other nationality		NO
Parent acquires other nationality		NO
Resumption of previous nationality		NO
Service to foreign state	(*But possible revocation of naturalisation for conviction related to crimes against the national interest*)	NO (*exception*)

Event	Law	**Consequence of event is loss of nationality**
Other attribution of nationality		NO (*but see naturalisation and birth*)
(Punitive) deprivation	Revocation of naturalisation for conviction related to crime against national interest	POSSIBLE

Special considerations

General attitude toward multiple nationality
There is no restriction on multiple nationality acquired at birth, according to foreign law. The Brazilian Constitution was amended in 1994 such that naturalisation elsewhere would not result in automatic deprivation of Brazilian nationality, but only in cases that amount to an individual desire to abandon Brazilian nationality. There are no fundamental distinctions between multiple and mono-nationals, although naturalised citizens cannot hold certain government offices.

Recognition of Multiple Nationality
Brazilian diplomatic and consular practice does not distinguish among Brazilians on the basis of multiple nationality, and offers the same services to all Brazilian nationals abroad.

*Canada[8]

Nationality category or status
Only one, and no technical distinction between nationality and citizenship.

Attribution/acquisition of nationality

Event	Law	Condition is renunciation/ loss of other nationality
Birth	In Canada (except to diplomat et al parents)	NO
	Foundlings deemed to be born in Canada	
	Overseas to Canadian parent	
Naturalisation	Upon fulfilment of requirements	NO
Adoption	Not automatic, only after permanent residence	
Legitimation	(see birth)	
Marriage	Not automatic	

---

[8] CANADA: *Citizenship Act* (updated to 3 March 2006), Department of Justice – Canada (internet), http://laws.justice.gc.ca/en/c–29/228322.html, consulted 7 April 2006; *Citizenship Regulations*, 1993 (updated to 21 February 2006), Department of Justice – Canada (internet), http://laws.justice.gc.ca/en/c–29/sor–93–246/73752.html, consulted 7 April 2006; *Dual citizenship*, Department of Citizenship and Immigration Canada (internet), http://www.cic.gc.ca/english/citizen/dualci%5Fe.html, consulted 1 April 2007; *Bill C-18 Key changes*, http://www.cic.gc.ca/english/policy/c18-changes.html, consulted 1 August 2003; *Dual citizenship: What travelers should know*, Department of Foreign Affairs and International Trade (internet), http://www.voyage.gc.ca/main/pubs/dual_citizenship-en.asp, consulted 7 April 2006; *Frequently asked questions*, Department of Foreign Affairs and International Trade (internet), http://www.voyage.gc.ca/main/before/faq-en.asp, consulted 7 April 2006; "Canada. Votes and migrants", The Economist, 10 June 2000, 43; "Sir, how dare you! It's a matter of honour", The Sydney Morning Herald, 20 June 2001, 13; Campbell and Meek, eds., *International immigration and nationality law*; Gerard-René de Groot, "Loss of nationality: a critical inventory", in *Rights and duties of dual nationals. Evolution and prospects*, ed. David A. Martin and Kay Hailbronner, 201–299, (The Hague: Kluwer Law International, 2003); Donald Galloway, "Citizenship rights and non-citizens: a Canadian perspective", in *Citizenship in a global world. Comparing citizenship rights for aliens*, ed. Atsushi Kondo, 176–195, (Houndmills (UK): Palgrave, 2001); J. Donald Galloway, "The dilemmas of Canadian citizenship law", *Georgetown Immigration Law Journal* (1999) vol. 13, no. 2, 201–231; José Woehrling, "Les politiques de la citoyenneté au Canada et au Québec", in *La citoyenneté européenne*, ed. Christian Philip and Panayotis Soldatos, 27–56, (Montréal: Université de Montréal, 2000).

Event	Law	Condition is renunciation/ loss of other nationality
Resumption	Fulfilment of requirements	NO
State service	Ministerial discretion for services of exceptional value	NO
Parent acquires nationality	No direct effect – nautralisation	
Spouse acquires nationality	No direct effect – naturalisation	
Registration	Former women citizens deprived of nationality upon marriage	NO
Special considerations	Ministerial discretion in conferring citizenship in cases of hardship	NO

Withdrawal/loss of nationality

Event	Law	Consequence of event is loss of nationality
Renunciation	Of right if: adult, lives outside Canada, and has or will receive another nationality, no mental disability – understands significance	YES
Attribution at birth conditional	If birth overseas and parent also born outside Canada, loss at age 28 unless application to retain, has residence in Canada within certain time-frame, or has close connection to Canada	YES
Naturalisation elsewhere		NO
Adoption by a foreigner		NO
Marriage to a foreigner		NO
Spouse acquires other nationality		NO
Parent acquires other nationality		NO
Resumption of previous nationality		NO
Service to foreign state		NO

Event	Law	Consequence of event is loss of nationality
Other attribution of nationality		NO
(Punitive) deprivation	Revocation of any obtention, retention, renunciation or resumption of citizenship for fraud	POSSIBLE

General attitude toward multiple nationality

Canada's Department of Citizenship and Immigration states that Canadian law "makes it possible to have two or more citizenships and allegiances at the same time for an indefinite period . . . Whenever you are in a country that recognizes you as a citizen, its laws take priority over the laws of any other country of which you are a citizen. International treaties may, however, allow exceptions to this rule". A bill tabled in 2002 proposed to restrict citizenship of those born abroad to two generations, but did not act on a 1994 Parliamentary Committee's opinion that Canadians naturalised abroad might be deprived of Canadian nationality, indicating that the latter should be seen more in relation to the almost concurrent referendum related to the status of Québec as part of Canada, and political rejection of dual nationality for Québecois in the context of an independent Québec.

Recognition of Multiple Nationality

Canada may attempt to assist its multiple nationals even in their other countries of nationality, but warns its citizens that this may be impossible and viewed as outside interference in an internal matter. Canada advises that its citizens should always use Canadian passports and obtain visas even for other countries of citizenship, and has concluded several consular treaties that provide for international protection according to use of passport and issuance of an appropriate visa, thus allowing its citizens potentially to be treated as foreigners in certain situations. There is no obligation on citizens to use a Canadian passport to enter Canada, but citizens are advised that it is the only document that will guarantee their entry.

Chile[9]

Nationality category or status
Only one, and the Constitution distinguishes specifically between nationality and citizenship.

Attribution/acquisition of nationality

Event	Law	Condition is renunciation/ loss of other nationality
Birth	In Chile (except to transient foreign parents or those in foreign state service – children of these groups may exercise right of option)	NO
	Overseas to Chilean parent, provided that one parent or grandparent obtained Chilean nationality by birth in Chile, naturalisation, or special naturalisation (conditions)	
Naturalisation	Upon fulfillment of requirements	NO
Adoption	Not automatic – naturalisation possible (conditions)	
Legitimation	See birth	
Marriage	No automatic effect	
Resumption		

---

[9] CHILE: *Constitución Política de la República de Chile*, 8 August 1980 (last modified 25 August 2001), *Código Civil*, 16 May 2000 (updated to 24 July 2001), **UNHCR (internet)**; *Reformas constitucionales Ley Nº 20.050 en materia de nacionalidad*, Consulate General of Chile in New York (internet), http://www.chileny.com/00tramites.html, consulted 25 May 2005; *Reformas artículo XI–XIII*, Consulate General of Chile in New York (internet), http://www.chileny.com/00tramites.html, consulted 25 May 2005; *Aprobadas reformas constitucionales: dos articulados benefician a los chilenos en el exterior*, Consulate General of Chile in New York (internet), http://www.chileny.com/01noticias.html, consulted 25 May 2006; *Chilenos en el exterior*, Ministerio de Relaciones Exteriores, August 2005 (internet), http://www.gobiernodechile.cl/chilenos_exterior/registro_chilenos_exterior.pdf, consulted 25 May 2006; *Convenio de doble nacionalidad con Chile (Chile-España)*, 24 May 1958, Ministerio de Trabajo y Asuntos Sociales, Secretaría de Estado de Inmigración y Emigración – España (internet), http://extranjeros.mtas.es/es/normativa_jurisprudencia/Internacional/doblenac/CHILE.pdf, consulted 25 May 2006; *La nacionalidad, después de la reforma* (internet), http://www.chile.com/tpl/articulo/detalle/ver.tpl?cod_articulo=70870, consulted 25 May 2006; *¿Cómo se puede solicitar la ciudadanía chilena?*, Ministerio del Interior de Chile (internet), http://www.tramitefacil.gov.cl/1481/article-47207.html, consulted 27 May 2006.

Event	Law	Condition is renunciation/ loss of other nationality
State service		
Parent acquires nationality		
Spouse acquires nationality		
Registration / Option	Right of option for nationality for those born in Chile who did not acquire nationality at birth because parents were foreign diplomats or only had transient presence	NO
Special considerations		

Withdrawal/loss of nationality

Event	Law	Consequence of event is loss of nationality
Renunciation	Possible only upon previous naturalisation abroad	YES
Attribution at birth conditional	No provision	
Naturalisation elsewhere		NO
Adoption by a foreigner		NO
Marriage to a foreigner		NO
Spouse acquires other nationality		NO
Parent acquires other nationality		NO
Resumption of previous nationality		NO
Service to foreign state	Service to Chile's enemies or allies during an international war	POSSIBLE
Other attribution of nationality		NO

| | | **Consequence of event is** |
Event	**Law**		**loss of nationality**
(Punitive) deprivation	Cancellation of naturalisation possible; special naturalizations may be revoked by law; service to Chile's enemies or allies during an international war	POSSIBLE

Special considerations

General attitude toward multiple nationality
Chile revised its Constitutional provisions on attribution and loss of nationality in 2005, making loss of nationality possible only upon express renunciation in cases of naturalisation abroad. The Constitution's provisions requiring express renunciation of previous nationality as a condition of naturaliation in Chile and for loss of Chilean nationality in most cases of naturalisation abroad were eliminated. Those who previously lost Chilean nationality as a consequence of naturalisation abroad can apply to have the official records of loss of nationality changed, with retroactive effect, and are thus held never to have lost their Chilean nationality. The changes were billed as benefiting Chileans resident overseas. Multiple nationals are not otherwise the subject of special provisions, but the Presidency is limited to Chileans by birth. Likewise, rights of citizenship can be exercised by citizens born overseas or by virtue of special naturalisation only upon one year's residence. Whereas nationality can be lost only be express renunciation, deprivation of citizenship is possible. Foreign residents who live in Chile for at least five years may be allowed to take part in suffrage.

Recognition of Multiple Nationality
Chilean multiple nationals must enter and depart Chile on Chilean travel documents.

*People's Republic of China[10]

Nationality category or status
Only one, although Chinese citizens who are officially Hong Kong or Macao permanent residents arguably belong to different categories of Chinese nationality, as they would be returned to those territories, and Chinese nationality legislation is interpreted differently in their regard (see the section on Hong Kong herein).

---

[10] CHINA: *Law of the People's Republic of China on the Protection of the Rights and Interests of Returned Overseas Chinese and the Family Members of Overseas Chinese*, 1 January 1991; *Rules for the Implementation of the Law of the People's Republic of China on the Control of the Exit and Entry of Citizens*, 26 December 1986; *Law of the People's Republic of China on the Control of the Exit and Entry of Citizens*, 1 February 1986; *Provisional Measures for the Control of Chinese Citizens Entering and Leaving the Regions of Hong Kong and Macao for Personal Reasons*, 25 December 1986; *Nationality Law of the People's Republic of China – China Law No. 71*, 10 September 1980, **UNHCR (internet)**; *Nationality Law of the People's Republic of China* (adopted at the Third Session of the Fifth NPC, promulgated by Order no. 8 of the Chairman of the Standing Committee of the NPC and effective 10 September 1980), in Immigration Department of the Hong Kong Special Administrative Region of the People's Republic of China: *Naturalization as a Chinese national. Nationality law of the People's Republic of China. A guide for applicants*, vol. ID874A (Hong Kong: Immigration Department of the Hong Kong Special Administrative Region of the People's Republic of China, 2001); *China (including the Hong Kong Special Administrative Region), A guide for Canadian visitors*, Department of Foreign Affairs and International Trade (internet), http://www.voyage.gc.ca/main/pubs/china-en.asp, consulted 7 April 2006; *Deputy Director General Wei Wei of the Department of Consular Affairs of the Ministry of Foreign Affairs Accepts an Interview with the China Youth Daily on the Issue of Consular Protection*, 28 December 2005, Ministry of Foreign Affairs of the PRC (internet), http://www.fmprc.gov.cn/eng/zxxx/t228775.htm, consulted 7 April 2006; *Guide to China's Consular Protection and Services Overseas*, 16 June 2004, Embassy of the PRC in the Kingdom of the Netherlands (internet), http://www.china-embassy.nl/eng/xwdt/t137432.htm, consulted 7 April 2006; *Table of Consular conventions and Agreements Between China and Foreign Countries*, 18 May 2004, Embassy of the PRC in the Republic of Estonia (internet), http://www.chinaembassy.ee/eng/lsqw/lsxx/t111172.htm, consulted 7 April 2006; *Consular information sheet. China*, 13 September 2005, United States Department of State (internet), http://travel.state.gov/travel/cis_pa_tw/cis/cis_1089.html, consulted 7 April 2006; *Minjian xiuxian huiyiti "shuangshi jianyi" yu quxiao zhuanzheng*, Duoweixinwen (internet), www.chinesenewsnet.com, consulted 1 August 2003; "China: Returnees. No place like home", Far Eastern Economic Review, 15 June 2000, 72–75; Tung-Pi Chen, "The nationality law of the People's Republic of China and the overseas Chinese in Hong Kong, Macao and South-east Asia", *New York Law School Journal of International and Comparative Law* (1984) vol. 5, 281–325; Jerome Alan Cohen and Hungdah Chiu, *People's China and international law. A documentary study*, vol. 1 (Princeton, NJ: Princeton University Press, 1973); Jerome Alan Cohen and Shao-Chuan Leng, "The Sino-Indian dispute over the internment and detention of Chinese in India", in *China's practice of international law: some case studies*, ed. Jerome Alan Cohen, 268, (Cambridge, MA: Harvard University Press, 1972);

Attribution/acquisition of nationality

Event	Law	Condition is renunciation/ loss of other nationality
Birth	In China to a Chinese parent	NO
	In China to stateless parents (or of uncertain nationality) and who have settled in China	
	Overseas to a Chinese parent (unless parent has settled abroad and child acquires foreign nationality automatically at birth)	
Naturalisation	Upon fulfilment of requirements	YES
Adoption	Unclear if automatic – probably	NO
Legitimation	(see birth: law does not address paternity in rel. to nationality)	
Marriage	Not automatic – may lead to facilitated naturalisation	
Resumption	Possible upon fulfillment of requirements	YES
State service		
Parent acquires nationality	No direct effect – may lead to facilitated naturalisation	
Spouse acquires nationality	No direct effect – may lead to facilitated naturalisation	
Special considerations		

George Ginsburgs, "The 1980 nationality law of the People's Republic of China", *American Journal of Comparative Law* (1982) vol. 30, 459–498; Shao-Chuan Leng and Hungdah Chiu, eds., *Law in Chinese foreign policy: Communist China and selected problems of international law* (Dobbs Ferry, NY: Oceana Publications, Inc., 1972); Sasmojo, ed., *Menjelesaikan masalah dwikewarganegaraan RI-RRT* (Jakarta: Penerbit Djambatan, 1959); Sheng Yu, "China's nationality law and the principles of international law", in *Selected articles from the Chinese Yearbook of International Law*, ed. Chinese Society of International Law, 204–219 (Beijing: China Translation and Publishing Corp., 1983); Wang Keju, "Basic principles of the nationality law of the People's Republic of China", in *Selected Articles from the Chinese Yearbook of International Law*, ed. Chinese Society of International Law, 220–239, (Beijing: China Translation and Publishing Corp., 1983).

Withdrawal/loss of nationality

Event	Law	Consequence of event is loss of nationality
Renunciation	Possible if: have foreign relatives; settled abroad; other legitimate reasons; but not if in government or military service. In any case subject to government approval	YES
Attribution at birth conditional	No provision	
Naturalisation elsewhere	And settlement abroad, or settlement abroad and any voluntary acquisition of foreign nationality	YES
Adoption by a foreigner	Probably no effect	NO
Marriage to a foreigner		NO
Spouse acquires other nationality		NO
Parent acquires other nationality		NO
Resumption of previous nationality	Any voluntary acquisition of foreign nationality (but see naturalisation and renunciation)	YES
Service to foreign state		
Other attribution of nationality	Any voluntary acquisition of foreign nationality	YES
(Punitive) deprivation		
Special considerations		

General attitude toward multiple nationality

Chinese law never recognises foreign nationality, although it does not prevent multiple nationality at birth in China or upon birth overseas if the parents have not settled abroad. Some countries warn their citizens that Chinese practice does not always uniformly reflect the provisions of the Nationality Law: naturalisation abroad should provoke loss of Chinese nationality, but for certain persons who are deemed to have left China while not fulfilling all legal requirements, an official renunciation process is required. Likewise, children of Chinese nationals born outside China acquire Chinese nationality unless their parents have "settled abroad", reportedly also a definition that allows for flexibility in interpretation. Use of another country's passport, however, reportedly usually guarantees recognition of that country's right to consular protection of the individual concerned. Historically, in relation to overseas Chinese, the PRC's practice seems characterised by reassurance to various countries that naturalisation abroad would provoke expatriation in China, while demonstrating strong resistance to any forced naturalisation of Chinese citizens in those countries. A major conference in June 2003 planning policy-related objectives over the next ten years, in which a former Minister of Information and current members of the National People's Congress participated, signifying some level of state involvement and approval, concluded that China should introduce multiple nationality for its citizens who reside overseas within ten years.

Recognition of Multiple Nationality
The Nationality Law states that the PRC does not recognise dual nationality for any Chinese national, and Chinese consular practice is to emphasise that any voluntary acquisition of a foreign nationality results in loss of Chinese nationality, and thus no diplomatic or consular protection. With respect to multiple nationality produced at birth, the policy of non-recognition seems to mean that China would attempt to protect its nationals in any case, although no evidence could be found of such practice. Regarding exit and entry, Chinese law states that citizens must use Chinese documents with proper endorsements. The treaty on dual nationality with Indonesia of 1955 was unilaterally abrogated by Indonesia in 1969. Various consular agreements with other nations provide for recognition of foreign nationality upon use of a passport with a valid visa, and several informal agreements regarding choice of nationality of children born with dual nationality may still be applied (for example, Mongolia).

Colombia[11]

Nationality category or status
Only one, but the Constitution distinguishes between nationality and citizenship specifically, providing that citizenship is lost when nationality is renounced.

Attribution/acquisition of nationality

Event	Law	Condition is renunciation/ loss of other nationality
Birth	In Colombia to a Colombian parent or parent born in Colombia	NO
	In Colombia to foreign parents one of whom was domiciled in Colombia at the time of birth	
	To a Colombian parent abroad and registered with authorities or later domiciled in Colombia	
Naturalisation	Upon fulfillment of conditions	NO
Adoption		
Legitimation		
Marriage	Facilitated naturalisation	
Resumption	Possible two years after loss (conditions)	NO

---

[11] COLOMBIA: *Constitución Política de la República de Colombia de 1991* (as amended until 2005), Base de Datos Políticos de las Américas (internet), http://pdba.georgetown.edu/ Constitutions/Colombia/col91.html, consulted 15 May 2006; *Ley 43 de 1993 – Nacionalidad* (1 February 1993), *Decreto 4000/04 Visas: nuevas normas sobre expedición de visas, control de extranjeros y migración* (27 December 2004), *Ley 649 de 2001* (27 March 2001), *Decreto 1869 de 1994* (3 August 1993), *Decreto 286 de 1993* (10 February 1993), **UNHCR (internet)**; *Ley 638 de 2001*, Secretaria del Senado de Colombia (internet), http://www.secretariasenado. gov.co/leyes/L0638001.htm, consulted 15 May 2005; *Decreto 3541*, 26 December 1980, Centro de Información Migratoria para América Latina (internet), http://www.cimal.cl/cimal/interior/ legislacion_migratoria/colombia/decretos/d_3541_80.htm, consulted 15 May 2006; *Nacionalidad colombiana por adopción*, *Recuperación de la nacionalidad colombiana*, *Renuncia a la nacionalidad colombiana*, Ministerio de Relaciones Exteriores de la República de Colombia (internet), http://portal.minrelext.gov.co/portal/?MIval=po_tr_co_obtener_nacionali- dad&id_tramite=7, consulted 15 May 2006; *Doble nacionalidad*, Consulado General de Colombia en Chicago (internet), http://www.consulcolombia.us/doble.php, consulted 15 May 2006; *Nacionalidad Colombiana*, Consulado General de Colombia en Sydney (internet), http://www. consuladodecolombiasydney.org.au/SServicio07.htm, consulted 21 May 2006.

Event	Law	**Condition is renunciation/ loss of other nationality**
State service Parent acquires nationality	Minor children may be naturalised with parent	
Spouse acquires	No direct effect	
Registration	Facilitated naturalisation possible for various categories (Latin Americans, Caribbean citizens, members of indigenous tribes on border, Spaniards)	
Special considerations	Those naturalised during minority must confirm desire to be Colombian upon attaining majority (conditions)	

Withdrawal/loss of nationality

Event	Law	**Consequence of event is loss of nationality**
Renunciation	Possible for multiple nationals or if about to acquire foreign nationality (obligations owed persist notwithstanding loss)	YES
Attribution at birth conditional	No provision	
Naturalisation elsewhere		NO
Adoption by a foreigner		NO
Marriage to a foreigner		NO
Spouse acquires other nationality		NO
Parent acquires other nationality		NO
Resumption of previous nationality		NO
Service to foreign state		NO
Other attribution of nationality		NO

Event	Law	**Consequence of event is loss of nationality**
(Punitive) deprivation	Possible revocation of naturalisation for fraud, crimes commited before naturalisation	POSSIBLE
	Possible deprivation for naturalised citizens for crimes against the existence and security of the state and the constitutional order	

Special considerations

General attitude toward multiple nationality
Colombia's 1991 Constitution introduced a "principle of dual nationality" whereby Colombians who are naturalised abroad do not thereby lose Colombian nationality, and persons naturalised in Colombia are not obliged to renounce their previous nationality. Renunciation of nationality in the form of a simple oath or affirmation upon naturalisation elsewhere is held to be ineffective. The Constitution provides that Colombian multiple nationals may be subject to laws limiting their assumption of political positions in government. It states that multiple nationals may not be members of Congress, with the exception of Colombians by birth. The Nationality Act provides that Colombians by birth who acquire another nationality do not lose civil and political rights given them by the Constitution and law. Naturalised Colombians are, however, barred from becomnig President, Vice President, Senator, certain judicial appointments, Attorney General, Foreign or Defense Minister, Officer in the Armed Forces, director of security or intelligence services, among other positions. If they are also multiple nationals, they are also barred from being members of Congress, and ministers and directors of administrative departments. The Constitution also provides that former Colombians who renounced nationality can be tried and sentenced for treason should they act against Colombian interests in a war against Colombia. It further provides that naturalised Colombians and foreigners domiciled in Colombia may not be obliged to take up arms against their country of origin. Likewise, Colombians naturalised abroad may not be forced to take up arms against their "new" country of nationality. A 1979 treaty regulating dual nationality with Spain which provides for resumption of the original nationality upon acquisition of domicile and fulfilment of other conditions was modified by an Additional Protocol in 1998. The Protocol recognises that Colombians and Spaniards no longer lose their nationality upon naturalisation overseas, and provides that persons affected by the 1979 treaty can recover their civil and political rights in the country concerned by simple notification. It stipulates that Colombian-Spanish dual nationals may not invoke one nationality against the other country of nationality.

Recognition of Multiple Nationality
Colombian multiple nationals must enter and depart Colombia using Colombian travel documents, and identify themselves as Colombians in all civil and political acts.

*Cook Islands[12]

Nationality category or status

The Cook Islands does not have its own legislation on nationality, and all Cook Islanders are New Zealand nationals (citizens). The Joint Centenary Declaration between New Zealand and the Cook Islands confirms the Cooks' independent statehood, but states that its people will retain New Zealand citizenship, "upholding the fundamental values on which that citizenship is based". The Declaration stipulates that "[t]he Government of the Cook Islands will accord New Zealand citizens preferential consideration in respect of entry into and residence in the Cook Islands", confirming the Cooks' capacity to enact nationality legislation of its own, which is as yet only expressed in terms of residency (or for example in qualification of electors). Nonetheless, at the time of the Declaration (June 2001) the New Zealand Prime Minister declared that nothing stood in the way of the Cooks declaring "full independence", and media reports claimed that should the Cooks seek admission to the United Nations or the Commonwealth, that New Zealand citizenship might be lost. The popular consensus and within government in the Cook Islands is reportedly to maintain the citizenship link to New Zealand, above and beyond any other aspirations. Although New Zealand legislation on nationality is separate from Cook Islands' legislation on permanent residence, the provisions below relate to New Zealand citizenship. Those related to Cook Islands permanent residence are added *in italics*. References to "New Zealand" are defined to include the Cook Islands, Niue and Tokelau.

---

[12] COOK ISLANDS: *Citizenship Act 1977 (last amended 2005)*, No. 61, Statutes of New Zealand, 8 March 2006, Parliamentary Counsel Office, http://www.legislation.govt.nz/browse_vw.asp?content-set=pal_statutes, consulted 8 April 2006; *Citizenship-Raraunga*, The Department of Internal Affairs (internet), http://www.citizenship.govt.nz/diawebsite.nsf/wpg_URL/Services-Citizenship-Index?OpenDocument, consulted 8 April 2006; *New Zealand Citizens*, Ministry of Foreign Affairs and Trade (internet), http://www.mfat.govt.nz/nzcitizens.html, consulted 8 April 2006; *New Zealand-Cook Islands: Joint Centenary Declaration*, June 2001, Ministry for Foreign Affairs and Trade (internet), http://www.mfat.govt.nz/foreign/regions/pacific/cookislandseclaration/cooksdec.html, consulted 7 April 2006; *Cook Islands Country Paper*, March 2006, Ministry of Foreign Affairs and Trade, http://www.mfat.govt.nz/foreign/regions/pacific/country/cookislandspaper.html, consulted 8 April 2006; "Laws of the Cook Islands 1994. Constitution, statutes and subsidiary legislation", vol. 2 (Rarotonga: Legislative Service of the Cook Islands, 1994); Rosemary Gordon and Anthony Angelo, "Laws of the Cook Islands. Indexes, Constitution, supplement, statutes 1994–1997", (Rarononga: The Crown in right of the Cook Islands, 1997). *Constitution Amendment (No. 9) Act 1980–81*, in "Laws of the Cook Islands", (Rarotonga); Campbell and Meek, eds., *International immigration and nationality law*; Paul Spoonley, "Aliens and citizens in New Zealand", in *Citizenship in a global world. Comparing citizenship rights for aliens*, ed. Atsushi Kondo, 158–175, (Houndmills (UK): Palgrave, 2001); "Cook Islands: Kiwis to Cook Islands: Full independence whenever you want", PINA Nius Online, 13 June 2001 (internet); "Cook Islands puts New Zealand citizenship first", PINA News Online, 14 June 2001 (internet); "New Zealand Minister invited to attend celebrations in Cook Islands", PACNEWS, 19 January 2001 (internet), held by author; "Kiwis float plan for joint citizenship", The Australian, 10 August 2000, 1.

Attribution/acquisition of nationality

Event	Law	Condition is renunciation/ loss of other nationality
Birth	In New Zealand (all references to NZ include the Cook Islands, Niue and Tokelau) to at least one New Zealand parent or permanent resident (or parent entitled to reside permanently in the Cook Islands, Niue or Tokelau)	NO
	In New Zealand if otherwise stateless	
	Overseas to New Zealand parent who is in govt/public service (citizen by birth)	
	Overseas to a New Zealand parent who is a citizen otherwise than by descent (additionally, ministerial discretion in grant to children of citizens by descent if in public interest)	
	In the Cook Islands to a Cook Islands parent	
Naturalisation	Fulfilment of requirements (including for citizens by descent)	NO
	Application for Cook Islands permanent residence upon fulfillment of requirements	
Adoption	Child deemed born at place and time of adoption (conditions)	NO
	Adoption outside NZ by NZ citizen other than by descent (conditions)	
	By a Cook Islands parent	
Legitimation	(see birth)	
Marriage	Not automatic – facilitated naturalisation	
Resumption	For those who renounced, only via naturalisation provisions	NO
State service		
Parent acquires	No direct effect – facilitated naturalisation possible	

APPENDIX

Event	Law	Condition is renunciation/ loss of other nationality
Spouse acquires nationality	No direct effect – facilitated naturalisation possible	
Registration	Persons born prior to 1 January 1978 to NZ mother citizen by birth	NO
Special considerations	Ministerial discretion in granting citizenship to stateless persons	

Withdrawal/loss of nationality

Event	Law	Consequence of event is loss of nationality
Renunciation	Possible if adult of full capacity who is multiple national, but may be declined if resident in NZ or NZ in state of war	YES
Attribution at birth conditional	No provision	
Naturalisation elsewhere	(Deprivation possible if adult acquires foreign nationality by voluntary act (not marriage) and commits acts against NZ, or exercises other rights/ duties contrary to NZ interests)	NO (but deprivation possible)
Adoption by a foreigner		NO
Marriage to a foreigner		NO
Spouse acquires other nationality		NO
Parent acquires other nationality		NO
Resumption of previous nationality		NO
Service to foreign state	(see naturalisation elsewhere)	NO
Other attribution of nationality	(see naturalisation elsewhere)	NO
(Punitive) deprivation	For citizenship by naturalisation, registration or grant: fraud in acq.	YES
Special considerations	*Cook Islands permanent residence acquired by grant of certificate may be lost upon three years absence*	

General attitude toward multiple nationality

New Zealand accepts multiple nationality for its citizens. The NZ Citizenship Act provides that loss of citizenship does not result in the discharge of obligations owed while still a citizen. No distinction is made on the basis of multiple nationality.

Recognition of Multiple Nationality

New Zealand nationals may use foreign passports to enter and depart New Zealand, and may even be provided with resident return visas should they wish. There does not appear to be a difference in the exercise of international protection on the basis of multiple nationality.

Costa Rica[13]

Nationality category or status
Only one, and the Constitution creates a distinction between nationality and citizenship.

Attribution/acquisition of nationality

Event	Law	Condition is renunciation/ loss of other nationality
Birth	In Costa Rica to a Costa Rican parent	NO
	Overseas to Costa Rican parent citizen by birth and registered by parent while a minor or by him/herself before age 25	
	In Costa Rica to foreign parents and registered by parent while a minor or by him/herself before age 25	
	Foundling	
Naturalisation	Upon fulfillment of requirements	NO
Adoption		
Legitimation		
Marriage	If woman thereby loses her previous nationality, otherwise facilitated naturalisation	NO
Resumption		
State service	By naturalisation, if honorary nationality granted by Legislative Assembly	

---

[13] COSTA RICA: *Constitución Política de la República de Costa Rica*, 7 November 1949 (as amended until 1995), **UNHCR (internet)**; *Convenio de doble nacionalidad con Costa Rica (Costa Rica – España)*, 8 June 1964, Ministerio de Trabajo y Asuntos Sociales, Secretaría de Estado de Inmigración y Emigración – España (internet), http://extranjeros.mtas.es/es/ normativa_jurisprudencia/Internacional/doblenac/COSTA_RICA.pdf, consulted 25 May 2006; *Protocolo adicional entre el Reino de España y la República de Costa Rica modificando el Convenio de Doble Nacionalidad de 8 de junio de 1964, hecho «ad referendum» en Madrid*, 23 October 1997 (internet), http://www.intermigra.info/semiex/archivos/legislacion/cdn_08_01.htm, consulted 25 May 2006; *Al ingresar a un país extranjero*, Ministerio de Relaciones Exteriores y Culto, Servicio Exterior (internet), http://www.rree.go.cr/servicio-exterior/index.php?stp=61&langtype=&SID=, consulted 25 May 2006.

Event	Law	Condition is renunciation/ loss of other nationality
Parent acquires nationality	Minor children acquire automatically with parent	NO
Spouse acquires nationality		
Registration		
Special considerations		

Withdrawal/loss of nationality

Event	Law	Consequence of event is loss of nationality
Renunciation	Not possible – Costa Rican nationality cannot be lost and no deprivation is possible	NO
Attribution at birth conditional	No provision	
Naturalisation elsewhere		NO
Adoption by a foreigner		NO
Marriage to a foreigner		NO
Spouse acquires other nationality		NO
Parent acquires other nationality		NO
Resumption of previous nationality		NO
Service to foreign state		NO
Other attribution of nationality		NO
(Punitive) deprivation	Costa Rican nationality cannot be lost and no deprivation is possible – citizenship can be suspended by judicial decision	NO
Special considerations		

General attitude toward multiple nationality

Costa Rica accepts multiple nationality for its citizens. Naturalisation abroad does not provoke loss of Costa Rican nationality, and loss of previous nationality is not a condition of naturalisation in Costa Rica. Multiple nationals are not subject to special provisions, but naturalised citizens cannot vote until one year after naturalisation, or be elected deputies of the Legislative Assembly or appointed as a government Minister until ten years' residence in Costa Rica after having obtained nationality. The Convention on Dual Nationality with Spain of 8 June 1964 was revised by an additional protocol in 1997, allowing for those who had taken advantage of the Convention to opt for its application to cease with respect to them, without losing either of the two nationalities.

Recognition of Multiple Nationality

Costa Rica's advice to its citizens should they have troubles abroad does not mention multiple nationality, only that Costa Rican consuls will aid Costa Rican nationals in all ways possible.

Cyprus[14]

Nationality category or status

Only one, and no distinction between nationality and citizenship.

Attribution/acquisition of nationality

Event	Law	Condition is renunciation/ loss of other nationality
Birth	In Cyprus to a Cypriot parent (including deceased parent) unless one parent illegal entry (conditions)	NO
	Overseas to a Cypriot parent (including deceased parent) and birth registered within two years (conditions)	
Naturalisation	Upon fulfillment of conditions	POSSIBLE (*exceptions*)
	(*the government has latitude to require renunciation as a condition of naturalisation in any case or class of cases*)	
Adoption	Adoption according to relevant law of personal status – see birth	
Legitimation	Legitimation according to relevant law of personal status – see birth	
Marriage	Facilitated registration possible (conditions)	

---

[14] CYPRUS: *Republic of Cyprus Citizenship Law*, 1967, as amended until 1999 (internet), http://www.uniset.ca/nold/cypnaten.pdf, consulted 25 May 2006; *Information for overseas and repatriated Cypriots – Matters of citizenship*, Ministry of Foreign Affairs of the Republic of Cyprus (internet), http://www.mfa.gov.cy/mfa/mfa.nsf/OverseasUsefulInfoDisplay?OpenForm& InfoID=FD535E468ACD070BC2256B7600225034, consulted 25 May 2006; *Information for overseas and repatriated Cypriots – Entry and stay in Cyprus*, Ministry of Foreign Affairs of the Republic of Cyprus (internet), http://www.mfa.gov.cy/mfa/mfa.nsf/OverseasUsefulInfoDisplay? OpenForm&InfoID=08AB0A320E4266B0C2256B760022D556, consulted 25 May 2006; *Registration of persons of Cypriot origin as citizens of the Republic of Cyprus and acquisition of the Cypriot citizenship by naturalisation*, Embassy of Cyprus in Sweden (internet), http://www.cyprusemb.se/Dbase/cypemb/registration_of_persons.asp, consulted 25 May 2006; *European Bulletin on Nationality – Cyprus*, 18 October 2002, Council of Europe (internet), http://www.coe.int/T/E/Legal_Affairs/Legal_co-operation/Foreigners_and_citizens/Nationality/ Documents/Bulletin/Cyprus%20E.pdf, consulted 25 May 2006.

		Condition is renunciation/ loss of other nationality
Event	**Law**	
Resumption	Possible registration upon Minister's approval	
State service		
Parent acquires nationality	Child may be registered as a citizen (conditions)	
Spouse acquires nationality		
Registration	Possible for various categories, including: those born to Cypriot mothers between 1960–1999, upon reaching full age; persons descended from persons born in Cyprus between 1914–1960 and resident there; Commonwealth/foreign citizens of Cypriot origin; certain spouses, widows, widowers of citizens or persons with right to citizenship (conditions)	NO
Special considerations		

Withdrawal/loss of nationality

		Consequence of event is loss of nationality
Event	**Law**	
Renunciation	Possible if of full age and capacity and multiple national (may be refused in wartime or if aim is to avoid military service or criminal prosecution – conditions)	YES
Attribution at birth conditional	No provision	
Naturalisation elsewhere		NO
Adoption by a foreigner		NO
Marriage to a foreigner		NO
Spouse acquires other nationality		NO

Event	Law	**Consequence of event is loss of nationality**
Parent acquires other nationality		NO
Resumption of previous nationality		NO
Service to foreign state		NO
Other attribution of nationality		NO
(Punitive) deprivation	For naturalised citizens: fraud in acquisition; disloyal/disaffected; assistance to enemy in wartime; certain sentence within five years of naturalisation; continuous residence abroad for seven years not in government service or no annual registration at Consulate (conditions) For citizens by registration: fraud in acquisition	YES

Special considerations

General attitude toward multiple nationality
Cyprus states that it accepts dual citizenship. Although the government leaves itself latitude to make exceptions, renunciation of foreign nationality is not specifically a condition of naturalisation, and naturalisation abroad does not provoke loss of Cypriot nationality. Persons of Cypriot descent are considered "Overseas Cypriots", and are accorded facilitated registration as nationals. They "may enter Cyprus without a visa and work in Cyprus without formalities for an unlimited perid of time". Certain government-related positions require Cypriot citizenship, but multiple nationality is not a bar.

Czech Republic[15]

Nationality category or status

Only one, and no technical distinction between nationality and citizenship.

Attribution/acquisition of nationality

Event	Law	Condition is renunciation/ loss of other nationality
Birth	To a Czech parent	NO
	In the Czech Republic to stateless parents, at least one of whom has permanent residence	
	Foundling under 18, except when proved acquired another nationality at birth)	
Naturalization	Upon fulfillment of requirements	YES (*exceptions*)
	(*Exceptions to the requirement that foreign nationality be lost as a condition of naturalisation can include: refugees; if cannot secure release or on unreasonable terms; would expose applicant or family to persecution; person's acquisition of nationality would benefit Czech Republic in*	

---

[15] CZECH REPUBLIC: *Constitution of the Czech Republic*, 16 December 1992 (as amended until 2002), Parliament of the Czech Republic (internet), http://www.psp.cz/cgi-bin/ eng/docs/laws/constitution.html, consulted 25 May 2006; *Act No. 40/1993 on gaining and losing citizenship of the Czech Republic*, 29 December 1992, Parliament of the Czech Republic (internet), http://www.psp.cz/cgi-bin/dee/docs/laws/1993/40_index.html, consulted 25 May 2006; *Law No. 194 changing the Law No. 40/1993 Coll. on acquisition and loss of the citizenship of the Czech Republic in the reading of later regulations*, 29 July 1999, *Act No. 216 concerning travel documents and travel abroad*, 15 May 1991 (as amended 26 April 1996), **UNHCR (internet)**; *European Bulletin on Nationality – Czech Republic*, 28 July 2004, Council of Europe (internet), http://www.coe.int/t/e/legal_affairs/legal_co-operation/foreigners_and_ citizens/nationality/documents/bulletin/Czech%20Republic%202004%20E.pdf, consulted 25 May 2006; *Citizenship*, Czech Consulate General in New York (internet), http://www. mzv.cz/wwwo/default.asp?ido=12886&idj=2&amb=114, consulted 25 May 2006; *Adoption in the Czech Republic*, Czech Consulate General in New York (internet), http://www.mzv.cz/ wwwo/default.asp?ParentIDO=7331&ido=8071&amb=114&idj=2, consulted 25 May 2006.

Event	Law	Condition is renunciation/ loss of other nationality
	terms of science, culture, sports, society; over 20 years' residence; certain former nationals – conditions).	
Adoption	By Czech parent	NO
Legitimation	Upon determination of paternity (conditions)	NO
Marriage	Facilitated naturalisation possible	
Resumption	Facilitated naturalisation possible (condition of renunciation may be waived)	
State service	Facilitated naturalisation possible (condition of renunciation may be waived if person's acquisition of nationality would benefit Czech Republic in terms of science, culture, sports, society)	
Parent acquires nationality	Children under 15 may be included in parent's naturalisation – foreign spouse must agree to child's loss of foreign nationality (conditions)	
Spouse acquires nationality	Spouses may make joint application for naturalisation	
Registration/ (Declaration)	Possible for certain categories including certain citizens of Czechoslovakia and their children, descendants; certain long-term permanent residents of Czechoslovakia including children under 15, certain former Czechoslovak nationals – conditions)	NO
Special considerations	Legal guardian may apply for child under 15 to acquire by naturalisation	

Withdrawal/loss of nationality

Event	Law	Consequence of event is loss of nationality
Renunciation	Possible if not permanent resident and multiple national or about to acquire foreign nationality – married couples may file jointly and parent may include	YES

Event	Law	**Consequence of event is loss of nationality**
	child under 15 with consent of other parent (conditions)	
Attribution at birth conditional	No provision	
Naturalisation elsewhere	*(Exceptions include when nationality obtained in connection with marriage; Czech nationals who were nationals of Czecholslovakia prior to 1993 who acquire Slovakian nationality)*	YES *(exception)*
Adoption by a foreigner		NO
Marriage to a foreigner	Acquisition of a spouse's foreign nationality in connection with marriage (even voluntary naturalisation abroad) does not provoke loss of Czech nationality	NO
Spouse acquires other nationality	No automatic effect	NO
Parent acquires other nationality	Parent's loss of Czech nationality may be extended to minor children; any voluntary acquisition of foreign nationality, including on parent's authorisation during minority	YES
Resumption of previous nationality	Any voluntary acquisition of foreign nationality not linked to marriage or when automatic acquisition	YES
Service to foreign state		
Other attribution of nationality	Any voluntary acquisition of foreign nationality not linked to marriage or when automatic acquisition	YES
(Punitive) deprivation		
Special considerations		

General attitude toward multiple nationality

The Czech Republic retains a principle of avoidance of multiple nationality, to which several exceptions apply. The Constitution declares that "[n]obody may be deprived of his or her citizenship against his or her will", however any voluntary act that leads to acquisition of foreign nationality with the exception of acquisition in connection with marriage, or when nationality is attributed automatically at birth, leads to loss of Czech nationality. Loss of previous nationality is a condition of naturalisation, with certain exceptions. The Czech Republic is party to several agreements discouraging the production of, or regulating, multiple nationality (United States, Hungary, Poland, Bulgaria, Mongolia, certain successor states of the USSR).

Recognition of Multiple Nationality
The Czech Republic applies a principle of exclusivity of nationality, and does not take foreign nationality into account with regards to its nationals. Czech nationals must use Czech travel documents to travel abroad.

East Timor[16]

Nationality category or status
Only one, and no technical distinction between nationality and citizenship.

Attribution/acquisition of nationality

Event	Law	Condition is renunciation/ loss of other nationality
Birth	In East Timor to father or mother born in East Timor (original citizen)	NO
	In East Timor to unknown or stateless parents or whose citizenship is not known (original citizen)	
	Overseas to East Timorese parent (original citizen – possible conditions)	
	See registration/declaration	
Naturalisation	Upon fulfillment of requirements (conditions)	NO
Adoption	Upon full adoption of child by East Timorese parent	NO
Legitimation		
Marriage	Automatic if loss of prior nationality upon marriage – otherwise facilitated acquisition	NO

---

[16] EAST TIMOR: *Constituição da República Democrática de Timor-Leste*, 20 May 2002, *Constitution of the Democratic Republic of East Timor*, 20 May 2002, *Lei No. 9/2002 da Nacionalidade*, 5 November 2002, *Law no. 9/2002 on Citizenship*, 5 November 2002, **UNHCR (internet)**; *Address by H.E. Dr. José Ramos-Horta Senior Minister and Minister of Foreign Affairs and Cooperation, to the 59th Session of the UN Commission on Human Rights*, 18 March 2003, Ministry of Foreign Affairs and Cooperation Timor-Leste (internet), http://www. mfac.gov.tp/media/spc030318.html, consulted 7 May 2006; *Indonesia* in "UNHCR Global Report 2003", United Nations High Commissioner for Refugees (internet), http://www.unhcr.org/cgi-bin/texis/vtx/home/opendoc.pdf?id=40c6d74e0&tbl=PUBL, consulted 7 May 2006; Mark Dodd, "Harmony falters in no-man's land", Sydney Morning Herald, 21 February 2000, 8; Kerry Carrington, Stephen Sherlock and Nathan Hancock, "The East Timorese Asylum Seekers: Legal Issues and Policy Implications Ten Years On – Current Issues Brief no. 17 2002–03", Parliament of Australia Parliamentary Library (internet), http://www.aph.gov.au/library/pubs/CIB/2002-03/03cib17.htm, consulted 7 May 2006.

Event	Law	Condition is renunciation/ loss of other nationality
Resumption	If parents renounced on behalf of minor child, may resume as adult (conditions)	NO
	Possible if renounced citizenship (conditions)	
State service	Parliament may grant special naturalisation	NO
Parent acquires nationality	Possible for minor or disabled child upon request by parent, and child may opt for other citizenship when adult	NO
Spouse acquires nationality		
Registration (Declaration)	Birth in East Timor to a foreign parent and declaration when over age 17 of will to acquire nationality (original citizen)	NO
Special considerations		

Withdrawal/loss of nationality

Event	Law	Consequence of event is loss of nationality
Renunciation	Possible upon acquisition of foreign nationality	YES
	Possible if born overseas of East Timorese parents and has foreign nationality, upon declaration when adult	
Attribution at birth conditional	No provision	
Naturalisation elsewhere		NO
Adoption by a foreigner		NO
Marriage to a foreigner		NO
Spouse acquires other nationality		NO

Event Law		Consequence of event is loss of nationality
Parent acquires other nationality		NO
Resumption of previous nationality		NO
Service to foreign state	*(Naturalised citizen loses upon: foreign army service unless specifically authorized by agreement with other state; if "exercises functions of sovereignty in favour of a foreign state" without permission from Government)*	NO *(exception)*
Other attribution of nationality		NO
(Punitive) deprivation	For naturalised citizen only: conviction for criminal offense against external state security; fraud in acquisition of citizenship	POSSIBLE
Special considerations	Nullity or annulment of marriage does not affect citizenship of spouse who married in good faith	

General attitude toward multiple nationality

East Timor accepts multiple nationality for its citizens, but does not recognise any foreign nationality its nationals may possess. East Timor's first nationality law does not make naturalisation conditional on loss of prior nationality, and does not deprive East Timorese who are naturalised elsewhere of their nationality. The Act appears to exclude from naturalisation Indonesians who settled in East Timor between 1975 and 1999, as it excludes persons who settled in East Timor "as a result of transmigration policy or foreign military occupation" from the definition of "usual or regular resident", which is one of the conditions for naturalisation. Estimates state that over 230,000 East Timorese returned to East Timor in the years following 1999, when they fled or were driven into the neighboring Indonesian province of Nusa Tenggara Timur. Following East Timor's independence, Indonesia withdrew its nationality from East Timorese in East Timor. In 2003 an Indonesian presidential decree gave the remaining East Timorese in Indonesia the option of registering as Indonesian citizens, or as East Timorese citizens with valid Indonesian residence permits, but continued its policy of avoidance of multiple nationality.

Recognition of Multiple Nationality

The Citizenship Act (2002) states specifically that "[a]ny other citizenship granted to an East Timorese national shall not be recognised nor shall it be effective in the internal legal framework". As regards conflicts between foreign citizenships, the act states that "[w]here foreign citizenships come into conflict, citizenship of the State on whose territory the person holding multi-citizenship has his or her usual residence or, in the absence of such residence, citizenship of the state with which he or she has closer links shall prevail.

Ecuador[17]

Nationality category or status
Only one, and no distinction between nationality and citizenship (the Constitution specifies that use of the term "nationality" in foreign laws and international instruments is to be read as "citizenship" and that "rights of citizenship" should be read as "political rights".

Attribution/acquisition of nationality

Event	Law	Condition is renunciation/ loss of other nationality
Birth	In Ecuador	NO
	Overseas to an Ecuadorian parent citizen by birth overseas on state/ international service or temporarily abroad, unless express opposition	
	Overseas to an Ecuadorian parent citizen by birth, upon domicile in Ecuador and declaration	
	Overseas to an Ecuadorian parent citizen by birth, and between 18–21 declare desire to be Ecuadorian, notwithstanding residence overseas	
Naturalization	Upon fulfillment of requirements	NO
Adoption	By Ecuadorian during minority – by naturalisation	
Legitimation	See birth	

---

[17] ECUADOR: *Constitución Política de la República de Ecuador*, 1998, *Ley de Extranjería*, 23 July 2001, *Ley N° 276 Ley de Naturalización*, 2 April 1976, *Reglamento a la Ley de Naturalización*, 28 July 1985, **UNHCR (internet)**; *De la doble nacionalidad, Reconocimiento de nacionalidad Ecuatoriana por nacimiento, Recuperación de la nacionalidad Ecuatoriana*, Ministerio de Relaciones Exteriores de Ecuador (internet), http://www.mmrree.gov.ec/mre/ documentos/pol_internacional/migratoria%20consular/doblenacionalidad.htm, consulted 25 May 2006; *Declaración de nacionalidad Ecuatoriana por naturalización*, Ministerio de Relaciones Exteriores del Ecuador (internet), http://www.mmrree.gov.ec/mre/documentos/pol_interna-cional/migratoria%20consular/declaracion%20nacionalidad.htm, cosulted 25 May 2006; *Convenio de doble Nacionalidad con Ecuador (España-Ecuador)*, 4 March 1964 (includes modifying Protocol of 25 August 1995), Ministerio de Trabajo y Asuntos Sociales, Secretaría de Estado de Inmigración y Emigración – España (internet), http://extranjeros.mtas.es/es/nor-mativa_jurisprudencia/Internacional/doblenac/ECUADOR.pdf, consulted 25 May 2006.

Event	Law	Condition is renunciation/ loss of other nationality
Marriage	No automatic acquisition	
Resumption	Possible for those who previously lost citizenship upon naturalisation abroad	
State service	Facilitated naturalisation possible	
Parent acquires nationality	Children acquire by naturalisation	
Spouse acquires nationality		
Registration		
Special considerations		

Withdrawal/loss of nationality

Event	Law	Consequence of event is loss of nationality
Renunciation	No express general provision.	YES
	Child naturalised with parents during minority may make express renunciation of nationality upon reaching majority	
	Child adopted by Ecuadorian during minority may declare wish not be retain Ecuadorian nationality upon reaching majority (conditions)	
Attribution at birth conditional	(Birth overseas to an Ecuadorian parent does not necessarily lead to nationality – see birth; child may declare desire to be Ecuadorian between 18–21 notwithstanding residence overseas, or upon acquisition of domicile in Ecuador and declaration)	
Naturalisation elsewhere		NO
Adoption by a foreigner		NO
Marriage to a foreigner		NO
Spouse acquires other nationality		NO

Event	Law	**Consequence of event is loss of nationality**
Parent acquires other nationality		NO
Resumption of previous nationality		NO
Service to foreign state		NO
Other attribution of nationality		NO
(Punitive) deprivation	Naturalisation may be revoked	
Special considerations		

General attitude toward multiple nationality
The 1998 Constitution changed Ecuador's attitude toward multiple nationality. It states specifically that naturalisation abroad no longer causes loss of Ecuadorian nationality; loss of previous nationality is no longer a condition of naturalisation in Ecuador. The Constitution also contains a provision allowing for resumption of nationality by those who lost it previously upon previous naturalisation abroad.

Recognition of Multiple Nationality
The Constitution's article that stipulates that Ecuadorians do not lose nationality upon naturalisation abroad also states that the state should attempt to protect Ecuadorians who are abroad. Ecuadorians must use Ecuadorian travel documents to enter and depart the country.

*Egypt[18]

Nationality category or status
Only one, and no technical distinction between nationality and citizenship.

Attribution/acquisition of nationality

Event	Law	Condition is renunciation/ loss of other nationality
Birth	To an Egyptian father or an Egyptian mother (but not implemented if the father is Palestinian)	NO
	In Egypt to unknown parents (Foundlings), until proven otherwise	
Naturalisation	Upon fulfillment of requirements	NO

[18] EGYPT: _Decree No. 12025 of the Year 2004 Concerning Certain Provisions Enforcing Law No. 154 of the Year 2004 on Amendment of Certain Provisions of Law No. 26 of the Year 1975 Concerning the Egyptian Nationality_, 25 July 2004; _Law No. 26 for 1975 concerning Egyptian Nationality_, 29 May 1975, _Constitution of the Arab Republic of Egypt_, 22 September 1971, **UNHCR (internet)**; _Authorization of Foreign Citizenship, Arab Republic of Egypt_, Ministry of Foreign Affairs (internet), http://www.mfa.gov.eg/frames.asp?id=05, consulted 1 August 2003; _Emigration and Sponsoring Egyptians Abroad Law No. 111 of the year 1983_, Ministry of Manpower and Emigration (internet), http://www.emigration.gov.eg/MigrationLaw/EgyptianMigration Law.aspx, consulted 8 April 2006; _Facilities offered by the Ministry of the Interior to Egyptian Nationals Living Abroad_, Ministry of Manpower and Emigration (internet), http://www.emigration.gov.eg/GovernmentalServices/Interior.aspx, consulted 8 April 2006; _The facilities offered by the military forces for the Egyptian residents abroad_, Ministry of Manpower and Emigration (internet), http://www.emigration.gov.eg/GovernmentalServices/Defence.aspx, consulted 8 April 2006; _Consular information sheet – Egypt_, United States Department of State (internet), http://travel.state.gov/travel/cis_pa_tw/cis/cis_1108.html, consulted 7 April 2006; Reem Leila, "Egyptian at last?", Al-Ahram Weekly On-line, 2–8 October 2003, no. 658 (internet), http://weekly.ahram.org.eg/2003/658/eg7.htm, consulted 8 April 2006; Amira Howeidy, "Egyptian to the core", Al-Ahram Weekly On-line, 11–17 January 2001, no. 516 (internet), http://weekly.ahram.org.eg/2001/516/eg2.htm, consulted 8 April 2006; "A hundred years of fortitude", The Economist, 27 November 1999, 45; Ibrahim Abdul-Karim Alghasi, "Die Staatsangehörigkeit in den Bundesstaaten, im Staatenbund und in der Staatengemeinschaft, angeführt als Beispiel: Die Staatsangehörigkeit in den arabischen Staaten", dissertation presented at the Julius-Maximilians-Universität Würzburg, 1965; Thomas Oppermann and Ahmad Yousry, eds., _Das Staatsangehörigkeitsrecht der Arabischen Staaten_, vol. 15a, Sammlung Geltender Staatsangehörigkeitsgesetze (Frankfurt am Main: Alfred Metzner Verlag, 1964); Fouad Abdel-Moneim Riad, "Nationalité: Egypte", in Juris-Classeur Nationalité, ed. Michel J. Verwilghen and Charles L. Closset, Collection des Juris-Classeurs (Paris: Éditions du Juris-Classeur, 1985).

Event	Law	Condition is renunciation/ loss of other nationality
Adoption	(cases reportedly rare)	
Legitimation	(see birth)	
Marriage	Not automatic – facilitated naturalisation for wife of Egyptian	
Resumption	By woman who lost nationality upon marriage to foreigner	NO
	For those deprived of nationality (conditions)	
State service	By Presidential decree	NO
Parent acquires nationality	If children reside in Egypt, unless otherwise stateless after father's acquisition	NO
Spouse acquires nationality	Not automatic (provision only relates to wife deriving nationality from husband)	
Registration	Grant possible to various categories (birth, descent, residence)	NO
Special considerations	Birth abroad to Egyptian mother and father stateless or nationality unknown, if residence in Egypt and declaration within one year of majority, and no government objection	NO

Withdrawal/loss of nationality

Event	Law	Consequence of event is loss of nationality
Renunciation	Option if acquired through father's acquisition	YES
Attribution at birth conditional	No provision	
Naturalisation	(*If permission not obtained, no loss of Egyptian nationality. If permission obtained, results in loss, unless declaration of retention*)	NO (*exception*)
Adoption by a foreigner	(Essentially impossible procedure)	NO
Marriage to a foreigner	Not automatic – woman who marries alien may in any case elect to retain Egyptian nationality	NO

Event	Law	**Consequence of event is loss of nationality**
Spouse acquires other nationality	*(except if wife desires to lose Egyptian nationality and has received her husband's new nationality)*	NO *(exception)*
	Some deprivations may be extended to spouse	
Parent acquires other nationality	*(except minor children lose if acquire their father's new nationality, but may elect Egyptian nationality in the year after majority)*	NO *(exception)*
	Some deprivations may be extended to children	
Resumption of previous nationality	If children resume nationality lost after father's naturalisation	YES
	If wife acquired nationality after marriage to Egyptian husband, loses if resumes previous nationality, or if acquires another nationality by marriage	
Service to foreign state	Possible deprivation for foreign military service without government permission	POSSIBLE
	Possible deprivation for certain foreign government or international service and ignores order to quit	
Other attribution of nationality		NO
(Punitive) deprivation	For acquisition of nationality by fraud	YES
	If acquisition by naturalisation or marriage: for certain crimes, crimes against internal/external security, failure to reside in Egypt for two consecutive years and govt finds no acceptable reason	
	For anyone (see service to foreign state also): acquisition of foreign nationality without permission, residence abroad and work to undermine the state, assistance to enemy state; if a "zionist"	

General attitude toward multiple nationality

Egypt accepts and even recognises multiple nationality for its citizens, but exercises discretion over the extent and character of such recognistion. "Egyptian nationals seeking to acquire a foreign citizenship shall apply to the Egyptian consular mission in which area they reside. A procedure needs to be completed whereby they receive the necessary authorisation required by Egyptian authorities. The following documents are required to apply for such authorization: The applicant's birth certificate and his/her father's. A copy of the identity card. The military tripartite number for those requesting exemption from military service. The authorization is usually granted within one-month period from the date of application". If permission is received, and the applicant makes a declaration of retention of Egyptian nationality, the foreign nationality is recognised for certain purposes (see below). Should an Egyptian not seek permission, his foreign nationality is in any case not recognised, and he may be deprived of his Egyptian nationality although this is not automatic. Loss of previous nationality is not a condition of acquiring Egyptian nationality. Multiple nationals are exempt from military service, and barred from military and police academies.

Certain disabilities are imposed on naturalised citizens for a number of years, and a recent court decision held that multiple nationals could not be members of Parliament, reasoning that multiple nationals lack full loyalty to Egypt. Along general lines, Egyptian military officers and diplomats are reportedly barred from marrying foreigners. A major legislative change in 2004 gave women equal rights with men to transmit nationality to their children. Their incapacity (with certain exceptions) to transmit their nationality had reportedly left 80,000 children in Egypt ("many of them products of brief marriages to Gulf Arabs") stateless and thus excluded from many public benefits.

Recognition of Multiple Nationality
The Nationality Law provides that if permission to obtain a foreign nationality has been received, such nationality will be recognised by Egypt for certain purposes, when possessed alongside the Egyptian. Exemptions from military service may be secured, and foreign passports may be used to enter and depart the country, and may contain visas (thus providing access to diplomatic/consular protection). If an Egyptian identity document is produced with the foreign passport, the period of stay may be lengthened, but the individual will generally still be treated as a foreigner. In any case after six months' stay, the individual is subject to general rules on stay and departure (for example a father's permission for minor children to travel). Entry on an Egyptian passport or extended stay in any case means treatment as an Egyptian.

*Fiji[19]

Nationality category or status
Only one, and no technical distinction between nationality and citizenship.

Attribution/acquisition of nationality

Event	Law	Condition is renunciation/ loss of other nationality
Birth	In Fiji to a Fijian parent (unless one parent has diplomatic imm.)	NO
	Overseas to a Fijian parent, upon registration (conditions)	(but if multiple national, conditional attribution)
Naturalisation	Fulfilment of requirements	YES
Adoption	Adopted when under 18 by a Fijian parent, upon registration	YES
Legitimation	(see birth)	
Marriage	No effect	
Resumption	By registration	YES
State service		
Parent acquires nationality	If under 21, upon registration (conditions), also possible if over 21, upon registration (conditions)	YES
Spouse acquires nationality	Not automatic	
Registration	Various possibilities	YES (if applic. by adult)
Special considerations	Any application for registration made by an adult	YES

---

[19] FIJI: *Constitution of the Republic of the Fiji Islands*, 27 July 1998. Suva: Government Printing Office, 1998; *Citizenship Act* (no. 17 of 1998), *Citizenship Act (Amendment) Decree 2000*, Military Interim Government of Fiji Decree no. 8 2000, **UNHCR (internet)**; *The State v. The Registration Officer, Tailevu Fijian Provincial Constituency ex-parte Samuela Matawalu*, High Court of Fiji, HBJ 18 of 1995 (unreported case: M. D. Scott, Judge); *The Fijian Association v. Adi Litia Samanunu Cakobau, The Supervisor of Elections, The Attorney-General of Fiji*, High Court of Fiji, civil action no. 0250 of 1995 (unreported case, D. V. Fatiaki, Judge); "Govt monitors dissident group", Fiji's Daily Post, 22 September 1999, 3; Chandrasekharan, S., *FIJI: Ex PM Chaudhry's dilemma*, South Asia Analysis Group, 6 March 2003 (internet), http://www.saag.org/papers7/paper624.html, consulted 8 April 2006.

Event	Law	**Condition is renunciation/ loss of other nationality**
	If foreign law prevents renunciation of nationality must make declaration will not exercise benefits of that nationality (*but deprivation if exercise rights of foreign nationality*)	NO

Withdrawal/loss of nationality

Event	Law	**Consequence of event is loss of nationality**
Renunciation	Over age 21 and is a multiple national	YES
Attribution at birth conditional	If acquisition of foreign nationality while a minor, and does not forfeit such nationality before age 22.	YES
Naturalisation elsewhere	If voluntary acquisition of nationality	YES
Adoption by a foreigner	No direct effect, unless nationality thereby acquired voluntarily. If while a minor, must forfeit foreign nat. before age 22.	
Marriage to a foreigner	No effect, if foreign nationality attributed automatically	NO
Spouse acquires other nationality	No effect, if foreign nationality attributed automatically	
Parent acquires other nationality	No direct effect, unless nationality nationality thereby acquired, if a minor must forfeit by age 22, or lose Fijian nationality	
Resumption of previous nationality	Any voluntary acquisition of other nationality	YES
Service to foreign state	No effect unless voluntary acquisition of foreign nationality	
Other attribution of nationality	Any voluntary acquisition of foreign	YES
(Punitive) deprivation	Possible if:	POSSIBLE
	obtained by fraud, for citizens by registr. or naturalisation;	
	exercises foreign citizenship entitlement/ right after decl.	

Event	Law	**Consequence of event is loss of nationality**
Special considerations	Involuntary acquisition of foreign nationality does not result in loss, unless failure to renounce if required by govt or within 12 months of becoming aware of the attribution	YES

General attitude toward multiple nationality
Fiji's stated policy is that multiple nationality is not accepted. Of interest is the Constitutional provision that grants former citizens a right of entry and residence, and a right to resumption as long as any other nationality possessed is abandoned. One of the first demands of those who carried out the coup d'etat in May 2000 was reported to be the rejection of multiple nationality, as well as that the British government "repatriate all Indians from Fiji". The widely-reported, and incorrect, statement in 2002 by the Multi-Ethnic Affairs Minister that Indo-Fijians would soon have a right to Indian nationality in addition to their Fijian nationality, was reportedly not generally well-received by ethnic Fijians (see section on India herein). Loss of previous nationality is a condition of naturalisation or registration in Fiji, and even if a foreign nationality cannot be lost effectively, any exercise of rights or entitlements pursuant to a foreign nationality may lead to deprivation of Fijian nationality.

Recognition of Multiple Nationality
No evidence of any policy of protection overseas of any possible multiple nationals was found. As that category of persons will be small, due to the operation of legislation, this is basically a moot point.

Finland[20]

Nationality category or status

Only one category of nationality, and no technical distinction between nationality and citizenship. The Nationality Act defines citizenship as "a legislative bond between an individual and the State defining the individual's status in the state as well as the basic rights and duties existing between the individual and the state". The Act states that its provisions do not apply if a person would thereby become stateless.

Attribution/acquisition of nationality

Event	Law	Condition is renunciation/ loss of other nationality
Birth	To a Finnish mother	NO
	To a Finnish Father married to the mother (including if father deceased but citizen at time of death)	*(However multiple nationals retain Finnish nationality at age 22 only if they have a sufficient connection to Finnland (conditions)*
	To a Finnish father out of wedlock if child born in Finland and paternity established (including if father deceased but citizen at time of birth)	
	(To a Finnish father overseas – see by declaration)	
	In Finland and no other acquisition of citizenship at birth, or secondary right to acquire foreign citizenship	

---

[20] FINLAND: *Nationality Act 359/2003*, Unofficial translation Ministry of the Interior **UNHCR (internet)**; *Citizenship*, Directorate of Immigration (internet), http://www.uvi.fi/netcomm/content.asp?path=8,2477, consulted 23 April 2006; *Acquiring Finnish Citizenship*, Directorate of Immigration (internet), http://www.uvi.fi/netcomm/content.asp?path=8,2477,2549, consulted 23 April 2006; *Retaining Finnish Citizenship at the age of 22*, Directorate of Immigration (internet), http://www.uvi.fi/download.asp?id=Retaining+Finnish+citizenship+at+the+age+of+22;631;{8AB6F224-0D2A-49E6-9783-40AB7A9EEEEB}, consulted 23 April 2006; *Release from Finnish Citizenship*, Directorate of Immigration (internet), http://www.uvi.fi/download.asp?id=Release+from+Finnish+citizenship;635;{62BBDEC6-5D3C-4AA0-88BE-ECE30A1B843A}, consulted 23 April 2006; *Losing or being Released from Finnish Citizenship*, Directorate of Immigration (internet), http://www.uvi.fi/netcomm/content.asp?path=8,2477,2552, consulted 23 April 2006; *Publications*, Directorate of Immigration (internet), http://www.uvi.fi/netcomm/content.asp?path=2484&language=EN, consulted 23 April 2006; *Finnish citizenship*, Directorate of Immigration (internet), http://www.uvi.fi/download.asp?id=Finnish+citizenship;620;{D82F502B-112E-442A-BB4F-23BF82D0E996}, consulted 23 April 2006; *FAQ Multiple nationality*, Directorate of Immigration (internet), http://www.uvi.fi/netcomm/content.asp?path=8,2477,2553, consulted 23 April 2006.

Event	Law	**Condition is renunciation/ loss of other nationality**
	In Finland to refugee parents if no automatic or other acquisition of citizenship (conditions)	
	In Finland to parents (or mother out of wedlock) with unknown citizenship, and child not established a foreign citizen before age 5	
	Foundling, unless foreign citizenship established before age 5	
Naturalisation	Upon fulfillment of conditions	NO
Adoption	Of child under 12 by Finnish citizen upon valid adoption in Finland	NO
Legitimation	See birth	NO
	Upon parents' marriage, if man was Finnish citizen at child's birth and continues to be, and paternity established before marriage (or as of date when paternity established, if after the marriage, including if father deceased) – conditions	
Marriage	Not automatic – facilitated naturalisation (conditions)	
Resumption	Possible by declaration (conditions)	
State service		
Parent acquires nationality	Facilitated naturalisation possible (conditions)	
Spouse acquires nationality	No automatic effect	
Registration (Declaration)	Possible for certain aliens with Finnish fathers, adopted children over 12, persons between 18–23, former citizens, Nordic citizens (conditions)	NO
Special considerations	Children over 12 and their parent/ guardian are interviewed with respect to applications made on their behalf. Children over 15 and their parent/ guardian may object to applications.	

Withdrawal/loss of nationality

Event	Law	Consequence of event is loss of nationality
Renunciation	Possible if multiple national or about to acquire foreign nationality, and not if resides in Finland and aim is to escape obligation – must report on acquisition of citizenship (conditions)	YES
Attribution at birth conditional	*Multiple nationals retain Finnish nationality at age 22 only if they have a sufficient connection to Finland (conditions)*	POSSIBLE
Naturalisation elsewhere		NO
Adoption by a foreigner		NO
Marriage to a foreigner		NO
Spouse acquires other nationality		NO
Parent acquires other nationality		NO
Resumption of previous nationality		NO
Service to foreign state		NO
Other attribution of nationality		NO
(Punitive) deprivation	Fraud in acquisition	POSSIBLE
Special considerations	If father's paternity annulled and child acquired on basis of father's citizenship, loss discretionary (conditions)	POSSIBLE

General attitude toward multiple nationality

Finland states that it accepts multiple nationality in all situations, and that "[a] citizen of both Finland and another country is considered a Finnish citizen by the Finnish authorities whether he/she is in Finland and abroad. However, he/she will not automatically be considered a Finnish citizen by the authorities of other countries". Finland's acceptance of multiple nationality in the Nationality Act in force as of 1 June 2003 does, however, contain a specific condition that Finnish multiple nationals retain their Finnish nationality at age 22 only if they have a sufficient connection to Finnland. Various acts suffice to establish the requisite connection:

birth in Finland and residence there at age 22; residence in Finland or permanent residence and domicile in a Nordic country for seven years before age 22; after age 18 but before age 22 either giving notice of the desire to retain Finnish nationality, or having been issued a Finnish passport, or completed military/civil service in Finland. The Act provides that the authorities must make an effort to give Finnish multiple nationals information regarding retention of their nationality.

Recognition of Multiple Nationality

Finland states that its nationals have the right to protection abroad, but does not elaborate on specific policies regarding multiple nationals.

*France[21]

Nationality category or status
Only one, and no technical distinction between nationality and citizenship.

---

[21] FRANCE: *Code civil* (as of 7 January 1999), *Circulaire sur application de la loi MIS-SEFEN (Application de la loi n° 2003–1119 du 26 novembre 2003 relative à la maîtrise de l'immigration, au séjour des étrangers en France et à la nationalité)*, 1 January 2004, **UNHCR (internet)**; *Assistance Consulaire*, Ministère des Affaires Etrangères (internet), http://www.diplomatie.gouv.fr/voyageurs/etrangers/avis/conseils/savoir3.asp, consulted 1 August 2003; *La nationalité française*, 27 June 2005, Ministère des Affaires Etrangères (internet), http://www.diplomatie.gouv.fr/fr/les-francais-etranger_1296/vos-droits-demarches_1395/nationalite-francaise_5301/index.html, consulted 8 April 2006; *Statement by the Ministry of Foreign Affairs Spokesperson*, Paris, August 21, 2001, Ministère des Affaires Etrangères (internet), http://www.france.diplomatie.fr/actu/articletxt.gb.asp?ART=10878, consulted 1 August 2003; Daniel Bermond, "La nationalité française: und histoire à rebondissements (interview with Patrick Weil)", *Label France* (2003) vol. 49, Janvier-Mars, 34–36; Vincent Bonnet, "Les obstacles à l'acquisition de la nationalité française du conjoint et la question de la fraude", paper presented at the conference: "Être français aujourd'hui . . ." Premier bilan de la mise en oeuvre du nouveau droit de la nationalité, (Lyon: Presses universitaires de Lyon, 1995), 101–111; Rogers Brubaker, *Citizenship and nationhood in France and Germany* (Cambridge (Massachusetts): Harvard University Press, 1992); Christian Bruschi, "L'acquisition de la nationalité française à raison du mariage", paper presented at the conference: "Être français aujourd'hui . . ." Premier bilan de la mise en oeuvre du nouveau droit de la nationalité, (Lyon: Presses universitaires de Lyon, 1995), 81–88; Campbell and Meek, eds., *International immigration and nationality law*; de Groot, "Loss of nationality: a critical inventory"; Géraud de La Pradelle, "Dual nationality and the French citizenship tradition", in *Dual nationality, social rights and federal citizenship in the U.S. and Europe. The reinvention of citizenship*, ed. Randall Hansen and Patrick Weil, 191–212, (New York: Berghahn Books, 2002); Hugues Fulchiron, *La nationalité française, Que sais-je?* (Paris: Presses universitaires de France, 2000); Hugues Fulchiron and Savinien Grignon Dumoulin, "Nationalité: France", in *Juris-Classeur Nationalité – commentaire des traités internationaux et des législations nationales*, ed. Michel J. Verwilghen and Charles L. Closset, *Collection des Juris-Classeurs* (Paris: Éditions du Juris-Classeur, 1997); Benoît Guiguet, "Citizenship rights for aliens in France", in *Citizenship in a global world. Comparing citizenship rights for aliens*, ed. Atsushi Kondo, 71–99, (Houndmills (UK): Palgrave, 2001); Paul Lagarde, "Droit de la nationalité et droit de l'immigration. L'expérience française", in *Mélanges en l'honneur de Nicolas Valticos*, ed. René-Jean Dupuy, 663–672, (Paris: Éditions A. Pedone, 1999); Michel Moreau, "Nationalité française – propos en marge du rapport de la commission de la nationalité", paper presented at the conference: La condition juridique de l'étranger, hier et aujourd'hui, Katholieke Universiteit Nijmegen, 21–35, (Nimègue: Katholieke Universiteit, 1988); Patrick Weil, "The history of French nationality: a lesson for Europe", in *Towards a European nationality. Citizenship, immigration and nationality law in the EU*, ed. Randall Hansen and Patrick Weil, 52–68, (Houndmills: Palgrave, 2001); Patrick Weil, "L'histoire de la nationalité française: une leçon pour l'Europe", in *Nationalité et citoyenneté en Europe*, ed. Patrick Weil and Randall Hansen, *Collection "Recherches"*, 55–70, (Paris: Éditions La Découverte, 1999).

Attribution/acquisition of nationality

Event	Law	Condition is renunciation/ loss of other nationality
Birth	To a French parent	NO
	In France (or French territory) if one parent was born in France	
	In France to parent born in Algeria before 3 July 1962	
	In France if otherwise stateless	
	Foundling presumed to be child of French parent	
Naturalisation	Upon fulfillment of conditions	NO
Adoption	If full adoption (conditions) during minority; other conditions for "simple" adoption	NO
Legitimation	(as at birth)	NO
Marriage	Not automatic – facilitated acquisition	
Resumption	Possible in certain cases (varying conditions)	NO
State service	Facilitated naturalisation possible	
Parent acquires nationality	Resumption or acquisition of French nationality by parent: minor children included (conditions)	NO
Spouse acquires nationality	No direct effect – facilitated naturalisation possible	
Registration	Acquisition of nationality at age 18, if born in France to alien parents and resided in France for total of five years since age 11 (conditions)	NO
	Of minor child born in France to alien parents at age 13 (conds)	

Withdrawal/loss of nationality

Event	Law	Consequence of event is loss of nationality
Renunciation	Possible in certain cases – including if born overseas to one French parent,	YES

Event	Law	Consequence of event is loss of nationality
	adult residing abroad who acquires foreign nationality. Not possible if under 30 and subject to military obligations and only if not thereby stateless	
Attribution at birth conditional	No provision (*except if discovered foundling has foreign parents and would not be stateless*)	NO (*exception*)
Naturalisation elsewhere	(*except in relation to 1963 Council of Europe Convention, modified by 1993 Protocol*)	NO (*exception*)
Adoption by a foreigner	No direct effect	NO
Marriage to a foreigner	No direct effect	NO
Spouse acquires other nationality	No direct effect	NO
Parent acquires other nationality	(*If parent loses French nationality during child's minority – conditions*)	NO (*exception*)
Resumption of previous nationality		NO
Service to foreign state	Possible deprivation for foreign state or military service and ingnores order to resign such service	POSSIBLE
Other attribution of nationality	(*the Code states that French nationals who reside in a former département or territory, to whom nationality is not attributed upon independence, remain French (and minor children), implying loss of French nationality if other is attributed*)	NO (*exception*)
(Punitive) deprivation	Revocation of naturalisation for fraud, certain crimes	POSSIBLE
	Possible for multiple nationals who "behave as foreign nationals"	
	Possible if nationality acquired by naturalisation, adoption, residence, unless thereby stateless, for: conviction of crime against state or terrorism,	

Event	Law	**Consequence of event is loss of nationality**
	certain other crimes including related to military service, acts prejudicial to French interests	
Special considerations	Possible deprivation if nationality acquired by descent, never resided in France, nor did ancestors in past 50 years	POSSIBLE

General attitude toward multiple nationality
France accepts multiple nationality for its citizens, notwithstanding having ratified the 1963 Council of Europe Convention (although modified by the 1993 Protocol), and states that the possession of foreign nationality has no effects on French nationality. No distinction is made on the basis of multiple nationality in terms of the rights and obligations of citizenship, although France recognises the right of the other state of nationality to regard the individual in question as its national exclusively.

Recognition of Multiple Nationality
France warns its multiple nationals that they cannot be assured of consular protection in countries where they also possess nationality, but maintains an official position that such protection is justified due to the possession of French nationality. In relation to protection of dual nationals a Foreign Ministry spokesman stated [it is a problem] "that crops up in all relations with countries where there are dual nationals. In our eyes, they are French and so we are justified in granting them consular protection. But we know that in the eyes of the other country, they are not considered aliens but nationals. So these states maintain there are no grounds for having special rules for them. Consular protection in that case rests more on relations of courtesy, on the good relations that we may have with the state in question rather than on an official rule".

*Germany[22]

Nationality category or status
Only one, and no technical distinction between nationality and citizenship.

---

[22] GERMANY: *Staatsangehörigkeitsgesetz (zuletzt geändert durch das Gesetzes zur Änderung des Aufenthaltsgesetzes und weiterer Gesetze vom 14. März 2005)*, Beauftragte der Bundesregierung für Migration, Flüchtlinge und Integration (internet), http://www.einbuergerung.de/gesetz.pdf, consulted 8 April 2006; *Staatsangehörigkeitsrecht*, February 2005, Auswärtiges Amt (internet), http://www.auswaertiges-amt.de/www/de/willkommen/staatsangehoerigkeitsrecht/index_html, consulted 8 April 2006; *Einbürgerung: Fair. Gerecht. Tolerant.*, Beauftragte der Bundesregierung für Migration, Flüchtlinge und Integration (internet), http://www.einbuergerung.de/index2.htm, consulted 8 April 2006; *Konsularische Hilfe in* Notfällen, May 2004, Auswärtiges Amt (internet), http://www.auswaertiges-amt.de/www/de/laenderinfos/konsulat/notfallhilfe_html, consulted 8 April 2006; Peter Friedrich Bultmann, "Dual nationality and naturalisation policies in the German Länder", in *Dual nationality, social rights and federal citizenship in the U.S. and Europe. The reinvention of citizenship*, ed. Randall Hansen and Patrick Weil, 136–157 (New York: Berghahn Books, 2002); de Groot, "Loss of nationality: a critical inventory"; Nina Isabel Goes, *Mehrstaatigkeit in Deutschland*, ed. Ingolf Pernice, vol. 2, *Schriftenreihe Europäisches Verfassungsrecht* (Baden-Baden: Nomos Verlagsgesellschaft, 1997); Simon Green, "Citizenship policy in Germany: the case of ethnicity over residence", in *Towards a European nationality. Citizenship, immigration and nationality law in the EU*, ed. Randall Hansen and Patrick Weil 24–51 (Houndmills: Palgrave, 2001); Kay Hailbronner, "Citizenship rights for aliens in Germany", in *Citizenship in a global world. Comparing citizenship rights for aliens*, ed. Atsushi Kondo, 100–115 (Houndmills (UK): Palgrave, 2001); Kay Hailbronner, "Dopelte Staatsangehörigkeit", *Zeitschrift für Ausländerrecht und Ausländerpolitik* (1999) no. 2, 51–58; Kay Hailbronner, "Germany's citizenship law under immigration pressure", in *Dual nationality, social rights and federal citizenship in the U.S. and Europe. The reinvention of citizenship*, ed. Randall Hansen and Patrick Weil, 121–135 (New York: Berghahn Books, 2002); Kay Hailbronner, Günter Renner, and Christine Kreuzer, *Staatsangehörigkeitsrecht*, 3rd ed., vol. 55, *Beck'sche Kurz-kommentare* (München: Verlag C. H. Beck, 2001); Rainer Hausmann, "Doppelte Staatsbürgerschaft für Ausländer: Auswirkungen im Internationalen Privat- und Verfahrensrecht", paper presented at the conference: Hohenheimer Tage zum Ausländerrecht 1999 und 5. Migrationspolitisches Forum, Hohenheim, 1999); Hessisches Ministerium des Innern und für Sport, "Rundschreiben vom 23.10.2000–II A 11–04–20", *Informationsbrief Ausländerrecht* (2001) no. 1, 43; Rainer Hofmann, "German citizenship law and European citizenship: towards a special kind of dual nationality?", in *European citizenship. An institutional challenge*, ed. Massimo La Torre, *European Forum*, 149-165 (The Hague: Kluwer Law International, 1998); Hans-Detlef Horn, "Einbürgerungen durch die Länder ohne Zustimmungsvorbehalt des Bundes?", *Zeitschrift für Ausländerrecht und Ausländerpolitik* (2001) vol. 21, no. 3, 99–104; Martin A. Klein, *Zu einer Reform des deutschen Staatsangehörigkeitsrechts – eine kritische Betrachtung under Einbeziehung Frankreichs* (Frankfurt am Main: Peter Lang, 1999); Christine Kreuzer, "Double and multiple nationality in Germany after the Citizenship Reform Act of 1999", in *Rights and duties of dual nationals. Evolution and prospects*, ed. David A. Martin and Kay Hailbronner 347–359 (The Hague: Kluwer Law International, 2003); Günter Renner, "Was ist neu am neuen Staatsangehörigkeitsrecht?", *Zeitschrift*

APPENDIX

Attribution/acquisition of nationality

Event	Law	Condition is renunciation/ loss of other nationality
Birth	To a German parent (unless birth overseas to German parent born overseas with foreign residence, then only if registered within one year of birth, unless stateless)	NO
	In Germany to alien permanent resident parent (conditions)	NO (*conditional*)
	Foundling acquires German nationality	
Naturalisation	Fulfilment of requirements	YES (*exceptions*)

---

für Ausländerrecht und Ausländerpolitik (1999) no. 4, 154–163; Günter Saathoff and Malti Taneja, "Von der "doppelten" zur "optionalen" Staatsbürgerschaft – Werdegang und Ergebnis des Gesetzgebungsprozesses", paper presented at the conference: Hohenheimer Tage zum Ausländerrecht 1999 und 5. Migrationspolitisches Forum, Hohenheim, 1999; Klaus-Dieter Schnapauff, "The reform of the nationality law in the Federal Republic of Germany", *Law & European Affairs* (2000) no. 1–2, 81–87; Michael Silagi, "Minderheitenrecht und diplomatischer Schutz für Deutsche in Ost-, Ostmittel- und Südosteuropa. Historische Aspekte", in *Rechtsanspruch und Rechtswirklichkeit des europäischen Minderheitenschutzes*, ed. Dieter Blumenwitz, Gilbert H. Gornig, and Dietrich Murswiek, *Staats- und völkerrechtliche Abhandlungen der Studiengruppe für Politik und Völkerrecht* (Köln: Verlag Wissenschaft und Politik, 1998); Michael Silagi, *Vertreibung und Staatsangehörigkeit, Forschungsergebnisse der Studiengruppe für Politik und Völkerrecht* (Bonn: Kulturstiftung der deutschen Vertriebenen, 1999); Tade Matthias Spranger, "Der Verzicht von Mehr- und Doppelstaatern auf die deutsche Staatsangehörigkeit", *Zeitschrift für Ausländerrecht und Ausländerpolitik* (1999) no. 2, 71–74; Fritz Sturm and Gudrun Sturm, *Das deutsche Staatsangehörigkeitsrecht. Grundriss und Quellen* (Frankfurt am Main: Verlag für Standesamtswesen, 2001); Hans von Mangoldt, "Ius-sanguinis-Prinzip, Ius-soli-Prinzip und Mehrstaatigkeit: Umbrüche durch das Staatsangehörigkeitsreformgesetz", *Zeitschrift für Ausländerrecht und Ausländerpolitik* (1999) no. 6, 243–252; Hans von Mangoldt, "The right of return in German nationality law", *Tel Aviv University Studies in Law* (1997) vol. 13, 29–52; Astrid Wallrabenstein, *Das Verfassungsrecht der Staatsangehörigkeit* (Baden-Baden: Nomos Verlagsgesellschaft, 1999); Marianne Wiedemann, "Development of dual nationality under German law", in *Rights and duties of dual nationals. Evolution and prospects*, ed. David A. Martin and Kay Hailbronner, 335–345 (The Hague: Kluwer Law International, 2003); Andreas Zimmermann, "Staats- und völkerrechtliche Fragen der Reform des deutschen Staatsangehörigkeitsrechts", *IPRax Praxis des Internationalen Privat- und Verfahrensrechts* (2000) no. 3, 180–185; Kate Connolly, "France and Germany talking dual citizenship", The Sydney Morning Herald, 23 January 2003, 9; "Who's a German then", The Economist, 7 December 2002, 16; "German killer dies in US gas chamber", The Australian, 5 March 1999, 12; William Drozdiak, "Germany's new multicultural citizens", The Guardian Weekly, 13–19 January 2000, 27; "Both Turkish and German", The Economist, 6 February 1999, 12.

Event	Law	Condition is renunciation/ loss of other nationality
Adoption	If full adoption of a minor	NO
Legitimation	If recognised by formal procedure	NO
Marriage	Not automatic – facilitated naturalisation	YES (*exceptions*)
Resumption	Possible	YES (*exceptions*)
State service	Naturalization possible	YES (*exceptions*)
Parent acquires nationality	Not automatic – facilitated naturalisation possible	
Spouse acquires nationality	Not automatic –facilitated naturalisation possible	

Withdrawal/loss of nationality

Event	Law	Consequence of event is loss of nationality
Renunciation	Person who has or will acquire other nationality, not in government service, with consent, subject to possible obligations	YES
Attribution at birth conditional	Birth in Germany to foreign permanent resident parent and has other nationality, must declare before age 23 opts for German nationality and demonstrate loss of foreign nationality, or loses German nationality (also if no declaration made). Exceptions may be made. If discovered foundling of foreign descent, even after majority	YES (*exceptions*)
Naturalisation elsewhere		YES, (*but permission to retain possible*)
Adoption by a foreigner	If adoption valid at German law and other nationality acquired, unless remains related to German parent	YES
Marriage to a foreigner		NO
Spouse acquires other nationality		NO
Parent acquires other nationality	Not automatic. May apply for release.	NO

Event	**Law**	**Consequence of event is loss of nationality**
Resumption of previous nationality		YES (*but permission to retain possible*)
Service to foreign state	Possible automatic deprivation, for example for foreign military service of multiple national without permission	POSSIBLE
Other attribution of nationality	Not if involuntary attribution	YES
(Punitive) deprivation	Possible evocation of naturalisation for fraud	POSSIBLE

General attitude toward multiple nationality
Germany states that it does not favour possession of multiple nationality, but does not prevent it at birth if German nationality is attributed via *jus sanguinis*, and a relatively long list of exceptions applies to the rule that persons applying to be naturalised in Germany must renounce their previous nationality. Exceptions include: for elderly persons for whom loss of foreign nationality would present practical problems; for recognised refugees; when renunciation of nationality is impossible or made unreasonably difficult; if loss of foreign nationality would cause substantial economic or financial difficulties for the person concerned; if the foreign nationality is that of a European Union country. Exceptions apply equally to persons to whom German nationality was attributed by birth in Germany, and who wish to continue to possess their other nationality alongside the German beyond age 23. No distinctions are made on the basis of multiple nationality.

Recognition of Multiple Nationality
Germany informs its citizens that only limited, if any, consular assistance is possible to citizens in another country of nationality. It notes that officials of the other country concerned "regard you as their own national and will prohibit any consular 'interference' by German representatives abroad". German multiple nationals must enter and depart Germany on German travel documents.

Ghana[23]

Nationality category or status
Only one, and no distinction between nationality and citizenship.

Attribution/acquisition of nationality

Event	Law	Condition is renunciation/ loss of other nationality
Birth	To a Ghanaian parent or grandparent, including former citizens (includes posthumous children)	NO
	Foundling under eight	
Naturalisation	Upon fulfillment of requirements	NO
Adoption	Of child under 17 neither of whose parents is Ghanaian	NO
Legitimation		
Marriage	Possible registration	
Resumption	Automatic resumption if Ghanaian forced to renounce/lost citizenship upon marriage abroad, upon dissolution of marriage	NO
	If lost nationality as result of acquisition or possession of foreign nationality, automatic resumption if renounces that nationality; if lost nationality as a result of previous Ghanaian prohibition of dual nationality, may apply to resume	
State service	Possible registration	
Parent acquires nationality	Child can acquire by registration upon parent's registration or naturalisation	

---

[23] GHANA: *Constitution of the Republic of Ghana*, 7 January 1993 (last amended 1996), *Citizenship Act (Act 591)*, 2000, **UNHCR (internet)**; *Brochure on dual citizenship*, Ghana Permanent Mission – Geneva (internet), http://www.ghanamission.ch/mission6a.html, consulted 18 May 2006; *Dual citizenship*, Ghana Permanent Mission – Geneva (internet), http://www.ghanamission.ch/mission6.html, consulted 18 May 2006; *Travel advice for Ghana*, 31 March 2006, Australian Department of Foreign Affairs and Trade (internet), http://www.smartraveller.gov.au/zw-cgi/view/Advice/Ghana, consulted 25 May 2006; *Consular information sheet – Ghana*, 4 November 2005, United States Department of State (internet), consulted 18 May 2005.

Event	Law	**Condition is renunciation/ loss of other nationality**
Spouse acquires nationality		
Registration	Possible for various categories (spouses of citizens, widow/widower – conditions)	NO
Special considerations		

Withdrawal/loss of nationality

Event	Law	**Consequence of event is loss of nationality**
Renunciation	Possible if of full age and capacity and multiple national	YES
Attribution at birth conditional	No provision	
Naturalisation elsewhere		NO
Adoption by a foreigner		NO
Marriage to a foreigner		NO
Spouse acquires other nationality		NO
Parent acquires other nationality		NO
Resumption of previous nationality		NO
Service to foreign state		NO
Other attribution of nationality		NO
(Punitive) deprivation	Possible for citizens otherwise than by birth or adoption for activities inimical to state security or prejudicial to public morality or public interest; fraud in acquisition	POSSIBLE
Special considerations		

General attitude toward multiple nationality
The 1993 Constitution changed Ghana's previous attitude toward multiple nationality. It contains an article on "Dual Citizenship" that provides that "[a] citizen of Ghana may hold the citizenship of any other country in addition to his citizenship of Ghana". It stipulates that Ghanaian multiple nationals may not be appointed to the positions of ambassador; high commissioner; cabinet secretary; chief of defence staff or any service chief; inspector-general of police; commissioner of customs, excise and preventive service; director of immigration, and other offices specified by act of Parliament. Members of Parliament may also not be multiple nationals. The Citizenship Act adds the positions of supreme court justice; commissioner of value-added tax service, director-general of the Prison Service; chief fire officer, chief director of a ministry; the rank of colonel in the Army or equivalent in other security services. Loss of previous nationality is not a condition of naturalisation, and naturalisation abroad does not result in loss of Ghanaian nationality, although the Citizenship Act requires that Ghanaians must notify the government of any acquisition of foreign nationality.

Recognition of Multiple Nationality
The Citizenship Act states that "[a] citizen of Ghana who is also a citizen of any other counry shall whilst in Ghana be subject to the laws of Ghana as any othe citizen". It provides that regulations may be issued for "procedures relating to use of travel documents by holders of dual citizenship". Ghanaian multiple nationals may choose whether they use a Ghanaian or foreign travel document to enter and depart Ghana, but "it is an offence for a dual citizenship holder to use two passports interchangeably to deceive an immigration officer". Persons summarily convicted of this offence are subject to a fine and/or up to one year's imprisonment. Ghanaian "dual citizens are required to travel with their certificates of Dual Citizenship and only one passport of their choice". Ghanaians who enter Ghana on a Ghanaian passport "shall be permitted to remain in Ghana without limitation". Some countries advise their citizens that while Ghana recognises multiple nationality, their ability to provide consular assistance to dual nationals may be limited. Ghanaians who enter Ghana on a foreign passport may, however, have a better claim to be treated as foreigners while in the country.

Greece[24]

Nationality category or status
Only one, and no distinction between nationality and citizenship.

Attribution/acquisition of nationality

Event	Law	Condition is renunciation/ loss of other nationality
Birth	To a Greek parent	NO
	In Greece and no other acquisition of nationality, or child of unknown nationality	
Naturalisation	Upon fulfillment of conditions	NO
Adoption	Of child under age 18	NO
Legitimation	Of child under 18	NO
Marriage	No direct affect – facilitated naturalisation	
Resumption	Possible for categories including: ethnic Greeks born in Greece and nationals by birth who lost under previous legislation upon acquisition of foreign nationality and have since lost that nationality;	NO

---

[24] GREECE: *Law 2910/2001 Entry and stay of aliens in Greek territory. Acquisition of Greek citizenship by naturalisation and other provisions* (as amended 2003), **UNHCR (internet)**; *Code of Greek Nationality*, 1995 translation (internet), http://www.geocities.com/nationalite/greek-eng.txt, consulted 25 May 2006; *Greek citizenship*, Embassy of Greece in Ottawa (internet), http://www.greekembassy.ca/consular.html, consulted 25 May 2006; *Acquisition of Greek nationality by naturalisation*, Embassy of Greece – London (internet), http://www.greekembassy.org.uk/pages_en/citizenships.html, consulted 25 May 2006; *Travel advice for Greece*, 16 February 2006, Australian Department of Foreign Affairs and Trade (internet), http://www.smartraveller.gov.au/zw-cgi/view/Advice/Greece, consulted 25 May 2006; *Consular information sheet – Greece*, 10 February 2006, United States Department of State (internet), http://travel.state.gov/travel/cis_pa_tw/cis/cis_1127.html, consulted 25 May 2006; *European Bulletin on Nationality – Greece*, 4 June 2004, Council of Europe (internet), http://www.coe.int/T/E/Legal_Affairs/Legal_cooperation/Foreigners_and_citizens/Nationality/Documents/Bulletin/Greece%202004%20E.pdf, consulted 25 May 2006; *Naturalisation for spouses becomes an easy process*, November 1998, Law Offices Haroula Constandinidou (internet), http://www.constandinidou.gr/article2.en.html, consulted 25 May 2006; Konstantinos Tsitselikis, "Citizenship in Greece – present challenges for future changes" (internet), http://www.kemo.gr/archive/papers/Tsitselik.htm, consulted 25 May 2006.

Event	Law	Condition is renunciation/ loss of other nationality
	women who lost nationality upon marriage (conditions)	
State service	Ethnic Greeks acquire nationality by enlistment in armed forces or acceptance to military academies (conditions)	NO
Parent acquires nationality	Unmarried children under 18 are naturalised with parent	NO
Spouse acquires nationality	No direct effect	
Registration	Certain ethnic Greeks domiciled abroad may be recognised as Greek nationals, including parents and children (conditions)	

Special considerations

Withdrawal/loss of nationality

Event	Law	Consequence of event is loss of nationality
Renunciation	Possible if multiple national and adult living abroad; in advance of application for naturalisation abroad; acceptance of foreign public service position entailing acquisition of foreign nationality (not if subject to military obligations or criminal prosecution) – conditions	YES
Attribution at birth conditional	No provision	
Naturalisation elsewhere	Application may be made in advance to lose Greek nationality upon naturalisation abroad. Application to lose Greek nationalitiy after acquisition of foreign nationality granted for extraordinary reasons. (*Deprivation of nationality is possible.*)	NO (*exception*)
Adoption by a	If child under age 18 and acquires nationality of adoptive parents, parents may apply for loss (ministerial discretion – conditions)	POSSIBLE

Event	Law	**Consequence of event is loss of nationality**
Marriage to a foreigner		NO
Spouse acquires other nationality		NO
Parent acquires other nationality		NO
Resumption of previous nationality		NO
Service to foreign state	Application may be made in advance to lose Greek nationality upon acceptance of foreign public service position entailing acquisition of foreign nationality. Application to lose Greek nationalitiy after acquisition of foreign nationality granted for extraordinary reasons. (*Deprivation of nationality is possible.*) – conditions	NO (*exception*)
Other attribution of nationality		NO
(Punitive) deprivation	Possible upon intentional acquisition of foreign nationality; acceptance of foreign public service office and ignoring order to abandon office; while living abroad acts beneficial to foreign state but contrary to Greek interests	YES
Special considerations	Children naturalised with parent may declare they wish to abandon Greek nationality within one year from completing age 18 if of foreign ethnicity and retained previous nationality (conditions)	

General attitude toward multiple nationality
Greece accepts multiple nationality for its citizens. Loss of previous nationality is not a condition of naturalisation in Greece, and naturalisation abroad does not provoke loss of Greek nationality unless a specific application to that effect is made in advance (or afterwards in exceptional circumstances). Some countries warn their nationals that they may be required to do military service or complete other obligations when in Greece if they are Greek dual nationals or even elegible for Greek nationality, or considered Greek by Greek authorities. Dual nationality for the ethnic Greek minority in southern Albania is reportedly the subject of discussions between the two countries.

Recognition of Multiple Nationality

Greek law provides that "[p]ersons having more than one citizenships [sic], including Grek, shall be considered Greek citizens and shall have all the obligations and rights of Greek citizens. Persons having more than one citizenships [sic], excluding Greek, shall declare to the aliens' and immigration service their citizenship of preference, provided that they have obtained a passport or another travel document of the state concerned.

Guatemala[25]

Nationality category or status

Only one, although the Constitution states that nationals by birth in in one of the republics that constituted the Federation of Central America (considered by Guatemala to be: El Salvador, Honduras, Nicaragua, Guatemala, Costa Rica) or Belize, shall be considered Guatemalans by birth (*origen*) should they be domiciled in Guatemala and express a desire to be Guatemalan. They are not required to renounce prior nationality. The Nationality Act states that recognition as a Guatemalan in a determined "status" does not prevent being such in a "larger sense" as long as a legal basis exists. The Constitution creates a specific distinction between nationality and citizenship, defining citizens as Guatemalans who are 18 years of age or over. While nationals by birth (*origen*) may not be deprived of their nationality, citizenship may be suspended, lost or recovered by law. The Nationality Act defines Guatemalan nationality as the juridical-political link that exists between persons determined by the Constitution, and the State of Guatemala. Using wording from the *Nottebohm Case* in the International Court of Justice, the Act states that Guatemalan nationality "has as its basis a social fact of attachment and a connection of existence, interests and sentiments and implies reciprocal rights and obligations".

Attribution/acquisition of nationality

Event	Law	Condition is renunciation/ loss of other nationality
Birth	In Guatemala, including Guatemalan vessels and aircraft (not if parents diplomats)	NO
	Overseas to a Guatemalan parent	
Naturalisation	Upon fulfillment of conditions	YES (*exception: perhaps ineffective renunciation*)

---

[25] GUATEMALA: *Constitución Política de la República de Guatemala, 1985 con reformas de 1993*, 1985 (as amended until 1993), *Decreto número 1613 – Ley de Nacionalidad y sus reformas*, 29 October 1966 (as amended until 1996), *Decreto número 95-98 – Ley de Migración*, 26 November 1998, **UNHCR (internet)**; *Discurso de Canciller Gabriel Orellana Rojas pronunciado con ocasión de la revelación del busto del General Francisco Morazán el la Plaza de la Federación Centroamericana*, 30 April 2002, Ministerio de Relaciones Exteriores (internet), http://www.minex.gob.gt/discursos/disministerio/dis2002/disCancillerrevelacion-bustomorazan.htm, consulted 16 May 2006; *Procedimiento para la obtención de nacionalidad Guatemalteca por naturalización*, Ministerio de Relaciones Exteriores (internet), http://www.minex.gob.gt/nacionalidad/naturalizacion.htm, consulted 16 May 2006; *Obtención de la nacionalidad Guatemalteca*, Ministerio de Relaciones Exteriores (internet), http://www.minex.gob.gt/nacionalidad/nacionalidad.htm, consulted 16 May 2006; *Guatemaltecos nunca pierden nacionalidad*, Ministerio de Relaciones Exteriores (internet), http://www.minex.gob.gt/prensa/despliega.asp?Documento=163&Banner=&Texto1=&Texto2=, consulted 16 May 2006.

Event	Law	**Condition is renunciation/ loss of other nationality**
	(*An oath of renunciation of foreign nationality must be sworn – steps to ensure loss of foreign nationality may or may not be required- conditions*)	
Adoption		
Legitimation	For birth overseas various government depts. involved (conditions)	NO
Marriage	Facilitated naturalisation – automatic if loses other nationality upon marriage to Guatemalan (conditions)	
Resumption	Possible for those who renounced (conditions)	NO
State service	Facilitated naturalisation	
Parent acquires nationality	Children can be included in parents' naturalisation – must opt upon age of majority (conditions)	
Spouse acquires nationality	All acts must be done by individual him- or herself	
Registration	Nationals by birth in in one of the republics that constituted the Federation of Central America are be considered Guatemalans by birth (*origen*) should they be domiciled in Guatemala and express a desire to be Guatemalan	NO

Special considerations

Withdrawal/loss of nationality

Event	Law	**Consequence of event is loss of nationality**
Renunciation	Possible only when renunciation is a condition of voluntary naturalisation elsewhere	YES (*exception*)
	(*Otherwise nationality cannot be renounced or lost*)	
Attribution at birth conditional	No provision	
Naturalisation elsewhere		NO

Event	Law	Consequence of event is loss of nationality
Adoption by a foreigner		NO
Marriage to a foreigner		NO
Spouse acquires other nationality		NO
Parent acquires other nationality		NO
Resumption of previous nationality		
Service to foreign state		
Other attribution of nationality	Those naturalised during minority, if they do not exercise option of nationality upon attaining majority – naturalisation may be revoked (conditions)	YES
(Punitive) deprivation	Naturalization may be revoked for: activities against state security, public order or institutions; invoking foreign sovereignty; refusal to defend the state; fraud in acquisition; bad faith/ fraud in marriage (conditions)	
Special considerations	Guatemalans by naturalisation may lose nationality upon more than four years' residence abroad (conditions)	YES

General attitude toward multiple nationality
The Constitution provides that no Guatemalan by birth may be deprived of nationality, and naturalisation elsewhere does not provoke loss of Guatemalan nationality. Guatemalan nationality cannot be renounced, except in cases where renunciation is an express requirement of naturalisation elsewhere. In these cases the Nationality Act provides for a procedure for registration as a foreigner in Guatemala and loss of nationality. Otherwise, Guatemalans who use foreign nationality in Guatemala commit a criminal offense, as does any official who assists them. Army officers must be Guatemalan by birth and never have adopted foreign nationality.

Recognition of Multiple Nationality
The Nationality Act states that within Guatemala, no multiple or dual nationality of Guatemalans will be recognised, and no foreign rights of Guatemalans may be invoked against the state. In their other countries of nationality, however, Guatemalan multiple nationals may exercise rights and be subject to obligations of nationality. Guatemalans by birth who are multiple nationals may use their other country's travel document to enter and depart Guatemala.

*Hong Kong[26]
Special Administrative Region of the People's Republic of China (HKSAR)

Nationality category or status
There is technically only one Chinese nationality, but the PRC's Nationality Law is implemented differently in the HKSAR, according to Article 18 of, and Annex III to, the *Hong Kong Basic Law*, interpreted in accordance with the *Explanations of Some Questions by the Standing Committee of the National People's Congress Concerning the Implementation of the Nationality Law of the PRC in the HKSAR* (adopted at the 19th meeting of the Standing Committee of the NPC at the 8th NPC on 15 May 1986). Chinese nationality in relation to Hong Kong and rights of residence in the HKSAR are separate issues, but are linked here (exceptionally) for the purposes of this study.

---

[26] HONG KONG: *Joint Declaration of the Government of the United Kingdom of Great Britain and Northern Ireland and the Government of the People's Republic of China on the Question of Hong Kong*, 19 December 1984; *Basic Law of the Hong Kong Special Administrative Region of the People's Republic of China*, 1 July 1997, **UNHCR (internet)**; *Guide to Consular Protection and Services Outside Chinese Territory*, 1 March 2006, Immigration Department of the HKSAR (internet), http://www.immd.gov.hk/ehtml/topical_5_2.htm, consulted 8 April 2006; *Consular protection and right of abode in HK(SAR) for dual nationals*, Consulate General of the United States of America Hong Kong and Macau (internet), http://hongkong.usconsulate.gov/consular/acs/dualnationals.htm, consulted 8 April 2006; *Guide to China's Consular Protection and Services Overseas*, 16 June 2004, Embassy of the PRC in the Kingdom of the Netherlands (internet), http://www.chinaembassy.nl/eng/xwdt/t137432.htm, consulted 8 April 2006; *Table of Consular Conventions and Agreements Between China and Foreign Countries*, 18 May 2004, Embassy of the PRC in the Republic of Estonia (internet), http://www.chinaembassy.ee/eng/lsqw/lsxx/t111172.htm, consulted 8 April 2006; *Immigration Ordinance*, Hong Kong Ordinances (internet), http://www.hklii.org/hk/legis/en/ord/115/, consulted 8 April 2006; (a) Application for Hong Kong Special Administrative Region Passport. Notes for guidance and application form, vol. ID841A, (b) Application for verification of eligibility for permanent identity card, vol. ROP 145, (c) Declaration of change of nationality. A guide for applicants, vol. ID869A; (d) Information leaflet. Arrangements for entry to the Hong Kong Special Administrative Region (HKSAR) for overseas Chinese and Chinese residents of Taiwan, vol. ID 895A; (e) Naturalization as a Chinese national. Nationality law of the People's Republic of China. A guide for applicants; (f) Renunciation of Chinese nationality. Nationality law of the People's Republic of China. A guide for applicants, vol. ID877A; (g) Restoration of Chinese nationality. Nationality law of the People's Republic of China. A guide for applicants, vol. ID878A (Hong Kong: Immigration Department of the Hong Kong Special Administrative Region of the People's Republic of China, 2001); Immigration Department of the Hong Kong Special Administrative Region of the People's Republic of China, Right of abode in the Hong Kong Special Administrative Region, Third (revised) ed. (Hong Kong: Hong Kong Special Administrative Region Government, 2000); Andrew Byrnes and Johannes Chan, "The British Nationality (Hong Kong) Act 1990", in Public Law and Human Rights. A Hong Kong Sourcebook, ed. Andrew Byrnes and Johannes Chan, 74–80 (Hong Kong: Butterworths, 1993); Johannes M. M. Chan, "Hong Kong: an analysis of the British nationality proposals", Immigration and nationality law and practice (1990) vol. 4, 57–62; Frank Ching, "Chinese

Attribution/acquisition of Chinese nationality and the right of abode in Hong Kong

Event	Law	Condition is renunciation/ loss of other nationality
Birth	In Hong Kong to a Chinese (Hong Kong) parent	NO
	In Hong Kong to stateless parents, or when their nationality is uncertain, who have settled there	
	Overseas to (Hong Kong) Chinese parent	
Naturalisation	Upon fulfilment of requirements	YES
Adoption	No direct effect	
Legitimation	(see birth)	
Marriage	Not automatic	
Resumption	Possible upon conditions	YES
State service	Naturalisation for "other legitimate reasons"	YES
Parent acquires nationality	Not automatic – may apply for child's naturalisation	YES
Spouse acquires nationality	No effect	
Registration		

Withdrawal/loss of nationality

Event	Law	Consequence of event is loss of nationality
Renunciation	Possible if have foreign relatives; settled abroad; legitimate reasons; but	YES

nationality in the Basic Law", in The Basic Law and Hong Kong's future, ed. Peter Wesley-Smith and Albert H. Y. Chen (Hong Kong: Butterworths, 1988); G. B. Endacott, Government and people in Hong Kong 1841–1962 (Hong Kong: Hong Kong University Press, 1964); Robin M. White, "Hong Kong: nationality, immigration and the agreement with China", International and Comparative Law Quarterly (1987) vol. 36, 483–503; Robin M. White, "Nationality aspects of the Hong Kong settlement", Case Western Reserve Journal of International Law (1988) vol. 20, 225–251; Mason, Anthony, "Human rights in China and Hong Kong", lecture at The Australian National University, 21 August 2001, Canberra: ANU Centre for International and Public Law, 2001.

Event	Law	Consequence of event is loss of nationality
	application must be approved. Not possible for government and military personnel.	
Attribution at birth conditional	No provision	
Naturalisation elsewhere	(*Unless have made a declaration of change of nationality to the HKSAR Immigration Department*)	NO (*exception*)
Adoption by a foreigner	No effect unless has renounced nationality	NO
Marriage to a foreigner	No effect	NO
Spouse acquires other nationality	No effect	NO
Parent acquires other nationality	No automatic effect	NO
Resumption of previous nationality	By naturalised (Hong Kong) Chinese citizens	YES
Service to foreign state		
Other attribution of nationality	If settled abroad and acquisition is voluntary, but no effect if no declaration of change of nationality to Hong Kong Immigration Department	NO
(Punitive) deprivation	Possible for fraud in acquisition	POSSIBLE

General attitude toward multiple nationality
The Chinese Nationality Law states specifically that dual nationality is "not recognised" for any Chinese national. The foreign nationality of persons considered to be Chinese citizens is not recognised in Hong Kong, but tolerated in practice for Hong Kong Chinese who have acquired foreign nationality but do not file a Declaration of Change of Nationality with the Hong Kong Immigration Department – unlike mainland Chinese, they are not considered to have lost their Chinese nationality by being naturalised abroad. By virtue of this practice, their children become Hong Kong residents and Chinese citizens even if born overseas and concurrently acquiring another nationality.

Recognition of Multiple Nationality
No foreign diplomatic protection in Hong Kong or mainland China will be allowed for Chinese (Hong Kong) nationals, unless they file a Declaration of Change of Nationality, with certain exceptions: notwithstanding the general provision that multiple nationality will never be recognised, the PRC entered into an agreement with the United States stipulating that all US

citizens who enter Hong Kong on US passports will be considered US nationals for the purposes of consular protection, for up to 90 days. After such period, a Declaration of Change of Nationality must be filed with the Hong Kong Immigration Deparment for a right of protection to continue, if they are Chinese (Hong Kong) citizens. Other consular agreements have been entered into by the PRC with other countries.

Overseas, although Hong Kong Chinese citizens may not have lost their Chinese nationality for purposes related to Hong Kong notwithstanding possession of another nationality, it is unclear whether China's policy of non-recognition of multiple nationality leads to a policy whereby consular protection would be extended or not. The Ministry of Foreign Affairs states only that as Chinese citizens residing abroad automatically lose Chinese nationality upon naturalisation elsewhere (not the case for Hong Kong Chinese citizens) no protection can be enjoyed. It would seem that while protection would not be exercised against another state of nationality, in the case of third states this is less clear.

*Hungary[27]

Nationality category or status

Only one, and no technical distinction between nationality and citizenship.

Attribution/acquisition of nationality

Event	Law	Condition is renunciation/ loss of other nationality
Birth	To a Hungarian parent	NO
	In Hungary to resident stateless parents	
	Foundling	
Naturalisation	Upon fulfilment of requirements	NO
Adoption	May be naturalised immediately	NO
Legitimation	With retroactive effect from birth	NO
Marriage	Not automatic	
Resumption	If residing in Hungary and requirements fulfilled	NO

---

[27] HUNGARY: _Constitution of the Republic of Hungary_, 31 December 1990; _Act LV of 1993 on Hungarian Citizenship_, 1 October 1993; _Cabinet Decree 125/1993. (IX.22.) on the Execution of Act. LV. of 1993 on Hungarian Citizenship_, 1 October 1993; _Act LXII of 2001 on Hungarians Living in Neighboring Countries (adopted by Parliament on 19 June 2001)_, 1 January 2002, **UNHCR (internet)**; _Consular Service_, 23 June 2004, Government of Hungary Portal (internet), http://www.magyarorszag.hu/angol/orszaginfo/kulpolitika/konzuliszolgalat/consular.htm, consulted 8 April 2006; _Hungarian Minorities Abroad_, 5 August 2003, Government of Hungary Portal (internet), http://www.magyarorszag.hu/angol/orszaginfo/kulpolitika/hatarontulimagyarok/kisebbseg_a.html, consulted 8 April 2006; _Hungarian Certificate_, 23 June 2004, Government of Hungary Portal (internet), http://www.magyarorszag.hu/angol/orszaginfo/kulpolitika/hatarontulimagyarok/magyarigazolvany/certificate.html, consulted 8 April 2006; _The Hungarian Diaspora_, 5 August 2003, Government of Hungary Portal (internet), http://www.magyarorszag.hu/angol/orszaginfo/kulpolitika/hatarontulimagyarok/diaszpora/diszpora_a.html, consulted 8 April 2006; _Hungarians in the neighboring countries_, 5 August 2005, Government of Hungary Portal (internet), http://www.magyarorszag.hu/angol/orszaginfo/kulpolitika/hatarontulimagyarok/hatarontul/magyarok_a_szomszedos_orszagokban_a.html, consulted 8 April 2006; "Privilegien für Ausland-Ungarn abgebaut", Basler Zeitung, 31 May – 1 June 2003, 6; André Liebich, "Plural citizenship in post-Communist states", _International Journal of Refugee Law_ (2000) vol. 12, no. 1, 97–107; Ryszard W. Piotrowicz, "The Australian-Hungarian Consular Treaty of 1988 and the regulation of dual nationality", _The Sydney Law Review_ (1990) vol. 12, no. 2/3, 569–583; Michael A. Weinstein, "Hungary's Referendum on Dual Citizenship: A small victory for Europeanism" 13 December 2004, Global Policy Forum (internet), http://www.globalpolicy.org/nations/sovereign/sover/emerg/2004/1213hungaryref.htm, consulted 8 April 2006.

Event	Law	**Condition is renunciation/** **loss of other nationality**
State service		
Parent acquires nationality	No effect	
Spouse acquires nationality	No effect	
Registration	Grant upon declaration if certain previous deprivation	NO

Withdrawal/loss of nationality

Event	Law	**Consequence of event is** **loss of nationality**
Renunciation	If reside abroad and multiple national or will acquire foreign nationality	YES
Attribution at birth conditional	No provision	
Naturalisation elsewhere		NO
Adoption by a foreigner		NO
Marriage to a foreigner		NO
Spouse acquires other nationality		NO
Parent acquires other nationality		NO
Resumption of previous nationality		NO
Service to foreign state		NO
Other attribution of nationality		NO
(Punitive) deprivation	Revocation of citizenship if obtained through unlawful means, but not after ten years of award of citizenship	POSSIBLE

General attitude toward multiple nationality
Accepting the production of multiple nationality for its citizens, Hungarian policy statements on nationality and rights are more related to the situation of ethnic Hungarians outside

Hungary. The Constitution states that "[t]he Republic of Hungary recognizes its responsibilities toward Hungarians living outside the borders of the country and shall assist them in fostering their relations to Hungary". In 2001 the government provided ethnic Hungarian non-nationals in Slovakia, the Ukraine, Romania, Serbia, Croatia and Slovenia with the right to special identity cards providing facilitated entry into Hungary, and various entitlements. As of June 2003 over 650,000 persons had applied. The policy reportedly led to protests from neighbouring countries and the disapproval of the European Union. An agreement was reached with Romania in 2003 whereby many of the scheme's benefits would go to all Romanians, not just ethnic Hungarians. In 2004, however, the Government opposed a referendum forced upon it, on whether to give ethnic Hungarians a quasi-automatic right to apply for Hungarian citizenship (popularly known as a referendum on "dual citizenship". The referendum did not pass, with 38% of registered voters participating, of which 51% voted in favour. Multiple nationals are not treated differently from other nationals.

Recognition of Multiple Nationality
The Citizenship Act provides that Hungarian multiple nationals are regarded as Hungarian nationals for the purposes of the application of Hungarian law. Notwithstanding, Hungary has entered into various consular treaties that provide that its citizens will be treated as foreigners if they enter on foreign passports with appropriate entry visas. In relation to consular protection abroad, the Hungarian government cites the Constitutional provision (article 69(3)) whereby all Hungarian nationals have a right to protection while legally abroad, but adds that the 2001 Law on Consular Protection's provisions must take into account the requirements of international law and the rights of other states.

Iceland[28]

Nationality category or status

Only one, and no technical distinction between nationality and citizenship.

Attribution/acquisition of nationality

Event	Law	Condition is renunciation/ loss of other nationality
Birth	To an Icelandic mother	NO
	To an Icelandic father in wedlock (not if judicial separation when child conceived)	*(but see conditional attribution)*
	In Iceland to an Icelandic father out of wedlock under the Children's Act (conditions)	
	Foundling	
	(Child born abroad without domicile or residence in Iceland loses at age 22 unless thereby stateless – may apply to retain – conditions)	
Naturalisation	For various categories upon fulfillment of conditions	NO
Adoption	With permission of Icelandic authorities if child under 12 (conditions)	NO
Legitimation	Birth overseas to Icelandic father out of wedlock, father may apply before child 18 (conditions)	NO
Marriage	Facilitated naturalisation	NO
Resumption	Person who acquired Icelandic nationality at birth and domiciled in Iceland until age 18, then lost nationality, upon two years' domicile and declaration – children included (conditions)	NO

---

[28] ICELAND: *Iceland Nationality Act*, 23 December 1952 (as amended until 2003), Official Translation, Ministry of Justice and Ecclesiastical Affairs – Iceland (internet), http://eng.doms-malaraduneyti.is/laws-and-regulations/nr/114, consulted 7 May 2006; *Dual Citizenship*, Embassy of Iceland – Ottawa (internet), http://www.iceland.org/ca/the-embassy/consular-services/citizenship/, consulted 7 May 2006.

Event	Law	Condition is renunciation/ loss of other nationality
	Resumption upon declaration and domicile in Iceland for person who lost Icelandic citizenship and ever since citizen of Nordic country	
	Resumption by notification for certain category (conditions)	
	Facilitated naturalisation	
State service	Parliament may grant by statute	NO
Parent acquires nationality	Unmarried children under 18 of persons who acquire by notification, if has custody and domiciled in Iceland	NO
	Facilitated naturalisation	
Spouse acquires nationality		
Registration (Notification)	Domiciled and residing in Iceland continuously since age 11 (or if stateless age 13), notification in writing after 18 but before 20	NO
Special considerations		

Withdrawal/loss of nationality

Event	Law	Consequence of event is loss of nationality
Renunciation	Residence abroad and has or will become foreign national (conditions)	YES
Attribution at birth conditional	Child born abroad without domicile or residence in Iceland loses at age 22 unless thereby stateless – may apply to retain – conditions	YES
Naturalisation elsewhere		NO
Adoption by a foreigner		
Marriage to a foreigner		NO
Spouse acquires other nationality		NO

Event	Law	Consequence of event is loss of nationality
Parent acquires other nationality		NO
Resumption of previous nationality		NO
Service to foreign state		
Other attribution of nationality		NO
(Punitive) deprivation		NO
Special considerations	Children of Icelandic citizen who was born abroad and loses nationality at age 22, who acquired nationality on the basis of parent's nationality, lose at same time unless thereby stateless	

General attitude toward multiple nationality

The Icelandic Citizenship Act was amended in 2003 to enable citizens to retain Icelandic nationality upon naturalisation elsewhere. Renunciation of nationality is permitted in cases where a state does not "allow dual citizenship", but proof that the new nationality will be acquired once release is granted, must be submitted. Citizens who lost Icelandic nationality previously by operation of law upon being naturalised elsewhere may apply for their Icelandic nationality to be restored. Applicants must reside in Iceland or have previously resided in Iceland (detailed conditions) and resumption of Icelandic citizenship must not lead to loss of the other nationality. The provision that children born abroad must have been domiciled or have resided in Iceland prior to age 22 in order to retain Icelandic nationality, barring statelessness, may be circumvented by an application in advance to retain nationality. Ties to Iceland must, however, be shown.

*India[29]

Nationality category or status

Only one category of nationality: Indian Citizenship, however as of 2003 (amended in 2005) two categories of (municipal) citizenship: Indian Citizen (national), and Overseas Citizen of India (OCI). India restates its constitutional prohibition on dual nationality in announcements related to OCI status, and that OCI applicants must be foreign nationals. The United Kingdom has, however, stated that it will treat the status of OCI as that of possessing the nationality/citizenship of another state for purposes of British nationality law.

---

[29] INDIA: *Constitution of India*. 26 January 1950; *Citizenship Act*, no. 57, 30 December 1955 (as amended); *Citizenship Rules*, 7 July 1956; *Citizenship Amendment Act 2003*, 7 January 2004, *Citizenship (Registration of Citizens and Issue of National Identity Cards) Rules*, 2003, *Emigration Act*, 1983, no. 31 of 13 September 1983; *Citizenship (Pondicherry) Order*, 29 November 1962; *Foreigners (Restriction on Chinese Nationals) Order*, 25 October 1962; *Goa, Daman and Diu (Citizenship) Order*, 28 March 1962; *Dadra and Nagar Haveli (Citizenship) Order*, 1962, 1 January 1970, **UNHCR (internet)**; *Dual Citizenship – Overseas Citizenship of India (OCI)*, Ministry of Home Affairs (internet), http://www.mha.nic.in/oci/oci-main.htm, consulted 9 April 2006; *Scope of Overseas Citizenship of India Extended-Press Note*, 2 December 2005, Government of India Press Information Bureau (internet), http://www.mha.nic.in/press-release/pr021205.pdf, consulted 9 April 2006; *Salient Points of Citizenship Amendment Ordinance of 2005 Press Note*, 29 June 2005, Government of India Press Information Bureau (internet), http://pib.nic.in/release/release.asp?relid=9929, consulted 8 April 2006; *New Information on Indian Citizenship Laws-Implications for Elegibility for British Citizenship*, Home Office (internet), http://www.ind.homeoffice.gov.uk/ind/en/home/applying/british_nationality/new_information_on.html?, consulted 9 April 2006; *Registration and naturalisation other than under the British Nationality Act 1981 – Annex H – Indian Citizenship Law*, 27 January 2006, Home Office (internet), http://www.ind.homeoffice.gov.uk/ind/en/home/laws___policy/policy_instructions/nis/chapter_14/annex_h.html, consulted 9 April 2006; S. Chandrasekharan, *FIJI: Ex PM Chaudhry's dilemma*, 6 March 2003, South Asia Analysis Group (internet), http://www.saag.org/papers7/paper624.html, consulted 9 April 2006; Virginia Gidley-Kitchin, "Nationality joy for overseas Indians", BBC News, 9 January 2003 (internet), http://news.bbc.co.uk/1/hi/world/south_asia/2643149.stm, consulted 9 April 2006; *Dual citizenship limited to 7 nations, for now*, Rediff.com (internet), www.rediff.com/money/2003/jan/09 pbd3.htm, consulted 9 April 2006; *We do not want your riches, just the richness of your experience*, speech by Indian Prime Minister Atal Bihari Vajpayee's at the inaugural session of the First Pravasi Bharatiya Divas celebrations, 9 January 2003 (internet), http://www.rediff.com/money/2003/jan/09pbd4.htm, consulted 9 April 2006; *PM to NRIs: Panel on dual nationality question in pipeline*, The Hindustan Times, 13 November 1998 (internet), http://www.hindustantimes.com/nonfram/131198/detFRO03.htm, consulted 1 August 2003; (Lord) Bhikhu Parekh, *Why the Diaspora needs India*, 14 January 2003 (internet), http://www.rediff.com/news/2003/jan/08 spec1.htm, consulted 9 April 2006; *Dual citizenship to be granted to NRIs*, Press release of the High Commission of India in Ottawa, 6 May 2003 (internet), http://www.hciottawa.ca/news/pr/pr-030507.html, consulted 9 April 2006; S. K. Agrawala and M. Koteswara Rao, "Nationality and international law in Indian perspective", in *Nationality and international law in Asian perspective*, ed. Ko Swan Sik, 65–123 (Dordrecht: Martinus Nijhoff Publishers, 1990); Campbell

Attribution/acquisition of nationality

Event	Law	Condition is renunciation/ loss of other nationality
Birth	In India to Indian parent and other parent is not an illegal migrant, foreign (non-Indian citizen) diplomat, or enemy alien and birth in occupied territory	NO
	Overseas to Indian parent and birth is registered within one year, or with Central Government permission thereafter (conditions)	NO (*but parents must declare minor does not hold passport of another country*)
Naturalisation	Upon fulfilment of requirements	YES (*exceptions for persons who render certain distinguished service*)
Adoption	No direct effect	
Legitimation	(see birth)	
Marriage	No direct effect	
Resumption	Possible for certain categories	YES
State service	May lead to naturalisation	YES (*see exceptions above*)
Parent acquires nationality	No direct effect	
Spouse acquires nationality	No direct effect	
Registration	For certain categories (facilitated for Overseas Citizens of India)	YES

Special considerations

and Meek, eds., *International immigration and nationality law*; Cohen and Leng, "The Sino-Indian dispute over the internment and detention of Chinese in India"; Subhash C. Kashyap, *Citizens and the Constitution. (Citizenship values under the Constitution)* (New Delhi: Public-ations Division, Ministry of Information and Broadcasting, Government of India, 1997); Ranjit Malhotra, "Dual nationality for Indians: the need for a fresh debate", *Immigration and nation-ality law and practice* (1996) vol. 10, no. 2, 57–59; Meher K. Master, *Citizenship of India. Dual nationality and the Constitution*, ed. L. M. Singhvi (Calcutta: Eastern Law House, 1970).

Withdrawal/loss of nationality

Event	Law	Consequence of event is loss of nationality
Renunciation	If of full age and capacity. Government may withhold in wartime	YES
Attribution at birth conditional	Citizens by descent (birth outside India) are deprived of Indian nationality six months after attaining full age if they do not renounce other citizenship/ nationality	YES
Naturalisation elsewhere	If voluntary acquisition (except if India at war, until government confirms loss)	YES
Adoption by a foreigner	No direct effect (unless direct attribution of nationality thereby)	NO
Marriage to a foreigner	No direct effect	NO
Spouse acquires other nationality	No direct effect	NO
Parent acquires other nationality	Child has right of resumption	YES
Resumption of previous nationality		YES
Service to foreign state		
Other attribution of nationality	Any voluntary acquisition of foreign nationality (except in wartime)	YES
(Punitive) deprivation	Certain citizens by naturalisation or registration: for fraud in obtaining nationality, disloyalty, help to the enemy, certain sentences, residence abroad for 7 years if not student or in government or international service, and no annual registration	YES

Special considerations

General attitude toward multiple nationality
Indian policy toward multiple nationality has been characterised as "ambivalent", although provisions introduced in 2003 seem to harden opposition to multiple nationality. Although any voluntary acquisition of foreign nationality results in the loss of Indian nationality, and abandonment of foreign nationality is a condition of acquisition of Indian nationality, multiple nationality produced by birth in India is not prevented, but is not recognised. In 2003 the Citizenship Act was amended such that Indian citizens by descent (birth outside India to an Indian

parent) would lose their Indian nationality six months after attaining full age if they continued to possess another nationality. Inital government statements in 2002 that Indians would be allowed to acquire the nationality of specific countries, without losing their Indian nationality, proved untrue. Voluntary acquisition of another nationality still results in loss of Indian nationality. Rather, in 2003 the government amended the Citizenship Act to provide for what appears to be a new category of municipal citizenship, "Overseas Citizen of India" (OCI) to persons of Indian origin, including Indians who lose their nationality through naturalisation elsewhere. OCI applicants must come from a country that is characterised by India as "allowing dual citizenship in some form or other", the original list including Australia, Canada, Finland, France, Greece, Ireland, Israel, Italy, the Netherlands, New Zealand, Portugal, Cyprus, Sweden, Switzerland, the United Kingdom and the United States. A previous proposal had included Singapore, whose legislation would not be conducive to such a policy (see section on Singapore herein). In 2005 the Indian Government announced that the provision would be extended to all countries except Pakistan and Bangladesh, doing away with the criterion relating to other countries' acceptance of multiple nationality, then later ostensibly reinstating the provision in another announcement. Likewise, the government announced that certain administrative procedures to obtain the status would be eliminated, including an oath of allegiance, and declaration of property. OCIs are to be provided with a life-long multiple-entry multiple-purpose visa that reportedly gives them the same economic, financial and educational rights as non-resident Indian Citizens. They may, however, not acquire agriculture/plantation properties. OCIs do not enjoy the right to vote, hold certain high office, or be employed in the public service. The Indian government characterises the policy as a way to facilitate ties of ethnic Indians to India, and for them to "contribute towards the national goal of equitable development by generously contributing to national economy".

Recognition of Multiple Nationality
The foreign nationality of any Indian is not recognised in India. Numerous court cases have held that Indian nationality is lost merely by any evidence of possession of a foreign nationality, but a more recent case in the 1990s held that if Indian nationality had not been lost (the foreign nationality was acquired at birth concurrently with Indian nationality), non-recognition of foreign nationality dictates that Indian nationality be given full effect for purposes of entitlements in India.

*Indonesia[30]

Nationality category or status
Only one, with no technical distinction between nationality and citizenship.

Attribution/acquisition of nationality

Event	Law	Condition is renunciation/ loss of other nationality
Birth	To an Indonesian father (married)	NO
	To an Indonesian mother (unmarried)	(*Exception: unless other nationality is acted on or taken up, such as by applying for a passport, in which case YES*)
	To an Indonesian mother if father stateless, of unknown nationality, or child has no legal relationship to father	
	In Indonesia to stateless parents, or if child otherwise stateless	
	Foundlings	
Naturalisation	Upon fulfilment of requirements (not possible for married woman without husband)	YES
Adoption	By an Indonesian father of a child under age five	NO (*see exception above*)
Legitimation	Establishment of a legal relationship to Indonesian father before age 18 or marriage	NO (*see exception above*)

---

[30] INDONESIA: *Law No. 62 of 1958, Law on the Citizenship of the Republic of Indonesia*, 1 August 1958, **UNHCR (internet)**; *Consular Information Sheet-Indonesia*, 9 July 2004, United States Department of State (internet), http://travel.state.gov/travel/cis_pa_tw/cis/cis_1140.html, consulted 9 April 2006; Hellmuth Hecker, "Die Staatsangehörigkeit von Chinesen, die vor 1900 nach Niederländisch-Indien eingewandert sind, und ihrer Nachkommen", in *Gutachten zum internationalen Recht*, ed. Hellmuth Hecker, *Werkhefte des Instituts für Internationale Angelegenheiten der Universität Hamburg* (Hamburg, Frankfurt: Alfred Metzner Verlag GmbH, 1975); Ko Swan Sik and Teuku Moh. Rhadie, "Nationality and international law in Indonesian perspective," in *Nationality and international law in Asian perspective*, ed. Ko Swan Sik, 125–176 (Dordrecht: Martinus Nijhoff Publishers, 1990); *Undang-Undang No. 62 Tahun 1958 Tentang Kewarga-Negaraan Republik Indonesia*, Lembaga Bantuan Hukum (internet), http://www.lbh-apik.or.id/uu-62–58.htm, consulted 9 April 2006; Netherlands Council of the Institute of Pacific Relations, "The legal status of foreigners in Netherlands India", in *The legal status of aliens in Pacific countries*, ed. Norman MacKenzie (London: Oxford University Press, 1937; reprint, 1975); Sasmojo, ed., *Menjelesaikan masalah dwikewarganegaraan RI-RRT;* Sudargo Gautama, *Tafsiran undang-undang kewarganegaraan Republik Indonesia* (Bandung: Penerbit Alumni, 1983).

Event	Law	**Condition is renunciation/ loss of other nationality**
Marriage	Declaration by alien wife after one year of marriage	YES
Resumption	In certain cases	YES
State service	May lead to special naturalisation (government discretion)	NO
Parent acquires nationality	Unmarried minor children of married father/unmarried mother who acquires Indonesian nationality, who reside in Indonesia (unless otherwise stateless)	YES
Spouse acquires nationality	Husband's acquisition of Indonesian nationality extended to the wife automatically, unless she continues to possess foreign nationality	YES
Registration	Certain groups have right to petition for nationality	YES

Withdrawal/loss of nationality

Event	Law	**Consequence of event is loss of nationality**
Renunciation	By Indonesian spouse after one year of marriage to foreign spouse, unless stateless	YES
	By divorced wife who acquired Indonesian nationality by marriage, unless thereby stateless	
	By children who acquired nationality by adoption or parent's acquisition of Indonesian nationality, unless stateless (conditions)	
	May request if over 21, domiciled abroad, and not thereby stateless, but requires government approval	
Attribution at birth	No provision (see birth)	
Naturalisation elsewhere	Acquisition of other nationality of own free will (with certain exception if person is in Indonesia at the time)	YES
Adoption by a foreigner	Any recognition of parentage of an unmarried minor that leads to acquisition of foreign nationaltiy	YES

Event	Law	**Consequence of event is loss of nationality**
	Adoption of a child under five, unless thereby stateless	
Marriage to a foreigner	No effect on Indonsian husband. Automatic deprivation for Indonesian woman, unless thereby stateless.	DEPENDS (*see exception above*)
Spouse acquires other nationality	Spouse's loss of Indonesian nationality automatically affects other spouse, unless thereby stateless	YES
Parent acquires other nationality	Loss by married father/unmarried mother affects unmarried minor children, unless thereby stateless	YES
Resumption of previous nationality	Including not securing release from foreign nationality when required to by Indonesian law	YES
Service to foreign state	Foreign military, state or other international service without prior permission (conditions); oath or promise of loyalty to other state	YES
Other attribution of nationality	Any voluntary acquisition of foreign nationality	YES
(Punitive) deprivation	Any grant based on incorrect information may be withdrawn	POSSIBLE
Special considerations	Voting in certain foreign elections; possession of valid foreign passport; five years' residence abroad without periodic declaration of retention (as of age 18)	YES

General attitude toward multiple nationality
Indonesia states generally that it does not accept multiple nationality for its citizens, but does not prevent its production in relation to original acquisition of nationality (generally, birth). But if benefits or entitlements related to a foreign nationality are ever taken up, such as voting or application for a passport, Indonesian nationality is considered to have been lost.

Recognition of Multiple Nationality
Article 1 of the Concluding Regulations to the Citizenship Law states that "[a] citizen of the Republic of Indonesia who is within the territory of the Republic of Indonesia is considered to possess no other nationality". Due to the general practice outlined above, consular practice overseas is to extend protection to all those who are considered to possess Indonesian nationality, notwithstanding technical possession of foreign nationality, if benefits or entitlements related to the latter have not been used by the individual in question.

*Iran[31]

Nationality category or status
Only one, and no technical distinction between nationality and citizenship.

Attribution/acquisition of nationality

Event	Law	Condition is renunciation/ loss of other nationality
Birth	In Iran to Iranian father	NO
	In Iran to unknown parents	
	In Iran to alien parents, one of whom was born in Iran (unless possess father's nationality and declare – conditions)	
	In Iran to alien father and one year's residence after age 18	
	Outside Iran to Iranian father	
Naturalisation	Fulfilment of requirements	NO
Adoption		
Legitimation	(see birth)	
Marriage	Foreign women who marry Iranian men	NO
	Facilitated naturalisation for alien husbands of Iranian wives, if have children	

.

---

[31] IRAN: *Constitution of the Islamic Republic of Iran*, 24 October 1979, *Civil Code of the Islamic Republic of Iran* (as at 29 December 1985), **UNHCR (internet)**; *Consular information sheet – Iran*, 3 April 2006, United States Department of State (internet), http://travel.state.gov/travel/cis_pa_tw/cis/cis_1142.html, consulted 9 April 2006; *Travel advice-Iran*, 22 February 2006, Australian Department of Foreign Affairs and Trade (internet), http://www.dfat.gov.au/zw-cgi/view/Advice/Iran, consulted 9 April 2006; *Les conseils aux voyageurs pour: Iran*, 10 February 2006, Swiss Ministry of Foreign Affairs (internet), http://www.eda.admin.ch/travel/iran_f.html, consulted 9 April 2006; *Iran Parliament approves key bill aimed at attracting assets in exile*, 29 July 2003, Payvand's Iran News (internet), http://www.payvand.com/news/03/jul/1197.html, consulted 9 April 2006; Nancy Amoury Combs, "On children and dual nationality: Sabet and The Islamic Republic of Iran", *Leiden Journal of International Law* (2000) vol. 13, no. 1, 173–191; Hessisches Ministerium des Innern und für Sport, "Rundschreiben vom 23.10.2000–II A 11–04–20"; Peter E. Mahoney, "The standing of dual-nationals before the Iran-United States Claims Tribunal", *Virginia Journal of Internaional Law* (1984) vol. 24, no. 3, 695–728.

Event	Law	Condition is renunciation/ loss of other nationality
Resumption	In certain cases	NO
	Of right by Iranian woman who was deprived of nationality by automatic acquistion of husband's nationality upon marriage, after divorce, separation or husband's death	
State service	Naturalisation (special provisions)	NO
Parent acquires nationality	Also attributed to minor children of naturalised man, but children may opt for father's previous nationality within one year after turning 18	NO
Spouse acquires nationality	Also attributed to wife of naturalised man, but wife may opt for husband's previous nationality within one year	NO
Registration		
Special considerations	All persons who reside in Iran are considered to be Iranian nationals, unless their foreign nationality has been established (their foreign nationality documents have not been objected to by the Iranian government)	NO

Withdrawal/loss of nationality

Event	Law	Consequence of event is loss of nationality
Renunciation	If 25 or older, specificallyapproved by government (reportedly improbable), and possess property only as alien	YES
	Non-Iranian wife who acquired nationality by marriage may opt for her former nationality only after divorce or death of husband, but not as long as she has minor children, and she may then only possess property as allowed for aliens	
Attribution at birth conditional	No provision	
Naturalisation elsewhere	(But may lead to loss of property and disqualification from holding certain offices and government positions)	NO

	Event Law	Consequence of event is loss of nationality
Adoption by a foreigner		
Marriage to a foreigner	(*Except Iranian woman loses nationality if husband's nationality is imposed automatically upon marriage*)	NO (*exception*)
Spouse acquires other nationality	(Renunciation of nationality by Iranian husband does not affect wife)	NO
Parent acquires other nationality	(Renuncation of nationality by Iranian father does not affect children)	NO
Resumption of previous nationality		NO
Service to foreign state		
Other attribution of nationality		
(Punitive) deprivation	No provision	

General attitude toward multiple nationality

Iran does nothing to prevent the production of multiple nationality. Laws apparently do distinguish among persons on the basis of multiple nationality in that naturalisation elsewhere may lead to loss of property and disqualification from holding certain offices and positions, and naturalised citizens may not hold certain public offices or government positions. A bill was reportedly introduced in Parliament in 2003 that might allow for some recognition of foreign nationality held by Iranians, in certain cases.

Recognition of Multiple Nationality

Iran does not recognise possession of foreign nationality by its citizens. Nationals are required to enter and depart Iran on Iranian passports, and travel warnings caution citizens who may also be considered Iranian nationals in Iran, that protective services cannot be provided due to Iranian practice. Iranian nationals require an exit visa to depart the country.

*Ireland[32]

Nationality category or status

Only one, and no technical difference between nationality and citizenship, although the Citizenship Act's provision providing for mutual citizenship rights in relation to certain countries implies recognition of the difference. The Irish Constitution speaks of the Irish Nation in relation to the whole island of Ireland.

Attribution/acquisition of nationality

Event	Law	Condition is renunciation/ loss of other nationality
Birth	On the island of Ireland (including Irish ship or aircraft) to: an Irish parent, a parent entitled to Irish citizenship, a British citizen, a parent with permanent residency rights, a parent with British permanent residency rights, a parent who lawfully resided in Ireland for at least three of the four years immediately preceding (excludes time spent as refugee or studying, and diplomats)	NO

---

[32] IRELAND: *Irish Nationality and Citizenship Act*, 1956 (last amended 2004); *Irish Nationality and Citizenship Act*, 2004, *Constitution of Ireland*, 29 December 1937 (as at 20 November 2002), **UNHCR (internet)**; *Information Notice – Entitlement of children born on the Island of Ireland on or after 1 January 2005 to Irish Citizenship*, Department of Justice, Equality and Law Reform (internet), http://www.justice.ie/80256E010039C5AF/vWeb/flJUSQ67XFUS-en/ $File/Notice.pdf, consulted 9 April 2006; *Consular Services*, Department of Foreign Affairs of Ireland (internet), http://foreignaffairs.gov.ie/services/consular/02.asp, consulted 9 April 2006; *Ireland votes to end birth right*, 13 June 2004, BBC News (internet), http://news.bbc.co.uk/2/ hi/europe/3801839.stm, consulted 9 April 2006; "Citizenship Tourists", The Economist, 5 June 2004, 27; "Ireland. Honey pot", The Economist, 28 August 1999, 41; *Ireland and the Irish Abroad – Report of the Task Force on policy regarding Emigrants*, August 2002, Department of Foreign Affairs (internet), http://foreignaffairs.gov.ie/policy/emigrant_taskforce.asp, consulted 9 April 2006; Campbell and Meek, eds., *International immigration and nationality law;* de Groot, "Loss of nationality: a critical inventory"; Philippe de Patoul, Tony O'Connor, and John G. Fish, "Nationalité: Irlande", in *Juris-Classeur Nationalité*, ed. Michel Verwilghen and Charles L. Closset, *Collection des Juris-Classeurs* (Paris: Éditions du Juris-Classeur, 1984); Clive R. Symmons, "Irish nationality law", in *Towards a European nationality. Citizenship, immigration and nationality law in the EU*, ed. Randall Hansen and Patrick Weil, 273–312 (Houndmills: Palgrave, 2001); Brian Thompson, "Transcending territory: towards an agreed Northern Ireland?", in *Accommodating national identities. New approaches in international and domestic law*, ed. Stephen Tierney 233 (The Hague: Kluwer Law International, 2000).

Event	Law	Condition is renunciation/ loss of other nationality
	In Ireland if otherwise stateless	
	Foundlings deemed to have been born in Ireland to Irish parent	
	Overseas to an Irish parent who was born in Ireland, or Irish parent citizen by descent on government service	
	Overseas to Irish parent citizen by descent, if registered	
Naturalisation	Upon fulfilment of requirements	NO
Adoption	Automatic upon legal adoption by Irish national	NO
Legitimation	(see birth)	
Marriage	Post-nuptial citizenship possible unless Irish citizenship acq. by naturalisation, post-nuptial, or token of honour, otherwise	NO
	Not automatic – may lead to facilitated naturalisation	
Resumption	Former citizens born on the island of Ireland who renounced may resume nationality at any time	NO
State service	Citizenship as token of honour bestowed by govt	NO
Parent acquires nationality	Not automatic – may lead to facilitated naturalisation	
Spouse acquires nationality	Not automatic – may lead to facilitated naturalisation	
Registration	Upon birth overseas to Irish parent who is a citizen other than by birth in Ireland	NO
Special considerations	Someone born in Ireland and entitled to Irish citizenship is considered a citizen when he/she does any act that only an Irish citizen is entitled to do (Anglo-Irish accords)	

Withdrawal/loss of nationality

Event	Law	Consequence of event is loss of nationality
Renunciation	Possible for adult multiple national or person about to acquire foreign nationality, who lives abroad, but not in wartime	YES
Attribution at birth conditional	No provision (see special considerations above)	
Naturalisation elsewhere	For citizens by birth or registration	NO
	For citizens by naturalisation, unless acquisition automatic upon marriage	NO (*but Minister may revoke – discretionary*)
Adoption by a foreigner		NO
Marriage to a foreigner		NO
Spouse acquires other nationality	No loss of spouse's nationality affects spouse	NO
Parent acquires other nationality	No loss of parent's nationality affects children	NO
Resumption of previous nationality		NO (*ministerial discretion in naturalisation revocation*)
Service to foreign state		
Other attribution of nationality	No involuntary attribution of nationality by foreign state can lead to loss of Irish nationality	
(Punitive) deprivation	Revocation of naturalisation for: fraud; disloyalty; 7 years' residence abroad (except for those of Irish descent) unless annual declaration of intent to retain citizenship; nationality in a country at war with Ireland	YES
Special considerations		

General attitude toward multiple nationality
Ireland amended its Citizenship Act in 2004 following a popular referendum that voted to end its "pure" jus soli attribution of nationality at birth. According to the Citizenship Act all citizens are treated equally no matter how they acquired Irish citizenship. No distinctions seem to

be drawn on the basis of possession of multiple nationality, and Article two of the Irish Constitution mentions specifically that "the Irish nation cherishes its special affinity with people of Irish ancestry living abroad who share its cultural identity and heritage". The Citizenship Act states that "if a person ceases to be an Irish citizen the cesser of his citizenship shall not of itself operate to discharge any obligation, duty or liability undertaken, imposed or incurred before the cesser".

Recognition of Multiple Nationality
Although Irish practice is pragmatic in terms of recognising that protection of Irish nationals in other countries of nationality may not be possible, it may attempt to do so depending on the case. The Department of Foreign Affairs established a Task Force on Policy regarding Emigrants, not only to facilitate return and reintegration, but to recommend appropriate assistance to emigrants generally that might be provided abroad.

*Israel[33]

Nationality category or status
Only one, and no technical distinction between nationality and citizenship.

Attribution/acquisition of nationality

Event	Law	Condition is renunciation/ loss of other nationality
Birth	In Israel to Israeli parent	NO
	Overseas to Israeli parent who is a national by birth in Israel, return, residence (closed historical category) or naturalisation	
Naturalisation	Upon fulfilment of requirements	YES (*possible exemption*)
	Of spouse of Israeli national	NO

---

[33] ISRAEL: *Nationality Law*, 5712–1952, 14 July 1953 (last amended 1980); *The Law of Return*, 5710–1950, 5 July 1950; *Entry into Israel Law*, 5712–1952 **UNHCR (internet)**; *The Law of Return* 5710–1950, Israeli Knesset (internet), http://www.knesset.gov.il/laws/special/eng/return.htm, consulted 9 April 2006; *The Citizenship and Entry into Israel Law (temporary provision)* 5763–2003, Israeli Knesset (internet), http://www.knesset.gov.il/laws/special/eng/citizenship_law.htm, consulted 9 April 2006; *Acquisition of Israeli Nationality*, 4 August 1998, Ministry of Foreign Affairs of Israel (internet), http://www.mfa.gov.il/MFA/Facts+About+Israel/State/Acquisition+of+Israeli+Nationality.htm, consulted 9 April 2006; *Israeli legislation regarding Citizenship and Residence Rights for Palestinian Residents of the Territories*, 10 August 2003, Israel Ministry of Foreign Affairs (internet), http://www.mfa.gov.il/MFA/Government/Law/Legal+Issues+and+Rulings/Israeli%20Legislation%20regarding%20Citizenship%20and%20Resi, consulted 9 April 2006; James Meek, "Israelis alarmed by the 'influx of non-Jews'", The Guardian Weekly, 20–26 January 2000, 22; "Israel and human rights. When good men turn racist", The Economist, 19 Octrober 2002, 42; "America's Jews and Israel. Push and pull", The Economist, 24 March 2001, 95; Ed O'Loughlin, "Converting from Judaism requires faith", The Sydney Morning Herald, 28–29 December 2002, 11; James Bennet, International Herald Tribune, *Israel's fresh limit on Palestinians* (internet), http://www.iht.com/articles/104091.htm, consulted 1 August 2003; Campbell and Meek, eds., *International immigration and nationality law;* Ross Dunn, "Citizenship Israel's new weapon in war against suicide bombers", *The Sydney Morning Herald*, 7 August 2002, 10; Anis F. Kassim, "The Palestinian: from hyphenated citizen to integrated citizen", in *Yearbook of Islamic and Middle Eastern Law*, ed. Eugene Cotran and Chibli Mallat, 64–84 (London: Kluwer Law International Ltd., 1997); Claude Klein, "The right of return in Israeli law", *Tel Aviv University Studies in Law* (1997) vol. 13, 53–61; Asher Moaz, "Who is a convert?", *Justice* (1997) vol. 15, 11–15; Mazal Mualem and Jalal Bana, "Yishai revokes citizenship of Israeli Arab", *Ha'aretz* (internet), 10 September 2002; Joroen van Pottelberge, "The right of return in a changing world order", *Tel Aviv University Studies in Law* (1997) vol. 13, 311–325.

Event	Law	Condition is renunciation/ loss of other nationality
Adoption	According to Israeli law and parent is citizen or permanent resident, or adopted outside Israel and parents are citizens	NO
Legitimation	(see birth)	
Marriage	Not automatic – facilitated naturalisation	
Resumption	In certain situations	NO
State service	Facilitated naturalisation for military or assimilated service, or by child of applicant who died in such service	NO
	Discretionary naturalisation for furthering the state's security or interests by residents of territories occupied by Israeli army, and their family members	
Parent acquires nationality	Parent's naturalisation confers nationality on minor child who is resident of Israel or occupied territory, unl. other parent opposes	DEPENDS
Spouse acquires nationality	Not automatic – facilitated naturalisation, including possible exemption from requirement of loss of other nationality	
Registration	Birth in Israel of person who never had a nationality, may apply between 18–25, if resident for 5 consecutive years prior	NO
	Discretionary grant to minor resident, upon parents' application	
Special considerations	Law of Return for persons deemed to be "Jews" and their family members (not applicable for those with diplomatic/ cons immunity)	NO

Withdrawal/loss of nationality

Event	Law	Consequence of event is loss of nationality
Renunciation	Any non-resident adult, or parent on behalf of minor born outside Israel who	YES

Event	Law	**Consequence of event is loss of nationality**
	acquired nationality at birth, or parent on behalf of minor born in Israel (many conditions attached)	
	If resident, must cease to be resident, unless person is a Jewish immigrant, in which case may keep residency	
	All applications subject to approval.	
Attribution at birth conditional	No provision	
Naturalisation elsewhere	*(except if involves acquisition of the nationality of a "hostile state")*	NO *(exception)*
Adoption by a foreigner		NO
Marriage to a foreigner		NO
Spouse acquires other nationality		NO
Parent acquires other nationality	(Parent's loss of nationality affects child if other parent is not Israeli or resident – many other attached conditions)	NO
Resumption of previous nationality	*(except if involves acquisition of the nationality of a "hostile state")*	NO *(exception)*
Service to foreign state	Hostile state – see punitive deprivation	
Other attribution of nationality	Hostile state – see punitive deprivation	
(Punitive) deprivation	For: acquisition of citizenship under false pretenses; illegal departure and entry into hostile state; acquisition of citizenship of hostile state (deemed to have renounced nationality)	POSSIBLE
	Discretionary deprivation for any act "constituting a breach of allegiance to the State of Israel"	
Special considerations	Any loss of nationality does not exempt from duties or obligations owed prior to loss	

General attitude toward multiple nationality

Israel's Nationality Law contains a specific provision on "dual nationality and dual residence" that states "[s]ave for the purposes of naturalization, acquisition of Israel nationality is not conditional upon renunciation of a prior nationality".

Recognition of Multiple Nationality

The Nationality Law state that "[a]n Israel national who is also a foreign national shall, for the purposes of Israel law, be considered as an Israel national.

*Italy[34]

Nationality category or status
Only one, and no technical distinction between citizenship and nationality.

Attribution/acquisition of nationality

Event	Law	Condition is renunciation/ loss of other nationality
Birth	To an Italian parent	NO
	In Italy if would otherwise be stateless	
	Foundlings (absent proof of other citizenship)	
Naturalisation	Upon fulfilment of requirements	NO
Adoption	Attribution automatic if child is a minor	NO
	Conditions attached upon adoption by Italian of adult	
Legitimation	Judicial recognition or filiation of minor, or if right to maintenance established. If adult within one year by declaration	NO

---

[34] ITALY: *Act No. 91, Citizenship*, 5 February 1992, **UNHCR (internet)**; *Servizi consolari per il cittadino italiano all'estero*, Embassy of Italy in Canberra (internet), http://www. ambitalia.org.au/servizi_italiani_estero.htm, consulted 10 April 2006; "Important advice for Italian citizens resident in Australia. Italian national elections and referenda. Right of Italian citizens resident abroad to vote (Italian law no. 459/2001)", The Sydney Morning Herald, 22 January 2003, 4; Stefania Bariatti, *La disciplina giuridica della cittadinanza italiana*, vol. 2, *L'Italia e la vita giuridica internazionale* (Milano: Giuffrè Editore, 1996); Stefania Bariatti, "Nationalité: Italie", in *Juris-Classeur Nationalité*, ed. Michel Verwilghen and Charles L. Closset, *Collection des Juris-Classeurs* (Paris: Éditions du Juris-Classeur, 1994); Campbell and Meek, eds., *International immigration and nationality law*; Roberta Clerici, "Italian nationality and the situation of immigrants", paper presented at the conference: Citizenship and immigration, University of Milano, Law Faculty, 1996; de Groot, "Loss of nationality: a critical inventory"; Ferruccio Pastore, "Droit de la nationalité et migrations internationales: le cas italien", in *Nationalité et citoyenneté en Europe*, ed. Patrick Weil and Randall Hansen, *Collection "Recherches"*, 95–116 (Paris: Éditions La Découverte, 1999); Ferruccio Pastore, "Nationality law and international migration: the Italian case", in *Towards a European nationality. Citizenship, immigration and nationality law in the EU*, ed. Randall Hansen and Patrick Weil, 95–117 (Houndmills: Palgrave, 2001); Petriella, *El Convenio de Doble Ciudadanía entre la Argentina e Italia;* Massimo Siclari, "Gli effetti del matrimonio sulla cittadinanza della donna nella giurisprudenza della Corte Constituzionale Italiana", *La cominità internazionale* (1998) vol. 53, no. 3, 423–427.

	Event	Law	Condition is renunciation/ loss of other nationality
	Marriage	Not automatic – conditions and discretionary	
	Resumption	Possible upon fulfilment of conditions	NO
	State service	Possible	NO
	Parent acquires nationality	By minor children who live with relevant parent	NO
	Spouse acquires nationality	No automatic effect	
	Registration	If one ancestor within two generations was Italian by birth and military or public service (having declared intention); certain residence and declaration upon majority; certain residence	NO
		Birth in Italy to foreign parents and uninterrupted legal residence until majority, and declaration within year of majority	

Special considerations

Withdrawal/loss of nationality

	Event	Law	Consequence of event is loss of nationality
	Renunciation	Possible for multiple national if lives abroad	YES
		Possible upon declaration pursuant to judicial recognition or filiation by foreigner whose nationality is thereby acquired	
		Possible within one year of revocation of adoption when adoptee is adult, if not thereby stateless	
		Possible if nationality acquired while a minor by attribution of nationality to parent, upon majority, if not thereby stateless	
	Attribution at birth conditional	No provision	

Event	Law	Consequence of event is loss of nationality
Naturalisation elsewhere	Fined if fact not communicated to authorities	NO (*exceptions*)
	(*If voluntary acquisition of nationality of country while at war with Italy; ratification of 1963 Council of Europe treaty*)	
Adoption by a foreigner		NO
Marriage to a foreigner		NO
Spouse acquires other nationality		NO
Parent acquires other nationality		NO
Resumption of previous nationality	(but fined if fact not communicated to authorities)	NO
Service to foreign state	Possible deprivation unless obeys order of the Italian state to abandon the related service or office; military or public service (or office) in state at war with Italy if not obligatory	POSSIBLE
Other attribution of nationality	Fined if fact not communicated to authorities	NO
(Punitive) deprivation	(see service to foreign state)	
Special considerations	If nationality by adoption and adoption revoked, nationality is also lost if not thereby stateless	YES

General attitude toward multiple nationality

Italy accepts multiple nationality for its citizens, and warns them that multiple nationality or residence abroad does not necessarily exempt them from various requirements under municipal law. Acquisition of another nationality must be communicated to Italian authorities, or a fine is imposed.

Recognition of Multiple Nationality

Warnings are given to Italians traveling or resident abroad that if they are multiple nationals, they may not be able to receive protection from Italian consular officials.

*Ivory Coast[35]

Nationality category or status
Only one, and no technical distinction between nationality and citizenship.

Attribution/acquisition of nationality

Event	Law	Condition is renunciation/ loss of other nationality
Birth	In Ivory Coast to married parents, at least one a national	NO
	In Ivory Coast to unmarried parents, unless filiation legally proved to one or both alien parents	
	Outside Ivory Coast to married parents, at least one a national	
	Outside Ivory Coast when filiation is legally proved to one IC parent	
Naturalisation	Upon fulfilment of requirements	NO
Adoption	Of minor by at least one Ivory Coast national	NO
Legitimation	Birth in or outside Ivory Coast and legitimated by Ivory Coast parent	NO
Marriage	Of alien woman to Ivory Coast man, but she may decline before celebration of marriage if will retain her nationality.	NO

---

[35] IVORY COAST: *Act no. 1961–415 of 14 December 1961 promulgating the Ivory Coast Nationality Code* (as amended by Act no. 1972–852 of 21 December 1972), **UNHCR (internet)**; Constitution of the Republic of Côte d'Ivoire (Summary), 24 July 2000, Center for Human Rights University of Pretoria (internet), http://www.chr.up.ac.za/hr_docs/constitutions/ docs/CoteD'ivoire(english%20summary)(rev).doc, consulted 10 April 2006; Lane Hartill, "Clouding Ivory Coast's peace: *Ivoirité*", 27 January 2006, The Christian Science Monitor (internet), http://www.csmonitor.com/2006/0127/p07s02–woaf.html, consulted 10 April 2006; Todd Pittman, "Citizenship at Heart of Ivorian Conflict", 14 July 2005, The Independent Online – South Africa (internet), http://www.iol.co.za/index.php?set_id=1&click_id=68&art_id= qw112132728172R131, consulted 10 April 2006; Shravanti Reddy, "Ivory Coast activist who fought against citizenship restrictions is now in exile", 14 June 2003, Digital Freedom Network (internet), http://bobsonwong.com/dfn/news/ivory-coast/kamagate.htm, consulted 10 April 2006; "Côte d'Ivoire. The old enemies", The Economist, 29 July 2000. Ed O'Loughlin, "Doomed city a despot's folly in marble and gold", The Sydney Morning Herald, 11 November 2000, 25.

Event	Law	**Condition is renunciation/ loss of other nationality**
	Govt may block acquisition, and no acquisition if subject to expulsion or restricted residence order or marriage annulled	
	Facilitated naturalisation for husbands of IC women	
Resumption	Possible under certain conditions	NO
State service	Not automatic – facilitated naturalisation	NO
Parent acquires nationality	Minor children do as well, if born during marriage and father or widowed mother is naturalised, if born to unmarried parents if the parent exercising parental authority is naturalised, unless child is married or serving/served in the armed forces of the country of origin, and other conditions are met. Otherwise facilitated naturalisation.	NO
Spouse acquires nationality	No direct effect – facilitated naturalisation	
Registration		

Withdrawal/loss of nationality

Event	Law	**Consequence of event is loss of nationality**
Renunciation	May seek authorization to renounce if multiple national by operation of law	YES
	Possible by woman before marriage to alien, if thereby acquires his nationality	
Attribution at birth conditional	No provision – except that if Ivorian states at full age that she/he possesses a foreign nationality, Ivorian nationality is lost – subject to authorisation by government during 15 year period from registration	DEPENDS
Naturalisation elsewhere	*(If adult and voluntary acquisition; but subject to authorisation of loss by government for 15 year period from registration of loss)*	YES *(exception)*

Event	Law	**Consequence of event is loss of nationality**
Adoption by a foreigner		NO
Marriage to a foreigner	No direct effect	
Spouse acquires other nationality	If spouse deprived of nationality for behaviour as a national of a foreign country, other spouse may also be deprived	NO
	Punitive deprivation of spouse's nationality may be extended, if other spouse of foreign origin and has other nationality	
Parent acquires other nationality	If parent deprived of nationality for behaviour as a national of a foreign country, children may be deprived if other spouse is also	NO
	Punitive deprivation of parent's nationality may be extended, if children of foreign origin and have other nationality, and also extended to other spouse (parent) as well	
Resumption of previous nationality	*(If adult and voluntary acquisition; but subject to authorization of loss by govt for 15 year period from registration of loss)*	YES *(exception)*
Service to foreign state	Military or public service and does not resign when so directed by the Ivory Coast government, unless absolutely unable to do so	POSSIBLE
Other attribution of nationality	*(If adult and voluntary acquisition; but subject to authorization of loss by governmentt for 15 year period from registration of loss)*	YES *(exception)*
(Punitive) deprivation	Possible for behaviour as a foreign national, if that nationality actually possessed	POSSIBLE
	If not national by birth or descent, within 10 years of acquisition and 2 years of act: crimes against internal or external state security or state	

Event	Law	Consequence of event is loss of nationality
	institutions; act benefiting a foreign state and to the detriment of the Ivory Coast; certain conviction and sentence	
Special considerations	If marriage annulled by court order, wife not deemed to have acquired Ivory Coast nationality	YES
	Any statement by an adult as to possession of another nationality	

General attitude toward multiple nationality
Ivorian nationality/citizenship has been a major issue of disagreement in the recent north-south conflict, relating to who possesses and should possess Ivorian nationality. The questions have not centered around multiple nationality, but rather who is to be considered Ivorian, and whether Ivorians with certain foreign links (for example a parent born outside the country) should be allowed to hold public office. The Nationality Code provides that naturalised citizens may not hold certain public offices for prescribed periods of time, and the Constitution that both parents of candidates for President must have been native Ivorians. It is estimated that almost one third of Ivorians may have been born outside the country's borders, with many in the northern regions coming from Burkina Faso.

Recognition of Multiple Nationality
The law provides that with the exception of holding certain public offices by naturalised citizens, all Ivory Coast nationals are treated alike.

Jamaica[36]

Nationality category or status
Only one, and no technical difference between nationality and citizenship.

Attribution/acquisition of nationality

Event	Law	**Condition is renunciation/ loss of other nationality**
Birth	In Jamaica (unless parent enjoys diplomatic immunity and other parent not Jamaican, or parent is enemy alien and birth in place under occupation) Overseas to Jamaican father or mother (conditions)	NO
Naturalisation	Upon fulfillment of conditions	NO
Adoption	Legally adopted in Jamaica by Jamaican parent	NO
Legitimation		
Marriage	By registration (conditions)	
Resumption	Possible for citizens by birth, descent or adoption who renounced citizenship (conditions)	NO
State service	Possible by registration	
Parent acquires nationality	Possible by registration	
Spouse acquires nationality	By registration	

---

[36] JAMAICA: *Constitution of Jamaica*, 6 August 1962, **UNHCR (internet)**; *Jamaican Nationality Act*, 6 August 1962 (as amended until 1999), Ministry of Justice Jamaica (internet), http://www.moj.gov.jm/law, consulted 7 May 2006; *Citizenship*, Consulate General of Jamaica in New York (internet), http://www.congenjamaica-ny.org/citizenship.htm#Citizenship%20by%20 Adoption, consulted 7 May 2006; *Renunciation & Restoration of Jamaican Citizenship*, Consulate General of Jamaica in New York (internet), http://www.congenjamaica-ny.org/General%20 Info/renunciation.htm, consulted 7 May 2006; Cheryl Wynter, "Immigration should be high on agenda of Diaspora Conference – CBA President", 10 June 2004, Jamaica Information Service (internet), http://www.jis.gov.jm/foreign_affairs/html/20040609T090000–0500_2817_JIS_ IMMIGRATION__SHOULD__BE_HIGH_ON_AGENDA_OF_DIASPORA__CONFERENCE___ CBA_PRESIDENT.asp, consulted 7 May 2006; Phil Dinam, "Jamaicans.Com interview with the Consul General of Jamaica, C.P. Ricardo Allicock", 1 October 2005, Jamaicans.Com (internet), http://www.jamaicans.com/articles/primeinterviews/seconsulgeneralja.shtml, consulted 7 May 2006.

Event	Law	Condition is renunciation/ loss of other nationality
Registration	For certain categories upon fulfillment of conditions	NO
Special considerations		

Withdrawal/loss of nationality

Event	Law	Consequence of event is loss of nationality
Renunciation	If of full age and capacity and multiple national or about to acquire foreign nationality (may be withheld in wartime – conditions)	YES
Attribution at birth conditional	No provision	
Naturalisation elsewhere		NO
Adoption by a foreigner		
Marriage to a foreigner		NO
Spouse acquires other nationality		NO
Parent acquires other nationality		NO
Resumption of previous nationality		NO
Service to foreign state		
Other attribution of nationality		NO
(Punitive) deprivation	If registration or naturalisation obtained by fraud, false representation of concealment of any material fact	POSSIBLE
	Of citizenship by naturalisation for disloyalty/disaffection, aid to enemy in wartime, certain sentence, certain residence abroad without annual registration or notice (conditions)	
Special considerations		

General attitude toward multiple nationality
Jamaica accepts multiple nationality for its citizens, and the 1962 Nationality Act allowed for naturalisation without requiring loss of former nationality, and for Jamaicans to retain their nationality upon naturalisation elsewhere. The current version (it was amended in 1965, 1979, 1993, and 1999) maintains the provision that former nationals by birth, descent or adoption who renounced their citizenship may resume Jamaican citizenship. Should they not do so, they may return to Jamaica with permanent residence status, and legal facilities are available to assist their family members in acquiring residence. Jamaica's Consul-General in Miami was quoted in 2005 as advising Jamaicans who intend to reside in the United States to apply for US citizenship and register to vote, as a means to anchoring their rights in the USA. Rather than highlighting Jamaican consular or diplomatic protection for its citizens, he emphasized that American citizenship provided the best protection to Jamaicans in the United States, and that both countries "recognize dual citizenship". The President of the Caribbean Bar Association in South Florida gave the same advice, also emphasising Jamaica's "recognition" of "dual citizenship".

*Japan[37]

Nationality category or status

Only one, and no technical distinction between nationality and citizenship.

Attribution/acquisition of nationality

Event	Law	Condition is renunciation/ loss of other nationality
Birth	To a Japanese parent	NO
	In Japan if a foundling, or parents are stateless	*(but if multiple national, conditional)*
	(In Japan and stateless – only facilitated naturalisation)	
Naturalisation	Upon fulfilment of requirements	YES
Adoption	Not automatic – facilitated naturalisation possible	
Legitimation	If child under 20 and relevant parent a Japanese national at time of birth, upon	NO

[37] JAPAN: *The Nationality Law (Law no. 147 of 1950, as amended 1952, 1984, 1993)*, Tokyo: Ministry of Justice Civil Affairs Bureau, 1997; *Constitution of Japan*, 3 november 1946, *Immigration Control and Refugee Recognition Act*, 1951 (amended 2001), Office **UNHCR (internet)**; Ministry of Justice (Japan), *The choice of nationality*, brochure provided by the Consulate General of Japan in Sydney, 1 August 2003; Ministry of Justice (Japan), *Choosing nationality* (unofficial translation), Embassy of the United States in Japan (internet), http://tokyo.usembassy.gov/e/acs/tacs-7118b.html, consulted 10 April 2006; "Key ruling on Japan Nationality", 29 March 2006, BBC News (internet), http://news.bbc.co.uk/2/hi/asiapacific/4858448.stm, consulted 10 April 2006; *Petition in support of multiple nationality*, presented in the Japanese Diet, 4 March 2002 (internet), http://www.kouenkai.org/~ist/seigan-e.htm, consulted 1 August 2003; "Investigating Fujimori's regime", The Economist 23 December 2000, 20; "Hunted by the past", The Sydney Morning Herald, 14–15 September 2002, 29; "Fujimori's choice", The Australian, 29 November 2000, 11; "Protest Perus gegen japanische Einbürgerung", Neue Zürcher Zeitung Online, 20 Julz 2001 (internet), http://www.nzz.ch/2001/07/20/al/page-article7J5SJ.html, consulted 1 August 2003; "No end to discrimination for suffering minorities", The Sydney Morning Herald, 2 December 2000, 19; "Japan ponders economic rescue by immigrants", Guardian Weekly, 12–18 August 1999, 16; Campbell and Meek, eds., *International immigration and nationality law*; Kiyoshi Hosokawa, "Japanese nationality in international perspective", in *Nationality and international law in Asian perspective*, ed. Ko Swan Sik, 177–253 (Dordrecht: Martinus Nijhoff Publishers, 1990); Atsushi Kondo, "Citizenship rights for aliens in Japan", in *Citizenship in a global world. Comparing citizenship rights for aliens*, ed. Atsushi Kondo, 8–30 (Houndmills: Palgrave, 2001).

Event	Law	Condition is renunciation/ loss of other nationality
	notification, and parent is at that time a national	
		(*but if multiple national, conditional*)
Marriage	Not automatic – facilitated naturalisation possible	
Resumption	Facilitated naturalisation possible	YES
	By notification to govt in certain cases	
State service	Facilitated naturalisation possible	
Parent acquires nationality	Not automatic – facilitated naturalisation possible	
Spouse acquires nationality	Not automatic – facilitated naturalisation possible	
Registration		
Special considerations	If person to be naturalised is unable to secure release from foreign nationality, requirement may be waived if has family relationship with national, or exceptional circumstances present	NO

Withdrawal/loss of nationality

Event	Law	Consequence of event is loss of nationality
Renunciation	Possible by multiple nationals	YES
Attribution at birth (and otherwise) conditional	Must choose between Japanese and other nationality before age 22, or within two years if acquired after age 22. Japanese nationaltiy may be lost if declaration to preserve is not made. If declaration for Japanese nationality is made and foreign nationality kept, may be deprived of Japanese nationality if occupy public office in other country reserved to its nationals and govt finding that this contracts option for Japanese nat.	YES (*although not necessarily effective*)
Naturalisation elsewhere	If upon voluntary act	YES

Event	Law	**Consequence of event is loss of nationality**
Adoption by a foreigner	No direct effect	
Marriage to a foreigner	No direct effect	
Spouse acquires other nationality	No direct effect	
Parent acquires other nationality	No direct effect	
Resumption of previous nationality		YES
Service to foreign state		
Other attribution of nationality	Any exercise of an option of foreign nationality	YES
(Punitive) deprivation		

General attitude toward multiple nationality
Multiple nationality is not favoured, and Japan states that it follows a policy of "unique" nationality. Although multiple nationals by birth or other original attribution (not by an act of free will) are required to opt for Japanese or foreign nationality at age 22, if they choose Japanese nationality, renunciation of the other nationality is not verified, although an oath must be taken that the other nationality has been renounced. The Nationality Law contains a specific provision that should the other nationality nevertheless continue to be possessed in fact, only holding of a public office reserved to nationals provides the government with the ability to deprive the person in question of Japanese nationality. There are increasing public calls for Japan to provide for retention of nationality upon naturalisation abroad, and to eliminate the condition of renunciation for those who apply for naturalisation. Prior to 1985, if a declaration was not made, it was assumed that an option had been exercised in favour of Japanese nationality.

Recognition of Multiple Nationality
Japanese nationals must enter and depart Japan using a Japanese passport. In terms of international protection, Japanese practice is to regard all nationals as potential recipients of such protection, notwithstanding possession of another nationality.

*Kenya[38]

Nationality category or status

Only one, and no technical distinction between nationality and citizenship.

Attribution/acquisition of nationality

Event	Law	**Condition is renunciation/ loss of other nationality**
Birth	In Kenya to Kenyan parent (unless father diplomat, or citizen of country at war with Kenya and birth is in occupied territory)	NO (_but if multiple national conditional attribution until age 21_)
	Outside Kenya if father is Kenyan	
Naturalisation	Upon fulfilment of requirements	YES
Adoption		
Legitimation	(If father Kenyan on date of birth)	
Marriage	Of foreign woman to Kenyan man, may apply for registration	YES
Resumption	Possible registration or naturalisation	YES
State service		
Parent acquires nationality	No direct effect – may lead to registrationa or naturalisation	
Spouse acquires nationality	No direct effect – may lead to registration or naturalisation	
Registration nationality	Various categories of persons, upon fulfilment of requirements	YES (_if no proof of loss registration cancelled_)

---

[38] KENYA: _Constitution of Kenya_, 11 December 1963; _Kenya Citizenship Act_, Cap 170, 12 December 1963, **UNHCR (internet)**; Campbell and Meek, eds., _International immigration and nationality law_; Hellmuth Hecker, _Das Staatsangehörigkeitsrecht des anglophonen Afrika_, vol. 38, _Sammlung geltender Staatsangehörigkeitsgesetze_ (Frankfurt am Main: Alfred Metzner Verlag, 1981); Stephen N. Ndegwa, "Citizenship amid economic and political change in Kenya", _Africa Today_ (1998) vol. 45, no. 3–4, 351–368.

Withdrawal/loss of nationality

Event	Law	Consequence of event is loss of nationality
Renunciation	Only multiple nationals may renounce, but may be refused if Kenya at war or contrary to public policy	YES
Attribution at birth conditional	Any multiple national who does not renounce other nationality before age 21	YES
Naturalisation elsewhere	Any voluntary act other than marriage	YES
Adoption by a foreigner	No direct effect – but if thereby multiple national, must renounce other nationality before age 21 to retain Kenyan	NO (_but possible conditional retention_)
Marriage to a foreigner	(if involuntary acquisition of foreign nationality)	NO
Spouse acquires other nationality	(if nationality thereby attributed and is deemed involuntary acquisition)	NO
Parent acquires other nationality	No direct effect – but if thereby multiple national, must renounce other nationality before age 21 to retain Kenyan	NO (_possibly conditional_)
Resumption of previous nationality		YES
Service to foreign state	(see punitive deprivation)	
Other attribution of nationality	Any voluntary attribution, except if under age 21 (when must renounce other nationality in order to retain Kenyan)	YES
(Punitive) deprivation	For Citizens by registration or naturalisation for: disloyalty; assisting the enemy in war; certain crimes/ sentences; 7 years residence abroad and not in state or international service and no annual regisration; fraud in acquisition	POSSIBLE
Special considerations	If required to renounce other nationality and are unable to do so due to foreign legislation/practice, requirement waived, for as long as so prevented	

General attitude toward multiple nationality

Kenya states that it neither permits nor recognises multiple nationality. Kenyan nationality produced at birth is withdrawn automatically at age 21 if a foreign nationality is possessed.

*Republic of Korea[39]

Nationality category or status
Only one, and no technical distinction between nationality and citizenship.

Attribution/acquisition of nationality

Event	Law	Condition is renunciation/ loss of other nationality
Birth	To ROK father or mother	NO
	To an ROK father who died before subject's birth	(*see conditional attribution below – if dual national must opt before age 22*)
	In ROK to stateless or unknown parents	
	Foundlings presumed to have been born in ROK	
Naturalisation	Upon fulfilment of requirements	YES (*must renounce foreign nationality within six months of acquisition – exceptions*)
Adoption	Not automatic – facilitated naturalisation	
Legitimation	Of minor by ROK parent – see birth (with conditions)	
Marriage	Not automatic – facilitated naturalisation	YES (*exceptions*)

---

[39] KOREA (ROK): *Constitution of the Republic of Korea*, 17 July 1948 (amended 29 October 1987), *Law No. 16, Nationality Act*, 20 December 1948 (last amended 20 January 2004), *Enforcement Decree of the Nationality Act*, Wholly amended by Presidential Decree 15807, 5 June 1998, *Act on the Immigration and Legal Status of Overseas Koreans* (wholly amended as of 30 December 2000), **UNHCR (internet)**; *Travel Advice-Republic of Korea*, 16 March 2006, Department of Foreign Affairs and Trade Australia (internet), http://www.smartraveller.gov.au/zw-cgi/view/Advice/South_Korea, consulted 10 April 2006; "Kim laments MPs' rejection of woman as PM", The Sydney Morning Herald, 2 August 2002, 9; "The Region", Far Eastern Economic Review, 6 September 2001, 20; *Consular information sheet-Republic of Korea*, 9 August 2005, United States Department of State (internet), http://travel.state.gov/travel/cis_pa_tw/cis/cis_1018.html, consulted 10 April 2006; Campbell and Meek, eds., *International immigration and nationality law*; Hyo Sang Chang, "Nationality in divided countries: a Korean perspective", in *Nationality and international law in Asian perspective*, ed. Ko Swan Sik, 255–308 (Dordrecht: Martinus Nijhoff Publishers, 1990); Louis Kim-Ukkon, "Nationalité: Corée (République de)", in *Juris-Classeur Nationalité*, ed. Michel J. Verwilghen and Charles L. Closset, *Collection des Juris-Classeurs* (Paris: Éditions Juris-Classeur, 1997).

Event	Law	Condition is renunciation/ loss of other nationality
Resumption	Possible (with exceptions, such as if renounced nationality to avoid military service, state security, public welfare)	YES (*exceptions*)
State service	Facilitated naturalisation	YES (*exceptions*)
Parent acquires nationality	Minor child of naturalised person is naturalised at same time as parent	YES (*exceptions*)
Spouse acquires nationality	No automatic effect	

Withdrawal/loss of nationality

Event	Law	Consequence of event is loss of nationality
Renunciation	By multiple national but not if thereby avoiding military service	YES
Attribution (at birth) conditional	Dual nationals are required to opt between ROK and foreign nationality before age 22 or after completion of military service obligations (Korean nationality cannot be abandoned to avoid military service), but if no option is made it is unclear whether Korean nationality is automatically withdrawn if the subject's name remains on the Korean Family Census Register	
Naturalisation elsewhere	Any voluntary acquisition of foreign nationality	YES
Adoption by a foreigner	If nationality thereby acquired, unless declares desire to keep ROK nationality within six months after acquisition of foreign nationality	YES (Depends)
Marriage to a foreigner	If nationality thereby acquired, unless declares desire to keep ROK nationality within six months after acquisition of foreign nationality	YES (Depends)
Spouse acquires other nationality	If spouse acquires foreign nationality, unless declares desire to keep ROK nationality within six months after acquisition of foreign nationality	YES (Depends)

Event	Law	Consequence of event is loss of nationality
Parent acquires other nationality	If parent acquires foreign nationality, unless declares desire to keep ROK nationality within six months after acquisition of foreign nationality	YES (Depends)
Resumption of previous nationality	(considered naturalisation abroad)	YES
Service to foreign state		
Other attribution of nationality	Acquisition of foreign nationality by legitimation leads to loss of ROK nationality, unless subject declares desire to keep ROK nationality within six months after acquisition of foreign nationality	YES (Depends)
(Punitive) deprivation	If after six months of acquisition of Korean nationality have not lost foreign nationality	YES
Special considerations	Any alien who acquires ROK nationality and does not lose other nationality within 6 months is automatically deprived of ROK nationality unless government permission. ROK nationality can be reinstated if foreign nationality is lost within one year of the loss of ROK nationality	YES
	If Korean nationality was acquired by marriage, then another nationality acquired after anulment or divorce	

General attitude toward multiple nationality

The ROK's policy is not to accept multiple nationality for its citizens. It does not prevent its production at birth, but forces a choice of nationality later in life. The Nationality Act provides that dual nationals (whether Korean nationality was acquired by birth or otherwise under the Nationality Act) shall select between foreign and Korean nationality by age 22, or if over 22, within two years. Both opting for Korean nationality (requiring renunciation of foreign nationality) and opting for foreign nationality ("willingness to abandon the nationality of the ROK") require reporting to the Minister of Justice, however, and it remains unclear whether avoidance of the obligation means that ROK nationality is still possessed. There are indications that Korean authorities treat persons whose names appear on the Korean Family Census Register as possessing ROK nationality, notwithstanding the non-exercise of the option, and the provision that seems to result in automatic deprivation if no option is exercised. The Nationality Act specifically obliges public officials to notify the Ministry of Justice should they find people who have legally lost Korean nationality. Male multiple nationals are not permitted to renounce ROK nationality until completion of compulsory military service or receipt of a special exemption. Any person losing Korean nationality must transfer related rights to a Korean national within three years. Both ROK nationals and foreign nationals of Korean origin may apply for the status of Overseas Korean, which entails certain rights and entitlements, but is not possession of Korean nationality.

Recognition of Multiple Nationality

The Republic of Korea does not recognise any multiple nationality of its citizens, although the Nationality Act refers to "dual nationals" and contemplates certain situations in which dual nationality is tolerated through express government consent. Article two of the Constitution states that "[i]t is the duty of the State to protect citizens residing abroad as prescribed by law". Korean citizens must travel in and out of the ROK on Korean documents.

*Latvia[40]

Nationality category or status

Only one, and no technical differentiation between nationality and citizenship. Although the category and status of *Former USSR Citizens who are not citizens of Latvia or any other state* arguably cannot be classified as a type of nationality, it may provide cause for reflection in this regard.

Attribution/acquisition of nationality

Event	Law	Condition is renunciation/ loss of other nationality
Birth	Anywhere to two Latvian parents	NO
	In Latvia to one Latvian parent*	*(but in certain cases * if parents agree may opt for child only to possess other nationality)*
	Outside Latvia to one Latvian parent, if both parents or parent living with the child permanently reside in Latvia*	

---

[40] LATVIA: *The Procedure for the Acceptance and Review of the Application on the Recognition of a Child to Be a Citizen of Latvia*, Regulations of The Cabinet of Ministers no. 32, 1999, *The procedure for documenting loss and and restoration of the citizenship of Latvia*, Regulations of the Cabinet of Ministers No. 13, Legal Acts, 2001, *Citizenship Law* (amendments to 22 June 1998), The Naturalization Board of Latvia (internet), http://www.np.gov.lv/ index.php?en=akti_en&saite=akti_en.htm, consulted 11 April 2006; *Law of Stateless Persons*, 2 March 2004, *Law on the Status of Former USSR Citizens Who Are Not Citizens of Latvia or Any Other State*, 9 May 1995; *Law on Citizenship* (last amended 1995); *Resolution of the Supreme Council on Conditions for the Recognition of Republic of Latvia Citizens' Rights to Persons Who Resided Within Latvia Before August 1, 1914 and Their Descendants*, 29 October 1992; *Constitution of the Republic of Latvia*, 15 February 1922 (last amended 30 April 2002), **UNHCR (internet)**; "Charlemagne. Andris Berzins, a hard-pressed Latvian", The Economist, 24 June 2000, 70; "Latvia votes for Europe", The Economist, 10 October 1998, 59; Lowell W. Barrington, "The making of citizenship policy in the Baltic states", Georgetown Immigration Law Journal (1999) vol. 13, no. 2, 159–199; Juris Bojars, "The citizenship regulation of the Republic of Latvia", Humanities and Social Sciences: Latvia (1995) vol. 1, no. 6, 4–28; British Helsinki Human Rights Group, "Nationalism and citizenship in Latvia", East European Human Rights Review (2000) vol. 6, no. 1/2, 1–31; Hellmuth Hecker, "Staatsangehörigkeitsfragen in völkerrechtlichen Verträgen osteuropäischer Staaten", Archiv des Völkerrechts (1992) vol. 30, no. 3, 326–354; Liebich, "Plural citizenship in post-Communist states"; Artis Pabriks, "Citizenship and rights of minorities in Latvia", Humanities and Social Sciences: Latvia (1994) vol. 1, no. 2, 60–67; Ineta Ziemele, "The citizenship issue in the Republic of Latvia", in Citizenship and nationality status in the new Europe, ed. Síofra O'Leary and Teija Tiilikainen, 187–204 (London: Sweet & Maxwell, 1998).

Event	Law	Condition is renunciation/ loss of other nationality
	Outside Latvia to one Latvian parent when both parents reside abroad, only if both parents agree to acquisition	
	Anywhere to one Latvian parent, if other parent is stateless or unknown	
	Foundlings and children without parents living in Latvian boarding schools and orphanages	
Naturalisation	Upon fulfilment of requirements	YES
Adoption	Of minor children (conditions)	YES
Legitimation	See birth	
Marriage	Not automatic – facilitated naturalisation possible	
Resumption	By naturalisation (conditions)	YES
	Of right, in certain cases related to adoption, parental decisions, judicial error, or illegal deprivation	NO
State service	Upon Parliamentary decision	YES
Parent acquires nationality	Minor children of naturalised parent who permanently reside in Latvia, or parents agree	YES
Spouse acquires nationality	No effect – may lead to facilitated naturalisation	
Registration	Of certain former citizens and their descendants, except if acquired another nationality after 1990	NO
Acknowledgment	Birth in Latvia of stateless person or certain "non-citizen" to stateless or non-citizen parent(s)/adoptor – "acknowledgment of citizenship" after certain time period (with conditions), must be before age 18	YES

Withdrawal/loss of nationality

Event	Law	Consequence of event is loss of nationality
Renunciation	Of right by a person who has or will acquire nationality, subject to military service and other obligations due	YES
Attribution at birth conditional	No provision	
Naturalisation elsewhere	Court may revoke if acquistion of other nationality without renunciation	POSSIBLE
Adoption by a foreigner	No automatic loss	NO
Marriage to a foreigner		NO
Spouse acquires other nationality	No deprivation of nationality affects other spouse	NO
Parent acquires other nationality	No deprivation of nationality affects children	NO
Resumption of previous nationality	(possible depending on mode of acquisition – see naturalisation elsewhere)	YES
Service to foreign state	Possible deprivation if without government (Cabinet) permission, but not of dual national if resides outside Latvia	POSSIBLE
Other attribution of nationality		
(Punitive) deprivation	For providing false information in acquisition of citizenship	YES

General attitude toward multiple nationality

Latvia does not prevent dual nationality at birth, and allows the status for certain persons and their descendants who were forced to leave Latvia after 1940 and who reclaimed Latvian nationality before 1995. The Law on Citizenship provides that the granting of Latvian citizenship should not lead to multiple nationality, but also that a citizen of Latvia who is considered to be a national of a foreign country according to its laws is only considered to be Latvian for purposes of legal relations with the state. It stipulates that citizens are equal, no matter how their nationality was acquired.

Recognition of Multiple Nationality

The Law on Citizenship contains an article that provides for the protection abroad of all citizens.

Luxembourg[41]

Nationality category or status
Only one, and no distinction between nationality and citizenship.

Attribution/acquisition of nationality

Event	Law	Condition is renunciation/ loss of other nationality
Birth	To a Luxembourg parent, and parentage established by age 18, parent citizen when parentage established, or citizen when deceased (conditions)	NO (*see conditional attribution and special considerations under loss*)
	In Luxembourg to unknown parents (foundling presumed to be born in Luxembourg)	
	In Luxembourg to stateless parent(s) and therefore stateless	
	(*See conditional attribution re. birth overseas and special considerations under loss re. multiple nationals*)	
Naturalisation	Upon fulfillment of conditions	YES (*exception*)

---

[41] LUXEMBOURG: *Loi de 22 février 1968 sur la nationalité lexembourgeoise*, as amended until 2001, Memorial – Journal Officiel du Grand-Duché de Luxembourg, Recueil de legislation, 26 October 2001, **UNHCR (internet)**; *La nationalité luxembourgeoise*, Le gouvernement du Grand-Duché de Luxembourg (internet), http://www.gouvernement.lu/publications/luxembourg/nationalite_luxembourgeoise/index.html, consulted 7 May 2006; *Remise d'un rapport sur les effets juridiques de la double nationalité au ministre de la Justice Luc Frieden*, 14 January 2004, Le Gouvernement du Grand-Duché de Luxembourg (internet), http://www.gouvernement.lu/salle_presse/actualite/2004/01/14frieden/index.html, consulted 7 May 2006; *Interview avec le ministre de la Justice Luc Frieden sur la double nationalité*, RTL Télé Lëtzebuerg, 14 January 2004, Le Gouvernement du Grand-Duché de Luxembourg (internet), http://www.gouvernement.lu/salle_presse/Interviews/20040114frieden_rtl/index.html, consulted 7 May 2006; Francis Delpérée and Michel Verwilghen, "Citoyenneté multiple et nationalité multiple au Grand-Duché de Luxembourg", Janvier 2004, Le Gouvernement du Grand-Duché de Luxembourg (internet), http://www.gouvernement.lu/salle_presse/communiques/2004/01/14rapport/rapport.pdf, consulted 7 May 2006; *Assistance consularie*, Ministère des Affaires étrangères – Luxembourg (internet), http://www.mae.lu/mae.taf?IdNav=323, consulted 7 May 2006; *Second report on Luxembourg adopted on 13 December 2002 and made public on 8 July 2003, CRI (2003) 38*, Council of Europe (internet), http://www.coe.int/t/e/human_rights/ecri/1–ecri/2–country-by-country_approach/Luxembourg/Luxembourg_CBC_2en.asp, consulted 7 May 2006; "Proibição de dupla nacionalidade impede portugueses de votar", Público, 10 July 2005, 21.

Event	Law	**Condition is renunciation/ loss of other nationality**
	(exceptions include: loss not possible, non-cooperation of foreign authorities, if recognised refugee, exemption by Chamber of Deputies)	
Adoption	"Full" adoption of child – child <u>obtains</u> nationality (conditions)	NO
	Child under age 18 by "simple" adoption, if stateless, or if thereby loses foreign nationality, <u>obtains</u> nationality	YES
Legitimation	Before age 18 and parent citizen when legitimated (including posthumous children – conditions) – see birth	
Marriage	Acquisition by option possible	
Resumption	Possible for Luxembourgers by birth (conditions)	YES
	By woman who lost nationality in relation to foreign marriage	NO
State service	Facilitated naturalisation possible	YES *(exception)*
	(exceptions include: loss not possible, non-cooperation of foreign authorities, if recognised refugee, exemption by Chamber of Deputies)	
Parent acquires nationality	Child under age 18 whose parent or adopter who is legal guardian acquires or resumes nationality, <u>obtains</u> nationality	
	Child under age 18 whose parent or adopter who is legal guardian obtained nationality as subject of "full" adoption, <u>obtains</u> nationalty	
Spouse acquires	When spouses are naturalised together – facilitated naturalisation possible for one spouse	
	Spouse of person who acquires or resumes nationality may acquire by option	
Registration/ Option	Open to those: born in Luxembourg; born abroad to a former-national by	YES *(exception)*

Event	Law	**Condition is renunciation/ loss of other nationality**
	birth; born abroad to a foreign parent and completed all of obligatory schooling in Luxembourg; spouses of nationals or those who acquire/resume nationality; children subject of "simple" adoption who did not lose their previous nationality; a foreigner over age 18 whose parent(s) when the child reached that age were his/her legal guardians and acquired or resumed nationality (conditions)	
	(exceptions include: loss not possible, non-cooperation of foreign authorities, if recognised refugee)	
Special considerations		

Withdrawal/loss of nationality

Event	Law	**Consequence of event is loss of nationality**
Renunciation	Possible if over 18 and multiple national or about to acquire foreign nationality (extended to minor children if they also receive/possess foreign nationality, unless one parent continues to be Luxembourger)	YES
Attribution at birth conditional	Luxembourgers born overseas and multiple nationals with uninterrupted residence abroad after age 18 must declare within 20 years the desire to retain nationality; after declaration a new twenty-year period begins (exception if national or spouse abroad on state/international service) – conditions	POSSIBLE
Naturalisation elsewhere	Any voluntary acquisition of foreign nationality when over age 18 (extended to minor children if they also receive/possess foreign nationality, unless one parent continues to be Luxembourger)	YES

Event	Law	Consequence of event is loss of nationality
Adoption by a foreigner	If minor child thereby acquires adopter's foreign nationality, unless one parent continues to be Luxembourger	YES
Marriage to a foreigner		NO
Spouse acquires other nationality		NO
Parent acquires other nationality	Parent's renunciation or voluntary acquisition of foreign nationality when over age 18 is extended to minor children if they also receive/possess foreign nationality, unless one parent continues to be Luxembourger	YES
Resumption of previous nationality	Any voluntary acquisition of foreign nationality when over age 18 (extended to minor children if they also receive/possess foreign nationality, unless one parent continues to be Luxembourger)	YES
Service to foreign state	See deprivation	
Other attribution of nationality	Any voluntary acquisition of foreign nationality when over age 18 (extended to minor children if they also receive/possess foreign nationality, unless one parent continues to be Luxembourger)	YES
(Punitive) deprivation	Possible for nationals otherwise than by descent at birth for: fraud in acquisition; non-observance of citizenship obligations; exercise of foreign rights or obligations; certain criminal convictions. Spouse and minor children of person deprived may renounce (conditions)	POSSIBLE
Special considerations	Luxembourg multiple nationals over age 18, who make a declaration to a foreign official of wish to conserve foreign nationality, or who upon notification by Luxembourg minister of justice fail to renounce within two years foreign nationality or make declaration of wish to conserve Luxembourg	YES

			Consequence of event is
-------	-----		**loss of nationality**
Event	**Law**		

nationality should renunciation not be
possible, lose nationality (exception if
national or spouse abroad on state/
international service)

Child loses nationality if parentage
disproved before age 18, unless other
parent is Luxembourger (conditions)

Children who aquired nationality by birth
in Luxembourg lose it if proven before
age 18 that they possess foreign
nationality (conditions)

General attitude toward multiple nationality
Luxembourg policy does not favour multiple nationality for its citizens, but multiple nationality produced automatically at birth is accepted. Nevertheless, Luxembourg multiple nationals
born abroad and with uninterrupted residence abroad must make an official declaration of their
desire to conserve Luxembourg nationality at least once every twenty years after turning 18.
Loss of previous nationality is a condition of naturalisation in Luxembourg, with a few exceptions, and any voluntary acquisition of foreign nationality results in the loss of Luxembourg
nationality. The government commissioned a report on citizenship and multiple nationality in
2003 aimed at discussing the issue, but has remained opposed to multiple nationality for
Luxembourgers. Luxembourg's opposition to multiple nationality is cited by immigrants who
make up 40 percent of the population as an impediment to integration and political participation. This is so particularly among the Portuguese community of about 70,000 persons, of a
total population of c. 450,000.

Recognition of Multiple Nationality
Luxembourg's advice on consular assistance states that consular protection cannot be officially
assured to citizens who also possess the nationality of the country in which they are travelling.

*Malaysia[42]

Nationality category or status
Only one, and there is no technical distinction between nationality and citizenship.

Attribution/acquisition of nationality

Event	Law	Condition is renunciation/ loss of other nationality
Birth	In Malaysia to a Malaysian parent citizen or permanent resident	NO
	Overseas to a Malaysian father either born in Malaysia or in government service abroad, and birth registered within one year	
	In Malaysia and child would otherwise be stateless	
Naturalisation	Upon fulfilment of requirements	YES (but not necessarily effective renunciation)
Adoption	Child may be registered as citizen	
Legitimation	(see birth)	
Marriage	Not automatic – possible by registration	
Resumption	Possible in certain cases	YES (not nec. effective)
State service		
Parent acquires nationality	Not automatic – possible by registration	
Spouse acquires nationality	No direct effect – possible by registration	

---

[42] MALAYSIA: *Federal Constitution*, 31 August 1957 (as amended 1995), *Second schedule to the Constitution*, **UNHCR (internet)**; *Consular Services*, Ministry of Foreign Affairs Malaysia, 6 March 2006 (internet), http://www.kln.gov.my/english/Fr-services.html, consulted 12 April 2006; *Consular Information Sheet Malaysia*, United States Department of State, 20 December 2005 (internet), http://travel.state.gov/travel/cis_pa_tw/cis/cis_960.html, consulted 12 April 2006; Campbell and Meek, eds., *International immigration and nationality law*; Visu Sinnadurai, "Nationality and international law in the perspective of the Federation of Malaysia", in *Nationality and international law in Asian perspective*, ed. Ko Swan Sik, 309–333 (Dordrecht: Martinus Nijhoff, 1990).

Event	Law	Condition is renunciation/ loss of other nationality
Registration	Various categories and conditions – registration as right	YES (but not necessarily effective renunciation)
	Government may register anyone under 21 at its discretion	

Withdrawal/loss of nationality

Event	Law	Consequence of event is loss of nationality
Renunciation	If over 21, or married woman, and has or will acquire foreign nationality, except government may refuse in wartime	YES
Attribution at birth conditional	No provision	
Naturalisation elsewhere	May be deprived of nationality for any voluntary acquisition of nationality (except marriage)	POSSIBLE – discretionary
Adoption by a foreigner		NO
Marriage to a foreigner	Woman citizen by registration by be deprived if acquires (new) husband's nationality	POSSIBLE
Spouse acquires other nationality		NO
Parent acquires other nationality	Children of parent deprived of nationality may also lose, if not thereby stateless	POSSIBLE
Resumption of previous nationality	(deprivation possible)	POSSIBLE
Service to foreign state	Possible deprivation (conditions) if no prior approval, and not thereby stateless	POSSIBLE
Other attribution of nationality	If voluntary acquisition – possible deprivation	
(Punitive) deprivation	Revocation of registration or naturalisation for fraud	POSSIBLE
(only possible if not thereby stateless)	Deprivation of citizens by registration or naturalisation for disloyalty, assistance to the enemy, certain sentences for crimes,	

Event	Law	**Consequence of event is loss of nationality**
	service to other govt., exercise of foreign political rights, residence abroad for five years and not in govt service or no annual registration with consulate and declaration	
	Deprivation possible for exercise of foreign rights or entitlements	
	If woman acquired nationality by registration upon marriage, and marriage disolved	

General attitude toward multiple nationality

Malaysia states that it does not recognise or permit dual nationality. It issued a joint communiqué with the People's Republic of China in 1974 in which it affirmed that it does not recognise multiple nationality. Malaysia does, however, not automatically withdraw Malaysian nationality from multiple nationals in most situations. The provisions on nationality in the Constitution leave the government considerable latitude to deprive nationals of Malaysian nationality if they acquire a foreign nationality voluntarily or exercise rights associated with such nationality. An oath of renunciation of foreign nationality is a condition of naturalisation and registration, but this is does not necessarily amount to an effective loss of foreign nationality. Rights and entitlements accrue to all citizens regardless of any possible multiple nationality.

Recognition of Multiple Nationality

No foreign nationality of a Malaysian citizen is recognised, and any use or citation of such nationality may be cited as grounds for deprivation of Malaysian nationality.

*Mexico[43]

Nationality category or status

One only, but the Mexican Constitution creates a legal distinction between nationality and citizenship (political rights), which nationals receive at age 18 and if they lead an honest life, "modo honesto de vivir".

Attribution/acquisition of nationality

Event	Law	Condition is renunciation/ loss of other nationality
Birth	In Mexico (including on Mexican war/ civil ships or aircraft)	NO
	Overseas to Mexican parent who was born in Mexico or was naturalised	
	Foundling presumed to be born in Mexico to Mexican parents, unless proven otherwise	
Naturalisation	Upon fulfilment of requirements	YES
Adoption	No automatic effects	
Legitimation	(see birth)	

---

[43] MEXICO: *Constitución política de los Estados Unidos Mexicanos*, 1917, last modified 21 September 2000; *Ley de nacionalidad*, 23 January 1998, **UNHCR (internet)**; *Constitución política de los Estados Unidos Mexicanos*, 1917, last modified 27 September 2004, Base de Datos Políticos de las Américas (internet), http://pdba.georgetown.edu/Constitutions/Mexico/mexico2004.html, consulted 12 April 2006; Carlos Arellano García, "Los peligros de la doble nacionalidad", paper presented at the conference: La doble nacionalidad, Ciudad de México, 1995; Campbell and Meek, eds., *International immigration and nationality law*; de Groot, "Loss of nationality: a critical inventory"; Víctor Carlos García Moreno, "La propuesta sobre doble nacionalidad", paper presented at the conference: La doble nacionalidad, Ciudad de México, 1995; Paula Gutierrez, "Mexico's dual nationality amendments: they do not undermine U.S. citizens' allegiance and loyalty or U.S. political sovereignty", *Loyola of Los Angeles International and Comparative Law Journal* (1997) vol. 19, no. 4, 999–1026; Jones-Correa, *Under two flags: dual nationality in Latin America and its consequences for the United States*; Pablo Lizarraga Chavez, "Creating a United States-Mexico political double helix: the Mexican government's proposed dual nationality amendment", *Stanford Journal of International Law* (1997) vol. 33, no. 1, 119–151; Antonio Tenorio Adame, "La doble nacionalidad", paper presented at the conference: La doble nacionalidad, Ciudad de México, 1995; "Mexico's elections. El Norte gets a voice", The Economist, 5 July 2003, 36. "Mexico and the United States. Half an enchilada", The Economist, 25 January 2003, 41; "The tragedy of Elian", The Economist, 8 April 2000, 33; "Mexico. Fox's Pepsi challenge", The Economist, 19 February 2000, 45.

Event	Law	Condition is renunciation/ loss of other nationality
Marriage	Not automatic – residence and fulfillment of requirements	
Resumption	Possible if Mexican national by birth, who was previously deprived of nationality due to naturalisation abroad	NO
State service		
Parent acquires nationality	No direct effect – facilitated naturalisation possible	
Spouse acquires nationality	No direct effect	
Registration		

Withdrawal/loss of nationality

Event	Law	Consequence of event is loss of nationality
Renunciation	(*Not possible for those born in Mexico*)	YES (*exception*)
Attribution at birth conditional	No provision	
Naturalisation elsewhere	National by birth in Mexico (*loss only for naturalised citizens*)	NO (*exception*)
Adoption by a foreigner	No direct effect	NO
Marriage to a foreigner		NO
Spouse acquires other nationality	No loss of a Mexican spouse's nationality affects spouse	NO
Parent acquires other nationality	No loss of a Mexican parent's nationality affects children	NO
Resumption of previous nationality	(for naturalised citizens)	YES
Service to foreign state	Possible loss of citizenship rights only, for use of foreign noble titles, decorations or titles, foreign government service without permission, assistance to foreigner or foreign government against Mexican interests	NO

		Consequence of event is
Event	**Law**	**loss of nationality**
Other attribution of nationality	Any voluntary acquisition of nationality by naturalised citizen	
(Punitive) deprivation	Not possible for Mexicans by birth	NO
	Naturalisation revoked for fraud, accepting foreign titles of nobility, using a foreign passport, mention in public documents as a foreigner, five years' residence abroad	YES

General attitude toward multiple nationality

Longstanding opposition to the possession of multiple nationality by Mexicans was reversed in the mid-1990s, with constitutional and legislative amendments that create a specific regime in relation to the possession of foreign nationality. The issue was traditionally a sensitive one: President Vicente Fox was barred from contesting the 1994 presidential election on the basis of mixed Mexican-Spanish parentage alone. The legislative change reportedly initially resulted in only a lukewarm response by Mexicans abroad. The Mexican Constitution specifically reserves certain public and government positions to Mexican-born mono-nationals, while legislation provides for a means to be regarded as a mono-national under Mexican law in order to occupy such posts, involving swearing an oath of renunciation of foreign nationality and no performance of any act pursuant to such nationality (actual proof of loss does not seem to be required, however). Along these lines, the Constitution recognises that multiple nationals may be treated differently in terms of the exercise of the rights of citizenship, and authorises laws aimed at avoiding conflicts related to multiple nationality. In peacetime, no alien may serve in the army, the police, or public security forces, as well as in certain positions such as captains or pilots, but multiple nationals are not defined as aliens or "extranjeros". Recent legislative changes allow Mexicans to vote in elections from overseas.

Recognition of Multiple Nationality

Mexicans must use proof of Mexican nationality to enter and depart Mexico, notwithstanding possession of any foreign nationality. All Mexican multiple nationals are treated exclusively as Mexicans for purposes involving Mexican law, and must act as Mexicans in relation to legal acts in Mexico, legal acts outside Mexico involving Mexican capital, legal persons and property, or related credit, toward which no protection of a foreign government will be allowed. If such is sought, the underlying thing is subject to loss (confiscation) in favour of the state.

*Morocco[44]

Nationality category or status

Only one, and no technical distinction between nationality and citizenship.

Attribution/acquisition of nationality

Event	Law	Condition is renunciation/ loss of other nationality
Birth	To a Moroccan father	NO
	To a Moroccan mother if the child's father is unknown	
	In Morocco to a Moroccan mother and a stateless father	
	In Morocco to unknown parents, unless parentage is established while a minor and thereby not stateless – Foundlings are presumed to have been born in Morocco	
Naturalisation	Upon fulfillment of requirements	NO
Adoption		
Legitimation	During minority by a Moroccan father (conditions)	NO
Marriage	Not automatic – declaration (conditions)	

---

[44] MOROCCO: *Constitution of the Kingdom of Morocco*, 13 September 1996, *Dahir n° 1–58–250 du 21 safar 1378 portant code de la nationalité marocaine*, 6 septembre 1958, **UNHCR (internet)**; *Guide douanier des marocains résidents a l'étranger*, Ministère de la communication, Royaume du Maroc (internet), http://www.mincom.gov.ma/french/mdlm/guide_douan/français/index.htm, consulted 12 April 2006; *Consular information sheet-Morocco*, 10 March 2006, United States Department of State (internet), http://travel.state.gov/travel/cis_pa_tw/cis/cis_975.html, consulted 12 April 2006; "Calls to reconsider discrimination against women in Nationality Code", 19 June 2004, Politics (Morocco) (internet), http://www.arabicnews.com/ansub/Daily/Day/040619/2004061917.html, consulted 12 April 2006; "Gender, Citizenship, and Nationality Programme – Legal Study Morocco", December 2002, United Nations Development Program, Programme on Governance in the Arab Region (internet), http://www.pogar.org/publications/gender/nationality/morocco-legal-f.pdf, consulted 12 April 2006; "Jews in the Arab world. Memories, mostly", The Economist, 27 April 2002, 47; *Human rights and arbitrary deprivation of nationality. Report of the Secretary General*, United Nations Economic and Social Council, Commission on Human Rights, 13 January 2000 (internet), http://www.unhchr.ch/Huridocda/Huridoca.nsf/0/486c1e0f2e7904eb80256887004fa764?Opendocument, consulted 12 April 2006; Oppermann and Yousry, eds., *Das Staatsangehörigkeitsrecht der Arabischen Staaten*.

Event	Law	**Condition is renunciation/ loss of other nationality**
Resumption	Possible for certain groups (native-born Moroccans)	NO
State service	Facilitated naturalization	
Parent acquires nationality	Unmarried minor children of those reintegrated also acquire	NO
	Unmarried minor children of those naturalised also acquire (if 16 or over have option to renounce between 18 and 20)	
	Minor children of those acquiring as per "special conditions"	
Spouse acquires nationality	Not automatic	
Registration		
Special considerations	Birth in Morocco to a Moroccan mother and an alien father, who while residing in Morocco, may declare desire to acquire nationality in the two years before majority, unless govt opposes	NO
	Birth in Morocco to alien parents born after 1958 and declares desire to acquire nationality in the two years before majority, unless govt opposes	
	Birth in Morocco to alien father who was also born in Morocco, if father from majority Arab/Muslim country and is Arab/Muslim, unless government opposes	

Withdrawal/loss of nationality

Event	Law	**Consequence of event is loss of nationality**
Renunciation	Adult who has voluntarily acquired foreign nationality, upon authorization	YES
	Adult or minor multiple national, upon authorization	
	Woman who automatically acquires her husband's nationality upon marriage,	

Event	Law	Consequence of event is loss of nationality
	and received authorization prior to marriage	
	Certain children naturalised with parents, between 18–20	
Attribution at birth conditional	No provision	
Naturalisation elsewhere	(*Loss only if authorized to renounce*)	NO (*exception*)
Adoption by a foreigner		
Marriage to a foreigner	No automatic effect	NO
Spouse acquires other nationality	Deprivation of husband's nationality may be extended to wife if of foreign origin and not thereby stateless	
Parent acquires other nationality	Loss of nationality by parent upon renunciation extends to minor children who reside with him/her, except for women before marriage, and if specified also in cases of deprivation	
	Deprivation of father's nationality may be extended to children if of foreign origin and not thereby stateless, but only if mother (wife) also deprived	
Resumption of previous nationality		NO
Service to foreign state	Deprivation six months after issuance of injunction to leave foreign state or military service, if ignored	POSSIBLE
Other attribution of nationality		NO
(Punitive) deprivation	Revocation of naturalisation for fraud	POSSIBLE
	Except for Moroccans by birth, deprivation possible for offense to sovereign; crime against internal/external state security; certain crime/sentence; refusal to complete military obligations; assistance to foreign state harmful to Morocco – all acts having taken place within ten years of acquisition	

General attitude toward multiple nationality
Morocco does not oppose multiple nationality for its citizens, and does not distinguish among citizens on the basis of multiple nationality. Certain disabilities are only imposed on naturalised citizens for a number of years after their naturalisation. Morocco reportedly offers Israelis descended from Moroccan parents the option of returning to Morocco, and nationality.

Recognition of Multiple Nationality
Foreign nationality is not recognised, and all Moroccan nationals are held to the same standards. Entry and exit must be with Moroccan travel documents.

*The Netherlands[45]

Nationality category or status
Only one, and no technical distinction between nationality and citizenship.

Attribution/acquisition of nationality

Event	Law	Condition is renunciation/ loss of other nationality
Birth	To a Dutch parent, if married	NO
	To a Dutch mother, if unmarried (see also legitimation)	
	Foundling presumed to be child of Dutch national	

---

[45] THE NETHERLANDS: *Tekst van de Rijkswet op het Nederlanderschap zoals deze is komen te luiden op grond van de Rijkswet van 21 december 2000 (STB. 618) en de Rijkswet van 18 april 2002 (STB. 222)*, Staatsblad van het Koninkrijk der Nederlanden, (2003) 113; *Netherlands Citizenship Act*, 1985, **UNHCR (internet)**; *Information on dual nationality*, 18 February 2006, The Royal Netherlands Embassy Washington DC (internet), http://www. netherlands-embassy.org/article.asp?articleref=AR00001778EN, consulted 12 April 2006; *Netherlands Nationality Act (RWN) – Amendments of 1 April 2003*, Vertegenwoordigingen van het Koninkrijk der Nederlanden (internet), http://www.netherlands.org.au/assets/7545folder %20RRWN%20Engels.doc, consulted 12 April 2006; *Consular assistance abroad*, Ministerie van Buitenlandse Zaken (internet), http://www.minbuza.nl/default.asp?CMS_ITEM=34716C 70AA7B46D28CA42BC6294F4F1CX1X48501X01, consulted 12 April 2006; *Dutch Nationality*, Ministerie van Buitenlandse Zaken (internet), http://www.minbuza.nl/default.asp?CMS_ ITEM=AF9532E21DA3474DBCE836516126293BX1X60309X98, consulted 12 April 2006; *Amended Netherlands Nationality Act to enter into force*, 31 March 2003, Ministerie van Justitie (internet), http://www.justitie.nl/english/press/press_releases/archive/archive_2003/Amended_ Netherlands_Nationality_Act.asp, consulted 12 April 2006; *IND Residence Wizard*, Ministerie van Justitie (internet), http://www.ind.nl/EN/verblijfwijzer/, consulted 12 April 2006; *Campbell and Meek*, eds., *International immigration and nationality law*; Gerard-René de Groot, "Access to citizenship for aliens in the Netherlands", in *Citizenship in a global world. Comparing citizenship rights for aliens*, ed. Atsushi Kondo, 31–46 (Houndmills (UK): Palgrave, 2001); de Groot, "Loss of nationality: a critical inventory"; Kees Groenendijk and Eric Heijs, "Immigration, immigrants and nationality law in the Netherlands, 1945–98", in *Towards a European nationality. Citizenship, immigration and nationality law in the EU*, ed. Randall Hansen and Patrick Weil, 143–172 (Houndmills: Palgrave, 2001); T. P. Spijkerboer, "Transnationaliteit in de nieuwe Vreemdelingenwet en de gewijzigde Rijkswet op het Nederlanderschap", *Rechtsgeleerd Magazijn Themis* (2001) no. 6, 163–170; C.A. Groenendijk, *Dual nationality in the Netherlands: pragmatism and stability*, 12 January 1999 (internet), http://migration.unikonstanz.de/ content/center/events/de/events/mpf5/mpf5–groenendijk.htm, consulted 12 April 2006; Peter Fray, "Death of Dutch innocence sends a shiver through Europe", The Sydney Morning Herald, 8 May 2002, 1; H. U. Jessurun d'Oliveira, "Onze koningin heeft twee nationaliteiten. Kan dat nog wel?", *HP/De Tijd*, 16 December 2005, 22–28.

Event	Law	Condition is renunciation/ loss of other nationality
	To a parent domiciled in the Netherlands at the time of the child's birth, who was also born to a parent then domiciled in the Netherlands, provided the child is also domiciled in the Netherlands (conditions)	
Naturalisation	Upon fulfilment of requirements	YES (*exceptions*)
	(*exceptions include if married to Dutch citizen, born in NL, refugee, lived in NL for uninterrupted five years before age 18*) – conditions	
Adoption	Of minor child upon judicial decision (conditions)	NO
Legitimation	Of minor after birth – child may acquire by option if in care of legitimator for over three uninterrupted years after acknowledgement	NO
	If acknowledged by Dutch father before birth, child acquires at birth	
	Judicial declaration of paternity (conditions)	
Marriage	No automatic effect	
Resumption	Possible for various persons who lost Dutch nationality (conditions) by option or naturalisation	NO (*exceptions*)
State service		
Parent acquires nationality	May be naturalised with parent (conditions)	YES (*exceptions*)
	Children of parent who acquires by option may acquire at same time (conditions)	NO (*former Dutch nationals*)
Spouse acquires nationality	No direct effect	
Registration/ Option	Various categories of persons may acquire Dutch nationality by option (conditions)	DEPENDS
Special considerations	Children over 12 years old are consulted about decisions affecting them	

**Withdrawal/loss of nationality**

Event	Law	**Consequence of event is loss of nationality**
Renunciation	Always possible for multiple nationals or persons who will acquire another nationality	YES
Attribution at birth conditional		
Naturalisation elsewhere	*(Unless nationality acquired is that of country where born and lives, or lived there as minor for 5 years, or is spouse's nationality – these exceptions do not apply to all countries, including Austria, Belgium, Denmark, Luxembourg, Norway)*	YES *(exceptions)*
Adoption by a foreigner	If child has or acquires another nationality	YES *(exceptions)*
	(if legitimised by a foreigner)	(NO)
Marriage to a foreigner		NO
Spouse acquires other nationality		NO
Parent acquires other nationality	If acquisition of NL nationality was via parent, parent loses NL nationality and child acquires for nationality	YES
Resumption of previous nationality		YES
Service to foreign state	No effect	
Other attribution of nationality	If naturalised person doesn't renounce other nationality	YES
(Punitive) deprivation	Possible for any fraudulent acquisition of Dutch nationality up to 12 years after grant, even if subject is thereby rendered stateless	POSSIBLE
Special considerations	Dutch multiple nationals who reside outside the Netherlands or the EU for ten years lose Dutch nationality. In order to retain nationality, subject must either live in NL/EU for one year or be issued with a new passport before the	YES

Event	Law	Consequence of event is loss of nationality
	ten year period expires. A new ten year period starts the day a new passport or proof of Dutch nationality is issued.	
	If foundling is proven to have foreign nationality by birth, within five years of date found, then	YES

General attitude toward multiple nationality

Dutch law is selectively accepting of multiple nationality, and has been changed at various points over the past twenty years (last in 2003) in relation to the effects of naturalisation elsewhere, and the conditions of naturalisation in the Netherlands, as far as possession or retention of another nationality. The country's practice has been characterised as "pragmatic", especially in relation to considerations related to immigration. A large group of naturalised citizens reportedly come from countries where renunciation of nationality is made difficult in a practical sense (Morocco, for example). Dutch multiple nationals who live outside the Netherlands or the EU for ten years lose their Dutch nationality by operation of law, however they can avoid this simply by keeping their passport valid – each renewal amounts to restarting the clock on the ten year period.

Recognition of Multiple Nationality

The Netherlands exercises protection on behalf of its nationals notwithstanding any multiple nationality, although it advises citizens that this may not always be possible in other countries of nationality. In the Netherlands, nationals are considered to possess only Netherlands' nationality, and foreign nationality is not recognised in that sense.

New Zealand[46]

Nationality category or status
Only one and no difference between nationality and citizenship.

Attribution/acquisition of nationality

Event	Law	Condition is renunciation/ loss of other nationality
Birth	In New Zealand to at least one New Zealand parent or permanent resident (or parent entitled to reside permanently in the Cook Islands, Niue or Tokelau)	NO
	In New Zealand if otherwise stateless	
	Overseas to New Zealand parent who is in govt/public service (citizen by birth)	
	Overseas to a New Zealand parent who is a citizen otherwise than by descent (additionally, ministerial discretion in grant to children of citizens by descent if in public interest)	
Naturalisation	Fulfilment of requirements (including for citizens by descent)	NO
Adoption	Child deemed born at place and time of adoption (conditions)	NO
	Adoption outside NZ by NZ citizen other than by descent (conditions)	
Legitimation	(see birth)	
Marriage	Not automatic – facilitated naturalization	

---

[46] NEW ZEALAND: *Citizenship Act 1977 (last amended 2005)*, No. 61, Statutes of New Zealand, 8 March 2006, Parliamentary Counsel Office, http://www.legislation.govt.nz/browse_ vw.asp?content-set=pal_statutes, consulted 8 April 2006; *Citizenship-Raraunga*, The Department of Internal Affairs (internet), http://www.citizenship.govt.nz/diawebsite.nsf/wpg_ URL/Services-Citizenship-Index?OpenDocument, consulted 8 April 2006; *New Zealand Citizens*, Ministry of Foreign Affairs and Trade (internet), http://www.mfat.govt.nz/nzcitizens.html, consulted 8 April 2006; Campbell and Meek, eds., *International immigration and nationality law*; Paul Spoonley, "Aliens and citizens in New Zealand", in *Citizenship in a global world. Comparing citizenship rights for aliens*, ed. Atsushi Kondo, 158–175, (Houndmills (UK): Palgrave, 2001); "Kiwis float plan for joint citizenship", The Australian, 10 August 2000, 1.

Event	Law	Condition is renunciation/ loss of other nationality
Resumption	For those who renounced, only via naturalisation provisions	NO
State service		
Parent acquires nationality	No direct effect – facilitated naturalisation possible	
Spouse acquires nationality	No direct effect – facilitated naturalisation possible	
Registration	Persons born prior to 1 January 1978 to NZ mother citizen by birth	NO
Special considerations	Ministerial discretion in granting citizenship to stateless persons	

Withdrawal/loss of nationality

Event	Law	Consequence of event is loss of nationality
Renunciation	Possible if adult of full capacity who is multiple national, but may be declined if resident in NZ or NZ in state of war	YES
Attribution at birth conditional	No provision	
Naturalisation elsewhere	Deprivation possible if adult acquires foreign nationality by voluntary act (not marriage) and commits acts against NZ, or exercises other rights/duties contrary to NZ interests	NO *(but deprivation possible)*
Adoption by a foreigner		NO
Marriage to a foreigner		NO
Spouse acquires other nationality		NO
Parent acquires other nationality		NO
Resumption of previous nationality		NO
Service to foreign state	(see naturalisation elsewhere)	NO

Event	Law	**Consequence of event is loss of nationality**
Other attribution of nationality	(see naturalisation elsewhere)	NO
(Punitive) deprivation	For citizenship by naturalisation, registration or grant: fraud in acq.	YES

Special considerations

General attitude toward multiple nationality
New Zealand accepts multiple nationality for its citizens. The NZ Citizenship Act provides that loss of citizenship does not result in the discharge of obligations owed while still a citizen. No distinction is made on the basis of multiple nationality.

Recognition of Multiple Nationality
New Zealand nationals may use foreign passports to enter and depart New Zealand, and may even be provided with resident return visas should they wish. There does not appear to be a difference in the exercise of international protection on the basis of multiple nationality.

*Nigeria[47]

Nationality category or status
Only one, and no technical distinction between nationality and citizenship.

Attribution/acquisition of nationality

Event	Law	Condition is renunciation/ loss of other nationality
Birth	In Nigeria to a Nigerian parent (or if has Nigerian grandparent)	NO
	Outside Nigeria to a Nigerian parent	
Naturalisation	Upon fulfilment of requirements	NO (*exception*)
	(*except must effectively renounce any nationality not acquired at birth*)	
Adoption		
Legitimation	(see birth)	
Marriage	Not automatic – by registration (conditions)	
Resumption	Registration possible (conditions)	
State service	Facilitated naturalisation possible	
Parent acquires nationality		
Spouse acquires nationality	No direct effect – registration possible (conditions)	
Registration	Various categories (born outside Nigeria and has Nigerian grandparent) (*except must effectively renounce any nationality not acquired at birth*)	NO (*exception*)

[47] NIGERIA: *Constitution of the Federal Republic of Nigeria*, 1999 (internet), http://www. nigeria-law.org/ConstitutionOfTheFederalRepublicOfNigeria.htm#Chapter_3, consulted 12 April 2006; *Dual Nationality – Adults*, British High Commission Nigeria (internet), http://www.british highcommission.gov.uk/servlet/Front?pagename=OpenMarket/Xcelerate/ShowPage&c=Page&cid= 1107298150374, consulted 12 April 2006; Hecker, *Das Staatsangehörigkeitsrecht des anglo-phonen Afrika*; Arthur V. J. Nylander, *The nationality and citizenship laws of Nigeria* (Lagos: University of Lagos, 1973).

Withdrawal/loss of nationality

Event	Law	Consequence of event is loss of nationality
Renunciation	Possible if of full age, may be withheld in wartime or if against public policy	YES
Attribution at birth conditional	No provision	
Naturalisation elsewhere	*(except, if not a citizen by birth, acquisition or retention of nationality of country where not citizen by birth)*	NO *(exception)*
Adoption by a foreigner		NO
Marriage to a foreigner		NO
Spouse acquires other nationality		NO
Parent acquires other nationality		NO
Resumption of previous nationality	*(if a national of that country by birth)*	NO *(condition)*
Service to foreign state		NO
Other attribution of nationality	If involuntary	NO
(Punitive) deprivation	Of naturalised citizens upon certain criminal sentences (conditions)	POSSIBLE
	Of naturalised or registered citizens for disloyalty, assistance to enemy in wartime (according to court proceedings or inquiry)	

Special considerations

General attitude toward multiple nationality

Nigeria accepts certain multiple nationality of its citizens, in relation to nationality acquired at birth: it does not require renunciation of such nationality as a condition of naturalisation, and does not deprive its nationals by birth of Nigerian nationality should they acquire a foreign nationality. It may be remarked that this represents a considerable change from past practice, which required effective renunciation of foreign nationality by age 22, in order for Nigerian nationality to be retained. No distinction is made on the basis of multiple nationality, but naturalised and registered citizens may not hold certain public office for a prescribed period of time after acquisition of citizenship.

Recognition of Multiple Nationality

Nigerian multiple nationals must travel in and out of Nigeria on Nigerian travel documents. No evidence was found of specific practice recognising multiple nationality.

Norway[48]

**Nationality category or status**
Only one, and no distinction between nationality and citizenship.

**Attribution/acquisition of nationality**

Event	Law	**Condition is renunciation/ loss of other nationality**
Birth	To a Norwegian father in wedlock (including if deceased – conditions)	NO (*but see conditional attribution*)
	To a Norwegian mother	
	Foundlings considered Norwegian until contrary information received	
	Children born abroad and living abroad lose nationality at age 22 if have always lived overseas and unless apply to retain – includes their children unless (conditions)	
Naturalization (Application)	Application to Directorate of Immigration or County Governor's Office, for certain categories upon fulfillment of conditions	YES
Adoption	By Norwegian national in Norway of child under 12 – automatic	NO
	By Norwegian national overseas of child under 12, if Governmental Office	

---

[48] NORWAY: *Norwegian Nationality* Act, 1951 (as amended to 1989), **UNHCR (internet)**; *Norwegian Citizenship*, Utlendingsdirektoratet – Norwegian Directorate of Immigration (internet), http://www.udi.no/upload/Publikasjoner/EngPublications/Norwegian%20citizenship.pdf, consulted 7 May 2006; *Citizenship*, http://www.udi.no/upload/Faktaark/Engelsk/engstb0512%20pdf.pdf, consulted 7 May 2006; *Circular 35/2005 – Section 6 fourth paragraph, cf second paragraph of the Norwegian Nationality Act relating to adoptive children*, Utlendingsdirektoratet (internet), http://www.udi.no/templates/Rundskriv.aspx?id=6683, consulted 7 May 2006; *Circular 41/ 2004 – Section 6 fourth paragraph cf second paragraph of the Norwegian Nationality Act – adoptive children living abroad*, Utlendingsdirektoratet (internet), http://www.udi.no/templates/ Rundskriv.aspx?id=5480, consulted 7 May 2006; *Circular 62/2001 – Section 2a of the Norwegian Nationality Act – paternity pursuant to foreign legislation*, Utlendingsdirektoratet (internet), http://www.udi.no/templates/Rundskriv.aspx?id=6831, consulted 7 May 2006; *Diplomatic Protection – Statement by Norway, 1 November 2004, Report of the International Law Commission*, Norwegian Mission to the UN (internet), http://www.norway-un.org/Norwegian Statements/CommitteeMeetings/diplomatic.htm, consulted 7 May 2006.

Event	Law	Condition is renunciation/ loss of other nationality
	for Youth and Adoption consents in advance – automatic	
	By Norwegian national of child between 12–18 and child consents, by notification to County Governor's Office or Norwegian mission abroad	
Legitimation	If parents marry before child reaches 18 and is unmarried, see birth	NO
	Birth to unmarried Norwegian father, child under 18, and if over 12 gives consent – by notification to County Governor's Office or Norwegian mission abroad (conditions)	
Marriage	Not automatic – facilitated application	
Resumption	Possible by application or notification depending on category	
State service		
Parent acquires nationality	Children may be included in parents' application for nationality, or unmarried children living in Norway in registration (conditions)	
Spouse acquires nationality		
Registration (Notification)	(Conditions) Notification via County Governor's Office for: (a) lived in Norway since 16 or younger and for at least five years; (b) Nordic national by birth, livd in Norway for 7 years and no criminal record, and at least 18, (c) lost Norwegian nationality and then only national of Nordic country, (d) between 18–21 residence for total often years, and permanently resided 5 years before application, (e) acquired Norwegian nationality at birth and lived in Norway until 18, then lost nationality, may resume upon living in Norway for two years	NO (*exception*)
	(*Categories (d) and (e) must renounce other nationality*)	
Special considerations		

Withdrawal/loss of nationality

Event	Law	Consequence of event is loss of nationality
Renunciation	Possible if reside overseas permanently and have or will acquire other nationality – not possible if reside permanently in Norway	YES
Attribution at birth conditional	Children born abroad and living abroad lose nationality at age 22 if have always lived overseas and unless apply to retain – includes their children unless stateless (conditions)	YES
Naturalisation elsewhere		YES
Adoption by a foreigner	If thereby acquire nationality	YES
Marriage to a foreigner	(Unless voluntary acquisition of foreign nationality)	NO (*exception*)
Spouse acquires other nationality		NO
Parent acquires other nationality	Unmarried children under 18 who acquire foreign nationality due to acquisition by parent, parent has custody, and other parent not Norwegian	YES
Resumption of previous nationality	If voluntary acquisition of foreign nationality	YES
Service to foreign state	If thereby acquires foreign nationality	YES
Other attribution of nationality	Any voluntary acquisition of foreign nationality	YES
(Punitive) deprivation		
Special considerations		

General attitude toward multiple nationality

Norway states that it does not accept dual nationality for its citizens. It does, however, tolerate certain exceptions: multiple nationality acquired at birth by descent, birth to Norwegian parents in a country where *jus soli* is applied, if upon being naturalised relinquishing a previous nationality is not possible, and upon certain other grant of Norwegian nationality. Norwegians who acquire foreign nationality voluntarily are deprived of their nationality, however, and loss of previous nationality is a condition of naturalisation in Norway. Norwegians who were born and are living abroad are deprived of nationality at age 22 (along with their children, unless thereby stateless) if they have always lived abroad and have not applied to retain their nationality. If the parent from whom Norweign nationality was derived was also born and is living abroad, ties to Norway determine whether nationality may be retained. Norway states that its multiple nationsls are considered Norwegian nationals "on par with other Norwegian nationals in every respect". The government warns that "it may be difficult for the Norwegian authorities to provide you with diplomatic assistance when you are in the other country where you are a national". In a statement on behalf of the Nordic countries to the International Law Commission, Norway's representative said that "a State may exercise diplomatic protection also on behalf of a foreign national, lawfully and habitually residing in that State, and which in this State's judgement clearly is in need of protection without necessarily formally qualifying for status as a refugee". Should Norwegian multiple nationals be subject to compulsory military service (other than in Norway), Norwegian norms hold that this should be done in the country of permanent residence.

Recognition of Multiple Nationality
Norway states specifically that its dual nationals may hold a foreign passport, but that no Norwegian permits will be placed in foreign travel documents.

Paraguay[49]

Nationality category or status
Only one, and the Constitution specifically distinguishes between nationality and citizenship.

Attribution/acquisition of nationality

Event	Law	Condition is renunciation/ loss of other nationality
Birth	In Paraguay	NO
	Overseas to Paraguayan parent in state service	
	Overseas to Paraguayan parent upon assuming permanent residence (effected by declaration by legal representative while a minor, or personal declaration when over 18)	
	Foundlings	
Naturalisation	Upon fulfillment of requirements	NO
Adoption		
Legitimation		
Marriage	No automatic effect	
Resumption		
State service	Honorary nationality conferred by act of Congress	NO
Parent acquires nationality		
Spouse acquires nationality		

---

[49] PARAGUAY: *Constitution of the Republic of Paraguay*, 20 June 1992, **UNHCR (internet)**; *Constitución de la República de Paraguay*, 25 August 1967, Base de Datos Políticos de las Américas (internet), http://pdba.georgetown.edu/Constitutions/Paraguay/para1967.html, consulted 25 May 2006; *Convenio de doble Nacionalidad con Paraguay (España-Paraguay)*, 25 June 1959, Ministerio de Trabajo y Asuntos Sociales, Secretaría de Estado de Inmigración y Emigración – España (internet), http://extranjeros.mtas.es/es/normativa_jurisprudencia/Internacional/doblenac/PARAGUAY.pdf, consulted 25 May 2006; *Protocolo adicional entre el Reino de España y la República del Paraguay modificando el Convenio de doble nacionalidad de 25 de junio de 1959, hecho «ad referendum» en Asunción el 26 de junio de 1999* (internet), http://www.lexureditorial.com/boe/0104/07286.htm, consulted 25 May 2006.

Event	Law	**Condition is renunciation/ loss of other nationality**
Registration		
Special considerations		

Withdrawal/loss of nationality

Event	Law	**Consequence of event is loss of nationality**
Renunciation	Possible	YES
Attribution at birth conditional	No provision	
Naturalisation elsewhere	(*Only naturalised Paraguayans lose nationality upon naturalisation elsewhere, not the native-born*) Native Paraguayans' rights of citizenship are suspended upon naturalisation elsewhere	NO (*exception*)
Adoption by a foreigner		NO
Marriage to a foreigner		NO
Spouse acquires other nationality		NO
Parent acquires other nationality		NO
Resumption of previous nationality	Any voluntary acquisition of foreign nationality by a naturalized Paraguayan	YES
Service to foreign state		NO
Other attribution of nationality	Any voluntary acquisition of foreign nationality by a naturalized Paraguayan	POSSIBLE
(Punitive) deprivation	Naturalised Paraguayans may lose upon unfustified absence from Paraguay for over three years, upon judicial decision	POSSIBLE

Special considerations

General attitude toward multiple nationality
The 1992 Constitution changed the country's approach to multiple nationality, eliminating the provision that naturalisation elsewhere provokes loss of nationality in all cases. It contains an article entitled "On multiple nationality" which stipulates that multiple nationality may be

allowed by international treaty by reciprocity. Nonetheless, Paraguayan legislation allows for the production of multiple nationality: no native-born Paraguayan may be deprived of nationality, but may voluntarily renounce it. Naturalisation abroad only provokes loss of Paraguayan nationality if it was obtained by naturalisation. Renunciation of previous nationality is not a condition of naturalisation in Paraguay. Naturalised persons receive rights of citizenship two years after naturalisation. The 1959 Convention on Dual Nationality with Spain was modified by an additional protocol in 1999.

Peru[50]

Nationality category or status
Only one, and no distinction between nationality and citizenship.

Attribution/acquisition of nationality

Event	Law	Condition is renunciation/ loss of other nationality
Birth	In Peru	NO
	Overseas to Peruvian parent citizen by birth and registered during minority, but no more than three generations of birth abroad (conditions)	
	See right of option	
	Foundlings	
Naturalisation	Upon fulfillment of conditions	YES
Adoption		
Legitimation		
Marriage	Not automatic – by right of option (conditions)	
Resumption	Possible for Peruvians by birth who renounced nationality, upon fulfillment of conditions (conditions)	NO

---

[50] PERU: *Constitución Política del Perú*, 1993, *Ley no. 26574 – Ley de la nacionalidad*, 3 January 1996, *Ley 27532 – Ley modificatoria de la ley de nacionalidad*, 17 October 2001, **UNHCR (internet)**; *Decreto supreme no. 004–97–IN – Reglamento de la Ley de Nacionalidad*, Consulado General del Peru en Francfort del Meno (internet), http://www.conperfrankfurt.de/ leyes.htm, consulted 4 May 2006; *La nacionalidad peruana*, Consulado General del Peru en Francfort del Meno (internet), http://www.conperfrankfurt.de/nacionalidad.htm, consulted 4 May 2006; *Convenio de doble Nacionalidad con Perú (España-Perú)*, 16 May 1959 Ministerio de Trabajo y Asuntos Sociales, Secretaría de Estado de Inmigración y Emigración – España (internet), http://extranjeros.mtas.es/es/normativa_jurisprudencia/Internacional/doblenac/PERU.pdf, consulted 7 May 2006; *Baruch Ivcher Bronstein v. Peru*, Judgment of 6 February 2001, Inter-American Court of Human Rights, (internet), http://www.corteidh.or.cr/seriec_ing/ seriec_74__ing.doc, consulted 19 March 2006; Philip Brasor, "Espíritu de regimens corruptos latente en el Japón", (translated from The Japan Times, 10 August 2003), Ministerio de Relaciones Exteriores del Perú (internet), http://www.rree.gob.pe/portal/enlaces.nsf/0/9dac 610a7f12f5c805256e8a005eea5a?OpenDocument, consulted 4 May 2006; "Good to be back", South China Morning Post, 6 December 2000.

Event	Law	Condition is renunciation/ loss of other nationality
State service	Naturalisation by Conressional legislative resolution	NO
Parent acquires nationality		
Spouse acquires nationality	Possible by right of option	
Registration (Right of option)	Possible for various categories upon fulfillment of conditions, including upon marriage to a Peruvian, or for the child of Peruvian parent born abroad and over age 18	NO
Special considerations		

Withdrawal/loss of nationality

Event	Law	Consequence of event is loss of nationality
Renunciation	Possible if over 18 and express renunciation before Peruvian authorities – parents may not do on behalf of children	YES
Attribution at birth conditional		NO
Naturalisation elsewhere		NO
Adoption by a foreigner		NO
Marriage to a foreigner		NO
Spouse acquires other nationality		NO
Parent acquires other nationality		NO
Resumption of previous nationality		NO
Service to foreign state		NO
Other attribution of nationality		NO

Event	Law	**Consequence of event is loss of nationality**
(Punitive) deprivation		NO
Special considerations	Peruvian nationality may only be lost by express declaration to Peruvian authorities	

General attitude toward multiple nationality

Peru accepts certain multiple nationality for its citizens. The Constitution provides that Peruvian nationality can only be lost by express renunciation before Peruvian authorities, however loss of previous nationality is a condition of naturalisation. The Nationality Act contains a chapter on dual nationality, which states that: Peruvians by birth who adopt foreign nationality do not lose Peruvian nationality, with the exception of express renunciation before Peruvian authorities; multiple nationals are to exercise rights and obligations of the nationality where they are domiciled; naturalised citizens who are dual nationals do not possess the exclusive rights that Peruvian citizens by birth possess; Peruvians by birth who possess dual nationality do not thereby lose the exclusive rights they possess as citizens by birth. A treaty allowing for, and regulating, dual nationality with Spain is in force. The Nationality Act was amended in 2001 in order to eliminate any possibility of deprivation of nationality by the state or by operation of law, and requiring express renunciation in all cases. This was most likely a consequence of the *Ivcher Bronstein Case* before the Inter-American Court of Human Rights, in which the Court found that Peru's deprivation of Bronstein's nationality had violated the Inter-American Convention on Human Rights. The case of former Peruvian President Alberto Fujimori, whom Japan confirmed as possessing Japanese nationality after he left office, was a major source of friction between the countries.

*Philippines[51]

Nationality category or status
Only one, and no technical distinction between nationality and citizenship.

Attribution/acquisition of nationality

Event	Law	Condition is renunciation/ loss of other nationality
Birth	To a Filipino parent	NO
Naturalisation	Upon filfilment of requirements; must receive "permission" from state of nationality – unclear whether must be effective renunciation	YES (*but not necessarily effective renunciation*)
	Facilitated naturalisation for persons born in Philippines	NO

---

[51] THE PHILIPPINES: *Citizenship Retention and Re-acquisition Act of 2003*, Republic Act No. 9225, Republic of the Philippines Government Portal (internet), http://www.gov.ph/ laws/RA9225.pdf, consulted 12 April 2006; *Rules Governing Philippine Citizenship under Republic Act (RA) No. 9225 and Administrative Order (A.O.) No. 91, Series of 2004*, Republic of the Philippines Government Portal (internet), http://www.gov.ph/faqs/dualcitizenship_irr.asp, consulted 12 April 2006; *Administrative Naturalization Act of 2000, Republic Act 9139*, Chan Robles Virtual Law Library (internet), http://www.chanrobles.com/republicactno9139.html, consulted 12 April 2006; *An Act providing for the repatriation of Filipino women who have lost their Philippine citizenship by marriage to aliens and of natural born Filipinos*, Republic Act 8171, 23 October 1995; *Constitution of the Republic of the Philippines*, 2 February 1987; *Presidential Decree No. 836, Granting Citizenship to Deserving Aliens and for Other Purposes*, 3 December 1975, *Commonwealth Act No. 63, Providing for the ways in which Philippine Citizenship may be Lost or Acquired (as amended)*, October 1936 amended 1977, *Commonwealth Act No. 473, Act to Provide for the Acquisition of Philippine Citizenship by Naturalization*, June 1939 amended 1977, *Act Providing the Manner in Which the Option to Elect Philippine Citizenship Shall be Declared by a Person Whose Mother is a Filipino Citizen*, June 1941, *Republic Act No. 530, Making Additional Provisions for Naturalization*, June 1950, **UNHCR (internet)**; *Dual Citizenship FAQ*, Republic of the Philippines Government Portal (internet), http://www. gov.ph/faqs/dualcitizenship.asp, consulted 12 April 2006; Tito Guingona, *On dual citizenship*, Press Statement by the Secretary, 20 December 2001, Department of Foreign Affairs Philippines (internet), http://www.dfa.gov.ph/archive/speech/guingona/dualcitizenship.htm, consulted 12 April 2006; Irene R. Cortes and Raphael Perpetuo M. Lotilla, "Nationality and international law from the Philippine perspective", in *Nationality and international law in Asian perspective*, ed. Ko Swan Sik, 335–422 (Dordrecht: Martinus Nijhoff Publishers, 1990); Dan Albert S. de Padua, "Ambiguous allegiance: multiple nationality in Asia", *Philippine Law Journal* (1985) vol. 60, no. 2, 239–267; Leon T. Garcia, *Problems of citizenship in the Philippines* (Hong Kong: Commercial Press Printing Works, 1949).

Event	Law	Condition is renunciation/ loss of other nationality
Adoption	Not automatic	
Legitimation	(see birth)	
Marriage	Not automatic – facilitated naturalisation possible	
Resumption	Possible for natural born Filipinos	NO
State service	Possible	
Parent acquires nationality	Child acquires as a consequence of parentage, if minor, and residing in the Philippines	NO
	Minor unmarried children of natural-born Filipinos who resume nationality	NO
Spouse acquires nationality	Facilitated naturalisation	
Registration		

Withdrawal/loss of nationality

Event	Law	Consequence of event is loss of nationality
Renunciation	Only if express renunciation by adult	YES
Attribution at birth conditional	No provision	
Naturalisation elsewhere	*(if involves subscribing an oath of allegiance)*	YES *(condition) – natural born can resume*
Adoption by a foreigner		
Marriage to a foreigner	(unless deemed to have renounced)	NO
Spouse acquires other nationality		NO
Parent acquires other nationality		NO
Resumption of previous nationality	(if naturalisation that involves previous nationality subscribing an oath of allegiance)	YES
Service to foreign state	Possible if without consent of govt	POSSIBLE

		Consequence of event is
Event	**Law**	**loss of nationality**
	unless allied country (conditions), and voluntary. No deprivation for any involuntary military service	
Other attribution of nationality		
(Punitive) deprivation	Revocation of naturalisation possible for: fraud, returning to reside permanently in country of origin or other country, acts against national security	POSSIBLE
Special considerations		

General attitude toward multiple nationality
The Philippines' Constitution provides specifically that "[d]ual allegiance of citizens is inimical to the national interest and shall be dealt with by law". Filipino practice has, however, been characterised as "ambivalent" toward multiple nationality acquired at birth, and the Department of Foreign Affairs stated in 2001 that growing demands from Filipinos resident overseas for multiple nationality meant that the government was studying ways to address the problem, stating that "dual citizenship . . . is a challenge whose time has come", and distinguishing citizenship from allegiance. In 2003 the Philippines' Congress enacted legislation that permits natural born citizens (born of a Filipino parent) to resume their Philippine nationality after having lost it upon naturalisation abroad, upon application and by taking an oath (no loss of foreign nationality is required). Philippines' law and policy does not exclude multiple nationality acquired at birth, and depending on judicial interpretation, the requirement that candidates for naturalisation must seek permission from their countries of nationality, combined with a loyalty oath of allegiance, may be seen as requiring effective loss of foreign nationality as a condition of naturalisation, or not. The 2003 Act that allows "natural born" former citizens to resume Philippine nationality as dual nationals contains specific provisions regarding the exercise of political rights, limiting Philippine dual nationals in relation to holding public office should they occupy certain positions in their other country of nationality.

Recognition of Multiple Nationality
Filipino practice is reportedly to adopt a low-key approach to consular protection, especially in countries where vast numbers of Filipino workers are employed, and to build constructive relations with authorities as opposed to confrontation.

Poland[52]

Nationality category or status
Only one, and no distinction between nationality and citizenship.

Attribution/acquisition of nationality

Event	Law	Condition is renunciation/ loss of other nationality
Birth	To Polish parents	NO
	To a Polish parent and the other parent is unknown, of undetermined citizenship, or stateless	
	In Poland to unknown parents, parents of unknown citizenship, or stateless parents (includes foundling)	
	To a Polish parent and foreign citizen (within three months of birth parents may declare child only to acquire foreign parent's nationality – if parents disagree they may submit for court adjudication. Such foreign child may between 16 and six months of majority request Polish nationality – conditions)	

---

[52] POLAND: *Constitution of the Republic of Poland*, April 1997, *Law on Polish Citizenship*, 15 February 1962, **UNHCR (internet)**; *Polish citizenship*, Consulate General of the Republic of Poland in New York (internet), http://www.polishconsulateny.org/index.php?p=43, consulted 25 May 2006; *Repatriation as a form of acquiring Polish citizenship*, 19 April 2005, Ministry of Interior and Administration (internet), http://www.mswia.gov.pl/index_eng_wai.php?dzial= 16&id=27, consulted 25 May 2006; *European Bulletin on Nationality – Poland*, 19 September 2004, Council of Europe (internet), http://www.coe.int/t/e/legal_affairs/legal_co-operation/ foreigners_and_citizens/nationality/documents/bulletin/Poland%20E%202004.pdf, consulted 25 May 2006; *Citizenship*, Embassy of the Republic of Poland in Washington, DC (internet), http://www.polandembassy.org/Links/consular/Citizenship.htm, consulted 25 May 2006; *Dual nationality*, United States Diplmatic Mission to Warsaw (internet), http://usembassy.state.gov/ poland/dual_nationality-408cda12d248a.html, consulted 25 May 2006; *Travel advice for Poland*, 10 May 2006, Australian Department of Foreign Affairs and Trade (internet), http:// www.smartraveller.gov.au/zw-cgi/view/Advice/Poland, consulted 25 May 2006; Agata Górny, Aleksandra Grzymała-Kazłowska, Piotr Koryś, Agnieszka Weinar, "Multiple citizenship in Poland", Institute for Social Studies Warsaw University (internet), http://www.iss.uw.edu.pl/osrodki/cmr/ wpapers/pdf/053.pdf, consulted 25 May 2006.

Event	Law	Condition is renunciation/ loss of other nationality
Naturalisation	Upon fulfillment of conditions *(grant may depend on submission of evidence of loss)*	DEPENDS
Adoption		
Legitimation	Possible if under 16, if over with child's consent (conditions)	
Marriage	No automatic effect – possible by declaration *(grant may depend on submission of evidence of loss)*	DEPENDS
Resumption	Possible for various categories, including loss upon marriage to foreigner; Poles who emigrated to Israel between 1958–1984 and their descendants *(grant may depend on submission of evidence of loss)*	DEPENDS
State service	Facilitated naturalisation possible	
Parent acquires	When both parents acquire children also acquire. When only one parent acquires, children included if under that parent's authority, other parent is Polish, other parent consents	NO
Spouse acquires nationality		
Registration	Certain resident stateless persons can be declared to be Polish nationals – can be extended to their children (conditions)	
Special considerations	Certain persons of Polish ethnic origin may apply for repatriation from Armenia, Azerbaijan, Georgia, Kazakhstan, Kyrgyzstan, Tajikistan, Uzbekistan, and the "Asian part of the Russian Federation" (conditions)	

Withdrawal/loss of nationality

Event	Law	Consequence of event is loss of nationality
Renunciation	"Permission to renounce" nationality may be made upon application for acquisition of foreign nationality	YES
Attribution at birth conditional	No provision	
Naturalisation elsewhere	Only provokes loss of nationality upon specific application for loss	NO (*exception*)
Adoption by a foreigner		NO
Marriage to a foreigner		NO
Spouse acquires other nationality		NO
Parent acquires other nationality	Parent's loss of Polish nationality upon application in acquisition of foreign citizensip is extended to children if other parent has no parental authority, is not Polish, or consents – children over 16 must consent (conditions)	NO (*exception*)
Resumption of previous nationality		NO
Service to foreign state		NO
Other attribution of nationality		NO
(Punitive) deprivation		NO
Special considerations		

General attitude toward multiple nationality
Poland accepts multiple nationality for its citizens. Naturalisation abroad does not result in loss of Polish nationality unless a specific application is made requesting such loss ("permission to change citizenship"). The Constitution provides that nationality can only be lost by voluntary renunciation.

Recognition of Multiple Nationality
Poland does not recognise multiple nationality and treats its nationals as Poles only. The Citizenship Act stipulates that "a person who is a Polish citizen under Polish law cannot be recognised at the same time as a citizen of another state". In order to be recognised as a foreign citizen, an application for "permission for change of citizenship" must be submitted and

accepted, entailing the loss of Polish nationality. The Constitution provides that Polish citizens have the right to protection by the state when abroad. Poles must enter and depart Poland on Polish travel documents, except when consular agreements provide otherwise. Some countries advise their citizens that they may be unable to provide consular assistance to dual nationals in Poland.

*Portugal[53]

Nationality category or status

Only one, deemed to be acquired either "originally" or "non-originally", and no technical distinction between nationality and citizenship.

Attribution/acquisition of nationality

Event	Law	Condition is renunciation/ loss of other nationality
Birth	In Portugal to Portuguese parent	NO
	In Portugal to alien parents at least one of whom has been legally present in Portugal for at least five years (conditions), unless in diplomatic service	

---

[53] PORTUGAL: *Constitution of the Portuguese Republic*, 25 April 1976 (as revised 1997); *Loi sur la nationalité – no. 37/1981*, 3 October 1981; *Decree-Law No. 59/1993*, 3 March 1993, **UNHCR (internet)**; José Bento Amaro, "SEF contra nova lei da nacionalidade", Público, 30 June 2005, 8; Campbell and Meek, eds., *International immigration and nationality law*; de Groot, "Loss of nationality: a critical inventory"; Fernandes, *O direito da igualdade entre Portugal e Brasil*; Miguel Galvão Teles and Paulo Canelas de Castro, "Portugal and the right of peoples to self-determination", *Archiv des Völkerrechts* (1996) vol. 34, no. 1, 2–46; Moura Ramos, "La double nationalité et les liens spéciaux avec d'autres pays. Les développements et les perspectives au Portugal"; Rui Manuel Moura Ramos, "Migratory movements and nationality law in Portugal", in *Towards a European nationality. Citizenship, immigration and nationality law in the EU*, ed. Randall Hansen and Patrick Weil, 214–229 (Houndmills: Palgrave, 2001); Rui Manuel Moura Ramos, "Nationalité, plurinationalité et supranationalité en droit Portugais", *Archiv des Völkerrechts* (1996) vol. 34, no. 1, 96–119; Ella Rule, "Portuguese nationality law in outline", *Tolley's Immigration and Nationality Law and Practice* (1996) vol. 10, no. 1, 12–15; Nuno Sá Lourenço and Helena Pereira, "Lei da nacionalidade alterada pelo Governo a pensar nos ilhos de imigrantes", Público, 8 July 2005, 20; *A nova lei da nacionalidade, Data: 06–03–2006*, Alto Commissariado para a Imigração e Minorias Étnicas (internet), http://www.acime.gov.pt/modules.php?name=News&file=print&sid=1253, consulted 17 April 2006; *Nacionalidade Portuguesa. Folheto informativo*, Alto Commissariado para a Imigração e Minorias Étnicas (internet), http://www.oi.acime.gov.pt/docs/rm/Brochuras/nacionalidade.pdf, consulted 12 April 2006; *Perguntas Frequentes (FAQ). Nacionalidade Portuguesa*, Alto Commissariado para a Imigração e Minorias Étnicas (internet), http://www.acime.gov.pt/modules.php?name=FAQ&myfaq=yes&id_cat=4&categories=Nacionalidade+Port.#719, consulted 12 April 2006; *Nacionalidade portuguesa*, Secretaria de Estado das Comunidades Portuguesas (internet), http://www.www.secomunidades.pt/poios/nacional.html, consulted 1 August 2003; *Situação militar*, Consulado de Portugal em Santos (internet), http://www.consuladodeportugal-santos.org.br/situacao_militar.htm, consulted 12 April 2006.

Event	Law	Condition is renunciation/ loss of other nationality
	In Portugal to alien parents also born in Portugal (conditions)	
	In Portugal, if otherwise stateless, or a foundling	
	Overseas to Portuguese parent, if parent in state service, or if child is registered or declares desire to be Portuguese	
Naturalisation	Upon fulfilment of requirements (various categories)	NO
Adoption	If full adoption, automatic acquisition	NO
Legitimation	Only produces effects during child's minority (see birth)	NO
Marriage	Not automatic – acquisition by declaration (conditions), also applies to de-facto unions	NO
Resumption	Minor who lost nationality through parents' decision	NO
	Woman who lost nationality previously upon marriage to an alien	
	Those deprived previously upon acquisition of other nationality	
State service	Facilitated naturalisation possible	
Parent acquires nationality	Children may acquire by declaration	NO
Spouse acquires nationality	No direct effect – facilitated acquisition possible	
Registration		

Withdrawal/loss of nationality

Event	Law	Consequence of event is loss of nationality
Renunciation	Always possible for multiple nationals	YES
Attribution at birth conditional	No provision (except registration if born abroad)	
Naturalization elsewhere		NO

Event	Law	Consequence of event is loss of nationality
Adoption by a foreigner		NO
Marriage to a foreigner		NO
Spouse acquires other nationality		NO
Parent acquires other nationality		NO
Resumption of previous nationality		NO
Service to foreign state	(*see punitive deprivation*)	NO (*exception*)
Other attribution of nationality		NO
(Punitive) deprivation	Possible for those who acquire nationality after birth (by judicial decree within one year of acquisition) for a refusal to recognise a tie to Portugal, crimes entailing a sentence over three years, voluntary foreign state or military service.	POSSIBLE
Special considerations	Nationality lost by foundling if discovered is child of foreign parents and not stateless	YES

General attitude toward multiple nationality
Portugal allows its citizens to possess multiple nationality, but recognises Portuguese nationality alone for the purposes of Portuguese law. Article 4 of the Portuguese Constitution provides that "[a]ll persons are Portuguese citizens who are regarded as such by law or under international convention". In terms of conflicts of law, the Nationality Law recognises that multiple nationality may be possessed, and states that "[s]i quelqu'un possède deux ou plusieurs nationalités, dont l'une est la nationalité portugaise, celle-ci est la seule, qui, à l'égard de la loi portugaise, doit être prise en considération". Foreigners are defined as those who lack Portuguese nationality.

Recognition of Multiple Nationality
Only Portuguese nationality is acknowledged in Portugal, and in-principle protection may be exercised on behalf of all nationals, regardless of multiple nationality. Portugal informs non-Portuguese multiple nationals that they will be treated as nationals of their place of habitual residence, or if none exists, of the state to which they have the closest connection.

*Romania[54]

Nationality category or status
Only one, and no technical distinction between nationality and citizenship.

Attribution/acquisition of nationality

Event	Law	Condition is renunciation/ loss of other nationality
Birth	In Romania to a Romanian parent	
	Abroad to a Romanian parent	
	Foundlings whose parentage is unknown	NO
Naturalisation	Upon fulfillment of requirements	NO
Adoption	Of a minor by two Romanian parents	NO
	Of a minor by one Romanian parent	
	Of a minor by parents only one of whom is Romanian, by agreement, and consent of the child at age 14	
Legitimation	(see birth)	
Marriage	No direct effect – facilitated naturalisation	
Resumption	Possible for various groups	NO
State service	Possible, by Parliament	NO
Parent acquires nationality	If parent resumes/acquires nationality, minor children also, with consent of child if 14 or over (court to decide if spouse opposes)	NO
Spouse acquires nationality	No direct effect	
Registration		

---

[54] ROMANIA: *Romanian Constitution*, 8 December 1991 (internet), http://www.oefre. unibe.ch/law/icl/ro00000_.html, consulted 17 April 2006, *Loi de la citoyenneté roumaine*, 5 April 1991; *Décret-loi concernant quelques dispositions qui se referent a la citoyenneté roumaine*, 11 May 1990, **UNHCR (internet)**; Octavian Capatina, "Nationalité: Roumanie", in *Juris-Classeur Nationalité*, ed. Michel J. Verwilghen and Charles L. Closset, *Collection des Juris-Classeurs* (Paris: Éditions du Juris-Classeur, 1996); Liebich, "Plural citizenship in post-Communist states".

Withdrawal/loss of nationality

Event	Law	Consequence of event is loss of nationality
Renunciation	Adult, no criminal accusation or involvement, no debts (unless provides related guarantees), for serious reasons	YES
Attribution at birth conditional	No provision	
Naturalisation elsewhere		NO
Adoption by a foreigner	*(except if adoptive parent request loss of child's citizenship, and child will receive parent's nationality. If adoption revoked child is considered never to have lost Romanian nationality)*	NO *(exception)*
Marriage to a foreigner	No direct effect	NO
Spouse acquires other nationality	Any loss or deprivation of spouse's nationality does not affect other spouse	NO
Parent acquires other nationality	*(Any loss or deprivation of parent's nationality does not affect children, except if both parents renounce nationality and leave the country with the child (if child 14 or over only if consents))*	NO *(exception)*
Resumption of previous nationality		NO
Service to foreign state	*(Possible deprivation if enrolment abroad in armed forces of state at war with Romania or with which has no diplomatic relations)*	POSSIBLE
Other attribution of nationality		NO
(Punitive) deprivation	*No deprivation possible if nationality acquired at birth*	NO
	While abroad commission of acts against Romania's interests; for fraud in acquisition of nationality	YES
Special considerations	*No deprivation possible if nationality acquired at birth*	

Event	Law	Consequence of event is loss of nationality
	If adoption revoked, minor child considered never to have been Romanian if resides abroad or leaves to reside abroad	YES
	If foundling's parent identified as foreign national	

General attitude toward multiple nationality
The 1991 Citizenship Law is mostly silent as to multiple nationality, but notwithstanding a specific provision that all citizens are equal, stipulates that access to civil or military public office "is granted to persons whose citizenship is only and exclusively Romanian and whose domicile is in Romania". The Constitution provides that citizenship acquired by birth cannot be withdrawn. Honorary citizens enjoy all rights of citizenship, except to be elected to, or serve in, public office.

Recognition of Multiple Nationality
The Constitution provides that all citizens enjoy the state's protection while abroad, but in practice, protection of multiple nationals seems to be on a case-by-case basis. In Romania, Romanian law exclusively is applied to multiple nationals.

*Russian Federation[55]

Nationality category or status

There is only one, and no technical distinction between nationality and citizenship (in terms of citizenship rights).

Attribution/acquisition of nationality

Event	Law	Condition is renunciation/ loss of other nationality
Birth	To two Russian parents	NO
	To a Russian parent and the other parent is stateless or missing	
	To a Russian parent and an alien, if otherwise stateless	
	In the Russian Federation to a Russian parent and an alien	
	In the Russian Federation to alien or stateless parents, if otherwise stateless	
	Foundling (if parents unidentified six months after found)	
Naturalisation	Upon fulfilment of requirements (*renunciation a condition unless applicable treaty provision, impossible*	YES (*exceptions*)

---

[55] RUSSIA: *Federal law on the legal position of foreign citizens in the Russian* Federation, no. 115–FZ of 25 July 2002, Federal *law on citizenship of the Russian Federation,* no. 62–FZ of 31 May 2002, **UNHCR (internet)**; William E. Butler, *Russian law* (Oxford: Oxford University Press, 1999); William E. Butler and Jane E. Henderson, eds., *Russian legal texts – the foundations of a rule-of-law state and a market economy* (The Hague: Simmonds & Hill; Kluwer Law International, 1998); George Ginsburgs, "Citizenship and state succession in Russia's treaty and domestic repertory", *Review of Central and East European Law* (1995) vol. 21, no. 5, 433–482; George Ginsburgs, "The "right to a nationality" and the regime of loss of Russian citizenship", *Review of Central and East European Law* (2000) vol. 26, no. 1, 1–33; Vassilij Jermolin, "Das Staatsangehörigkeitsrecht der Russischen Föderation (Russlands)", *Jahrbuch für Ostrecht* (1998) vol. 39, 41–53; Liebich, "Plural citizenship in post-Communist states"; Hans von Mangoldt, "Das Staatsangehörigkeitsrecht der Russischen Föderation im Lichte ihrer völkerrechtlichen Verpflichtungen", in *Russlands Reform auf dem Prüfstand,* ed. Dieter Blumenwitz and Silke Spieler, 11–37 (Bonn: Kulturstiftung der deutschen Verbriebenen, 1997); "Turkmenistan. Time to choose", The Economist, 5 July 2003, 27; "Russia's imperial yearning", The Economist, 24 June 2000, 65; *Dual Nationality,* US Consulate St. Petersburg, (internet), http://stpetersburg.usconsulate.gov/citizen_dual.htm, consulted 17 April 2006.

Event	Law	Condition is renunciation/ loss of other nationality
	to renounce, child of Russian parent or guardian)	
Adoption	Of minor child by Russian citizen (conditions)	NO
Legitimation	(see birth)	
Marriage	No direct effect – facilitated naturalisation	
Resumption	Facilitated naturalisation (conditions)	YES
State service	Facilitated naturalisation	NO
Parent acquires nationality	If both parents acquire or single parent acquires, during minority	DEPENDS
Spouse acquires nationality	No direct effect – facilitated naturalisation possible	
Registration		

Withdrawal/loss of nationality

Event	Law	Consequence of event is loss of nationality
Renunciation	Possible of individual's free will, but not if obligations owed, involved or sentenced in criminal matter, or if thereby stateless	YES
Attribution at birth conditional	No provision	
Naturalisation elsewhere		NO
Adoption by a foreigner	(*unless adoptive parent/s apply for renunciation and child not thereby stateless*) – conditions	NO (*exception*)
Marriage to a foreigner		NO
Spouse acquires other nationality		NO
Parent acquires other nationality	Possible for parent to renounce child's citizenship – conditions	NO (*exceptions*)
	If parent/s lose Russian citizenship, minor children do as well, unless one	

Event	Law	**Consequence of event is loss of nationality**
	parent still citizen, or if not thereby stateless	
Resumption of previous nationality		DEPENDS
Service to foreign state		NO
Other attribution of nationality		DEPENDS
(Punitive) deprivation	Acquisition reversed for fraud in obtention	YES
Special considerations	In any territorial change citizens must be given the option of retaining Russian citizenship	

General attitude toward multiple nationality
The Russian Constitution provides that all citizens are to be treated the same in Russia, and that they may not be deprived of their citizenship, or the right to change it. Whereas the Soviet Union's practice was to attempt to eliminate or reduce multiple nationality, current Russian practice is reportedly to negotiate bi-lateral treaties related to multiple nationality. The Russian Constitution states that multiple nationality is permitted, but the Citizenship Law stipulates that multiple nationality (foreign nationality) will not be recognised unless a treaty applies. Russian law defines a foreign citizen as "anyone who is not a citizen of the Russian Federation".

Recognition of Multiple Nationality
The Citizenship Law specifically provides that "[a] citizen of the Russian Federation who also possesses another citizenship shall be regarded by the Russian Federation as a citizen of the Russian Federation only, except for the cases specified in an international treaty . . . or federal law. The acquisition of another citizenship by a citizen of the Russian Federation shall not entail termination of the citizenship of the Russian Federation". The law also stipulates that Russian citizens are to be extended protection and assistance abroad, and makes no distinction on the basis of multiple nationality. Russians must enter and depart on Russian passports/travel documents.

Samoa[56]

Nationality category or status
Only one, and no distinction between nationality and citizenship.

Attribution/acquisition of nationality

Event	Law	Condition is renunciation/ loss of other nationality
Birth	In Samoa to a Samoan parent	NO
	In Samoa (or on Samoan ship or aircraft) and otherwise stateless and unable to obtain citizenship of another state, Minister may grant	
	Overseas to a Samoan citizen otherwise than by descent or who has resided in Samoa for at least three years (child is citizen by descent)	
Naturalisation	See registration	NO
Adoption		
Legitimation		
Marriage	Not automatic – facilitated registration (conditions)	
Resumption		
State service		
Parent acquires nationality		
Spouse acquires nationality		

[56] SAMOA: *The Constitution of the Independent State of Samoa* (as at 2 March 2001), *Citizenship Act 2004*, **UNHCR (internet);** *Government Response to Report of the Government Administration Committee on Parliamentary Petition 2002/44 of Dr George Paterson Barton Vaitoa Sa and 100,000 others – Presented to the House of Representatives Pursuant to Standing Order 251*, New Zealand Ministry of Foreign Affairs and Trade (internet), http://www.mfat.govt.nz/foreign/regions/pacific/generalinfo/policy/samoagovtresponse.html, consulted 4 May 2006; *Aliens and citizens*, Encyclopedia of New Zealand (internet), http://www.teara.govt.nz/NewZealanders/NewZealandPeoples/Citizenship/3/en, consulted 4 May 2006; "Select Committee on Foreign Affairs Submissions on the Citizenship (Western Samoa) Bill 1982", (Wellington: New Zealand Parliament, 1982).

Event	Law	**Condition is renunciation/ loss of other nationality**
Registration	By permanent residence (conditions)	
	By marriage to a Samoan (conditions)	
Special considerations		

Withdrawal/loss of nationality

Event	Law	**Consequence of event is loss of nationality**
Renunciation	Possible if multiple national, or about to become a national of a state that does not permit "dual citizenship" (only effective when other nationality confirmed)	YES
Attribution at birth conditional	No provision	
Naturalisation elsewhere		NO
Adoption by a foreigner		NO
Marriage to a foreigner		NO
Spouse acquires other nationality		NO
Parent acquires other nationality		NO
Resumption of previous nationality	*(For citizens by registration (permanent residence and marriage), possible deprivation upon two year continuous residence abroad, and if unlikely to reside in Samoa in the future)*	NO (*exception*)
Service to foreign state		
Other attribution of nationality		
(Punitive) deprivation	For disloyalty or disaffection toward Samoa (not possible for citizens by birth or descent)	YES

		Consequence of event is
Event	**Law**	**loss of nationality**

For citizens by registration (permanent residence and marriage), possible deprivation upon two year continuous residence abroad, and if unlikely to reside in Samoa in the future

If citizenship obtained by means of fraud, false representation, concealment of material fact or mistake

Special considerations

General attitude toward multiple nationality

The Citizenship Act of 1972 provided for loss of Samoan citizenship upon voluntary acquisition of foreign nationality, swearing an oath of allegiance, voluntary enlistment in foreign armed forces without approval, voluntarily exercising foreign rights of citizenship, or using a foreign passport to travel. The Oath of Allegiance also entailed renouncing rights, powers and privileges by virtue of foreign nationality. These provisions were deleted in the Citizenship Act 2004. The 2004 Act does not make loss of foreign citizenship a condition of naturalisation, and does not withdraw citizenship from Samoans who are naturalised elsewhere. It makes specific reference to dual nationality in the provision on renunciation, allowing renunciation for citizens who are multiple nationals or who seek to adopt the nationality of a state that does not permit dual nationality – the norm appears to indicate that should such state "allow" multiple nationality, renunciation would not be permitted.

*Singapore[57]

Nationality category or status
Only one. No technical differentiation between citizenship and nationality.

Attribution/acquisition of nationality

Event	Law	Condition is renunciation/ loss of other nationality
Birth	In Singapore to a Singaporian parent, unless father has diplomatic immunity, or was an enemy alien and birth in place under occupation, (child is citizen by birth)	NO *(see conditional attribution)*
	In Singpore, at government discretion (child is citizen by birth)	
	Outside Singapore to a Singaporian parent and birth is registered within one year, but not if parent is citizen by registration and and child acquires nationality of country where born, and not if parent is citizen by descent who did not lawfully reside in Singapore for aggregate 5 years before birth or 2 years during 5 years immediately preceding birth	
	Foundlings deemed citizens by birth	
Naturalisation	Upon fulfilment of requirements	NO *(see policy)*
Adoption	Upon legal adoption	NO *(but conditional attribution possible)*
Legitimation	(see birth)	

---

[57] SINGAPORE: *Singapore Constitution and schedules*, 16 September 1963 (as of November 1996), **UNHCR (internet)**; *Constitution of the Republic of Singapore* (as revised 2004), The Attorney-General's Chambers Singapore (internet), http://statutes.agc.gov.sg/non_version/cgi-bin/cgi_retrieve.pl?&actno=Reved-CONST&date=latest&method=part, consulted 17 April 2006; *Citizen Services*, Immigration and Checkpoints Authority (internet), http://app.ica.gov.sg/serv_citizen/citizenship/app_citizen.asp, consulted 17 April 2006; Campbell and Meek, eds., *International immigration and nationality law*; Cohen and Chiu, *People's China and international law. A documentary study*; M. Sornarajah, "Nationality and international law in Singapore", in *Nationality and international law in Asian perspective*, ed. Ko Swan Sik, 423–452 (Dordrecht: Martinus Nijhoff, 1990).

Event	Law	Condition is renunciation/ loss of other nationality
Marriage	Not automatic – facilitated registration	
Resumption	Possible for certain categories, by registration	NO (*see policy*)
State service	Facilitated naturalisation/registration possible – discretion	
Parent acquires nationality	Children of citizens – via registration (conditions)	
Spouse acquires nationality	Facilitated registration possible – conditions	
Registration	Fulfilment of requirements for various categories: citizens' wives, landed permanent residents, children of citizens, others (conditions)	NO (*see policy*)

Withdrawal/loss of nationality

Event	Law	Consequence of event is loss of nationality
Renunciation	Any citizen over 21, or married woman under 21 may renounce, if has or will acquire other nationality; govt may withhold if at war or if subject to military service, subject to obligations owed	YES
Attribution at birth conditional	Singaporians by descent are deprived of nationality at age 22 unless swear loyalty oath, and if government requires, divest themselves of foreign nationality	POSSIBLE (*government discretion*)
Naturalisation elsewhere	Deprivation discretionary if voluntary acquisition of foreign nationality as adult	POSSIBLE
Adoption by a foreigner		
Marriage to a foreigner	(*Deprivation discretionary if nationality thereby acquired*)	NO (*exception*)
Spouse acquires other nationality		NO
Parent acquires other nationality	(*If nationality obtained via parent, and parent loses nationality, may be*	NO (*exception*)

Event	Law	Consequence of event is loss of nationality
	deprived if citizen by registration – conditions)	
Resumption of previous nationality	Deprivation discretionary if voluntary acquisition of foreign nationality as adult	POSSIBLE
Service to foreign state	Citizens by naturalisation may be deprived of citizenship if such service without authorisation	POSSIBLE
Other attribution of nationality	Any voluntary acquisition as adult gives rise to discretionary deprivation	POSSIBLE
(Punitive) deprivation	For citizens by naturalisation or registration: if fraud or mistake in acquisition or certain sentence within 5 years but not if stateless, activities prejudicial to security, public order, against essential services or peace, criminal acts	POSSIBLE
		(government discretion)
	For naturalised citizens: disloyalty/ disaffection or assistance to enemy, certain foreign govt service without permission, 5 years' continuous residence abroad unless annual registration or in government service (conditions), but not if thereby stateless	
	Woman citizen by registration upon marriage, when marriage dissolved within two years	
Special considerations	Discretionary deprivation upon use of foreign citizenship rights	

General attitude toward multiple nationality

The Singaporian Constitution appears intolerant of multiple nationality, but in fact allows for it while leaving the government considerable leeway with regard to individual citizens' Singaporian nationality and their ties to foreign states. Singaporians by descent are deprived of nationality at age 22 unless they swear a loyalty oath, and if the government requires, unless they divest themselves of foreign nationality. The "Oath of renunciation, allegiance, and loyalty" upon naturalisation or registration requires only the non-exercise of rights, powers and privileges to which one may be entitled by foreign citizenship, not a divestiture of nationality as such. But the exercise of such rights may lead to loss of Singaporian nationality. The Constitution allows the Government to deprive citizens of nationality should they acquire foreign nationality or exercise foreign rights of citizenship, but does not mandate deprivation.

Recognition of Multiple Nationality

Singapore does not recognise any multiple nationality of its citizens, and may use evidence of such nationality, or in particular the use of related entitlements or rights, as grounds for deprivation of Singaporian nationality. Extension of international protection also appears to be discretionary, likely a reflection of the policy toward multiple nationality generally.

Slovenia[58]

Nationality category or status
Only one, and no distinction between nationality and citizenship.

Attribution/acquisition of nationality

Event	Law	Condition is renunciation/ loss of other nationality
Birth	To Slovenian parents	NO
	In Slovenia to a Slovenian	
	Overseas to a Slovenian parent and a stateless parent	
	Overseas to a Slovenian parent and child otherwise stateless	
	Overseas to a Slovenian parent and a foreign parent, if registered before age 18/36, or if permanently settles in Slovenia before age 18 with citizen parent – requires child's consent if over 14 (conditions)	
	In Slovenia to parents who are unknown, of unknown citizenship, or stateless – includes foundling (conditions)	
Naturalisation	Upon fulfillment of conditions	YES (*exceptions*)
	(*possible exceptions include: renunciation impossible; those who emigrated from Slovenia or of certain Slovenian ancestry; requirement may be waived upon application; marriage to Slovene; recognised refugee; offers certain benefits to state – conditions*)	

[58] SLOVENIA: *Citizenship of the Republic of Slovenia Act, officially revised text* (as 2002), Ministry of the Interior – Slovenia (internet), http://www.mnz.gov.si/index.php?id=4097&L=1, consulted 26 May 2006; *Citizenship of the Republic of Slovenia – procedure for the granting and cessation of citizenship*, Ministry of the Interior – Slovenia (internet), http://www.mnz.gov. si/index.php?id=4097&L=1, consulted 26 May 2006; *European Bulletin on Nationality – Slovenia*, 2 September 2004, Council of Europe (internet), http://www.coe.int/t/e/legal_affairs/ legal_cooperation/foreigners_and_citizens/nationality/documents/bulletin/Slovenia%20E%202004. pdf, consulted 25 May 2006.

Event	Law	Condition is renunciation/ loss of other nationality
Adoption	Leads to grant of nationality by birth if "full " adoption – requires child's consent if over 14 (conditions)	NO
	(If not "full" adoption child under 18 who lives with adoptive parents and they request, may acquire by naturalisation – conditions)	
Legitimation	See birth	
Marriage	Not automatic – facilitated naturalisation possible	
Resumption	Facilitated naturalisation possible	
State service	Facilitated naturalisation possible	
Parent acquires nationality	Children under 18 may be naturalised with parent, if resident; if over 14 must consent (conditions)	
Spouse acquires nationality		
Registration		
Special considerations		

Withdrawal/loss of nationality

Event	Law	Consequence of event is loss of nationality
Renunciation/ Discharge	Release possible at age 18 for multiple national (or about to acquire foreign nationality) who lives abroad and has no military/other obligations (may be rejected if not in state's interest – conditions)	YES
	Parent(s) may request release for child under 18 (conditions) Renunciation possible by adult multiple national born and resident abroad, before age 25 (special conditions for minor children)	
Attribution at birth conditional	No provision	

Event	Law	Consequence of event is loss of nationality
Naturalisation elsewhere		NO
Adoption by a foreigner	When "full" adoption of child under 18 by foreigner or Slovenian who has applied for release, upon parent's request – requires child's consent if over 14 (conditions)	POSSIBLE
Marriage to a foreigner		NO
Spouse acquires other nationality		NO
Parent acquires other nationality	If parents' naturalisation repealed, children under 18 naturalised with them may also lose	NO
Resumption of previous nationality	(Revocation of naturalisation for fraud, or no loss of foreign citizenship)	
Service to foreign state	See deprivation	
Other attribution of nationality		NO
(Punitive) deprivation	Slovenian multiple nationals who reside abroad may be deprived for membership in organizations aimed at overthrowing the state; member of foreign intelligence service and jeopardizes/harms interests; certain criminal offenses; refusal to fulfill obligations	POSSIBLE
	Revocation of naturalisation for fraud, or no loss of foreign citizenship without grant of exception to keep	
Special considerations	Parents of child who acquired nationality by birth in Slovenia (parents were unknown, of unknown citizenship, or stateless – includes foundling), may request nationality be withdrawn if child under 18, if discovered parents are foreign citizens	

General attitude toward multiple nationality

Slovenia tolerates multiple nationality to a large extent: it is not prevented when produced at birth, and naturalisation abroad does not result in loss of Slovenian nationality. Although loss of previous nationality is a condition of naturalisation in Slovenia, several exceptions apply, and the condition may be waived at the government's discretion.

Recognition of Multiple Nationality

The Citizenship Act provides that "[o]n the territory of the Republic of Slovenia, a citizen of the Republic of Slovenia, who also has the citizenship of a foreign country, shall be considered a citizen of the Republic of Slovenia, unless otherwise stipulated by international agreement".

*South Africa[59]

Nationality category or status
Only one, and no technical differentiation between nationality and citizenship.

Attribution/acquisition of nationality

Event	Law	Condition is renunciation/ loss of other nationality
Birth	In South Africa to citizen or permanent resident parents (if one parent is a diplomat or not a permanent resident, the other must be a citizen) – citizen by birth	NO
	Overseas to South African parent in govt/int'l service – citizen by birth	
	Foundling (citizen by birth)	
	Overseas to a South African parent and birth registered	
	Overseas to permanent resident who has a certificate of resumption (conditions) – citizen by descent	

---

[59] SOUTH AFRICA: *South Afriacan Citizenship Act*, 6 October 1995, South African Government Online (internet), http://www.gov.za/gazette/acts/1995/a88–95.htm, consulted 17 April 2006; *South African Citizenship Amendment Act*, 1997, South African Government Online (internet), http://www.info.gov.za/gazette/acts/1997/a69–97.pdf, consulted 17 April 2006; *South African Citizenship Amendment Act*, 2004, South African Government Online (internet), http://www.info.gov.za/gazette/acts/2004/a17–04.pdf, consulted 17 April 2006; *Statement on the South African Citizenship Amendment Act (2004)*, 11 November 2004, South African Government Online (internet), http://www.info.gov.za/speeches/2004/04111114451003.htm, consulted 17 April 2006; *If you are arrested or jailed overseas*, Department of Foreign Affairs of South Africa, (internet), http://www.dfa.gov.za/consular/arrest.htm, consulted 18 April 2006; Campbell and Meek, eds., *International immigration and nationality law*; G. Erasmus, "South African citizenship in a constitutional context", *Journal for Juridical Studies* (1998) vol. 23, no. 2, 1–19; C. R. D. Halisi, "Citizenship and populism in the new South Africa", *Africa Today* (1998) vol. 45, no. 3–4, 423–438; Raylene Keightley, "The child's right to a nationality and the acquisition of citizenship in South African law", *South African Journal on Human Rights* (1998) vol. 14, 411–429; Kiran Lalloo, "Citizenship and place: spatial definitions of oppression and agency in South Africa", *Africa Today* (1998) vol. 45, no. 3–4, 439–460; Wolf B. van Lengerich, "Das Staatsbürgerschaftsrecht Südafrikas unter besonderer Berücksichtigung der ehemaligen Homelands", *Verfassung und Recht in Übersee* (2001), no. 3, 361–386.

Event	Law	Condition is renunciation/ loss of other nationality
Naturalization	Upon fulfilment of requirements (must declare foreign nationality)	NO
Adoption	By citizen, and born in South Africa (citizen by birth)	NO
	By citizen, and born outside South Africa (citizen by descent)	
Legitimation	(see birth)	
Marriage	Not automatic	
Resumption	If loss of citizenship due to previous acquisition of foreign nationality or residence in an African country	NO (*must declare foreign nationality*)
State service	Possible – facilitated naturalisation – discretion	NO
Parent acquires nationality	No direct effect – facilitated naturalisation possible	
Spouse acquires nationality	Not automatic – facilitated naturalisation possible	
Registration		

Withdrawal/loss of nationality

Event	Law	Consequence of event is loss of nationality
Renunciation	If has or will acquire foreign nationality	YES
Attribution at birth conditional	No provision	
Naturalisation elsewhere	(*No loss if minor, and only for voluntary act. In principle loss, but may apply in advance to retain citizenship*)	YES (*exception*)
Adoption by a foreigner		
Marriage to a foreigner		NO
Spouse acquires other nationality		NO

Event	Law	Consequence of event is loss of nationality
Parent acquires other nationality	Loss of nationality by parent extended to children, if other parent is not South African	YES (*exception*)
	Any deprivation may be extended to minors, if born abroad	
Resumption of previous nationality	In principle loss, but may apply in advance to retain citizenship	YES (*exception*)
Service to foreign state	(see deprivation)	POSSIBLE
Other attribution of nationality	If voluntary acquisition, must apply in advance to retain citizenship	
(Punitive) deprivation	If naturalisation obtained by fraud	POSSIBLE
	Of multiple national's citizenship for certain sentence, if in public interest	

General attitude toward multiple nationality

South Africa accepts multiple nationality for its citizens, although its laws provide the government with the means to deprive multiple nationals of their South African citizenship in cases where the individual is seen to act against the public interest. The Citizenship Act provides that any loss of citizenship does not result in the discharge of duties owed. It was amended in 1997 to allow citizens to use foreign passports if approval was sought and received, and to provide for resumption of citizenship in certain cases of prior deprivation. It was further amended in 2004 such that permission is no longer required to use foreign passports overseas, and South Africans cannot be deprived of their citizenship for using the citizenship of a foreign country. It is, however, an offence for adult South Africans to enter or depart South Africa on a foreign passport. Likewise, it is an offence to use foreign nationality or citizenship to gain advantage or avoid a responsibility or duty in South Africa.

Recognition of Multiple Nationality

The Department of Foreign Affairs warns South Africans that "[i]f you are a dual national in the country of your other nationality the assistance which South African consular representatives can give you may be limited. That is, even if you are a South African citizen but you also possess the nationality of the country in which you have been detained or arrested. It is possible, however, that the local authorities will allow the consular representative to assist you. You should ask for access to your consular representative in such circumstances and press the prison, court or police authorities for such access to the greatest extent". As of 2004, South African citizens may use foreign passports to travel abroad, but must enter and depart South Africa on South African passports/travel documents.

*Spain[60]

Nationality category or status

One only, with two forms of acquisition, originally at, or derivatively after, birth. No distinction is made between nationality and citizenship.

---

[60] SPAIN: *Ley 36/2002, de 8 de octubre, de modificación del Código Civil en materia de nacionalidad*, Ministerio de Asuntos Exteriores y de Cooperación de España (internet), http://www.mae.es/NR/rdonlyres/E49AA180–B25E-4973–AD5B-CAC5FBB1E38A/184/leyna cionalidadpdf1.pdf, consulted 18 April 2006; "Derechos y libertades de los extranjeros en España (Ley Orgánica 4/2000, reformada por la Ley Orgánica 8/2000)", Biblioteca de Legislación. Madrid: Civitas, 2001; "Código civil, actualizada a septiembre 2000". Biblioteca de Legislación. Madrid: Civitas, 2000; Aurelia Álvarez Rodríguez, *Guía de la nacionalidad española* (Madrid: Ministerio de Trabajo y Asuntos Sociales, 1996); Aurelia Álvarez Rodríguez, *Nacionalidad y emigración* (Madrid: La Ley, 1990); Juan Aznar Sánchez, *La doble nacionalidad* (Madrid: Editorial Montecorvo, 1977); Campbell and Meek, eds., *International immigration and nationality law*; Elena Cano Bazaga, *Adopción internacional y nacionalidad española* (Madrid: Mergablum, 2001); de Groot, "Loss of nationality: a critical inventory"; Castor M. Díaz Barrado, "La protección de Españoles en el extranjero. Práctica constitucional", in *Cursos de derecho internacional de Vitoria-Gasteiz*, ed. Departamento de Estudios Internacionales y Ciencia Política y la Facultad de Derecho Universidad del País Vasco, 286–291 (Bilbao: Servicio Editorial Universidad del País Vasco, 1993); Echezarreta Ferrer, ed., *Legislación sobre nacionalidad*; José María Espinar Vicente, *La nacionalidad y la extranjería en el sistema jurídico español* (Madrid: Editorial Civitas, 1994); Carlos Esplugues Mota, Guillermo Palao Moreno, and Manuel de Lorenzo Segrelles, *Nacionalidad y extranjería* (València: Tirant Lo Blanch, 2001); José Carlos Fernández Rozas, *Derecho español de la nacionalidad* (Madrid: Editorial Technos, 1987); Jacinto Gil Rodríguez, *La nacionalidad española y los cambios legislativos – significado y alcance de las disposiciones transitorias de la Ley 18/1990, de 17 de diciembre* (Madrid: Editorial Colex, 1993); Francisco Javier Moreno Fuentes, "Migration and Spanish nationality law", in *Towards a European nationality. Citizenship, immigration and nationality law in the EU*, ed. Randall Hansen and Patrick Weil, 118–142 (Houndmills: Palgrave, 2001); Susana Salvador Gutiérrez, *Manual práctico sobre nacionalidad* (Granada: Editorial Comares, 1996); Jaume Saura Estapà, *Nacionalidad y nuevas fronteras en europa* (Madrid: Marcial Pons, 1998); Juan Soroeta Liceras, "La problemática de la nacionalidad de los habitantes de los territorios dependientes y el caso del Sahara Occidental", *Anuario de Derecho Internacional* (1999) vol. 15, 645–676; *Travel Advice Spain*, 9 March 2006, Australian Department of Foreign Affairs and Trade (internet), http://www.smartraveller.gov.au/zw-cgi/view/Advice/Spain, consulted 18 April 2006; *Españoles en el extranjero*, Ministerio de Asuntos Exteriores y de Cooperación (internet), http://www.mae.es/es/MenuPpal/Consulares/Servicios+Consulares/Españoles+en+el+extranjero/, consulted 18 April 2006; *Nacionalidad*, 13 June 2005, Ministerio de Asuntos Exteriores y de Cooperación (internet), http://www.mae.es/es/MenuPpal/Consulares/Servicios+Consulares/A+Extranjeros/Nacionalidad/, consulted 18 April 2006.

Attribution/acquisition of nationality

Event	Law	Condition is renunciation/ loss of other nationality
Birth	To a Spanish parent	NO
	In Spain to a parent also born in Spain (except diplomats)	*(but see conditional attribution)*
	In Spain if otherwise stateless	
	Foundling presumed to be of Spanish descent	
Naturalisation	Upon fulfilment of requirements	YES *(but certain countries excepted, and not effective renunciation)*
Adoption	By at least one Spanish parent as a minor (original acqisition)	NO
	If as an adult, see option	
Legitimation	(see birth) – if filiation established after majority, see option	
Marriage	Not automatic – option after one year of marriage	
Resumption	Possible for all cases of loss (conditions – some cases attract government discretion)	NO
State service		
Parent acquires nationality	Not automatic – facilitated naturalisation possible	
Spouse acquires nationality	Not automatic – facilitated naturalisation possible	
Option	Have parent who was Spanish (by origin) and who was born in Spain; Person is/was subject to *patria potestad* of a Spaniard; Adult adoption; Legitimation/birth in Spain determined when adult (conditions)	YES *(certain countries excepted, and ineffective renunciation requirement)*
Residence	And – Birth in Spain (conditions); those who had option of nationality but did not exercise it; person subject to tutelage/guardianship of Spaniard or Spanish institution (conditions);	

Event	Law	**Condition is renunciation/ loss of other nationality**
	marriage (conditions); widow/widower (conditions); birth abroad to Spanish parent or grandparent (nationality of origin)	

Withdrawal/loss of nationality

Event	Law	**Consequence of event is loss of nationality**
Renunciation	Possible if adult who is multiple national and resides permanently abroad, but not if Spain at war	YES
Conditional Attribution	If reside permanently abroad and use exclusively other nationality attributed during minority, lose Spanish nationality three years from majority, except in wartime and not in relation to certain Ibero-American and other countries, and not if make declaration of wish to conserve nationality, and not if Spain at war	POSSIBLE (*exceptions noted*)
	Those born and permanently residing abroad who receive Spanish nationality through a parent who was also born abroad, who possess the nationality of their country of residence, lose Spanish nationality three years from majority if they do not declare their desire to conserve it, but not if Spain at war	
Naturalisation elsewhere	Provokes loss three years after act if permanently residing abroad, but not if Spain at war, or if in a specified country, and not if make declaration of wish to conserve nationality	POSSIBLE (*exceptions noted*)
Adoption by a foreigner		NO
Marriage to a foreigner		NO
Spouse acquires other nationality		NO

Event Law		Consequence of event is loss of nationality
Parent acquires other nationality		NO
Resumption of previous nationality	If voluntary acquisition	YES (*with exceptions*)
Service to foreign state	Possible deprivation for naturalised citizens (including by option or residence), for military service or exercise of political office where such service is expressly forbidden by the Spanish Government	POSSIBLE
Other attribution of nationality	Any voluntary acquisition of foreign nationality provokes loss three years after act if residing abroad, but not if Spain at war, in specified countries, or if make declaration of wish to conserve	POSSIBLE
(Punitive) deprivation	Revocation of nationality by naturalisation, option or residence for (1) fraud in acquisition, but not extended to innocent third-party derivatives, (2) if during three year period use exclusively the nationality renounced when acquiring Spanish nationality	YES
Special considerations	Possible loss of nationality if adult resides abroad and only uses other nationality which was attributed before majority (conditions) If foundling discovered not of Spanish descent, even as adult	YES

General attitude toward multiple nationality

Spain tolerates the multiple nationality of its citizens. Spain's attitude toward multiple nationality is ostensibly built around a series of conventions with various countries, which provide for dual nationality, involving at any given time an active and a passive nationality for questions of application of law. Conventions exist with Chile, Peru, Paraguay, Nicaragua, Guatemala, Bolivia, Ecuador, Costa Rica, Honduras, the Dominican Republic, Argentina, Colombia, and there has been an exchange of notes with Venezuela providing for reciprocal rights of nationality between the two countries. In relation to conditions and consequences of acquisition and loss of nationality generally, Spain's *Código Civil* exempts all Latin American countries, as well as Portugal, the Philippines, Andorra and Equatorial Guinea from the relevant provisions. Naturalisation abroad provokes loss of nationality with the exception of the above-listed countries, however only if the subject resides permanently overseas, and loss can be avoided by making a declaration of desire to conserve Spanish nationality. Likewise, renunciation of foreign nationality is a condition of naturalisation, but such renunciation does not have to be effective. No difference is apparent in terms of the treatment of multiple nationals.

Recognition of Multiple Nationality

Spain does not recognise foreign nationality of its nationals, and various countries warn their nationals who are also Spanish nationals that they may be unable to provide them with consular protection in Spain. Spanish practice is to avoid consular protection of multiple nationals in another country of nationality if this is considered to be their "effective" nationality, although such protection is in no way excluded, depending on the gravity of the circumstances. Thus protection was attempted on behalf of many incarcerated persons in various South American countries in the mid-twentieth century, and in many cases was extended to those who seemed possibly to be Spaniards, without further proof of nationality and notwithstanding any multiple nationality. In certain situations of humanitarian distress, even a circumstantial tie to Spain was deemed sufficient to attempt measures in favour of certain persons.

Sweden[61]

Nationality category or status
Only one, and no distinction between nationality and citizenship.

Attribution/acquisition of nationality

Event	Law	Condition is renunciation/ loss of other nationality
Birth	To a Swedish mother	NO
	To Swedish father married to child's mother (even if father deceased)	
	To a Swedish father in Sweden (even if father deceased)	
	Foundling	
	(*See also Registration/Notification and Legitimation*)	
	If child born abroad, never domiciled in Sweden, never been in Sweden in circumstances indicating link to Sweden, loses nationality at age 22, unless prior application to retain, or unless thereby stateless – not applicable to Nordic countries	
Naturalisation	Upon fulfillment of conditions	NO
Adoption	Child under 12 adopted by Swedish citizen if child is from Nordic country or adopted by certain decision (conditions)	NO
Legitimation	Upon marriage of Swedish man to foreign woman, their child who is an unmarried minor born before the marriage	NO
Marriage	Not automatic – facilitated naturalisation	NO

---

[61] SWEDEN: *The Swedish Citizenship Act* (entry into force: 1 July 2001) **UNHCR (internet)**, *Dual citizenship*, Embassy of Sweden Canberra (internet), http://www.swedenabroad.com/pages/general____27944.asp, consulted 23 April 2006; *Swedish citizenship*, Swedish Migration Board – Migrationsverket (internet), http://www.migrationsverket.se/english/emedborg/emedborg.html, consulted 23 April 2006.

Event	Law	Condition is renunciation/ loss of other nationality
Resumption	Possible for various categories (conditions)	NO
	By notification upon taking up residence	
	in Sweden for former citizen who became citizen of Nordic country (conditions)	
State service		
Parent acquires nationality	If alien who has sole custody or joint custody with a Swedish citizen becomes citizen by notification, or parents who share custody of child become citizens by notification at same time, unmarried domiciled children under 18 acquire (conditions)	NO
	If parent naturalised, possible for children to acquire at same time	
	If former citizen who became citizen of Nordic country resumes citizenship by notification, extended to children (conditions)	
Spouse acquires nationality	No direct effect	
Registration (Notification)	Child born abroad to father who held Swedish citizenship since birth of the child, upon notification by the father before age 18. If child over 12 and foreign national must give consent, unless impeded (conditions)	NO
	Birth in Sweden and stateless since birth, upon notification by guardian before age 5, if child permanent resident and domiciled in Sweden	
	Upon notification by guardian for permanent resident child under 18 domiciled in Sweden for 5 years (3 years if stateless). If child is over 12 and a foreign national must give consent, unless impeded (conditions)	
	Alien at least 18 but not yet 20, if permanent resident and domiciled since age 13, or age 15 if stateless	

Event	Law	Condition is renunciation/ loss of other nationality
	Possible for citizens of Nordic countries (conditions)	
Special considerations		

Withdrawal/loss of nationality

Event	Law	Consequence of event is loss of nationality
Renunciation	If is or will become foreign citizen, and not domiciled in Sweden. If domiciled in Sweden possible denial if special grounds (conditions)	YES
Attribution at birth conditional	If child born abroad, never domiciled in Sweden, never been in Sweden in circumstances indicating link to Sweden, loses nationality at 22, unless prior application to retain, or unless thereby stateless – not applicable to Nordic countries (conditions)	POSSIBLE
Naturalisation elsewhere		NO
Adoption by a foreigner		NO
Marriage to a foreigner		NO
Spouse acquires other nationality		NO
Parent acquires other nationality	(see special considerations)	NO
Resumption of previous nationality		NO
Service to foreign state		
Other attribution of nationality		NO
(Punitive) deprivation		
Special considerations	Swede born abroad who loses nationality at age 22 (see conditional	YES

		Consequence of event is
Event	**Law**	**loss of nationality**

attribution), loss extended to his/her
children if acquired nationality through
him/her, unless other parent Swedish
and nationality also derived from that
parent, and unless stateless

General attitude toward multiple nationality

Sweden amended its nationality legislation in 2001 to permit multiple nationality for its citizens, abandoning its former practice of avoiding multiple nationality. Swedes who are naturalised abroad do not lose their Swedish nationality, and loss of foreign citizenship is no longer a condition of naturalisation in Sweden. The government cites promotion of integration and full civic participation as well as what it calls practical advantages as having led to the change of policy, such as the ability of migrants to work in, visit, or return to their countries of origin, and preservation of ties to Swedish emigrants.

Recognition of Multiple Nationality

The Swedish government warns its citizens that "only a person with exclusively Swedish citizenship can count on full Swedish legal protection abroad. If you are a citizen of an additional country besides Sweden, the other country regards you as a citizen only of that country. Thus Sweden has little chance of helping a person who gets into trouble in that particular country".

*Switzerland[62]

Nationality category or status
One only, and no technical distinction between nationality and citizenship. The latter is conceived of at federal, cantonal and municipal levels.

Attribution/acquisition of nationality

Event	Law	Condition is renunciation/ loss of other nationality
Birth	To a Swiss parent, if couple is married	NO
	To Swiss mother, if unmarried	
	(See legitimation regarding birth to Swiss father)	
	Foundling	

---

[62] SWITZERLAND: *Bundesgesetz über Erwerb und Verlust des Schweizer Bürgerrechts vom 29. September 1952*, as of 6 December 2005, (internet), www.admin.ch/ch/d/sr/1/141.0.de.pdf, consulted 18 April 2006; Margrith Bigler-Eggenberger, "Bürgerrechtsverlust durch Heirat: Ein dunkler Fleck in der jüngeren Schweizer Rechtsgeschichte", *Recht* (1999) vol. 2, 33–42; Campbell and Meek, eds., *International immigration and nationality law*; Pierre Corboz, "Nationalité: Suisse", in *Juris-Classeur Nationalité*, ed. Michel J. Verwilghen and Charles L. Closset, *Collection des Juris-Classeurs* (Paris: Éditions du Juris-Classeur, 1997); de Groot, "Loss of nationality: a critical inventory"; Rainer Hofmann, "Einbürgerungspraxis und -probleme ausgewählter Staaten und die jeweilige Anwendung des Übereinkommens über die Verringerung der Mehrstaatigkeit", paper presented at the conference: Doppelte Staatsbürgerschaft – ein europäischer Normalfall?, Berlin, 1989; Jakob Maag, "Der konsularische und diplomatische Schutz des Auslandschweizers", dissertation presented at the Universität Zürich, 1953; Günter Renner, "Einheitliche Staatsangehörigkeit in der Familie. Nationaler Befund – internationaler Vergleich", paper presented at the conference: Hohenheimer Tage zum Ausländerrecht 1999 und 5. Migrationspolitisches Forum, Hohenheim, 1998; Roland Schärer, "La nouvelle Convention européenne sur la nationalité et le droit suisse", paper presented at the conference: Mélanges édités à l'occasion de la 50ème Assemblée générale de la Commission Internationale de l'État Civil, Neuchâtel, 1997; F. Sturm and G. Sturm, "Erwerb des Schweizer Buergerrechts durch Kinder einer Schweizer Mutter", *Das Standesmt* (1986) vol. 39, no. 2, 29–34; "Avoid problems on returning home", *Swiss Review* (2003) no. 3 June, 8; "Boy, 11, on molest charge", The Australian, 23 October 1999, 19; "Exercising political rights made easier", Swiss Review, (2002) no. 5 October, 12; "Emergency support", Swiss Review (2001) no. 3 July, 9; "Requirements for acquiring a Swiss passport", Swiss Review (2001) no. 1 February, 9; *Diplomatic Protection*, Federal Department of Foreign Affairs (DFA) (internet), http://www.eda.admin.ch/sub_dipl/e/home/thema/intlaw/diplo.html, consulted 19 April 2006; *Consular Protection*, Federal Department of Foreign Affairs (DFA) (internet), http://www.eda.admin.ch/sub_dipl/e/home/thema/intlaw/consu.html, consulted 19 April 2006.

Event	Law	Condition is renunciation/ loss of other nationality
	If child born abroad and a multiple national, must be registered with Swiss authorities before age 22 or loses nationality – thereafter may apply for resumption (conditions)	
Naturalisation	Upon fulfilment of requirements	NO
Adoption	Of minor child – automatic acquisition	NO
Legitimation	Minor foreign child receives Swiss nationality as if attributed at birth upon legitimation by Swiss father	NO
Marriage	Not automatic – facilitated naturalisation	
Resumption	Possible (conditions) for various persons	NO
State service	Possible	NO
Parent acquires nationality	Legitimised child's children automatically acquire	NO
	Children usually included in parent's naturalisation	
Spouse acquires nationality	Not automatic – facilitated naturalisation	
Registration	Facilitated naturalisation for various categories (conditions)	NO

Withdrawal/loss of nationality

Event	Law	Consequence of event is loss of nationality
Renunciation	Possible if non-resident multiple national or not thereby stateless	YES
Attribution at birth conditional	If child born abroad and a multiple national, must be registered with Swiss authorities before age 22 or loses nationality – thereafter may apply for resumption (conditions)	POSSIBLE
Naturalisation elsewhere		NO
Adoption by a foreigner	If minor has or thereby acquires foreign nationality (unless maintains or establishes via adoption a legal	POSSIBLE

		Consequence of event is
Event	**Law**	**loss of nationality**
	relationship to a Swiss parent) he or she loses Swiss nationality – if adoption revoked, no loss	
Marriage to a foreigner		NO
Spouse acquires other nationality		NO
Parent acquires other nationality	(*But if Swiss nationality via parent and parent expressly renounces Swiss nationality during the child's minority, child also loses if non-resident and multiple national or not thereby stateless. If child is over 16, must agree to any renunciation*)	NO (*exception*)
Resumption of previous nationality		NO
Service to foreign state	(see punitive deprivation)	NO
Other attribution of nationality		NO
(Punitive) deprivation	Revocation of naturalisation for fraud within five years of acquisition	POSSIBLE
	Acts against national interest/ reputation, if multiple national	
Special considerations	Foundling loses nationality if descent established during minority, and not thereby stateless	YES
	If parent-child relationship to Swiss parent from whom child derived nationality is revoked, child loses Swiss nationality if not stateless	
	If Swiss multiple national child born abroad does not register with Swiss authorities before age 22, his/her children also lose nationality	

General attitude toward multiple nationality

Switzerland has long accepted multiple nationality for its citizens, and in 1992 eliminated the condition that applicants for naturalisation divest themselves of foreign nationality. There is no distinction made among citizens in terms of rights on the basis of multiple nationality, although certain entitlements, such as financial assistance abroad, may not be provided to multiple nationals in their other country of nationality. Entitlements in Switzerland accrue to all citizens. All citizens are liable for conscription until age 25, but those permanently resident abroad are exempt.

Recognition of Multiple Nationality

Express recognition of multiple nationality is possible in Switzerland in various ways. Swiss citizens may enter and depart the country using foreign passports. Although Swiss officials warn citizens that they may not be able to be protected in their other countries of nationality, such protection is not excluded if allowed by the other country. The Swiss Foreign Ministry states that "when the life or health of a dual national Swiss is in danger (notably in cases of torture, degrading treatment or detention in inhuman conditions), Swiss representatives will be expected to do everything in their power to ensure their protection. Swiss representatives are also expected to intervene in cases where the course of justice is being unduly delayed or where justice is being denied".

*Syria[63]

Nationality category or status
Only one, and no technical distinction between nationality and citizenship.

Attribution/acquisition of nationality

Event	Law	Condition is renunciation/ loss of other nationality
Birth	To a Syrian father	NO
	In Syria to a Syrian mother and unknown father	
	In Syria to unknown parents or of unknown nationality	
	Foundling deemed born in Syria	
	In Syria if otherwise stateless	
Naturalisation	Upon fulfillment of requirements	NO
Adoption		
Legitimation	(see birth)	
Marriage	Of alien woman to Syrian man	NO
Resumption	By woman who lost upon marriage to alien, at his death	NO
	For persons deprived of nationality	

---

[63] SYRIA: *The Nationality Act*, November 1969 (last amended 1972), *Decision No. 576 of 5 October 1970* (Expatriate Citizen Certificate), *Circular 2 of 19 January 1982 – Legal Provisions applicable to the entry and residence of Syrian and non-Syrians and no Syrian Arabs and Aliens*, January 1982, **UNHCR (internet)**; *Syria – Constitution*, 13 March 1973 (internet), http://www.oefre.unibe.ch/law/icl/sy00000_.html, consulted 18 April 2006; Alghasi, "Die Staatsangehörigkeit in den Bundesstaaten, im Staatenbund und in der Staatengemeinschaft, angeführt als Beispiel: Die Staatsangehörigkeit in den arabischen Staaten"; Uri Davis, *Citizenship and the State – a comparative study of citizenship legislation in Israel, Jordan, Palestine, Syria and Lebanon* (Reading (UK): Garnet Publishers, 1997); Oppermann and Yousry, eds., *Das Staatsangehörigkeitsrecht der Arabischen Staaten*. United States Office of Personnel Management Investigations Service, "Citizenship laws of the world", March 2001 (internet); *Travel Advice – Syria*, 7 February 2006, Department of Foreign Affairs and Trade Australia (internet), http://www.smartraveller.gov.au/zw-cgi/view/Advice/Syria, consulted 18 April 2006; *Consular Information Sheet – Syria*, 3 April 2006, United States Department of State (internet), http://travel.state.gov/travel/cis_pa_tw/cis/cis_1035.html, consulted 18 April 2006.

Event	Law	Condition is renunciation/ loss of other nationality
State service		
Parent acquires nationality	By children of woman who lost nationality upon marriage to alien, at father's death (conditions)	NO
	Children acquire with father	
Spouse acquires nationality	Wife acquires with husband, if agrees, or is of Syrian origin	NO
Registration		

Withdrawal/loss of nationality

Event	Law	Consequence of event is loss of nationality
Renunciation	Reportedly very difficult; not permitted for those of military age	YES
Attribution at birth conditional	No provision	
Naturalisation elsewhere	Recognised if permission obtained; if not, deprivation possible, but foreign nationality usually not recognized	NO
Adoption by a foreigner		
Marriage to a foreigner	If Syrian woman marries alien and voluntary acquisition of his nationality	YES (*condition*)
Spouse acquires other nationality	(*Wife loses automatically upon husband's naturalisation elsewhere, if thereby acquires nationality, unless declares desire to retain Syrian nationality*)	YES (*exception*)
Parent acquires other nationality	(*Children lose automatically upon father's acquisition of foreign nationality, if they thereby acquire nationality, but may request reinstatement upon majority (conditions)*)	YES (*exception*)
Resumption of previous nationality	By woman who acquired Syrian nationality upon marriage, upon divorce – (conditions)	YES
Service to foreign state	Unauthorised voluntary foreign military service may lead to deprivation	POSSIBLE

Event	Law	**Consequence of event is loss of nationality**
Other attribution of nationality	Must seek permission for voluntary acquisition	
(Punitive) deprivation	For acquisition of nationality by fraud	
	Foreign government service and failure to abandon when so instructed; any assistance to country at war with Syria; illegal departure for country at war with Syria	
	For certain naturalised persons: if in state security interests	
	Certain refusal to return when instructed, upon residence abroad	POSSIBLE
Special considerations	Deprivation if woman acquired nationality upon marriage, upon divorce and subsequent marriage to alien	YES

General attitude toward multiple nationality
Syria accepts multiple nationality for its citizens, but states that multiple nationals are always considered Syrians first. Syrian multiple nationals resident abroad may be permitted to stay in the country for up to three months without becoming subject to military service, but various countries advise their citizens to seek related guarantees from Syrian authorities before initiating travel.

Recognition of Multiple Nationality
Syria does not recognise multiple nationality. Some countries warn their nationals who are also Syrian nationals that they may not be able to benefit from consular protection in Syria, due to the opposition from Syrian authorities. Minors always require their father's permission to depart the country, and women may likewise be subject to control by their families. Husbands may prevent their wives from departing Syria, notwithstanding any foreign or multiple nationality they may possess.

*Taiwan[64]

Nationality category or status

Technically only one category of nationality, although passports may be issued to certain categories of persons defined as "overseas Chinese" who have permanent residence rights in foreign countries, and are not necessarily entitled to enter and reside in Taiwan. There is no technical distinction between nationality and citizenship.

Attribution/acquisition of nationality

Event	Law	Condition is renunciation/ loss of other nationality
Birth	To a Taiwanese parent	NO
	Foundling	
Naturalisation	Upon fulfillment of requirements	YES (*proof required, but certain exceptions*)
Adoption	Automatic if legal adoption	NO
Legitimation	Recognitition of minor children by father, if unmarried	NO
Marriage	Not automatic – by naturalisation	YES
Resumption	By woman who lost upon marriage to alien if widowed or divorced	DEPENDS

---

[64] TAIWAN: As stated in chapter one, the inclusion of Taiwan or the "Republic of China" as its authorities call the territory does not imply an opinion as to its legal nature or condition, or the validity of the effects of Taiwan's practice on the survey herein in relation to international law. The territory's inclusion here is for purposes of comparison and historical and practical interest. See: *Information on Taiwanese passports*, 1 August 2001, *Taiwan: Nationality Laws (2000 – February 2004)*, February 2004 **UNHCR (internet)**; *Emergency services to ROC citizens abroad*, Bureau of Consular Affairs, Ministry of Foreign Affairs (internet), http://www.boca.gov.tw/ct.asp?xItem=1640&CtNode=163&mp=2, consulted 19 April 2006; *Passport Act*, Bureau of Consular Affairs, Ministry of Foreign Affairs (internet), http://www.boca.gov.tw/ct.asp?xItem=1293&CtNode=96&mp=2, consulted 19 April 2006; *Compulsory military service in Taiwan*, American Institute in Taiwan (internet), http://www.ait.org.tw/en/uscitizens/military.asp, consulted 19 April 2006; Campbell and Meek, eds., *International immigration and nationality law*; Hungdah Chiu, "Nationality and international law in Chinese perspective—with special reference to the period before 1950 and the practice of the administration in Taipei", in *Nationality and international law in Asian perspective*, ed. Ko Swan Sik, 27–64 (Dordrecht: Martinus Nijhoff Publishers, 1990); *Qiu* Bincun, *Hua qiao shuang chong guoji zhi zhi ben zhenli* (Taibei: Xin sheng chu ban she, 1957). See generally (internet), http://www.gio.gov.tw, consulted 19 April 2006.

Event	Law	Condition is renunciation/ loss of other nationality
	Possible if lost otherwise, but not by naturalised citizen (conditions)	
State service	Naturalization possible	YES (*but may be waived*)
Parent acquires nationality	Naturalization may be extended to children (conditions)	YES
Spouse acquires nationality	Naturalization may be extended to spouse (conditions)	
Registration		

Withdrawal/loss of nationality

Event	Law	Consequence of event is loss of nationality
Renunciation	Upon application to government if over 20, and not possible if of military age (up to age 40), in military or civilian office or service	YES
Attribution at birth conditional	No provision	
Naturalisation elsewhere	(*if not considered national by birth*)	NO (*exception*)
Adoption by a foreigner	Legitimation by foreign parent	YES
Marriage to a foreigner		NO
Spouse acquires other nationality		NO
Parent acquires other nationality		NO
Resumption of previous nationality		POSSIBLE
Service to foreign state		POSSIBLE
Other attribution of nationality		NO
(Punitive) deprivation	Possible for various acts. Revocation of naturalisation for fraud	POSSIBLE
Special considerations		

General attitude toward multiple nationality

Multiple nationality is generally accepted, except for persons applying for naturalisation in Taiwan, who are required to divest themselves of foreign nationality, if possible. Naturalisation abroad does not provoke loss of nationality for citizens by birth. The law does not distinguish between citizens on the basis of multiple nationality, although naturalised citizens may not be elected to certain public office until ten years after their naturalisation.

Recognition of Multiple Nationality

Notwithstanding possession of another nationality, a national must in principle use a Taiwanese passport to enter and depart. Use of a foreign passport with a valid entry visa is, however, not an offence and foreign consular protection may be allowed in certain cases. Such use will not allow the bearer of a foreign passport to avoid military obligations owed as a national, however. Taiwan states that it may exercise protection over citizens, notwithstanding any multiple nationality, although this may not be possible in practice. "Emergency services are available to any ROC citizen staying in a foreign country, whose personal life and safety is threatened due to an accident or an incident that damaged personal rights and interests. Such individuals may contact the nearest ROC Embassy, Consulate and Representative Office".

*Thailand[65]

Nationality category or status
Only one, and no technical distinction between nationality and citizenship.

Attribution/acquisition of nationality

Event	Law	Condition is renunciation/ loss of other nationality
Birth	To a Thai parent	NO
	In Thailand, unless to alien parents not permanent/legal residents, or to alien parents with diplomatic immunity or employed by such person	*(but if born to alien father and has his nationality also, possibly conditional)*
Naturalisation	Upon fulfilment of requirements (*except if makes use of foreign nationality may be deprived, of Thai*)	NO (*exception*)
Adoption		
Legitimation	(upon recognition by father)	NO
Marriage	By alien woman married to Thai husband, at government's discretion	NO
Resumption	For woman who renounced upon marrige to alien if marrige disolved	NO
	Minor who lost nationality with his parents	
	Facilitated naturalisation possible for certain others (conditions)	
State service	Facilitated naturalisation possible	NO
Parent acquires nationality	Minor children domiciled in Thailand – facilitated naturalisation possible (but possible conditional attribution)	NO (*conditional attribution*)

---

[65] THAILAND: *Constitution of the Kingdom of Thailand*, 11 October BE 2540 (AD 1997); *Nationality Act (no. 3)*, 9 April BE 2535 (AD 1992); *Nationality Act (no. 2)*, 26 February BE 2535 (AD 1992); *Nationality Act*, 21 July BE 2508 (AD 1965) **UNHCR (internet)**; *Consular Information*, The Royal Thai Embassy Washington, DC (internet), http://www.thaiembdc.org/con-sular/con_info/con_inf.htm, consulted 19 April 2006; Sompong Sucharitkul, "Thai nationality in international perspective", in *Nationality and international law in Asian perspective*, ed. Ko Swan Sik, 453–491 (Dordrecht: Martinus Nijhoff Publishers, 1990); "Natural rights. Citizenship by birth", *Far Eastern Economic Review*, 20 August 1998, 62.

Event	Law	Condition is renunciation/ loss of other nationality
	Other facilitated naturalisation for adult children	
Spouse acquires nationality	Facilitated naturalisation possible	NO
Registration nationality	Birth in Thailand to alien parents, at government's discretion	

Withdrawal/loss of nationality

Event	Law	Consequence of event is loss of nationality
Renunciation	Possible by woman marrying an alien and will acquire his nationality	YES
	Possible by multiple national, or if naturalised citizen	
Attribution at birth conditional	If has alien father's nationality, or naturalised with parent, must renounce Thai nationality by age 21 if desires to retain other nationality	POSSIBLE
Naturalisation elsewhere		YES
Adoption by a foreigner		NO
Marriage to a foreigner		NO
Spouse acquires other nationality		NO
Parent acquires other nationality	(revocation of naturalised parent's nationality may be extended to minor children) – loss may be extended to children, who may resume as adults	YES
Resumption of previous nationality	(possible deprivation if use of former nationality)	POSSIBLE
Service to foreign state	(possible deprivation for certain nationals)	POSSIBLE
Other attribution of nationality		NO
(Punitive) deprivation	Woman who acquired nationality by	POSSIBLE

| | | **Consequence of event is** |
| **Event** | **Law** | **loss of nationality** |

marriage to Thai, for fraud, acts against
state security or public good/morals,
insults to the nation

Birth in Thailand to alien father:
revocation of nationality possible for:
certain residence as adult in father's
country of origin, use or interest in his
father's or other foreign nationality; acts
against state interests, public order,
good morals; insults to the nation

Child born in Thailand granted
nationality at government discretion,
government may deprive for security
reasons

Naturalised citizens: fraud, use of
former (other) nationality, certain
residence abroad without Thai domicile,
acts against state security or interests,
public order, good morals; retention of
nationality of country at war with
Thailand

Special considerations

General attitude toward multiple nationality
Thailand does not recognise multiple nationality for its citizens, but does not prevent its production at birth. Although the law stipulates that Thai nationality must be renounced by age 21
in order to retain foreign nationality, there do not appear to be consequences for non-renunci-
ation or a provision for automatic deprivation if this is not done; this is left to the government's discretion. Rather than interpreting the provision as attempting to regulate a foreign
nationality, it seems that such foreign nationality will not be recognised if Thai nationality is
still possessed.

Recognition of Multiple Nationality
Thailand does not recognise the effects of foreign nationality for the purposes of Thai law, and
it appears that protection on behalf of multiple nationals would not normally be exercised.

Tonga[66]

Nationality category or status

Only one, Tongan nationality. The Nationality Act does not speak of citizenship, but of Tongan subjects.

Attribution/acquisition of nationality

Event	Law	Condition is renunciation/ loss of other nationality
Birth	In Tonga to a Tongan father	NO
	In Tonga to a Tongan mother out of wedlock	
	Overseas to a Tongan father born in Tonga	
Naturalisation	Upon fulfillment of conditions – at the King's "absolute discretion"	NO
Adoption		
Legitimation		
Marriage	Of an alien woman to a Tongan upon declaration and oath (conditions)	NO
Resumption	Possible for children who lost citizenship when father ceased to be a Tongan subject, upon declaration within one year after age 16	NO
	For all others at the King's "absolute discretion"	
State service		
Parent acquires nationality	Children under 16 of a Tongan who has resumed nationality who reside with him/her	NO

---

[66] TONGA: *Constitution of Tonga*, December 1988 (as amended until 1991), *Passport Act (Act relating to passports and certificates of identity), Cap 61*, November 1964 (as amended until 1988), **UNHCR (internet)**; *Chapter 59 – Nationality*, in "Laws of Tonga comprising all Laws, Acts, Ordinances and subsidiary legislation in force on the 31st day of December, 1988", 1988 revised edition, Volume II (Reading: The Eastern Press, 1989); Barbie Dutter, "Tongans hunting a 'natural-born fool' and $40m", The Sun Herald, 7 October 2001, 56; Michael Field, "Jester fools island kingdom", The Fiji Times, 20 October 2001, 8; "Tonga's democracy movement push for the amendment of Tonga's nationality act", Pacnews, 31 February 2001.

Event	Law	Condition is renunciation/ loss of other nationality
	Children under 16 may be included in parent's naturalisation – "if [His Majesty] thinks fit"	
Spouse acquires nationality	No automatic effect	
Registration		
Special considerations		

Withdrawal/loss of nationality

Event	Law	Consequence of event is loss of nationality
Renunciation	No provision	
Attribution at birth conditional	No provisoin	
Naturalisation elsewhere	Naturalization or other voluntary and formal act abroad and not under disability	YES
Adoption by a foreigner		
Marriage to a foreigner	Tongan woman who marries and alien and exercises a right to acquire husband's nationality – (upon husband's death or dissolution of marriage she may resume by naturalisation without residency requirement)	YES
Spouse acquires other nationality	No automatic effect	
Parent acquires other nationality	(If Tongan father ceases to be a Tongan subject, his children under 16 also lose, unless they do not receive another citizenship by naturalisation)	
Resumption of previous nationality	Naturalization or other voluntary and formal act abroad and not under disability	YES
Service to foreign state		

Event	Law	**Consequence of event is loss of nationality**
Other attribution of nationality	Naturalization or other voluntary and formal act abroad and not under disability	YES
(Punitive) deprivation	Revocation of naturalisation for fraud or false representation	

Special considerations

General attitude toward multiple nationality
The Nationality Act provides that subjects who lose their nationality are not thereby "discharged from any obligation duty or liability in respect of any act done before he ceased to be a Tongan subject". It dictates loss of Tongan nationality upon naturalisation abroad, but does not make loss of former nationality a condition of naturalisation in Tonga. It provides that registers should be kept of persons who have resumed nationality and who have been naturalised. Tonga reportedly engaged in a scheme to sell passports to investors from 1983–1991, many to Hong Kong Chinese. The scheme initially involved only a travel document without right of abode, but was amended when various countries declined to recognise the passports issued thereunder. Press reports state that takers included former Philipines President Ferdinand Marcos his family members, and General Motors Vice President Michael Nyland. More recently in 2001, a public petition was launched to allow Tongans naturalised abroad to retain their nationality. It specifically refers to the fact that persons can be naturalised in Tonga while remaining multiple nationals.

Recognition of Multiple Nationality
The Passport Act provides that Tongans "desiring to leave the Kingdom for parts beyond the seas" must apply for a passport or for travel to certain countries, a certificate of identity. The norm regarding certificates of identity applies also to residents of Tonga born in Tonga. The Act specifies that it is an offence for a Tongan to leave Tonga without a passport or certificate of identity obtained from the Minister of Police.

Trinidad and Tobago[67]

Nationality category or status

Only one, and no distinction between nationality and citizenship.

Attribution/acquisition of nationality

Event	Law	Condition is renunciation/ loss of other nationality
Birth	Birth in Trinidad and Tobago to a T/T parent (unless parent diplomat or enemy alien in place under occupation – conditions)	NO
	Overseas to T/T parent (including if deceased) born in Trinidad and Tobago (child is citizen by descent)	
	Overseas to a T/T parent on government service	
Naturalisation	Upon fulfillment of conditions	NO
Adoption	Under T/T law by T/T father in wedlock or mother outside wedlock	NO
Legitimation	Subsequent marriage of parents leads to treatment as legitimate at birth	
Marriage	Not automatic – registration or naturalisation possible (conditions)	
Resumption	Possible for various categories, including persons who lost citizenship	NO

---

[67] TRINIDAD AND TOBAGO: *Constitution of the Republic of Trinidad and Tobago*, August 1976 (as revised until 2000), 2003, Parliament of Trinidad and Tobago (internet), http://www.ttparliament.org/Docs/constitution/ttconst.pdf, consulted 5 May 2006; *Citizenship Act of the Republic of Trinidad and Tobago*, July 1976 (as amended until 1981), **UNHCR (internet)**; *An Act to amend the Citizenship of the Republic of Trinidad and Tobago Act, Chap. 1:50*, no. 63 of 2000, Parliament of Trinidad and Tobago (internet), http://www.ttparliament.org/bills/acts/2000/a2000–63.pdf, cosulted 5 May 2006; *Frequently asked questions*, Trinidad and Tobago High Commission Ottawa (internet), http://www.ttmissions.com/faq.html, consulted 24 April 2006; "Trinidad. Pandaymonium", The Economist, 7 December 2000; *Too late to turn back, Gypsy*, Trinicenter (internet), http://www.trinicenter.com/TrinidadandTobagoNews/Nov/Gypsy.htm, consulted 24 April 2006; Kim Johnson, "The case against Gypsy and Chaitan", Trinicenter, 17 December 2000 (internet), http://www.trinicenter.com/TrinidadandTobagoNews/Dec/thecase.htm, consulted 24 April 2006.

Event	Law	Condition is renunciation/ loss of other nationality
	previously by naturalisation abroad (conditions)	
State service	Facilitated registration possible for various categories (conditions)	NO
Parent acquires nationality	Children of former citizens whose citizenship is restored can also acquire	NO
Spouse acquires nationality		
Registration (Application)	Birth overseas to a T/T/ parent citizen by descent, but not if T/T parent also acquired nationality by application (conditions)	NO
	Possible for various categories	
Special considerations		

Withdrawal/loss of nationality

Event	Law	Consequence of event is loss of nationality
Renunciation	Possible (conditions)	YES
Attribution at birth conditional	No provision	
Naturalisation elsewhere	For citizens by birth or descent	
	(*Citizens by naturalisation or registration lose nationality*)	NO (*exception*)
Adoption by a foreigner		NO
Marriage to a foreigner		NO
Spouse acquires other nationality		NO
Parent acquires other nationality		NO
Resumption of previous nationality		NO

Event	Law	**Consequence of event is loss of nationality**
Service to foreign state		NO
Other attribution of nationality		NO
(Punitive) deprivation	For citizen by registration or naturalisation for fraud, false representation or concealment of material particular	YES
Special considerations		

General attitude toward multiple nationality

Trinidad and Tobago's attitude toward multiple nationality has changed completely over time. Under the 1976 Constitution dual nationality was ostensibly completely discouraged. In 1980 the norm that children born overseas had to relinquish their foreign nationality upon attaining the age of majority or lose their T/T nationality, was revoked. In 1988 the Citizenship Act was amended to allow citizens by birth or descent to acquire another nationality without losing their Trinidadian. Former citizens who had lost nationality could have it restored. In 2000, the Act was further amended such that loss of foreign nationality is no longer a condition of naturalisation. Those who have their nationality restored are also considered to have reacquired their Trinidadian nationality as of the day it had previously been lost. The Constitution bars Trinidad and Tobago citizens who have voluntarily become citizens of another country or made a related declaration of allegiance, from being elected as a member of the House of Representatives (this does not apply to all multiple nationals, as persons who have become citizens of Trinidad and Tobago by naturalisation or registration are not included in the norm).

Recognition of Multiple Nationality

Trinidadian and Tobagonian multiple nationals may enter and depart the country on foreign travel documents.

*Turkey[68]

Nationality category or status
Only one, and no technical distinction between nationality and citizenship.

Attribution/acquisition of nationality

Event	Law	Condition is renunciation/ loss of other nationality
Birth	To a Turkish parent	
	In Turkey if otherwise stateless	NO
Naturalisation	Upon fulfilment of requirements	NO
Adoption	Not automatic, unless child otherwise stateless or parents unknown	
Legitimation	If paternity can be proved or is recognized	NO
Marriage	Automatic if foreign spouse loses nationality upon marriage or stateless,	NO

---

[68] TURKEY: *Constitution*, 1982; *Law No. 4112 Amendments to the Turkish Citizenship Act of 7 June 1995*, *Law No. 403 Amendments to the Turkish Citizenship Law*, 13 February 1981, *Loi sur l'acquisition de la nationalité turque, no. 403*, 11 February 1964, **UNHCR (internet)**; *Dual nationality*, Embassy of the United States of American in Ankara (internet), http://ankara. usembassy.gov/dual_nationality.html, consulted 19 April 2006; *European Bulletin on Nationality – Turkey*, 14 September 2004, Council of Europe (internet), http://www.coe.int/T/E/Legal_ Affairs/Legal_co-operation/Foreigners_and_citizens/Nationality/Documents/Bulletin/Turkey%20E %202004.pdf, consulted 19 April 2006; Tugrul Ansay, "Die Behandlung von Doppelstaatern in der Türkei", paper presented at the conference: Hohenheimer Tage zum Ausländerrecht 1999 und 5. Migrationspolitisches Forum, Hohenheim, 1999; de Groot, "Loss of nationality: a critical inventory"; Nuray Eksi, "Consequences of dual nationality for employment, property ownership and other rights and duties under Turkish law", in *Rights and duties of dual nationals. Evolution and prospects*, ed. David A. Martin and Kay Hailbronner 375–382 (The Hague: Kluwer Law International, 2003); Nuray Eksi, "Political rights of dual nationals in Turkish law", in *Rights and duties of dual nationals. Evolution and prospects*, ed. David A. Martin and Kay Hailbronner, 153–156 (The Hague: Kluwer Law International, 2003); Riva Kastoryano, "Türken mit deutschem Pass: Sociological and political aspects of dual nationality in Germany", in *Dual nationality, social rights and federal citizenship in the U.S. and Europe. The reinvention of citizenship*, ed. Randall Hansen and Patrick Weil, 158–175 (New York: Berghahn Books, 2002); Kemal Kirisci, "Disaggregating Turkish citizenship and immigration practices", *Middle Eastern Studies* (2000) vol. 36, no. 3, 1–22; Christian Rumpf, "Citizenship and multiple citizenship in Turkish law", in *Rights and duties of dual nationals. Evolution and prospects*, ed. David A. Martin and Kay Hailbronner, 361–373 (The Hague: Kluwer Law International, 2003).

Event	Law	Condition is renunciation/ loss of other nationality
	otherwise three year waiting period after marriage	
Resumption	Facilitated naturalisation for various categories of persons	NO
State service	Facilitated naturalisation possible	NO
Parent acquires nationality	Facilitated naturalisation possible, in some cases automatic acquisition	NO
Spouse acquires nationality	Facilitated naturalisation possible, in some cases option to acquire	NO
Registration		
Special considerations		

Withdrawal/loss of nationality

Event	Law	Consequence of event is loss of nationality
Renunciation	Right for certain minors two years within age of majority	YES
	Right for woman who acquired nationality at marriage, within three years of marriage ending, if not thereby stateless	
	Otherwise, must be adult who has or will acquire another nationality, subject to government discretion (men not subject to military obligs)	
Attribution at birth conditional	No provision	
Naturalisation elsewhere	*(conditional upon permission by government before naturalisation – discretionary power of authorities)*	NO *(conditional)*
Adoption by a foreigner		NO
Marriage to a foreigner	*(Except a woman acquiring foreign nationality by marriage, if she declares that she accepts her husband's nationality, then)*	NO *(exception)*

Event	Law	Consequence of event is loss of nationality
Spouse acquires other nationality		NO
Parent acquires other nationality	(*Except if paternity is denied, the child of a foreign mother loses Turkish nationality, unless it would be stateless*)	NO (*exception*)
Resumption of previous nationality	(*if permission received in advance*)	NO (*conditional*)
Service to foreign state	Possible deprivation if service conflicts with Turkey's interests and individual doesn't obey order to abandon	POSSIBLE
Other attribution of nationality	If involuntary; if voluntary acquisition, permission must be sought in advance	NO (*condition*)
(Punitive) deprivation	Revocation of naturalisation: fraud, desertion, remaining abroad when summoned to return	POSSIBLE
	Possible deprivation upon refusal to return to defend country in case of war, or to complete military service	
Special considerations	Possible deprivation after acquisition of foreign nationality and seven years' residence abroad without evidence of link	YES

General attitude toward multiple nationality

The Turkish Constitution provides for in-principle jus sanguinis attribution of nationality, and that no one may be deprived of nationality except for disloyal acts toward Turkey. Turkey's laws provide for the potential production of multiple nationality at birth, upon naturalisation in Turkey, and upon acquisition of a foreign nationality, in the last case if permission is applied for and received before the naturalisation takes place. Men subject to military service obligations are excused from such if they have performed such service in the country where they reside, and exemptions from military service are possible for various reasons, except in wartime. No distinction is made among citizens on the basis of multiple nationality

Recognition of Multiple Nationality

The legal status of multiple nationals is no different from other nationals in Turkish law, and Turkey may choose to exercise protection of multiple nationals abroad as in the case of mono-nationals, depending on the acquiesecne of the other state concerned. In this sense, foreign nationality is not recognised in terms of the attribution of benefits or entitlements – Turks are treated as Turks, notwithstanding any multiple nationality. Accordingly, the Turkish government reportedly does not allow multiple nationals to contact consular officials of their other country of nationality upon arrest. Turkish nationals must use Turkish passports to enter and depart Turkey.

Tuvalu[69]

Nationality category or status
Only one, and no distinction between nationality and citizenship.

Attribution/acquisition of nationality

Event	Law	Condition is renunciation/ loss of other nationality
Birth	In Tuvalu to a Tuvaluan parent (not if diplomat, enemy in wartime – conditions) – citizen by birth	NO
	Overseas to a Tuvaluan parent (including deceased parent – conditions) – citizen by birth	
	(Foundling considered born in Tuvalu)	
Naturalisation	Upon fulfillment of conditions	YES
Adoption	Possible by registration	
Legitimation		
Marriage	By registration	
Resumption	Possible for women who lost nationality upon marriage (conditions)	YES
	Possible for those who lost nationality under previous requirement to renounce foreign nationality (conditions)	
	Otherwise by facilitated registration or naturalisation	
State service		
Parent acquires nationality	Possible by registration	
Spouse acquires nationality	Possible by registration	

---

[69] TUVALU: *Constitution of Tuvalu*, September 1986 (revised as of 1990), **UNHCR (internet)**; *Chapter 98 – Citizenship*, in "The Laws of Tuvalu containing the Ordinances and Subsidiary Legislation thereunder in force on the 31st day of December 1982 together with certain Orders in Council and other Provisions relating to Tuvalu", Revised Edition 1982, Volume III (London: Eyre and Spottiswoode, 1983).

Event	Law	**Condition is renunciation/ loss of other nationality**
Registration	Possible for various categories upon fulfillment of conditions, including spouses upon marriage to a Tuvaluan, or when a spourse has acquired Tuvaluan nationality	YES
Special considerations		

Withdrawal/loss of nationality

Event	Law	**Consequence of event is loss of nationality**
Renunciation	Possible if of full age and capacity, and multiple national or to about to acquire foreign nationality – requires prior written consent of Prime Minister in wartime	
Attribution at birth conditional	(Provision in Citizenship Act superseded by Constitution for citizens by birth – see remarks below)	
Naturalisation elsewhere	No deprivation of citizenship for persons who became citizens at independence, or citizens by birth	NO (*exception*)
	(*Citizens by naturalisation or registration may lose nationality upon any voluntary obtention of foreign nationality – conditions*)	
Adoption by a foreigner		NO
Marriage to a foreigner	(*Citizens by naturalisation or registration may lose nationality upon any voluntary obtention of foreign nationality – conditions*)	NO (*exception*)
Spouse acquires other nationality	(*Citizens by naturalisation or registration may lose nationality upon any voluntary obtention of foreign nationality – conditions*)	NO (*exception*)
Parent acquires other nationality	(*Citizens by naturalisation or registration may lose nationality upon any voluntary obtention of foreign nationality – conditions*)	NO (*exception*)

Event	Law	**Consequence of event is loss of nationality**
Resumption of previous nationality	For citizens by naturalisation or registration, if voluntary act	POSSIBLE
Service to foreign state	Citizens by registration or naturalisation who make oath of allegiance, entry/ service in armed forces without express approval of Prime Minister, voting in election or accepting elective office, unless under compulsion (conditions)	POSSIBLE (*exception*)
Other attribution of nationality	For citizens by naturalisation or registration, if voluntary act	POSSIBLE
(Punitive) deprivation	Citizens by registration or naturalisation who exercise a right pursuant to foreign nationality, unless exercised inadvertently or under compulsion (conditions)	POSSIBLE
	Fraud in obtention of citizenship by naturalisation or registration (conditions)	
	For citizen by naturalisation who does not make Tuvalu permanent home, not financially self-supporting, other matters (conditions)	

Special considerations

General attitude toward multiple nationality
The 1986 Constitution provides that Parliament may not deprive Tuvaluans who became citizens at independence or who are citizens by birth, of their nationality. It does, however, allow Parliament to legislate "for the maintenance of a register of citizens of Tuvalu who are also citizens or nationals of another country". Notwithstanding its provisions that go against the Constitution's dictates as regards loss of nationality, the Citizenship Act of 1979 is still in force. It provides that persons who are citizens by operation of law (by birth under the Act) are deprived of Tuvaluan nationality if they fail to renounce any foreign nationality by age 20. The Act must thus be interpreted in light of the Constitution's rules, which take precedence. The Act also required all citizens to renounce foreign nationality by 1 October 1981, or by age 20. Decisions related to any deprivation of Tuvaluan nationality are made by a Citizenship Committee. The Nationality Act requires candidates for naturalisation to relinquish previous nationality, but provides that a declaration suffices should this not be possible.

*United Kingdom[70]

Nationality category or status
There appear to be five separate categories of British nationality: British Citizen; British Overseas Territories Citizen; British Overseas Citizen; British National (Overseas), and British Subject. British Overseas Citizens, British Nationals (Overseas) and British Subjects cannot transmit their nationality and constitute closed-off groups, and are thus not covered in separate sections. British Overseas Territories Citizens, with the exception of those related to the

---

[70] UNITED KINGDOM: *British Overseas Territories Act 2002*, Office of Public Sector Information (internet), http://www.opsi.gov.uk/acts/acts2002/20020008.htm, consulted 20 April 2006; *Immigration, Asylum, and Nationality Act 2006*, Office of Public Sector Information (internet), http://www.opsi.gov.uk/acts/acts2006/20060013.htm, consulted 20 April 2006; *Help for dual nationals*, Foreign and Commonwealth Office (internet), http://www.fco.gov.uk/servlet/Front?pagename=OpenMarket/Xcelerate/ShowPage&c=Page&cid=1098377478962, consulted 20 April 2006; Byrnes and Chan, "The British Nationality (Hong Kong) Act 1990"; Campbell and Meek, eds., *International immigration and nationality law*; Chan, "Hong Kong: an analysis of the British nationality proposals"; Robin Cook, *Foreword to Partnership for Progress and Prosperity: Britain and the Overseas Territories*, Foreign & Commonwealth Office (internet), http://www.fco.gov.uk/servlet/Front?pagename=OpenMarket/Xcelerate/ShowPage&c=Page&cid=1018028164839, consulted 20 April 2006; de Groot, "Loss of nationality: a critical inventory"; Laurie Fransman, *British nationality law* (London: Butterworths, 1998); Laurie Fransman, "The case for reform of nationality law in the United Kingdom", in *Citizenship and nationality status in the new Europe*, ed. Síofra O'Leary and Teija Tiilikainen, 123–147 (London: Sweet & Maxwell, 1998); Randall Hansen, "The dog that didn't bark: dual nationality in the United Kingdom", in *Dual nationality, social rights and federal citizenship in the U.S. and Europe. The reinvention of citizenship*, ed. Randall Hansen and Patrick Weil, 179–190 (New York: Berghahn Books, 2002); Randall Hansen, "Doppelte Staatsangehörigkeit im Vereinigten Königreich von Grossbritannien und Nordirland", paper presented at the conference: Hohenheimer Tage zum Ausländerrecht 1999 und 5. Migrationspolitisches Forum, Hohenheim, 1999; Randall Hansen, "From subjects to citizens: immigration and nationality law in the United Kingdom", in *Towards a European nationality. Citizenship, immigration and nationality law in the EU*, ed. Randall Hansen and Patrick Weil, 69–94 (Houndmills: Palgrave, 2001); Zig Layton-Henry, "Patterns of privilege: citizenship rights in Britain", in *Citizenship in a global world. Comparing citizenship rights for aliens*, ed. Atsushi Kondo, 116–135 (Houndmills (UK): Palgrave, 2001); Ian A. Macdonald and Nicholas Blake, *The new nationality law* (London: Butterworths, 1982); Nicola Piper, *Racism, nationalism and citizenship – ethnic minorities in Britain and Germany* (Aldershot: Ashgate, 1998); Mark Roberti, *The fall of Hong Kong. China's triumph & Britain's betrayal.* (New York: John Wiley & Sons, Inc., 1996); Colin Warbrick, "Current legal developments", *International and Comparative Law Quarterly* (1988) vol. 37, no. 4, 983–1012; White, "Hong Kong: nationality, immigration and the agreement with China"; Robin M. White, "Nationality and the British Empire: historical doubts and confusions on the status of the inhabitants", *Hong Kong Law Journal* (1989) vol. 19, 10–42; White, "Nationality aspects of the Hong Kong settlement"; "Freedom and anti-terrorism. Coming quietly", The Economist, 1 March 2003, 51; *Consular protection*, British Embassy Tel Aviv (internet), http://www.britemb.org.il/Consular/ConsularProtection.html, consulted 20 April 2006; "Sorry old chap, but you're just not British enough", The Sun-Herald, 17 June 2001, 66.

"Sovereign Base Areas of Akrotiri and Dhekelia", were given the rights of British Citizenship in 2002 and therefore are also not covered separately. *The following thus applies only to British Citizens.*

Attribution/acquisition of nationality

Event	Law	Condition is renunciation/ loss of other nationality
Birth	In UK if parent is British Citizen or legally settled in UK	NO
	In UK if parents unknown (foundling)	
	Overseas if parent is British Citizen other than by descent, or citizen in state/EU service	
	Overseas if parent is British Citizen by descent, whose parent was a British Citizen otherwise than by descent, and who spent at least three years in the UK	
Naturalisation	Upon fulfillment of requirements	NO
Adoption	By court order	NO
Legitimation	(see birth)	NO
Marriage	Not automatic	
Resumption	Possible once if nationality was renounced, otherwise discretionary	NO
State service	Facilitated naturalisation possible	NO
Parent acquires nationality	No direct effect – minor children may be registered as citizens	
Spouse acquires nationality	No direct effect – naturalisation	
Registration	Birth Overseas to parent who is British Citizen by descent whose parent was British Citizen by descent, if parent and child spend three years in the UK	NO
	Of children of person to be naturalised	

Withdrawal/loss of nationality

Event	Law	Consequence of event is loss of nationality
Renunciation	Possible	YES

Event	Law	Consequence of event is loss of nationality
Attribution at birth conditional	No provision	
Naturalisation elsewhere		NO
Adoption by a foreigner		NO
Marriage to a foreigner		NO
Spouse acquires other nationality		NO
Parent acquires other nationality		NO
Resumption of previous nationality		NO
Service to foreign state		
Other attribution of nationality		NO
(Punitive) deprivation	Revocation of naturalisation or registration for fraud, disloyalty, certain sentences, collaborating with the enemy	POSSIBLE
	If satisfied that "deprivation is conducive to the public good"	
Special considerations	If discovered that a foundling is of foreign origin, even after majority	YES

General attitude toward multiple nationality
The UK accepts multiple nationality for its citizens, its policy having been described at various times as "indifferent" to the situation. Hansen posits that such acceptance is related to a view that dual nationality is a means to promote the integration of immigrants, maintain ties to emigrants, and promote British interests abroad, and that multiple nationality "creates no meaningful problems for the UK". He points out the Britain's first citizenship in 1948 was "essentially plural in character", including the United Kingdom, colonies, and dominions.

Recognition of Multiple Nationality
British citizens are warned that the UK may not undertake consular protection on their behalf in other countries of nationality, even if they entered that country using a British passport, and consular advice as well as the UK Claims Rules state that such efforts will only be undertaken in exceptional cases of specific urgency or need, or special humanitarian reason. The UK advises its dual nationals that when they are in third countries they should "seek consular assistance from the country on whose passport you are travelling". Britons may enter and depart the UK on foreign passports, but are treated in any case as UK citizens for purposes of UK law.

*United States of America[71]

Nationality category or status

There are two categories of nationality in the United States: US Citizen and US Non-citizen national, the latter category restricted to persons born in or who have a connection to American Samoa or Swains Island. Certain inhabitants of the Commonwealth of the Northern Mariana Islands who are US citizens via treaty arrangements between the two countries may opt for non-citizen national status instead of US citizenship should they so choose. Non-citizen nationals are granted rights of entry and permanent residence in the United States, and may choose to become citizens at any time in the United States.

---

[71] UNITED STATES: *Immigration and Nationality Act 1952*, updated to 5 January 2006, US Citizenship and Immigration Services (internet), http://www.uscis.gov/lpBin/lpext.dll/inserts/slb/ slb-1/slb-20?f=templates&fn=document-frame.htm#slb-act, consulted 20 April 2006; *Constitution of the United States of America, September 1787* (last amended 7 May 1992), **UNHCR (internet)**; Christine L. Agnew, "Expatriation, double taxation, and treaty override: who is eating crow now?", *The University of Miami Inter-American Law Review* (1996) vol. 28, no. 1, 69–94; Candice Lewis Bredbenner, *A nationality of her own – women, marriage, and the law of citizenship* (Berkeley: University of California Press, 1998); Campbell and Meek, eds., *International immigration and nationality law;* Jerry A. Dagrella, "Wealthy Americans planning to renounce their citizenship to save on taxes have a new problem to consider: this time Congress means business", *The Transnational Lawyer* (2000) vol. 13, no. 2, 363–390; de Groot, "Loss of nationality: a critical inventory"; Gutierrez, "Mexico's dual nationality amendments: they do not undermine U.S. citizens' allegiance and loyalty or U.S. political sovereignty"; Michael Robert W. Houston, "Birthright citizenship in the United Kingdom and the United States: a comparative analysis of the Common Law basis for granting citizenship to children born of illegal immigrants", *Vanderbilt Journal of Transnational Law* (2000) vol. 33, no. 1, 693–738; Jon B. Hultman, "Administrative denaturalization: is there 'nothing you can do that can't be [un]done'?", *Loyola of Los Angeles Law Review* (2001) vol. 34, no. 2, 895–935; Michael Jones-Correa, "Under two flags: dual nationality in Latin America and its consequences for naturalization in the United States", in *Rights and duties of dual nationals. Evolution and prospects*, ed. David A. Martin and Kay Hailbronner, 3403–333 (The Hague: Kluwer Law International, 2003); Joppke, "The evolution of alien rights in the United States, Germany, and the European Union"; Alain Levasseur, "La nationalité américaine: aspects juridiques", in *La citoyenneté européenne*, ed. Christian Philip and Panayotis Soldatos, 59–79 (Montréal: Université de Montréal, 2000); Susan Martin, "The attack on social rights: U.S. citizenship devalued", in *Dual nationality, social rights and federal citizenship in the U.S. and Europe. The reinvention of citizenship*, ed. Randall Hansen and Patrick Weil, 215–232 (New York: Berghahn Books, 2002); Jeffrey R. O'Brien, "U.S. dual citizen voting rights: a critical examination of Aleinikoff's solution", *Georgetown Immigration Law Journal* (1999) vol. 13, no. 2, 573–595; Elizabeth Olson, International Herald Tribune, *U.S. to test expat cybervoting*, 25 July 2003 (internet), http://www.iht.com/articles/2003/07/25/vote_ed3_.php, consulted 20 April 2006; Karin Scherner-Kim, "The role of the oath of renunciation in current U.S. nationaltiy policy – the enforce, to omit, or maybe to change?", *The Georgetown Law Journal* (2000) vol. 88, no. 2, 329–379; Peter J. Spiro, "Questioning barriers to naturalization", *Georgetown Immig-*

Attribution/acquisition of nationality

Event	Law	**Condition is renunciation/ loss of other nationality**
Birth	In USA (includes Puerto Rico, Guam, US Virgin Islands, and by agreement the Northern Mariana Islands, internal waters and airspace), except to heads of state and government, diplomats, members of army of occupation, or aboard foreign public vessel within territorial limits	NO
	Overseas to two US citizen parents in wedlock, one of whom resided in the USA at some point	
	Overseas to one US citizen parent in wedlock who was present in the USA for five years prior to child's birth, two of which were after age 14 (military, government, or international service abroad included)	

---

ration Law Journal (1999) vol. 13, no. 1, 479–519; *Possible loss of U.S. citizenship and foreign military service*, US Department of State, July 1998 (internet), http://travel.state.gov/law/ citizenship/citizenship_780.html, consulted 20 April 2006; *Advice about possible loss of U.S. citizenship and seeking public office in a foreign state*, US Department of State, January 2005 (internet), http://travel.state.gov/law/citizenship/citizenship_779.html, consulted 20 April 2006; *Certificates of Non-Citizen Nationality*, US Department of State (internet), http://travel.state. gov/law/citizenship/citizenship_781.html, consulted 20 April 2006; *Citizenship and Nationality*, US Department of State (internet), http://travel.state.gov/law/citizenship/citizenship_782.html, consulted 20 April 2006; *Dual nationality*, US Department of State (internet), http://travel.state. gov/travel/cis_pa_tw/cis/cis_1753.html, consulted 20 April 2006; *Renunciation of U.S. citizenship*, US Department of State (internet), http://travel.state.gov/law/citizenship/citizenship_776.html, consulted 20 April 2006; *Renunciation of U.S. citizenship by persons claiming a right of residence in the United States*, US Department of State, May 1998 (internet), http://travel.state.gov/ law/citizenship/citizenship_777.html, consulted 20 April 2006; David Weissbrodt, *Immigration law and procedure in a nutshell*, Second ed., Nutshell (St. Paul: West Publishing Co., 1989); "The New Americans. A survey of the United States", The Economist, 11 March 2000, supplement; "Civil liberties and terrorism. A question of freedom", The Economist, 8 March 2003, 35; "Moves to curtail birthrights of babies born in American Samoa", PACNEWS, 18 March 2002 (internet), held by author; Margaret Graham Tebo, "Closing the door" (2002) ABA Journal, September, 43; "US accused of abandoning its own to justify entering WWII", The Sydney Morning Herald, 31 July 2002, 9; "Lexington. Treasonous reflections", The Economist, 15 December 2001, 34.

Event	Law	Condition is renunciation/ loss of other nationality
	Overseas to US citizen mother out of wedlock, and mother was physically present in USA continuously for 12 months at some point prior to child's birth	
	Overseas to US citizen father out of wedlock: father was present in the USA for five years prior to child's birth, two of which were after age 14 (military, government, or international service abroad included); blood relationship established; father a US citizen at child's birth (unless deceased; father agrees in writing to support child until age 18; child legitimated while a minor: written acknowledgment of paternity, court adjudication of paternity, or legitimation under law of child's residence or domicile	
Naturalisation	(*The citizenship oath requires renunciation of foreign nationality, but no steps are required to be taken to ensure actual loss*)	NO (*exception*)
Adoption	Facilitated naturalisation (conditions)	NO
Legitimation	(see birth)	
Marriage	No effect – facilitated naturalisation possible	
Resumption	By naturalisation (*renunciation does not have to be effective*)	NO (*exception*)
State service	Possible facilitated naturalisation	
Parent acquires nationality	No direct effect	
Spouse acquires nationality	No direct effect	
Registration	Facilitated naturalisation for various categories	

Withdrawal/loss of nationality

Event	Law	Consequence of event is loss of nationality
Renunciation	Possible only outside United States, if voluntary and result of free choice, even if thereby stateless, in which case US would accept that the person could be deported to the United States	YES
Attribution at birth conditional	No provision	
Naturalisation elsewhere	*(except if accompanied by specific intent to relinquish US nationality)*	NO *(exception)*
Adoption by a foreigner		NO
Marriage to a foreigner		NO
Spouse acquires other nationality		NO
Parent acquires other nationality	*(except if parent's naturalisation is revoked and child claims nationality through parent)*	NO *(exception)*
Resumption of previous nationality	*(Possible deprivation, if voluntary acquisition of nationality accompanied by specific intent to relinquish US nationality)*	NO *(exception)*
Service to foreign state	*(Possible deprivation, if accompanied by specific intent to relinquish US nationality)*	NO *(exception)*
Other attribution of nationality	*(Possible deprivation, if accompanied by specific intent to relinquish US nationality)*	NO *(exception)*
(Punitive) deprivation	Revocation of naturalisation for fraud, "illegal acquisition", conviction for certain crimes, etc.	POSSIBLE
	If certain proscribed acts are accompanied by an intent to relinquish citizenship (treason, war against the state, etc.)	

General attitude toward multiple nationality

The United States tolerates multiple nationality for its citizens, although this acceptance is characterised in qualified terms: "[t]he U.S. Government recognizes that dual nationality exists but does not encourage it as a matter of policy because of the problems it may cause. Claims of other countries on dual national U.S. citizens may conflict with U.S. law, and dual nationality may limit U.S. Government efforts to assist citizens abroad. The country where a dual national is located generally has a stronger claim to that person's allegiance. However, dual nationals owe allegiance to both the United States and the foreign country. They are required to obey the laws of both countries. Either country has the right to enforce its laws, particularly if the person travels there". Although US law provides that various acts such as naturalisation in a foreign country constitute "expatriating acts" potentially leading to loss of American nationality, in order for deprivation of nationality to take place, these acts must be accompanied by a specific intent to lose US nationality, thus making loss highly improbable without an expression of individual will. Likewise, the requirement that a candidate for naturalisation in the US renounce foreign nationality amounts to the swearing of an oath of loyalty, and no demonstration of actual or effective loss of nationality is required. The US maintains that any obligations owed, including related to taxation and military service, persist beyond any loss of US nationality.

Recognition of Multiple Nationality

US citizens must use a US passport to enter and depart the United States, although use of a foreign passport in other situations is not prohibited. Although the US warns its citizens that they may not be able to be protected in other countries where they are considered nationals, it maintains a right of protection in all cases where an individual is a US citizen.

*Uruguay[72]

Nationality category or status

Only one, but Uruguayan law specifically distinguishes between "natural citizens" and persons who possess "legal citizenship". Whereas the former cannot be lost, the latter may be. Uruguayan legislation uses the term "nationality" for nationality acquired at birth, and the term "legal citizenship" for both rights of citizenship, as well as nationality acquired by grant or naturalisation or certain acquisition subsequent to birth.

Attribution/acquisition of nationality

Event	Law	Condition is renunciation/ loss of other nationality
Birth	In Uruguay (natural citizen)	NO
	Overseas to Uruguayan parent, upon taking up residence and registration in the Civic Register (Registro Cívico), unless parent also born overseas (natural citizen)	
Naturalisation	Upon fulfillment of requirements (becomes a legal citizen)	NO
Adoption	(see birth)	
Legitimation	(see birth)	
Marriage	Not automatic – naturalisation	
Resumption	(if legal citizen)	NO
State service	Possible, from General Assembly (legal citizenship)	NO
Parent acquires nationality	Not automatic – acquisition of citizenship rights upon majority, but nationality probably acquired with parent, although unclear	
Spouse acquires nationality	Not automatic – naturalisation procedure and acquisition of citizenship rights	
Registration		

---

[72] URUGUAY: *Constitución de la Republica Oriental del Uruguay*, November 1966 (last amended 8 December 1996); *Ley no. 16.021, Se establece que tienen la calidad de nacionales de la Republica Oriental del Uruguay, los hombres y mujeres nacidos en cualquier punto del territorio de la Republica*, 27 April 1989, **UNHCR (internet)**; *Nacionalidad de origen*, Base de Datos Políticos de las Américas, 1998 (internet), http://pdba.georgetown.edu/Comp/Nacionalidad/ nacionalidad.html, consulted 20 April 2006; Jones-Correa, *Under two flags: dual nationality in Latin America and its consequences for the United States.*

Withdrawal/loss of nationality

Event	Law	Consequence of event is loss of nationality
Renunciation	No provision	NO
Attribution at birth conditional	No provision (see birth)	
Naturalisation elsewhere	Legal citizens only are deprived of nationality (but not if keep ties with Uruguay such as residence)	DEPENDS (*exceptions*)
	Only loss of political rights by natural citizens, which can be recovered by entry and inscription in civic register. Natural citizens can never be deprived of nationality	NO
Adoption by a foreigner		NO
Marriage to a foreigner		NO
Spouse acquires other nationality		NO
Parent acquires other nationality		NO
Resumption of previous nationality	By legal citizen, if considered naturalisation (but not if keeps ties with Uruguay, such as residence)	YES (*exceptions*)
Service to foreign state		NO
Other attribution of nationality	If considered subsequent naturalisation of legal citizen, but not if keeps ties to Uruguay, such as residence	YES (*exceptions*)
(Punitive) deprivation	Suspension of citizenship rights only –	NO

General attitude toward multiple nationality

Multiple nationality has long been accepted in Uruguay. Nationality acquired at birth is not lost by attribution of another nationality and can never be renounced. There are no distinctions made among citizens, although citizenship rights can be suspended, and "legal" citizens are treated differently from "natural" citizens in certain respects. Although legal citizenship acquired by those not born in Uruguay or to Uruguayans can be lost by subsequent naturalisation elsewhere, this is reportedly not the case when ties to Uruguay are maintained.

Recognition of Multiple Nationality

Uruguayans may use foreign passports to enter and depart Uruguay, but are always treated as Uruguayans. Consular protection is reportedly exercised on behalf of multiple nationals in all cases, although it is recognised that this may not be possible in another country of nationality, or in cases where foreign passports have been used rather than Uruguayan passports.

APPENDIX

Vanuatu[73]

Nationality category or status
Only one, and no technical distinction between citizenship and nationality.

Attribution/acquisition of nationality

Event	Law	**Condition is renunciation/ loss of other nationality**
Birth	To a ni-Vanuatu parent	NO (*but see conditional attribution*)
Naturalisation	Upon fulfillment of conditions	YES
Adoption	Upon adoption by ni-Vanuatu father in wedlock, or mother out of wedlock (conditions)	NO (*but see conditional attribution*)
Legitimation		
Marriage	Woman married to a ni-Vanuatu husband – by registration	YES
Resumption	By woman who lost nationality upon acquiring foreign nationality during marriage, if marriage has broken down (conditions)	YES
State service	Honorary citizenship upon advice of Prime Minister	DEPENDS
Parent acquires nationality	Children may be included in father's naturalisation	NO (*but see conditional attribution*)
Spouse acquires nationality	Wife may be included in husband's naturalisation if she wishes	YES
Registration	Possible for various categories (conditions)	YES (*see conditional attribution*)
Special considerations		

---

[73] VANUATU: *Constitution of the Republic of Vanuatu*, July 1980 (as amended 1983), **UNHCR (internet)**; *Chapter 112 – Citizenship*, in "The Laws of The Republic of Vanuatu", revised edition 1988, Volume II (Portsmouth: Grosvenor Press, 1988); "Chinese yen for Vanuatu passports", Far Eastern Economic Review, 5 April 2001, 10.

Withdrawal/loss of nationality

Event	Law	Consequence of event is loss of nationality
Renunciation	By persons of full age and capacity if multiple national or about to acquire nationality (requires consent during war – conditions)	YES
Attribution at birth conditional	Must renounce foreign nationality within three months of age 18 or lose ni-Vanuatu nationality by operation of law	YES
Naturalisation elsewhere	Any voluntary act or agreement to become a citizen/national, or statement of allegiance	YES
Adoption by a foreigner		
Marriage to a foreigner	If thereby acquire foreign nationality	YES
Spouse acquires other nationality		
Parent acquires other nationality		
Resumption of previous nationality		
Service to foreign state	Voluntary service or entry into foreign armed forces except with express approval of Prime Minister in Council (conditions)	YES
	Voting in foreign elections or accepting foreign elective office	
Other attribution of nationality		
(Punitive) deprivation	Obtention of nationality by false representation, fraud (conditions)	YES
	Possible for citizens by naturalisation upon sentence of ten or more years' imprisonment	
Special considerations		

General attitude toward multiple nationality

Vanuatu's Constitution contains a specific provision on "avoidance of dual nationality", mandating automatic loss of nationality upon acquisition or maintenance of a foreign nationality or citizenship, or within three years of attaining age 18. Upon independence from the United Kingdom and France in 1980 persons who had four grandparents who belonged to a ni-Vanuatu tribe or indigenous community as well as persons of ni-Vanuatu ancestry who had no nationality, became citizens automatically. Persons of ni-Vanuatu ancestry who were nationals of another state were provided with an opportunity to apply for citizenship, however with the express provision that Vanuatu citizenship would automatically lapse if the foreign nationality had not been renounced within three months of attribution of ni-Vanuatu citizenship, or within three months of reaching age 18. The Citizenship Act mandates that registers be kept of all those who become citizens, regain citizenship, and who lose or renounce citizenship. Allegations that various Vanuatu honorary consuls in Asia might have sold regular and diplomatic passports to mainland Chinese surfaced in the 1990s.

Recognition of Multiple Nationality

The Constitution provides that "[t]he Republic of Vanuatu does not recognise dual nationality". The Citizenship Act provides that naturalized citizens lose ni-Vanuatu citizenship by using a foreign passport to cross any national boundary.

*Venezuela[74]

Nationality category or status
Only one, but the Venezuelan Constitution distinguishes between nationality and citizenship specifically, the former being a prerequisite for the latter, which is defined as the possession and use of political and other rights.

Attribution/acquisition of nationality

Event	Law	Condition is renunciation/ loss of other nationality
Birth	In Venezuela	NO
	Overseas to Venezuelan parents by birth	
	Overseas to Venezuelan parent by birth, upon taking up residence or declaration of desire to be Venezuelan	
	Overseas to Venezuelan parent by naturalisation, and establishes residence in Venezuela before age 18 and declares wish to be Venezuelan before age 25	
Naturalisation	Upon fulfilment of requirements (conditions)	NO
Adoption	(see naturalisation)	
Legitimation	(see birth)	
Marriage	Not automatic – facilitated naturalisation	
Resumption	By Venezuelans by birth upon two years' residence and declaration	NO
	By naturalised citizens only upon fulfilment of same requirements for naturalisation (conditions)	
State service	Facilitated naturalisation possible	NO

---

[74] VENEZUELA: *Ley de Nacionalidad y Ciudadanía*, 1 July 2004 (Gaceta Oficial Número 37.971), *Constitución de la Republica Bolivariana de Venezuela*, 29 December 1999, **UNHCR (internet)**; *Nacionalidad de origen*, Base de Datos Políticos de las Américas, 1998 (internet), http://pdba.georgetown.edu/Comp/Nacionalidad/nacionalidad.html, consulted 20 April 2006; *Dirección General de Relaciones Consulares*, Ministerio de Relaciones Exteriores, República Bolivariana de Venezuela (internet), http://www.mre.gov.ve/consular/index.htm, consulted 22 April 2006.

Event	Law	Condition is renunciation/ loss of other nationality
Parent acquires nationality	Naturalisation with parent, or facilitated naturalisation (conditions)	NO
Spouse acquires nationality	No direct effect – facilitated naturalisation possible	
Registration		

Withdrawal/loss of nationality

Event	Law	Consequence of event is loss of nationality
Renunciation	Possible for nationals by birth, but only valid when obtain other nationality	YES
	Possible for nationals by naturalisation only if opt for, will acquire, or have acquired another nationality	
Attribution at birth conditional	No provision (see conditions related to birth overseas)	
Naturalisation elsewhere		NO
Adoption by a foreigner		NO
Marriage to a foreigner		NO
Spouse acquires other nationality		NO
Parent acquires other nationality		NO
Resumption of previous nationality		NO
Service to foreign state	Suspension of rights of citizenship possible for accepting foreign political functions or honours, or military service, without prior authorization from the National Assembly	
Other attribution of nationality		NO

Event	Law	Consequence of event is loss of nationality
(Punitive) deprivation	No revocation, suspension or privation of nationality possible for Venezuelans by birth	POSSIBLE
	For Venezuelans by naturalisation only revocation by judicial sentence, for fraud, prejudicial acts, acts that affect integrity, sovereignty or independence, acts that prejudice state security, acts that diminish institutions or public authorities, acts that incite disobedience to public institutions or the Constitution	

General attitude toward multiple nationality

The Venezuela Constitution stipulates that Venezuelan nationality is not lost by exercising an option for, or acquiring, a foreign nationality. It places an obligation on the state to reach international treaties with respect to nationality with the countries that border Venezuela, as well as those countries whose citizens are granted facilitated naturalisation: Spain, Portugal, Italy, and Latin-American and Caribbean countries. The Nationality and Citizenship Act (2004) provides that Venezuelan multiple nationals have the same rights and duties as Venezuelans who are mono-nationals, except as provided in the Constitution and by law. Although all Venezuelan are treated fundamentally on the same basis, the Constitution does incapacitate multiple nationals and naturalised citizens in certain respects. Only Venezuelans by birth who are not multiple nationals may hold various high office (President, Vice President, President and Vice President of the National Assembly, judges of the Supreme Court, and others). Additional restrictions apply to naturalised citizens that do not apply to multiple nationals. The 2004 Act provides that renunciation of nationality is not a condition of naturalization in Venezuela, but that should candidates for naturalisation desire to renounce their other nationality, they should declare this when beginning the naturalisation procedure.

Recognition of Multiple Nationality

All citizens seem to be provided the same rights to protection abroad, irrespective of multiple nationality. The Nationality and Citizenship Act (2004) provides that Venezuelan multiple nationals must use Venezuelan documents to enter, remain, and exit Venezuela, and identify themselves as Venezuelans in all civil and political acts.

***Zimbabwe**[75]

Nationality category or status

Only one, and no technical distinction between nationality and citizenship (although the category of "honorary citizenship" exempts the holder from military service and other obligations, while excluding him or her from electoral rights and the capacity to transmit nationality).

Attribution/acquisition of nationality

Event	Law	Condition is renunciation/ loss of other nationality
Birth	In Zimbabwe to a Zimbabwean parent (citizen by birth)	
	Abroad to Zimbabwean parent lawfully ordinarily resident in Zimbabwe, or abroad on government service and birth is registered (citizen by birth)	NO *(but conditional attribution)*
	Abroad to Zimbabwean parent citizen otherwise than by descent and birth registered (citizen by descent)	
Naturalisation	Upon fulfillment of requirements	YES
Adoption	Child may acquire by registration if adoptive father Zimbabwean or if single adoption by Zimbabwean mother	YES *(any attribution conditional)*
Legitimation	(see birth)	YES *(conditional)*
Marriage	Not automatic – by registration	
Resumption	Possible (conditions)	YES

---

[75] ZIMBABWE: *Citizenship of Zimbabwe Act*, 1 December 1984 (as of 1990); *Constitution of Zimbabwe*, 18 April 1980 (as of 1996) **UNHCR (internet**; *Information for Australian Citizens who hold Zimbabwe Citizenship*, Department of Foreign Affairs and Trade Australia (internet), http://www.citizenship.gov.au/info/zimbabwe.htm, consulted 22 April 2006; *Zimbabwe – Country Reports on Human Rights Practices 2005*, 8 March 2006, US Department of State (internet), http://www.state.gov/g/drl/rls/hrrpt/2005/61600.htm, consulted 22 April 2006; "Zimbabwe. Friends say stop", The Economist, 9 December 2000; "Zimbabwe. While you looked the other way", The Economist, 13 October 2001, 47; "Mugabe's foes demand extension in voting", The Sydney Morning Herald, 11 March 2002, 7; "Obituary. Sir Garfield Todd", The Economist, 19 October 2002, 82; "He was Rhodesia's conscience", The Sydney Morning Herald, This life, 31 October 2002, 32; "Dual citizens told to hand in passports", The Sydney Morning Herald, 15 May 2000, 12; "White's voting rights cut", The Dominion (Wellington, New Zealand), 27 May 2000, 5; Hecker, *Das Staatsangehörigkeitsrecht des anglophonen Afrika*.

Event	Law	Condition is renunciation/ loss of other nationality
State service	Honorary citizenship	NO
Parent acquires nationality	Parent may apply for minor child's registration	YES
Spouse acquires nationality	No direct effect	
Registration	Of certain categories of persons (conditions)	YES
Special considerations	Birth in Zimbabwe to married father or unmarried mother who subsequently becomes permanent resident ("by bush")	YES (*conditional*)

Withdrawal/loss of nationality

Event	Law	Consequence of event is loss of nationality
Renunciation	By adults of sound mind	YES
(*unless national of country at war "declared or not"*)	Parent or guardian on behalf of minor child	
	By other person on behalf of citizen under legal disability	
Attribution at birth conditional	If foreign nationality is possessed, automatic deprivation one year after majority, unless renounced	YES
Naturalisation elsewhere	Voluntary acquisition (including if naturalisation is "deemed to have been granted")	YES
Adoption by a foreigner		
Marriage to a foreigner	(*If foreign nationality thereby acquired, one year after the date of the marriage, unless renounced*)	YES (*condition*)
Spouse acquires other nationality	No direct effect	
Parent acquires other nationality	Minor children citizens by registration only	YES
Resumption of previous nationality		YES

Event	Law	**Consequence of event is loss of nationality**
Service to foreign state	(see punitive deprivation)	
Other attribution of nationality	Any voluntary acquisition of foreign nationality (excluding marriage)	YES
	Any other attribution of nationality provokes loss one year after the acquisition, unless renounced	
(Punitive) deprivation	If citizenship by registration or naturalisation and foreign nationality not renounced one year after registration, fraud in acquisition, disloyalty or disaffection, acts prejudicial or likely to be prejudicial to public safety/order, assistance to the enemy, certain sentences/convictions	POSSIBLE
	For citizens by registration, 7 years' absence (conditions)	

General attitude toward multiple nationality

The Citizenship Act contains a specific prohibition on dual nationality, stating that "*no citizen of Zimbabwe who is of full age and sound mind shall be entitled to be a citizen of a foreign country*". The provision is backed by comprehensive norms to deprive any multiple national of Zimbabwean nationality past age 19, by which time any foreign nationality acquired automatically or otherwise must be lost, or deprivation of Zimbabwean nationality is automatic. Although deprivation of nationality is in all cases automatic, the Act allows for the President to exempt individuals from any of its provisions, including those related to the prohibition on multiple nationality. The government has reportedly often made use of the Citizenship Act's discretion and open provisions to deprive, or threaten to deprive, various citizens of their nationality, because they have been deemed to possess another nationality, although they may in fact not. It was reported that up to 86,000 Zimbabweans may in fact possess United Kingdom nationality of right. During elections in 2002, a presidential decree, later ruled unconstitutional by courts, prevented many persons, usually whites, from voting, if they could not prove that they had renounced any possible multiple nationality, or that they were not eligible for another country's nationality. The Act likewise contains a provision that failure to return to Zimbabwe in any five-year period results in loss of nationality. It was amended in 2003 such that the renunciation provision does not apply to persons born in Zimbabwe with parents from South African Development Community (SADC) countries or who were born in SADC countries of Zimbabwean parents.

Recognition of Multiple Nationality

Zimbabwe doesnot recognize multiple nationality, except for the purpose of depriving citizens of their Zimbabwean nationality. There is no evidence of diplomatic/consular protection of any de-facto multiple nationals. Use of a foreign passport to enter or leave Zimbabwe indicates loss of Zimbabwean nationality for all but under 19 year-olds who acquired foreign nationality by operation of law.

Bibliography*

PUBLICATIONS

Abiew, Francis Kofi. The evolution of the doctrine and practice of humanitarian intervention. The Hague: Kluwer Law International, 1999.

Abu-Laban, Yasmeen. "Reconstructing an inclusive citizenship for a new millennium: globalization, migration and difference", International Politics (2000) vol. 37, no. 4, 509–26.

Agence France Presse. "Royal cheesed off in Danish blue", The Australian, 7 February 2002, 7.

Agnew, Christine L. "Expatriation, double taxation, and treaty override: who is eating crow now?", The University of Miami Inter-American Law Review (1996) vol. 28, no. 1, 69–94.

Agrawala, S. K., and M. Koteswara Rao. "Nationality and international law in Indian perspective", in Nationality and international law in Asian perspective, edited by Ko Swan Sik. Dordrecht: Martinus Nijhoff Publishers, 1990, 65–123.

Alcorn, Gay. "Locked away in Guantanamo Bay", The Age, 22 May 2002 (internet), http://www.theage.com.au/articles/2002/05/21/1021882051530.html, consulted 1 April 2006.

Aleinikoff, T. Alexander, and Douglas Klusmeyer. Citizenship policies for an age of migration. Washington, DC: Carnegie Endowment for International Peace, 2002.

——. "Plural nationality: facing the future in a migratory world", in Citizenship today. Global perspectives and practices, edited by T. Alexander Aleinikoff and Douglas Klusmeyer. Washington: Carnegie Endowment for International Peace, 2001, 63–88.

Aleinikoff, T. Alexander, and Rubén Rumbaut. "Terms of belonging: are models of membership self-fulfilling prophecies?", Georgetown Immigration Law Journal (1998) vol. 13, no. 1, 1–24.

Alghasi, Ibrahim Abdul-Karim. "Die Staatsangehörigkeit in den Bundesstaaten, im Staatenbund und in der Staatengemeinschaft, angeführt als Beispiel: Die Staatsangehörigkeit in den arabischen Staaten", dissertation presented at the Julius-Maximilians-Universität Würzburg. Würzburg: Julius-Maximilians-Universität, 1965.

---

* This bibliography does not include references to sources of national legislation and policy used to compile the Appendix on national legislation. These are listed separately, in the endnotes to the Appendix.

Allen, William B. "The truth about citizenship: an outline", Cardozo Journal of International and Comparative Law (1996) vol. 4, no. 2, 355–372.

Alpher, Joseph, and Khalil Shikaki. "Concept paper: The Palestinian refugee problem and the right of return", Middle East Policy (1999), vol. 6, no. 3, 167–189.

Altmaier, Peter. "Integration als Gestaltungsaufgabe. Zur aktuellen Diskussion über die Reform des Staatsangehörigkeitsrechts", paper presented at the conference: Hohenheimer Tage zum Ausländerrecht 1999 und 5. Migrationspolitisches Forum, Hohenheim 1999. Edited by Klaus Barwig and Gisbert Brinkmann, Kay Hailbronner, Bertold Huber, Christine Kreuzer, Klaus Lörcher, Christoph Schumacher. Hohenheim: Nomos Verlagsgesellschaft, 1999, 133–138.

Álvarez Rodríguez, Aurelia. Guía de la nacionalidad española. Madrid: Ministerio de Trabajo y Asuntos Sociales, 1996.

——. Nacionalidad y emigración. Madrid: La Ley, 1990.

Ansay, Tugrul. "Die Behandlung von Doppelstaatern in der Türkei", paper presented at the conference: Hohenheimer Tage zum Ausländerrecht 1999 und 5. Migrationspolitisches Forum, Hohenheim 1999. Edited by Klaus Barwig and Gisbert Brinkmann, et al. Hohenheim: Nomos Verlagsgesellschaft, 1999, 199–205.

Arellano García, Carlos. "Los peligros de la doble nacionalidad", paper presented at the conference: La doble nacionalidad, Ciudad de México 1995. Ciudad de México: Miguel Ángel Porrúa Librero-Editor, 1995, 59–121.

Arendt, Hannah. "200 Jahre Amerikanische Revolution", in Zur Zeit. Politische Essays, edited by Marie Luise Knott. Berlin: Rotbuch-Verlag, 1986.

——. "Home to Roost: A Bicentennial Address", New York Review of Books (25 June 1975), 3–6.

——. The origins of totalitarianism. New York: Harcourt, Brace & Company, 1973.

——. A report on the banality of evil. Eichmann in Jerusalem. New York: Penguin Books, 1964.

"Argentinean commander refuses to accept the service of a Dutch soldier", 7 July 1998, Hellenic Resources Network (internet), http://www.hri.org/news/Cyprus/tcpr/1998/98-07-08.tcpr.html, consulted 25 May 2006.

Arlović, Mato. "Croatian citizenship and the peaceful reintegration of Eastern Slavonia, Baranja and Western Srijem", Croatian Critical Law Review (1998) vol. 3, no. 3, 271–284.

Arnaoutoglou, Ilias. Ancient Greek laws. A sourcebook. London: Routledge, 1998.

Arnell, P. "The case for nationality based jurisdiction", International and Comparative Law Quarterly (2001) vol. 50, 955–962.

Aron, Raymond. "Kann es eine multinationale Staatsbürgerschaft geben?", in Transnationale Staatsbürgerschaft, edited by Heinz Kleger. Frankfurt: Campus Verlag, 1997, 23–41.

"Asylum seekers to swear allegiance", The Age, 8 February 2002, 9.

Aznar Sánchez, Juan. La doble nacionalidad. Madrid: Editorial Montecorvo, 1977.

Bachellier, Marie-Noëlle. "Rapport de synthèse sur la nationalité", paper presented at the conference: Nationalité, minorités et succession d'états en europe de l'est, Prague, 22–24 September 1994. Edited by Emmanuel Decaux and Alain Pellet. Cedin Paris X Nanterre Cahiers Internationaux. Paris: Montchrestien, 1996, 49–61.

Baker, Mark. "Fiery tug-of-war over Angkor Wat", The Sydney Morning Herald, 31 January 2003, 7.

Baldwin, Suzy (ed.). "Getty fortune brought grief, then grace. Sir J. Paul Getty II, Philanthropist", The Sydney Morning Herald, 24 April 2003, 38.

Barbalet, J. M. Citizenship. Rights, struggle and class inequality. Edited by Frank Parkin, Concepts in the social sciences. Stony Stratford (UK): Open University Press, 1988.

Barbieri Jr., William A. Ethics of citizenship. Durham: Duke University Press, 1998.

Bariatti, Stefania. La disciplina giuridica della cittadinanza italiana. Vol. 2, L'Italia e la vita giuridica internazionale. Milano: Giuffrè Editore, 1996.

——. "Nationalité: Italie", in *Juris-Classeur Nationalité*, edited by Michel Verwilghen and Charles L. Closset. Paris: Éditions du Juris-Classeur, 1994.

Barrière, Louis-Augustin. "À propos de la pluralité des nationalités", paper presented at the conference: *"Être français aujourd'hui . . ." Premier bilan de la mise en oeuvre du nouveau droit de la nationalité*, Lyon 1995. Edited by Hugues Fulchiron. Lyon: Presses Universitaires de Lyon, 1995, 197–203.

Barrington, Lowell W. "The making of citizenship policy in the Baltic states", Georgetown Immigration Law Journal (1999) vol 13, no. 2, 159–199.

——. "Nations, states, and citizens: an explanation of the citizenship policies in Estonia and Lithuania", Review of Central and East European Law (1995) vol. 21, no. 2, 103–48.

Bartlett, Katharine T. "Feminist legal methods", in *Feminist legal theory – readings in law and gender*, edited by Katharine T. Bartlett and Rosanne Kennedy. Boulder: Westview Press, 1991, 370–403.

Bartlett, Katharine T., and Rosanne Kennedy. "Introduction", in *Feminist legal theory – readings in law and gender*, edited by Katharine T. Bartlett and Rosanne Kennedy. Boulder: Westview Press, 1991, 1–11.

Bar-Yaacov, Nissim. Dual nationality. London: Stevens & Sons Ltd., 1961.

Baty, Théodore. "La double nationalité est-elle possible?", Revue de droit international et de législation comparée (1926) vol. 7, 622–632.

Baubök, Rainer, and Dilek Çinar. "La législation sur la nationalié et la naturalisation en Autriche", in *Nationalité et citoyenneté en Europe*, edited by Patrick Weil and Randall Hansen. Paris: Éditions La Découverte, 1999, 265–80.

——. "Nationality law and naturalisation in Austria", in *Towards a European nationality. Citizenship, immigration and nationality law in the EU*, edited by Randall Hansen and Patrick Weil. Houndmills: Palgrave, 2001, 255–72.

Baudez, Marcel. Essai sur la condition des étrangers en Chine. Paris: A. Pedone, 1913.

BBC News. "Albright tipped for Czech Presidency", 28 February 2000 (internet), http://news.bbc.co.uk/1/hi/world/ europe/659215.stm, consulted 29 March 2006.

——. "Briton William Beausire 'returns' to haunt Pinochet", 1998 (internet), http://news.bbc.co.uk/1/hi/special_report/1998/10/98/the_pinochet_file/201678.stm, consulted 22 July 2003.

——. "Switzerland calls for Pinochet extradition", 1998 (internet), http://www.bbc.co.uk/1/hi/uk/201994.stm, consulted 22 July 2003.

Beaud, Olivier. "The question of nationality within a federation: a neglected issue in nationality law", in *Dual nationality, social rights and federal citizenship in the U.S. and Europe. The reinvention of citizenship*, edited by Randall Hansen and Patrick Weil. New York: Berghahn Books, 2002, 314–30.

Beedham, Brian. "A survey of the new geopolitics. The road to 2050. False heaven", The Economist, 31 July 1999, 4–7.

Bendix, Ludwig. Fahnenflucht und Verletzung der Wehrpflicht durch Auswanderung. Edited by Georg Jellinek and Gerhard Anschütz, Staats- und völkerrechtliche Abhandlungen. Leipzig: Verlag von Duncker & Humblot, 1906.

Benedek, Wolfgang. "Nationality decrees in Tunis and Morocco (Advisory Opinion)", in *Encyclopedia of Public International Law*, edited by Rudolf Bernhardt and Max Planck Institute for Comparative Public Law and International Law. Amsterdam: Elsevier, 1981, 510–11.

Bennet, James. "Israel's fresh limit on Palestinians", International Herald Tribune, 2003 (internet), http://www.iht.com/articles/104091.htm, consulted 1 August 2003.

Berlingò, Salvatore. "Cadre général proposé aux rapporteurs nationaux", paper presented at the conference: *Citizens and believers in the countries of the European Union. A double membership to the test of secularization and globalization*, Università per Stranieri, Reggio Calabria (Italy) 1998. Milano: Dott. A. Giuffrè Editore, 1998, 1–4.

Berman, Nathaniel. "The Nationality Decrees Case, or, of intimacy and consent", Leiden Journal of International Law (2000) vol. 13, no. 1, 265–295.

Bermond, Daniel. "La nationalité française: und histoire à rebondissements (interview with Patrick Weil)", Label France (2003) vol. 49, Janvier-Mars, 34–36.

Bernhardt, Rudolf, ed. Encyclopedia of public international law. Vol. 4. Amsterdam: Elsevier, 2000.

Bernier, Ivan. International legal aspects of federalism. London: Longman Group Ltd., 1973.

Bertossi, Christophe. Les frontières de la citoyenneté en europe – nationalité, résidence, appartenance. Paris: L'Harmattan, 2001.

Bhabha, Jacqueline, and Sue Shutter. Women's movement: women under immigration, nationality and refugee law. Stoke-on-Trent: Trentham Books, 1994.

Bickerton, Ian. "Dutch murders result in tighter terrorism laws", Financial Times, 15 July 2005, 2.

Biehler, Gernot. "Ausländerrecht und jüdische Emigration aus der früheren Sowjetunion", in *Staat – Souveränität – Verfassung*. Festschrift für Helmut Quaritsch zum 70. Geburtstag, edited by Dietrich Murswiek, Ulrich Storost and Heinrich A. Wolff. Berlin: Duncker & Humblot, 2000, 265–83.

Bigler-Eggenberger, Margrith. "Bürgerrechtsverlust durch Heirat: Ein dunkler Fleck in der jüngeren Schweizer Rechtsgeschichte", Recht (1999) vol. 2, 33–42.

Binyon, Michael. "Mob boss outsmarted KGB, ripped off Jews. The Mr Biggest of the Moscow underworld has had a chequered career", The Australian, 24 August 1999, 12.

Bishop, Matthew. "Globalisation and tax. The mystery of the vanishing taxpayer", The Economist, 29 January 2000, Insert 1–18.

Blackman, Jeffrey L. "State successions and statelessness: the emerging right to an effective nationality under international law", Michigan Journal of International Law (1998) vol. 19, 1141–1194.

Blackshield, Tony, George Williams, and Brian Fitzgerald. Australian constitutional law and theory. Commentary and materials. Annandale (NSW): The Federation Press, 1996.

Blaser, Pierre Michel. "La nationalité et la protection juridique internationale de l'individu", dissertation presented at the Université de Neuchâtel, 1962. Lausanne: Imprimerie Rencontre, 1962.

Blumenwitz, Dieter. "Die minderheitenschutzrechtlichen Anforderungen der EU hinsichtlich des Beitritts der ost- und ostmitteleuropäischen Staaten", in *Fortschritte im Beitrittsprozess der Staaten Ostmittel-, Ost und Südosteuropas zur Europäischen Union. Regelungen und Konsequenzen für die deutschen Volksgruppen und Minderheiten*, edited by Dieter Blumenwitz, Gilbert H. Gorr and Dietrich Murswiek. Köln: Verlag Wissenschaft und Politik, 1999, 25–36.

Bojārs, Juris. "The citizenship regulation of the Republic of Latvia", Humanities and Social Sciences: Latvia (1995) vol. 1, no. 6, 4–28.

Bökel, Gerhard. "Zur Situation ausländischer Jugendlicher – eine Zukunft in Deutschland?", Zeitschrift für Ausländerrecht und Ausländerpolitik (März 1998) no. 2, 51–54.

Boll, Alfred Michael. "Nationality and obligations of loyalty in international and municipal law", The Australian Year Book of International Law (2004) vol. 24, 37–63.

——. "The Asian values debate and its relevance to international humanitarian law", International Review of the Red Cross (2001) vol. 841, 45–58.

Bommes, Michaèl. "Migration and ethnicity in the national welfare-state", in *Migration, citi-*

zenship and ethno-national identities in the European Union, edited by Marco Martiniello. Aldershot: Avebury, 1995, 120.

Bonnet, Vincent. "Les obstacles à l'acquisition de la nationalité française du conjoint et la question de la fraude", paper presented at the conference: "Être français aujourd'hui . . . Premier bilan de la mise en oeuvre du nouveau droit de la nationalité", Lyon 1995. Edited by Hugues Fulchiron. Lyon: Presses Universitaires de Lyon, 1995, 101–111.

Bosniak, Linda. "Denationalizing citizenship", in Citizenship today. Global perspectives and practices, edited by T. Alexander Aleinikoff and Douglas Klusmeyer. Washington: Carnegie Endowment for International Peace, 2001, 237–52.

——. "Multiple nationality and the postnational transformation of citizenship", in Rights and duties of dual nationals. Evolution and prospects, edited by David A. Martin and Kay Hailbronner. The Hague: Kluwer Law International, 2003, 27–48.

Boudreaux, Richard. "Fallen rock star flies home to face the music in sex scandal", The Sydney Morning Herald, 23 December 2002, 7.

Bourbousson, Edouard. Traité général de la nationalité dans les cinq parties du monde. Paris: Recueil Sirey, 1931.

Bradsher, Keith. "China formally arrests Hong Kong reporter as spy", International Herald Tribune, 6–7 August 2005, 2.

Braga, Sevold. "Zur Dogmatik des Staatsangehörigkeitsrechts", in Völkerecht – Recht der Internationalen Organisationen – Weltwirtschaftsrecht – Law of Nations – Law of International Organizations – World's Economic Law – Festschrift für Ignaz Seidl-Hohenveldern – Liber amicorum honouring Ignaz Seidl-Hohenveldern, edited by Karl-Heinz Böckstiegel, Hans-Ernst Folz, Jörg Manfred Mössner and Karl Zemanek. Köln: Carl Heymanns Verlag, 1988, 35–49.

Bredbenner, Candice Lewis. A nationality of her own – women, marriage, and the law of citizenship. Berkeley: University of California Press, 1998.

Breunig, Günter. Staatsangehörigkeit und Entkolonisierung. Die Abgrenzung des Staatsvolkes bei der Verselbständigung der frankophonen Staaten Schwarzafrikas unter völkerrechtlichen Gesichtspunkten, Schriften zum Völkerrecht. Berlin: Duncker & Humblot, 1974.

Bribosia, Emmanuelle, Emmanuelle Dardenne, Paul Magnette, and Anne Weyembergh, eds. Union européenne et nationalités. Bruxelles: Bruylant, 1999.

Bribosia, Emmanuelle and Emmanuelle Dardenne. "Citoyenneté – Droits fondamentaux – Libre circulation des personnes, asile, immigration: Bilan après le Traité d'Amsterdam", in L'Année Sociale 97. Bruxelles: Université Libre de Bruxelles, 1998, 307–325.

"Bring Hicks, Habib home to justice", The Sydney Morning Herald, 10 May 2002, 12.

British Helsinki Human Rights Group. "Nationalism and citizenship in Latvia", East European Human Rights Review (2000) vol. 6, nos. 1 and 2, 1–31.

Brochmann, Grete. European integration and immigration from third countries. Oslo: Scandinavian University Press, 1996.

Broughton, Philip Delves. "Picasso not the patriot he painted", The Sydney Morning Herald, 19 May 2003, 10.

Brown, Bartram S. "Nationality and internationality in international humanitarian law", Stanford Journal of International Law (1998) vol. 34, no. 2, 347–406.

Brown, DeNeen L. and Dana Priest. "Chretien protests deportation of Canadian", The Washington Post, 6 November 2003, A24.

Browne, Thomas. "The case of allegiance to a King in possession", in Classics of English legal history. New York: Garland Publishing, Inc., 1978, 1690.

Brownlie, Ian. Principles of public international law. Fifth ed. Oxford: Clarendon Press, 1998.

——. "The relations of nationality in public international law", The British Yearbook of International Law (1963) vol. 39, 284–364.

Brubaker, Rogers. Citizenship and nationhood in France and Germany. Cambridge (Massachusetts): Harvard University Press, 1992.

Brubaker, William Rogers. "Citizenship and naturalization: policies and politics", in *Immigration and the politics of citizenship in Europe and North America*, edited by William Rogers Brubaker. Lanham: University Press of America, 1989, 99–127.

——. "Introduction", in *Immigration and the politics of citizenship in Europe and North America*, edited by William Rogers Brubaker. Lanham: University Press of America, 1989, 1–27.

Bruschi, Christian. "L'acquisition de la nationalité française à raison du mariage", paper presented at the conference: *"Être français aujourd'hui . . . Premier bilan de la mise en oeuvre du nouveau droit de la nationalité"*, Lyon 1995. Edited by Hugues Fulchiron. Lyon: Presses Universitaires de Lyon, 1995, 81–88.

Bučar, Ana, and Mirjana Miličič. "Case analysis in the Republic of Slovenia", Croatian Critical Law Review (1998) vol. 3, no. 1–2, 215–220.

Bultmann, Peter Friedrich. "Dual nationality and naturalisation policies in the German Länder", in *Dual nationality, social rights and federal citizenship in the U.S. and Europe. The reinvention of citizenship*, edited by Randall Hansen and Patrick Weil. New York: Berghahn Books, 2002, 136–57.

Bundesministerium der Finanzen (Ministry of Finance, Germany). "Leistungen der öffentlichen Hand auf dem Gebiet der Wiedergutmachung – Stand 31. Dezember 2004", 2004 (internet), http://www.bundesfinanz ministerium.de/cln_04/nn_3792/DE/Finanz__und__Wirtschaftspolitik/ Vermoegensrecht__und__Entschaedigungen/Kriegsfolgen__und__Wiedergutmachung/8391.html, consulted 29 March 2006.

Butler, William E. Russian law. Oxford: Oxford University Press, 1999.

Butler, William E., and Jane E. Henderson, eds. Russian legal texts – the foundations of a rule-of-law state and a market economy. The Hague: Simmonds & Hill; Kluwer Law International, 1998.

James Button, "Secret Tory lender is Australian", The Sydney Morning Herald, 28 March 2006 (internet), http://www.smh.com.au/articles/2006/03/27/1143441083323.html, consulted 28 March 2006.

Byrnes, Andrew, and Johannes Chan. "The British Nationality (Hong Kong) Act 19900", in *Public Law and Human Rights. A Hong Kong Sourcebook*, edited by Andrew Byrnes and Johannes Chan. Hong Kong: Butterworths, 1993, 74–80.

Cairncross, Frances. "The longest journey. A survey of migration", The Economist, 2 November 2002, Insert.

"Câmara delega 31 competências em Fátima Felgueiras", Diário de Notícias (Lisbon), 24 November 2005 (internet), http://dn.sapo.pt/2005/11/24/nacional/camara_delega_competencias_ fatima_fe.html, consulted 28 March 2006.

Campbell, Dennis, and Susan Meek, eds. International immigration and nationality law. Vol. 1. The Hague: Kluwer Law International, 2001.

"Canada warns on tough new US law", The Sydney Morning Herald, 1 November 2002, 9.

Cançado Trindade, Antônio Augusto. Tratado de direito internacional dos direitos humanos. Vol. 1. Porto Alegre: Sergio Antonio Fabris Editor, 1997.

——. Tratado de direito internacional dos direitos humanos. Vol. 2. Porto Alegre: Sergio Antonio Fabris Editor, 1999.

Cano Bazaga, Elena. Adopción internacional y nacionalidad española. Madrid: Mergablum, 2001.

Capatina, Octavian. "Nationalité: Roumanie", in *Juris-Classeur Nationalité*, edited by Michel J. Verwilghen and Charles L. Closset. Paris: Éditions du Juris-Classeur, 1996.

Caporal, Stéphane. "Citoyenneté et nationalité en droit public interne", paper presented at the conference: *De la citoyenneté*, Faculté de droit et des sciences politiques de Nantes, 3–5 November 1993. Edited by Geneviève Koubi. Nantes: LITEC, 1993, 59–68.

Carens, Joseph H. "Citizenship and civil society: what rights for residents?", in *Dual nationality, social rights and federal citizenship in the U.S. and Europe. The reinvention of citizenship*, edited by Randall Hansen and Patrick Weil. New York: Berghahn Books, 2002, 100–18.

——. "Why naturalization should be easy: a response to Noah Pickus", in *Immigration and citizenship in the twenty-first century*, edited by Noah M. J. Pickus. Lanham: Rowman & Littlefield, 1998, 141–46.

Carrington, Kerry, Stephen Sherlock and Nathan Hancock, "The East Timorese asylum seekers: legal issues and policy implications ten years on", Current Issues Brief no. 17 2002–03, Parliament of Australia Parliamentary Library (internet), http://www.aph.gov.au/library/pubs/CIB/2002–03/03cib17.htm, consulted 7 May 2006.

Carter, Stephen L. The dissent of the governed. A meditation on law, religion, and loyalty. Cambridge, Massachusetts: Harvard University Press, 1998.

Cassese, Antonio. International law. Oxford: Oxford University Press, 2001.

Castles, Stephen, and Gianni Zappalà. "The rights and obligations of immigrant citizens and non-citizens in Australia", in *Citizenship in a global world. Comparing citizenship rights for aliens*, edited by Atsushi Kondo. Houndmills (UK): Palgrave, 2001, 136–57.

Castro, F. de. "La nationalité la double nationalité et la supra-nationalité", Recueil des cours, Académie de droit international, (1962) vol. 102 (1961), no. 1, 515–634.

Chan, Johannes. "Nationality", in *Human Rights in Hong Kong*, edited by Raymond Wacks. Hong Kong: Oxford University Press, 1992, 470–508.

Chan, Johannes M. M. "Hong Kong: an analysis of the British nationality proposals", Immigration and nationality law and practice (1990) vol. 4, 57–62.

——. "The right to a nationality as a human right. The current trend towards recognition", Human Rights Law Journal (1991) vol. 12, no. 1–2, 1–14.

Chang, Hyo Sang. "Nationality in divided countries: a Korean perspective", in *Nationality and international law in Asian perspective*, edited by Ko Swan Sik. Dordrecht: Martinus Nijhoff Publishers, 1990, 255–308.

Chang, Jaw-ling Joanne. "Settlement of the Macao issue: distinctive features of Beijing's negotiating behavior", Case Western Reserve Journal of International Law (1988) vol. 20, 253–278.

Charlesworth, Hilary. "The sex of the state in international law", in *Sexing the subject of law*, edited by Ngaire Naffine and Rosemary J Owens. Sydney: LBC, 1997, 251–68.

Charlesworth, Hilary, and Christine Chinkin. The boundaries of international law – a feminist analysis. Edited by Dominic McGoldrick, Melland Schill Studies in International Law. Manchester: Manchester University Press, 2000.

Chen, Tung-Pi. "The nationality law of the People's Republic of China and the overseas Chinese in Hong Kong, Macao and South-east Asia", New York Law School Journal of International and Comparative Law (1984) vol. 5, 281–325.

Chesterman, John, and Brian Galligan. Citizens without rights. Aborigines and Australian citizenship. Cambridge, United Kingdom: Cambridge University Press, 1997.

——, eds. Defining Australian citizenship – selected documents. Carlton South (Victoria): Melbourne University Press, 1999.

Ching, Frank. "Chinese nationality in the Basic Law", in *The Basic Law and Hong Kong's future*, edited by Peter Wesley-Smith and Albert H. Y. Chen. Hong Kong: Butterworths, 1988.

Chiu, Hungdah. "Nationality and international law in Chinese perspective – with special reference to the period before 1950 and the practice of the administration in Taipei", in *Nationality and international law in Asian perspective*, edited by Ko Swan Sik. Dordrecht: Martinus Nijhoff Publishers, 1990, 27–64.

Clark, Bruce. "A survey of Greece. Roll out the welcome mat", The Economist, 12 October 2002, Supplement, 7.

Clerici, Roberta. "Italian nationality and the situation of immigrants", paper presented at the conference: *Citizenship and immigration*, University of Milano, Law Faculty, 1996. Edited by Vincenzo Ferrari, Thomas Heller, Elena de Tullio. Milano: Dott. A. Giuffrè Editore, 1998, 45–52.

———. "Recenti orientamenti di alcuni stati europei nei confronti della doppia cittadinanza", in *Collisio Legum. Studi di diritto internazionale privato per Gerardo Broggini*. Milano: Dott. A. Giuffrè Editore, 1997, 101–18.

Closa, Carlos. "Das Konzept der Staatsbürgerschaft in den Verträgen der Europäischen Union", in *Transnationale Staatsbürgerschaft*, edited by Heinz Kleger. Frankfurt: Campus Verlag, 1997, 191–207.

———. "EU citizenship at the 1996 IGC", in *Dual nationality, social rights and federal citizenship in the U.S. and Europe. The reinvention of citizenship*, edited by Randall Hansen and Patrick Weil. New York: Berghahn Books, 2002, 293–313.

Close, Paul. Citizenship, Europe and change. London: Macmillan Press, 1995.

Coates, Austin. A Macao Narrative. Hong Kong: Oxford University Press, 1978.

Cochrane, George. "Honesty the best policy", The Sun-Herald, 3 November 2002, 8.

Cockburn, Alexander. Nationality: or the law relating to subjects and aliens, considered with a view to future legislation. London: William Ridgway, 1869.

Cogordan, George. La nationalité au point de vue des rapports internationaux. Paris: L. Larose, Libraire-Éditeur, 1879.

Cohen, Jerome Alan, and Hungdah Chiu. People's China and international law. A documentary study. Vol. 1. Princeton, NJ: Princeton University Press, 1973.

Cohen, Jerome Alan, and Shao-Chuan Leng. "The Sino-Indian dispute over the internment and detention of Chinese in India", in *China's practice of international law: some case studies*, edited by Jerome Alan Cohen. Cambridge, MA: Harvard University Press, 1972, 268.

Čok, Vida. "New Yugoslav citizenship", Yugoslav Law (1997) vol. 24, no. 2, 143–159.

Combs, Nancy Amoury. "On children and dual nationality: Sabet and The Islamic Republic of Iran", Leiden Journal of International Law (2000) vol. 13, no. 1, 173–191.

"A Constitution for the European Union", The Economist, 28 October 2000, 16.

"Comunidades Fórum de luso-eleitos", Correio da Manhã (Lisbon), 6 April 2005, 33.

Cook, Robin. "Foreword to Partnership for Progress and Prosperity: Britain and the Overseas Territories". Foreign & Commonwealth Office, 17 March 1999 (internet), http://www.fco.gov.uk/servlet/Front?pagename=OpenMarket/Xcelerate/ShowPage&c=Page&cid=1018028164839, consulted 2 April 2006.

Corboz, Pierre. "Nationalité: Suisse", in *Juris-Classeur Nationalité*, edited by Michel J. Verwilghen and Charles L. Closset. Paris: Éditions du Juris-Classeur, 1997.

Córdova, Roberto. "Report on multiple nationality", Yearbook of the International Law Commission (1960) vol. 1954, no. II, 42–52.

———. "Report on the elimination or reduction of statelessness", Yearbook of the International Law Commission (1959) vol. 1953, no. II, 167–195.

——. "Second report on the elimination or reduction of statelessness", Yearbook of the International Law Commission (1959) vol. 1953, no. II, 196–199.

——. "Third report on the elimination or reduction of statelessness", Yearbook of the International Law Commission (1960) vol. 1954, no. II, 26–42.

Corsi, Cecilia. "Diritti fondamentali e cittadinanza", Diritto Pubblico (2000) vol. 1, 793–816.

Cortes, Irene R. and Raphael Perpetuo M. Lotilla. "Nationality and international law from the Philippine perspective", in Nationality and international law in Asian perspective, edited by Ko Swan Sik. Dordrecht: Martinus Nijhoff Publishers, 1990, 335–422.

Costa-Lascoux, Jacqueline. "'Devenir français aujourd'hui . . .' Réflexion sur la sociologie des naturalisations", paper presented at the conference: "Être français aujourd'hui . . ." Premier bilan de la mise en oeuvre du nouveau droit de la nationalité, Lyon 1995. Edited by Hugues Fulchiron. Lyon: Presses Universitaires de Lyon, 1995, 137–159.

Council of Europe. Explanatory report on the Additional protocol to the Convention of 6 May 1963 on the reduction of cases of multiple nationality and military obligations in cases of multiple nationality. Strasbourg: Council of Europe, 1978.

——. Explanatory report on the protocol amending the Convention of 6 May 1963 on the reduction of cases of multiple nationality and military obligations in cases of multiple nationality. Strasbourg: Council of Europe, 1978.

Crawford, James. The Creation of States in International Law. Oxford: Clarendon Press, 1979.

——. "Decisions of British Courts during 1974–1975. Case No. 7. R. v. Secretary of State for the Home Department, ex parte Thakrar", The British Year Book of International Law (1977) vol. 47, 352–356.

——. The International Law Commission's articles on state responsibility. Introduction, text and commentaries. Cambridge: Cambridge University Press, 2002.

Cuniberti, Marco. "Espulsione dello straniero e libertà constituzionali", Diritto Pubblico (2000) no. 1.

——. La cittadinanza – Libertà dell'uomo e libertà del cittadino nella constituzione italiana. Vol. 18, Diritto e Istituzioni Richerche Dirette da Giorgio Berti. Verona: Casa Editrice Dott. Antonio Milani, 1997.

Cuttler, S. H. The law of treason and treason trials in later medieval France. Cambridge: Cambridge University Press, 1981.

Czaplinski, Wladyslaw. "Réactions relatives à la première partie", paper presented at the conference: Nationalité, minorités et succession d'états en europe de l'est, Prague, 22–24 September 1994. Cedin Paris X Nanterre Cahiers Internationaux 10. Edited by Emmanuel Decaux and Alain Pellet. Paris: Montchrestien, 1996, 63–66.

Dagrella, Jerry A. "Wealthy Americans planning to renounce their citizenship to save on taxes have a new problem to consider: this time Congress means business", The Transnational Lawyer (2000) vol. 13, no. 2, 363–390.

Dahm, Georg, Jost Delbrück, and Rüdiger Wolfrum. "Kapitel 14: Der einzelne in seinem Verhältnis zum Staat: Die Staatsangehörigkeit", in Völkerrecht. I: Die Grundlagen. Die Völkerrechtssubujekte. Teilband 2. Berlin: Walter de Gruyter, 2002, 17–103.

D'Amato, Gianni. "Gelebte Nation und Einwanderung. Zur Trans-Nationalisierung von Nationalstaaten durch Immigrantenpolitik am Beispiel der Schweiz", in Transnationale Staatsbürgerschaft, edited by Heinz Kleger. Frankfurt: Campus Verlag, 1997, 132–157.

Davis, Madeleine. The Pinochet case. London: Institute of Latin American Studies, 2000.

Davis, Uri. Citizenship and the State – a comparative study of citizenship legislation in Israel, Jordan, Palestine, Syria and Lebanon. Reading (UK): Garnet Publishers, 1997.

de Burlet, Jacques. Nationalité des personnes physiques et décolonisation. Bruxelles: Établissements Émile Bruylant, 1975.

de Cruz, Peter. Comparative law in a changing world. Second ed. London: Cavendish Publishing Ltd., 1999.

de Groot, Gerard-René. "Access to citizenship for aliens in the Netherlands", in Citizenship in a global world. Comparing citizenship rights for aliens, edited by Atsushi Kondo. Houndmills (UK): Palgrave, 2001, 31–46.

——. "The European Convention on Nationality: a step towards a ius commune in the field of nationality law", Maastricht Journal of European and Comparative Law (2000) vol. 7, no. 2, 117–157.

——. "Loss of nationality: a critical inventory", in Rights and duties of dual nationals. Evolution and prospects, edited by David A. Martin and Kay Hailbronner. The Hague: Kluwer Law International, 2003, 201–299.

——. "The relationship between the nationality legislation of the member states of the European Union and European citizenship", in European citizenshp. An institutional challenge, edited by Massimo La Torre. The Hague: Kluwer Law International, 1998, 115–147.

——. "Towards a European Nationality Law", Electronic Journal of Comparative Law, vol. 8.3, October 2004 (internet), http://www.ejcl.org/83/art83–4.html, consulted 1 March 2006.

——. Staatsangehörigkeitsrecht im Wandel – eine rechtsvergleichende Studie über Erwerbs- und Verlustgründe der Staatsangehörigkeit. Köln: Carl Heymanns Verlag KG, 1989.

De La Brière, Yves. "La condition juridique de la Cité du Vatican", in Recueil des Cours. Paris: Librairie du Recueil Sirey, 1930, 114–163.

de La Pradelle, Géraud. "Des changements territoriaux et les effets sur les questions de nationalité", Austrian Journal of Public and International Law (1995) vol. 49, 81–88.

——. "Die doppelte Staatsangehörigkeit im französischen Recht", paper presented at the conference: Hohenheimer Tage zum Ausländerrecht 1999 und 5. Migrationspolitisches Forum, Hohenheim 1999. Edited by Klaus Barwig and Gisbert Brinkman et al. Hohenheim: NomosVerlagsgesellschaft, 1999, 221–227.

——. "Dual nationality and the French citizenship tradition", in Dual nationality, social rights and federal citizenship in the U.S. and Europe. The reinvention of citizenship, edited by Randall Hansen and Patrick Weil. New York: Berghahn Books, 2002, 191–212.

——. "Les conséquences des nouvelles règles de nationalité sur la condition des individus", paper presented at the conference: Nationalité, minorités et succession d'états en europe de l'est, Prague, 22–24 September 1994. Edited by Emmanuel Decaux and Alain Pellet. Paris: Montchresitien, 1996, 25–39.

de Lapradelle, Albert. "Introduction", in Emmerich De Vattel, The law of nations or the principles of natural law applied to the conduct and to the affairs of nations and of sovereigns. Washington: Carnegie Institution of Washington, 1916.

de Morsier, Gaston. "Étude sur la nationalité des enfants mineurs et spécialement des enfants illégitimes", thesis presented at the Université de Genève, 1895. Genève: Imprimerie Jules-Guillaume Rick, Maurice Reymond & Cie., 1895.

de Padua, Dan Albert S. "Ambiguous allegiance: multiple nationality in Asia", Philippine Law Journal (1985) vol. 60, no. 2, 239–267.

de Patoul, Philippe, Tony O'Connor, and John G. Fish. "Nationalité: Irlande", in Juris-Classeur Nationalité, edited by Michel Verwilghen and Charles L. Closset. Paris: Éditions du Juris-Classeur, 1984.

de Vasconcellos, Paulo. "Fátima Felgueiras 'vive uma vida normal e já não fala mais em voltar", Público (Lisbon), 6 May 2005, 18.

"Dealing with traitors",The Economist, 13 August 2005, 12–13.

Dean, Hartley. Welfare, law and citizenship. London: Prentice Hall Harvester Wheatsheaf, 1996.

Debard, Thierry. "La citoyenneté européenne et le traité d'Amsterdam", in *La citoyenneté européenne*, edited by Christian Philip and Panayotis Soldatos. Montréal: Université de Montréal, 2000, 263–267.

Defense Security Service (USA). Adjudicative guidelines for determining elegibility for access to classified information, 1997, (internet), http://www.dss.mil.nf/adr/adjguid/adjguidT.htm, consulted 7 July 2003.

——. Allegiance test, 1997 (internet), http://www.dss.mil/nf/adr/alleg/allegT.htm, consulted 7 July 2003.

——. Foreign influence test, 1997 (internet), http://www.dss.mil/nf/adr/forinfl/forinflT.htm, consulted 7 July 2003.

——. Foreign preference test, 1997 (internet), http://www.dss.mil/nf/adr/forpref/forprefT.htm, consulted 7 July 2003.

Degan, Vladimir-Djuro. "Commentaires", paper presented at the conference: *Nationalité, minorités et succession d'états en europe de l'est*, Prague, 22–24 September 1994. Edited by Emmanuel Decaux and Alain Pellet. Paris: Montchrestien, 1996, 67–69.

Degen, Manfred. "Perspektiven einer umfassenden Zuwanderungspolitik in der EG?", in *Zuwanderungspolitik in Europa*, edited by Hubert Heinelt. Opladen: Leske & Budrich, 1994, 162–175.

Del Vecchio, Anna Maria. "Alcuni rilievi in tema di nazionalità e di cittadinanza nel contesto internazionale", Rivista internazionale dei diritti dell'uomo (1997) vol. 10, no. 1, 7–24.

——. "La considerazione del principio di effettività nel vincolo di nazionalità e di cittadinanza doppia o plurima (e problematiche relative)", Rivista internazionale dei diritti dell'uomo (2000) vol. 13, no. 1, 11–31.

——. "Problematische derivanti dan vincolo di cittadinanza a livello internazionale (con particolare referimento alla cittadinanza originaria «Iure Soli» e «Iure Sanguinis»)", Rivista internazionale dei diritti dell'uomo (1998) vol. 11, no. 1, 669–693.

Delpérée, Francis. "De la commune à l'Europe. L'émergence d'une citoyenneté multiple", in *De l'étranger au citoyen*, edited by Paul Magnette. Paris: De Boeck & Larcier, 1997, 135–44.

——. "La citoyenneté multiple", Annales de droit de Louvain 1996 (1996) no. 1, 261–273.

Delupis, Ingrid. Bibliography of international law. Epping, Essex: Bowker, 1975.

Department of Immigration & Multicultural & Indigenous Affairs (Australia), "Loss of Australian citizenship on acquisition of another citizenship. Discussion paper on Section 17 of the Australian Citizenship Act 1948", June 2001 (internet), http://www.citizenship.gov.au/0601paper/index.htm, consulted 3 April 2006.

"Deportations planned", International Herald Tribune, 14–15 May 2005, 6.

Deutsche Botschaft – Embajada Alemana Santiago. "Hoja informativa sobre la nacionalidad alemana", (internet), http://www.santiago.diplo.de/es/04/Konsularischer__Service/Merkblatt__Staatsangeh_C3_B6rigkeit.html, consulted 30 May 2006.

Devine, Miranda. "We should stand up for our country", The Sun-Herald, 13 October 2002, 15.

Díaz Barrado, Castor M. "La protección de Españoles en el extranjero. Práctica constitucional", in *Cursos de derecho internacional de Vitoria-Gasteiz*, edited by the Departamento de Estudios Internacionales y Ciencia Política y la Facultad de Derecho Universidad del País Vasco. Bilbao: Servicio Editorial Universidad del País Vasco, 1993, 286–291.

Díaz García, Nieves. La reforma de la nacionalidad. Comentario a la Ley 18/1990, de 17 de diciembre. Madrid: Editorial Civitas, 1991.

Dieckhoff, Albrecht D. (Freiherr von). Fehlerhaft erworbene Staatsangehörigkeit im Völkerrecht. (Fall Nottebohm). Vaduz: Liechtensteiner Volksblatt, 1956.

Diggs, Dudley. "The vnlawfvlnesse of subjects taking up armes against their soveraigne, in what case soever. Together with an answer to all objections scattered in their severall bookes. And a proofe, that notwithstanding such resistance as they plead for, were not damnable, yet the present warre made upon the King is so, because those cases, in which onely some men have dared to excuse it, are evidently not now; His Majesty fighting onely to preserve himselfe, and the rights of the subjects" (1643), in Classics of English legal history in the modern era. New York: Garland Publishing, Inc. 1978.

Dimitrijevic, Voijn. "The fate of non-members of dominant nations in post-communist European countries", paper presented at the conference: Nationalité, minorités et succession d'états en europe de l'est, Prague, 22–24 September 1994. Edited by Emmanuel Decaux and Alain Pellet. Paris: Montchresitien, 1996, 139–162.

Dingu-Kyrklund, Elena. "Citizenship rights for aliens in Sweden", in Citizenship in a global world. Comparing citizenship rights for aliens, edited by Atsushi Kondo. Houndmills: Palgrave, 2001, 47–70.

"Displaced people. When is a refugee not a refugee?", The Economist, 3 March 2001, 21–23.

Doehring, Karl. "Mehrfache Staatsangehörigkeit im Völkerrecht, Europarecht und Verfassungsrecht", in Staat-Souveränität-Verfassung. Festschrift für Helmut Quaritsch zum 70. Geburtstag, edited by Dietrich Murswiek, Ulrich Storost and Heinrich A. Wolff. Berlin: Duncker & Humblot, 2000, 255–264.

Doling, Hilary. "Shock for dual nationals", The Sun-Herald, 20 January 2002, 6 (Travel).

Dominicé, Christian. "La personnalité juridique internationale du CICR", in Etudes et essais sur le droit internationale humanitaire et sur les principes de la Croix-Rouge en l'honneur de Jean Pictet. Studies and essays on international humanitarian law and Red Cross principles in honour of Jean Pictet, edited by Christophe Swinarski. Genève: Comité international de la Croix-Rouge. Martinus Nijhoff Publishers, 1984, 663–73.

Donner, Ruth. The regulation of nationality in international law. Second ed. Irvington-on-Hudson (USA): Transnational Publishers Inc., 1994.

"Doppelte Staatsbürgerschaft – ein europäischer Normalfall?", Conference organised by: Veranstaltung des Bündnis Türkischer Einwanderer e.V., 30. May 1989, Universität Hamburg. Edited by Ulrich Büschelmann. Berlin: Senatsverwaltung für Gesundheit und Soziales Berlin, 1989, 175–193.

Dugger, Celia W. "'Brain drain' is damaging world's poorest countries, study shows", International Herald Tribune, 26 October 2005, 3.

du Granrut, Claude. La citoyenneté européenne. Une application du principe de subsidiarité. Paris: Librairie Générale de Droit et de Jurisprudence, 1997.

Dubois, Bernhard. Die Frage der völkerrechtlichen Schranken landesrechtlicher Regelung der Staatsangehörigkeit. Vol. 314, Abhandlungen zum Schweizerischen Recht. Bern: Verlag Stämpfli & Cie., 1955.

Dunn, Frederick Sherwood. The diplomatic protection of Americans in Mexico. New York: Columbia University Press, 1933.

Dunn, Ross. "Citizenship Israel's new weapon in war against suicide bombers", The Sydney Morning Herald 2002, 10.

"Dupla cidadania complica relações entre Ancara e Berlim", Público (Lisboa), 13 April 2005, 17.

Dutoit, Bernard, and Simon Affolter. La nationalité de la femme mariée. Vol. 1: Europe de l'Est et pays de l'ex-URSS, Supplément 1989–1997. Genève: Librairie Droz, 1998.

Dutoit, Bernard, and Catherine Blackie. La nationalité de la femme mariée. Vol. 3: Amérique, Asie, Océanie, Supplément 1980–1992. Genève: Librairie Droz, 1993.

Dutoit, Bernard, Daniel Dumusc, Yves Gonset, and Hélène Marie-de Riedmatten. La nationalité de la femme mariée. Vol. 2: Afrique. Genève: Librairie Droz, 1976.

Dutoit, Bernard, Daniel Gay, and Terrence Vandeveld. La nationalité de la femme mariée. Vol. 3: Amérique, Asie, Océanie. Genève: Librairie Droz, 1980.

Dutoit, Bernard, and Denis Masmejan. La nationalité de la femme mariée. Vol. 2: Afrique, Supplément 1976–1990. Genève: Librairie Droz, 1991.

Dutoit, Bernard, and Christine Sattiva Spring. La nationalité de la femme mariée. Vol. 1: Europe – supplément 1973–1989. Genève: Librairie Droz, 1990.

Dutter, Barbie. "Tongans hunting a 'natural-born fool' and $40m", The Sun-Herald, 7 October 2000, 56.

Dzialoszynski, Salo. "Die Bancroft-Verträge", dissertation presented at the Königlichen Friedrich-Wilhelms-Universität zu Breslau, 1913. Breslau: Königlichen Friedrich-Wilhelms-Universität, 1913.

"An earlier foreign war. They fought Franco, in Abe's name", The Economist, 3 May 2003, 33.

Echezarreta Ferrer, María Teresa, ed. Legislación sobre nacionalidad. Third ed. Madrid: Tecnos, 1999.

Edwards, R. Randle, Louis Henkin, and Andrew J. Nathan. Human rights in contemporary China. New York: Columbia University Press, 1986.

Eggerton (Baron Ellesmere and Viscount Brackley), Thomas. "The speech of the Lord Chancellor of England, in the Eschequer Chamber, touching the Post-nati" (1609), in Classics of English legal history in the modern era. New York: Garland Publishing, Inc., 1978.

Ehrlich, Kurt. "Über Staatsangehörigkeit – zugleich ein Beitrag zur Theorie des öffentlich-rechtlichen Vertrages und der subjektiven öffentlichen Rechte", dissertation presented at the Universität Zürich, 1929. Aarau (Switzerland): Graphische Werkstätten H. R. Sauerländer & Co., 1929.

Eichhofer, André. "Die Aufnahme jüdischer Emigranten aus der ehemaligen Sowjetunion als Kontingentflüchtlinge (mit Berücksichtigung des Zuwanderungsgesetzes)", paper presented at the Universität Trier Institut für Rechtspolitik, 2002 (internet), http://www.irp.uni-trier.de/13_Eichhofer.pdf, consulted 29 March 2006.

Ekşi, Nuray. "Consequences of dual nationality for employment, property ownership and other rights and duties under Turkish law", in Rights and duties of dual nationals. Evolution and prospects, edited by David A. Martin and Kay Hailbronner. The Hague: Kluwer Law International, 2003, 375–382.

———. "Political rights of dual nationals in Turkish law", in Rights and duties of dual nationals. Evolution and prospects, edited by David A. Martin and Kay Hailbronner. The Hague: Kluwer Law International, 2003, 153–156.

Elias, O. A., and C. L. Lim. The paradox of consensualism in international law. Vol. 31, Developments in international law. The Hague: Kluwer Law International, 1998.

Elkin, M. "Court gives Spanish judiciary right to try any foreign genocide", El País (English edition with the International Herald Tribune), 6 October 2005, 1.

Endacott, G. B. Government and people in Hong Kong 1841–1962. Hong Kong: Hong Kong University Press, 1964.

Erasmus, G. "South African citizenship in a constitutional context", Journal for Juridical Studies (1998) vol. 23, no. 2, 1–19.

Ersbøll, Eva. "Le droit de la nationalité en Scandinavie: Danemark, Finlande et Suède", in *Nationalité et citoyenneté en Europe*, edited by Patrick Weil and Randall Hansen. Paris: Éditions La Découverte, 1999, 239–263.

———. "Nationality law in Denmark, Finland and Sweden", in *Towards a European nationality. Citizenship, immigration and nationality law in the EU*, edited by Randall Hansen and Patrick Weil. Houndmills: Palgrave, 2001, 230–54.

Espinar Vicente, José María. La nacionalidad y la extranjería en el sistema jurídico español. Madrid: Editorial Civitas, 1994.

Esplugues Mota, Carlos, Guillermo Palao Moreno, and Manuel de Lorenzo Segrelles. Nacionalidad y extranjería. València: Tirant Lo Blanch, 2001.

Euripides. "The Medea", in *Euripides I*, edited by David Greene and Richmond Lattimore. Chicago: University of Chicago Press, 1955, 56–108.

———. "The Medea" (excerpt from), Refugees (2000) vol. 3, no. 120, cover.

European Commission for Democracy through Law. "Consequences of state succession for nationality". Strasbourg: Council of Europe, 1996.

European Union. "Citizenship of the Union. Diplomatic and consular protection", 2003 (internet), http://europa.eu.int/scadplus/leg/en/lvb/l14010a.htm, consulted 8 August 2003.

Ewing, Alfred Cyril. The individual, the state, and world government. New York: The Macmillan Company, 1947.

Farber, Daniel A., and Suzanna Sherry. Beyond all reason – the radical assault on truth in American law. New York: Oxford University Press, 1997.

"Fate for former Portuguese soldiers unclear", Dili Suara Timor Lorosae, 16 March 2005 (author's translation from Indonesian).

Fatouros, A. A. "National legal persons in international law", in *Encyclopedia of Public International Law*, edited by Rudolf Bernhardt and Max Planck Institute for Comparative Public Law and International Law. Amsterdam: Elsevier, 1987, 495–501.

"Fear of China. China crisis", The Economist, 7 June 2003, 59.

Feer, Robert Ernest. "Die mehrfache Staatsangehörigkeit natürlicher Personen", dissertation presented at the Universität Zürich, 1955.

Ferayoli, Luidgi. "Beyond sovereignty and citizenship. For a world constitutionalism", Savremenno Pravo [Contemporary Law] (1995) vol. 6 [in Bulgarian].

Fernandes, Anacleto de Magalhães. O direito da igualdade entre Portugal e Brasil. São Paulo: Editôra Juriscrédi Ltda., 1972.

Fernández Marcane, Luis. Contribución al estudio de la doble nacionalidad de los hijos de Españoles nacidos en América. La Habana: Imprente "El Siglo XX", 1924.

Fernández Rozas, José Carlos. Derecho español de la nacionalidad. Madrid: Editorial Technos, 1987.

Field, Michael. "Jester fools island kingdom", Fiji Times Weekend, 20 October 2001, 8.

Fionda, Julia. "Legal concepts of childhood: an introduction", in *Legal concepts of childhood*, edited by Julia Fionda. Oxford: Hart Publishing, 2001, 3–17.

Firth, Anson. "The status of aliens in Malaya, Fiji, Fanning and Washington Islands, and Tonga", in *The legal status of aliens in Pacific countries*, edited by Norman MacKenzie. London: Oxford University Press, 1937. Reprint, 1975, 182–89.

Flathman, Richard E. Political obligation. Edited by Michael Walzer, Studies in political theory. New York: Atheneum, 1972.

Flournoy, Richard W., Jr., and Manley O. Hudson, eds. A collection of nationality laws of various countries as contained in constitutions, statutes and treaties. London: Oxford University Press, 1929. Reprint, Littleton: Fred B. Rothman & Co., 1983.

Føllesdal, Andreas. "The future soul of Europe: nationalism of just patriotism? A critique of David Miller's Defence of Nationality", Journal of Peace Research (2000) vol. 37, no. 1, 503–518.

Foot, Rosemary. Rights beyond borders. The global community and the struggle over human rights in China. Oxford: Oxford University Press, 2000.

Franck, Thomas M. "Multiple citizenship: autres temps, autres moeurs", in *Mélanges en l'honneur de Nicolas Valticos*, edited by René-Jean Dupuy. Paris: Éditions A. Pedone, 1999, 149–158.

Frankenberg, Günter. "The grammar of exclusion: the legal construction of the own and the other in German law", Tel Aviv University Studies in Law (2000) vol. 15, 9–22.

Fransman, Laurie. British nationality law. London: Butterworths, 1998.

——. "The case for reform of nationality law in the United Kingdom", in *Citizenship and nationality status in the new Europe*, edited by Síofra O'Leary and Teija Tiilikainen. London: Sweet & Maxwell, 1998, 123–147.

——. "The new infidels", The Sydney Morning Herald, 11–12 May 2002, 36.

Fray, Peter, and Kelly Burke. "Archbishop tongue-lashed for tilt at the London boss", The Sydney Morning Herald, 22 January 2003, 1, 8.

Friedländer, Saul. Nazi Germany and the Jews. Volume I: The years of persecution: 1933–1939. New York: HarperCollins Publishers, 1997.

Friedman, Lawrence M. "Ethnicity and citizenship", paper presented at the conference: *Citizenship and Immigration*, University of Milano Law Faculty, 1996. Edited by Vincenzo Ferrari and Thomas Heller, Elena de Tullio. Milano: Dott. A. Giuffrè Editore, 1998, 65–78.

Friedman, Thomas. "Fear for the voice of democracy when power speaks louder", The Sydney Morning Herald, 5 August 2002, 13.

Fukuyama, Francis. The end of history and the last man. New York: Free Press, 1992.

Fulchiron, Hugues. La nationalité française, Que sais-je? Paris: Presses universitaires de France, 2000.

——. "Le cadre de la manifestation de volonté", paper presented at the conference: *"Être français aujourd'hui . . ." Premier bilan de la mise en oeuvre du nouveau droit de la nationalité*, Lyon, 1995. Lyon: Presses Universitaires de Lyon, 1996, 19–30.

——. "Rétablissement du droit du sol et réforme du droit de la nationalité (Commentaire de la loi no 98–170 du 16 mars 1998)", Journal du droit international (1998) vol. 125, no. 1, 343–388.

Fulchiron, Hugues, and Savinien Grignon Dumoulin. "Nationalité: France", in *Juris-Classeur Nationalité – commentaire des traités internationaux et des législations nationales*, edited by Michel J. Verwilghen and Charles L. Closset. Paris: Éditions du Juris-Classeur, 1997.

"The functionality of citizenship", (1997) Harvard Law Review, vol. 110, no. 8, 1814–1831.

Galbraith, Peter W. "Croatian citizenship and peaceful reintegration", Croatian Critical Law Review (1998) vol. 3, no. 3, 263–270.

Galligan, Brian, and John Chesterman. "Aborigines, citizenship and the Australian Constitution: did the Constitution exclude Aboriginal people from citizenship?", Public Law Review (1997) vol. 8, no. 1, 45–61.

Galloway, Donald. "Citizenship rights and non-citizens: a Canadian perspective", in *Citizenship in a global world. Comparing citizenship rights for aliens*, edited by Atsushi Kondo. Houndmills (UK): Palgrave, 2001, 176–195.

Galloway, J. Donald. "The dilemmas of Canadian citizenship law", Georgetown Immigration Law Journal (1999) vol. 13, no. 2, 201–231.

Galvão Teles, Miguel, and Paulo Canelas de Castro. "Portugal and the right of peoples to self-determination", Archiv des Völkerrechts (1996) vol. 34, no. 1, 2–46.

Gans, Chaim. Philosophical anarchism and political disobedience. Cambridge: Cambridge University Press, 1992.

García Amador, F. V. "International responsibility", Yearbook of the International Law Commission (1957) vol. 1956, no. II.

García Haro, Ramón. La nacionalidad en América Hispana. Vol. 29, Biblioteca de la "Revista general de Legislación y Jurisprudencia". Madrid: Editorial Reus, 1922.

Garcia, Leon T. Problems of citizenship in the Philippines. Hong Kong: Commercial Press Printing Works, 1949.

García Moreno, Víctor Carlos. "La propuesta sobre doble nacionalidad", paper presented at the conference: La doble nacionalidad, Ciudad de México 1995. Ciudad de México: Miguel Ángel Porrúa Librero-Editor, 1995, 173–181.

García, Soledad. "European Union identity and citizenship", in European citizenship and social exclusion, edited by Maurice Roche and Rik van Berkel. Aldershot: Ashgate, 1997, 201–212.

Gardner, J. P., ed. Citizenship – The White Paper. London: The British Institute of International and Comparative Law, 1997.

Garot, Marie-José. "A new basis for European citizenship: residence?", in European Citizenship. An institutional challenge, edited by Massimo La Torre. The Hague: Kluwer Law International, 1998, 229–248.

Gattini, Andrea. "Diritto al nome e scelta del nome nei casi di plurima cittadinanza", Rivista di Diritto Internazionale (1996) vol. 79, 93–109.

Genoni, Maurizio A. M. Die Notwehr im Völkerrecht. Vol. 48, Schweizer Studien zum internationalen Recht. Zürich: Schulthess Polygraphischer Verlag, 1987.

German Marshall Fund Project on Dual Nationality. "Recommendations of the German Marshall Fund Project on Dual Nationality", in Rights and duties of dual nationals. Evolution and prospects, edited by David A. Martin and Kay Hailbronner. The Hague: Kluwer Law International, 2003, 385–388.

Gerwien, Tanja. "The citizenship problems of the Baltic states in the light of public international law", mémoire presented at the Université de Genève, Institut Universitaire de Hautes Études Internationales, 1996.

Gil Rodríguez, Jacinto. La nacionalidad española y los cambios legislativos – significado y alcance de las disposiciones transitorias de la Ley 18/1990, de 17 de diciembre. Madrid: Editorial Colex, 1993.

Gilchrist, Michelle, and Stefanie Balogh. "Visa rules lure young to Britain", The Weekend Australian, 21–22 June 2003, 2.

Ginsburgs, George. "The 1980 nationality law of the People's Republic of China", American Journal of Comparative Law (1982) vol. 30, 459–498.

——. "Citizenship and state succession in Russia's treaty and domestic repertory", Review of Central and East European Law (1995) vol. 21, no. 5, 433–482.

——. "Option of nationality in Soviet treaty practice, 1917–1924", The American Journal of International Law (1961) vol. 55, 919–946.

——. "The 'right to a nationality' and the regime of loss of Russian citizenship", Review of Central and East European Law (2000) vol. 26, no. 1, 1–33.

Gläser, Karl. Erwerb und Verlust der Staatsangehörigkeit in Hispano-Amerika. Edited by Richard Schmidt, Abhandlungen des Instituts für politische Auslandskunde an der Universität Leipzig. Leipzig: Universitätsverlag von Robert Noske, 1930.

Gnatzy, Thomas. "Zuwanderungssteuerung in den »klassischen« Einwanderungsländern USA,

Kanada und Australien", Zeitschrift für Ausländerrecht und Ausländerpolitik (2001) no. 6, 243–253.

Goes, Nina Isabel. Mehrstaatigkeit in Deutschland. Edited by Ingolf Pernice. Vol. 2, Schriftenreihe Europäisches Verfassungsrecht. Baden-Baden: Nomos Verlagsgesellschaft, 1997.

Golden, Tim. "Unapologetic American who spied for Cuba gets 25 years' jail", The Sydney Morning Herald, 18 October 2002, 12.

Goldlust, John. Understanding citizenship in Australia. Edited by Heather Kelly, Understanding series. Canberra: Australian Government Publishing Service, 1996.

Goodin, Robert E. "What is so special about our countrymen?", Ethics (1988) vol. 98, no. 4, 663–686.

Goodwin-Gill, Guy. International law and the movement of persons between states. Oxford: Clarendon Press, 1978.

Gornig, Gilbert H. "Niederlassungsfreiheit in den Europäischen Gemeinschaften im Lichte des Rechts auf die Heimat", in *Der Beitritt der Staaten Ostmitteleuropas zur Europäischen Union und die Rechte der deutschen Volksgruppen und Minderheiten sowie der Vertriebenen*, edited by Dieter Blumenwitz, Gilbert H. Gornig and Dietrich Murswiek. Köln: Verlag Wissenschaft und Politik, 1997, 119–144.

Goscha, Christopher E. "Annam and Vietnam in the new Indochinese space 1887–1945", in *Asian forms of the nation*, edited by Stein Tønnesson and Hans Antlöv. Richmond (UK): Curzon, 1996, 93–130.

Gravers, Mikael. "The Karen making of a nation", in *Asian forms of the nation*, edited by Stein Tønnesson and Hans Antlöv. Richmond (UK): Curzon, 1996, 237–269.

Grawert, Rolf. Staat und Staatsangehörigkeit – Verfassungsgeschichtliche Untersuchung zur Entstehung der Staatsangehörigkeit. Vol. 17, Schriften zur Verfassungsgeschichte. Berlin: Duncker & Humblot, 1973.

Gray, Christopher J. "Cultivating citizenship through xenophobia in Gabon, 1960–1995", Africa Today (1998) vol. 45, no. 3–4, 389–410.

Green, L.C. The contemporary law of armed conflict. Manchester: Manchester University Press, 1993.

Green, Simon. "Citizenship policy in Germany: the case of ethnicity over residence", in *Towards a European nationality. Citizenship, immigration and nationality law in the EU*, edited by Randall Hansen and Patrick Weil. Houndmills: Palgrave, 2001, 24–51.

——. "La politique de la nationalité en Allemagne – la prédominance de l'appartenance ethnique sur la résidence", in *Nationalité et citoyenneté en Europe*, edited by Patrick Weil and Randall Hansen. Paris: Éditions La Découverte, 1999, 29–54.

Groelsema, Robert J. "The dialectics of citizenship and ethnicity in Guinea", Africa Today (1998) vol. 45, no. 3–4, 411–422.

Groenendijk, Kees. "Doppelte Staatsangehörigkeit und Einbürgerung in den Niederlanden: Pragmatismus und soziale Stabilität", paper presented at the conference: *Hohenheimer Tage zum Ausländerrecht 1999 und 5. Migrationspolitisches Forum*, Hohenheim 1999. Edited by Klaus Barwig and Gisbert Brinkmann, Kay Hailbronner, Bertold Huber, Christine Kreuzer, Klaus Lörcher, Christoph Schumacher. Hohenheim: Nomos Verlagsgesellschaft, 1999, 189–197.

Groenendijk, Kees, and Eric Heijs. "Immigration, immigrants and nationality law in the Netherlands, 1945–98", in *Towards a European nationality. Citizenship, immigration and nationality law in the EU*, edited by Randall Hansen and Patrick Weil. Houndmills: Palgrave, 2001, 143–172.

——. "Immigration, immigrés et législation sur la nationalité aux Pays-Bas (1945–1998)", in

Nationalité et citoyenneté en Europe, edited by Patrick Weil and Randall Hansen. Paris: Éditions La Découverte, 1999, 145–175.

Grönvall, Filip, and Kustavi Kaila. "Lagberedningens förslag till lag om utlännings antagande till Finsk medborgare jämte motiv". Helsingfors: Finlands Senats Tryckeri, 1918.

Grotius, Hugo. De jure belli ac pacis libri tres (The three books on the law of war and peace). Translated by Francis W. Kelsey. 1646 ed. Vol. 2. Oxford: Clarendon Press, 1925.

——. De jure belli ac pacis libri tres (The three books on the law of war and peace). Translated by Francis W. Kelsey. 1646 ed. Vol. 3. Oxford: Clarendon Press, 1925.

Guiguet, Benoît. "Citizenship and nationality: tracing the French roots of the distinction", in *European citizenship. An institutional challenge*, edited by Massimo La Torre. The Hague: Kluwer Law International, 1998, 95–111.

——. "Citizenship rights for aliens in France", in *Citizenship in a global world. Comparing citizenship rights for aliens*, edited by Atsushi Kondo. Houndmills (UK): Palgrave, 2001, 71–99.

Gutierrez, Paula. "Mexico's dual nationality amendments: they do not undermine U.S. citizens' allegiance and loyalty or U.S. political sovereignty", Loyola of Los Angeles International and Comparative Law Journal (1997) vol. 19, no. 4, 999–1026.

Hagedorn, Heike. "Administrative systems and dual nationality: the information gap", in *Rights and duties of dual nationals. Evolution and prospects*, edited by David A. Martin and Kay Hailbronner. The Hague: Kluwer Law International, 2003, 183–200.

Hailbronner, Kay. "Citizenship rights for aliens in Germany", in *Citizenship in a global world. Comparing citizenship rights for aliens*, edited by Atsushi Kondo. Houndmills (UK): Palgrave, 2001, 100–115.

——. "Dopelte Staatsangehörigkeit", Zeitschrift für Ausländerrecht und Ausländerpolitik, (1999) no. 2, 51–58.

——. "Doppelte Staatsangehörigkeit", paper presented at the conference: *Hohenheimer Tage zum Ausländerrecht 1999 und 5. Migrationspolitisches Forum*, Hohenheim 1999. Edited by Klaus Barwig and Gisbert Brinkmann, Kay Hailbronner, Bertold Huber, Christine Kreuzer, Klaus Lörcher, Christoph Schumacher. Hohenheim: Nomos Verlagsgesellschaft, 1999, 97–114.

——. "Germany's citizenship law under immigration pressure", in *Dual nationality, social rights and federal citizenship in the U.S. and Europe. The reinvention of citizenship*, edited by Randall Hansen and Patrick Weil. New York: Berghahn Books, 2002, 121–135.

——. "Mehrfache Staatsangehörigkeit und Einbürgerung in der Bundesrepublik Deutschland", in *Vom Ausländer zum Bürger – Problemanzeigen im Ausländer-, Asyl- und Staatsangehörigkeitsrecht – Festschrift für Fritz Franz und Gert Müller*, edited by Klaus Barwig, Gisbert Brinkmann, Bertold Huber, Klaus Lörcher and Christoph Schumacher. Baden-Baden: Nomos Verlagsgesellschaft, 1994, 393–407.

——. "Rights and duties of dual nationals: changing concepts and attitudes", in *Rights and duties of dual nationals. Evolution and prospects*, edited by David A. Martin and Kay Hailbronner. The Hague: Kluwer Law International, 2003, 19–26.

Hailbronner, Kay, Günter Renner, and Christine Kreuzer. Staatsangehörigkeitsrecht. 3rd ed. Vol. 55, Beck'sche Kurz-kommentare. München: Verlag C. H. Beck, 2001.

Halisi, C. R. D. "Citizenship and populism in the new South Africa", Africa Today (1998) vol. 45, no. 3–4, 423–438.

Halisi, C. R. D., Paul J. Kaiser, and Stephen N. Ndegwa. "Guest editors' introduction: the multiple meanings of citizenship – rights, identity, and social justice in Africa", Africa Today (1998) vol. 45, no. 3–4, 337–350.

Hall, Stephen. Nationality, migration rights and citizenship of the Union. Dordrecht: Martinus Nijhoff Publishers, 1995.

Hammar, Tomas. "State, nation, and dual citizenship", in *Immigration and the politics of citizenship in Europe and North America*, edited by William Rogers Brubaker. Lanham: University Press of America, 1989, 81–95.

Hannappel, Wolfgang. Staatsangehörigkeit und Völkerrecht – Die Einwirkung des Völkerrechts auf das Staatsangehörigkeitsrecht in der Bundesrepublik Deutschland. Edited by Dieter Henrich, Erik Jayme and Fritz Sturm. Vol. 27, Schriftenreihe der Wissenschaftlichen Gesellschaft für Personenstandswesen und Werwandte Gebiete M. B. H. Frankfurt am Main: Verlag für Standesamtswesen, 1986.

Hanne, Gottfried, Eva-Clarita Onken, and Norbert Götz. "Ethnopolitik", in *Handbuch Baltikum heute*, edited by Heike Graf and Manfred Kerner. Berlin: Berlin Verlag Arno Spitz GmbH, 1998, 299–334.

Hansen, Randall. "The dog that didn't bark: dual nationality in the United Kingdom", in *Dual nationality, social rights and federal citizenship in the U.S. and Europe. The reinvention of citizenship*, edited by Randall Hansen and Patrick Weil. New York: Berghahn Books, 2002, 179–190.

——. "Doppelte Staatsangehörigkeit im Vereinigten Königreich von Grossbritannien und Nordirland", paper presented at the conference: *Hohenheimer Tage zum Ausländerrecht 1999 und 5. Migrationspolitisches Forum*, Hohenheim 1999. Edited by Klaus Barwig and Gisbert Brinkmann, Kay Hailbronner, Bertold Huber, Christine Kreuzer, Klaus Lörcher, Christoph Schumacher. Hohenheim: Nomos Verlagsgesellschaft, 1999, 207–219.

——. "From subjects to citizens: immigration and nationality law in the United Kingdom", in *Towards a European nationality. Citizenship, immigration and nationality law in the EU*, edited by Randall Hansen and Patrick Weil. Houndmills: Palgrave, 2001, 69–94.

——. "Le droit de l'immigration et de la nationalité au Royaume-Uni – des sujets aux citoyens", in *Nationalité et citoyenneté en Europe*, edited by Patrick Weil and Randall Hansen. Paris: Éditions La Découverte, 1999, 71–94.

Hansen, Randall, and Patrick Weil. "Introduction. Dual citizenship in a changed world: immigration, gender and social rights", in *Dual nationality, social rights and federal citizenship in the U.S. and Europe. The reinvention of citizenship*, edited by Randall Hansen and Patrick Weil. New York: Berghahn Books, 2002, 1–15.

——. "Introduction: citizenship, immigration and nationality: towards a convergence in Europe?", in *Towards a European nationality*, edited by Randall Hansen and Patrick Weil. Houndmills: Palgrave, 2001, 1–23.

——, eds. Dual nationality, social rights and federal citizenship in the U.S. and Europe. New York: Berghahn Books, 2002.

Hart, Herbert Lionel Adolphus. The concept of law. Second ed. Oxford: Clarendon Press, 1994.

——. "The concept of law – postcript." edited by Penelope A. Bulloch and Joseph Raz, 238–76. Oxford: Clarendon Press, 1994.

Hausmann, Rainer. "Doppelte Staatsbürgerschaft für Ausländer: Auswirkungen im Internationalen Privat- und Verfahrensrecht", paper presented at the conference: *Hohenheimer Tage zum Ausländerrecht 1999 und 5. Migrationspolitisches Forum*, Hohenheim 1999. Edited by Klaus Barwig und Gisbert Brinkmann, Kay Hailbronner, Bertold Huber, Christine Kreuzer, Klaus Lörcher, Christoph Schumacher. Hohenheim: Nomos Verlagsgesellschaft, 1999, 163–188.

Heater, Derek. "Citizenship: a remarkable case of sudden interest", Parliamentary Affairs (1991) vol. 44, 140–156.

Hecker, Hellmuth. Das Staatsangehörigkeitsrecht des anglophonen Afrika. Vol. 38, Sammlung geltender Staatsangehörigkeitsgesetze. Frankfurt am Main: Alfred Metzner Verlag, 1981.

———. Das Staatsangehörigkeitsrecht des nicht-anglophonen Afrika. Vol. 39, Sammlung geltender Staatsangehörigkeitsgesetze. Frankfurt am Main: Alfred Metzner Verlag, 1982.

———. Das Staatsangehörigkeitsrecht von Australien und Ozeanien. Vol. 37, Sammlung geltender Staatsangehörigkeitsgesetze. Frankfurt am Main: Alfred Metzner Verlag GmbH, 1980.

———. "Die Doppelstaaterverträge des Ostblocks", WGO Monatshefte für Osteuropäisches Recht (1986), 273–83.

———. "Die Staatsangehörigkeit in Bosnien und Herzegowina seit dem Friedensabkommen von Dayton/Ohio", WGO Monatshefte für Osteuropäisches Recht (1996), 105–13.

———. "Die Staatsangehörigkeit in der Republik Moldau", WGO Monatshefte für Osteuropäisches Recht (1998) 269–275.

———. "Die Staatsangehörigkeit von Chinesen, die vor 1900 nach Niederländisch-Indien eingewandert sind, und ihrer Nachkommen", in Gutachten zum internationalen Recht, edited by Hellmuth Hecker. Hamburg, Frankfurt: Alfred Metzner Verlag GmbH, 1975.

———. "Doppelstaatigkeit, Bancroft-Verträge und Osteuropa", WGO Monatshefte für Osteuropäisches Recht (2000), 409–430.

———. "Staatsangehörigkeitsfragen in völkerrechtlichen Verträgen osteuropäischer Staaten", Archiv des Völkerrechts (1992) vol. 30, no. 3, 326–354.

———. "Verträge über Staatsangehörigkeitsfragen vor Gründung (1918–1922) und nach Zerfall der Sowjetunion (ab 1990)", Archiv des Völkerrechts (1997) vol. 35, 73–115.

Hegi, René. "La nationalité de la femme mariée." Thesis presented at the Université de Lausanne, 1954. Lausanne: Imprimerie La Concorde, 1954.

Heilman, Bruce. "Who are the indigenous Tanzanians? Competing conceptions of Tanzanian citizenship in the business community", Africa Today (1998) vol. 45, no. 3–4, 369–388.

Heller, Thomas C. "Change and convergence: is American immigration still exceptional?", in Citizenship in a global world. Comparing citizenship rights for aliens, edited by Atsushi Kondo. Houndmills (UK): Palgrave, 2001, 196–224.

Helton, Arthur C. "Preface to the collected papers from the conference: citizenship status of citizens of the former SFR Yugoslavia after its dissolution", Croatian Critical Law Review (1998) vol. 3, no. 1–2, 1–7.

Helton, Arthur C., and Elena Popović. "State building and avoiding individual hardships: a model agreement on citizenship", Croatian Critical Law Review (1998) vol. 3, no. 3, 337–351.

Hepp, Michael. "Wer Deutscher ist, bestimmen wir . . .", in Die Ausbürgerung deutscher Staatsangehöriger 1933–45 nach den im Reichsanzeiger veröffentlichen Listen, edited by Michael Hepp. München: K G Saur, 1985, xxv–xl.

———, ed. Expatriation lists as published in the 'Reichsanzeiger' 1933–45 (Die Ausbürgerung deutscher Staatsangehöriger 1944–45 nach den im Reichsanzeiger veröffentlichten Listen). Vol. 1. München: K G Saur, 1985.

Hessisches Ministerium des Innern und für Sport. "Rundschreiben vom 23.10.2000–II A 11–04–20", Informationsbrief Ausländerrecht (2001), no. 1, 43.

Hevener, Natalie Kaufman. International law and the status of women. Boulder: Westview Press, 1983.

Hiss, Eduard. Geschichte des neuern Schweizerischen Staatsrechts. Vol. 3. Basel: Verlag von Helbing & Lichtenhahn, 1938.

Höcker-Weyand, Christine. "Zum neuen jugoslawischen Staatsangehörigkeitsgesetz", WGO Monatshefte für Osteuropäisches Recht (1997), 93–113.

Hofmann, Rainer. "Einbürgerungspraxis und -probleme ausgewählter Staaten und die jeweilige Anwendung des Übereinkommens über die Verringerung der Mehrstaatigkeit", paper presented at the conference: *Doppelte Staatsbürgerschaft – ein europäischer Normalfall?*, Berlin 1989. Berlin: Senatsverwaltung für Gesundheit und Soziales Berlin, 1989, 66–102.

——. "German citizenship law and European citizenship: towards a special kind of dual nationality?", in *European citizenship. An institutional challenge*, edited by Massimo La Torre. The Hague: Kluwer Law International, 1998, 149–165.

——. "Overview of nationality and citizenship in international law", in *Citizenship and nationality status in the new Europe*, edited by Síofra O'Leary and Teija Tiilikainen. London: Sweet & Maxwell, 1998, 5–19.

Hofverberg, Stig. "Om framtida vandel vid prövning av naturalisationsärenden", Förvaltningsrättslig Tidskrift (1998) vol. 61, no. 5, 239–253.

Hollifield, James F. Immigrants, markets, and states – the political economy of postwar Europe. Cambridge (USA): Harvard University Press, 1992.

Holzgrefe, J. L., ed. Humanitarian intervention. Ethical, legal and political dilemmas. Cambridge: Cambridge University Press, 2003.

Hong Kong Special Administrative Region Government, Home Affairs Bureau, "Second report on the Hong Kong Special Administrative Region of the People's Republic of China in the light of the International Covenant on Civil and Political Rights", Hong Kong: Government Logistics Department, No. 2256256, 2005.

Horn, Hans-Detlef. "Einbürgerungen durch die Länder ohne Zustimmungsvorbehalt des Bundes?". Zeitschrift für Ausländerrecht und Ausländerpolitik (2001) vol. 21, no. 3, 99–104.

Hörnig, Ernst Otto. "Die mehrfache Staatsangehörigkeit in Rechtsprechung, Verwaltung und Gesetzgebung. Eine rechtsvergleichende Studie", dissertation presented at the Eberhard-Karls-Universität zu Tübingen, 1939. Bleicherode am Harz, 1939.

Hosokawa, Kiyoshi. "Japanese nationality in international perspective", in *Nationality and international law in Asian perspective*, edited by Ko Swan Sik. Dordrecht: Martinus Nijhoff Publishers, 1990, 177–253.

Houston, Michael Robert W. "Birthright citizenship in the United Kingdom and the United States: a comparative analysis of the Common Law basis for granting citizenship to children born of illegal immigrants", Vanderbilt Journal of Transnational Law (2000) Vol. 33, no. 1, 693–738.

Hudson, Manley O., and Richard W. Flournoy Jr. "Nationality – Responsibility of states – Territorial waters, drafts of conventions prepared in anticipation of the first conference on the codification of international law, The Hague 1930", The American Journal of International Law (1929) vol. 23 Supplement.

Hultman, Jon B. "Administrative denaturalization: is there 'nothing you can do that can't be [un]done'?", Loyola of Los Angeles Law Review (2001) vol. 34, no. 2, 895–935.

"Human-rights course offers a close look at worldwide violations", University of Chicago Magazine (1998) December, 8–9.

Içduygu, Ahmet, Yilmaz Çolak, and Nalan Soyarik. "What is the matter with citizenship? A Turkish debate", Middle Eastern Studies (1999) vol. 35, no. 4, 187–208.

Illiano, Cesar. "Argentina orders arrest of 46 over war crimes", The Sydney Morning Herald, 26–27 July 2003, 15.

"Immigrants in the Netherlands. Fortuynism without Fortuyn", The Economist, 30 November 2002, 46.

Immigration Department of the Hong Kong Special Administrative Region of the People's Republic of China. Application for Hong Kong Special Administrative Region Passport. Notes for guidance and application form. Vol. ID841A. Hong Kong: Immigration Department of the Hong Kong Special Administrative Region of the People's Republic of China, 2001.

——. Application for verification of eligibility for permanent identity card. Vol. ROP 145. Hong Kong: Immigration Department of the Hong Kong Special Administrative Region of the People's Republic of China, 2001.

——. Declaration of change of nationality. A guide for applicants. Vol. ID869A. Hong Kong: Immigration Department of the Hong Kong Special Administrative Region of the People's Republic of China, 2001.

——. Information leaflet. Arrangements for entry to the Hong Kong Special Administrative Region (HKSAR) for overseas Chinese and Chinese residents of Taiwan. Vol. ID 895A. Hong Kong: Immigration Department of the Hong Kong Special Administrative Region of the People's Republic of China, 2001.

——. Naturalization as a Chinese national. Nationality law of the People's Republic of China. A guide for applicants. Vol. ID874A. Hong Kong: Immigration Department of the Hong Kong Special Administrative Region of the People's Republic of China, 2001.

——. Renunciation of Chinese nationality. Nationality law of the People's Republic of China. A guide for applicants. Vol. ID877A. Hong Kong: Immigration Department of the Hong Kong Special Administrative Region of the People's Republic of China, 2001.

——. Restoration of Chinese nationality. Nationality law of the People's Republic of China. A guide for applicants. Vol. ID878A. Hong Kong: Immigration Department of the Hong Kong Special Administrative Region of the People's Republic of China, 2001.

——. Right of abode in the Hong Kong Special Administrative Region. Third (revised) ed. Hong Kong: Hong Kong Special Administrative Region Government, 2000.

"Implementing the Framework Convention for the Protection of National Minorities", paper presented at the conference: *Implementing the Framework Convention for the Protection of National Minorities*, Flensburg, Germany 1998. Edited by Martín Estébanez, María Amor, Kinga Gál. Flensburg: European Centre for Minority Issues, 1998.

Inrikesdepartementet (Sweden). Medborgarskap och identitet. Delbetänkande av 1997 års medborgarskapskommitté, Statens offentliga utredningar 1997: 162. Stockholm: Fritzes, 1997.

International Law Association, Committee on Diplomatic Protection of Persons and Property. "First Report, 69th Conference of the ILA". London: International Law Association, 2000, 604–630.

International Law Association, Committee on Feminism and International Law. "Final report on women's equality and nationality in international law", in *Sixty-ninth Conference of the International Law Association*, edited by A. H. A. Soons and Christopher Ward. London: International Law Association, 2000, 248–304.

International Law Commission. "252nd meeting. Nationality, including statelessness (item 5 of the agenda) A/CN.4/83, A/CN.4/84)", Yearbook of the International Law Commission (1954) no. I, 52–57.

——. "Report of the Commission to the General Assembly on the work of its fiftieth session", Yearbook of the International Law Commission (2001) vol. 1998, no. II, Part 2.

——. Report of the Commission to the General Assembly on the work of its fifty-first session, 1999 (internet), http://www.un.org/law/ilc/sessions/51/51sess.htm, consulted 1 April 2003.

——. "Report of the Commission to the General Assemby on the work of its forty-ninth session", Yearbook of the International Law Commission (2000) vol. 1997, no. II, Part 2.

——. "Report of the International Law Commission to the General Assembly", Yearbook of the International Law Commission (1959) vol. 1953, no. II, 219–230.

——. "Report of the International Law Commission to the General Assembly", Yearbook of the International Law Commission (1960) vol. 1954, no. II, 140–149.

——. Report of the International Law Commission to the General Assembly, Fifty-fourth session. New York: United Nations General Assembly, Official Records, Fifty-seventh session, Supplement No. 10 (A/57/10), 2002.

——. Report of the International Law Commission to the General Assembly, Fifty-second session. New York: United Nations General Assembly Official Records, Fifty-fifth session, Supplement No. 10 (A/55/10), 2000.

——. Report of the International Law Commission to the General Assembly, Fifty-sixth session. New York: United Nations General Assembly Official Records, Fifty-ninth session, Supplement No. 10 (A/59/10), 2004, 38–44.

——. Report of the International Law Commission to the General Assembly, Fifty-third session. New York: United Nations General Assembly, Official Records, Fifty-sixth session, Supplement No. 10 (A/56/10), 2001.

International Olympic Committee. "Olympic Charter, in force as from 1 September 2004", 2006 (Internet), http://multimedia.olympic.org/pdf/en_report_122.pdf, consulted 28 March 2006.

Ishmael, Safraz W., Guyana news and information, "The beginning of the Guyana-Venezuela border dispute" (internet), http://www.guyana.org/features/guyanastory/chapter52.html, consulted 5 July 2003.

Jackson, Vicki C. "Citizenship and federalism", in *Citizenship today. Global perspectives and practices*, edited by T. Alexander Aleinikoff and Douglas Klusmeyer. Washington: Carnegie Endowment for International Peace, 2001, 124–182.

"Jakarta warns citizens", The Sydney Morning Herald, 2–3 November 2002, 13.

Jalal, P. Imrana. Law for Pacific women: a legal rights handbook. Suva: Fiji Women's Rights Movement, 1998.

Jellinek, Hansjörg. Der automatische Erwerb und Verlust der Staatsangehörigkeit durch völkerrechtliche Vorgänge, zugleich ein Beitrag zur Lehre von den Staaten sukzession. Edited by Carl Bilfinger. Vol. 27, Beiträge zum ausländischen öffentlichen Recht und Völkerrecht. Berlin: Carl Heymanns Verlag, 1951.

Jenkins, Gareth, Al-Ahram Weekly. "Turkey threatened by a scarf", 20–26 May 1999 (internet), http://www.ahram.org.eg/weekly/1999/430/re6.htm, consulted 13 September 2002.

Jenkins, Jim. "My time in the long lens of the Syrian security police", The Australian, 10 February 2003, 15.

Jennings, Robert, and Arthur Watts. "Oppenheim's International Law". London: Longman, 1992.

Jermolin, Vassilij. "Das Staatsangehörigkeitsrecht der Russischen Föderation (Russlands)", Jahrbuch für Ostrecht (1998) vol. 39, 41–53.

Jessup, Philip C. "Non-universal international law", Columbia Journal of Transnational Law (1973) vol. 12, no. 1, 415–429.

Jessurun d'Oliveira, H. U. "Onze koningin heeft twee nationaliteiten. Kan dat nog wel?", *HP/De Tijd*, 16 December 2005, 22–28.

Joint Committee on Foreign Affairs and Defence (Australia). "Dual nationality (Report from the Joint Committee on Foreign Affairs and Defence)". Canberra: Parliament of Australia, 1976.

Jones Correa, Michael. "Seeking shelter: immigrants and the divergence of social rights and citizenship in the United States", in *Dual nationality, social rights and federal citizenship in the U.S. and Europe. The reinvention of citizenship*, edited by Randall Hansen and Patrick Weil. New York: Berghahn Books, 2002, 233–63.

——. "Under two flags: dual nationality in Latin America and its consequences for naturalization in the United States", in *Rights and duties of dual nationals. Evolution and prospects*, edited by David A. Martin and Kay Hailbronner. The Hague: Kluwer Law International, 2003, 303–33.

——. "Under two flags: dual nationality in Latin America and its consequences for the United States", 2003 (internet), http://www.fas.harvard.edu/~drclas/publications/papers.html#, consulted 23 June 2003.

Joppke, Christian. "The evolution of alien rights in the United States, Germany, and the European Union", in Citizenship today. Global perspectives and practices, edited by T. Alexander Aleinikoff and Douglas Klusmeyer. Washington: Carnegie Endowment for International Peace, 2001, 36–62.

"Jordan and its Palestinians. The queen outmatched", The Economist, 7 December 2002, 46.

Joseph, Cuthbert. "Diplomatic protection and nationality. The Commonwealth of Nations", doctoral thesis presented at the Université de Genève, Institut Universitaire de Hautes Études Internationales, 1968.

——. Nationality and diplomatic protection. Leyden: A. W. Sijthoff, 1969.

Juárez Pérez, Pilar. Nacionalidad estatal y ciudadanía europea. Madrid: Marcial Pons, Ediciones Jurídicas y Sociales S. A., 1998.

Juss, Satvinder S. Immigration, nationality and citizenship. London: Mansell, 1993.

——. "Nationality law, sovereignty, and the doctrine of exclusive domestic jurisdiction", Florida Journal of International Law (1994) vol. 9, no. 2, 219–240.

Kadende-Kaiser, Rose M., and Paul J. Kaiser. "Identity, citizenship, and transnationalism: Ismailis in Tanzania and Burundians in the Diaspora", Africa Today (1998) vol. 45, no. 3–4, 461–480.

Kalman, Matthew. "How Jews were swindled of Haider estate", The Sydney Morning Herald 11 February 2000, 10.

Kalshoven, Frits. Constraints on the waging of war. Geneva: International Committee of the Red Cross, 1991.

Kammann, Karin. Probleme mehrfacher Staatsangehörigkeit unter besonderer Berücksichtigung des Völkerrechts. Vol. 398, Europäische Hochschulschriften (European University Studies) – Series II. Frankfurt am Main: Peter Lang, 1984.

Kaplan, Marion A. Between dignity and despair. Jewish life in Nazi Germany. New York, Oxford: Oxford University Press, 1998.

Karamanoukian, Aram. Les étrangers et le service militaire. Paris: Editions A. Pedone, 1978.

Kashyap, Subhash C. Citizens and the Constitution. (Citizenship values under the Constitution). New Delhi: Publications Division, Ministry of Information and Broadcasting, Government of India, 1997.

Kassim, Anis F. "The Palestinian: from hyphenated citizen to integrated citizen", in Yearbook of Islamic and Middle Eastern Law, edited by Eugene Cotran and Chibli Mallat. London: Kluwer Law International Ltd., 1997, 64–84.

Kastoryano, Riva. "Türken mit deutschem Pass: Sociological and political aspects of dual nationality in Germany", in Dual nationality, social rights and federal citizenship in the U.S. and Europe. The reinvention of citizenship, edited by Randall Hansen and Patrick Weil. New York: Berghahn Books, 2002, 158–175.

"Kaunda 'Stateless'", The Sydney Morning Herald, 2 April 1999, 8.

"Keeping out Li Ka-shing", The Economist, 3 May 2003, 54.

Keightley, Raylene. "The child's right to a nationality and the acquisition of citizenship in South African law", South African Journal on Human Rights (1998) vol. 14, 411–429.

Keith-Reid, Robert, and Mere Tuqiri. "Whispers. Funny business", Pacific, February 2002, 9.

Kelsen, Hans. Beiträge zur Kritik des Rechtsgutachtens über die Frage der Österreichischen Staatsbürgerschaft des Fürsten von Thurn und Taxis. Zagreb: Jugoslovenska Stampa, 1924.

Kerber, Linda K. No constitutional right to be ladies – women and the obligations of citizenship. New York: Hill and Wang, 1988.

Keskin, Hakkı. "Staatsbürgerschaft im Exil", paper presented at the conference: *Doppelte Staatsbürgerschaft – ein europäischer Normalfall?*, Berlin 1989. Edited by Ulrich Büschelmann. Berlin: Senatsverwaltung für Gesundheit und Soziales, 1989, 43–54.

Killerby, Margaret. "Steps taken by the Council of Europe to promote the modernization of the nationality laws of European states", in *Citizenship and nationality status in the new Europe*, edited by Síofra O'Leary and Teija Tiilikainen. London: Sweet & Maxwell, 1998, 21.

Kim-Ukkon, Louis. "Nationalité: Corée (République de)", in *Juris-Classeur Nationalité*, edited by Michel J. Verwilghen and Charles L. Closset. Paris: Éditions Juris-Classeur, 1997.

Kinzer, Stephen. "Scarf MP loses citizenship", Sydney Morning Herald, 17 May 1999, 8.

Kirişci, Kemal. "Disaggregating Turkish citizenship and immigration practices", Middle Eastern Studies (2000) vol. 36, no. 3, 1–22.

Klampfer, Friderik. "Does membership in a nation as such generate any special duties?", in *Nationalism and ethnic conflict. Philosophical perspectives*, edited by Nenad Miscevic. Chicago: Open Court Publishing Company, 2000, 219–238.

Kleger, Heinz. "Einleitung: Ist eine politische Mehrfachidentität möglich", in *Transnationale Staatsbürgerschaft*, edited by Heinz Kleger. Frankfurt: Campus Verlag, 1997, 9–20.

——, ed. Transnationale Staatsbürgerschaft. Edited by Axel Honneth, Hans Joas and Claus Offe. Vol. 38, Theorie und Gesellschaft. Frankfurt am Main: Campus Verlag, 1997.

Klein, Claude. "The right of return in Israeli law", Tel Aviv University Studies in Law (1997) vol. 13, 53–61.

Klein, Martin A. Zu einer Reform des deutschen Staatsangehörigkeitsrechts – eine kritische Betrachtung unter Einbeziehung Frankreichs. Frankfurt am Main: Peter Lang, 1999.

Klusmeyer, Douglas. "Introduction", in *Citizenship today. Global perspectives and practices*, edited by T. Alexander Aleinikoff and Douglas Klusmeyer. Washington: Carnegie Endowment for International Peace, 2001, 1–14.

Knapp, Blaise. "Nottebohm Case (preliminary objection)", in *A digest of the decisions of the International Court*, edited by Krystyna Marek. The Hague: Martinus Nijhoff, 1978, 390–398.

——. "Nottebohm Case (second phase)", in *A digest of decisions of the International Court*, edited by Krystyna Marek. The Hague: Martinus Nijhoff, 1978, 400–418.

Knežević, Gašo. "Acquisition of citizenship according to the citizenship law of the Federal Republic of Yugoslavia (with special regard to transitional provisions)", Croatian Critical Law Review (1998) vol. 3, no. 1–2, 227–241.

Knop, Karen. "Relational nationality: on gender and nationality in international law", in *Citizenship today. Global perspectives and practices*, edited by T. Alexander Aleinikoff and Douglas Klusmeyer. Washington: Carnegie Endowment for International Peace, 2001, 89–124.

Knop, Karen, and Christine Chinkin. "Remembering Chrystal Macmillan: Women's equality and nationality in international law", Michigan Journal of International Law (2001) vol. 22, no. 4, 523–585.

Ko Swan Sik. De meervoudige nationaliteit. Leiden: A. W. Sijthoff's Uitgeversmaatschappij N.V., 1957.

——, ed. Nationality and International Law in Asian Perspective. Dordrecht: Martinus Nijhoff Publishers, 1990.

Ko Swan Sik, and Teuku Moh. Rhadie. "Nationality and international law in Indonesian perspective", in *Nationality and international law in Asian perspective*, edited by Ko Swan Sik. Dordrecht: Martinus Nijhoff Publishers, 1990, 125–176.

Ko Swan Sik, and J. Van Rijn van Alkemade. "Nationalité: Pays-Bas", in *Juris-Classeur Nationalité*, edited by Michel J. Verwilghen and Charles L. Closset. Paris: Éditions du Juris-Classeur, 1984.

Koch, Ida Elisabeth. "Retssikkerhed i forbindelse med erhvervelse af indfødsret ved lov – retlige og/eller politiske hindringer", Juristen (1999) vol. 81, 26–42.

Koch, Tony. "Fleeced by UK over pensions", The Courier-Mail, 21 June 2003, 25.

Koessler, Maximilian. "'Subject,' 'Citizen,' 'National,' and 'Permanent Allegiance'", Yale Law Journal (1947) vol. 56, 58–76.

Kohler, Lotte, and Hans Saner, eds. Hannah Arendt Karl Jaspers Correspondence 1926–1969. New York: Harcourt Brace Jovanovich, 1992.

Kondo, Atsushi. "Citizenship rights for aliens in Japan", in Citizenship in a global world. Comparing citizenship rights for aliens, edited by Atsushi Kondo. Houndmills: Palgrave, 2001, 8–30.

——. "Conparative citizenship and aliens' rights", in Citizenship in a global world. Comparing citizenship rights for aliens, edited by Atsushi Kondo. Houndmills: Palgrave, 2001, 225–235.

——, ed. Citizenship in a global world. Comparing citizenship rights for aliens. Houndmills (UK): Palgrave, 2001.

Koolen, Ben. "Kommunalwahlrecht für Ausländer in den Niederlanden 1990–1998", Zeitschrift für Ausländerrecht und Ausländerpolitik (1999) no. 2, 79–84.

Koslowski, Rey. "Challenges of international cooperation in a world of increasing dual nationality", in Rights and duties of dual nationals. Evolution and prospects, edited by David A. Martin and Kay Hailbronner. The Hague: Kluwer Law International, 2003, 157–182.

——. "EU-interne Migration, Staatsbürgerschaft und Politische Union", in Transnationale Staatsbürgerschaft, edited by Heinz Kleger. Frankfurt: Campus Verlag, 1997, 209–242.

Kotalakidis, Nikolaos. Von der nationalen Staatsangehörigkeit zur Unionsbürgerschaft – die Person und das Gemeinwesen. Edited by Peter Behrens, Thomas Bruha, Harald Jürgensen, Gert Nicolaysen, Karl-Ernst Schenk and Thomas Straubhaar. Vol. 29, Schriftenreihe des Europa-Kollegs Hamburg zur Integrationsforschung. Baden-Baden: Nomos Verlagsgesellschaft, 2000.

Kowal-Wolk, Tatjana. Die sowjetische Staatsbürgerschaft– Insbesondere ihr Erwerb und Verlust. Series II ed. Vol. 297, Europäische Hochschulschriften (European University Series). Frankfurt am Main: Peter Lang, 1982.

Krause, Jason. "Casting a wide net. Search Engines Yahoo and Google Tussle With Foreign Courts Over Content", ABA Journal November (2002), 20.

Kremmer, Christopher. "Nowhere to run", The Sydney Morning Herald, 16–17 June 2001, 31.

Kreuzer, Christine. "Double and multiple nationality in Germany after the Citizenship Reform Act of 1999", in Rights and duties of dual nationals. Evolution and prospects, edited by David A. Martin and Kay Hailbronner. The Hague: Kluwer Law International, 2003, 347–359.

——. Staatsangehörigkeit und Staatensukzession. Vol. 132, Schriften zum Völkerrecht. Berlin: Duncker & Humblot, 1998.

Kulturdepartementet (Sweden). Svenskt medborgarskap. Slutbetänkande av 1997 års medborgarskapskommitté, Statens offentliga utredningar 1999:34. Stockholm: Fritzes, 1999.

Kymlicka, Will. Multicultural citizenship – a liberal theory of minority rights. Oxford: Clarendon Press, 1995.

La Legión. "Los requisitos para alistarse en La Legión", 2003 (internet), http://www.lalegion.com/ser/requisitos.htm, consulted 21 July 2003.

Lagarde, Paul. "Droit de la nationalité et droit de l'immigration. L'expérience française", in Mélanges en l'honneur de Nicolas Valticos, edited by René-Jean Dupuy. Paris: Éditions A. Pedone, 1999, 663–672.

——. "Nationalité et filiation: leur interaction dans le droit comparé de la nationalité", paper presented at the conference: Nationalité et status personnel – leur interaction dans les traités *internationaux et dans les législations nationales*, Louvain-la-Neuve (Belgium), 1982. Edited by Michel Verwilghen. Louvain-la-Neuve: Émile Bruylant, 1984, 475–508.

Lague, David. "Hong Kong. Interim report. After five years of mainland sovereignty, Beijing signals that it wants a more hands-on role", Far Eastern Economic Review, 11 July 2002, 20.

Laitin, David D., and Roland Grigor Suny. "Armenia and Azerbaijan: thinking a way out of Karabakh", Middle East Policy (1999) vol. 7, no. 1, 145–176.

Lalloo, Kiran. "Citizenship and place: spatial definitions of oppression and agency in South Africa", Africa Today (1998) vol. 45, no. 3–4, 439–460.

Lamont, Leonie. "Deported rapist faces execution in China", The Sydney Morning Herald, 2 July 2003, 3.

———. "State clears Boeing for discrimination pass", The Sydney Morning Herald, 1 April 2005 (internet), http://www.smh.com.au/news/National/State-clears-Boeing-for-discrimination-pass/2005/03/31/1111862537239.html?oneclick=true, consulted 25 March 2006.

Lanham, David. Cross-border criminal law. Melbourne: FT Law & Tax Asia Pacific, 1997.

Lauterpacht, Hersch. International law and human rights. London: Stevens, 1950.

Lawrence, T. J. The principles of international law. Edited by Percy H. Winfield. 7th ed. London: Macmillan & Co., 1895.

Lawyers Committee for Human Rights. Wrongs and rights. A human rights analysis of China's revised Criminal Law. New York: Lawyers Committee for Human Rights, 1998.

Layton-Henry, Zig. "Patterns of privilege: citizenship rights in Britain", in *Citizenship in a global world. Comparing citizenship rights for aliens*, edited by Atsushi Kondo. Houndmills (UK): Palgrave, 2001, 116–135.

Lazarova Trajkovska, Mirjana. "Continuity and efficiency in the regulation of citizenship in the Republic of Macedonia", Croatian Critical Law Review (1998) vol. 3, no. 1–2, 187–190.

Le Grand, Chip. "Pragmatism takes hold in nationality stakes. Adopting a new country is a common occurrence in world tennis", The Weekend Australian, 20–21 January 2001, 34.

Legomsky, Stephen H. "Dual nationality and military service: strategy number two", in *Rights and duties of dual nationals. Evolution and prospects*, edited by David A. Martin and Kay Hailbronner. The Hague: Kluwer Law International, 2003, 79–126.

Lehmann, Hans Georg. "Act und Ächtung politischer Gegner im Dritten Reich. Die Ausbürgerung deutscher Emigranten 1933–45", in *Die Ausbürgerung deutscher Staatsangehöriger 1933–45 nach den im Reichsanzeiger veröffentlichen Listen*, edited by Michael Hepp. München: K. G. Saur, 1985, ix–xxiii.

Lehr, Ernest. La nationalité dans les principaux états du globe (acquisition, perte, recouvrement). Paris: A. Pedone, 1909.

Leng, Shao-Chuan, and Hungdah Chiu, eds. Law in Chinese foreign policy: Communist China and selected problems of international law. Dobbs Ferry, NY: Oceana Publications, Inc., 1972.

Lessing, Juan A. Problemas del derecho de nacionalidad. (Proposiciones de reforma). Buenos Aires: Tipografica Editora Argentina, 1946.

Levasseur, Alain. "La nationalité américaine: aspects juridiques", in *La citoyenneté européenne*, edited by Christian Philip and Panayotis Soldatos. Montréal: Université de Montréal, 2000, 59–79.

Levi, Margaret. Consent, dissent, and patriotism. Cambridge: Cambridge University Press,1997.

Levie, Howard S. "Prisoners of war in international armed conflicts", International Law Studies – US Naval War College (c. 1977) vol. 59.

Levitt, Peggy. "Variations in transnational belonging: lessons from Brazil and the Dominican Republic", in *Dual nationality, social rights and federal citizenship in the U.S. and Europe.*

The reinvention of citizenship, edited by Randall Hansen and Patrick Weil. New York: Berghahn Books, 2002, 264–289.

Liebich, André. "Plural citizenship in post-Communist states", International Journal of Refugee Law (2000) vol. 12, no. 1, 97–107.

Liénard-Ligny, Monique. "Le droit de la nationalité en Belgique et au Luxembourg", in *Nationalité et citoyenneté en Europe*, edited by Patrick Weil and Randall Hansen. Paris: Éditions La Découverte, 1999, 199–220.

——. "Loi du 1er mars 2000 modifiant certaines dispositions relatives à la nationalité belge (M.B., 5 avril 2000, p.10.560)", Actualités du droit (2000) no. 1, 469–474.

——. "Nationality law in Belgium and Luxembourg", in *Towards a European nationality. Citizenship, immigration and nationality law in the EU*, edited by Randall Hansen and Patrick Weil. Houndmills: Palgrave, 2001, 193–213.

Lizarraga Chavez, Pablo. "Creating a United States-Mexico political double helix: the Mexican government's proposed dual nationality amendment", Stanford Journal of International Law (1997) vol. 33, no. 1, 119–151.

Loehr, Friedrich. "Passports", in *Encyclopedia of Public International Law*, edited by Rudolf Bernhardt and Max Planck Institute for Comparative Public Law and International Law. Amsterdam: Elsevier, 1985, 428–431.

Longley, Clifford. "American justice on trial", The Tablet (2002), 2.

Löwer, Wolfgang. "Doppelte Staatsbürgerschaft als Gefahr für die Rechtssicherheit", paper presented at the conference: *Doppelte Staatsbürgerschaft – ein europäischer Normalfall?*, Berlin 1989. Edited by Ulrich Büschelmann. Berlin: Senatsverwaltung für Gesundheit und Soziales, 1989, 149–174.

Maureen Lynch, "The people who have no country . . .", *International Herald Tribune*, 18 February 2005.

Maag, Jakob. "Der konsularische und diplomatische Schutz des Auslandschweizers", dissertation presented at the Universität Zürich, 1953. Zürich: Juris-Verlag, 1953.

Macdonald, Ian A., and Nicholas Blake. The new nationality law. London: Butterworths, 1982.

MacKinnon, Catharine A. "Feminism, Marxism, method, and the state: toward feminist jurisprudence", in *Feminist legal theory – readings in law and gender*, edited by Katharine T. Bartlett and Rosanne Kennedy. Boulder: Westview Press, 1991, 181–200.

Magnus, Julius, ed. Tabellen zum internationalen Recht. Zweites Heft. Staatsangehörigkeitsrecht. Berlin: Verlag von Franz Vahlen, 1926.

Mahoney, Peter E. "The standing of dual-nationals before the Iran-United States Claims Tribunal", Virginia Journal of Internaional Law (1984) vol. 24, no. 3, 695–728.

Makarov, Alexander N. Deutsches Staatsangehörigkeitsrecht – Kommentar. Frankfurt am Main: Alfred Metzner Verlag, 1966.

Makarov, Alexandre N. "Le droit d'option en cas de double nationalité dans les conventions internationales", Nederlands Tijdschrift voor Internationaal Recht (1959) vol. VI, July (special issue), 194–202.

Malhotra, Ranjit. "Dual nationality for Indians: the need for a fresh debate", Immigration and nationality law and practice (1996) vol. 10, no. 2, 57–59.

Manasian, David. "Digital dilemmas. A survey of the internet society. Power to the people", The Economist, 25 January 2003, 13–15.

Mann, Michael. "Ruling class strategies and citizenship", in *Citizenship today. The contemporary relevance of T. H. Marshall*, edited by Martin Bulmer and Anthony M. Rees. London: UCL Press Ltd., 1996, 125–144.

Mansell, Wade. "Pure law in an impure world", in *The critical lawyers' handbook 2*, edited by Paddy Ireland and Per Laleng. London: Pluto Press, 1997, 30–45.

Manuh, Takyiwaa. "Ghanaians, Ghanaian Canadians, and Asantes: citizenship and identity among migrants in Toronto", Africa Today (1998) vol. 45, no. 3–4, 481–494.

Marcos, P and X. Hermida, "Galician premier takes election bandwagon to Buenos Aires", El País (English supplement to the International Herald Tribune), 10 May 2005, 3.

Marek, Krystyna. "Case concerning rights of nationals of the United States of America in Morocco", in A digest of decisions of the International Court, edited by Krystyna Marek. The Hague: Martinus Nijhoff, 1978, 348–372.

Marinho, Ilmar Penna. Tratado sôbre a nacionalidade. 4 vols. Vol. 4. Rio de Janeiro: Departamento de Imprensa Nacional, 1961.

Marshall, Tyler. "HK subversion bill sparks alarm on human rights", The Sydney Morning Herald, 15–16 February 2003, 21.

Martin, David A. "Introduction: the trend toward dual nationality", in Rights and duties of dual nationals. Evolution and prospects, edited by David A. Martin and Kay Hailbronner. The Hague: Kluwer Law International, 2003, 3–18.

——. "New rules for dual nationality", in Dual nationality, social rights and federal citizenship in the U.S. and Europe. The reinvention of citizenship, edited by Randall Hansen and Patrick Weil. New York: Berghahn Books, 2002, 34–60.

Martin, David A., and Kay Hailbronner, eds. Rights and duties of dual nationals. Evolution and prospects. The Hague: Kluwer Law International, 2003.

Martin, Susan. "The attack on social rights: U.S. citizenship devalued", in Dual nationality, social rights and federal citizenship in the U.S. and Europe. The reinvention of citizenship, edited by Randall Hansen and Patrick Weil. New York: Berghahn Books, 2002, 215–232.

Masing, Johannes. Wandel im Staatsangehörigkeitsrecht vor den Herausforderungen moderner Migration. Tübingen: Mohr Siebeck, 2001.

Master, Meher K. Citizenship of India. Dual nationality and the Constitution. Edited by L. M. Singhvi. Calcutta: Eastern Law House, 1970.

McCormack, Timothy. "The use of force", in Public international law. An Australian perspective, edited by Sam Blay, Ryszard Piotrowicz and B. Martin Tsamenyi. Melbourne: Oxford University Press, 1997, 238–270.

McLean, Renwick, International Herald Tribine. "Spanish Parliament to weigh Catalan autonomy", 4 November 2005 (internet), http://www.iht.com/articles/2005/11/03/news/spain.php, consulted 19 December 2005.

McNair (Lord). International law opinions. Vol. 2. Cambridge: Cambridge University Press, 1956.

McNeill, William H. Polyethnicity and national unity in world history. The Donald G. Creighton lectures. Toronto: University of Toronto Press, 1986.

Mearsheimer, John J. The tragedy of great power politics. New York: Norton, 2001.

Medvedović, Dragan. "Federal and republican citizenship in the former SFR Yugoslavia at the time of its dissolution", Croatian Critical Law Review (1998) vol. 3, no. 1–2, 21–56.

Meehan, Elizabeth. Citizenship and the European Community. London: SAGE Publications, 1993.

——. "Staatsbürgerschaft und die Europäische Gemeinschaft", in Transnationale Staatsbürgerschaft, edited by Heinz Kleger. Frankfurt: Campus Verlag, 1997, 42–62.

Meessen, Karl Matthias. Die Option der Staatsangehörigkeit. Vol. 38, Schriften zum Öffentlichem Recht. Berlin: Duncker & Humblot, 1966.

——. "Option of nationality", in Encyclopedia of Public International Law, edited by Rudolf Bernhardt and Max Planck Institute for Comparative Public Law and International Law. Amsterdam: Elsevier, 1985, 424–428.

Mesojedec-Prvinšek, Alenka, and Slavko Debelak. "Citizenship and legal continuity after the declaration of independence of the Republic of Slovenia", Croatian Critical Law Review (1998) vol. 3, no. 1–2, 191–214.

Messerli, Patricia. "Swiss Guard at Swiss Abroad Day", Swiss Review (2002) vol. 4, 12–13.

Meyer, Josh. "Fear over US-born extremists is brewing", Los Angeles Times, 1 August 2005 (internet), http://www.hvk.org/articles/0805/1.html, consulted 28 March 2006.

Meyer, P. "Cour d'appel de Ouagadougou. 1er décembre 1995", Revue burkinabè de droit (1996) vol. 30, no. 2, 287–304.

Meyler, Bernadette. "The gestation of birthright citizenship, 1868–1898 states' rights, the law of nations, and mutual consent", Georgetown Immigration Law Journal (2001) vol. 15, no. 3, 519–562.

"Migration boom", The Australian, 3 November 2000, 8.

Miklavič-Predan, Neva. "Ethnic cleansing through the revocation of citizenship rights in the Republic of Slovenia", Croatian Critical Law Review (1998) vol. 3, no. 1–2, 221–225.

Mikulka, Vàclav. "L'incidence des règles internationales de la nationalité", paper presented at the conference: Nationalité, minorités et succession d'états en europe de l'est, Prague, 22–24 September 1994. Edited by Emmanuel Decaux and Alain Pellet. Paris: Montchrestien, 1994, 11–23.

Mill, John Stuart. "On Liberty" (1858), in Readings in social and political philosophy, edited by Robert M. Stewart. New York: Oxford University Press, 1986, 110–141.

Miller, David. "The ethical significance of nationality", Ethics (1998) vol. 98, no. 4, 647–662.

——. On nationality, Oxford Political Theory. Oxford: Clarendon Press, 1995.

Mišković-Prodanović, Dubravka. "Obtaining Croatian citizenship: findings of the Civic Committee on Human Rights", Croatian Critical Law Review (1998) vol. 3, no. 1–2, 145–152.

Mittlebeeler, Emmet V. African custom and western law. The development of the Rhodesian Criminal Law for Africans. New York: Africana Publishing Company, 1976.

Moaz, Asher. "Who is a convert?", Justice (1997) vol. 15, 11–15.

Moon, Parker Thomas. "Preface", in The diplomatic protection of Americans in Mexico, edited by Frederick Sherwood Dunn. New York: Columbia University Press, 1933, v–vii.

Moore, John Bassett. A digest of international law as embodied in diplomatic discussions, treaties and other international agreements, international awards, the decisions of municipal courts, and the writings of jurists, and especially in documents, published and unpublished, issued by Presidents and Secretaries of State of the United States, the opinions of the Attorneys-General, and the decisions of courts, Federal and State. 8 vols. Vol. 3. Washington: Government Printing Office, 1906.

Moore, Matthew. "FBI joins inquiry into US murders in Papua", The Sydney Morning Herald, 17 January 2003, 9.

Moore, Matthew, Linda Morris, and Deborah Cameron. "Don't keep us in dark, says angry Jakarta", The Sydney Morning Herald, 1 November 2002, 1.

Moreau, Gérard. "Préface", paper presented at the conference: "Être français aujourd'hui... Premier bilan de la mis en oeuvre du nouveau droit de la nationalité, Lyon 1995. Edited by Hugues Fulchiron. Lyon: Presses Universitaires de Lyon, 1995, 5–9.

Moreau, Michel. "Nationalité française – propos en marge du rapport de la commission de la nationalité", paper presented at the conference: La condition juridique de l'étranger, hier et aujourd'hui, Katholieke Universiteit Nijmegen (Nimègue) 1988. Nijmegen: Faculteit der Rechtsgeleerdheid, Katholieke Universiteit Nijmegen, 1988, 21–35.

Moreira, Augusto. "Fátima Felgueiras acusada de 28 crimes", Público (Lisbon), 30 April 2004, 2.

Moreno Fuentes, Francisco Javier. "La migration et le droit de la nationalité espagnole", in *Nationalité et citoyenneté en Europe*, edited by Patrick Weil and Randall Hansen. Paris: Éditions La Découverte, 1999, 117–144.

——. "Migration and Spanish nationality law", in *Towards a European nationality. Citizenship, immigration and nationality law in the EU*, edited by Randall Hansen and Patrick Weil. Houndmills: Palgrave, 2001, 118–142.

Morin, Jacques-Yvan. "La citoyenneté européenne comparée avec la citoyenneté dans les unions de type fédéral", in *La citoyenneté européenne*, edited by Christian Philip and Panayotis Soldatos. Montréal: Université de Montréal, 2000, 95–112.

Motomura, Hiroshi. "Alienage classifications in a nation of immigrants: three models of 'permanent' residence", in *Immigration and citizenship in the twenty-first century*, edited by Noah M. J. Pickus. Lanham: Rowman & Littlefield, 1998, 199–222.

Moura Ramos, Rui Manuel. "La déclaration commune Sino-Portugaise dans la perspective du droit international", in *Mélanges en hommage Michel Waelbroeck*, edited by Marianne Dony. Bruxelles: Bruylant, 1999, 97–109.

——. "La double nationalité et les liens spéciaux avec d'autres pays. Les développements et les perspectives au Portugal", Revista de direito e economia (1990–1993) vols. 16–19, 577–605.

——. "Migratory movements and nationality law in Portugal", in *Towards a European nationality. Citizenship, immigration and nationality law in the EU*, edited by Randall Hansen and Patrick Weil. Houndmills: Palgrave, 2001, 214–229.

——. "Mouvements migratoires et droit de la nationalité au Portugal dans le dernier demi-siècle", in *Nationalité et citoyenneté en Europe*, edited by Patrick Weil and Randall Hansen. Paris: Éditions La Découverte, 1999, 221–238.

——. "Nationalité, plurinationalité et supranationalité en droit Portugais", Archiv des Völkerrechts (1996) vol. 34, no. 1, 96–119.

Mualem, Mazal. "I'm not Israeli, says Arab stripped of citizenship", Ha'aretz, 12 September 2002, 2.

Mualem, Mazal, and Jalal Bana. "Yishai revokes citizenship of Israeli Arab", Ha'aretz, 10 September 2002.

Muhibić, Esad. "Citizenship as a human right in Bosnia Herzegovina: wartime and current practice", Croatian Critical Law Review (1998) vol. 3, no. 1–2, 89–98.

Müller, Kaspar. "Das Problem der mehrfachen Staatsangehörigkeit", dissertation presented at the Universität Köln, Hohen Rechtswissenschaftlichen Fakultät, 1927.

Muminović, Edin. "Problems of citizenship laws in Bosnia and Herzegovina", Croatian Critical Law Review (1998) vol. 3, no. 1–2, 71–87.

Munro, Catherine. "Playing on the right for Italy", The Sydney Morning Herald, 2 April 2006 (internet), http://www.smh.com.au/news/world/on-the-right-wing/2006/04/01/11434413-78366.html#, consulted 2 April 2006.

Mutharika, A. Peter. The regulation of statelessness under international law. June 1989 ed. Dobbs Ferry: Oceana Publications, Inc., 1989.

Muzak, Gerhard. "Notstandshilfe und Staatsbürgerschaft. Neuerlicher Versuch einer verfassungskonformen Lösung", Zeitschrift für Arbeitsrecht und Sozialrecht (2001) no. 1, 1–7.

Nafziger, James A. R. "The general admission of aliens under international law", American Journal of International Law (1983) vol. 77, no. 4, 804–847.

Ndegwa, Stephen N. "Citizenship amid economic and political change in Kenya", Africa Today (1998) vol. 45, no. 3–4, 351–368.

Neff, Stephen C. The rights and duties of neutrals. A general history. Manchester: Manchester University Press, 2000.

Nesbit, E. "Caesars dialogve or a familiar communication containing the first institution of a subiect, in allegiance to his soveraigne" (1601). Amsterdam: Theatrvm Orbis Terrarvm Ltd., 1972.

Netherlands Council of the Institute of Pacific Relations. "The legal status of foreigners in Netherlands India", in *The legal status of aliens in Pacific countries*, edited by Norman MacKenzie. London: Oxford University Press, 1937. Reprint, 1975, 240–261.

Neubecker, Friedrich Karl. "Thronfolgerecht und fremde Staatsangehörigkeit. Ist die Zuge-hörigkeit eines regierenden deutschen Fürsten zu einem fremden Staatsverband vereinbar mit den Normen des Staats- und Völkerrechts?", dissertation presented at the Königliche Friedrich-Wilhelms-Universität zu Berlin, Juristische Fakultät, 1897.

Newman, John Henry. A letter addressed to his Grace the Duke of Norfolk on occasion of Mr. Gladstone's recent expostulation. London: B M Pickering, 1875.

News.com.au. "Hicks 'significant al-Qaeda links'", 2003 (internet), http://www.news.com.au/n/print-page/0,6093,6730709,00.html, consulted 27 July 2003.

Niyonzima, Matthias. "Burundi: débat au sujet de la double nationalité", African journal of international and comparative law (1995) vol. 7, 895–905.

Nylander, Arthur V. J. The nationality and citizenship laws of Nigeria. Lagos: University of Lagos, 1973.

O'Brien, Jeffrey R. "U.S. dual citizen voting rights: a critical examination of Aleinikoff's solu-tion", Georgetown Immigration Law Journal (1999) vol. 13, no. 2, 573–595.

O'Connell, D. P. "The Crown in the British Commonwealth", The International and Com-parative Law Quarterly (1957) vol. 6, no. 1, 103–125.

ODIN. Ministry of Defence (Norway). "Norwegian Defence Facts and Figures 2002. G. Military Service. 1. Compulsory Service", 2002 (internet), http://odin.dep.no/fd/english/publ/veiledninger/010011–120027/index-hov007–b-n-a.html, consulted 10 May 2003.

O'Donnell, Lynne. "Family fears knock of deportation", The Weekend Australian, 4–5 May 2002, 13.

Oeter, Stefan. "Effect of nationality and dual nationality on judicial cooperation, including treaty regimes such as extradition", in *Rights and duties of dual nationals. Evolution and prospects*, edited by David A. Martin and Kay Hailbronner. The Hague: Kluwer Law International, 2003, 55–77.

Ohmae, Kenichi. "A world no longer round. The new frontier is shifting fundamental life assumptions", The Australian, 26 July 2000, 36.

Okafor, Obiora Chinedu. Re-defining legitimate statehood, Developments in international law. The Hague: Martinus Nijhoff Publishers, 2000.

Okonkwo, C. O. Okonkwo and Naish on criminal law in Nigeria. London: Sweet & Maxwell, 1980.

O'Laughlin, Bridget. "Class and the customary: the ambiguous legacy of the indigenato in Mozambique", African Affairs (2000) vol. 99, no. 394, 5–42.

O'Leary, Síofra. The evolving concept of community citizenship – from the free movement of persons to Union citizenship. The Hague: Kluwer Law International, 1996.

Olson, Elizabeth, International Herald Tribune. "U.S. to test expat cybervoting", 2003 (inter-net), http://www.iht.com/articles/104098.html, consulted 26 June 2003.

Omejec, Jasna. "Initial citizenry of the Republic of Croatia at the time of the dissolution of legal ties with the SFRY, and acquisition and termination of Croatian citizenship", Croatian Critical Law Review (1998) vol. 3, no. 1–2, 99–127.

——. "Introduction", Croatian Critical Law Review (1998) vol. 3, no. 1–2, 9–18.

——. "Legal requirements for acquiring Croatian citizenship by naturalization", Zbornik. Pravnog Fakulteta U Zagrebu (1996) vol. 46, no. 5, 489–519.

"On trial: Hicks and Australians' rights", The Sydney Morning Herald, 8 July 2003, 10.

"Opening the door. Whom to let in to the richer countries and why", The Economist, 2 November 2002, 11.

Oppenheim, L. International law. A treatise, edited by Hersch Lauterpacht. London: Longmans, Green & Co., 1948.

Oppermann, Thomas, and Ahmad Yousry, eds. Das Staatsangehörigkeitsrecht der Arabischen Staaten. Vol. 15a, Sammlung Geltender Staatsangehörigkeitsgesetze. Frankfurt am Main: Alfred Metzner Verlag, 1964.

Orfield, Lester B. "The legal effects of dual nationality", The George Washington Law Review (1949) vol. 17, no. 4, 427–445.

Organization of American States. Inter-American treaties and conventions: signatures, ratifications, and deposits with explanatory notes. Washington DC: Organization of American States, General Secretariat, 1993.

"Outward bound. Do developing countries gain orlose when their brightest talents go abroad?", The Economist, 28 September 2002, 24–26.

Pabriks, Artis. "Citizenship and rights of minorities in Latvia", Humanities and Social Sciences: Latvia (1994) vol. 1, no. 2, 60–67.

Paenson, Isaac. Manual of the terminology of public international law (law of peace) and international organizations. Brussels: Bruylant, 1983.

Papassiopi-Passia, Zoe. "The Greek nationality law in a nutshell", Revue hellénique de droit international (1998) vol. 51, no. 2, 501–519.

Parliament of Australia, Department of the Parliamentary Library. "Dual citizenship in Australia. Current issues brief 2000–01", 2001 (internet), http://www.aph.gov.au/library/pubs/cib/2000–01/01cib05.htm, consulted 7 July. 2003.

Parry, Clive, ed. A British digest of international law. Vol. 5. London: Stevens & Sons, 1965.

Parry, Clive, John P. Grant, Anthony Parry, and Arthur D. Watts, eds. Encyclopaedic dictionary of international law. New York: Oceana Publications Inc., 1986.

Partsch, Karl Joseph. "Nations, Peoples", in Encyclopedia of Public International Law, edited by Rudolf Bernhardt and Max Planck Institute for Comparative Public Law and International Law. Amsterdam: Elsevier, 1993, 511–515.

Pastore, Ferruccio. "Droit de la nationalité et migrations internationales: le cas italien", in Nationalité et citoyenneté en Europe, edited by Patrick Weil and Randall Hansen. Paris: Éditions La Découverte, 1999, 95–116.

———. "Nationality law and international migration: the Italian case", in Towards a European nationality. Citizenship, immigration and nationality law in the EU, edited by Randall Hansen and Patrick Weil. Houndmills: Palgrave, 2001, 95–117.

Pejić, Jelena. "The international legal aspects of citizenship", Croatian Critical Law Review (1998) vol. 3, no. 3, 303–336.

Peled, Yoav. "Ethnische Demokratie und die rechtliche Konstruktion der Staatsbürgerschaft: Die arabischen Bürger des jüdischen Staates", in Transnationale Staatsbürgerschaft, edited by Heinz Kleger. Frankfurt: Campus Verlag, 1997, 160–185.

Pellonpää, Matti. Expulsion in international law. A study in international aliens law and human rights with special reference to Finland. Helsinki: Suomalainen Tiedeakatemia, 1984.

Pérez Vera, Elisa, and José-María Espinar y Vicente. "Nationalité: Espagne", in Juris-Classeur Nationalité, edited by Michel Verwilghen and Charles L. Closset. Paris: Éditions du Juris-Classeur, 1993.

Perry, Louise. "Mixed feelings on player hitting for both sides", The Australian, 5 November 2002, 5.

Peter-Ruetschi, Tina. "Betrachtungen zum Doppelbürgerrecht. Vorschläge zu einer Regelung auf europäischer Grundlage", paper presented at the conference: *Generalversammlung der Neuen Helvetischen Gesellschaft*, Zürich 1952. Zürich: Neue Helvetische Gesellschaft, 1952.

Petriella, Dionisio. El Convenio de Doble Ciudadanía entre la Argentina e Italia. Vol. 30. Buenos Aires: Asociación Dante Alighieri, 1988.

Petruševska, Tatjana. "Legal grounds for the acquisition and termination of citizenship of the Republic of Macedonia: the possibility of multiple citizenship and statelessness", Croatian Critical Law Review (1998) vol. 3, no. 1–2, 153–186.

Philipp, Christiane E., Max-Planck-Institut für ausländisches öffentliches Recht und Völkerrecht. "Deutsche Rechtsprechung in völkerrechtlichen Fragen 1993, IV. Staatsangehörigkeit. 1. Erwerb", 1993 (internet), http://www.mpil.de/publ/en/rspr93/r93_7.cfm, consulted 29 March 2006.

——. "Deutsche Rechtsprechung in völkerrechtlichen Fragen 1993. IV. Staatsangehörigkeit. 2. Mehrfache Staatsangehörigkeit", 1993 (internet), http://www.virtual-institute.de/en/rspr93/er93?8.cfm, consulted 10 April 2003.

Picciotto, Sol. "International law: the ligitimation of power in world affairs", in *The critical lawyers' handbook 2*, edited by Paddy Ireland and Per Laleng. London: Pluto Press, 1997, 13–29.

Pickus, Noah M. J. "Introduction", in *Immigration and citizenship in the twenty-first century*, edited by Noah M. J. Pickus. Lanham: Rowman & Littlefield, 1998, xvii–xxxiii.

——. "To make natural: creating citizens for the twenty-first century", in *Immigration and citizenship in the twenty-first century*, edited by Noah M. J. Pickus. Lanham: Rowman & Littlefield, 1998, 107–133.

Piggott, Francis. Nationality – including naturalization and English law on the high seas and beyond the realm. Vol. Part 1. London: William Clowes and Sons, Ltd., 1907.

Pintaric, Tomislav. "Das Staatsangehörigkeitsgesetz von Bosnien und Herzegowina", Jahrbuch für Ostrecht (1999) vol. XL, no. 1, 335–341.

Piotrowicz, Ryszard. "Victims of trafficking and de facto statelessness", Refugee Survey Quarterly (2002) vol. 21, Special Issue, 50–59.

Piotrowicz, Ryszard, and Stuart Kaye. Human rights in international and Australian law. Chatswood (Australia): Butterworths, 2000.

Piotrowicz, Ryszard W. "The Australian-Hungarian Consular Treaty of 1988 and the regulation of dual nationality", The Sydney Law Review (1990) Vol. 12, no. 2/3, 569–583.

Piper, Nicola. Racism, nationalism and citizenship – ethnic minorities in Britain and Germany. Aldershot: Ashgate, 1998.

Plumyène, Jean. Les nations romantiques – histoire du nationalisme – le XIXᵉ siècle. Paris: Fayard, 1979.

Pomoell, Jutta. European Union citizenship in focus, Forum Iuris. Helsinki: Faculty of Law University of Helsinki, 2000.

Preuss, Ulrich K. "Probleme eines Konzepts europäischer Staatsbürgerschaft", in *Transnationale Staatsbürgerschaft*, edited by Heinz Kleger. Frankfurt: Campus Verlag, 1997, 249–269.

Prieto-Castro y Roumier, Fermin. La nacionalidad múltiple. Madrid: Consejo Superior de Investigaciones Científicas Instituto "Francisco de Vitoria", 1962.

"Prisoner repatriation for humanity's sake", The Sydney Morning Herald, 4 October 2002, 10.

Prunes, Cândido. Opinião e Notícia, "O resgate da cidadania (italiana)", 9 December 2005 (internet), http://www.opiniaoenoticia.com.br/interna.php?mat=1814, consulted 27 March 2006.

Pufendorf, Samuel von. De jure naturae et gentium libri octo. Translated by C. H. Oldfather and W. A. Oldfather. 1688 ed. Vol. 2. Oxford: Clarendon Press, 1934.

——. De officio hominis et civis juxta legem naturalem libri duo (The two books on the duty of man and citizen according to the natural law). Translated by Frank Gardner Moore. 1682 ed. Vol. 2. New York: Oxford University Press, 1927.

Putman Tong, Rosemarie. Feminist thought: a more comprehensive introduction. Second ed. St. Leonard's (NSW): Allen & Unwin, 1998.

Qiu, Bincun. Hua qiao shuang chong guoji zhi zhi ben zhenli. Taibei: Xin sheng chu ban she, 1957.

Quermonne, Jean-Louis. "Citoyenneté et nationalité dans l'Union Européenne. Problèmes et perspectives", in De l'étranger au citoyen, edited by Paul Magnette. Bruxelles: De Boeck & Larcier S. A., 1997, 21–31.

Radaković, Mirjana. "A case report on the problems of establishing Croatian citizenship", Croatian Critical Law Review (1998) vol. 3, no. 1–2, 129–136.

Radan, Peter. The break-up of Yugoslavia and international law, Routledge Studies in International Law. London: Routledge, 2002.

Rafiqul Islam, M. "The nationality law and practice of Bangladesh", in Nationality and international law in Asian perspective, edited by Ko Swan Sik. Dordrecht: Martinus Nijhoff Publishers, 1990, 1–25.

Raik-Allen, Georgie. "They want to call Australia home again", The Sydney Morning Herald, 19 February 2002, 12.

Rakić, Vesna. "State succession and citizenship: the example of FR Yugoslavia", Croatian Critical Law Review (1998) vol. 3, no. 1–2, 57–67.

Randelzhofer, Albrecht. "Nationality", in Encyclopedia of Public International Law, edited by Rudolf Bernhardt and Max Planck Institute for Comparative Public Law and International Law. Amsterdam: Elsevier, 1985, 416–424.

Räthzel, Nora. "National politics and the consequences for European perspectives of new citizenship and migration policies: analysing discourses of the new right and their opponents in Germany", in Migration, citizenship and ethno-national identities in the European Union, edited by Marco Martiniello. Aldershot: Avebury, 1995, 144–161.

Ratner, Michael. "The Lords' decision in Pinochet III", in The Pinochet papers. The case of Augusto Pinochet in Spain and Britain, edited by Reed Brody and Michael Ratner. The Hague: Kluwer Law International, 2000, 33–51.

Ravet-Gobbe, Anne-Françoise. "Nationalité: Portugal", in Juris-Classeur Nationalité, edited by Michel J. Verwilghen and Charles L. Closset. Paris: Éditions du Juris-Classeur, 1983.

Reermann, Olaf. "Dual nationality and military service", in Rights and duties of dual nationals. Evolution and prospects, edited by David A. Martin and Kay Hailbronner. The Hague: Kluwer Law International, 2003, 127–134.

Rees, Anthony M. "T. H. Marshall and the progress of citizenship", in Citizenship today. The contemporary relevance of T. H. Marshall, edited by Anthony M. Rees and Martin Bulmer. London: UCL Press Ltd., 1996, 1–23.

"Remessas mundiais de emigrantes podem atingir 243 mil milhões de euros", Lusa: Agência de Notícias de Portugal, 2004 (internet), www.lusa.pt/print.asp?id=SIR-6189151, consulted 14 July 2004.

Renauld, Bernadette. "La loi du 1er mars 2000 modifiant certaines dispositions relatives à la nationalité belge", Revue belge de droit constitutionnel (2000) no. 1, 43–53.

Renner, Günter. "Einheitliche Staatsangehörigkeit in der Familie. Nationaler Befund – internationaler Vergleich", paper presented at the conference: Hohenheimer Tage zum Ausländerrecht 1999 und 5. Migrationspolitisches Forum, Hohenheim 1999. Edited by Klaus Barwig and Gisbert Brinkmann, Kay Hailbronner, Bertold Huber, Christine Kreuzer, Klaus Lörcher, Christoph Schumacher. Hohenheim: Nomos Verlagsgesellschaft, 1999, 149–161.

——. "Erste Anmerkungen zur Reform des Staatsangehörigkeitsrechts", paper presented at the conference: *Hohenheimer Tage zum Ausländerrecht 1999 und 5. Migrationspolitisches Forum*, Hohenheim 1999. Edited by Klaus Barwig and Gisbert Brinkmann, Kay Hailbronner, Bertold Huber, Christine Kreuzer, Klaus Lörcher, Christoph Schumacher. Hohenheim: Nomos Verlagsgesellschaft, 1999, 81–95.

——. "Mehr integration durch option gegen Mehrstaatigkeit?", paper presented at the conference: *Hohenheimer Tage zum Ausländerrecht 1999 und 5. Migrationspolitisches Forum*, Hohenheim 1999. Edited by Klaus Barwig and Gisbert Brinkmann, Kay Hailbronner, Bertold Huber, Christine Kreuzer, Klaus Lörcher, Christoph Schumacher. Hohenheim: Nomos Verlagsgesellschaft, 1999, 139–148.

——. "Was ist neu am neuen Staatsangehörigkeitsrecht?" Zeitschrift für Ausländerrecht und Ausländerpolitik (1999) no. 4 (Juli), 154–163.

Renshon, Stanley A., Center for Immigration Studies. "Dual citizens in America. An issue of vast proportions and broad significance", 2000 (internet), http://www.cis.org/articles/2000/back700.html, consulted 17 January 2003.

Renton, David. "The genuine link concept and the nationality of physical and legal persons, ships and aircraft", dissertation presented at the Universität Köln, Hohe Rechtswissenschaftliche Fakultät, 1975.

Republic of Turkey. Ministry of Foreign Affairs. "Deprivation of citizenship", 2001 (internet), http://www.mfs.gov.tr/grupa/ac/acd/acda/wtdepriv.htm, consulted 27 January 2001.

Rešković, Veronika. "Case analysis in the Republic of Croatia", Croatian Critical Law Review (1998) vol. 3, no. 1–2, 137–144.

Ress, Hans-Konrad, Max-Planck-Institut für ausländisches öffentliches Recht und Völkerrecht. "Deutsche Rechtsprechung in völkerrechtlichen Fragen 1994. IV. Staatsangehörigkeit. 2. Mehrfache Staatsangehörigkeit", 1994 (internet), http://www.virtual-institute.de/en/rspr94/ersp94_8.cfm, consulted 10 May 2003.

"Returning Afghans. No place like home", The Economist, 23 February 2002, 37.

"Reunited", The Economist, 18 February 2006, 61.

Reuter, Paul. "La personnalité juridique internationale du Comité international de la Croix-Rouge", in *Etudes et essais sur le droit internationale humanitaire et sur les principes de la Croix-Rouge en l'honneur de Jean Pictet. Studies and essays on international humanitarian law and Red Cross principles in honour of Jean Pictet*, edited by Christophe Swinarski. Genève: Comité international de la Croix-Rouge. Martinus Nijhoff Publishers, 1984, 783–791.

Reuter, Rudolf. Das Recht der Staatsangehörigkeit in Dänemark. Edited by A. Hegler, L. von Köhler, H. Pohl, C. Satrorius and A. Schötensack, Tübinger Abhandlungen zum Öffentlichen Recht. Stuttgart: Verlag von Ferdinand Enke, 1929.

Riad, Fouad Abdel-Moneim. "Nationalité: Egypte", in *Juris-Classeur Nationalité*, edited by Michel J. Verwilghen and Charles L. Closset. Paris: Éditions du Juris-Classeur, 1985.

Ribeiro, Nuno. "Eleições na Galiza serão decididas por 36 mil votos de emigrantes", Público (Lisbon), 28 June 2005, 16.

Riege, Gerhard. Die Staatsbürgerschaft der DDR. Berlin: Staatsverlag der Deutschen Demokratischen Republik, 1986.

Rights & Democracy International Centre for Human Rights and Democratic Development, and The International Centre for Criminal Law Reform and Criminal Justice Policy. International Criminal Court. Manual for the ratification and implementation of the Rome Statute. Vancouver: Rights & Democracy International Centre for Human Rights and Democratic Development, The International Centre for Criminal Law Reform and Criminal Justice Policy, 2000.

Riley, Mark, and Kelly Burke. "Casualty count. Dual citizenship sows confusion as death toll tops 6,000", The Sydney Morning Herald, 22–23 September 2001, 2.

Rittstieg, Helmut. "Doppelte Staatsangehörigkeit im Völkerrecht", paper presented at the conference: *Doppelte Staatsbürgerschaft – ein europäischer Normalfall?*, Berlin 1989. Edited by Ulrich Büschelmann. Berlin: Senatsverwaltung für Gesundheit und Soziales, 1989, 112–130.

——. "Staatsangehörigkeit, deutsche Leitkultur und die deutsch-türkischen Beziehungen", Informationsbrief Ausländerrecht (2001) no. 1, 23–29.

Robert, Jacques. "Préface", collection of papers presented at the conference: *De la citoyenneté*, Faculté de droit et des sciences politiques de Nantes, 3–5 November 1993. Edited by Geneviève Koubi. Nantes: LITEC, 1993, i–v.

Roberti, Mark. The fall of Hong Kong. China's triumph & Britain's betrayal. New York: John Wiley & Sons, Inc., 1996.

Roberts, Adam. "A survey of the Nordic region", The Economist, 14–20 June 2003, Survey.

Robinson, O. F. The criminal law of ancient Rome. London: Gerald Duckworth & Co. Ltd., 1995.

Roby, Henry John. Roman private law in the times of Cicero and of the Antonines. Vol. 1. Cambridge: Cambridge University Press, 1902.

Rode, Zvonko R. "Dual nationals and the doctrine of dominant nationality", The American Journal of International Law (1959) vol. 53, 139–144.

Rotblat, Joseph. "Preface", in *World citizenship: allegiance to humanity*, edited by Joseph Rotblat. London: Macmillan Press Ltd., 1997, vii–xvi.

Rothwell, Donald R. "When our citizens are left to rot", The Sydney Morning Herald, 15 May 2002, 15.

Rozakis, Christos L. "Le droit de la nationalité en Grèce", in *Nationalité et citoyenneté en Europe*, edited by Patrick Weil and Randall Hansen. Paris: Éditions La Découverte, 1999, 177–197.

——. "Nationality law in Greece", in *Towards a European nationality. Citizenship, immigration and nationality law in the EU*, edited by Randall Hansen and Patrick Weil. Houndmills: Palgrave, 2001, 173–192.

Rubenstein, Kim. "Citizenship and the Constitutional Convention debates: a mere legal inference", Federal Law Review (1997) vol. 25, no. 2, 295–316.

——. "Citizenship in Australia: unscrambling its meaning", Melbourne University Law Review (1995) vol. 20, 503–527.

Rubio-Marín, Ruth. Immigration as a democratic challenge – citizenship and inclusion in Germany and the United States. Cambridge: Cambridge University Press, 2000.

Rule, Ella. "Portuguese nationality law in outline", Tolley's Immigration and Nationality Law and Practice (1996) vol. 10, no. 1, 12–15.

Rumpf, Christian. "Citizenship and multiple citizenship in Turkish law", in *Rights and duties of dual nationals. Evolution and prospects*, edited by David A. Martin and Kay Hailbronner. The Hague: Kluwer Law International, 2003, 361–373.

Ruthe, Walter. "Die organische Auffassung vom Staat und der Staatsangehörigkeit und die Frage der doppelten Staatsangehörigkeit", dissertation presented at the Universität Rostock, Rechts- und Wirtschaftswissenschaftliche Fakultät, 1938. Düsseldorf, 1938.

Ruzié, David. "Citoyenneté et nationalité dans l'Union Européenne", in *Vorträge, Reden und Berichte aus dem Europa-Institut – Sektion Rechtswissenschaft*, edited by Georg Ress and Torsten Stein. Saarbrücken: Europa-Institut Universität des Saarlandes, 1994, 3–19.

Saathoff, Günter, and Malti Taneja. "Von der "doppelten" zur "optionalen" Staatsbürgerschaft – Werdegang und Ergebnis des Gesetzgebungsprozesses," paper presented at the conference:

Hohenheimer Tage zum Ausländerrecht 1999 und 5. Migrationspolitisches Forum, Hohenheim 1999. Edited by Klaus Barwig and Gisbert Brinkmann, Kay Hailbronner, Bertold Huber, Christine Kreuzer, Klaus Lörcher, Christoph Schumacher. Hohenheim: Nomos Verlagsgesellschaft, 1999, 123.

Saba, Jean S. L'Islam et la nationalité. Paris: Librairie de Jurisprudence Ancienne et Moderne, 1931.

Salam, Nawaf A. "The emergence of citizenship in Islamdom", Arab Law Quarterly (1997) vol. 12, 125–147.

Salvador Gutiérrez, Susana. Manual práctico sobre nacionalidad. Granada: Editorial Comares, 1996.

Sandifer, Durward V. "A comparative study of laws relating to a nationality at birth and to loss of nationality", The American Journal of International Law (1935) vol. 29, 248–279.

Santulli, Carlo. Irrégularités internes et efficacité internationale de la nationalité. Paris: Université Panthéon-Assas Paris-2, 1995.

Sasmojo, ed. Menjelesaikan masalah dwikewarganegaraan RI-RRT. Jakarta: Penerbit Djambatan, 1959.

Sauerwald, Christine. Die Unionsbürgerschaft und das Staatsangehörigkeitsrecht in den Mitgliedstaaten der Europäischen Union. Edited by Dieter Blumenwitz. Vol. 66, Schriften zum Staats- und Völkerrecht. Frankfurt am Main: Peter Lang, 1996.

Saunier, Philippe. "Citoyenneté et droit international", paper presented at the conference: *De la Citoyenneté*, Nantes 1993. Edited by Geneviève Koubi. Nantes: LITEC, 1993, 31–37.

Saura Estapà, Jaume. Nacionalidad y nuevas fronteras en europa. Madrid: Marcial Pons, 1998.

Savage, David G. "Holding pattern. High Court limits immigrants' detention rights, setting stage for terrorism cases", ABA Journal (2003) July, 22.

Schade, Horst. "Mehrstaatigkeit – neue Entwicklungen im Europarat", in *Vom Ausländer zum Bürger – Problemanzeigen im Ausländer-, Asyl- und Staatsangehörigkeitsrecht*, edited by Klaus Barwig, Gisbert Brinkmann, Bertold Huber, Klaus Lörcher and Christoph Schumacher. Baden-Baden: Nomos Verlagsgesellschaft, 1994, 408–410.

Schärer, Roland. "The European Convention on Nationality", German Yearbook of International Law (1997) vol. 40, 438–459.

——. "La nouvelle Convention européenne sur la nationalité et le droit suisse", paper presented at the conference: *Mélanges édités à l'occasion de la 50ème Assemblée générale de la Commission Internationale de l'État Civil*, Neuchâtel 1997. Berne: Section Suisse de la Commission Internationale de l'État Civile; Office Fédéral de la Justice, Berne, 1997, 65–78.

Scherner-Kim, Karin. "The role of the oath of renunciation in current U.S. nationaltiy policy – to enforce, to omit, or maybe to change?", The Georgetown Law Journal (2000) vol. 88, no. 2, 329–379.

Schindler, Dietrich, and Jiří Toman, eds. The laws of armed conflicts. A collection of conventions, resolutions, and other documents. Third ed. Dordrecht: Martinus Nijhoff Publishers, 1988.

Schjoldager, Harald, ed. The Norwegian Penal Code. London: Sweet & Maxwell Limited, 1961.

Schlesinger, Rudolf B., Hans W. Baade, Peter E. Herzog, and Edward M. Wise. Comparative law – cases – texts – materials. Sixth ed, University Casebook Series. New York: Foundation Press, 1998.

Schleunes, Karl A., ed. Legislating the Holocaust. The Bernhard Loesener memoirs and supporting documents. Boulder: Westview Press, 2001.

Schmidt-Duvoisin, Isabelle. "Ten years of postal voting for Swiss Abroad. Interview with OSA President Georg Stucky", Swiss Review (2002) July, 9.

Schmidt-Jortzig, Edzard. Staatsangehörigkeit im Wandel. Vortrag: 9. März 1998. Vol. 234, Juristische Studiengesellschaft Karlsruhe Schriftenreihe. Heidelberg: C. F. Müller Verlag, 1997.

Schnapauff, Klaus-Dieter. "Bosniak on the postnational transformation of citizenship", in *Rights and duties of dual nationals. Evolution and prospects*, edited by David A. Martin and Kay Hailbronner. The Hague: Kluwer Law International, 2003, 49–51.

——. "The reform of the nationality law in the Federal Republic of Germany", Law & European Affairs (2000) no. 1–2, 81–87.

——. "Zur Reform des deutschen Staatsangehörigkeitsrechts", paper presented at the conference: *Hohenheimer Tage zum Ausländerrecht 1999 und 5. Migrationspolitisches Forum*, Hohenheim 1999. Edited by Klaus Barwig and Gisbert Brinkmann, Kay Hailbronner, Bertold Huber, Christine Kreuzer, Klaus Lörcher, Christoph Schumacher. Hohenheim: Nomos Verlagsgesellschaft, 1999, 69–80.

Schnapper, Dominique. Qu'est-ce que la citoyenneté? Paris: Gallimard, 2000.

Schuck, Peter H. Citizens, strangers, and in-betweens – essays on immigration and citizenship. Boulder: Westview Press, 1998.

——. "Citizenship in federal systems", The American Journal of Comparative Law (2000) vol. 48, no. 2, 195–226.

——. "Plural citizenships", in *Dual nationality, social rights and federal citizenship in the U.S. and Europe. The reinvention of citizenship*, edited by Randall Hansen and Patrick Weil. New York: Berghahn Books, 2002, 61–99.

Schulze, Georg. "Die Bedeutung des Militärdienstes für Verlust und Erwerbung der Staatsangehörigkeit", dissertation presented at the Königlichen Bayerischen Julius-Maximilians-Universität, Hohen rechts- und staatswissenschaftlichen Fakultät, Würzburg: 1910.

Schwartz, Gustav. Das Recht der Staatsangehörigkeit in Deutschland und im Ausland seit 1914. Edited by Heinrich Titze and Martin Wolff, Rechtsvergleichende Abhandlungen. Berlin: Verlag von Julius Springer, 1925.

Sciolino, Elaine. "Visions of a Union: Europe Gropes for an Identity", The New York Times, 15 December 2002, 11.

Scott, James Brown, and Victor M Maúrtua. Observations on nationality. New York: Oxford University Press, 1930.

Scott, Leisa. "Dark secrets, white lies", The Weekend Australian Magazine, 2 March 2002.

Seagrave, Sterling. Lords of the rim. The invisible empire of the Overseas Chinese. London: Transworld Publishers, 1995.

Secretary of State for the Home Department. "British nationality law – discussion of possible changes." London: Report presented to the Parliament of the United Kingdom of Great Britain and Northern Ireland, 1977.

"Selected bibliography on state succession and nationality", (1995) Austrian Journal of Public and International Law, vol. 49, 105–08.

Senate Legal and Constitutional References Committee (Australia). Discussion paper on a system of national citizenship indicators. Canberra: Parliament of the Commonwealth of Australia, 1995.

Shachar, Ayelet. "Whose republic?: citizenship and membership in the Israeli polity", Georgetown Immigration Law Journal (1999) vol. 13, no. 2, 233–272.

Sharrock, David. "Spanish welcome migrants", The Australian, 15 January 2003, 9.

Shaw, Malcolm N. International law. Fourth ed. Cambridge: Cambridge University Press, 1997.

Shearer, Ivan A. "Jurisdiction", in *Public international law. An Australian perspective*, edited by Sam Blay, Ryszard Piotrowicz and B. Martin Tsamenyi. Melbourne: Oxford University Press, 1997, 161–192.

———. "Non-extradition of nationals", The Adelaide Law Review (1966), 273–309.

———. Starke's international law. 11th ed. London: Butterworths, 1994.

Sheng, Yu. "China's nationality law and the principles of international law", in *Selected articles from the Chinese Yearbook of International Law*, edited by Chinese Society of International Law. Beijing: China Translation and Publishing Corp., 1983, 204–219.

Sherlock, William. "The case of the allegiance due to sovereign powers, stated and resolved, according to scripture and reason, and the principles of the Church of England, with a more particular respect to the oath, lately enjoyned, of allegiance to their present majesties, K. William and Q. Mary" (1691), in *Classics of English legal history in the modern era*. New York: Garland Publishing, Inc., 1978.

———. "A vindiction of the case of allegiance due to sovoraign powers, in reply to an answer to a late pamphlet, intituled, obedience and submission to the present government, demonstrated from Bishop Overal's Convocation-Book; with a postscript in answer to Dr Sherlock's case of allegiance" (1691), in *Classics of English legal history in the modern era*. New York: Garland Publishing, Inc., 1978.

Siclari, Massimo. "Gli effetti del matrimonio sulla cittadinanza della donna nella giurisprudenza della Corte Constituzionale Italiana", La cominità internazionale (1998) vol. 53, no. 3, 423–427.

Sieber, J. Das Staatsbürgerrecht im internationalen Verkehr, seine Erwerbung und sein Verlust. Vol. 1. Bern: Verlag von Stämpfli & Cie., 1907.

Silagi, Michael. "Anmerkung (BVerwG, Urteil vom 27. März 1990 – BVerwG 1 C 5.87)", Das Standesamt (1990) no. 11, 340–343.

———. "Anmerkung (VG Berlin, Urteil vom 27. Oktober 1986 – VG 2 A 39.85)", Das Standesamt (1987) no. 5, 144–146.

———. "Das Einbürgerungsprivileg des § 13 StAG", Zeitschrift für Ausländerrecht und Ausländerpolitik (2001) vol. 21, no. 3, 104–111.

———. "Minderheitenrecht und diplomatischer Schutz für Deutsche in Ost-, Ostmittel- und Südosteuropa. Historische Aspekte", in *Rechtsanspruch und Rechtswirklichkeit des europäischen Minderheitenschutzes*, edited by Dieter Blumenwitz, Gilbert H. Gornig and Dietrich Murswiek. Köln: Verlag Wissenschaft und Politik, 1998, 77–97.

———. Vertreibung und Staatsangehörigkeit, Forschungsergebnisse der Studiengruppe für Politik und Völkerrecht. Bonn: Kulturstiftung der deutschen Vertriebenen, 1999.

Simmons, A. John. Moral principles and political obligations. Princeton: Princeton University Press, 1979.

Simson, Gerhard, ed. Das schwedische Kriminalgesetzbuch vom 21. Dezember 1962. Berlin: Walter de Gruyter, 1976.

Sinnadurai, Visu. "Nationality and international law in the perspective of the Federation of Malaysia", in *Nationality and international law in Asian perspective*, edited by Ko Swan Sik. Dordrecht: Martinus Nijhoff, 1990, 309–333.

Sipkov, Ivan. "Settlement of dual nationality in European communist countries", The American Journal of International Law (1962) vol. 56, 1010–1019.

Skehan, Craig. "Nauru Inc: the scheme to privatise a nation", The Sydney Morning Herald, 1–2 March 2003, 6.

"Slapping Egypt's wrist", The Economist, 24 August 2002, 11.

"Slave-ships in the 21st century?", The Economist, 21 April 2001, 42.

Smis, Stefaan, and Kim Van der Borght. The American Society of International Law. "ASIL Insights. Belgian Law concerning the Punishment of Grave Breaches of International Humanitarian Law: A contested law with uncontested objectives", 2003 (internet), http://www.asil.org/insights/insigh112.htm, consulted 4 July 2003.

Smith, David M, and Maurice Blanc. "Some comparative aspects of ethnicity and citizenship in the European Union," in *Migration, citizenship and ethno-national identities in the European Union*, edited by Marco Martiniello. Aldershot: Avebury, 1995, 70–91.

Sokolewicz, Zofia. "Staatsbürgerschaft und Nationalität: ein polnisches oder europäisches Dilemma?", in *Nation, Ethnizität und Staat in Mitteleuropa*, edited by Urs Altermatt. Wien: Böhlau Verlag, 1996, 88–101.

"The soldier's tale", The Economist, 16 July 2005, 50.

Sonnenberger, Hans Jürgen. "Anerkennung der Staatsangehörigkeit und effektive Staatsangehörigkeit natürlicher Personen im Völkerrecht und im Internationalen Privatrecht", paper presented at the conference: *20. Tagung der Deutschen Gesellschaft für Völkerrecht*, Tübingen, 1987. Vol. 29, Berichte der Deutschen Gesellschaft für Völkerrecht. Heidelberg: C. F. Müller Juristischer Verlag GmbH, 1987, 9–36.

Sornarajah, M. "Nationality and international law in Singapore", in *Nationality and international law in Asian perspective*, edited by Ko Swan Sik. Dordrecht: Martinus Nijhoff, 1990, 423–452.

Soroeta Liceras, Juan. "La problemática de la nacionalidad de los habitantes de los territorios dependientes y el caso del Sahara Occidental", Anuario de Derecho Internacional (1999) vol. 15, 645–676.

Sowell, Thomas. Migrations and cultures. A world view. New York: Basic Books, 1996.

Soysal, Yasemin Nuho_lu. Limits of citizenship – migrants and postnational membership in Europe. Chicago: The University of Chicago Press, 1994.

Spijkerboer, T. P. "Transnationaliteit in de nieuwe Vreemdelingenwet en de gewijzigde Rijkswet op het Nederlanderschap", Rechtsgeleerd Magazijn Themis (2001) no. 6, 163–170.

Spiliopoulou Åkermark, Sia. Human rights of minority women – a manual of international law. Mariehamn (Finland): The Åland Islands Peace Institute, 2000.

Spiro, Peter J. "Dual nationality and the meaning of citizenship", Emory Law Review (1997) vol. 46, no. 4, 1412–1485.

——. Embracing dual nationality. Washington: Carnegie Endowment for International Peace, 1998.

——. "Embracing dual nationality", in *Dual nationality, social rights and federal citizenship in the U.S. and Europe. The reinvention of citizenship*, edited by Randall Hansen and Patrick Weil. New York: Berghahn Books, 2002, 19–33.

——. "Political rights and dual nationality", in *Rights and duties of dual nationals. Evolution and prospects*, edited by David A. Martin and Kay Hailbronner. The Hague: Kluwer Law International, 2003, 135–152.

——. "Questioning barriers to naturalization", Georgetown Immigration Law Journal (1999) vol. 13, no. 1, 479–519.

Spoonley, Paul. "Aliens and citizens in New Zealand", in *Citizenship in a global world. Comparing citizenship rights for aliens*, edited by Atsushi Kondo. Houndmills (UK): Palgrave, 2001, 158–175.

Spranger, Tade Matthias. "Der Verzicht von Mehr- und Doppelstaatern auf die deutsche Staatsangehörigkeit", Zeitschrift für Ausländerrecht und Ausländerpolitik (1999) no. 2, 71–74.

Steiner, Henry J., and Philip Alston. International human rights in context – law politics morals. Second ed. Oxford: Oxford University Press, 2000.

Strauss, Roland Alfred. Das Verbot der Rassendiskriminierung: Völkerrecht, internationales Übereinkommen und schweizerische Rechtsordnung. Vol. 72, Schweizerische Studien zum internationalen Recht. Zürich: Schulthess, 1991.

Struycken, A. V. M. "Acquisition et perte de la nationalité néerlandaise", paper presented at the conference: *La condition juridique de l'étranger, hier et aujourd'hui*, Katholieke Universiteit Nijmegen (Nimègue), 9–11 May 1988. Nijmegen: Fakulteit der Rechtsgeleerdheid Katholieke Universiteit, 1988, 3–19.

Stülken, Gustav. "Die mehrfache Staatsangehörigkeit", dissertation presented at the Universität zu Göttingen, 1934. Quackenbrück, 1934.

Sturm, F., and G. Sturm. "Erwerb des Schweizer Buergerrechts durch Kinder einer Schweizer Mutter", Das Standesmt (1986) vol. 39, no. 2, 29–34.

Sturm, Fritz, and Gudrun Sturm. Das deutsche Staatsangehörigkeitsrecht. Grundriss und Quellen. Frankfurt am Main: Verlag für Standesamtswesen, 2001.

Sucharitkul, Sompong. "Thai nationality in international perspective", in *Nationality and international law in Asian perspective*, edited by Ko Swan Sik. Dordrecht: Martinus Nijhoff Publishers, 1990, 453–491.

Sudargo Gautama. Tafsiran undang-undang kewarganegaraan Republik Indonesia. Bandung: Penerbit Alumni, 1983.

Sundberg-Weitman, Brita. Discrimination on grounds of nationality. Free movement of workers and freedom of establishment under the EEC treaty. Amsterdam: North-Holland Publishing Company, 1977.

Svilanovic, Goran. "The new law on Yugoslav citizenship: procedural provisions and practice", Croatian Critical Law Review (1998) vol. 3, no. 1–2, 243–259.

Swinarski, Christophe. "La notion d'un organisme neutre et le droit international", in *Etudes et essais sur le droit internationale humanitaire et sur les principes de la Croix-Rouge en l'honneur de Jean Pictet. Studies and essays on international humanitarian law and Red Cross principles in honour of Jean Pictet*, edited by Christophe Swinarski. Genève: Comité international de la Croix-Rouge. Martinus Nijhoff Publishers, 1984, 819–835.

Symmons, Clive. "Le droit de la nationalité en Irlande", in *Nationalité et citoyenneté en Europe*, edited by Patrick Weil and Randall Hansen. Paris: Éditions La Découverte, 1999, 307–328.

Symmons, Clive R. "Irish nationality law", in *Towards a European nationality. Citizenship, immigration and nationality law in the EU*, edited by Randall Hansen and Patrick Weil. Houndmills: Palgrave, 2001, 273–312.

Taylor, Greg. "Citizenship rights and the Australian Constitution", Public Law Review (2001) vol. 12, no. 3, 205–229.

Tenorio Adame, Antonio. "La doble nacionalidad", paper presented at the conference: *La doble nacionalidad*, Ciudad de México 1995. Ciudad de México, Miguel Ángel Porrúa Librero-Editor, 1995, 131–137.

Terra. "Cambio legislación ibérica. Unos 400.000 argentinos podrán ser ciudadanos españoles", 2003 (internet), http://www3.terra.com.ar/canales/informaciongeneral/60/60672.html, consulted 11 July 2003.

"The French lesson", The Economist, 13 August 2005, 25–26.

The Lockman Foundation. "New American Standard Bible, Acts of the Apostles, Chapters 22, 23, 25", 2003 (internet), http://www.biblegateway.com/bible?language=english&version=NASB&showxref=no&passage=Acts+22 (and following), consulted 8 July 2003.

Thomas, Ph. J. Introduction to Roman law. Deventer: Kluwer Law and Taxation Publishers, 1986.

Thompson, Brian. "Transcending territory: towards an agreed Northern Ireland?", in *Accommodating national identities. New approaches in international and domestic law*, edited by Stephen Tierney. The Hague: Kluwer Law International, 2000, 233.

Thränhardt, Dietrich. "Entwicklungslinien der Zuwanderungspolitik in EG-Mitgliedsländern", in

Zuwanderungspolitik in Europa. Nationale Politiken- Gemeinsamkeiten und Unterschiede, edited by Hubert Heinelt. Opladen: Leske & Budrich, 1994, 33–63.

Tichenor, Daniel J. "Membership and American social contracts: a response to Hiroshi Motomura", in *Immigration and citizenship in the twenty-first century*, edited by Noah M. J. Pickus. Lanham: Rowman & Littlefield, 1998, 223–227.

"Timorenses perdem dupla nacionalidade", Diário de Notícias (Lisbon), 16 February 2004, 1, 20.

Todorov, Todor. "Grazdanstvo po rozdenie po cl 93, al 2 ot konstitucijata", Pravna Misali (1996) vol. 37, no. 4, 7–14.

Tomson, Edgar. Das Staatsangehörigkeitsrecht des frankophonen schwarzen Afrika. Edited by Forschungsstelle für Völkerrecht und ausländisches öffentliches Recht der Universität Hamburg. Vol. 28, Sammlung Geltender Staatsangehörigkeitsgesetze. Frankfurt am Main: Alfred Metzner Verlag, 1967.

Tönnies, Ferdinand. Community and civil society. Translated by José Harris and Margaret Hollis. Edited by José Harris. Cambridge: Cambridge University Press, 2001.

Torcia, Charles E. Wharton's criminal law. Vol. 4. Rochester, NY: The Lawyers Co-operative Publishing Co., 1981.

Torpey, John. The invention of the passport – surveillance, citizenship and the state. Cambridge: Cambridge University Press, 2000.

"Traitors ahoy, and it's driving the Kiwis cuckoo", The Sydney Morning Herald, 19 February 2003, 1.

Tønnesson, Stein, and Hans Antlöv. "Asia in theories of nationalism and national identity", in *Asian forms of the nation*, edited by Stein Tønnesson and Hans Antlöv. Richmond (UK): Curzon, 1996, 1–39.

Turetsky, David. "Citizenship, diversity, and pluralism: Canadian and comparative perspectives", edited by Alain C. Cairns. Montreal: McGill-Queen's University Press, 2000, 277–286.

Udgave, Tredje. Nordiske Statsborgeres sociale Rettigheder under ophold i andet nordisk land. København: Den nordiske socialpolitiske Komité efter henstilling fra Nordisk Råd, 1963.

United Nations. Laws concerning nationality, United Nations Legislative Series. New York: United Nations, 1954.

——. United Nations national competitive recruitment examination. NCRE Frequently asked questions, 2006 (internet), http://www.un.org/Depts/OHRM/examin/exam.htm, consulted 28 March 2006.

United Nations, Département des affaires économiques et sociales. "Nationalité de la femme mariée". New York: United Nations, 1963.

United Nations, Economic and Social Council, Commission on Human Rights. "Implementation of the Programme of Action for the Second Decade to Combat Racism and Racial Discrimination. Report by Mr. Maurice Glélé-Ahanhanzo, Special Rapporteur on contemporary forms of racism, racial discrimination, xenophobia and related intolerance, submitted pursuant to Commission on Human Rights resolutions 1993/20 and 1995/12", E/CN.4/ 1996/72. Geneva: Fifty-second session, 1996.

——. "Letter dated 25 March 1996 from the Permanent Representative of Turkey to the United Nations Office at Geneva addressed to the Chairman of the Commission on Human Rights", E/CN.4/1996/153. Geneva, 1996.

——. "The rights of non-citizens". E/CN.4/1999/4–E/CN.4/Sub.2/98/45.-30 Sept. 98. Geneva: Subcommission on Prevention of Discrimination and Protection of Minorities, 50th session, Geneva, 3–28 August 1998, 79.

——. "Situation of migrant workers and members of their families", E/CN.4/1998/2. E/CN.4/Sub.2/97/50. Geneva: Sub-Commission on the Prevention of Discrimination and Protection of Minorities, 25th meeting, Geneva, 21 August 1997, 19.

——. "World Conference against Racism, Racial Discrimination, Xenophobia and Related Intolerance", E/CN.4/2001/2. E/CN.4/Sub.2/00/46. Geneva: Sub-Commission on the Promotion and Protection of Human Rights, 17th meeting, 11 August 2000, 19.

United Nations, General Assembly. "Letter dated 21 October 1992 from the Chargé d'affaires a.i. of the Permanent Mission of Yugoslavia to the United Nations addressed to the Secretary-General. Annex: Joint declaration made at Geneva on 20 October 1992 by the President of Croatia and the President of Yugoslavia", A/47/572. Geneva: Forty-seventh session, 1992.

United Nations, Global Commission on International Migration. "Report", October 2005 (internet), http://www.gcim.org/en/finalreport.html, consulted on 1 March 2006.

United Nations, High Commissioner for Refugees (UNHCR). Citizenship and prevention of statelessness linked to the disintegration of the Socialist Federal Republic of Yugoslavia. Vol. 3 No. 1, European Series. Geneva: UNHCR Regional Bureau for Europe, 1997.

——. Citizenship in the context of the dissolution of Czechoslovakia. Vol. 2 No. 4, European Series. Geneva: UNHCR Regional Bureau for Europe, 1996.

United Nations, Secretariat. "Survey of the problem of multiple nationality prepared by the Secretariat", Yearbook of the International Law Commission (1960) vol. 1954, no. II, 52–111.

United States Census Bureau. "Difference in population by race and hispanic or latino origin for the US: 1990 and 2000", 2004 (internet), http://www.census.gov/population/cen2000/phc-t1/tab04.pdf, consulted 1 March 2006

United States Congress. "Hearing before the Subcommittee on International Relations of the Committee on Foreign Affairs House of Representatives One Hundred Second Congress, First Session, June 25, 1991". Washington: U.S. Government Printing Office, 1991.

United States Department of State. "Advice about possible loss of U.S. citizenship and seeking public office in a foreign state", 2003 (internet), http://travel.state.gov/foreign_public_office.html, consulted 10 May 2003.

——. "Certificates of Non-Citizen Nationality", 2003 (internet), http://travel.state.gov/noncit_cert.html, consulted 9 July 2003.

——. "Dual nationality", 2002 (Internet), http://travel.state.gov/dualnationality.html, consulted 28 October 2002.

——. "Renunciation of U.S. citizenship by persons claiming a right of residence in the United States", 2003 (internet), http://travel.state.gov/pr_renun.html, consulted 10 May 2003.

——. "Saudi Arabia. International religious freedom report", 2002 (internet), www.state.gov/g/drl/rls/irf/2002/14012.html, consulted 21 November 2002.

United States Office of Personnel Management, Investigations Office. "Citizenship laws of the world", 2001 (internet), www.opm.gov/extra/investigate/IS-01.pdf, consulted 23 June 2003.

Uribe Ireguí, Luis Fernando. "Tesis de Grado", presented at the Pontífica Universidad Javeriana (Colombia), 1977.

"US visitors may be fingerprinted", The Sydney Morning Herald, 27 August 2002, 3.

van Creveld, Martin. The rise and decline of the State. Cambridge: Cambridge University Press, 1999.

van Lengerich, Wolf B. "Das Staatsbürgerschaftsrecht Südafrikas unter besonderer Berücksichtigung der ehemaligen Homelands", Verfassung und Recht in Übersee (2001) no. 3, 361–386.

van Panhuys, H. F. The rôle of nationality in international law – an outline. Leyden: A. W. Sythoff, 1959.

van Pottelberge, Joroen. "The right of return in a changing world order", Tel Aviv University Studies in Law (1997) vol. 13, 311–325.

Vashkevich, Alexander. "Ten years of Belarussian citizenship: success or failure?", in *The twentieth world congress of the International Association for Philosophy of Law and Social Philosophy.* Amsterdan, 2001.

Vattel, Emmerich de. The law of nations or the principles of natural law applied to the conduct and to the affairs of nations and of sovereigns. Translated by Charles G. Fenwick. 1758 ed. Vol. 3. Washington: The Carnegie Institution of Washington, 1916.

——. Le droit des gens ou principes de la loi naturelle. 1758 ed. Vol. 1. Washington: The Carnegie Institution of Washington, 1916.

——. Le droit des gens ou principes de la loi naturelle. 1758 ed. Vol. 2. Washington: The Carnegie Institution of Washington, 1916.

Verlag für Standesamtswesen GmbH. Ausländisches Staatsangehörigkeitsrecht. Edited by Verlag für Standesamtswesen GmbH. Vol. 6, Kleine Fachbibliothek für Verwaltung und Recht. Frankfurt am Main: Alfred Metzner Verlag, 1955.

——. Ausländisches Staatsangehörigkeitsrecht. 2 vols., Leitfaden für die Standesbeamten. Baden-Baden: Verlag für Behördenbedarf, 1955.

Viñas Farré, Ramón. "Régimen de la nacionalidad y de la extranjería en el derecho andorrano", paper presented at the conference: XVI Jornadas de la Asociación Española de Profesores de Derecho Internacional y Relaciones Internacionales, Andorra 1995. Edited by Alegría Borrás. Barcelona: Marcial Pons, Ediciones Jurídicas y Sociales, 1995, 163.

Visek, Richard C. "Creating the ethnic electorate through legal restorationism: citizenship rights in Estonia", Harvard International Law Journal (1997) vol. 38, no. 2, 315–373.

von Mangoldt, Hans. "Anerkennung der Staatsangehörigkeit und effektive Staatsangehörigkeit natürlicher Personen im Völkerrecht und im Internationalen Privatrecht", paper presented at the conference: 20. Tagung der Deutschen Gesellschaft für Völkerrecht, Tübingen, 1987. Vol. 29, Berichte der Deutschen Gesellschaft für Völkerrecht. Heidelberg: C. F. Müller Juristischer Verlag GmbH, 1987, 37–97.

——. "Das Staatsangehörigkeitsrecht der Russischen Föderation im Lichte ihrer völkerrechtlichen Verpflichtungen", in *Russlands Reform auf dem Prüfstand*, edited by Dieter Blumenwitz and Silke Spieler. Bonn: Kulturstiftung der deutschen Verbriebenen, 1997, 11–37.

——. "Ius-sanguinis-Prinzip, Ius-soli-Prinzip und Mehrstaatigkeit: Umbrüche durch das Staatsangehörigkeitsreformgesetz", Zeitschrift für Ausländerrecht und Ausländerpolitik (1999) no. 6, 243–252.

——. "Migration ouvrière et double nationalité. La situation allemande", Revue critique de droit international privé (1995) vol. 84, no. 4, 671–693.

——. "The right of return in German nationality law", Tel Aviv University Studies in Law (1997) vol. 13, 29–52.

von Rauchhaupt, Fritz. W. "Erwerb und Verlust der Staatsangehörigkeit in Ibero-Amerika", Ibero-Amerika (1928) vol. D, no. 4, 59–62; 79–81.

"Vote, sweet vote", The Economist, 26 June 2004, 58.

Vrabiescu Kleckner, Simone-Marie, ed. The Penal Code of the Romanian Socialist Republic. London: Sweet & Maxwell, 1976.

Walker, Andrew. "Rupert Murdoch: Bigger than Kane", BBC News, 31 July 2002 (internet), http://news.bbc.co.uk/1/ hi/uk/2162658.stm, consulted 28 March 2006.

Wallrabenstein, Astrid. Das Verfassungsrecht der Staatsangehörigkeit. Baden-Baden: Nomos Verlagsgesellschaft, 1999.

Wang, Keju. "Basic principles of the nationality law of the People's Republic of China", in *Selected Articles from the Chinese Yearbook of International Law*, edited by Chinese Society of International Law. Beijing: China Translation and Publishing Corp., 1983, 220–239.

Warbrick, Colin. "Current legal developments", International and Comparative Law Quarterly (1988) vol. 37, no. 4, 983–1012.

Weber, Max. "On the concept of citizenship", in *Max Weber on charisma and institution building*, edited by Shmuel N. Eisenstadt. Chicago: University of Chicago Press, 1968.

Weil, Patrick. "Access to citizenship: a comparison of twenty-five nationality laws", in *Citizenship today. Global perspectives and practices*, edited by T. Alexander Aleinikoff and Douglas Klusmeyer. Washington: Carnegie Endowment for International Peace, 2001, 17–35.

———. "The history of French nationality: a lesson for Europe", in *Towards a European nationality. Citizenship, immigration and nationality law in the EU*, edited by Randall Hansen and Patrick Weil. Houndmills: Palgrave, 2001, 52–68.

———. "L'histoire de la nationalité française: une leçon pour l'Europe", in *Nationalité et citoyenneté en Europe*, edited by Patrick Weil and Randall Hansen. Paris: Éditions La Découverte, 1999, 55–70.

Weil, Patrick, and Randall Hansen. "Citoyenneté, immigration et nationalité: vers la convergence européenne", in *Nationalité et citoyenneté en Europe*, edited by Patrick Weil and Randall Hansen. Paris: Éditions La Découverte, 1999, 9–28.

———, eds. Nationalité et citoyenneté en Europe. Paris: Éditions La Découverte et Syros, 1999.

Weinstock, Daniel. "National partiality: confronting the intuitions", in *Nationalism and ethnic conflict. Philosophical perspectives*, edited by Nenad Miscevic. Chicago: Open Court Publishing Company, 2000, 133–155.

Weis, Peter. Nationality and statelessness in international law. Alphen aan den Rijn: Sijthoff & Noordhoff, 1979.

Weissbrodt, David. Immigration law and procedure in a nutshell. Second ed, Nutshell. St. Paul: West Publishing Co., 1989.

Whitbeck, Harris, Cable News Network (CNN). "Struggling economy fuels Argentine emigration", 2003 (internet), http://www.cnn.com/2001/WORLD/americas/07/23/argentina.migration/, consulted 5 July 2003

White, Robin M. "Hong Kong: nationality, immigration and the agreement with China", International and Comparative Law Quarterly (1987) vol. 36, 483–503.

———. "Nationality and the British Empire: historical doubts and confusions on the status of the inhabitants", Hong Kong Law Journal (1989) vol. 19, 10–42.

———. "Nationality aspects of the Hong Kong settlement", Case Western Reserve Journal of International Law (1998) vol. 20, 225–251.

Whiteman, Marjorie M. Digest of international law. 15 vols. Vol. 6. Washington: Department of State, 1968.

Wiedemann, Marianne. "Development of dual nationality under German law", in *Rights and duties of dual nationals. Evolution and prospects*, edited by David A. Martin and Kay Hailbronner. The Hague: Kluwer Law International, 2003, 335–345.

Wiener, Antje. 'European' citizenship practice – Building institutions of a non-state. Boulder: Westview Press, 1998.

Wilkinson, Isambard. "Job, house, plane trip – just the ticket to viva España", The Sydney Morning Herald, 4–5 January 2003, 8.

Witte, Hubert. "Die mehrfache Staatsangehörigkeit, ihre Entstehung, sowie Versuche und Möglichkeiten ihrer Beseitigung", dissertation presented at the Bayerischen Friedrich-Alexanders-Universität Erlangen, Hohen philosophischen Fakultät, 1928.

Wittram, Reinhard. Das Nationale als europäisches Problem – Beiträge zur Geschichte des Nationalitätsprinzips. Göttingen: Vandenhoeck & Ruprecht, 1954.

Woehrling, José. "Les politiques de la citoyenneté au Canada et au Québec", in *La citoyenneté européenne*, edited by Christian Philip and Panayotis Soldatos. Montréal: Université de Montréal, 2000, 27–56.

Wolfrum, Rüdiger. "Völkerrechtliche Rahmenbedingungen für die Einwanderung", in *Einwanderungsrecht – national und international. Staatliches Recht, Europa- und Völkerrecht*, edited by Thomas Giegerich and Rüdiger Wolfrum. Opladen: Leske & Budrich, 2001, 20–35.

Woodhouse, Diana, ed. The Pinochet case. A legal and constitutional analysis. Oxford: Hart Publishing, 2000.

World Air Sports Federation. "Sporting Code. Chapter 8. Licences", 2004 (internet), http://www.fai.org/sporting_code/scg_c8.asp, consulted 28 March 2006.

World Chess Federation. "Handbook. C. General rules and recommendations for tournaments. 5. General rules for participation in FIDE events", (internet), http://www.fide.com/official, consulted 28 March 2006.

Wyler, Eric. "La règle dite de la continuité de la nationalité dans le contentieux international", thesis (thèse) presented at the Université de Genève, Institut Universitaire de Hautes Études Internationales, 1989.

Ylänkö, Maaria. "Le droit de la nationalité finlandaise", in *Nationalité et citoyenneté en Europe*, edited by Patrick Weil and Randall Hansen. Paris: Éditions La Découverte, 1999, 281–306.

Zagar, Mitja. "Nationality, Citizenship and Protection of Ethnic Minorities: the Case of the Republic of Slovenia", paper presented at the conference: *Nationalité, minorités et succession d'états en europe de l'est*, Prague, 22–24 September 1994. Cedin Paris X Nanterre Cahiers Internationaux 10. Edited by Emmanuel Decaux and Alain Pellet. Paris : Montchrestien, 1996, 249.

Zappalà, Gianni, and Stephen Castles. "Citizenship and immigration in Australia", Georgetown Immigration Law Journal (1999) vol. 13, no. 2, 273–316.

Ziccardi Capaldo, Giuliana, ed. Repertory of decisions of the International Court of Justice (1947–1992). Vol. 1. Dordrecht: Martinus Nijhoff, 1995.

Ziemele, Ineta. "The citizenship issue in the Republic of Latvia", in *Citizenship and nationality status in the new Europe*, edited by Síofra O'Leary and Teija Tiilikainen. London: Sweet & Maxwell, 1998, 187–204.

Zilbershats, Yaffa. "Reconsidering the concept of citizenship", Texas International Law Journal (2001) vol. 36, no. 4, 689–734.

Zimmermann, Andreas. "Europäisches Gemeinschaftsrecht und Staatsangehörigkeitsrecht der Mitgliedstaaten unter besonderer Berücksichtigung der Probleme mehrfacher Staatsangehörigkeit", Europarecht (1995) no. 1, 54–70.

——. "Staats- und völkerrechtliche Fragen der Reform des deutschen Staatsangehörigkeitsrechts", IPRax Praxis des Internationalen Privat- und Verfahrensrechts (2000) no. 3, 180–185.

LEGISLATION AND CASES

Acquisition of Polish nationality, Advisory Opinion no. 7, September 15, 1923, Permanent Court of International Justice, Series B, No. 7, 6–26, in *World Court Reports*, edited by Manley O. Hudson. Dobbs Ferry, New York: Oceana Publications, Inc., 1969, 237–252.

Advisory opinion OC-4/84 of January 19, 1984. Proposed amendments to the naturalization provision of the Constitution of Costa Rica. Requested by the Government of Costa Rica,

Inter-American Court of Human Rights, 1984 (internet), http://www.corteidh.or.cr/ seriea_ing/seriea_04_ing.doc, consulted 28 March 2006.

Baruch Ivcher Bronstein v. Peru, Judgment of 6 February 2001, Inter-American Court of Human Rights, (internet), http://www.corteidh.or.cr/seriec_ing/seriec_74__ing.doc, consulted 19 March 2006.

Basic Law of the Federal Republic of Germany (23 May 1949). Wiesbaden: Press and Information Office of the Federal Republic of Germany, 1977.

Beschluss vom 21.8.2000 – 10 E 2124–98, Verwaltungsgericht Giessen, Informationsbrief Ausländerrecht (2001) no. 1, 37.

British Overseas Territories Act 2002, Office of Public Sector Information, 2006 (internet), http://www.opsi.gov.uk/ ACTS/acts2002/20020008.htm, consulted 29 March 2006.

Bundesgesetz über Erwerb und Verlust des Schweizer Bürgerrechts vom 29. September 1952 (Stand 6 Dezember 2005), Confoederatio Helvetica -Authorities of the Swiss Confederation, 2006 (internet), www.admin.ch/ch/d/sr/1/141.0.de.pdf, consulted 2 April 2006.

Canevaro Case, 12 May 1912, Permanent Court of Arbitration, (1912) Scott Reports, vol. 1, 284–296.

Case No. A/18 concerning the question of jurisdiction over claims of persons with dual nationality, 6 April 1984, Iran-United States Claims Tribunal, (1984) International Legal Materials, vol. 23, 489.

Castillo Petruzzi et al. Case, Judgment of 30 May 1999, para. 102, Inter-American Court of Human Rights, (internet), http://www.corteidh.or.cr/seriec_52_ing.doc, consulted 19 March 2006.

Chinn Case, 12 December 1934, Permanent Court of International Justice, (1934) Annual Digest and Reports of Public International Law Cases, 312.

Constitución Política de la República de Colombia de 1991 (as amended until 2005), Base de Datos Políticos de las Américas (internet), http://pdba.georgetown.edu/Constitutions/ Colombia/col91.html, consulted 15 May 2006.

Constitution of the Republic of the Fiji Islands, 27 July 1998. Suva: Government Printing Department Fiji, 1998.

"Constitution of Saint Vincent and the Grenadines, 26 July 1979", in *The Laws of Saint Vincent and the Grenadines in force on the 1st January 1991*, edited by John Kingsley Havers. 8 vols., vol. 1. Kingstown: Government of Saint Vincent and the Grenadines, 1979, 71–74.

Erste Verordnung zum Reichsbürgergesetz. 14. November 1935. (1935) Reichsgesetzblatt, no. 1, 1333.

Flegenheimer Claim, 20 September 1958, Italian-United States Conciliation Commission, (1958) International Law Reports, vol. 25, 91.

Gaygusuz v. Austria, 1996, European Court of Human Rights (internet), http://cmiskp.echr.coe. int/tkp197/view.asp?item=1&portal=hbkm&action=html&highlight=Gaygusuz%20%7C%20Aus tria&sessionid=6516400&skin=hudoc-en, consulted 4 April 2006.

"Gesetz über den Widerruf von Einbürgerungen und die Aberkennung der deutschen Staatsangehörigkeit. Vom 14. Juli 1933. Verordnung zur Durchführung des Gesetzes über den Widerruf von Einbürgerungen und die Aberkennung der deutschen Staatsangehörigkeit. Vom 26. Juli 1933", in *Die Ausbürgerung deutscher Staatsangehöriger 1933–45 nach den im Reichsanzeiger veröffentlichen Listen*, edited by Michael Hepp. München: K. G. Saur, 1985, XLI–XLIII.

"Gesetz über die Staatsangehörigkeit von Bosnien und Herzegowina vom 16. Dezember 1997", in *Jahrbuch für Ostrecht*, edited by Friedrich-Christian Schroeder, Martin Fincke and Dieter Pfaff. München: Verlag C. H. Beck, 1999, 397–406.

"Gesetz vom 5. Juni 1991 über die Staatsangehörigkeit der Republik Moldau", in *WGO Monatshefte für Osteuropäisches Recht* (1998) vol. 40, edited by Otto Luchterhandt and Günther H. Tontsch. Hüthig: C. F. Müller, 1998, 276–86.

"*Grundgesetz für die Bundesrepublik Deutschland vom 23 Mai 1949*", in *Verfassung des Landes Hessen und Grundgesetz für die Bundesrepublik Deutschland mit einer Einführung und Karten von Hessen und Deutschland.* Bad Homburg: Verlag Dr. Max Gehlen, 1963.

Jong Kim Koe v. Minister for Immigration & Multicultural Affairs [1997] 306 FCA (Federal Court of Australia).

Kawakita (Tomoya Kawakita) v United States, United States Supreme Court, (1952) 343 U.S. 717.

Lay Kon Tji v. Minister for Immigration & Ethnic Affairs [1998] 1380 FCA.

Lembaga Bantuan Hukum. "Undang-Undang No. 62 Tahun 1958 Tentang Kewarga-Negaraan Republik Indonesia", 1958 (internet), http://www.lbh-apik.or.id/uu-62–58.htm, consulted 7 July 2003.

"Ley 32–2002, de 5 de julio, de modificación de la Ley 17/1999, de 18 de mayo, de Régimen del Personal de las Fuerzas Armadas, al objeto de permitir el acceso de extranjeros a la condición de militar profesional de tropa y marinería", 2003 (internet), http://www.lalegion. com/ser/ley_32_2002.htm, consulted 21 July 2003.

Lori Berenson Mejía v. Perú, Sentencia de 25 de noviembre de 2004, Inter-American Court of Human Rights, (internet), http://www.corteidh.or.cr/seriec_119_esp.doc, para. 91, consulted 19 March 2006.

MacKenzie v. Hare, United States Supreme Court, (1915) 239 U.S. 299.

Mavrommatis Concessions Case, 30 August 1924, Permanent Court of International Justice, (1924) Series A, no. 2, 12.

Mergé Claim, Italian-United States Conciliation Commission, (1955) International Law Reports, vol. 22, 443.

Nationality Decrees Issued in Tunis and Morocco (Advisory Opinion), Permanent Court of International Justice, (1923) Series B, No. 4.

Nottebohm Case (second phase), 6 April 1955, International Court of Justice, (1955) I.C.J. Reports, 4.

The Oscar Chinn Case, Permanent Court of International Justice, 12 December 1934, (1934) World Court Reports, vol. 3, 416.

Panevezys-Saldutiskis Railway Case, Permanent Court of International Justice, (1939) Series A/B, vol. 76, 16.

Perez v Brownell, United States Supreme Court, (1958) 356 U.S. 44.

Polites v The Commonwealth, High Court of Australia, (1945) 70 CLR 60.

Prosecutor v Dusko Tadic, Appeals Chamber of the International Tribunal for the Prosecution of Persons Responsible for Serious Violations of International Humanitarian Law Committed in the Territory of the Former Yugoslavia since 1991, 15 July 1999 (internet), http://www.un. org/icty/tadic/appeal/judgement/index.htm, consulted 1 August 2003.

"*Reichsbürgergesetz. Vom 15. September 1935* (Reichsgesetzblatt (RGBl.) I (1935): 1146", in *Der Nationalsozialismus. Dokumente 1933–1945*, edited by Walther Hofer. Frankfurt am Main: Fischer Bücherei, 1957, 284.

Reparation for injuries suffered in the service of the United Nations, 11 April 1949, International Court of Justice, (1949) Annual Digest of Reports of Public International Law Cases, vol. 16, 318.

Rush v Commissioner of Police, Federal Court of Australia (2006) FCA 12 (23 January 2006).

Salem Case, 8 June 1932, United States-Egypt Special Arbitral Tribunal, (1932) U.N. Reports, vol. 2, 1161.

'*SRRP*' and *Minister for Immigraiton and Multicultural Affairs* [2000] AATA 878 (Administrative Appeals Tribunal of Australia).

The State v Ratu Timoci Silatolu and Josefa Nata, 26 March 2002, High Court of Fiji (Criminal action no. misc. HAM 002 of 2002, Andrew Wilson, Judge, unreported*)*.

Sue v Hill and Another, High Court of Australia, (1999) 163 ALR 648.

Swedish Penal Code, 21 December 1962 (entry into force: 1 January 1965), Chapters 19 and 22, as of 1 May 1999, Government Offices of Sweden (internet), http://www.sweden.gov.se/content/1/c6/02/77/77/cb79a8a3.pdf, consulted 19 March 2006.

Urteil vom 4. April 1996 – OVG 5 B 60.93 (Land Berlin gegen Alfred M. Boll), 4 April 1996, Oberverwaltungsgericht Berlin (Meinhardt, Ehricke, Wahle, Böttcher, Drews, Judges, unreported case).

Urteil vom 27. März 1990 – BVerwG 1 C 5.87, 27 March 1990, Bundesverwaltungsgericht (1990) Das Standesamt, vol. 11, 337.

Urteil vom 27. Oktober 1986 – VG 2 A 39.85, 27 October 1986, Verwaltungsgericht Berlin, (1987) Das Standesamt, no. 5, 142.

TREATIES AND INTERNATIONAL RESOLUTIONS

Additional Protocol to the Convention on the Reduction of Cases of Multiple Nationality and Military Obligations in Cases of Multiple Nationality, 24 November 1977, entry into force: 17 October 1983. Council of Europe, European Treaty Series, no. 96 (internet), http://conventions.coe.int/treaty/EN/cadreprincipal.htm, consulted 13 August 2003.

Charter of the United Nations, 26 June 1945 (internet), www.un.org/charter, consulted 1 August 2003 (entry into force: 24 October 1945).

Convenção sôbre dupla nacionalidade entre o Brasil e Portugal, in Tratado sôbre nacionalidade, edited by Ilmar Penna Marinho. Rio de Janeiro: Departamento de Imprensa Nacional, 1961, 557–58.

Convention concernant l'échange d'informations en matière d'acquisition de nationalité, 1964. Commission internationale de l'état civil (internet), http://perso.wanadoo.fr/ciec-sg/ListeConventions.html, consulted 23 April 2003.

Convention on Certain Questions Relating to the Conflict of Nationality Laws, 12 April 1930, (1937) 179 LNTS 89, no. 4137 (entry into force: 1 July 1937).

Convention on the nationality of married women, 20 February 1957, (1958) 309 UNTS 66, no. 4468 (entry into force: 11 August 1958).

Convention on reduction of cases of multiple nationality and military obligations in cases of multiple nationality, 6 May 1963, (1968) 634 UNTS 221, no. 9065 (entry into force: 28 March 1968).

Convention on the reduction of statelessness, 30 August 1961, 989 UNTS 175, no. 14458, (entry into force: 13 December 1975).

Convention relating to the status of stateless persons, 28 September 1954, (1960) 360 UNTS 130, no. 5158 (entry into force: 6 June 1960).

"*Convention (IV) Respecting the Laws and Customs of War on Land*, Signed at The Hague, 18 October 1907. Annex to the Convention. Regulations Respecting the Laws and Customs of War on Land", in *The laws of armed conflicts. A collection of conventions, resolutions and other documents*, edited by Dietrich Schindler and Jirí Toman. Dordrecht: Martinus Nijhoff Publishers, 1907, 69–98.

Council of Europe. "*La nationalité des conjoints de nationalités différentes et la nationalité des enfants nés dans le mariage* – Résolutions (77) 12 et (77) 13 adoptées par le Comité des Ministres du Conseil de l'Europe le 27 mai 1977 et Exposés des motifs". Strasbourg: Council of Europe, 1977.

Declaration on the human rights of individuals who are not nationals of the country in which they live, 13 December 1985, United Nations General Assembly Resolution 40/144. UN Document Series ST/DPI. New York: United Nations, 1985.

European convention on nationality, 6 November 1997, ETS 166, Council of Europe, (entry into force: 1 March 2000).

"Final Act, Seventh International Conference of American States, Montevideo, Uruguay, 3–26 December 1933", American Journal of International Law (1933) vol. 28 Supplement (1933) 52–64. Concord (USA): The Rumford Press, 1934.

Geneva Convention relative to the protection of civilian persons in time of war, 12 August 1949 (entry into force: 21 October 1950), in *The Geneva Conventions of August 12 1949*. Geneva: International Committee of the Red Cross, 1991.

International Convention on the Elimination of All Forms of Racial Discrimination, United Nations General Assembly Resolution 2106 (XX), 21 December 1965 (internet), http://www.unhchr.ch/html/menu3/b/d_icerd.htm, consulted 1 August 2003.

International Covenant on Civil and Political Rights, 1966. United Nations (internet), http://www.hrweb.org/legal/cpr.html, consulted 1 August 2003.

Optional protocol to the Vienna convention on consular relations concerning acquisition of nationality, 24 April 1963, (1967) 596 UNTS 469, no. 8639 (entry into force: 19 March 1967).

Optional protocol to the Vienna convention on diplomatic relations concerning acquisition of nationality, 18 April 1961, (1964) 500 UNTS 223, no. 7311 (entry into force: 24 April 1964).

Protocol amending the Convention on the reduction of cases of multiple nationality and military obligations in cases of multiple nationality, 24 November 1977, ETS 95, Council of Europe (entry into force: 8 September 1978).

Protocol relating to a certain case of statelessness, 12 April 1930, (1937) 179 LNTS 115, no. 4138, (entry into force: 1 July 1937).

Protocol relating to military obligations in certain cases of double nationality, 12 April 1930, (1937) 178 LNTS 229, no. 4117 (entry into force: 25 May 1937).

Second protocol amending the Convention on the reduction of cases of multiple nationality and military obligations in cases of multiple nationality, 2 February 1993, ETS 149, Council of Europe, (entry into force: 24 March 1995).

Special protocol concerning statelessness, 12 April 1930, (not yet in force).

Universal Declaration of Human Rights, United Nations General Assembly Resolution 217 A (III), 10 December 1948 (internet), www.un.org/rights/50/decla.htm, consulted on 1 August 2003.

Vienna convention on diplomatic relations, 18 April 1961, (1964) 500 UNTS 95, no. 7310 (entry into force: 24 April 1964).

Index

Developments in International Law

26. S.P. Sharma: *Territorial Acquisition, Disputes and International Law*. 1997
ISBN 90-411-0362-7
27. V.D. Degan: *Sources of International Law*. 1997   ISBN 90-411-0421-6
28. Mark Eugen Villiger: *Customary International Law and Treaties*. A Manual on the Theory and Practice of the Interrelation of Sources. Fully Revised Second Edition. 1997   ISBN 90-411-0458-5
29. Erik M.G. Denters and Nico Schrijver: *Reflections on International Law from the Low Countries*. In Honour of Paul de Waart. 1998   ISBN 90-411-0503-4
30. Kemal Baslar: *The Concept of the Common Heritage of Mankind in International Law*. 1997   ISBN 90-411-0505- 0
31. C.L. Lim and O.A. Elias: *The Paradox of Consensualism in International Law*. 1998
ISBN 90-411-0516-6
32. Mohsen Mohebi: *The International Law Character of the Iran-United States Claims Tribunal*. 1998   ISBN 90-411-1067-4
33. Mojmir Mrak: *The Succession of States*. 1999   ISBN 90-411-1145-X
34. C.L. Lim and Christopher Harding: *Renegotiating Westphalia*. Essays and Commentary on the European and Conceptual Foundations of Modern International Law. 1999   ISBN 90-411-1250-2
35. Kypros Chrysostomides: *Republic of Cyprus*. A Study in International Law. 2000
ISBN 90-411-1338-X
36. Obiora Chinedu Okafor: *Re-Defining Legitimate Statehood*. International Law and State Fragmentation in Africa. 2000   ISBN 90-411-1353-3
37. Rein Müllerson: *Ordering Anarchy*. International Law in International Society. 2000
ISBN 90-411-1408-4
38. Joshua Castellino: *International Law and Self-Determination*. The Interplay of the Politics of Territorial Possession with Formulations of Post-Colonial 'National' Identity. 2000   ISBN 90-411-1409-2
39. Oriol Casanovas: *Unity and Pluralism in Public International Law*. 2001
ISBN 90-411-1664-8
40. Roberto C. Laver: *Falklands/Malvinas Case*. Breaking the Deadlock in the Anglo-Argentine Sovereignty Dispute. 2001   ISBN 90-411-1534-X
41. Guido den Dekker: *The Law of Arms Control*. International Supervision and Enforcement. 2001   ISBN 90-411-1624-9
42. Sandra L. Bunn-Livingstone: *Juricultural Pluralism vis-à-vis Treaty Law*. State Practice and Attitudes. 2002   ISBN (hb) 90-411-1779-2
ISBN (pb) 90-411-1801-2
43. David Raic: *Statehood and the Law of Self-Determination*. 2002
ISBN 90-411-1890-X
44. L. Ali Khan: *Theory of Universal Democracy*. Beyond the End of History. 2003
ISBN 90-411-2003-3
45. Antony Anghie, Bhupinder Chimni, Karin Mickelson and Obiora Okafor (eds.): *The Third World and International Order. Law, Politics and Globalization*. 2003
ISBN 90-411-2166-8
46. Stéphane Beaulac: *The Power of Language in the Making of International Law*. The Word Sovereignty in Bodin and Vattel and the Myth of Westphalia. 2004
ISBN 90-04-13698-3
47. Sienho Yee: *Towards an International Law of Co-progressiveness*. 2004
ISBN 90-04-13829-3

48. C.G. Weeramantry: *Universalising International Law*. 2004   ISBN 90-04-13838-2
49. R.P. Anand: *Studies in International Law and History*. 2004   ISBN 90-04-13859-5
50. Gerard Kreijen: *State Failure, Sovereignty and Effectiveness*. 2004
ISBN 90-04-13965-6
51. Nico Schrijver and Friedl Weiss (eds.): *International Law and Sustainable Development*. 2004   ISBN 90-04-14173-1
52. Markus Burgstaller: *Theories of Compliance with International Law*. 2004
ISBN 90-04-14193-6
53. L.J. van den Herik: *The Contribution of the Rwanda Tribunal to the Development of International Law*. 2005   ISBN 90-04-14580-X
54. Roda Verheyen: *Climate Change Damage and International Law*. 2005
ISBN 90-04-14650-4
55. E. Milano: *Unlawful Territorial Situations in International Law*. Reconciling Effectiveness, Legality and Legitimacy. 2006   ISBN 90-04-14939-2
56. L.A. Khan: *A Theory of International Terrorism*. Understanding Islamic Militancy. 2006   ISBN 90-04-15207-5
57. Alfred M. Boll: *Multiple Nationality and International Law*. 2006
ISBN 90-04-14838-8

MARTINUS NIJHOFF PUBLISHERS – LEIDEN / BOSTON